Critical Companion to Contemporary Marxism

Historical Materialism Book Series

More than ten years after the collapse of the Berlin Wall and the disappearance of Marxism as a (supposed) state ideology, a need for a serious and long-term Marxist book publishing program has risen. Subjected to the whims of fashion, most contemporary publishers have abandoned any of the systematic production of Marxist theoretical work that they may have indulged in during the 1970s and early 1980s. The Historical Materialism book series addresses this great gap with original monographs, translated texts and reprints of "classics."

Haymarket Books is proud to be working with Brill Academic Publishers (http://www.brill.nl) and the journal *Historical Materialism* to republish the Historical Materialism book series in paperback editions. Current series titles include:

Alasdair MacIntyre's Engagement with Marxism: Selected Writings 1953–1974
Edited by Paul Blackledge and Neil Davidson

Althusser: The Detour of Theory, Gregory Elliott

Between Equal Rights: A Marxist Theory of International Law, China Miéville

The Capitalist Cycle, Pavel V. Maksakovsky, Translated with introduction and commentary by Richard B. Day

The Clash of Globalisations: Neo-Liberalism, the Third Way, and Anti-globalisation, Ray Kiely

Critical Companion to Contemporary Marxism, Edited by Jacques Bidet and Stathis Kouvelakis

Criticism of Heaven: On Marxism and Theology, Roland Boer

Exploring Marx's Capital: Philosophical, Economic, and Political Dimensions, Jacques Bidet

Following Marx: Method, Critique, and Crisis, Michael Lebowitz

The German Revolution: 1917–1923, Pierre Broué

Globalisation: A Systematic Marxian Account, Tony Smith

Impersonal Power: History and Theory of the Bourgeois State,
Heide Gerstenberger, translated by David Fernbach

Lenin Rediscovered: What Is to Be Done? *In Context*, Lars T. Lih

Making History: Agency, Structure, and Change in Social Theory, Alex Callinicos

Marxism and Ecological Economics: Toward a Red and Green Political Economy, Paul Burkett

A Marxist Philosophy of Language, Jean-Jacques Lecercle and Gregory Elliott

The Theory of Revolution in the Young Marx, Michael Löwy

Utopia Ltd.: Ideologies of Social Dreaming in England 1870–1900, Matthew Beaumont

Western Marxism and the Soviet Union: A Survey of Critical Theories and Debates Since 1917
Marcel van der Linden

Critical Companion to Contemporary Marxism

Edited by Jacques Bidet and Stathis Kouvelakis

Haymarket Books
Chicago, Illinois

First published in 2005 by Brill Academic Publishers, The Netherlands

Published in paperback in 2009 by
Haymarket Books
P.O. Box 180165
Chicago, IL 60618
773-583-7884
www.haymarketbooks.org
ISBN: 978-1-608460-30-4

Trade distribution:
In the U.S., Consortium Book Sales, www.cbsd.com
In the UK, Turnaround Publisher Services, www.turnaround-psl.com
In Australia, Palgrave Macmillan, www.palgravemacmillan.com.au
In all other countries, Publishers Group Worldwide, www.pgw.com

Cover design by Ragina Johnson. Cover image by Olga Rozanova, 1917.

This book was published with the generous support of the Lannan Foundation and the Wallace Global Fund.

Printed in Canada by union labor.

10 9 8 7 6 5 4 3

Library of Congress Cataloging-in-Publication Data is available.

Contents

Figures

Introduction: Marxism, Post-Marxism, Neo-Marxisms

Jacques Bidet and Stathis Kouvelakis

Periodically proclaimed to be dead, or on its way back, Marxism and, more generally, references to Marx are an integral part of contemporary culture. A broad view capable of taking the slightest distance indicates that even today, more than two decades after the eruption of the last 'crisis' of Marxism and at a time when the régimes officially identified with it belong to history, reference to Marx is in no sense ephemeral – mere residue of a period that is now past – or a local phenomenon, confined to a few geographical and cultural zones or countries. Marxism is demonstrating its persistence, its productivity and its capacity to adapt to contexts and conjunctures. Such is the statement of fact that guided us in the choices governing the production of this book: to indicate the diverse forms – emulating the famous mole of history, they are often subterranean – through which that reference has shaped, and continues to shape, the theoretical debates of the last three decades.

Thus, in this *Companion*, readers will not find a series of entries corresponding to notions or authors, but a set of chapters offering a broad sense of the main axes (themes, theoretical schools and currents, major authors) around which debates from the 1970s and 1980s onwards have been structured. This perspective is not exhaustive; and different choices could have been made.[1]

---

[1] *Note to the English language edition*: six of the chapters in the *Dictionnaire Marx contemporain* (Presses Universitaires de France, 2001) were not included in this edition, either because they were unsuitable for an anglophone publication, or because they had already appeared in English elsewhere. Chapters 17–25, 28, 29, 32, 33 and 35 were newly commissioned for this edition, whilst Chapters 3 and 16 were substantially revised and updated. The Editors regret that their very ambitious hopes of covering a range of other themes, such as Marxist feminism, geographical-historical materialism (particularly the work of David Harvey), literary and cultural criticism (especially the contributions of Terry Eagleton), new debates in crisis theory (such as

It certainly leaves aside various important geo-cultural zones and some readers are bound to find it Eurocentric. However, our aim was not to provide a guide to the main concepts of Marxism or an encyclopaedic survey of Marxism. Others, before us, have done that to great effect: we shall simply mention Tom Bottomore's *Dictionary of Marxist Thought* (Basil Blackwell, Oxford 1983), Georges Labica's and Gérard Bensussan's *Dictionnaire critique du marxisme* (Presses Universitaires de France, Paris 1985), and the *Historisch-Kritisches Wörterbuch des Marxismus* directed by Wolfgang Fritz Haug (ten volumes, Argument Verlag, Berlin 1994–). And the present volume in no way claims to replace these works, which are indispensable for any reader or researcher interested in Marxism and its history. For our part, what we have sought to do is to pinpoint, and sometimes to disclose, the main *tendencies*, the lines of demarcation or flight, which *today* mark the field of reference to Marx; and the type of effect produced by this reference in the intellectual culture of our time, over and above the question (no doubt crucial) of the future of 'Marxism' as such.

From this initial decision several imperatives follow, which imposed themselves in the selection and organisation of the material that makes up this *Critical Companion of Contemporary Marxism*.

First and foremost, we wanted to demonstrate the displacement of the 'centre of gravity' of Marxist work, which has migrated from the lands where it was traditionally affirmed in the initial postwar decades – namely, southern Europe and Latin America – towards the anglophone world (and especially its universities), which in our time has become the centre of theoretical production referring to Marx. This involves a major transformation in the 'becoming-a-world' of Marx's thought, to use Henri Lefebvre's phrase. It requires an in-depth analysis, some elements of which we shall suggest, both in terms of theoretical and historical *balance-sheets* ('Prefigurations') and, throughout the book, of sketches that seek to construct a *cartography* of Marxism today, which is surprising in many respects. The constellations outlined thus simul-

---

that regarding Robert Brenner's theses), and so forth could not be realised in the time available. However, they hope that these chapters might be added in future editions of this *Companion*. The panoramic survey of journals included in the French edition also could not be updated and included here but, again, may appear in future editions.

taneously convey a diversification of the philosophical identity of Marxism, its integration into new social and political contexts, and its confrontation with what are in part historically unprecedented subjects – for example, the issue of the so-called 'globalisation' of the economy, changes in the labour process and production, generalised urbanisation, the effects of the revolution brought about by information and communication technologies, the new forms of racist violence, of cultural and military imperialism, of male domination, and of the ecological threat.

We have also sought to illuminate the interface between 'Marxism' and its other – that is to say, to indicate the ways in which Marx is present in what constitutes a kind of environment of Marxism and which, far from being external to it, is its very condition of existence, regardless of whether this is recognised. From Foucault to Bourdieu, and from Habermas to Deleuze, from theoreticians of postcolonialism to a international relations, a set of figures have established themselves, a multiplicity of configurations has developed and become firmly rooted in various political and intellectual contexts, attesting to the vitality of the Marxian reference.

It will perhaps be asked if we are still dealing with 'Marxism' here. Much has been said recently about 'post-Marxisms' and 'neo-Marxisms'. Although it is not always easy to distinguish between the two, they are differentiated in principle in as much as the one seems to proclaim the exhaustion of the Marxist paradigm, whereas the other introduces problematics which, while maintaining a special relationship with certain ideas derived from Marx, reinterpret them in new contexts or combine them with different traditions. The notion of neo-Marxism is opposed to that of some quintessential Marxism, inscribed in the empyrean of ideas. And, in reality, historically accredited Marxism indeed appears always to have lived off incessant restructuring and innovation, constantly finding in the surrounding culture, in perspectives generated outside its conceptual space and through the breaks that their integration involved, the conditions for its renewal. With the upheavals that marked the end of the twentieth century, any idea of orthodoxy has been shattered. The 'crisis of Marxism' has released a variety of more or less fleeting currents, schools, groups and unique individual trajectories, translated into shifting reclassifications in the theoretical field. The old lines of demarcation have in the main ceased to operate. It seemed to us that the moment had come to attempt to take stock, and to try to pinpoint some of the main themes and tracks in a vast landscape. We felt encouraged to do so by the complete absence of such a cartography in the French literature – an absence that is not without consequences in a debate which is too often enclosed in the national cultural space.

Exploring the *new* tendencies, we have certainly neglected some worthy and significant work, developed on more traditional foundations. Other *figures* might have featured, such as Lacan, alongside Foucault and Althusser. Moreover, different organisational options would doubtless have brought out different sorts of intellectual phenomena. For example, had we opted for a presentation by *disciplines*, readers would have got a better sense both of some massive regressions, like that of Marxist historiography in France (with notable exceptions, such as, *inter alia*, Guy Bois's works on the Middle Ages, research in the 'history of concepts' or on the French Revolution); and of the complexity and singularity of the relationship to Marx that can be assumed by the various forms of knowledge – sociological, economic, juridical, and so on – whose rigour implies specialisation in their scientific criteria, and which experience some difficulty relating to a theorisation of general ambition like that of Marxism. Entering into the subject via major 'problematics' seemed to us to be the way to show precisely how, in different fashions, this kind of junction was sought. We have aimed at a meaningful outline, stimulating debate and confrontation, rather than encyclopaedic exhaustiveness.

The index of ideas which, as it was being constructed, greatly surprised the editors of this book, makes it clear that contemporary Marxisms speak new languages, that they find expression only through a broad spectrum of concepts deriving from philosophies and forms of knowledge foreign to the classics, and which today mark its communication with shared critical thinking. However, this does not entail the erasure of the distinguishing characteristics involved in the analysis of societies in terms of class, exploitation, political and cultural domination, and imperialism.

* * *

Obviously, this work owes much to the work over fifteen years of the editorial team of the journal *Actuel Marx*, one of whose constant concerns has been to take the measure of reworkings of Marxism throughout the world, in different national cultures, in a new era, and in the context of a new civilisation.

We hope that this map will make it possible to get a better sense of what is at stake – which is not only theoretical – in the debates that animate a significant part of the contemporary intellectual field and thereby contribute to that knowledge of the world which is so essential to those who wish to change it.[2]

[2] We must thank all those who have helped us during this long task: Annie Bidet-Mordrel and Pascale Arnaud, who have participated in a whole host of ways in this undertaking; Sebastian Budgen, who has generously put his vast knowledge of anglophone Marxism at our disposal; our remarkable translators; Dorothée Rousset, who followed the work from beginning to end; Annie Dauphin, for her participation in giving effect to the questionnaire; Gérard Raulet, director of the UPRESA 8004, Contemporary Political Philosophy, for his concern for our project; Jean-Marc Lachaud; Christine Vivier; Emmanuel Renault; Roberto Nigro; and finally Sébastien Mordrel, who took responsibility for producing the text of the French edition. *Note on the English language edition*: the Introduction and Chapters 1–16, 20, 26, 27, 31, 34, 36–40 were translated by Gregory Elliott, who the Editors would like to take this opportunity to thank. Others who contributed to this edition should also be mentioned: Cinzia Arruzza, Ande de Cannes, David Fernbach, G.M. Goshgarian, Marie-José Gransard, Gonso Pozo-Martin, Guido Starosta, Peter Thomas, Alberto Toscano and Nicolas Vieitlescazes.

Prefigurations

Chapter One

A Key to the *Critical Companion to Contemporary Marxism*

Jacques Bidet

A *Companion* for a different world

This *Companion*, which bears the stamp of the major crisis experienced by Marxism over the last three decades, also aims to attest to the renewal it has undergone in the last ten years.

Crisis of socialism, crisis of Marxism

The crisis of Marxism that marked the end of the twentieth century is scarcely comparable with those that preceded it at the turn of the previous century. The latter affected the doctrine of what was still only a *movement* (working-class, socialist), one mainly confined to Europe, and which as yet only expressed hopes for an alternative. The current crisis affects a world which this movement, having become *state power*, helped fashion in significant measure. In what was called the Communist sphere, where official doctrine claimed to be rooted in Marxism, it supposedly defined the socio-economic order. In the capitalist sphere, much of the institutional architecture of society, inspired by socialism, had become popular to such an extent that it seemed to be inscribed in the naturally progressive course of history and to be set gradually to win over the whole world, thanks to the emergence of the new nation-states issued from liberation struggles. And, throughout most of the world, authoritarian régimes faced movements inspired by Marxism ranged against them. Up until the 1970s, capitalism could appear to be historically doomed by the gradual increase in the constraints weighing on it, by the nationalisation of economies, and by the assertion of social logics that challenged purely private capitalist interests.

The 'crisis of Marxism' is the calling into question of this optimistic view of the world and future history. It is not reducible to the collapse of the USSR and the evolution of China, where models prevailed which, in the eyes of most of those identifying with Marxism, had long since been exhausted. It is more general and more profound. Along with the former Third World, it affects all developed capitalist countries, particularly those of Europe, whose institutions of a socialist orientation, constructed in the course of a century and once so powerful and resonant – and sometimes going well beyond the 'social state', especially in their economic dimension – are gradually being dismantled, in a process that nothing seems capable of checking.

The obvious question facing Marxists is *why* things are thus. According to the type of hypothesis offered by 'historical materialism', such a reverse cannot be explained exclusively by political developments – by the implementation of the neoliberal project, conceived as a machination or *conspiracy* on the part of capitalist élites. The old adage according to which, at a certain point, the development of the 'productive forces' calls into question the existing 'social relations', is especially pertinent here. This does not mean that starting from a new technological age we can deduce a new social and political régime, which is its expression. The intertwining of the two orders is more complex: the 'productive forces', *as they have developed in the context of capitalism and in the uneven world system*, have ended up undermining, albeit in highly uneven fashion, the national form that prevailed in the modern world and perverting its content. New *potentialities* (deriving, in particular, from easier communications and transport, the immediacy and ubiquity of information, and the growing importance of immaterial production) have emerged, which form the basis for various political, economic, and military projects. In concrete terms, the new technological era has favoured those capitalist firms of the imperialist centre able to operate as transnationals within the world system in their pursuit of profit, distributing production here, research there, and financial management somewhere else again. The transnationals have acquired the power to dominate the states of the centre and their directive bodies, and to corrupt and dissolve those of the periphery. Consequently, national authorities – the institutional site of projects of a socialist orientation – find themselves neutralised as they come under the control of new bodies, whose political function is to dismantle the old institutions and open up national territories to a globalised neoliberal economy.

In these circumstances, it is the *predictive* power of Marxism that seems to be affected – its ability to define a different type of society, to which capitalism itself supposedly leads via the development of its contradictions. We are no longer dealing with a crisis *within Marxism*, between various interpretations, provoking expulsions and splits (which Marxism, as used to be said in optimistic former days, lived off). We face a crisis that involves Marxism's very existence, capped as it is by the disappearance of the institutions, party or other, that officially referred to it, and by its erasure from the cultural sphere, the collective memory, and individual imaginations.

Naturally, in the public mind the most spectacular aspect of the crisis was the disappearance of the USSR and the socialist bloc. Among professed Marxists, this massive upheaval was not exactly experienced as a crisis, since that major historical experiment had issued in a new form of class society, which had long been the object of their criticism. Instead, it took the form of disappointment in the inability of these régimes to reform themselves in any way, if only in a social-democratic direction. Only a few optimists regarded this as a 'liberation of Marxism' and the chance of a new beginning – a sublimation, no doubt, of their relief. The Chinese mutation was less of a cause for surprise, since it inscribed this continent in a common logic, where modern class confrontation, with its antagonistic projects, persists, even if it assumes specific forms.

In reality, Marxist morale is affected by something more profound and more general. It is the gradual destruction, within nation-states, of everything that was constructed in the name of socialism, with Marxism as a major theoretical reference-point: an economy in part under collective control, with multiple public services in education, health, information and communication, transport, research and culture. It is the privatisation of all aspects of social existence, the private appropriation of all sources of wealth, and the establishment of a world order in which the logic of profit, backed by military domination, holds exclusive sway. It is the consignment of the greatest number once again to the domination of capitalist power and thus to the cycle of poverty or insecurity. It is the crisis of any prospect for the social and political emancipation of humanity as a whole. Put in command by the insatiable pursuit of profit, it is the collective irresponsibility whose most visible sign is its powerlessness to curb the destruction of nature.

The resistance and resurgence of Marxism

The paradox is this: at the same time as Marxism's predictive power seems to be infirmed, its *analytical* power appears intact. And, in so far as it retains a capacity to interpret the new course of the world, it is also capable of intervening in it. To understand its reverses and defeats in its own language is already to possess resources with which to resist and to conceive new offensives – if this language is legitimate, at any rate. As we intend to demonstrate, Marxism does indeed supply interpretative perspectives for the great changes – social, political, cultural, anthropological – that are underway. And this is why it is – or can be – mobilised wherever social and popular struggles unfold against economic or bureaucratic domination, male domination, imperial power, and the commodification of nature and cultures. And it is what imparts acuteness, power, and potential universality to the prospect of an alternative globalisation, which is beginning to emerge as a common horizon.

As yet, this analytical power has not found expression in a general prospective vision, making it possible to give new life to the modern movement for emancipation, to bring about a convergence between the movements that are emerging. The precondition for this is unquestionably that Marxism should prove able to interpret its own shortcomings and to reconstruct itself by drawing on what is around it. To this end, while referring to the various chapters of this *Companion*, I offer some reflections below that refer to the perspective I have sought to develop in my recent trilogy, whose aim is precisely to reconstruct Marxism.[1]

The crisis and the alternative – this is what is at stake in this *Companion*, which is certainly to be taken as an academic reference work, permitting ready

[1] See Bidet 1999, 2000, and 2004. Various translations of these works are underway, particularly in English and Chinese.

access to the new forms, structures, and hypotheses that have been developed in Marxism. However, these figures and configurations are not restricted to a collection of what professes to be 'Marxist' today. The most important authors we present, from Bourdieu, via Habermas and Foucault, to Derrida, can in no way be identified as Marxists. Such figures, along with others, simply seem to us to be indispensable to any reconstruction. They represent other elements in our culture, which cannot be assimilated to Marxism, but which are nevertheless precious to us. Accordingly, this *Companion* aims to participate in a reconsideration and reconstruction of Marx's legacy, in reformulating a theory for the present.

For a re-generative grammar of Marxism

The official presuppositions of modernity

A first aspect of the crisis, directly related to the collapse of the communism derived from the Third International, concerns the issue of democracy. It was all too clear that if democratic forms had been neglected in the construction of 'socialism' in the USSR, China, and elsewhere, this was not some careless mistake on the part of history, or simply because the revolutionaries had betrayed revolutionary ideals. It was related to the very economic-political form of the societies constructed in the name of socialism. With the collapse of official communisms, an ever more radical issue than that of democracy has thus come back onto the Marxist agenda: the *issue of right* in general. Not, in the first instance, the issue of morality, but that of right, the just and the unjust, the foundation of a legitimate political and social order. Here, an engagement with liberalism was inevitable, particularly with those forms of it renewed by authors like Rawls and Habermas, which have proved capable of at least articulating the *claims* of modernity: that of basing all our relations on liberty and equality and of consigning them, in the last instance, to the requirements of a relationship of discursive communication. Particularly in the Anglo-American world, Marxism itself has sometimes been treated as one 'theory of justice' among others, striving for supremacy, capable of adding economic and social liberties to those that already exist; or it has been invoked as a utopia, as the declaration of a future society.

All this can be related to those elements in Marx's Marxism that are bound up with Enlightenment traditions of the social contract and political economy, Rousseau and Adam Smith. Moreover, in a sense, it is indeed to these traditions that Marx pays homage at the start of *Capital*, when he begins his exposition by referring to what constitutes the presupposition of the modern form of society. Marx begins by considering that which, officially at least, presents itself as the most general feature of capitalist society: market relations of production, based on exchange, in which everyone *eo ipso* considers the other as a free, equal, and rational individual, and thereby enjoys the status of citizen in a polity based on the social contract. Marx then shows how, in reality, this framework of production for exchange, in so far as it is generalised, turns labour-power itself into a commodity, bought by capitalists with a view to profit – that is to say, at a lower price than the value it will produce. Thereafter, social relations can no longer be analysed as simple relations of exchange between individuals, because they are at the same time relations of exploitation between classes with conflicting interests. And the class that is economically dominant is also the class which is politically dominant, in a state whose institutions, in this respect, are non-contractual, are such as to reproduce and maintain the class structure. The aim of the remainder of *Capital* is to demonstrate that this form of society is historically transient, leading to its own supersession. In fact, it has an irresistible tendency to the concentration of capital, such that large firms gradually replace small ones, to the point where the working class, increasingly numerous, educated, and organised by the production process itself, becomes capable of taking over management of it and replacing the logic of the market by democratically organised planning, so that a logic of concerted discourse can henceforth replace the blind mechanisms of the market.

It might be thought that there is much truth in Marx's analysis. And we have seen that during the twentieth century the working class, allied with other categories of wage-earner and elsewhere with peasant masses, demonstrated its ability to promote alternatives to capitalism, to impose limits on the omnipotence of the logic of the capitalist market, to establish non-market conditions for the employment of labour-power, and to appropriate in a national form a proportion of the production of goods and especially services. Even so, when attempts were made to substitute the 'organised' (or planned) form of society for the 'market' form in the USSR and China, it displayed a similar tendency to generate class relations, which in some respects were even more regressive. On the other hand, far from it being possible to envisage a utopia in which the market can simply be replaced by organised direction, *market* and *organisation*, these *two poles* of rational co-ordination on a social scale, function (as Marx saw, in least in the case of the market) as the two *class factors* constitutive of class relations in the modern era. These two factors are certainly not of the same nature. And the struggle for emancipation, which aims at forms of discursive, self-managerial, and associative co-operation, naturally looks for support to democratic (particularly national) to direction, *organisation, against the capitalist market*. Nevertheless, market and organisation are to be taken as *two poles*, correlative and co-imbricated, in all social structuration, from the firm to the state, giving rise in their interaction to a specific 'class-form'.

The specificity of these two poles in the modern era, however, is that each of them is identified, officially at least, with the same principles of liberty and equality, which supposedly govern the relation of 'each to each' and the relationship 'between all' (or 'from each to all and from all to each'). The market, where everyone decides freely with respect to others, theoretically excludes any duress by one person against another. The constraints of the organisation, including those of the firm, are supposedly neutralised by the fact that in principle people only pertain to it voluntarily, can withdraw from it, and that it is subject to rules which citizens supposedly develop together. These two modes of co-ordination are *in conflict* with one another, in the sense that what is constructed in the organisational mode is withdrawn in the market order, and vice versa. But they are, at the same time, *mutually imbricated* in the social whole: while constantly on the labour market, modern workers are organised by the firm, which is an organisation on a market that is itself organised to a considerable extent. In this sense, the *Rechtsstaat* is the instance that supposedly presides over the democratic arbitration between these two modes of co-ordination. It is itself an *organisation*, but one which presents itself as ensuring the power of collective deliberation, of an equal say between the 'voices' of citizens.

The bipolar matrix (market-organisation) of rational *economic* co-ordination thus presents another, *juridico-political* aspect, which is itself bi-polar. In this respect, the two poles are not only mutually imbricated, but *mutually imply* one another. In fact, a free and equal relationship between each person can only exist if it is based on a free and equal relationship between all, and vice versa. Such, in its complexity, is what it seems to me appropriate to call the 'metastructure of modernity', to which any modern structural form necessarily refers. And as we can see, it possesses an inherently *critical* character. In fact, in such a matrix no social *law* (no distribution of tasks, powers or property within the social space, from the family to the state), imposed on society in the name of nature or some transcendent principle, can exist, but only *rules*, which members reach agreement over. No alleged natural law, such as a 'law of the market', can be imposed on the deliberation of citizens, who are the sole judges of the collective order. Nor can there be any putatively rational organisation that does not respect the free relationship between persons. As we shall see, it remains the case that this modern *claim* is only ever present in amphibological fashion, articulated by the dominated as a requirement to be realised, and by the dominant as already existing, as a good to be defended – a sublimated expression of their privileges.

Marx reveals this amphibology in remarkable fashion. He begins his exposition in *Capital* with a theoretical description of what he regarded as the most general figure of the modern form of society: the logic of market relations between putatively free and equal partners, to which he devotes part one of Volume One. This is the basis, he explains, on which we can define what capitalism proper is: a society where labour-power is itself a commodity – which transforms so-called market society into a (commodity) capitalist society. And his objective was to show how the historical tendencies of this structure made it possible to conceive revolutionary strategies. For him, it was a question of going beyond the reign of the capitalist *market*, based on private property, through a collective appropriation of the means of production, leading to an *organisation* of production negotiated between all. It was a question of abolishing the market along with capital. And, although he refrained from futuristic constructions, he traced a path from market to organisation, which, with the abolition of capitalist property, would lose the despotic character it has in private firms. Yet it is clear that this historical schema must be revised. For the general matrix of modernity, which must form the starting-point, is in fact (as we have seen) more complex, containing *two poles* – that of market inter-individuality and that of organisational centricity – according to these *two aspects* – that of economic-rational co-ordination and that of politico-juridical order. If we wish to resume Marx's endeavour, these are the terms, so it seems to me, in which we must correct and expand the abstract general figure with which the analysis starts (and to which it regularly reverts). It will be understood that such a metastructural figure is strictly 'aporetic': on its own, it does not open up any 'royal road'. In itself, it is simply the form in which the problems of modernity are posed and to which anything that *claims to be* modern – that is to say, acceptable to us today – necessarily refers.

Thus, readers will find in this Companion *a fair number of highly distinct problematics referring to this moment of the 'claim' of modernity. It is to be found in the form of ideology, in the Althusserian terms of 'interpellation', or in the hauntology whereby Derrida presents the spectre who announces and denounces, threatens and promises, disappears and always 'returns'. It is equally present, albeit in contrasting terms, in the positive programme of rationalisation proposed by the regulation school, in American radicalism, or in the elaboration of 'models of socialism'. It is wholly explicit in Habermas's project, to be realised in a 'communicative' society. It is transcended in hope in liberation philosophies and theologies.*

The social and economic structure of capitalism

Better than anyone else, Marx showed how this universe of the *claims* of modernity does not coincide with the actual *reality* of the modern world. The egalitarian *metastructure* of commodity exchange, with which he begins his systematic exposition at the start of *Capital*, certainly possesses some reality in his eyes. But it actually only exists in the form of its converse in the actual *structure*. He reveals this inversion by means of two conjoint initiatives. On the one hand, he elaborates a 'critique of political economy' – of the *market* as the universal principle of the economic order; on the other, he develops a 'critique of politics' – of the *social contract* allegedly realised by the institutions of constitutional democracy – in a context where, more generally, any modern 'organisation' supposedly rests on a delegation of the authority that everyone has over themselves. His analysis always comes back to registering that the *official reference-points* of the capitalist modern world in no sense represent its essence, but its phenomenon – understood as that aspect of itself which this essence allows to appear, as that which it claims to be. The peculiarity of modernity is certainly the *claim* that the totality of relations between free and equal individuals is only conceived in a contractual form, which is indissociably private equal exchange and equal citizenship. But such a claim is only ever formulated in forms of society where market and organisation are already transformed into class factors, into vectors of class relations. And, in this sense, liberty and equality are *always already* 'transformed into their opposites'. They are definitely not mere appearances, sheer ideological smoke screens. For the fact that in any dealing one must invoke the liberty and equality of all is a constitutive critical feature of modern society, which confers on it its revolutionary character. But this society, like those that preceded it, is to be understood as a class society, which is neither free nor equal, but which nevertheless exhibits the peculiarity that class relations are constituted on the basis of the two major forms of rational social co-ordination – market and organisation – with their correlative claim of liberty-equality.

Marx focused analysis on demonstrating that underlying the appearances of wage-labour exchange is concealed exploitation. But he also disclosed that this is not realised by the simple relationship between *wage-earners* and *owners* of the means of production. For it always assumes the intervention of the other pole of the dominant class – that of the manager, the *organiser*, who directs, having supposedly been chosen for his competence. The power of 'competence' (supposed, professed, qualified) is of a different kind from that of ownership and extends far beyond private production, since it is equally deployed in the public sphere of administration and culture and, in truth, throughout society.

Marx was unable to complete a study of modern class structure, of which he nevertheless set out the main elements. If we wish to take up his outline today, we must in particular appreciate that the dominant class comprises two poles, one based on the market and on ownership, the other on organisation and 'competence' – two poles that are at once complementary and comparatively antagonistic. Like ownership, competence too is socially defined and recognised by means of specific titles (degrees, etc.). This bipolarity governs the existence of two distinct poles of hegemony, to which we can relate the pair of 'Right' (more on the side of ownership and the market) and 'Left' (more on the side of organisations and their competences) – a pair whose content varies enormously from one capitalist society to another (republicans and democrats here, conservatives and social democrats elsewhere), is always fluid and problematic, and preserves itself only by misrepresenting itself, with each pole being hegemonic only to the extent that it can in some way represent the other within itself and thus pass itself off as guarantor of the general interest.

For its part, the exploited class is correlatively distributed into various fractions, according to whether the exploitation and domination they endure proceed more or less directly from the *market* factor, the *organisational-hierarchical* factor, or *both* at once. Thus, we have *self-employed* workers (farmers, artisans, shopkeepers), *public-sector* wage-earners (workers in central or local administration, with or without the status of 'civil servant'), and *private-sector* wage-earners (workers and employees). Finally, the modern class factors (market/organisation), unlike earlier communitarian forms, structurally define an *exterior* comprising all those who are rejected by the capitalist market as lacking any regularly employable skill for the purposes of profit. These two structural factors are thus such as to generate a growing mass of the *excluded*, 'without' work, income, qualification, roof, abode, or recognised identity and yet, in this very margin, invariably prey to super-exploitation – not to mention the immigrants 'without papers', who are simultaneously subject to what will be called 'systemic' domination. Social relations between the sexes, bound up with the other major social function – the family – directed (at least in developed capitalism) not towards production, but towards the biological reproduction of the species, are closely interwoven with class relations, evolving with the variation in modes of production. The interplay of class factors, which in particular generates partial and illusory affinities between the 'self-employment' and ownership, as between 'civil servants' and competence, determines the obstacles that have to be surmounted for the class of the exploited to discover its *unity* and prove capable of an *alliance* politics (we shall see which later).

While outlining the sociological and juridical aspects of the capitalist form of society, Marx himself mainly set out its economic dimension. He showed how this society is reproduced and revealed the logic whereby it gives rise to accumulation. His analysis is mainly directed to a study of the market mechanisms peculiar to capitalism. It culminates in capitalism's structural tendency to cyclical crisis, attesting to its instability, to the menaces that constantly hang over it, which it eludes only by accentuating its contradictions; and, correlatively, in the prospects for its universal diffusion (particularly through colonial conquest). Yet it can be deemed inadequate. Certainly, Marx strongly emphasised the tendency to oligopolistic concentration, which for him was a prelude to the decline of the market. However, he failed – and this cannot be attributed solely to the era in which he wrote – to consider the potentialities of the capitalist structure starting from the other pole: organisation. On the one hand, he proved unable to take full account of the fact that this structure, given its 'metastructural matrix', materialises as such first of all in the form of the nation-state, which possesses a genuine potential to determine, organise, and regulate the capitalist market. On the other hand, he was unable clearly to envisage or examine the fact that in this framework a growing percentage of production – particularly services – could, as a result of the growing power of the wage-earning classes and their impact on the social order, be carried out in non-market form, in a publicly organised form, *without this entailing an exit from capitalism* – in a context where, correlatively, within the dominant class the pole of managers and, more broadly, of qualified competence, would come to occupy an important position (and even, under 'real socialism', come to represent the totality of this class).

Nevertheless, Marx identified the essential character of capitalism remarkably well. At the centre of his approach, an in some sense *quantitative* analysis of exploitation, which explains how class division occurs and is reproduced, how capital is accumulated, leads into a *qualitative* analysis of the *logic* of capitalism. His thesis is that capitalist production is not identical with production in general, or only with market production or the 'market economy'. Not only is it, like every form of exploitation, geared towards the extraction of a *surplus-product* from the producer. But it is very specifically geared towards the accumulation of *profit*, a purely *abstract* wealth (in reality, accumulation of a private social power over production), whatever the consequences for human beings, cultures, and nature. This is the root of the ecological and cultural critique, the most radical there is, articulated by Marxism.

To this it must be added that Marx's analysis, which mainly consists in the theoretical construction of the *structure* of capitalism (the main ideal type for an understanding of the modern world, according to Weber), offers, if not a sure way of comprehending capitalism's overall evolution and its historical *tendency* towards an end-point, then at least the most significant outline of the kind of investigation required for that purpose. It is also the analysis that makes it possible to pose the question of the *beginning* of capitalism in the West, starting out from the aleatory conditions in which it emerged. Marx, whose works pertain more directly to economics or sociology than historiography, nevertheless bequeathed historians an enormous work programme, since it is only on the basis of a definition of the *structure* of a form of society that one can examine its *origins*, its *development*, and its *end*.

Various chapters in this Companion *refer to the structural form, economic and sociological, of capitalism, drawing on Marx's analysis while contributing new dimensions to it – particularly by way of a more concrete examination of the features that characterise its current form. As regards more general issues, the stimulus in part derives from non-Marxist sociology. Thus, Bourdieu endeavoured to expand the concept of social 'reproduction', analysed by Marx in terms of production and capitalist market ownership, and which he redeploys to the other pole – that of 'competence', recognised in its arbitrariness through the very process of its production. Reproduction is not understood here, any more than it is in Marx, as a transmission to inheritors, but as the reproduction of a structure of domination. An analogous theme is developed by Erik Olin Wright in the idiom of analytical Marxism. A similar expansion underlies the problematic proposed by Gérard Duménil and Dominique Lévy, in the broad panorama they offer us which reveals the rise of a 'capitalo-cadrism'. On this basis they interpret the history of capitalism, with its successive switches marking an alternation between market dominance ('finance') and organisational dominance ('cadres'). Among other things, Foucault's work clarifies the fact that modernity is characterised not only by the generalisation of private relations, but equally by an organisational mesh which similarly counts in the emergence of the forms of affirmation and subjection of modern subjectivity. The historians of modernity are naturally widely called upon here. And sociologists also obviously have a large part to play when it comes to defining the characteristics of the current phase of capitalism, whether in the schema of neoliberalism and universal deregulation, or 'post-Fordism' and the 'postmodern flexibilisation' of labour-power. Nor will readers be surprised to find a chapter which roots the ecological critique of contemporary society in Marx's analysis; or another devoted to the sociological studies produced by feminism.*[2]

The world-system, the planet, and humanity

The concepts of social *structure*, class relations, and corresponding state authority are insufficient to define capitalism. They are simply those that determine it in the framework of the nation-state, characteristic of the modern form of society. But this nation-state precisely emerges as one state among others of the same kind, in a totality that progressively takes the form of a

---

[2] [*Editorial note*: the chapter on feminism included in the *Dictionnaire Marx contemporain* was a translation of a chapter by Stevi Jackson in Gamble (ed.) 1999. Despite many efforts, the editors were not able to secure a replacement chapter written specifically for the *Companion*.]

'state system'. Capitalism is thus at once (class) *structure* and (world) *system* – a particular historical structure of the nation-state and a particular historical system formed by the set of nation-states. The systemic totality is distinct from the structural totality in that it is not organised by a state. It does not embody a reference to a *putatively* collective power, exercised by supposedly equal partners. Nor is not realised by the domination of one class over another. The relation between nations, as modern theoreticians of the contract (from Hobbes to Kant) bluntly put it, is a 'state of war'. The capitalist market relation operates in it without encountering the *claim* of a supposedly collective, supra-national democratic government that regulates and possibly plans. Between nations, it is combined with a pure relationship of force, with the asymmetrical power of the nations of the centre over the periphery, limited by the mechanism of alliances and the strength of any resistance.

Obviously, none of this was wholly foreign to Marx. However, for want of a sufficiently complete theorisation of the *structure* – particularly of the relation between the economy and the capitalist state, between the two poles of structural domination (market and organisation), and hence also between its two aspects (economic and juridico-political) – Marx was unable to articulate structure and system adequately. Lenin's genius consisted, among other things, in taking up the issue of capitalism in its global dimension, starting from the world system. Yet imperialism still figures in his work as a (final) 'phase' of capitalism. The Third-Worldists of the 1960s developed a more adequate picture, which elevated the concepts of the system to the same epistemological level as the structure. As asymmetry within the world system, imperialism is as old as capitalism itself, in the sense that the capitalist system emerges as a multiplicity of nation-states, as a totality within which the states forming the centre dominate the periphery and the surrounding space. Thus, in different balances of forces, the same capitalism develops as wage-labour in the centre and slavery in the periphery, as (relative) civil peace within the Western nations, as war between them, and as colonial subjugation and extermination.

It is at this global level of the system and its development that the conditions for globalisation, neoliberal policy, the resistance to them, and the movement for an alternative globalisation are to be analysed. It is also at this total systemic level that the ecological crisis provoked by capitalism is most obvious, particularly as a result of the refusal of the leading powers to abandon the logic of profit, which is also a logic of the ineluctable destruction of the nature around us.

At this level too we begin to perceive the emergence, in the very long term, of a form of capitalist *world state*, encompassing and determining existing state entities, without bringing about their disappearance – and this in a perverse relationship with the *world system*, whose centre, unable to avoid the reproduction on an ultimate scale of a social form similar to the nation-state, seeks to colonise it for its benefit. The very relative legitimacy of the UN, for example, when it cannot be ignored, is instrumentally invoked, albeit with uneven success, to legitimate the most arbitrary enterprises of the imperialist centre. However, nothing will prevent the relation between the world-systemic centre and the world-state centre – two variable-geometry institutional conglomerations – emerging, in an oscillation between complicity and conflict, as the 'principal contradiction' of capitalism.

An important section of this Companion *is thus given over to the problematic of the capitalist totality. Hence the articles devoted to theories of the world-system, postcolonialism, the analysis of economic neoliberalism presented by Duménil and Lévy, the advances in Anglo-American Marxism highlighted by Alex Callinicos, and, once again, Jean-Marie Harribey's article on ecology.*

Tendencies and practices, Marxism and history

Marx's specificity consists in the fact that he not only described the *structure* of modern capitalist society, but also situated it in a general schema of history in line with the analytical grid of historical materialism, that he analysed its specific *tendencies*. It consists in the fact that he sought to elucidate the preconditions for its *end* and for the establishment of a *superior form* of society.

This stance on the future, sketched on the basis of the present, is not reducible either to an optimistic *evolutionism* diagnosing the 'revolution' as a natural phenomenon, in itself inevitable but whose advent can be hastened; or to a *normative* posture basing political action on a firm belief in a just order to be established. It can only be understood in terms of a *dialectic*, in which what is and what should be are not external to one another. Marx describes the actual *tendency* of capitalism to produce its own 'gravediggers'. But the task of this new class, the universal class of workers, seems to him to involve actually implementing, by means of production collectively determined by equals, what modern society *proclaims* – equality and liberty – without being able to *realise* it under capitalism. In fact, it can only assert itself as the universal class, sounding the death knell of class society, by meeting this expectation. This does not entail it conforming to values inscribed in the empyrean of the modern world, but means it responding to the imperatives that are actually operative as imperatives.

In reality – and we have seen why – these claims on the part of modernity could not be adequately realised in the form of the 'concerted-plan' régime, and still less when it was taken literally, as under collectivism. Yet they remain the reference-point. Modernity cannot but *promise* more every day. But it does so via the modern class factors of market and organisation, in the conditions of a class relation that inverts the outcome. The march towards emancipation is therefore to be conceived as a class struggle for a classless society on these two fronts.

However, those below know from experience that the two poles, and the two components of the dominant class corresponding to them, are not of the same kind. They know that 'organised' co-ordination, in so far the form of public deliberation can be imparted to it, can be imbued with self-managerial or associative co-responsibility and with discursive communication to a far greater extent than can 'market' co-ordination. And that is why the workers' movement has regularly privileged an *alliance* with this pole (competence) of the dominant class against the other, endeavouring to uncouple and hegemonise it.

The class struggle for a classless society is, in a sense, a struggle in the name of the claims made by modernity. But this does not boil down to achieving what capitalism only promises. In fact, such claims do not exist, have no determinate substantive content, outside of the struggles that generate them historically as principles without which societies cannot legitimately be governed. They would merely be insubstantial abstractions in the absence of social struggles, which alone impart concrete content to them. Thus, liberty-equality acquires a new content when women's struggle wrests universal suffrage or some right from the patriarchy, when trade unions force firms to recognise them, when homosexuality gets itself acknowledged as of equal value, when oppressed peoples drive out the colonisers or free themselves from their economic and cultural dominion. To decline the major figures of logic, the promise of the *universal* is meaningful only in and through its *particular* contents, the outcome of *singular* acts and events. The metastructural claims with which, emulating Marx in *Capital*, the exposition must begin, are only ever posited in their concrete content through such *practices*, which are always to be construed as 'struggles for recognition'. These practices emerge in the framework of determinate social *structures*, constitutive of a particular form of society (they are quite simply inconceivable elsewhere). But they are not to be understood as mere reflections of these structural forms. They only open up definite spaces of possibility, which alter as their *tendencies* unfold historically.

What is specific about the struggle of the exploited in the modern form of society is that, in as much as it exists, it is contrary to the *logic* of capital, which is that of modern class power: the *abstraction* of profit, abstract wealth, and the destruction of 'concrete' wealth. It is directed towards the use-values whose use is truly 'valuable' for all. That is why such struggle, as it develops, increasingly emerges in its cultural and ecological dimensions. It is organised by critical forces that are always resurgent within culture, by 'avant-gardes' which are regularly there at the appointed hour, even though, of necessity, they cannot be foreseen.

Thus, in the dialectical form represented by the *circle* 'metastructure/structures/practices' – a circle because metastructural claims are only ever given in practices – is formulated the Marxian concept of the modern class struggle. However, we cannot, in the name of this dialectical form, invoke a 'dialectic of history', a historical teleology. The dialectic is what makes it possible to transcend the ontological naivety which counter-poses structure to metastructure as what is to what should be, the real to the ideal, the balance of forces to legitimate values. It thus makes it possible to tackle the actual social process realistically. But its discourse is only acceptable within the limits of this definite object. It does not authorise the counter-position of 'man' to 'nature' (of which he only forms a part) as 'subject' to 'object'; or the conception of a dialectical development which is the dynamic of history itself, as the realisation of man and humanity. For history does not possess this teleological character, this subjective intention towards an end. That pertains exclusively to the designs that human beings, individually or collectively, can formulate, and which history carries off in a flux, of which we can only seek to analyse the tendencies.

More precisely, *practices* can only be conceived in determinate social *structures*, and always with reference to metastructural *claims*. But they only emerge in conformity with the objective *tendencies* of these structures, which constantly alter the relations between the productive forces and relations of production and, therewith, the projects that can be envisaged. And this in the swarm of *overdeterminations* and *discrepancies* whereby past forms never stop interfering, and being reinterpreted, in the present; in the *uncertainty* of *conjunctures*, by way of unforeseeable *events*, whose consequences are invariably incalculable. Hegel's dialectical lesson is thus inscribed in Spinoza's materialist lesson, as human action in a history that is ultimately natural. This is a Marxism of finitude: men do not make history.

And yet they act in it. No one has a monopoly on action in history. But the great mass of the exploited and the oppressed have every reason to demand their share of it, and constantly to refashion the project of 'changing the world'. No historical failure will be able to dispossess them of their capacity to project a future in accordance with their self-proclaimed dignity. Technological changes have been used by neoliberalism to destroy the mechanisms of solidarity constructed over generations of political confrontation and social invention. They can be summoned as witnesses against the great projects referred to as 'socialism' and 'communism'. In reality, however, embodied in increasingly intellectual forms of work, demanding ever more intellectual exchange, communication, and mutual responsibility (particularly in the face of the dangers that production now poses for the future of the human species and its environment), they are such as to reawaken, on an ever broader canvas, modern struggles for emancipation, eliciting unprecedented capacities to 'see them through to a conclusion'. And that is why the revolution never dies or why, at any rate, its death cannot be anticipated in the horizon of modernity.

There is thus a whole series of articles in this Companion *that aims to extend the principles required to analyse practices in the age of capitalism. There are also texts that provide bearings in the debate which seeks to make it possible to think together the dialectical heritage represented by the Frankfurt school and Gramscian traditions, and which underlies controversies over the theoretical status of* Capital *(through authors as varied as Kôzô Uno, Helmut Reichelt, or Hans-Georg Backhaus), and the materialist exigencies reformulated by Althusser, in a Spinozist tradition exempli-*

fied by Gilles Deleuze and also taken up by Toni Negri, but to which the intersecting reflections of G.A. Cohen and Jon Elster on historical materialism also attest in their different way. And a large portion of it, naturally, is devoted to cultural criticism, from Adorno and Lefebvre to Raymond Williams and Fredric Jameson.

Chapter Two

The Crises of Marxism and the Transformation of Capitalism

Stathis Kouvelakis

> In order to arrive at a sound assessment of the change that has occurred in ideas, we must take account of the transformation that capitalism itself has undergone.[1]

Among the reasons why Marxism is a strange, even disconcerting, intellectual object is, not least, the occurrence and recurrence of its 'crises'. The term 'crisis', much overused, requires some introductory discussion, however. In what follows, the formula 'crisis of Marxism' is to be construed in a resolutely 'subjective' sense – at the antipodes, for example, of the usage when economic crises are involved. Thus, we can only speak of a 'crisis of Marxism' as a unique moment in which something rather unusual in the history of ideas occurs (have Platonists ever been heard to speak of a 'crisis of Platonism' or Kantians of a 'crisis of Kantianism'?). What this suggests is that a category of agents who identify themselves as 'Marxists' declare that they live their relationship to this theoretical object in the form of a 'crisis'. In other words, 'crises of Marxism' are conjunctures when the statement that 'there is a crisis of Marxism'

---

[1] Sorel 1982, pp. 237–8.

is predominantly internal – when this statement serves, in other words, to designate the experience of 'Marxists' when they define their own relationship to this referent.

From this self-referential definition follow several consequences, which are less seemingly tautological. First of all, the 'crises of Marxism' are definitely not the same as the 'deaths of Marxism', periodically proclaimed from an external and, in general, openly polemical standpoint. The latter pertain to a quite different logic, in other words, to the 'spectral' dimension of the presence of Marxism in history. What these exorcism sessions tell us is essentially that, like the dead who are feared not to be at rest, Marxism never stops haunting our present (how else are we to explain the repetition-compulsion that drives such ritual putting to death?). They also tell us that every 'death' of Marxism will invariably be followed by its 'return'[2] on the occasion of a changed conjuncture, like the one we are doubtless currently witnessing.

In a way, Marxism escapes the spectral repetition of death and resurrection only to enter into crisis, and this is something that gives it a rather disturbing resemblance to psychoanalysis and the 'natural' sciences (compare with the 'crisis of physics' at the beginning of the nineteenth century, concomitant, moreover, with the first crisis of Marxism).[3] Is this a merely formal analogy? It would appear not, in so far as, like the natural sciences and psychoanalysis, Marxism can only be defined as a combination of theory/practice stamped by a radical historicity, and not as a doctrinal corpus formed *sub specie aeternitatis*, or rather, let us say that it only presents itself thus as a result of certain conjunctures. In this connection, 'crises' are moments when, generating 'controversies' that witness a confrontation between contradictory theses, the discrepancies internal to the theory/practice mix are paraded in the full light of day and pose the question of a wholesale reorganisation of the theoretico-practical configuration.

Now – and this is where the convergence with the natural sciences ends – it is completely illusory to think that the 'crises of Marxism' are simple transitional moments, separating two more or less stable states of theory/practice –

---

[2] For a development of this theme, see Kouvélakis 2000.

[3] Lenin begins the section of Chapter 5 of *Materialism and Empirio-Criticism* entitled 'The Crisis in Modern Physics', with this quotation from 'the famous French physicist Henri Poincaré': 'there are "signs of a serious crisis" in physics': Lenin 1968, p. 252. On this episode, see Lecourt 1973.

whether this transition is conceived in the manner of a succession of paradigms enjoying consensus in the scientific community (T.S. Kuhn's 'scientific revolutions'); or as the crossing of internal thresholds of scientificity thanks to repeated 'epistemological breaks' (the French tradition of Bachelard and Canguilhem). This is because Marxism is *constitutively*, from Marx's contribution itself, including the internal discrepancies, limits and incompletion of his *œuvre*, crisis theory. This is an effect of, and reaction to, the shock wave that the founding event of modernity (the French Revolution and its repercussions) set off in the sphere of theory and culture. A reflection of the original crisis of bourgeois society and emergent capitalism, whose absolute equivalence with the actuality of uninterrupted revolution it posited, Marxism is such, above all, in that it duplicates the crisis within the impurity of its theoretico-practical configuration. Inseparable from an imperative of 'scientificity' (which no real Marxism, not even the most ferociously 'anti-positivist', has been able to do without), Marxism conceived this in a wholly original manner (on this point, only psychoanalysis sustains comparison, as Althusser judiciously noted),[4] since in the final analysis it refers to nothing other than an intrinsically agonistic field, a *tendency struggle* – a struggle that focuses in itself, via the mechanism of displacement of lines of demarcation and its capacity to reformulate problems, the historicity and productivity of the theory. The Marxist theoretico-practical mix can only assert itself as the bearer of the 'spirit of scission' (Sorel) immanent in the capitalist order in so far as it (re)constitutes itself as a 'scissile science',[5] irreducibly divided into a multiplicity of tendencies, governed by a relationship of mutual interdependence that takes the form of confrontation.

'Fin-de-siècle' crises?

Despite its abstract character, this brief reminder of the constitutive dimension of the crisis of Marxism is necessary in order to place the conjunctures of particular crises in historical perspective. This is especially so for the two crises which, separated by about a century (end of the nineteenth century and of twentieth century), define a historical cycle of Marxism, whose effects

[4] See Althusser 1991.
[5] See Althusser 1991 and the discussion of this notion in Balibar 1991, pp. 80–9.

have not been exhausted. In these two cases, what is immediately striking on comparison of the inaugural texts (Masaryk and Bernstein for the crisis of the nineteenth century, Althusser for that of the twentieth) is the repetition of what seems like the symptomatology peculiar to the processes called crises of Marxism. We find the same inaugural observation of a crisis in the concrete forms of proletarian politics (the schizophrenia of German Social Democracy, torn between an unconsciously reformist practice and an impotent revolutionary discourse; the crisis of the workers' movement suffering in the long term the effects of the embodiment of twentieth-century revolutions as states). There is the same disquiet faced with the realisation of the unfinished and internally contradictory character of Marx's *œuvre*, even in the cornerstone of the theory – the *magnum opus, Capital*.[6] There is the same doubt about the actuality of the revolution, especially as regards its subjective conditions (the historical mission vested in the proletariat).[7] The same protest too against the primacy attributed to the 'economy' by historical materialism and against a 'determinist' and 'necessitarian' vision of social dynamics.[8] The same proclamation as well of the regenerative character and creative potential of the crisis for Marxism itself.

This last point is worth emphasising, given how forcefully it is asserted among authors who can scarcely be suspected of displaying any desire for

---

[6] Even before Volume Three of *Capital* appeared, Conrad Schmidt had launched the debate on the validity of the law of value – a debate that took off again after its publication, in particular with the interventions of Engels, Sombart and Böhm-Bawerk on the compatibility between Volumes One and Three. Generally speaking, the camp hostile to orthodoxy – with the (doubtful) exception of Labriola (see Bidet 1988) – was favourable to challenging the labour theory of value (compare Bernstein 1961, pp. 24ff, Sorel 1982, pp. 145–9, and Labriola 1934, pp. 25–9). For a general overview, see Besnier 1976. A century later, at the moment when he began to speak of a crisis of Marxism, Althusser cited the 'fictitious' character of the unity of the order of exposition in *Capital* as a first example of the 'contradictions' internal to Marx's *œuvre* (Althusser 1979, pp. 232–4).

[7] Bluntly summarising the dominant interpretation of Engels's 'political testament' within the Second International, Masaryk asserted that in it Engels pronounced 'the futility of revolution' and a rallying to 'political and parliamentary tactics' (Masaryk 1898, p. 515). Bernstein, who remained ambiguous as to the utopian or straightforwardly undesirable character of revolution, in any event sharply challenged the thesis of a proletariat that was homogeneous and revolutionary by nature (Bernstein 1961, pp. 6–12). To say the least, the 'anti-classist' and 'anti-essentialist' vigour of present-day post-Marxism (see, for instance, Laclau and Mouffe 1985) is not without precedent.

[8] This is another significant point of convergence between Bernstein and Sorel (compare Bernstein 1961, pp. 103–6 and Sorel 1982, pp. 106–9, 150–63). The importance of these themes in the post-Marxist vision of the 'plurality' and 'dispersion' constitutive of the social needs no emphasis (Laclau and Mouffe 1985, *passim*).

orthodoxy. Thus, at the very moment when he declares himself 'fully conscious that [he] differs in several important points from the ideas to be found in the theory of...Marx and Engels',[9] Bernstein defines his approach as a 'revision *in* Marxism',[10] and even as a contribution to it as a 'theory of modern society'.[11] Refusing to amalgamate 'revisionism' – a term with which he identifies – with the project of 'superseding Marx',[12] his aim is to revive the 'critical spirit' inspired by Kant,[13] and break with the 'scholasticism' of 'orthodoxy',[14] by rectifying, via the requisite updating, the 'gaps' and 'residues of utopianism'[15] that burden the theory founded by Marx.

Close on his heels, Sorel, who warmly applauded Bernstein's critique of the orthodoxy of Engels and Kautsky and even regarded it as a 'work of rejuvenation of Marxism' and a 'return to the Marxist spirit',[16] discerned in the 'crisis' and 'decomposition of Marxism', 'a great advance',[17] the beginning of a period of secularisation of the doctrine.[18] To the great displeasure of his trans-Alpine friend and interlocutor, Labriola, he carried on brandishing these terms.[19] 'Purged' of 'everything that is not specifically Marxist',[20]

---

[9] Bernstein 1961, p. 3.

[10] 'As regards theory, it would be more accurate to speak of a revision in Marxism than of an anti-Marxist revision' (quoted in Lidtke 1976, p. 349).

[11] Bernstein 1961, p. 4.

[12] Bernstein 1961, p. 213 (translation modified).

[13] 'It is not a matter of going back to the letter of what the Königsberg philosopher wrote, but to the fundamental principle of his work: the critical spirit' (Bernstein 1961, pp. 223–4; translation modified). The famous last chapter of his book ('Ultimate Aim and Tendency') has as its sub-title 'Kant against Cant'. However, Lidtke stresses that while being steeped in the neo-Kantian climate of the epoch, Bernstein never took this to its ultimate consequences (Lidtke 1976, p. 375).

[14] Bernstein 1961, p. 4 (translation modified).

[15] Bernstein 1961, pp. 25, 210.

[16] Sorel 1982, p. 182.

[17] 'The current crisis of scientific socialism marks a great advance: it facilitates the progressive movement by emancipating thinking from its shackles': Sorel 1982, p. 91.

[18] Sorel 1982, p. 215.

[19] 'Sorel has delivered himself body and soul to the *crisis of Marxism*, treats of it, expounds it, comments on it with gusto whenever he gets an opportunity': Labriola 1934, p. 179. Labriola, a careful and profound critic of Sorel, Masaryk, and Bernsteinian revisionism, while never conceding the legitimacy of the 'crisis of Marxism', nevertheless accepted the need for a 'direct and genuine revision of the problems of historical science' (Labriola 1970, p. 293). He rejected orthodoxy and revisionism alike and argued that '[s]ince this theory is, in its very essence, critical, it cannot be continued, applied, and improved, unless it criticises itself' (Labriola 1934, p. 29). Labriola's term for this theory was 'critical communism' (Labriola 1966, p. 244).

[20] Sorel 1982, p. 252.

this 'other' secularising decomposition would render Marxism once again adequate to the practice of proletarian self-organisation, concretely embodied in revolutionary syndicalism.[21] Even Masaryk, the typical positivist scholar with vaguely 'progressive' and socialist tendencies, concluded the article that publicly launched the debate on the 'crisis of Marxism' by interpreting it as the beginning of a possible renewal, if not of Marxism, then at least of socialism, which was bound to be reborn on the very basis of capitalist relations and their continued effects.[22]

In proclaiming Marxism's entry into crisis towards the end of the 1970s, and in banking on the liberating aspects of this performative statement, Althusser (as we can see) was hardly breaking new ground, contrary to what he himself seemed to think.[23] This amnesia, however, which is no real cause for surprise in an author who never attached much importance to anything outside his own extraordinarily selective and Gallocentric reading of Marx, is accompanied by an omission of a different order. Althusser, in fact, comes to 'officially launch' the crisis of Marxism without a single mention of what Marxism is the intellectual Other of: *capitalism*. There is merely a passing reference to the 'paradox' of the different paths being followed by the Communist parties in the context of 'unprecedented levels...[in]...the struggles of the working class and of the people', combined with 'the most serious crisis which imperialism has ever known'.[24] And then we pass onto serious matters: the 'theoretical

[21] 'In acting, the workers fashion real social science; they follow the paths that correspond to Marx's basic, essential theses': Sorel 1982, p. 90. Some three decades later, in a much darker context, Karl Korsch drew conclusions that were rather similar to Sorel's as regards the outcome of the 'crisis of Marxism' (Korsch 1973, pp. 166–7).

[22] Given the decline in the terms of intellectual debate that has occurred, especially in France, after two decades of violent anti-Marxist campaigns, it is worth quoting the conclusion of this article, written a little over a century ago: 'Even if Marxism was completely flawed, socialism would not collapse. It has real foundations in the clear defects of today's social organization, in its injustice and immorality, in the great material, intellectual and moral poverty of the masses. Hence the opponents of socialism would be mistaken if they thought that this crisis could be of much use to them. On the contrary, it can provide new forces for socialism, if its leaders march boldly towards the truth. This is what I feel obliged to say after having signalled the facts' (Masaryk 1898, p. 528).

[23] Whether in the text of his public intervention at the Venice conference, or in an unpublished text where he takes up the question of the crisis of Marxism (Althusser 1994a, pp. 359–66), Althusser suggests that the term has been brandished solely 'by the enemies of the labour movement', with the aim of 'intimidat[ing]' Marxists, by announcing the 'collapse' and 'death' of their theory (Althusser 1979, p. 225).

[24] Althusser 1979, p. 226.

crisis within Marxism'.[25] To say the least, the proposed reconstruction of that crisis is strange, since, having 'started in the 1930s', it went completely unnoticed by the author of *For Marx*. Althusser, loyal to his habits, was silent about the other diagnoses of a 'crisis of Marxism' issued during this period (Korsch as early as 1931 and Henri Lefebvre in 1958).[26] Moreover, after some reflections on the effects of Stalinism that are as schematic as they are unoriginal, the text lingers over the 'discovery' that Althusser seems to have made at this moment: the existence of 'lacunae', and even 'enigmas', in Marx's *œuvre* (the order of exposition of *Capital*, the state, or the problem of the working-class organisation). Althusser, however, would only dedicate a single unfinished, posthumous text to these issues.[27] In all this, at any rate, capitalism remains obstinately and utterly off-stage. As for the references to the 'struggles of the masses' scattered throughout, these are more like a ritual incantation than an analysis – if only in outline – of some concrete situation or practice.

The contrast with the crisis of the nineteenth century is, in this respect, truly arresting. A mere glance at the introductory texts suffices to indicate the acute understanding which, notwithstanding their divergent conclusions, Bernstein, Sorel or Luxemburg demonstrated as regards the overdetermination of the crisis of Marxism by extra-theoretical factors. To put it differently, if the crisis of politics that refers to Marx, above all, that of the organisations of the workers' movement, is at the centre of the controversy, it is constantly and highly systematically related to these conditions. In other words, it is linked to the great transformation which capitalism underwent at the end of the century under the dual impact of working-class struggles and the revival of the

---

25 Althusser 1979, p. 228.

26 Korsch's text is comparatively well-known (cf. Korsch 1931). However, justice should be done to the lucidity of Lefebvre, who in that monument of twentieth-century Marxist literature *La Somme et le reste* delivered a pioneering analysis of the 'crisis of philosophy' (Lefebvre 1989, pp. 9–151), and in particular, of the 'crisis of Marxism', of which the 'crisis of philosophy' was only one aspect (p. 220). This analysis was accompanied by a long study of the concrete conjuncture of the rise of Gaullism, the paralysis of the Left and of the PCF, as well as by all sorts of theoretical material which led to the extraordinary productivity of Lefebvre's interventions throughout the subsequent decades – a work at the antipodes of Althusser's self-destructive and sterile 'silence'.

27 And which ends on an interrogative note that is eloquent as to Althusser's confusion at the time: 'for to speak of what politics might be involves giving one's opinion on the party. But what does one do in the party if not politics?' (Althusser 1994a, p. 512).

cycles of accumulation, involving the extension of suffrage, the transition to a 'monopoly' phase after the crisis of 1890–5, imperial expansion, changes in the role of the state, and so on).

This perception of the 'absolute' character of the crisis, as a moment when the discrepancies in the theory and in its forms of subjective existence impacted with the changing reality of their object, is not unrelated to the extraordinary *productivity* displayed by this 'original crisis' of Marxism. It showed a real capacity to reformulate and reorder the questions around which the Marxist theoretico-practical complex had been constructed, including interpretations of the 'economic' transformation of the system (the debate on 'capitalist collapse' and the new modes of accumulation); questions of strategy (the role of parliament and the mass strike, trade unions and co-operatives); conceptions of working-class organisation (party/class relations, the place of unions); and finally, assessments of the 'imperial' realities of the new stage of capitalism (militarism, colonial expansion, the national question).

If, as Gérard Bensussan notes, it is true that the outbreak of the First World War and the ensuing disaster in the working-class movement reveal the 'objective limits' of any 'optimistic and productive' interpretation of the crisis,[28] the idea that it was precisely during this crisis that the materials which made possible the 'reversal' of the disaster into a revolutionary offensive were being prepared,[29] appears no less justified.

The end of an era of crises?

In the light of the comparison, it does not seem exaggerated to reverse the usual perceptual schemata of contemporary history. It was not the crisis of the end of the nineteenth century that had '*fin-de-siècle* Wagnerian overtones',[30] but that of the end of twentieth century, harbinger of a crushing defeat of the subaltern classes, which set off a 'process of dis-emancipation'[31] of literally epochal significance. If the performativity of Althusser's text proved effective, it was precisely due to this fact. Far from being confined, as the first optimistic

[28] Bensussan 1985, p. 263.

[29] If only in gradually clearing the way for a 'left critique' of orthodoxy, on bases that were much clearer than those of Sorel or even Labriola.

[30] Anderson 1983, p. 66.

[31] Tosel 1996, pp. 9–10.

commentators had it, to a 'regional crisis of Latin Marxism', bound up with the ebbing of the mass Communist parties and the failure of Eurocommunism,[32] the 'break' in the history of the working-class movement diagnosed in the European context of 1977 marked the beginning of a general mutation of conjuncture. This is so, even if, as regards the current topography of Marxism, the process proved uneven, releasing new zones of influence centred on the anglophone world.[33]

It remains the case that if Althusser opened the crisis, he also frustrated its unfolding and productivity, as a result of a narrow, theoreticist vision of its deep springs, of an absence of historical sense both at the level of Marxist theory and of the working-class movement. This is not unconnected to the 'depthlessness' characteristic of postmodern consciousness according to Fredric Jameson,[34] and even of a tone of 'pathos' – the very thing for which, in a familiar mechanism of 'projective displacement', he criticises the Gramsci of the *Prison Notebooks* and even Lenin in this same text.[35] All this, conveying a disarray in the immediacy of a situation of defeat, had its specific weight in the form of the 'veritable *débandade*',[36] with its train of repentance, acts of despair, and the unleashing of nihilistic drives, taken by the retreat of Marxism in the Latin world, especially in France. But it is also true, as his correspondence of the time indicates, that Althusser was conscious of his own limits and, conversely, of the imperatives that the crisis was already placing on the agenda. Evoking a time when it would be necessary to be equipped with 'concrete knowledge in order to speak of such things as the state, the economic crisis, organizations, the "socialist" countries', he confessed:

> I don't possess this knowledge and it would be necessary, like Marx in 1852, to 'begin again at the beginning'. But it is far too late, given my age, fatigue, weariness, and also solitude.[37]

To grasp the distance that separates us from this conjuncture today, it is perhaps necessary to pose the question: where do we stand with respect to this

---

[32] This is the hypothesis advance by Perry Anderson in Anderson 1983, pp. 28–30, 68–81. See the balance-sheet drawn up by Alex Callinicos below, Chapter 4.

[33] This is certainly the least questionable part of Anderson's diagnosis.

[34] Jameson 1991.

[35] Althusser 1979, p. 235.

[36] Anderson 1983, p. 32.

[37] Althusser 1994b, p. 528.

solitude? Does its echo resonate in silence and nothingness? Or does it open onto another solitude, which Althusser also had in mind[38] – the creative, liberating solitude of a Machiavelli? Without claiming to offer a definitive answer to that question, the hypothesis that I am advancing at least seeks to impart some consistency to the alternative terms of the question. In essence, the 'crisis of Marxism' is already behind us, which is by no means necessarily reassuring for Marxism. The more 'open' the period we are living through, without excluding new defeats that could lead to a definitive disintegration, is preparing at least some of the conditions required for a new 'encounter' between Marxism and mass practice and, therewith, a comprehensive radical theoretical reconstruction.

Like its inaugural act (Venice, November 1977), the end of the last crisis of Marxism can be dated with precision. It began twelve years later, nearly to the day, in Berlin, and ended in 1991 in Moscow, with the collapse of the USSR. A grand finale of the capitalist restructuring was underway since the mid-1970s under the sign of neoliberalism. The end of the states identifying with Marx and socialism put an end also to the conditions of the crisis of Marxism in two respects, which can be conveniently designated 'subjective' and 'objective'.

Subjectively, the end of the embodiment of twentieth-century revolutions in states delivered the *coup de grâce* to the organisations of the working-class movement, and the mass practices, that referred to it, even if in critical or openly oppositional fashion. With Stalinism and its descendents there also disappeared the various 'anti-Stalinisms'. In reality, the shock wave of 1989–91 affected the whole of the working-class movement, with social democracy, rapidly joined by substantial sections of the Communist parties, reacting to the removal of the 'Communist' obstacle by abandoning what had formed the basis of its identity and by rallying to the management of the new order, particularly in its imperialist dimension. The persistence of Communist parties, or parties directly derived from them, significant above all in the countries of the 'periphery', should not induce illusions. The 'international Communist movement' now belongs irrevocably to the past and this very persistence, even in the forms of the most open nostalgia, is not to be explained so much as of residues of the past, but much more as the result of, or as a reaction to,

[38] See Althusser 1999.

the new sociopolitical realities created by capitalist restructuring on a world scale.

In these conditions, it is hardly surprising to register the disappearance of any possible 'orthodoxy', but also the concomitant disappearance of any 'heresy' or 'heterodoxy', given that these notions clearly presuppose one another. This unquestionably involves a major break with any previous state of crisis of Marxism, where what was at issue in large part consisted precisely in simultaneously redefining the terms of an 'orthodoxy' and a 'revisionism'. Both of them refer to the shared reality of a Marxism that had become the ideological and doctrinal reference for mass organisations and state structures. Such an observation certainly licenses no triumphalism, since it appears to signal the end of any relationship between Marxism and organised forms of collective practice, without its future seeming to be any more assured in existing public institutions, especially higher education.[39] But, and this is the reverse side of any 'vacuum', it leaves the question of an encounter between a 'reconstructed' Marxism and the new forms of emancipatory struggle that neoliberal capitalism carries within it entirely open.

From this simultaneous collapse of orthodoxies and heresies likewise derives the other striking feature of the current 'exit from crisis': the absence of meaningful 'controversy' within the space that continues to recognise itself in the Marxist constellation (with one exception that will be dealt with below). It is as if the 'thousand Marxisms' to which André Tosel politely refers,[40] coexisted in a pacific landscape from which the need to generate controversy seems strangely absent. Given Marxism's status as a 'scissile science', a status that crisis conjunctures have amply confirmed, this surely involves an alteration of great significance, with ambiguous and unstable effects. An effect of attenuation unquestionably predominates insofar as it is in a struggle between tendencies that the productivity of Marxism finds its very principle, the cohesion of the theory, its only legitimate source. This explains, moreover, why the pacification of the theoretical field in question is strictly complementary to its

[39] In particular, this is the viewpoint of Étienne Balibar, who, abandoning his habitual aporetic and ambivalent formulations, categorically asserts: 'The century-long cycle to which I have referred (1890–1990) *certainly* marks the end of *any* mutual attachment between Marx's philosophy and an organization of *whatever kind*, and hence, *a fortiori*, between that philosophy and a State' (Balibar 1995, p. 118, my emphasis).

[40] See his contribution below, Chapter 3.

extreme fragmentation. On the other hand, if the validity of the hypothesis of the end of a historical cycle is accepted, then it is the mode of conflictuality of the previous period that has expired, precisely on account of its constitutive function. We would then be witnessing something like the end of the 'crisis-form' of Marxism, inseparable from the end of a certain 'party-form'.

In this case, the trend that is currently emerging could be interpreted as a slow reconstruction 'from cold' of the theoretical problematic, in conditions not simply of defeat – the *whole* history of Marxism, beginning with that of Marx, unfolds under the sign of defeat[41] – but through a mutation in the very status of Marxism as a theoretico-practical complex. The condition is one of maximum dissociation between activist groups adapting 'pragmatically' to a fragmentary practice, and a theory entrenched in some academic islands, where it struggles to persuade people that social transformation refers to anything other than, for example, an expansion of Habermasian communicative action or Rawlsian principles of justice.

The crisis of the new century

More profoundly, however, the hypothesis of a change of historical cycle is corroborated 'objectively' by the transformation of capitalism that certainly predated the dramatic reverse of 1989–91, but to which the latter imparted an irresistible force. The real strength of Bernstein's revisionism, archetype of all the 'post-Marxisms' of the subsequent century, consisted not so much in the 'purely' theoretical force of his arguments but in his perception of the inevitability of changes in the politics of the working-class organisations induced by the 'passive revolution' of capitalism underway in the imperialist period, particularly in its dual aspect of an enhanced capacity for sociopolitical compromises within the countries of the 'centre' and the extension of colonial violence, sustained by militarist escalation, to the outside and the periphery. Bernstein could thus allow himself to shelve the two pillars of working-class theory and practice in the nineteenth century. One is economic catastrophism, which justified the quietism of orthodoxy and which the economic growth fol-

[41] And not simply that – for this reason suspect – of a 'Western Marxism', guilty of damaging contact with bourgeois culture, as defined by Perry Anderson (1976).

lowing the crisis of 1890–5 seemed to have definitively liquidated.[42] The other is 'Blanquism', codename for the insurrectionary traditions of a working-class movement that was still widely infused with the memory of the Commune, the revolutions of 1848 and, perhaps above all,[43] of the Great Revolution and 1793. Bernstein wagered entirely on factors issued from the new equilibria of the system, which crystallysed the effects of its expanded reproduction and the conquests of popular struggle. Among these, was the dynamic of democratisation (which he deemed irrepressible) triggered by the extension of the suffrage in several European countries and by the abolition of the anti-socialist law in German; the strength of rapidly expanding co-operatives and trade unions; the expansion of the 'middle classes'; the increasing complexity of the social structure (especially the growing heterogeneity of the proletariat); and finally, the more prosaic but quite crucial element of the pacifying effect anticipated by the dominant classes because of the working-class movement's support for a policy of colonial expansion and defence of 'national interests'.[44]

There is no need to point out the extent to which, confronted with this resolutely offensive and prospective posture, conducted – under the sign of 'Marx...against Marx'[45] – by an executor of Engels's will possessed of great independent-mindedness and unquestionable intellectual honesty, the response of orthodoxy – Kautsky but also, initially, Luxemburg[46] (with the

---

[42] In this sense, Gustafsson's formulation, which is certainly one-sided, contains an important truth: 'the revisionist tendency of the 1890s was, in the last analysis, the consequence of the cyclical economic boom that started at the beginning of the decade' (Gustafsson 1976, pp. 275–6).

[43] As Eric Hobsbawm has stressed, throughout the nineteenth century, in the eyes of the revolutionary working-class movement it was 'Jacobinism' that appeared to furnish the key to the problem bequeathed by the defeats of 1848–50 (Hobsbawm 1990, pp. 40–1). In contrast, notwithstanding diametrically opposed motives, it was a shared desire to have done with the resonance of the Jacobin tradition that explains the considerable support Sorel gave to Bernstein, despite the latter's moderation and, more serious still, his praise for liberalism – supreme sin for the theoretician of revolutionary syndicalism. It is scarcely surprising to find the old refrain of the rejection of the 'Jacobin' conception of revolution resurfacing in 1980s post-Marxism (see Laclau and Mouffe 1985, pp. 177–8).

[44] Significantly, Bernstein concluded his eulogy of colonisation and German expansionism with the statement that '[t]he higher civilization ultimately can claim a higher right': Bernstein 1961, pp. 178–9.

[45] Bernstein 1961, p. 27.

[46] It should not escape us that *Reform or Revolution* (Luxemburg 1970, pp. 33–90) largely adopts the arguments of Kautsky, to whom Luxemburg was very close at this time, also personally. It was only from the debate on the mass strike, fuelled by the Belgian experience of 1902–3, and, later still, from the 1905 Russian revolution, that

exception – decisive, it is true – of the issue of militarism and colonialism) – could seem weak. Moreover, the perception of this first crisis of Marxism in the Latin world (Sorel, Labriola) offers ample evidence of this.

In this connection, the 'post-Marxism' constructed during the last crisis of Marxism, and which has found its bible in the work by Chantal Mouffe and Ernesto Laclau,[47] is a 'poor man's Bernsteinism', or, in other words, a revisionism that is unaware of itself in as much as it is mistaken as to both its novelty and its object. The results of the 'controversy' that it launched (the sole exception to the tendency to a pacification of the Marxist field)[48] soon appeared meagre enough, from the standpoint both of theoretical productivity and of the theory/practice relationship. On the one hand, the sophistication of the discourse around 'hegemony', 'multiple subject positions', and 'radical, plural democracy' cannot disguise an increasingly patent rallying-call to liberal common sense and to a state of fragmentation of social practices severely tested by a capitalist offensive. On the other hand, the stance of reaffirmation in the theory's core, albeit often judicious, and sometimes accompanied by nostalgia for a return to a mythical 'classical Marxism', has proved inadequate when confronted with the realities of the capitalism's new 'passive revolution',[49] and is just as cut off from collective practice as that advocated by 'neo-revisionism'. The latest episode in the cycle of the crises of Marxism ended with a rather disappointing balance-sheet.

During this time, capitalist restructuring has been following its course. The collapse of the 'socialist' states opens up vast zones of 'external' expansion for it. The dismantling of the social compromises of the Keynesian period opens up no less sizeable 'internal' zones of penetration. The working classes are undergoing the experience of a traumatic reproletarianisation on a world scale. Nation-states are enjoined to redeploy their forms of intervention in a way that is exclusively functional for the new requirements of accumulation,

---

the Left of the party (Luxemburg, Mehring, Liebknecht) gradually detached itself from the Kautskyite centre.

[47] Cf. Laclau and Mouffe 1985.

[48] See, in particular, Callinicos 1989, Geras 1990, and Wood 1998 [1986]. Significantly, both the 'neo-revisionist' literature and that of its opponents is exclusively anglophone – an additional indication of the displacement of the main zones of Marxism outside of Southern Europe.

[49] For a reading of capitalist transformation in the light of this Gramscian concept, see Kouvélakis 1996.

while a new imperialist order is being established that is now without any counterweight of the state variety. Faced with this reality, which resoundingly confirms the dialectic of continuity and discontinuity peculiar to capitalism, the question arises whether Fredric Jameson's thesis, according to which 'a postmodern capitalism will always call a postmodern Marxism into existence over and against itself',[50] has found initial confirmation?

Various facts prompt a response in the affirmative. Unnameable at the moment of its triumph, constantly veiled under the term of 'market economy', the system is increasingly referred to by its proper name. Few now doubt the relevance of the term 'capitalism' to refer to the reality that is now expanding on a planetary scale and the explosive contradictions that it harbours. It is not fortuitous if it is precisely in this conjuncture that Marxism has progressed in the direction of the 'cognitive mapping' for which Jameson called when he formulated his hypothesis on postmodernism as the cultural logic of late capitalism.[51] Whether in the recent works on the current crisis of capitalism always grasped in the historical medium-long *durée*, as those of Robert Brenner, Gérard Duménil and Dominique Lévy; or of the 'historico-geographical materialism' launched by David Harvey; or the approaches to the national phenomenon proposed by Benedict Anderson; or the study of postmodernism as the 'cultural logic of late capitalism' initiated by Jameson,[52] Marxism has unquestionably demonstrated a capacity to think the present which, while not supplying any guarantees for the future, offers the best refutation of prognoses of collapse or death.

There is something more, however: naming the system is in fact both a condition, and also a sign, which indicates that, subjectively speaking, something different has become possible. Not without being obliged to undertake the requisite labour of self-criticism, the experience of defeat is beginning to be superseded. The resumption of social struggles on a world scale, which was clear from the mid-1990s onwards (from Korea to Chiapas), including the December 1995 movement in France, the leftward turn in Latin America, or the extension of 'anti-globalisation' mobilisations in the wake of Seattle,

[50] Jameson 1993, p. 195.
[51] Jameson 1991, pp. 399–418.
[52] For references to these works, readers are referred to the Bibliography at the end of this volume.

doubtless marks the entry of the new capitalist order constructed under neoliberal hegemony into irreversible crisis. There is no doubt that the future of Marxism, which always pays a heavy price for its status of crisis theory *par excellence*, will be played out here, in the patient reconstruction of the conditions for the collective struggle for liberation.

Chapter Three

The Development of Marxism: From the End of Marxism-Leninism to a Thousand Marxisms – France-Italy, 1975–2005

André Tosel

Preliminary reflections

The inglorious end of Soviet Communism, the dissolution of the USSR, the victory of liberal democracy, and especially that of the capitalist world economy, seemed to mark the end of Marxism and close down any possibility of renewal. The hegemonic intellectual system in political, economic and social terms is liberalism (more or less social, or more or less neoliberal). Behind the anti-totalitarian defence of human rights, the market has imposed itself as the definitive institution of postmodernity. Marxism supposedly belongs to a past of errors and horrors. Such is the credo of the *la pensée unique*, of the world-view which, reversing the hopes of Gramsci, has become the common sense of the intelligentsia, and of business and political circles, and which is laid down as the religion of the individual with the full force of the means of communication. Hence, it supposedly remains to write an obituary column on the now definitive death of Marx and Marxisms and release thought to confront the 'the time of the end of the grand narrative of emancipation'.

But things are not so simple. The history of the years 1968–2005 is extremely uneven. While Marxism-Leninism sank ever deeper into irreversible crisis and moved towards its end, several major operations of theoretical reconstruction testified to the contradictory vitality of the hard core of Marx's *œuvre*. Between 1968 and 1977, the last attempts at a revival of Marxist theory in the tracks of the Third International, or on its margins, emerged. They involved proposals for intellectual, moral and political reform addressed to the Communist parties, whether in power or opposition, by theoreticians who were members of them. The *œuvre* of the great heretics and communist philosophers experienced a final, transient blaze. György Lukács (1885–1971) contributed his last great work, *Zür Ontologie des gesellschaftlichen Sein* (1971–3), while Ernst Bloch (1885–1977) published *Atheismus im Christentum* (1968), *Das Materialismus Problem. Seine Geschichte und Substanz* (1968), and *Experimentum Mundi* (1975). In Italy, publication of the original edition of the *Quaderni del carcere* (1975) of Antonio Gramsci facilitated a better appreciation of the philosophy of *praxis*, by differentiating it from the interpretation offered by Palmiro Togliatti (leader of the Italian Communist Party), and made it possible to assess its potential one last time. In France, Louis Althusser (1918–90) made the debate on a new extension of the materialist science of history and its forms a major element in the last international philosophico-political discussion of Marxism, with *Philosophie et philosophie spontanée des savants* and *Éléments d'autocritique*, both published in 1974. In fact, the shadow of 1968 held out the prospect of going beyond the old orthodoxy and even allowed for hopes that the project of an escape from Stalinism from the Left might be resumed, at a time when the issue of a revolutionary reformism centred on the rise of instances of radical democratisation was being posed. The *de facto* competition between these different models for reconstructing Marxist theory, nurtured by a re-reading of Marx, contradictory in their relationship to Hegel and the dialectic (which Hegel? Which dialectic?), marked by great heterogeneity in their references to elements of the philosophical or scientific tradition, divided in their assessment of liberalism. This competition between an ontology of social being, a critical utopia of the *not-yet*, a philosophy of *praxis*, and a philosophy of materialist intervention in the sciences and philosophy, represented a moment of great intensity which the over-hasty gravediggers of Marx affect to ignore.

It was accompanied by a great deal of research and the importance of Marx's contribution and the great Marxist heresies continued to make itself felt in historical and social science. But it was very brief. In fact, it still remained to explain what had occurred in the USSR and what had really become of the October 1917 revolution; to explain how – for reasons some of which were certainly external, but others internal – an *œuvre* of unprecedented, heterodox, revolutionary critical radicalism had been able to give rise to a dogmatism as sclerotic as Marxism-Leninism, with its laws of history and handful of 'dialectical' categories, open to all sorts of manipulation, a pathetic ideology legitimating a politics that was unaware of its true character, sealing the union between a philosophy that had once again become science of the sciences and a total Party-State. The inability of Soviet Communism to reform itself in a democratic direction, its deficiency as regards human and civil rights, its economic inefficiency in satisfying needs whose legitimacy it acknowledged – all this rendered it incapable of confronting the pitiless war of position that had been imposed on it since its foundation. The argument from the gulag became universal and wholly delegitimised Marx and the reconstructions of the Marxist heretics, subjecting them to the same verdict of infamy. Much of the Marxist intelligentsia, which had revelled in ruminating on Jean-Paul Sartre's thesis – that Marxism is unsurpassable as long as the moment of which it is the expression has not been surpassed (the thesis of *Search for a Method* of 1957, which became the introduction to *Critique of Dialectical Reason* in 1960)[1] – reckoned that the hour of liberation from the imposture of the century had struck. Most joined the ranks of liberalism and Karl Popper's falsificationist epistemology. The self-dissolution of the largest Communist party in Europe (the Italian), which abandoned the ambiguous principles of Eurocommunism to join the Euro-Left and take the name of Party of the Democratic Left, and the general crisis of strategy experienced by the Western Communist parties, which covered with a Marxist fundamentalism their rapprochement with classically social-democratic positions, all equated to the West-European equivalent of the implosion of the USSR after the fall of the Berlin Wall.

And yet, beneath this spectacular obliteration of a culture, free, pluralistic research continued. However, it had now lost one of its erstwhile major characteristics – its link with identifiable political forces and social actors (as compact as the working-class movement), which capitalist modernisation was in the process of violently dispersing. The disappearance of the party intellectual,

[1] See Sartre 1968, p. 7.

the fading of the figure of the intellectual as critical consciousness and the emergence of the figure of the intellectual as expert, did not represent an episode in the end of history, summoned to contemplate itself in the marriage between liberal-representative democracy and the sovereign market that had finally been effected. Marx continued to be the subject of topical re-readings and represented a moment in attempts to revive a critical theory commensurate with the new era, different from the reconstructive endeavours ventured by the great communist heretics of the previous period. Rather than an end of Marxism, what occurred was the diffuse and, above all, well-nigh impotent flowering of a thousand Marxisms, as the historian of the world economy Immanuel Wallerstein has nicely put it.[2] The problem is an adequate assessment of this situation, which frustrates the hopes of Marxism's undertakers.

The immediate cause of the paradoxical emergence of a thousand Marxisms is no mystery. It stems from the dynamic of global capitalism and the emergence of new contradictions, on the one hand, and from the unique status of Marx's thought, on the other. Let us begin with the second point. The fate of this thought, which (to adopt Henri Lefebvre's expression) became a world, is not comparable to that of any other philosophy. In the course of a century, it underwent developments that extended it to the human race and prior to its last crisis it had ended up, in its Leninist form, inspiring a third of humanity. If the hopes of emancipation it aroused were as boundless and overweening as the disillusionment caused by the terrible and terrifying defeat of the Bolshevik Revolution, and if we must not confuse Marx with Lenin, Lenin with Stalin, and Stalin with Mao Zedong, there remains an enormous bloc of ideas common to these Marxisms and their aberrations. Among them are the idea that it is possible to put an end to the domination and exploitation which stick to the capitalist mode of production like Nessus's shirt, or the idea that capitalist social being can be subject in its very immanence, in its economic, political, social and cultural forms, to a critique that will only end only when it does. This thinking, which is also a bloc of practices derived from Marx, developed in the context of extraordinary internal oppositions within these Marxisms, generating contradictory orthodoxies (Kautsky/Lenin, Stalin/reconstructive Marxist heresies, Tito/Mao, etc.). This development was

[2] See Wallerstein 1991.

always discontinuous, just as the relationship to Marx, whose unfinished work was only partially known, was always fragmentary. Each generation has had to discover its own Marx (to paraphrase the title of a famous article by the young Gramsci) and has also had to draw on a changing corpus. We need only think of the fact that Volumes Two and Three of *Capital* only became available at the end of the nineteenth century, that the 1844 *Economic and Philosophical Manuscripts* and *The German Ideology* were only accessible at the end of the 1930s, and that the major texts of 1858–63, including the *Grundrisse*, were only really usable and used after 1945. This régime of discontinuous development and recurrent crisis is thus the *de facto* norm for the existence of a body of thinking that has simultaneously altered the historico-social world. There would then be nothing to prevent us formulating the hypothesis that the deep crisis affecting Marxism from within is the very mode of existence and resurrection of the Marxist phoenix.

If it is wholly illegitimate to conclude that Marxism, which is fated to be transformed, and which only exists in the open-ended series of its forms, has arrived at its final end. We must go much further. The discontinuous existence of Marxism also stems from its specificity, which is that, before 1914, and again after 1917, it sought to tie itself to a real political movement. This movement, created by the contradictions of the capitalist socio-historical world, can only maintain itself in being when engaged in a 'revolutionary' transformation of the established order, embodied in the unwavering forms of practical resistance mounted by social forces subject to capitalist domination. If its global expansion up to 1991 – date of the end of the USSR – seems to give it some resemblance to a secular religion, with its orthodoxies and heresies, with its ineradicable divorce between utopian promise and practical fulfilment, it remains the case that Marxism has been more international than the most universal of religions, and in a different way. It was born out of the limits, contradictions and insufficiencies of the liberal order – that other secular religion. It may be that this liberal order in its neoliberal form only won a Pyrrhic victory in 1991. Certainly, this date clearly marks the end of a historical cycle that began in 1848 with the emergence of the social question and the national question. Third-International Marxism was not wrecked solely by its democratic deficit, which cancelled the prospect of a revolutionary outcome to the social question and a supersession of the crisis of liberalism. It was also broken by its internationalist deficit, by its inability to deal with the national question in the twentieth century in the context of the world economy. But it appears increasingly clear that the victory of globalised, rationalised capitalism, theoretically sanctioned and prepared by the hegemony of liberalism, issued in a new, unprecedented crisis of this new liberal order. The world economy is faced with the globalisation of a new social question, which betokens mass dis-emancipation and proletarianisation in the capitalist centres, and a decline (differentiated, obviously) in the living conditions of vast numbers of human beings, all of this accompanied by a staggering transfer of social wealth to what must be called a ruling class that is ever more concentrated and yet divided by the ruthless economic war its fractions are waging. This same world economy simultaneously confronts various national questions, often racialised into ethnic questions, and rooted in the transnational management of the international labour force and in the market's contradictory differentiation. The ambiguous current affirmation of a thousand Marxisms is thus the harbinger of the incipient, unprecedented crisis of the new liberal order and its forms of thought. Nothing is guaranteed – neither the historical capacity of these neo-Marxisms to think and transform this new period, nor the ability of liberalism to identify its crisis and control its results in a way that is compatible with the systemic imperatives of the capitalist mode of production. The thousand Marxisms likewise take an unprecedented form that will have to be examined, if only because the end of the coercive (and always provisional) unity of a Marxist orthodoxy renders their pluralism indeterminate. What, in fact, is the minimal consensus as to what may appropriately be called a legitimate Marxist interpretation, it being understood that this legitimacy is 'weak' in so far it has bid farewell to the prospect of becoming orthodoxy or even heresy? This is the very question posed by Eric Hobsbawm, one of the general editors of the most recent history of Marxism.[3]

In any event, one thing is certain: the period which began in 1991 is that not of the end of Marxism, but of the end of Marxism-Leninism as a single, dominant orthodoxy and, by a different token, of the great Marxist heresies, insofar as they were secretly haunted by hopes for the one true Marxism. Faced with the crisis that threatens the new liberal order at the point of its seeming triumph both over Soviet Communism and over all anti-systemic

[3] Hobsbawm 1982, pp. 36ff.

movements (the working-class movement and the national liberation and anticolonial movement, both of them stably integrated), Marx's thought retains an enormous critical potential on which the thousand Marxisms will be able to draw. For, as long as capitalism dominates, it demands a critique, dictated by capitalism's own self-criticism in its forms of existence. And Marxism will be able to be appealed to, transformed, reconstructed, reworked, in and through the renunciation, without any nostalgia, of the old certainties (on the ultimate fate of capitalism, the univocal forms of the old class struggle, the comparative merits of plan and market, the kinds of democracy required for a transition, the very meaning of this transition, the place and content of a labour freed from exploitation). Separated from the political practice of the old Communist parties, in search of a new, problematic link between theory and practice, the thousand Marxisms represent the fragile form of the broken, discontinuous continuity of the Marxist tradition. Once again, as Hobsbawm has pointed out, at some stage or other of their development they are vulnerable to the resurgence within them of a Marxist fundamentalism. A fundamentalism neurotically fixated on rehashing certain points identified with the hard core of the theory (the generic importance of the class struggle, not analysed in its current, displaced forms; denunciation of the exploitation of workers in ignorance of debates on the centrality of a labour that is in the process of becoming non-central; unqualified condemnation of what is alleged to be reformism or revisionism; scorn for the requisite rectification and reworking; abstract maximalism; and so on).

It will be difficult to conceive the unity of a capitalism reproduced in its mechanism of exploitation and transformed in its component parts and practices. It will also be difficult to reconstruct a link between the analysis of this capitalism and a politics of profound yet always specific changes; to reformulate hopes for a better society without once again wrapping it in the illusion of finally realising a perfect society; to impart to the inevitable eschatology the unquestionably reduced, but all the more militant form of a stubborn, always determinate struggle. It will be still more difficult to produce models that integrate a self-criticism of the historical experience supported by previous Marxisms and a critique of the forms of globalised capitalism. But the open crisis of liberalism is the objective foundation for the thousand Marxisms. Of itself, this crisis supplies no guarantee of success for the simultaneous supersession of the old Marxisms (plus the obsolete elements in Marx) and of liberalism.

But the task is on the agenda and it will be a history which the neo-Marxisms will make in the same way that human beings make their own history: it will be accomplished in determinate conditions and in unexpected forms.

The crisis of (and in) Marxism: problematic reconstructions and renunciations, 1975–89

This crisis exploded in the clear light of day at the end of the 1970s and was justified by the inability of Marxist theoreticians to illuminate the course of the twentieth century – to explain the evolution of the 'socialist' societies, their character and their structures, on the basis of historical materialism. Reference to the democratic deficit, denunciation of totalitarianism, insistence on the ambiguities of the Marxist theory of the state and law, renunciation of any necessitarian and finalistic philosophy of history, these reinforced the claims of social and political liberalism, rather than giving rise to positive, genuine theoretical reconstructions. If the former great heresies continued to fuel inter-Marxist debates, the latter lost their philosophical purchase outside of Marxist circles and were reduced to a secondary role. The hour of neo-positivism struck, as did that of several variations on hermeneutics (whether Heideggerian, postmodernist or otherwise) and of a return to various neo-Kantian or phenomenological philosophies of the subject (theological or otherwise). Marxist circles underwent a process of open or creeping disintegration, bound up with the marginalisation (France and Spain), social-liberal transformation (Italy), or implosion (Eastern Europe) of the Communist parties. This particular crisis formed part of the more general crisis of capitalism which, once the *trente glorieuses* of postwar reconstruction were over, had to counter the tendency for profit rates to fall through global competition, the management of a labour-force racialised and ethnicised by the reorganisation of nation-states, the restructuring of the dominant poles in the North, and the prosecution of a war of position against the 'socialist camp'. The true objective of what revealed itself ever more clearly to be a major offensive against the welfare state and the working-class movement, and an enterprise of financial recolonisation of the Third World, was ideologically draped in the flag of the human rights so cruelly flouted in the 'socialist' countries. The crisis of Marxism seemed to find a solution in social liberalism on the theoretical level and in a social-democratic strategy of social compromise at a political level. If the election of François Mitterrand to the presidency of the French Republic, or the electoral success of the PCI, or the good performance of the German SPD could temporarily convey this impression, the moment of a major neoliberal offensive had arrived, as indicated by the success of Mrs. Thatcher's Conservatives in Great Britain and Ronald Reagan's Republicans in the United States. The crisis of Marxism still concealed that of social liberalism, just as the crisis of Communism masked that of the social-democratic experience. More than the French 'New Philosophers' – André Glucksmann and Bernard-Henri Lévy – and even the much more substantial figure of Karl Popper, it was the great shadow of Friedrich von Hayek that dominated debates. In this context, Marxism rapidly lost its relative hegemony. Depending on their personal ethics, many philosophers and intellectuals renounced it with much ado or discretely distanced themselves from it. But the bill for the failure of the century had to be paid.

The positions subsequently adopted can be reduced to three: abandonment of Marxism; an attempt to return to Marx and a minimal Marx, in the hope of a reconstruction conducted with transplants from other intellectual currents; and the preservation of Marxism as a reserve for a critical utopia, while awaiting better days for a resumption of theory. Without being able to track this evolution in its entirety, I shall restrict myself to providing some samples of the crisis and its forms by studying a zone where Marxism had known an especially striking affirmation: France and Italy.

Post-Althusserianism, deconstruction and Marxist reformation in France

France is one of the countries where the crisis of Marxism was virulent. For legitimate reasons, the argument from the gulag defended by the 'New Philosophers' hit home. Certainly, what was merely a moralistic condemnation and a complete lack of any organic philosophical conception stood in for thought. But it presented the bill for the failure of Soviet Communism, its errors and its horrors. Althusserianism had had the merit of posing the issue of what the Third International represented. If recourse to Mao soon came to seem impossible, once the violence bound up with the Cultural Revolution became known, the pursuit of a mass politics in a developed country posed the question of a knowledge of the new forms of hegemony. The debate on humanism persisted for a while and gave rise to interesting research by a figure who (before distancing himself) was an official Communist philosopher, Lucien Sève. In *Man in Marxist Theory and the Psychology of Personality* (1968; third, expanded edition, 1974), he formulated the question of an anthropology centred on the use of time as an alternative to the employment of constrained time, and demonstrated the unavoidable character of reference to the formation of an expanded moral personality. Despite interesting remarks on the problem of contradiction, Sève's limit was that he continued to refer to a relatively conventional dialectical materialism, wavering between neo-Hegelianism and neo-Kantianism (*Une introduction à la philosophie marxiste*, published in 1980). Similarly, his critique of structuralism as an ideology of the eternity of a history that had become immobile posed the question of historicity in its singularity, without resorting to improbable laws of history, and emphasised the importance of forms as material logics (the *Structuralisme et dialectique* of 1984). But the finalistic structure and guarantees of the communist goal were retained in dogmatic fashion and compromised fertile intuitions as to the plurality of dialectics.

Other projects, more sensitive to the impasse of Marxism, were attempted in a French resumption of the philosophy of *praxis*. This was the moment when, in the paradoxical wake of the Althusserian critique, Gramsci enjoyed a certain significance in France and seemed capable of supporting the political science of a hegemony in the conditions of modern capitalism at the height of its Fordist phase (see the works of Jacques Texier, Christine Buci-Glucksmann, or André Tosel's *Praxis. Vers une refondation en philosophie marxiste*, which appeared in 1984). Other instances of reconstruction, which were more highly theoretical, also attempted balance-sheets, based on real attempts to expand knowledge of society, without managing to escape from a certain isolation despite their vitality. Such was the case of Henri Lefebvre (1901–91). While pursuing his analysis of the concrete forms of capitalist modernity (*Le droit à la ville*, of 1968 and *The Production of Space*, released in 1974), he identified the statist mode of production as the greatest obstacle to emancipation and sought to demonstrate Marxism's inability to confront this crux (*De l'État*, four volumes, published between 1975 and 1978). He also pondered the balance-sheet of Marxism as a world ideology and the elements of content and method that should be inherited from it. In 1980, *Une Pensée devenue monde* made it clear that capitalist globalisation had demonstrated both Marx's perspicacity and his failure, without having exhausted his reflection on historical possibility or the indispensable utopia of the project.

Amid the retreat of French Marxism, we should highlight the importance of the enterprise of Georges Labica (b. 1931), who, strongly marked by Althusser's politicism (*Marxism and the Status of Philosophy* [1976]), accomplished the difficult undertaking of the *Dictionnaire critique du marxisme* (1982 and 1985), in collaboration with Gérard Bensussan. This allowed the already attested multiplicity of Marxisms to reveal themselves and demonstrated the essential character of a theory that it was fashionable in Paris at the time to throw out of the window. This audit made it possible to fix the limits of the retreat of Marxist theory by transforming it into an intelligent retreat, as a basis for new treatment (of which Labica himself has provided some samples).

In this period of virulent delegitimisation of Marxism, a subterranean post-Althusserian (not anti-Althusserian) Marxism maintained itself which, although increasingly bereft of any organic relationship with organisational practice and politics, was able to develop in two directions. The first would lead to the ongoing discovery of the complexity of an unfinished *œuvre*, and the other, to the continuation of a certain theoretical productivity – and all this, in the face of various denials that the Althusserian seam was completely exhausted.

As regards the first, we may note the important contribution of Jacques Bidet (b. 1945), *Que faire du 'Capital'? Matériaux pour une refondation* (published in 1985 with a second edition printed in 2000),[4] which is a critical balance-sheet and general reinterpretation of Marx's masterpiece. Confirming certain Althusserian interpretations, Bidet shows how the Hegelian dialectic is both a support and an obstacle in the method of exposition of the Marxian critique and suggests a re-examination of all the system's categories – value, labour-power, classes, wage-labour, production, ideology, economy – while stressing that the aporiae of the quantitative conception of the labour theory of value can only be resolved through an indivisibly socio-political reading which makes it necessary to think through an effectively political economy of living labour. For his part, Jean Robelin (b. 1949) extends Althusser to track the theoretical vicissitudes of the socialisation of Marx and Engels's economics and politics

[4] For the English edition, see Bidet 2007.

in the practice of the Second and Third Internationals. *Marxisme et socialisation* (published in 1989) is, in fact, a historical critique of the communist idea and of the aporiae of its realisation from the standpoint of direct democracy and councils, regarded as the only pertinent level for the revolutionary articulation of practices. Alongside these fundamentals works, underground research on heretical Marxisms and their unexplored possibilities has developed, in a trend which includes works by Gérard Raulet, Michael Löwy, and Arno Münster on Bloch; work by Nicolas Tertulian on the late Lukács.

As regards the second post-Althusserian direction, there is the original contribution of Étienne Balibar (b. 1942) who, having clarified the basic concepts of historical materialism in his contribution to *Reading 'Capital'*, restarted work on decisive categories centred on the theme of real subsumption and sought to demonstrate the permanency of the class struggle ('Plus-value et classes sociales', in *Cinq études du matéralisme historique*, published in 1974). In these years, Balibar abandoned a dogmatic constructivism to practice a sort of theoretical experimentalism, aporetic in style, and to problematise the uncertainties of the Marxist theory of the state, the party, and ideology ('État, parti, idéologie', in *Marx et sa critique de la politique*, of 1979). On the basis of this re-reading of Marx, and after assimilating Immanuel Wallerstein's theses on the world economy, Balibar showed how the class struggle is bound up with the international management of labour-power; how it is doubly overdetermined by the production of national and ethnic imaginary identities; how the potential for resistance by working classes always risks being transformed and altered by nationalist and racist forms; and, finally, how nationalism and racism imply one another (*Race, Nation, Class: Ambiguous Identities*, with Immanuel Wallerstein, appeared in 1988). Balibar thereby creatively refutes all those who had rushed to conclude the exhaustion of the Althusserian stimulus, which he continues while maintaining a relationship with it that is at once critical and constructive (see the collection *Écrits pour Althusser*, of 1991). Thus continues the enterprise tragically interrupted by the suicide of Nicos Poulantzas (1936–80), who had sought in more abstract fashion to establish the general lines of a structural theory of political practice (*Political Power and Social Classes*, first published in 1968) and to rethink the state's functions in a relational conception of power (*State, Power, Socialism*, 1978).

Moving in the same direction, but in a sharply polemical relationship with Althusserianism, accused of ignoring the reality of the dynamic of the productive forces grasped in their singularity, is the research of Yves Schwartz. In *Expérience et connaissance du travail* (1988), he shows that through the repetition of the distance between prescribed work (the norms of capitalist productivity in their constant adjustment to the technological and social revolution in the labour process) and real work, human labour-power (or rather the productive act), conceived by its agents in the first person, focuses and reshapes the unexplored configurations of existence, history, thought and language. This approach makes it possible to open a discussion with other theoreticians like Jean-Marie Vincent, already author of *Fétichisme et société* (1973) and *La Théorie critique de l'École de Francfort* (1976). In *Abstract Labour: A Critique* (1987), he proposes a comparison between the Marxian critique of political economy and the Heideggerian deconstruction of technicist ontology, envisaging a prospect of action beyond productivism, centred on democracy understood as a transformation of action and an art of living. Finally, an attempt at a balance-sheet of the achievements and problems of historical materialism was attempted by Tony Andréani (1935), who in *De la société à l'histoire* (1989) simultaneously posed the issue of modes of production and of anthropology. The latter received an important contribution from Maurice Godelier (b. 1934), who gave his career as a Marxist ethnologist (*Horizon, trajets marxistes en anthropologie*, of 1973) a kind of systematisation in *The Mental and the Material* in 1984. The symbolic is co-constitutive of the social relationship in a way that differs according to social forms (we should not conflate the symbolic order bound up with societies in which kinship relations are the relations of production and societies where economic relations of production are directly determinant).

All these bodies of research propose a kind of critical re-reading of Marx and it would be appropriate to clarify the doctrinal minimum on which they concur in characterising themselves as 'Marxist'. In any event, even if the Pyrrhic victory of the 'socialist' new Left at the time consigned them to a limited readership, by establishing social-liberal theoreticians resigned to the eternity of capitalism; and if it briefly made people believe in the virtues of a politics of opinion, disconnected from any substantive critique of neocapitalist social relations, piloting so-called 'modernisation', they did more than simply resist. They explored the limits and impasses of this modernisation; in their fashion, they updated the anticapitalist passion of which the old Lukács spoke – and this in full awareness of the irrevocably dated, finished and unviable character of the organisational forms and strategies of historical Communism. Their own weakness precisely consisted in their separation from any political process capable of positively translating their critical substance.

The decomposition of the philosophy of *praxis* and returns to Marx in Italy

Italy is a unique case. The country of the largest and most liberal European Communist party, rich in a strong and distinctive Marxist tradition (that of Togliattian Gramscianism or the philosophy of *praxis*) experienced a rapid dissolution of this tradition. The declared strategy of conquering hegemony was ever more patently transformed into a simple democratic politics of electoral alliances. Historicism, which was more Togliattian than Gramscian, entered into an irreversible crisis. It had hitherto succeeded in combining, in a certain tension, the abstract, general perspective of a transformation of the capitalist mode of production and the definition of a policy of reforms that was supposed to realise the end of the process, and which found its confirmation in the real movement – that is to say, in the strength of the party and its mass reality. If this historicism spared Italian Marxism the experience of Stalinist diamat, and if it also long permitted it to avoid reverence for general historical laws, forecasting the conditions of possibility for a hegemonic revolutionary shift, it nevertheless ended up being diluted into a tactics bereft of any perspective, while the preservation of a link with the 'socialist camp' gave credence to the idea of a duplicity in the strategy itself.

At any rate, what was forgotten was that Gramsci had attempted to conceptualise a revival of the revolution in the West in a situation of passive revolution that assumed the reactivation of the popular masses and the construction of democratic situations going beyond the parliamentary framework.

This is why the Gramscian research still being conducted is obsessed by an increasingly liberal-democratic updating of the theory and reaches its limits when it steps beyond the analysis of the classic theme of modernity. Such was the case with the conference organised by the Istituto Gramsci, and published in 1977–8, *Politica e storia in Gramsci*. We must certainly take account of the work of the specialists who did so much to edit the *Quaderni* and clarify their internal structure and the dynamic of Gramsci's thought (among other,

V. Gerratana, N. Badaloni, G. Francioni, F. Lo Piparo, L. Paggi, G. Vacca), or to take the measure of historical materialism (G.M. Cazzaniga, M. Di Lisa, A. Gianquinto). Similarly, we must acknowledge the scholars who have continued to study Marx seriously in order to clarify the role of the real abstraction of labour (for example, R. Finelli and M. Mugnai), or who have resumed examination of the early works (F.S. Trincia) or of the 1861–3 *Manuscripts* (again, Badaloni). But, in fact, the philosophy of *praxis* lost the link with its analytical programme that had constituted its specificity. In some instances, (Biaggio De Giovanni to name but one) the tendency was for it to be drawn back to its actualist origins in Gentile's philosophy.

Corresponding to this dilution was the disappearance of the alternative line that had constituted a counter-weight to Gramscianism in the 1960s: the work of Galvano Della Volpe (1895–1968). The methodological call to conceive Marx's moral Galileanism in accordance with a Humean-Kantian scientific theory of determinate abstraction, and to abandon any Marxist-Hegelian dialectic as metaphysical speculation that made it impossible to envisage the determinate logic of a determinate object, was heeded only in its deconstructive aspect. Certainly, Della Volpeans like Mario Rossi (with his monumental study *Da Hegel a Marx*, appeared between 1960–70), or Umberto Cerroni (with such research in political theory as *La Libertà dei moderni*, in 1969, or *Teoria politica e socialismo*, in 1973), continued to produce work. But Della Volpe's scientific concerns were eventually translated into the language of Popper's fallibilist empiricism and turned into a polemic against Marx. Exemplary in this regard was the parabola of Lucio Colletti (1924–2000). His Marxist work is concentrated in *Hegel e il marxismo* (1969). Rejecting the Hegelian distinction between analytical understanding and dialectical reason, it defended the universality of the scientific method via hypothesis and experimentation. Marx, the scientist, had founded a sociology that explains the laws of the capitalist system by linking them to the generalisation of abstract labour and the reification this involves. The horizon of the theory was a struggle against this abstraction become reality, against this alienation-reification (which Della Volpe had missed). Liberation must result in a different set of laws. But very rapidly, Colletti rejected the scientificity of this sociology, which fashioned its unity on the labour theory of value, and separated the romantic critique of alienation from an objective approach. In particular, he questioned the theory of dialectical contradiction, which he replaced by real opposition. Things accelerated and the labour theory of value was rejected on the basis of the classic problem of the transformation of values into prices, which was highlighted by a generation of economists who had also reformulated Marx's critique downwards (C. Napoleoni, P. Garegnani, or M. Lippi). Having started out from an anti-revisionist and scientific (or scientistic) Marxism, Colletti left Marxism behind in stages, aligning himself with Popper, whose falsificationist epistemology and political options in favour of social engineering focused on social amelioration he defended. *A Philosophico-Political Interview* (1974), *Tra marxismo e no* (1979), and finally *Tramonto dell'ideologia* (1980) are the milestones on this road out of Marxism.

There was resistance, above all on the part of philosophers who had participated in the debate on the Galilean scientificity of the Marxist critique, immediately followed by the debate on historicism provoked by the reception of the Althusserian problematic. The road of the return to Marx crossed that of the reference to concrete utopia. The first road was followed by Cesare Luporini (1909–92); the second by Nicola Badaloni (1924–2005). In his 1974 collection *Dialettica e materialismo*, Luporini proposed to read Marx according to Marx. Criticising historicism with Althusser for its inability to think socio-historical forms and its tendency to flatten them out on the apparently continuous flow of tactical choices, he proposed to study the different modalities of transition to a different society within a model of the uneven development of the relations of production and the superstructures. He urged further research on the levels neglected by Marx, such as the critique of politics. His interventions in the 1980s led him to radicalise his position: the return to Marx beyond Marxisms amounted to registering the failure of the latter in the dual task of reflecting on the aporiae of socialism and the displacement in the relations of production of a now victorious neocapitalism. The stress on politics consisted in linking the theme of the dictatorship of the proletariat to an archaic phase of historical materialism dominated by the liberal opposition between civil society and the state. The mature phase of the doctrine thus lacked a political theory and this, so it was implied, could not be defined in such a dictatorship. Luporini went no further and ended his career without accepting the social-democratic normalisation of the PCI turned PDS.

For his part, Badaloni did not abandon the perspective opened up by his work of 1972, *Per il comunismo. Questioni di teoria*. In numerous important studies devoted to Marx and Gramsci among others (in particular, *Dialettica del capitale*, published in 1980), he proposed a radically democratic 'reconstruction' of the theory. The latter could not count on the exacerbation of the simple antagonism between capital and labour. It was a question of conceptualising the process by which social forces separated from hegemony can control the process of self-government that gives them mastery in the reconstitution of the elements hitherto subject to capital – or, constant capital, variable capital, and surplus-value. The communist perspective is anticipated in the possibility, which has become a reality, of free time. This does indeed involve a utopia, in that immediate political consequences are drawn from a long-term morphological forecast. But this utopia has its coherence and it has maintained an island of resistance in the rapid decomposition of Italian Marxism.

The same applies to the remarkable research of Ludovico Geymonat (1908–91), whose Marxist school in the theory of knowledge declined yet more rapidly, with a few exceptions (historians of science like A. Guerragio and F. Vidoni, or neo-empiricist philosophers like S. Tagliambe). Geymonat's main aim was to re-tie the threads of dialectical materialism, scarcely implanted in Italy, by showing that neo-positivist conventionalism and Leninist materialism could correct one another. While the former was able to define any theory as an operative construction, the second introduced the dimension of the process into theory and reminded it of its realism. Far from being naïve or pre-critical, the notion of reflection, once dialecticised, aimed to re-produce the various levels of reality in accordance with an indefinite process of successive deepening. Thus, theories could be regarded as the advanced point of an infinitely rectifiable knowledge, which had its basis in a vast scientific and technical inheritance (*Scienza e realismo*, appeared in 1977). Despite Geymonat's considerable efforts as organiser of a culture open to the sciences and permeated by the political imperatives of a revolutionary transformation (as attested by the monumental *Storia del pensiero filosofico e scientifico*, published between 1970 and 1978, and which proved very original in an Italian context largely uninterested in the rationality of the sciences), his school did not survive. Many of its members ended up rallying to Popperian theory and practice, thus following Colletti.

The exhaustion of Marxism-Gramscianism-Togliattism involves more than the return of many 'Marxists' to the bosom of social liberalism. We should also take into account an opposing current which left its imprint on the 1970s and conceived of itself as a return to revolutionary Marxism. We have in mind Italian *operaismo*, which framed the workers' and students' rebellion during the turbulent year 1969, extolling 'the great subjective revolution' against the objectivist determinism which characterised the Marxism of the Communist parties of the Third International, including the Italian Communist Party itself. This movement crystallised in 1961 around Raniero Panzieri, the founder of the journal *Quaderni rossi*. This trade-unionist theoretician contested the thesis of the development of the productive forces which underpinned the trade unions and promoted the role and interests of skilled 'professional' workers. He disputed the thesis of the neutrality of science, technology, and work organisation, elements which, it was claimed, had to be taken over from capitalism. These elements were said to be marked by capitalist social relations of production, and inscribed in the process of real subsumption which reduces the function of skilled work in favour of the unskilled work of the mass worker. Using some of Marx's important writings – the chapters from the first volume of *Capital* devoted to large-scale industry and 'Maschinerie', thus putting into circulation some little-known Marxian analyses – in particular the *Grundrisse* and the unpublished sixth chapter of *Capital*, Panzieri attempted to analyse the transformations of the capitalism of the period marked by Fordism. He singled out the mass worker, alienated by the subjective expropriation which separates him from the intellectual forces of production, a dominated worker who was also often an internal immigrant, as the paradoxical figure of a potentially revolutionary subject. Indeed, this unskilled worker could turn expropriation into a class struggle for autonomy, forcing reformist parties and corporatist trade unions to reconstruct themselves as political forces. Priority was given to the struggles of these new workers, who disrupted routine and relaunched the perspective of a political subjectivisation (see 'Surplus-Value and Planning' in the anthology of *Quaderni rossi* published in 1964).

According to Panzieri, Fordist capitalism plans the labour process of the factory and must extend this capitalist planning to a society dominated by competitive anarchy. The workers' struggle for autonomy could utilise such planning to appropriate and transvalue scientific knowledge and technology for its own purposes. Panzieri thus furnished the rudiments of a theory which had the incontestable merit of re-activating a certain Marxian conceptuality – particularly that developed in the chapter of the *Grundrisse* on machine industry and the formation of the workers' general intellect. Transformations in contemporary capitalism without fetishising a then flourishing welfare state. But the transition from the autonomous struggles of the mass worker to political struggle remained problematic, due to the PCI strategy aimed at uniting workers and the supposedly healthy parts of industrial capitalism and organising them against parasitical capitalism.

As Maria Turchetto shows in her study of Italian *operaismo* and its decline in this volume, *operaismo* came to an end over this issue. Thus Panzieri's two young collaborators, Mario Tronti and Antonio Negri, broke from him in 1963 in order to found a new, more political journal, *Classe operaia*. But they, in their turn, also parted company and set off down opposite paths.

Tronti maintained the view that the struggle for workers' autonomy could not succeed unless it was transformed into a political struggle waged by a political party able to defend the autonomy of politics – that is, to invest the state and transform it into an organisation capable of shape the class conflict. Thus he reunited Lenin and Schmitt. Such is the trajectory leading from *Operai e capitale* (1966) to *Sull'autonomia del politico* (1976).

Negri doubted the capacity of the state-form to transform production and found Tronti's rallying to the PCI unproductive; he regarded Tronti's hope of transforming it into a party which would shape the outcome of conflict as utopian. He remained faithful to the idea of class subjectivity, which he opposed to the subjectivity of Jacobin organisation, and he maintained the theme of a class composition denatured by the Communist search for a historical compromise. If capitalism was increasing its domination with a paradoxical planning which went beyond the working class to affect all aspects of society, thus radicalising 'social workers', it was crucial to deepen struggles by focusing them on the prospect of the end of work. It was necessary, Negri thought, to wager on a movement contrary to the one analysed by Panzieri, namely, a revolutionary version of the development of new productive forces that would economise labour-power. Such was Negri's thesis, which he has persistently maintained ever since. From initial texts such as *Proletari e stato. Per una discussione su autonomia operaia e compremesso storico* (1976) or *La forma Stato* (1977), through the study of the *Grundrisse*, *Marx oltre Marx* (1979) and his work on Spinoza *L'anomalia selvaggia* (1981), to the historical and speculative research on *Il potere constituente* (1993), Negri sees the failure of *operaismo* and his own life story (his prison sentence for terrorist activity) as so many proofs of the irreformability of the state machine and so many stages on the way to the constitution of the *general intellect* of the social multitudes who can be freed from work. A philosophy of plenary power is reinforced by an anti-modern theory of history. Negri wishes to inscribe himself in the subversive anti-modern movement of modernity – Machiavelli, the English Levellers, Spinoza, Marx and Lenin – against the dominant natural-law and contractualist current – Locke, Rousseau, Kant and even Hegel.

Marxo-Gramsciano-Togliattism had had its day. We must now introduce the theoretical victor who had proved capable of posing the questions of political theory that indicated the attrition of historicism and the hybrid character of a political theory suspended between an affirmation of parliamentary democracy and a critique of its impasses. I am referring to Norberto Bobbio, who in 1976 collected the various interventions made during a key debate that had opposed him to Marxist intellectuals in *Which Socialism?* – a debate that was extended in a discussion of the real meaning of Gramscian hegemony (*Egemonia, stato, partito e pluralismo in Gramsci*, published in 1977). Bobbio's theses were as follows. First, there was no Marxist political theory, only a critique of politics that had never answered the question it poses by specifying which social functions the socialist state should be responsible for. The historical response provided by the Soviet experience consisted in a centralising despotism involving a regression in terms of civil liberties. Obsessed by the issue of 'who governs?', Marxist theory had fetishised the party and had not broken new ground in inventing democratic power mechanisms and procedures. Secondly, the PCI's national road to socialism and theme of progressive democracy had indeed combined respect for political pluralism and the constitutional framework. But by retaining the reference to a soviet democracy, it had created uncertainty about the preservation of the institutions of liberty once power had been conquered. The real and imperfect democracy of the Western countries had certainly not checked the real centres of economic power, or developed forms of workers' participation in the management of capitalist firms. Conversely, however, the Party-State in the East had liquidated ethical, political and cultural pluralism, as well as its rules and procedures – that is to say, liberalism's most precious legacy. Thirdly, with the ambiguous exception of Gramsci, Marxist theoreticians had made no contribution to the problems of modern democracy, or posed the relevant questions: how could the private and public administrative institutions whose structural principle was hierarchical be transformed in a democratic direction? How could popular control be exercised when the autonomisation of technical skills was on the increase?

Italian Communism was unable to respond creatively to these questions and ended up drawing with the party leadership the conclusion that seemed self-evident to many at the time. Only a liberal-social natural-rights political theory can inform the action of mass parties, which are also reduced by certain sociological developments to operating as parties of opinion, focused on democratically agreed reforms that ameliorate the lot of the worst-off. In short, Italian Marxism by and large committed suicide, through a precipitation into social-liberal metamorphoses, and ended up accepting the liberalism of theories of justice derived from John Rawls, without even retaining the sense of tragic defects characteristic of Bobbio. An example of this development is the career of Salvatore Veca, long-time director of the Feltrinelli Foundation. Having started out from a resolute defence *à la* Della Volpe of the scientificity of Marx (*Saggio sul programma scientifico di Marx*, published in 1977), he became the effective introducer of Rawls and the liberalism of the Anglo-American Centre-Left (with *La Società giusta*, in 1982, and with *Una Filosofia pubblica*, four years later, where he develops a critique of Marx based on a condemnation of the guilty absence of a genuine theory of justice).

One might conclude that what died was only that which did not possess sufficient internal strength to resist and to reconstruct theoretical resources. This is the question posed by an atypical philosopher who, in these years of liquidation, was able to proceed to a balance-sheet of Marxism focused on Italy, which opened out into an examination of the major communist heretics – Bloch, the late Lukács, Althusser – and took account of the development of critical thinking in the West, with Nietzsche, Weber, and Heidegger. The philosopher in question is Costanzo Preve (b. 1943). In *La filosofia imperfetta. Una proposta di ricostruzione del marxismo contemporaneo* (1984), he pinpointed the nihilism peculiar to capitalist productivism as the instance that had contaminated Marxism and prevented it from reforming itself by settling accounts with a whole swathe of Western rationalism. The will to mastery was identified as the shadow of a voluntarist philosophy of history that risked dashing emancipatory intentions. Preve announced a reconstruction whose elements were to be borrowed from Bloch's hermeneutic ontology, Lukács's ontology of social being, and Althusser's anti-finalistic epistemology, with each element in some sense correcting the others. This programme awaits execution and, as we shall see, is problematic. But it remains highly distinct from the liquidations that were fashionable at the time and inspired by a desire to get to the heart of things.

But it is perhaps from what is best in the Italian historicist tradition that the most resolute resistance to the liberal and neoliberal wave has been forthcoming. The historian of philosophy Domenico Losurdo (b. 1941) undertook a counter-history of the liberal tradition, in numerous substantial works devoted to Kant, Hegel, Marx, and the history of freedom in the classical German philosophy of the nineteenth century (*inter alia, Tra Hegel e Bismarck. La rivoluzione del 1848 and la crisi della cultura tedesca*, published in 1983, and *Hegel, Marx e la tradizione liberale*, in 1988). He demonstrated that, far from coinciding with the hagiographical history of liberty, liberalism has always defined human rights as those of the private property owner, has denied the universality of the concept of man that it seemed to affirm, and was extended only under the pressure of class and mass struggles, which for their part were inspired by a subordinate tendency of modernity – the civic humanism or plebeian republicanism to which Rousseau, Hegel and Marx belonged. Historiographical resistance thus operates as a theoretical basis for reviving that tendency and Marxism, which is invited to proceed to its self-criticism.

The thousand Marxisms in search of their unity, 1989–2005

The fall of the Berlin Wall, followed by the end of the USSR, ushered in the phase of a thousand Marxisms, all of them faced with capitalist globalisation and the massive enterprise of dis-emancipation that accompanied it (dismantling of the welfare state, neocolonialism, rise of nationalism and ethnicism, aggravation of North-South contradictions) – and this at a time when global wealth continued to increase and labour productivity, rather than tabling the issue of the relationship between necessary labour-time and free time, translated into persistent unemployment and a new poverty. The end of the orthodoxies/heresies dialectic, once the inability of the Communist parties to reform themselves other than by imploding or becoming mere (social-) democratic parties had become obvious, posed the question of what united the plurality of research. Long desired, in the face of the violence of the Party-

State monolith, this pluralism made Marx and Marxisms available. If theoretical readings and essays could now develop, confronting one another on such crucial points as those of the labour theory of value and the market, the relative importance of the forces of production and the relations of production, the configuration of classes and the effectiveness of class struggle; if the crisis exceeded the single issue of the tendency for the profit rate to fall; if the critique of politics cannot conclude simply by forecasting the extinction of the state, but re-poses the question of democracy, its forms and procedures, and the same is true of law; if communism cannot be projected as a utopia involving the end of every known social form, or if it must be redefined as a constructible form assumed by 'the movement that abolishes the present state of things'; if all the above hold, then what does it mean to call oneself 'Marxist'? Where does the difference between Marxism and non-Marxism lie for each Marxism? The phase of a thousand Marxisms ushered in by the end of a whole cycle of struggles conducted by the working-class movement as an anti-systemic movement, and relayed at one time by anti-imperialist national-popular movement, represents the greatest fracture in the history of Marxism and dictates both a labour of mourning for a certain continuity and the task of thinking through a new unity.

The irreversible multiplicity of the present and future thousand Marxisms poses the issue of minimal theoretical agreement on the range of legitimate disagreements. Without anticipating, we may say that this consensus allowing for dissensus consists in two elements. The first element is an agreement on the theoretical possibility (rendered practically urgent by the persistence of an unnecessary, unjustifiable inhumanity) of an analysis of globalised capitalism and its forms, inscribed in, but not directly derivable from, the real submission of labour to capital. The second element is an agreement on historical hope in the real possibility of eliminating this inhumanity (whether it is called alienation, exploitation, domination, subjection, or manipulation of the powers of the multitude), and constructing determinate social forms that express the power or freedom of the multitude. If the second element is determinant, in the sense of the driving force, the first has a dominant function in that it ballasts utopia with its dimension of 'knowledge' and provides it with its condition of feasibility. The thousand Marxisms possess – and will possess – an epochal grasp of the time of capitalist globalisation only if they avoid the trap of Marxist fundamentalism (sheer repetition of the inhumanity of capitalism and generic appeals to the class struggle); and if they simultaneously carry out the work of critical memory as regards what became of Marx and Marxisms in the twentieth century and yield knowledge of the terrain of capitalist globalisation. The thousand Marxisms have – and will have – a capacity for understanding and altering the direction of the time only if they succeed in combining rigorous work in critically rediscovering the work of Marx and Marxisms and confronting the highpoints of philosophical and theoretical thought. Finally, they have a future in as much as the crisis that is rife in Marxism reveals itself ever more clearly to be simultaneously a crisis of the neoliberal order faced with the reality of vast processes of social dis-assimilation engendered by its seeming victory, and increasingly tempted to resort to forms of reactionary management of the dis-emancipation projected by its globalisation.

This work is already underway, for example, where the disintegration of Marxism has been most spectacular – in Italy. The marginality of Marxism cannot conceal the importance of the enterprise of Losurdo, who has now enriched his counter-history of liberalism in Western thought with an analysis of present-day liberal political forms (*Democrazia o bonapartismo. Trionfo e decadenza del suffragio universale*, of 1993), and offered an analysis of the political conjuncture in Italy that brings out the bond between neoliberalism, federalism and post-fascism (*La seconda repubblica. Liberismo, federalismo, post-fascismo*, in 1994), while also presenting a historical-theoretical balance-sheet of twentieth-century communism and Marxism, affirming the charge of liberation initially contained in the October Revolution while at the same time proceeding to a critique of the elements of abstract utopia in Marx as regards the state (*Marx e il balancio storico del Novecento*, published in 1993).

Losurdo has given his research a more systematic dimension by confronting head-on the revisionism which had obscured and distorted the comprehension of modern revolutions, in particular the Russian Revolution, preventing an equitable comparative analysis of historical processes. This revisionism united liberal currents – from Burke and Constant to Tocqueville, Mill, Croce, Hayek and Popper – with the line running from de Maistre to Chamberlain, Calhoun, and the Nazi and fascist theoreticians. This study, initiated in *Il revisionismo storico. Problemi e miti* (1996), was completed by a synthetic work, *Contrastoria del liberalismo* (2005), which defines liberalism as the philosophy of chosen people(s), masters of the modern world. It confronts the paradox of a doctrine which praises individual liberties, yet always contradicts this affirmation of universality with exception clauses. Thus excluded initially were wage-workers, assimilated to instruments of labour, and colonised peoples, identified as modern slaves, enemy nations excluded from the human race and categorised as inhuman. Liberalisms have always directly or indirectly justified social relationships of domination which actualised freedom. Losurdo does not restrict himself to deconstructing the liberal hagiography which has criminalised revolutionary attempts at emancipation. His black book of liberalism points to a tradition of radical liberalism which he argues we should take up (Diderot, Condorcet, Marx and Engels), yet which remains undefined. The lesson communists should learn from this history is not to flee history but to persevere in the analysis of social relations and their open contradictions. It would be wrong not to mention, as well, the work done by the historian of philosophy Losurdo in his study *Antonio Gramsci, dal liberalismo al 'communismo critico'* (1997) and his monumental *Nietzsche, il ribelle aristocratico. Biografia intelletuale e bilancio critico* (2002), which succeeds exactly where the Lukács of *The Destruction of Reason* fails – namely, in giving an account of the overwhelming power and ambiguities of the greatest of genealogists.

This work of theoretico-political historiography is directed to the two poles that form the spectrum of the thousand Marxisms: the pole of a good utopianism and the pole of an analysis based on a re-reading of Marx's key concepts. These two poles can be illustrated by recourse to examples that seem to belong to the previous phase, but which in reality are endowed with actuality in the new historical period – the pole represented by Walter Benjamin's final theses on the philosophy of history and that constituted by Anglo-Saxon analytical Marxism.

The thousand Marxisms in motion between conceptual deconstruction-reconstruction and utopia

It is impossible to take account of the thousand Marxisms that have developed between these two poles. We shall limit ourselves to a thematic selection of samples according to cultural-national context.

In Italy, where the collapse of Marxism was so profound, a revival seems to be in the offing. Sustained by the critical historiographical *œuvre* of Losurdo and a Marxist school of intellectual history (Guido Oldrini and Alberto

Burgio), various attempts at systematic reconstruction are in course. Two, in particular, stand out. The first is that of Giuseppe Prestipino (b. 1928) who, having started out from a historicism mixed with Della Volpeanism, has for many years been reformulating the theory of modes of production, conceived in terms of a logico-historical bloc. In any human society, the existence of an anthropologico-historical inheritance comprising distinct systems – productive, social, cultural, institutional – is presupposed. These systems can be combined in the course of history in different structures, or according to the dominant system in the theoretical model of a given formation. The thesis of an invariant dominance of the productive and/or social base over the cultural and institutional superstructure is peculiar to the bloc of initial modernity. Today, the developed modern bloc and an inceptive postmodern bloc are in competition. The first is dominated by the cultural element in the form of a comprehensive rationalisation, permeating all other domains, through the productivist discipline of labour, by following the (social) rules of the market and organising itself according to the (political) order of bureaucratic democracy. The second, which is still hypothetical, is dominated by the public institution, at its highest stage as an ethico-juridical, supra-state and supra-national system. Its task is to guide in hegemonic fashion (in the Gramscian sense) the other elements – that is to say, free cultural and scientific research, planetary social mobility established in a regime of real equality of opportunity and wealth, and technological production treated at last as a common property of human intelligence and 'descent' (*Da Gramsci a Marx. Il blocco logico-storico*, published in 1979, *Per un anthropologia filosofica*, in 1983, and *Modelli di strutture storiche. Il primato etico nel postmoderno*, in 1993). Prestipino has furnished a kind of conclusion to his research in a study (*Realismo e utopia* [2002]) which discusses both the Lukács of the *Ontology of Social Being* and Bloch in order to revisit the categories of the dialectic, such as the dialectic of logico-historical blocs. The de-anthropomorphising perspective of knowledge roots human activity in nature and life to allow us a better grasp of anthropogenesis and its particular categories, with their relations of conditioning, determination and succession. These themes deserve the kind of sustained attention that they have been denied for too long.

The second endeavour is that of Costanzo Preve. Having started out from a programme for a systematic reformulation of Marxist philosophy, on the Lukácsian basis of the ontology of social being, integrating the Blochian theme of ethical utopia, and centred on the theme of an Althusserian science of modes of production (*Il filo di Arianna,* in 1990), it faces the difficulties of a certain eclecticism. Taking account of the effective dominance of the nihilism inscribed in neocapitalism and reflected by the century's organic thinkers, Heidegger and Weber, Preve examines the major problems of universalism and individualism, seeking to eliminate from Marx certain aspects of Enlightenment thinking compromised by nihilism (*Il convitato di pietra. Saggio su marxismo e nihilismo,* which appeared in 1991; *Il planeta rosso. Saggio su marxismo e universalismo,* in 1992; and *L'assalto al cielo. Saggio su marxismo e individualismo,* in 1992). Preve's latest research finds him abandoning the programme of the ontology of social being and redefining a communist philosophy, criticising the notions of class-subject and the paradigm of labour and needs in a confrontation with theoreticians of postmodernity (*Il tempo della ricerca. Saggio sul moderno, il post-moderno e la fine della storia,* 1993). Finally compressing Marx's legacy into the critique of capitalism as destructive of the potentialities of human individuation initially liberated by it, Preve undertakes an anthropological reflection in order to identify the bourgeois-capitalist and archaeo-communist (the 'comrade') conceptions of human nature, in order to sketch a neo-communism as a community of individualities possessed of equal liberty (*L'eguale libertà. Saggio sulla natura umana,* published in 1994).

Finally, Preve attempts to reconstruct Marx's thought by radically separating it from historical Marxisms. With only a few exceptions (Korsch, Althusser, the later Lukács), these Marxisms sought to systematise, in a sterile manner, the necessarily incomplete thought of Marx. Marxism thought of itself as a triple synthesis of historicism, economism and utopianism. But this was in fact a triple denaturing of which we must rid ourselves. Historicism wraps theory in an illusory teleological grand narrative. Economism is a form of reductionism which takes the development of the forces of production as the sole evaluative criterion and ignores the articulated complexity of social totalities. Utopianism is the dream of a normative community where the plurality of human individualities must necessarily be subjected to an *a priori* model of socialisation. Such is the thesis of *Marx inattuale. Eredità e prospettiva* (2004). This critique implies the necessity of rehabilitating philosophical thought as such by posing the question of the possibility of communism in the light of an understanding of the nihilism which has run through Western thought since

Nietzsche, Weber, Schmitt and Heidegger. Preve accordingly offers a general philosophical reconstruction of twentieth-century thought as a transcendental condition in another little discussed book, *I tempi difficile* (1999). Here he re-opens the perspective of truth and discusses the key question of Marxian communism, that of the relations between individualism and universalism, in the context of a multilinear vision of history. A certain obscurity, or, rather, a dubious ambiguity, nevertheless persists: in these later texts, Preve seeks a mediation by way of a political proposal appealing to a national or 'nationalitarian' type, which is highly questionable to the extent that nationalitarianism turns into an apologia for a multiplicity of regionalisms that can hardly be characterised as universalistic.

In Italy, where the Party of Communist Refoundation is actively present, grouping together many militants who refused to accept the self-liquidation of the PCI into the PDS, we can still find scholars who engage with Marx. Thus, Alberto Burgio, whilst also intervening in questions of political theory (*Modernità del conflitto*, 1999), maintains, in *Strutture e catastrofi. Kant, Hegel, Marx* (2002), a classical dialectical tradition of interpretation quite close to Lucien Sève's. Roberto Finelli, for his part, identifies Marx's contribution with the theory of real abstractions (*Astrazione e dialettica dal romanticismo al capitalismo*, 1987) and shows that the materialism defended by Marx rests on a faulty understanding of the Hegelian theory of the subject, which only becomes itself in relation to alterity (*Un parricido mancato. Hegel e il giovane Marx*, 2004). Roberto Fineschi has undertaken a systematic study of *Capital* with *Ripartire da Marx. Processo storico ed economia politica nella teoria del 'Capitale'* (2001). Similarly, Gramscian research, brought to a halt with the 'liberal' mutation of the PCI, has been revived thanks to the International Gramsci Society, which has effectively replaced the Fondazione Istituto Gramsci with noteworthy contributions, such as those by Fabio Frosini and Franco Consiglio (*A. Gramsci. Filosofia e politica*, 1997), by Frosini again (*Gramsci e la filosofia. Saggio sui 'Quaderni de carcere'*, 2003), or by Giorgio Baratta (*La rose e i quaderni. Saggio sul pensiero di Antonio Gramsci*, 2000) and Domenico Losurdo.

Operaismo has made a stunning comeback thanks to its identification of globalisation as the indicated level for new analyses. Thus Antonio Negri, with *Empire* (2000) and *Multitude* (2004), both co-written with Michael Hardt, presents himself as a *Marx redivivus* who takes as his object of study the revolutionary transformation of capitalist globalisation. Although these works were celebrated by the international media as the Bible of the alterglobalisation movement, although their great merit is to integrate many of the findings of Anglo-Saxon research in a kind of portable encyclopedia; they proved capable of mobilising the enthusiastic, they were nonetheless shaped by the presuppositions of Negrian thought. Eulogies of communication technology and its determinism, a thoroughly positive metaphysics of power delegated to the multitude, the dilution of the notion of imperialism in an all-encompassing and indeterminable Empire – these features are more indicative of suggestive power rather than bearers of operational knowledge.

The insufficiently discussed work of the economist and theorist Gianfranco La Grassa, a collaborator of Costanzo Preve, with whom he published *La fine di una theoria* in 1996, proceeds in the opposite direction. Starting from a problematic inspired by Althusser and Bettelheim, author of thirty works on the Marxian critique of political economy and on economic theory, La Grassa became convinced of the analytical insufficiency of *Capital* (notably with regard to the theory of value). He seeks to develop a theory of the mode of production in the Althusserian sense of a science of society. The question of private property in the means of production is no longer central, for it has been displaced under contemporary capitalism, defined by a conflict of strategies between dominant social agents. These internal struggles are at once economic, political, ideological and cultural and lead to many more transformations than the struggles between the dominant and the dominated. As Althusser put it, to be a good materialist one must not tell oneself stories, including those about the existence and real power of a transmodal class supposedly capable of effecting a transition from the capitalist to a superior mode of production. These analyses inform, notably, *Lezioni sul capitalismo* (1996), *Il capitalismo oggi. Dalla proprietà al conflitto stratégico* (2004), *Gli strateghi del capitale. Una teoria del conflitto oltre Marx e Lenin* (2005). The struggles of the dominated persist and, with them, unexpected openings and possibilities. They provide the basis for a different anticapitalism which cannot be reduced to an ethical demand, but which has as its condition political vigilance armed with objective knowledge of the transformations underway.

In France, a change in the conjuncture seems to be emerging. Once the prospect of Communism had seemingly disappeared with the end of the USSR and its bloc, the reference to Marx ceased to be criminalised. Marx and Marxisms remain marginal, and lack academic recognition, but it is possible now to study them as intellectual classics. Journals, some already relatively old, such as *Actuel Marx*, founded by Jacques Bidet and Jacques Texier and now directed by Emmanuel Renault, or more recent, such as *Contretemps*, directed by Daniel Bensaïd, or *Multitudes*, close to Negri, and the successor to *Futur Antérieur* (long edited by the late Jean-Marie Vincent; Yann Moulier-Boutang is the editor of *Multitudes*), continue their critical activities, feature significant themes and even, as in the case of *Actuel Marx*, organise major conferences. Other older periodicals such as *La Pensée* (editor: Antoine Casanova) or *L'homme et la Société* (editor: Pierre Lantz) continue to occupy their niches.

These activities are not guided by research into the critical history of liberal thought like that of Domenico Losurdo in Italy. On the other hand, they are sustained by the renewal of an analysis of globalised capitalism of a Marxist orientation which has no counterpart in Italy (with the exception of La Grassa or Riccardo Bellofiore). Gérard Duménil and Dominque Lévy, in particular, have developed an original school of thought which studies the new forms of capitalism (*La dynamique du capital. Un siècle d'économie américaine*. 1996, *Crise et sortie de crise. Ordre et désordre néo-libéraux*. 2000). As in Italy, however, this work has not given rise to debates comparable to those which accompanied the publication of the texts of Althusser or Gramsci. The only debate of any note concerns Negri's theses in *Empire*, but these owe as much to passing fads or their rhetorical force as to their real novelty. There is no scientific community which is up to the task of discussing works and comparing and contrasting analyses. Scholars remain isolated and simply juxtapose their work to that of others. The previously cited journals are not sites of intellectual confrontation and their choices of book reviews are rather meagre. It is no longer a question of orthoxies nor of heresies; rather, separate and unquestioned *doxai* are ranged alongside one another. Certainly, it is better to have a thousand Marxisms than none at all, but this pluralism remains inert and has not (yet?) produced propositions that could make for a politically operative common sense.

We are dealing, then, with a centrifugal recovery which has neither had a snowball effect nor established a new school of thought and which is often marked by nostalgia and an inability to let go of the past. We can outline the conjuncture by situating current research in its degree of effective proximity and/or distance from the Marxian opus grasped in its complexity, and also from the heretical Marxisms of the communist movement (Lukács, Bloch, Gramsci, Althusser, or Adorno, Della Volpe, Lefebvre, etc.).

We should first note a certain resumption of philosophical-historical studies of Marx (and, to a lesser degree, Engels). They bear, first of all, on politics. Here, one might cite Miguel Abensour, *La Démocratie contre l'État* (1997), Antoine Artous, *Marx, l'État et la politique* (1999), Stathis Kouvelakis, *Philosophy and Revolution from Kant to Marx* (2001) – which happily renews the tradition of Auguste Cornu – Solange Mercier-Josa, *Entre Hegel et Marx* (1999), and, finally, Jacques Texier, *Révolution et démocratie chez Marx et Engels* (1998), which recasts the question referred to in its title. Engels was the subject of a very useful collective volume edited by Georges Labica and Mireille Delbraccio, *Friedrich Engels, savant et révolutionnaire* (1997). We should note that the classic question of democracy and/or revolution, which used to oppose communists to social democrats, has been displaced in favour of the issue as to what kind of democracy is possible or desirable after the self-dissolution of capitalist representative democracy? What kind of revolution can there be after the failure of Soviet Communism and the dead end of a certain type of violence? What should we adopt from the great ethico-political tradition of liberalism (cf. André Tosel. *Démocratie et libéralismes*, 1995)? All these studies are haunted by the possible renewal of a form of direct democracy capable of confronting structural conflict in the political field. This is the subject of a book by Jacques Rancière now considered a reference-point (*Disagreement*, 1995), which takes up a debate with the directive radicalism of Alain Badiou, who effectively responded in *Metapolitics* (1998) and reaffirmed the inevitability of violent rupture in *The Century* (2005), a reflection on the twentieth century. Rare indeed are those who insist on the need to cling to the perspective of revolution in the class struggle and who remind us that the democratic path, when the violence by the dominant reaches extreme forms, dictates the use of the revolutionary violence by the dominated as the only adequate response. This is Georges Labica's argument in *Démocratie et révolution* (2002).

The Marxian critique of political economy has been less thoroughly studied. Challenging theses which underline the importance of the critique of real abstractions in Marx (Jean-Marie Vincent, *Un autre Marx*, 2001), the analytical work of Jacques Bidet eliminates all dialectical residues in order to highlight the copresence within capital of a logic of ineliminable inter-individual contractuality (the market) and of central contractuality (the plan). These ideas are developed in Bidet's *Exploring Marx's 'Capital'* (new edition, 2000).

A philosophical approach has been sustained by specific studies bearing on one or another point of Marx's philosophical practice: Michel Vadée has systematically reconstructed the problematic of possibility in *Marx, penseur du possible* (1992); Isabelle Garo has done the same for representation in *Marx, critique de la philosophie* (2000); Henri Maler has interrogated the utopian dimension in two closely related works, *Congédier l'utopie? L'utopie selon Karl Marx* (1994) and *Convoiter l'impossible. L'utopie selon Marx malgré Marx* (1995). Emmanuel Renault has considered *Marx et l'idée de critique* (1995). Hervé Touboul, in a detailed study of *The German Ideology*, has dealt with *Marx et Engels et la question de l'individu* (2004). André Tosel, in his *Etudes sur Marx (et Engels). Vers un communisme de la finitude* (1996), has posed questions regarding the relationship between action and production in Marx and on the dialectical integration of the sciences. Franck Fischbach has re-examined, in a broader philosophical perspective, German idealism as an ontology of the act of production; he interprets Marx as a critic of the productivist apologia of production, and as a thinker of human beings' production of their selves by themselves. Marx is thus said to pursue Spinoza's enterprise by reinserting human and social productivity, which is productivity of a world, into the heart of natural and vital productivity (these theses are developed in *L'Être et l'acte. Enquête sur les fondements de l'ontologie moderne de la relation* (2002) and *La Production des hommes. Marx avec Spinoza* (2005)).

This interest in Marx beyond the Marxisms has not produced results which capable of making Marx an interlocutor of the thought of the twentieth century, and worthy of comparison with Heidegger or Wittgenstein, as both the later Althusser and Gérard Granel have proposed in a number of suggestive texts. The classic comparison with Hegel has not been renewed, except by Fischbach, and the connection with Spinoza has been rendered more complex, even confused. Bidet, Balibar, Negri and others invoke the latter, but is it in fact the same Spinoza? He remains rather a programme and an ambiguous token of recognition.

The great figures of twentieth-century Marxism have not received sustained attention, if we set aside the enigmatic references to the equally enigmatic notion of aleatory materialism in the later Althusser. Gramsci is unread other than by some incorrigible individuals. Lefebvre is still in purgatory, as is Sartre. Lukács has become an illustrious stranger despite the efforts of Nicolas Tertullian. Bloch has been the subject of a few studies (notably by Arno Münster, such as *L'utopie concrète d'Ernst Bloch. Une biographie.* 2001). Benjamin has been more extensively studied, by Münster (*Progrès et catastrophe. Walter Benjamin et l'histoire.* 1996), and also by Michael Löwy (*Fire Alarm: Reading Walter Benjamin's 'On the Concept of History'* 2001) and Daniel Bensaïd (*Walter Benjamin, sentinelle messianique*, 1990). The Frankfurt school has benefited from the interest of Germanophone philosophers such as Gérard Raulet. The watchword of a 'return to Marx beyond the Marxisms' has gone hand in hand with ignorance of the theoretical history of those Marxisms. It is symptomatic that Lenin, who used to count for so much, has not been the subject of any serious study, if we except Jean Robelin's *Marxisme et socialisation*, which has also been studiously ignored. We should not, therefore, tell ourselves stories about the radiant future of the thousand Marxisms. None of us is in a position to reforge Siegfried's sword, as Jean Robelin has sarcastically put it.

While it is true that the concern for philological and historical precision which characterises these lines of research should stimulate the translation into French of Marx's texts, in tandem with the publication of the new edition of the complete works of Marx and Engels (MEGA 2), it must also be said that the danger of Marxological 'exegeticism' looms large. Lucien Sève is right to ask 'Do we still need Marx?'. That is why it is important to consider work which has attempted to reply to the question by opening up avenues which go beyond historiography or merely indicative suggestions. Here we can take stock of those authors emblematic of the internal division wihich runs through the thousand Marxisms – namely Lucien Sève, Daniel Bensaïd, Jean Robelin, Jacques Bidet and Étienne Balibar. We have here a spectrum of theoretical positions which stretches from the assumption of Marx's usefulness to the rejection of numerous obsolete parts of the corpus and an exit from it in other directions. This reconstruction is a roll-call neither of honour nor horror, but, rather, an examination as to the real state of affairs. It hopes to help bring about a confrontation between authors who (with, of course, a few exceptions) scarcely engage in discussion with one another.

Lucien Sève is one of these exceptions. He discussed Althusser's theses in their time, criticising them for attributing an anti-dialectical conception of the epistemological break to Marx and denying the persistence of the problematic of alienation. Today, Sève discusses Bidet's positions, criticising him, too, for ignoring the dialectic. Sève thinks that most 'Marxist' interpretations of Marx rest, in reality, on partial or erroneous readings. He refuses to pass on too rapidly to distinguishing between the good Marx and the bad. In a certain sense, Sève retains all of Marx, after dusting him off a bit. He accepts the old framework of the articulation between historical materialism and dialectical materialism. The first lies, he says, on an ethico-political axis that opens out onto a re-affirmation of the legitimacy of the communist perspective. Class struggle is simultaneously ethical inasmuch as it is the abolition of alienations. Two works outline this theme: *Communisme, quel second souffle?* (1990) et *Commencer par les fins. La nouvelle question communiste* (1999).

Sève questions the autonomy of a socialist phase supposedly preparing the way for communism. The full development of capital in globalisation authorises a direct transition based on not only the central class struggle but also the mobilisation of all those who are ground down by capitalist exploitation. The democratic republic is the accomplished political form for this transition, a possibility that Lenin, according to Sève, did not exclude.

Today, dialectical materialism, likewise has an opportunity to rethink its categories, setting out from an enrichment of the category of contradiction. *De facto*, the natural sciences are the practical laboratory for this categorial productivity, which should no longer be conceived as a dialectic of nature raised to the level of a superscience. Sève gives concrete example of this immanent dialectic in *Dialectique et sciences de la nature*, written in collaboration with natural scientists (1998). Another work, *Emergence, complexité et dialectique* (2005), goes further down the same road and, engaging with the physics of non-linear phenomena and the biology of emergence, sketches the elaboration of these new categories, which can also be imported into the human sciences. Mediating these two lines of research is a reflection on the formation of the person and on bioethics (*Pour une critique de la raison bioéthique*, 1994).

The political polemics which challenged Sève's position, when he was the 'official philosopher' of the French Communist Party, contained a grain of truth, but they have so far prevented us from taking the measure of a coherent body of philosohical work. Sève announces in his programmatic book of 2004, *Penser avec Marx aujourd'hui. I. Marx et nous*, that he is in the process of undertaking a vast reading of Marx according to Marx. We shall wait and see.

With Daniel Bensaïd (b. 1946), we have a less conservative relationship to Marx, but one that is equally concerned to maintain the unity of a thought while also duly criticising it. *Marx for Our Times: Adventures and Misadventures of a Critique*, first published in 1995, re-elaborates Marx's thought on the basis of a triple critique. This thought is not a philosophy of the end of history, nor an empirical sociology of class that announces the inevitable victory of the proletariat, nor a universal science which carves out the path of inevitable progress that all peoples must follow in nature. The three critiques of historical reason, economic reason and speculative reason echo one another. Knowledge of the movements of capital frees the space for the idea of plurilinear temporalities, open to aleatory bifurcations and the category of possibility. The critique of political economy opens onto a specific ontology of social relations and their contradictions, but also onto all the other forms of oft-neglected conflictuality (gender, nationality, religion). Reason, finally, needs to recognise the supersession of a dominant model of scientificity and to be illuminated by the innovatory and dialectical thrust of scientific practices. Bensaïd is more open than Sève to the imperative of making the effort to understand the novelty of globalised capitalism and the concrete, especially political, conditions of the transformation of the world. In a work which is a pendant to the one just mentioned, *Le pari mélancolique* (1997), he takes into account the new spatio-temporal co-ordinates and the modifications in production and consumption in the context of a radical crisis of of the idea of progress. Communism is no longer thought of in positive Marxian fashion as the accomplishment of all the possibilities blocked by capitalist domination, but, rather, as an ethical and political effort to stave off impediments, to resist the threatening catastrophe. Bensaïd is closer to Benjamin or Péguy than Sève, and he defends a melancholic romanticism. It is the end of the certainties of all faiths; it is a Pascalean Marxism which wagers on resistance – as demonstrated by numerous texts, such as *Résistance. Essai de topologie générale* (2001), or *Les Irréductibles. Théorèmes de résistance à l'air du temps* (2001). The revolutionary perspective is rendered more complex, but remains an axis. It requires attention to the totality of popular and alterglobalist struggles, and a refinement of politics as a strategic art (this is the theme of *Un monde à changer. Mouvements et stratégies*, 2003). It necessitates vigilance against the return of wars which, with their claims to being ethically justified, are forging a new imperialism. A sense of urgency dominates all of Bensaïd's thinking, which conceives mass democratic struggles in the context of a new internationalism (*Un nouvel internationalisme,* 2003) and which is more sensitive than any competing body of thought to contingency and time (as *La Discordance des temps*, 1995, attests).

In Jacques Bidet, we find at one and the same time profound attention to the Marx of *Capital*, a considerable distance from Marx, and an enormous theoretical ambition which seeks to produce acontemporary but more comprehensive equivalent of the Marxian critique. In short, the desire for a *Marx redivivus*. A stringent reader of *Capital*, to which he devoted another volume in 2004 (*Explication et reconstruction du 'Capital'*), Bidet tracks down the weaknesses of Marx's masterpiece: the inadequacy of the theory of value, the impossibility of separating the market from its political forms and conditions, the ambiguities in the conception of law and freedom, and the need to preserve both inter-individual and central contractuality. This deconstructive enquiry opens out positively onto a reconstruction, or rather refoundation, of Marxism that sets itself up as an alternative to the euthanasia-reconstruction proposed by Habermas, yet complements Marx with a renewed form of contractualism (Bidet has devoted a perceptive study to Rawls: *John Rawls et la théorie de la justice,* 1995).

We must therefore take the measure of Bidet's *magnum opus*, *Théorie générale* (1999), which sets itself the task of formulating, in the unity of a single concept, a theory of modern society and a political philosophy which is both realistic and prescriptive. This conjunction of science and political doctrine is what Marx was aiming at in trying to think the world of real capitalism whilst at the same time trying to determine what is to be done. It is impossible to summarise a theory which rests on a complex intellectual organisation implying the separation of structures (the market, classes, the state) from the metastructure, which is the enunciation of modern social being by individuals who recognise each other as free and equal, yet a contradictory one divided between the discourses of domination and co-operation. This work deserves discussion that it has not received. Although one might baulk at the claim to generality, given the risk of a discourse from on high, such reservations can only be justified by a respectful analysis of the audacity of this attempt. Similarly, if one might be sceptical about the proposal of a communism identified with a world-state, a correlate of the world-system, which paradoxically realises an 'anarcho-Spinozist imperative', one must recognise the richness of a multidisciplinary enterprise which is capable of engaging the summits of contemporary thought (notably in a detailed critique of Habermasian discourse ethics or of the economics of conventions or regulation theory).

The long reflection of Étienne Balibar, begun when he was a very young man under the mentorship of Louis Althusser in the 1960s, took a noteworthy turn after *Race, Class, Nation* (1988). The death of the master and friend, following the personal catastrophe, the irreversible crisis of Soviet Communism, and the end of Maoism, obliged Balibar to engage in a labour of mourning which none of the other authors mentioned here has had to face. Without abjuring Marx, on whom he is a an expert and to whom he has devoted a substantial study – *The Philosophy of Marx* (1993) – Balibar renounced 'Marxism', which he regarded as an unproductive form of scholasticism. Moreover, he no longer considered as relevant the perspective of a communist revolution which would both surpass social democracy and outflank Stalinism on its left. There was no longer any reason to focus on the dictatorship of the proletariat that he had defended in 1976. Balibar believes that the Communist parties can no longer play a dynamic role because they conducted their struggles in a narrow nationalist and statist framework and because they cut themselves off from the modern masses due to their refusal to engage in grassroots politics. He maintains that they have completely failed to understand the social transformation wrought by globalisation, namely, the racist and 'nationalitarian' overdetermination of social conflict and the obsolescence of delegatory politics. If Althusser denounced what 'could no longer last' within the party – its clerico-military organisation and lack of a real strategy – Balibar arrived at the position, without declaring it publicly, that it was the historical communist party that could no longer last; that Marxism as a world-view was finished because it was incapable of accounting for its own history; and that all the attempts at reconstruction and refoundation (a return to Marx, or to Gramsci, or to Lenin) were without a future because they had not grasped the changes in the times and society.

A major work attests to this tacitly self-critical mutation, *La Crainte des masses. Politique et philosophie avant et après Marx* (1997), which many readers imagine to be a continuation of the essays in the reconstruction of historical materialism of the Althusserian period (1974). Heralded by *Les Frontières de la démocratie* (1992) et followed by *Droit de cité. Culture et politique en démocratie* (1998) and *Nous, citoyens d'Europe? Les frontières, l'Etat, le peuple* (2001), this investigation is based on a consideration of the unprecedented rise in violence inscribed in globalisation (policies of generalised apartheid implemented by capitalism that find their translation in an explosion of racisms, identitarian communitarianisms, cruel and endemic wars). The modern enunciation of *égaliberté* has to be considered as the ethico-political foundation for any analysis. First declared by the French Revolution, it was ignored by Marx, who pertinently analysed the conditions of politics while dissolving the historically produced norm in a purely ideological critique. Thus Marx's analysis cannot come to terms with the fact that subjective human action and social movements advance by mobilising the powers of the imagination and of life and by repressing norms. The conflicts of our modernity actualise the fear of the masses – the fear that the masses provoke in the state or in themselves; and the fear that the state arouses in them. Spinoza, Freud, and Foucault knew how to explore this conflictuality, which does not necessarily culminate in emancipation. More profoundly still, the political culture shared by Marx remains that of emancipation and social transformation, but ignores the background of minimal civility which is fundamentally that of non-violence. Only a politics that is democratic from top to bottom is capable of rethinking the possibilities of a universal, plural, cross-frontier community of right. It must stop referring exclusively to the resolvent power of the counter-violence that the oppressed counterpose to the different forms of violence of the dominant. This politics of civility bears within it the possibility of a universal which conjoins the spirit of revolt and the need for realistic intelligibility in the excessive conditions of our age. As we can see, Marx and Spinoza must learn to live with Hannah Arendt, the theorist of the superfluous human, and with Locke, the inventor of consciousness. From this point of view, ethico-political liberalism is untranscendable.

The same absence of religious respect and blind loyalty vis-à-vis the Marxisms and the aporiae of Marx may be observed in the case of Jean Robelin. The last student of Althusser, who recognised the importance of *Marxisme et socialisation* (1989), Robelin has been scandalously ignored by both the academic authorities as well as his comrades in 'Marxism', although he is the author of an important *œuvre* which has a real purchase on contemporary phenomena. He, too, has left behind the notion of Marxism as a world-view. His work is grounded in an analysis of the failure of Marxist socialisms as well as of Soviet Communism. He has highlighted its difficulties: the inadequacy of economism, organisational fetishism, the impasses of any general theory of the state, and the degeneration of critical communism into a teleological metaphysics of nature and of history. However, unlike Balibar, he has turned neither towards a normative theory of *égaliberté* nor a thematics of incontrovertible civility. He defends the relevance of the Marxian distinction between formal and real subsumption of labour, which the young Balibar magisterially underlined in his contribution to *Reading 'Capital'* in his Althusserian days. Robelin uses this as his guiding thread in analysing the transformations of politics, public and private law, international law, and social, productive, private, and communicational technology in works that are enriched with specific kinds of knowledge: *La petite fabrique du droit* (1994) and *Les Sagesses de l'art. Études de technologie sociale* (1998). Thus, law is a necessary expression of social relations; it functions politically and is always impure. The justice to which it refers can only result in divisive confrontations, without being able to constitute a foundational and transcendental order. Only a democracy that is really social and re-activates the experience of direct democracy, of the producers' and citizens' councils, can guarantee the functionning of juridicity via a confrontation between different conceptions of justice. Thus, far from being a form of aggression against *Dasein*, technique is the 'possibilisation' of things. It is not defined not as a subordination of ends to the simple rationality of means, but as a social technology which is realised through uses invested by social relations and the division of labour. Through it, human beings become the measure of all things, but, under capitalism, the possibilities of concrete freedom are inverted into vital impossibilities (the impossibility of working, living, escaping from interimperial wars or from the devastation of nature or the manipulation of human substance). The function of politics is to develop a democracy-process which makes these impossibilities impossible, not to realise the magnificent destiny of Humanity as a subject. More recently, Robelin has expanded his investigations to embrace thought and the form of reason, plunging as a materialist and pragmatist into the field of the metaphysics of the mind (*Esquisse d'une politique de l'esprit*, 2000). This is an *œuvre* whose time is still to come.

This review is incomplete. Other projects which seek to translate the Marxian critique into other fields deserve to be mentioned. Thus Yvon Quiniou has focused on morality (*Figures de la déraison politique*, 1995) and Jean Lojkine on the labour process (*Entreprise et société*, 1998). Yves Schwartz has produced a major work on work and industrious activities (*Travail et philosophie. Convocations mutuelles*, 1992). In philosophy in the strict sense, the defence of Marx and alterglobalisation proposed by Jacques Derrida (*Specters of Marx*, 1993) has played a noteworthy role.

Marx will not cease to haunt thought as long as capitalist globalisation renders both our being-in-the-world, and the very idea of a world shared in common, problematic. Do we still inhabit a world worthy of the name?

Today, from the point of view of the future of Marxism(s), it is the level of the world economy that is pertinent. The capacity to analyse it in its relationship to the real submission of labour, taken as the guiding thread, and to develop the skein of that thread, will constitute the immanent criterion of the importance of the thousand Marxisms. Acquiring this ability will oblige us to read both the known and the unknown Marx better; it will govern the development of Marxist 'science' in its confrontation with other forms of knowledge that will have to submit to the test of their critical transformation; it will revive examination of 'its' philosophy and the link between that science and that philosophy. The crisis of the neoliberal order has always been the negative precondition for a revival of Marxism. If the twentieth century was the short century that ran from capitalism to capitalism; if it opened with a catastrophic crisis which revealed the liberal-national order's fragility and potential for inhumanity, if it had at its centre the failure of the first attempt at communism, it did not close only with the crisis of Marxisms. It ended with the onset of a new crisis secreted in the barbarism of the new liberal order. This is where the thousand Marxisms discover the material for a new historical justification, the object of their analyses, and the occasion for their radical self-criticism, which is also the critique of the liberal order by itself. This is the terrain for the reconstitution of their positive precondition: the emergence of new social movements and new practices beyond the monstrous dead ends of the organisation of the State-Party, the possibility of forging a new link between theory and practice, whose forms cannot and must not be prejudged. Let us leave the last – and subsequent – word to the old Antonio Labriola: 'But what does the real novelty of the world which has made the imperfections of Marxism so very obvious consist in? There's the rub.'[5]

[5] Labriola 1975, p. 337.

Chapter Four

Whither Anglo-Saxon Marxism?

Alex Callinicos

François Truffaut famously suggested that once there was 'a certain incompatibility between the terms "cinema" and "Britain"'.[1] Till a generation ago one might have said the same about the words 'Marxism' and 'Anglo-Saxon'. Before the 1960s, the terrain was not completely barren, but the limited political influence of Marxism on the workers' movement the United States and Britain corresponded to the relative weakness of Marxism as a theoretical discourse in these countries.

The impact of the 1930s

The left radicalisation of the 1930s did produce some important contributions. In the US the early writings of Sidney Hook, notably *Towards an Understanding of Karl Marx*,[2] represented an intriguing encounter between the Hegelian Marxism of Lukács and Korsch and the left-liberal pragmatism of John Dewey. In Britain, the writings of John Strachey brilliantly publicised a version of Marxism close to that of the Communist Party and, in the domain of economic theory, a more original analysis willing to

[1] Truffaut 1978, p. 140.
[2] Hook 1933.

engage with the work of Hayek and Keynes. And Trotskyist writers produced some outstanding texts of historico-political analysis such as C.L.R. James's *The Black Jacobins* and Harold Isaacs's *The Tragedy of the Chinese Revolution*.

The 1930s had, moreover, some significant longer-term consequences. The Popular Front and the struggle against fascism was the formative political experience of a generation of young intellectuals some of whom, during the harsher climate of the Cold War, refused to abandon Marxism, and instead creatively developed it. The most important example is provided by the brilliant gallery of historians – among them Edward Thompson, Christopher Hill, Eric Hobsbawm, Rodney Hilton, and George Rudé – who emerged from the Communist Party of Great Britain after the Second World War. The CP Historians' Group provided in the late 1940s and early 1950s the milieu for a series of important debates that took as their starting point the Cambridge Marxist economist Maurice Dobb's *Studies in the Development of Capitalism* (1946). With the exception of Hobsbawm, all the leading figures left the CPGB after the Soviet suppression of the Hungarian Revolution of 1956. But, as independent socialist historians, they continued to develop a version of Marxism that sought to study history 'from below' – from the perspective of the oppressed and exploited – and to give the study of culture and representations a greater importance than had been accorded it in more orthodox approaches.

The American Marxist journal *Monthly Review* represented a somewhat analogous tendency the other side of the Atlantic. Under the guidance of figures such as Paul Sweezy, Paul Baran, and Harry Magdoff, *Monthly Review* practised a version of Marxism that was broadly sympathetic to the Communist régimes (notably those in the Third World, such as China and Cuba) but intellectually independent, for example in its development of an account of contemporary capitalism that distanced itself from the labour theory of value. The two groups clashed in the celebrated debate on the transition from feudalism to capitalism in the late 1940s precipitated by Sweezy's attack on Dobb's *Studies*.[3]

[3] See Hilton 1976.

Western Marxism and the 1960s generation

It is nevertheless fair to say that, before the 1960s, Marxism was marginal to the broader intellectual culture of the English-speaking world. One of the main preoccupations of *New Left Review (NLR)* under the editorship of Perry Anderson (1962–83) was the humiliating gap between the Western Marxism of Lukács and Gramsci, Adorno and Horkheimer, Sartre and Althusser, Della Volpe and Colletti, and the stunted growth in Britain. In a celebrated pair of interpretive essays, 'Origins of the Present Crisis' (1964) and 'Components of the National Culture (1968),[4] Anderson used a particular reading of Gramsci and Sartre, to present England as a case of abnormal capitalist development, in which a partially modernised aristocracy had succeeded in maintaining hegemony over both the main classes of industrial society: bourgeoisie and proletariat alike remained subaltern classes that had failed to develop their own hegemonic ideology. This specific pattern of class relations explained what Anderson claimed to be the peculiar backwardness of English intellectual culture by comparison with its continental counterparts: nowhere was there to be found a totalising analysis of society – neither a bourgeois sociology comparable to that of Weber or Durkheim nor a revolutionary Marxist critique.

Anderson's interpretation of English history was itself the subject of a devastating riposte by Thompson, 'The Pecularities of the English'.[5] But the quality of the arguments produced on both sides of this debate itself indicated that the poverty of British Marxism was a thing of the past. The fundamental force at work was political. The 1956 crisis in the Communist movement produced by Krushchev's secret speech and the Hungarian Revolution created a political space for a left independent of both Labourism – of course, dominant in the British workers' movement – and official Communism. *NLR* was one of the intellectual products of this New Left. The base of this Left was greatly expanded by a series of movements – for nuclear disarmament, against apartheid in South Africa, in solidarity with the struggle of the Vietnamese people – that folded into the more general contestation that Britain experienced, though on a more modest scale than the United States or continental Europe, at the end of the 1960s.

---

[4] Reprinted in Anderson 1992a.
[5] Reprinted in Thompson 1978.

The result was greatly to expand both the consumers and the producers of Marxist ideas. The generation of the 1960s provided much of the readership of the great mature works of the Marxist historians – Thompson's *The Making of the English Working Class* and *Whigs and Hunters*, Hill's *The World Turned Upside Down*, Hobsbawm's trilogy on the long nineteenth century.[6] Not least among the significance of these works was the model they offered for the radical young scholars who now began to enter an academy that, thanks to the expansion of higher education in the 1960s and 1970s, offered many more teaching posts.

One main thread in the ferment of debate that ensued concerned the kind of Marxism relevant to the needs of both political militants and socialist scholars (it was a characteristic of the radicalisation that most refused to distinguish between these two groups). In both Britain and the US this was issue was inseparable from that of the reception of forms of continental thought to which the intellectual cultures of these countries had hitherto been hostile. Perhaps because of the historical connection between the Frankfurt school and the American academy – reflected in the personal influence of Herbert Marcuse and Leo Lowenthal, who did not return from exile to Germany after the Second World War – it was this version of Western Marxism that proved most influential on American radicals.

In Britain, by contrast, it was Althusser's reconstruction of Marxism that formed the focus of debate. *NLR* and its publishing house New Left Books (later Verso) were particularly assiduous in publishing translations of Althusser's and his associates' writings, though for the *Review* he was merely one of a number of French and Italian Marxists whose works it sought to introduce to an English-speaking readership. The enthusiasm for Althusser was part of a broader reception of French structuralism and poststructuralism. In Britain, cultural studies had been launched in the late 1950s by New-Left intellectuals such as Raymond Williams and Stuart Hall. Compared therefore to the largely depoliticised reception of Lacan and Derrida in the US, where they were first taken up by literary critics at Yale, the various intellectual strands generated by Saussure's theory of language were received in Britain as contributions to a materialist analysis of culture and representations.

---

[6] Hobsbawm 1962, 1975 and 1987.

This reception of Western Marxism did not go uncontested. Once again Thompson and Anderson are emblematic figures. Thompson denounced the uncritical adoption of continental models in the name of a native English radical tradition dating back to the democratic revolutions of the seventeenth and eighteenth centuries. In an essay that showed his mastery of polemic to the full, 'The Poverty of Theory' (1978), he launched an all-out attack on Althusserian Marxism, which he excoriated for seeking to define experience out of theory and agency out of history.

Anderson was, by contrast, the chief figure responsible for importing the Continental Marxism Thompson reviled in order to remedy the defects of the native stock. Yet by the time 'The Poverty of Theory' appeared, Anderson had developed a more ambivalent position. In *Considerations of Western Marxism* (1976) he contrasted the Marxism of Adorno, Althusser, and Della Volpe – philosophical, preoccupied with ideology and aesthetics, alienated from practice – unfavourably with what he called (following Isaac Deutscher) classical Marxism, the tradition of Lenin, Luxemburg, and Trotsky, whose historical, political, and economic analyses were organically connected to their practical involvement in the workers' movement. Anderson's response to 'The Poverty of Theory' combined a reasoned defence of Althusser's contribution to Marxism with the espousal of a more materialist approach represented philosophically by G.A. Cohen's *Karl Marx's Theory of History* (1978), and politically by the Trotskyist movement.[7]

Anderson's evolution reflected the relative weight of Trotskyism in Anglophone left culture. While the Maoist groupuscules which dominated the American student movement at its height in the late 1960s and early 1970s had, if anything, a negative intellectual impact, the various strands of Trotskyism were a significant reference point. The writings of Isaac Deutscher during his later years in English exile were an important formative influence on the British New Left, and his great biography of Trotsky helped to increase the general intellectual prestige of Trotskyism. Ernest Mandel was an active contributor to left debates in the English-speaking world, and his economic writings – most notably *Late Capitalism* – were rapidly translated into English. Deutscher and Mandel were the chief influences on Anderson and the rest of the *NLR* team, but there were other signs of the vitality of English-speaking

[7] Anderson 1980.

Trotskyism, notably Tony Cliff's path-breaking analysis of Stalinist Russia as an instance of bureaucratic state capitalism, and the studies of postwar capitalism by his associates Michael Kidron and Chris Harman.

Crisis

By the early 1980s, Anderson could contrast the intellectual efflorescence of Marxism in the English-speaking world with the political and intellectual reaction that was gripping France after the *nouveaux philosophes* had led the generation of 1968 from Maoism to Cold-War liberalism.[8] The work of radical scholars such as the historian Robert Brenner and the sociologist Erik Olin Wright represented serious attempts systematically to connect theoretical reflection and empirical analysis. No doubt, serious weaknesses remained – certainly at the level of political strategy, but also theoretically with respect to such key issues as the analysis of gender and the problem of articulating market and plan in a socialist economy – but the future of 'Anglo-Marxism' seemed safe.

Alas, Anderson's analysis stands up better as a retrospective survey of the development of Marxist thought between the 1960s and the early 1980s than as a prediction of its future. Just as he was writing, the tide turned against Marxism in the English-speaking world. Once again, the decisive factor was a change in the political conjuncture. The advent of Margaret Thatcher and Ronald Reagan represented the beginning of major offensives against the workers' movements in Britain and the US that not only inflicted major defeats – above all, that of the British miners' strike of 1984–5 – but inaugurated the complex of neoliberal policies that by the 1990s had become a normative model for capitalism as a whole.

These reverses would have in any case produced a climate of pessimism and doubt on the intellectual Left. But more strictly theoretical problems also played their role in the unravelling of 'Anglo-Marxism'. Thus, in Britain, Althusserian Marxism self-destructed in the second half of the 1970s. An intensive exploration of the internal problems of the Althusserian system led some adepts first to renounce the notion of a general theory of history,

---

[8] Anderson 1983.

then the concept of mode of production, and finally Marxism *tout court*.[9] This rather arcane process was in fact symptomatic of a more general development. Whereas, at the height of the radicalisation in the late 1960s and early 1970s, French structuralism and what would later be called poststructuralism were embraced as forms of thought contributing to the renaissance of Marxism, by the end of the 1970s they were seem as constituting a major challenge to Marxism.

The writings of what might call 'Middle Foucault' – *Surveillir et punir, La Volonté de savoir*, and associated interviews and other texts on power-knowledge – were particularly important here. Detached from their immediate French context – the intense debates of the mid-1970s over the meaning of the Gulag – they played a broader theoretical role in the English-speaking world in helping philosophically to articulate a growing sense of the limitations of all forms of Marxism. The question of how to interpret gender oppression and other forms on non-class domination was particularly pressing. The belief that these forms could not be explained on the basis of the classical concepts of historical materialism – forces and relations of production, base and superstructure, exploitation and class, etc. – encouraged a quasi-Foucauldian view of society as a irreducible multiplicity of power-relations. Ernesto Laclau and Chantal Mouffe offered a particularly influential version of this view in *Hegemony and Socialist Strategy* (1985), which drew on the post-Althusserian debates as well as a peculiar reading of Gramsci to argue for a 'radical democratic' politics bringing together a plurality of different social movements.

The rise and fall of analytical Marxism

Yet it was in this very unpromising conjuncture of the 1980s that there emerged what might be considered the first Marxist theoretical current completely indigenous to the English-speaking world. The founding work of analytical Marxism is Cohen's *Karl Marx's Theory of History*, which represents one of the three main currents that went to make it up. Cohen, the product of a Communist-Party milieu in Quebec, but trained at Oxford in the techniques of post-war ordinary language philosophy, sought to use these techniques rigorously to articulate the conceptual structure of an orthodox historical materialism in

---

[9] See Hindess and Hirst 1974, Hindess and Hirst 1977, and Cutler et al. 1977–8.

which the development of the productive forces is the motor of social transformation. His main substantive thesis involved the elaboration of a conception of functional explanation that allowed him to argue that the production relations exist because of their tendency to develop the productive forces and the superstructure because of its tendency to stabilise these relations.

The elegance and originality of Cohen's treatment of historical materialism have permanently altered the terms on which discussion of Marx's work is conducted. More important perhaps than the content of Cohen's interpretation was the intellectual style it embodied – a combination of close acquaintance with Marx's writing with a careful attention to precision of statement and consequence of argument. Yet, surprisingly enough, the development of historical materialism did not for long provide the main focus of the group of philosophers and social scientists whose annual meetings represent the intellectual core of analytical Marxism. Cohen's critics were quick to seize on his reliance on the assumption that humans are 'somewhat rational' in order to justify the claim that the productive forces tend to develop through history. It was the attempt systematically to reconstruct Marxism on the basis of such an assumption that was pursued by the second, and arguably the dominant tendency within analytical Marxism.

'Rational-choice Marxism' was most systematically expounded by Jon Elster in *Making Sense of Marx* (1985). It rested on two theses: first, methodological individualism – social structures must be interpreted as the unintended consequence of individual actions; second, human actors must be regarded as instrumentally rational, in the sense of selecting the most efficient means for securing their ends. The first thesis was associated with the ideological offensive waged against Marxism by Popper and Hayek at the height of the Cold War; the second was a generalisation of an animating assumption of neoclassical economics. How could an approach with such anti-Marxist credentials come to be associated with an attempted reconstruction of Marxism?

In part this outcome was a consequence of the evolution of Marxist economic theory in the English-speaking world. The explosion of radical ideas at the end of the 1960s encouraged both the serious critical scrutiny of Marx's *Capital*, particularly by those influenced either by Althusser or by the German capital-logic school, and the attempt to develop the Marxist tradition of political economy by explaining why the Golden Age of postwar capitalism had come to an end. In the 1970s, however, these efforts became embroiled in prolonged debates about the internal coherence and explanatory power of Marx's value theory. Left-wing economists influenced by Piero Sraffa generalised from certain long-standing arguments about the transformation of values into prices of production and the theory of the tendency of the rate of profit to fall to argue that the labour theory of value was irrelevant to determining relative prices and an obstacle to understanding the actual behaviour of capitalist economies. The Sraffians' own crisis theory resembled Ricardo's theory that wages and profits are inversely related – hence they were commonly known as neo-Ricardians.

Some analytical Marxists – notably John Roemer and Philippe Van Parijs – took part in these debates on the neo-Ricardian side. But Roemer in particular went much further, embracing the neoclassical orthodoxy of which Sraffa had been such a subversive critic. In *A General Theory of Exploitation and Class* (1982), he sought to detach Marx's theory of exploitation from the labour theory of value and restate in terms of general equilibrium analysis and game theory. Since the latter both reduce social relations to the activities of optimising individuals, the rigour and imagination that Roemer displayed in using them to construct various formal models of exploitation seemed to demonstrate the fertility of a rational-choice approach.

The third current in analytical Marxism – represented chiefly by Wright and Brenner – enjoyed a somewhat oblique relationship to rational-choice Marxism. Wright drew on Roemer's theory of exploitation in his *Classes* (1985). But his own research was driven by a much more long standing preoccupation was systematically and empirically to test a carefully articulated Marxist theory of class whose original Althusserian influences remained visible even in the later versions. Both Wright and Brenner rejected methodological individualism. While the latter's interpretation of the origins of European capitalism laid great weight on the role of agency, in the shape of the class struggles between lord and peasant in the late mediaeval countryside, individual action was constrained by the 'rules of reproduction' imposed on social actors by their place in the structure of 'property relations' (as Brenner preferred to name the relations of production).

It is perhaps not surprising that, given the heterogeneity of analytical Marxism, its claim to be developing a distinctively Marxist understanding of the world proved to be quite short-lived. To some extent, this was a product of the contradictory internal logic of rational-choice Marxism itself. The labour theory of value and the theory of the falling rate of profit proved not to be the only item of Marxist thought that were deemed to be incompatible with the canons of rational-choice theory. The resulting intellectual vacuum encouraged some leading figures – notably Cohen and Roemer – to shift their intellectual focus towards normative political philosophy, and to become contributors to the debates provoked by the efforts of egalitarian liberals such as John Rawls, Ronald Dworkin, and Amartya Sen to develop a theory of justice that would give a prominent place to equality.[10]

There were internal reasons why this shift in focus should occur. A wide-ranging debate among English-speaking Marxist philosophers had drawn attention to Marx's tacit reliance in condemning capitalist exploitation on normative principles of justice that he denied possessing.[11] Roemer's attempts to reconstruct Marx's theory of exploitation led him to conclude that the injustice of exploitation did not derive from the appropriation of surplus labour but in the unjust initial distribution of productive assets responsible for this surplus extraction.[12] But such a view required some statement of egalitarian principles of justice in terms of which particular distributions could be evaluated. In Cohen's case, his attempt to articulate such principles seemed to be driven less by any such strict logic than by a more general sense that the most urgent task of socialist theory was to identify the normative preconditions of an egalitarian society. Thus, explaining his shift, he cites as a reason,

> which doesn't require that there is something wrong with historical materialism, is that I just don't think that it's terribly important, whereas I think that the normative questions are desperately important. The struggle at the intellectual level between capitalism and socialism as realizations of different normative orientations is immensely important for the future of socialist politics.[13]

---

[10] See Cohen 1989 and Cohen 1995 and Roemer 1995.
[11] See Geras 1985.
[12] Roemer 1986.
[13] Cohen 1996, pp. 12–13.

Is Marxism 'over'?

Cohen's move away from classical Marxism towards something more closely resembling utopian socialism was symptomatic of a more general sense of malaise. The impact of 1989 and 1991 – the East-European revolutions and the collapse of the Soviet Union – were undoubtedly of great importance, reinforcing the doubts and difficulties that had developed since the late 1970s. Even those Marxists critical of Stalinism often had hidden political capital invested in 'existing socialism': the existence of a viable state-run economic system, however authoritarian its political régime, offered a visible limit to the power and rationality of Western capitalism. Hence the fall of the Stalinist régimes demoralised the international Left well beyond the ranks of these régimes' organised political supporters in the Communist Parties. It was on this basis that Ronald Aronson argued that 'Marxism is over': 'By erasing its last, lingering hopes, the dissolution of the Soviet Union closes the eyes of the Marxian project.'[14]

In considering Aronson's claim in the Anglo-Saxon context it is necessary to draw a critical distinction.[15] Marxism has always operated in two registers. It is both an intellectual tradition and a political movement. The tension this implies is evident even in the name Engels sought to give it – scientific socialism. For sciences proceed according to protocols that respect the autonomy of theoretical research: propositions are scrutinised according to their heuristic power, empirical corroboration, logical consistency, and (occasionally) philosophical foundation. Socialism, by contrast, as a political movement must be judged by criteria of worldly success – mass support, political power, global extension. By proudly embracing the unity of theory and practice, Marxism submits itself to two standards of judgement.

Having drawn these unavoidable distinctions, I now wish to offer a hypothesis. Marxism has not been theoretically refuted, but has suffered several serious though not fatal political defeats. To assert that Marxism continues to be a viable and indeed a robust scientific research programme is not to deny that it suffers from a variety of anomalies, silences, and other limitations. It is simply to argue that none of its basic propositions have been refuted, let alone

[14] Aronson 1995, pp. 1, 69.
[15] This and the subsequent three paragraphs draw on Callinicos 1996, pp. 9–10.

replaced by those offered by a more powerful successor. This is, of course, a very strong claim, and one that I cannot make out in any detail here.[16] Indirect support for it is, however, provided by the current state of debate in the Western academy. It is not that there has been any decisive encounter between Marxism and its rivals in which the former was intellectually crushed. On the contrary, it is the most fashionable of these rivals, postmodernism, that has been subjected to such devastating theoretical criticism that the most interesting question about it is why ideas as bankrupt as these continue to exercise so widespread an influence.[17]

The intellectual retreat of Marxism is less a matter of outright defeat than of positions being abandoned, debates cut short, arguments left half way. Thus the early controversies among analytical Marxists over Cohen's interpretation of Marx represented competing attempts to articulate the conceptual structure of historical materialism. No ineluctable logic led from these arguments to the abandonment of classical Marxism. Rather, the antagonists lost interest and moved into the academic mainstream.

It is as if the defenders of a well-fortified stronghold were voluntarily to abandon it. There was, it is true, one area where Marxism has come under challenge, with the appearance of several powerful historical sociologies whose theoretical sources can be traced back ultimately to Max Weber.[18] These works offered wide-ranging theories of history that sought to establish that class exploitation is merely one among an irreducible plurality of forms of forms of domination, each of co-equal importance to the others. The appearance of the first volume of Mann's *The Sources of Social Power* apparently decided Anderson to abandon 'the intellectual world of the revolutionary left', since 'there now existed a developed analytical theory of the pattern of human development, exceeding in explanatory ambition and empirical detail any Marxist account'.[19]

But this seems like much too despairing a response. Once proper tribute has been paid to Mann's conceptual sophistication and historical range, the fact remains that a theory's strength is not primarily a matter of the amount of evidence it covers, but of how well it does so. Anderson's failure to draw this

[16] But see Callinicos 1983 and 1991.
[17] See Habermas 1987, Dews 1987, Callinicos 1989.
[18] Gellner 1989, Giddens 1981, Mann 1986 and 1993, and Runciman 1989.
[19] Anderson 1992b, p. xii.

distinction is particularly surprising since he was one of a number of writers who identified, from a Marxist perspective, major flaws in Mann's claim to have come up with a theory of history superior to Marx's.[20] It seems likely that Anderson's willingness to concede intellectual ground to neo-Weberian historical sociology was a symptom of a more general pessimism about the political prospects for the Left rather than a reflection of the demonstrable theoretical superiority of, say, Mann's work to classical historical materialism.

The transatlantic shift

Certainly the past two decades of crisis have seen some major contributions by English-speaking Marxists. They include one undeniable classic – G.E.M. de Ste Croix's *The Class Struggle in the Ancient Greek World* (1981), the work of a historian of the same generation as Hill and Hobsbawm, albeit formed in a different intellectual and political milieu, that of Oxford classical scholarship, on the one hand, and the Labour Party, on the other. Younger historians have also produced some important works – for example, Peter Linebaugh's *The London Hanged* (1991), Brenner's *Merchants and Revolution* (1993), and John Haldon's *Byzantium in the Seventh Century* (1997). Brenner has also contributed to the analysis of contemporary capitalism in his controversial study of the advanced economies since 1945.[21] In a similar mode is Wright's latest report from his ongoing comparative study of Western class structure.[22] These well-known texts are merely the tip of ice-berg: particularly in the United States, many Marxist scholars have simply ignored the grand apostasies of the past twenty years and carried on working in various areas of philosophy, political economy, sociology, and history.

This is a reflection of the fact that, as the huge wave of youth radicalistion that swept the US in the late 1960s and early 1970s receded, it deposited in its wake many of the participants lodged in niches within the vast university system. This has been one source of the 'culture wars' waged in the American academy over issues such as a race, gender, and sexual orientation. At its worst, the result has been a narcissistic, self-enclosed academic culture striking radical

[20] Anderson 1992b, Chapter 4; also Wickham 1988, Haldon 1993, and Callinicos 1995, pp. 110–28.
[21] Brenner 1998.
[22] Wright 1997.

postures and conducting arcane debates while, outside the campuses, the larger society moves in the opposite direction, as neoliberalism steers the state and economy, and the 'prison-industrial complex' expands remorselessly to process the casualties of an increasingly social-Darwinist capitalism. But the size and diversity of the university system has nevertheless provided spaces within which more serious Marxist and *marxisant* intellectuals can pursue their work according to a bewilderingly diversity of theoretical paradigms.

To some extent this is a repetition on a larger scale on what happened to the 1930s's generation from which figures such as Edward Thompson, Christopher Hill, Eric Hobsbawm, and Paul Sweezy sprang. There is, however, an important difference: the centre of gravity has shifted across the Atlantic. Thus, of the five leading figures associated with analytical Marxism, three – Roemer, Brenner, and Wright – are American, Cohen is a Canadian based at Oxford, and Elster is a Norwegian working in the US. It is not that there are no important British figures: the literary theorist Terry Eagleton has, for example, kept up for the past generation a dazzling performance in which he somehow manages to draw on such diverse sources as Althusser, Derrida, Trotsky, and Benjamin to produce a series of scintillating texts. But those British Marxists with an international reputation tend to write increasingly for an audience centred on the American academy and often to work there.[23]

The presence at UCLA of Anderson, an Anglo-Irish intellectual who has done more than anyone else to thematise the problem of a British Marxism, is symbolic of the process.

This phenomenon is part of a broader redistribution of intellectual power in the Western academy. For example, the dominance that the US has come to acquire in the domain of analytical philosophy in the era of Quine, Davidson, Rawls, Dworkin, Kripke, and Dennett is striking. The fact that Marxist theory has participating in the same process is a symptom of its integration in academic life. Today probably the two best-known Marxists in the English-speaking world are Eric Hobsbawm and Fredric Jameson. The first recalls an era that is now firmly in the past – Hobsbawm was formed by the experience of fascism and Popular Fronts in the 1930s, a loyal member of the British

[23] The US also acts as a conduit for communication with left intellectuals outside Europe. In East Asia, for example, radical milieux in countries such as South Korea and Taiwan have shown a healthy appetite for English-language Marxist texts that reach them largely via the US.

Communist Party till its collapse after 1989, apart from Thompson the most publicly active of the postwar historians, the practitioner of a subtle, even Jesuitical politics that may explain that he is the only Marxist to have been awarded the accolade of being made a Companion of Honour by the Queen.

Jameson, by contrast, is chiefly known for his celebrated essays on postmodernism.[24] These texts display an idiosyncratic Marxism at work, one that remarkably seeks to reconcile Althusser and Lukács by treating all the slips, elisions, and absences characteristic of ideological discourses as symptoms of the unrepresentable totality that constitutes the horizon of all human activity. It is the task of historical materialism to conceptualise this totality: thus Jameson's famous injunction: 'Always historicize!' might be transcribed: 'Always totalize!'.[25] This is an intellectual project working against the grain of the dominant tendency in discussions of postmodernism, which privileges fragmentation and uncertainty. Jameson's unapologetically totalising interpretation of postmodern art as the culture appropriate to a new epoch of global capitalism has recently won over at least one sceptic.[26] But, whatever one thinks of this interpretation as an historico-economic analysis, in its preoccupation with tracing the particularities of contemporary culture it is relatively easily recuperable within academic discourses that share none of Jameson's resolute materialism or his undiminished hostility to capitalism.

There is, then, a sense in which Anderson's earlier diagnosis of Western Marxism as an idealism that fled from a hostile world into the academy can be applied to contemporary English-speaking Marxism. It has been left to the pragmatist philosopher Richard Rorty to criticise 'the cultural Left' for effectively ignoring the sharp increase in socio-economic inequality over the past generation and to call a return to class politics.[27] This criticism does not apply to all left intellectuals: the work of Brenner and Wright, for example, has sought seriously to engage with the realities of contemporary capitalism. Beyond the academy, the heterodox Trotskyism inaugurated by Tony Cliff has represented a version of Marxism that seeks both to be analytically rigorous and to maintain the kind of systematic connection with political practice constitutive of the classical tradition. Chris Harman is perhaps the most

[24] See Jameson 1991.
[25] Jameson 1981, p. 9.
[26] See Anderson 1998.
[27] Rorty 1998 and Rorty 1999.

impressive exponent of this approach, producing a stream of books that span analysis of Stalinism (1974), historiography of the Left (1982 and 1988), political economy (1984), and, most recently, non-Eurocentric universal history (1999).

This still leaves a painful gap between theory and practice – between contemporary Marxists' capacity to offer critical analyses of the world in which they live and their ability to influence the development of that world. Understanding the source of this gap is a matter of critical political importance. Does it signify the demise of Marxism as a coherent intellectual and political project as Aronson, among many other left intellectuals, argues? Must we, rather, accept Jacques Bidet's and Jürgen Habermas's contrasting proposals to incorporate what was valid in Marx's critique of capitalism in a larger general theory of modernity? Does the current ineffectiveness of Marxist critique, as Jameson and Anderson suggest, reflect the inauguration of a new epoch of capitalist development that will eventually stimulate its socialist negation in some unimagined, unforeseeable form? Or, finally, are we already beginning to emerge from a period of severe but temporary defeats from the workers' movement, and entering an era when the new social struggles stimulated by neoliberalism will allow classical Marxism once again to become a material force?

I incline personally towards the last of these alternatives. The debate among the four options will not be quickly or decisively concluded. It is important that it is conducted in a way that avoids reliance on a misleading stereotype of a caricatured unitary 'Marxism' that typically combines the least attractive traits of the Second and Third Internationals. One positive consequence of the past twenty years of disorientation has been the recognition of what has been a fact at least since the Bernstein debate – that there is a plurality of Marxisms offering rival ways of carrying the tradition on. 1989 may have definitively killed off one such version – the Marxist-Leninist ideology that provided 'existing socialism' with its state religion. It does not follow that rival variants have also been disposed of – particularly those, stemming from Trotsky, that defined themselves in opposition to Stalinism. This does not mean one may take refuge in a dogmatised 'orthodoxy'. But not the least interesting feature of English-speaking Marxism over the past generation is the resources it offers for renewing the classical tradition.

Chapter Five

Old Theories and New Capitalism: The Actuality of a Marxist Economics

Gérard Duménil and Dominique Lévy

Introduction

Yes, capitalism undergoes a process of permanent change. Its capacity to plunge into enduring, profound crisis and then bounce back appears limitless. Each of these pulsations occurs at the cost of a renewal of certain aspects of its structure and dynamic. Which should surprise us more – the continuities or the ruptures? More clearly than in some of its previous phases, contemporary capitalism exhibits the basic characteristics that have defined it as such since it came into existence: private ownership of the means of production; concentration of income and wealth; exploitation at national and international levels; and a dynamic of change directed towards perpetuating the privileges of a minority. But other observations underline the extent of its transformation: new techniques of production and financial institutions; changes in property forms and managerial modes; the retreat of the working class in the advanced capitalist countries and the dissolution of old class boundaries into new intermediate strata; and so on. Are we already beyond capitalism?

What tools do we possess to master the paradoxical coexistence of continuity and change, to guide us in these developments? The thesis we wish to defend here is that, far from being obsolete, the tools identified by Marx in the mid-nineteenth century – by the Marx who was a theorist of capitalism – have still not been superseded and have not realised their full potential. The object of the present exercise, however, is not to elicit retrospective admiration, but to contribute to the renewal of an analytical framework.

In order to think the new starting from the old, two rules dictate themselves: first, grasping recent events in a historical perspective; and second, killing two birds with one stone – combining use of these tools and their refinement in a single intervention. If the concepts and analytical mechanisms that Marx bequeathed us are those most apt to supply us with the keys to the contemporary world, we must also know how to acknowledge their lacunae and defects – and the need for supplementation and reformulation.

This programme has only been very partially executed since the publication of the last volumes of *Capital*.[1] There are several reasons for this. In the developed capitalist countries, Marxist analysis has always been in a subordinate position, bereft of the resources required for its advance; and this is perhaps more than ever the case today. Where it was dominant, it was instrumentalised, put in the service of a party, whether conducting the revolutionary process or holding the reins of power. Next, we should remember, this is an arduous task! One of the characteristics of Marxist theory, which adds to its complexity, is the very general apprehension of social processes peculiar to it. If the economic theory is clearly defined by its concepts (commodity, value, capital, surplus-value, price, and so on), their deployment in empirical analysis necessarily draws us into the fields traditionally defined as sociological or political.

The two sections below elaborate on these themes: firstly, the tendencies and mechanisms that have emerged in world capitalism in the last decade or so pose a major analytical challenge; secondly, the concepts fashioned by Marx in the nineteenth century provide us with the keys – their utilisation requires and governs a deepening of them.

[1] See the major synthesis made in Howard and King 1989 and 1992.

A new phase of capitalism

If we must go straight to the heart of the matter and characterise the current operation of capitalism by way of its major features, two stand out. The first concerns the new tendencies of technical change and distribution. The second involves the neoliberal course of capitalism, in both its national characteristics (the rigour of its rules as regards the dominated classes and its service of the dominant classes) and its international features (the neoliberal phase of globalisation and its financial disorder). We shall consider them in turn. In this analysis, we shall tend to privilege, often implicitly, the examples of France and the United States.

Technical change and capital profitability

The structural crisis of the 1970s and 1980s followed a fall in the profitability of capital, which was itself an expression of the gradual deterioration in the conditions of technical change. The most obvious expression of this was the gradual slow-down in the growth in labour productivity. However, the quantitative output that can be achieved with the same mass of capital – what is called *capital productivity* (without any implication as to the ability of capital to *produce*) – is even more revealing: it began to diminish in absolute value. More and more capital was required to achieve the same output. From the first signs of these unfavourable trends, and with the help of the expanding wave of unemployment, wage growth was rapidly called into question (with more difficulty when it came to the social contributions entailed by state benefits, for obvious institutional reasons). Despite the low increase in labour costs, the profitability of capital continued on its downward slide until the mid-1980s.

The important point is that this trend has now been reversed on a long-term basis. Profits are increasing not only in absolute value, but relative to the stock of capital (this is what is measured by the profit rate).[2] In this respect, conditions are favourable for capital. On the one hand, although labour productivity is continuing to grow only slowly, capital productivity is now increasing. On the other hand, labour costs are still being contained. As this dynamic has

[2] The tendency for the rate of profit to rise has been evident for about twenty years, at least in the United States and the principal European countries. It is no more marked in the United States than Europe (Duménil and Lévy 2004, Chapter 3).

continued over the last fifteen years, it indicates the contours of a *new phase of capitalism*.

This is not the first time such a process has occurred. Going as far back as the statistical series allow, we can identify two phases of *declining* profit rates (from the end of the nineteenth century to the beginning of the twentieth, and from the initial postwar decades up to the 1980s); and two phases of *rising* profit rates (during the first half of the twentieth century and since the mid-1980s). Each lasted for some decades. The first and third, which are similar in many respects, resulted in equally similar structural crises: the crisis at the end of the nineteenth century and the crisis that began in the 1970s. The main symptoms of these crises were a slow-down in the accumulation of capital, and hence in growth; a correlative rise in unemployment; and greater instability (proliferating recessions). The crisis of 1929 interrupted the intermediary period, which was more auspicious, and of a different character.

The crisis at the end of the nineteenth century prompted a major transformation of capitalism. In the context of a crisis of competition (this was the era of trusts and cartels), the institutions of modern capitalism emerged: the large public limited company backed by modern finance – the institutional form of the separation between ownership and management. Large firms were managed by an enormous staff, extremely hierarchical in character, of managers and employees. This *managerial revolution* (a revolution in management in the broad sense)[3] underlay major efficiency gains in capital utilisation. Coupled with the growth in the number of public-sector managers and employees, this development created new social configurations, characteristic of twentieth-century capitalism. In a context of intense class struggle, it resulted in significant increases in workers' purchasing power.

In analysing the origin of the new course of technical change over the last twenty years, comparisons with the resolution of the structural crisis of the late nineteenth century are very useful. The new trends in technology and organisation, particularly what is often referred to as the *information revolution* or the *new economy*, bear a strong resemblance to the transformations at the beginning of the twentieth century. The changes of the last two decades

[3] These changes combined technology in the strict sense and organisation. The assembly line is the archetype, but management as a whole (commercial, financial) was transformed.

can be interpreted as a revolution in management, still in the very broad sense of the term,[4] in which computing and communications are the distinctive techniques. Somewhat schematically, we can say that, at the beginning of the twentieth century, management transformed production and marketing, whereas today it is transforming itself, enhancing its efficiency and reducing its own costs.

In tandem with this *restoration of capital profitability*, growth is reviving. Europe, which has been more heavily penalised by neoliberal policies (even more of a break with its previous practices than in the United States), is somewhat lagging behind on this path – hence the slow reduction in unemployment. That vast regions of the globe remain excluded is a major element in this picture requiring more detailed treatment. The global distribution of profits during this new phase appear far from equitable.

Neoliberalism – neoliberal globalisation – American hegemony

Neoliberalism corresponds to the reassertion of the power of finance – that is to say, of *capitalist property owners* (in a capitalism where ownership and management are separate). The contrast with the Keynesian (or social-democratic) years is marked. Then, the shareholder had become a partner of the managers, almost *on a par with the others* (workers and the state). Managers, whose autonomy had been greatly enhanced by the 1929 crisis, both in firms and in the state apparatuses, were reduced by property-owners to the role of agent of the maximisation of the firm's profit rate or stock-market value – an important inflexion in what has long been called *corporate governance*.

This resurgence of finance was secured following persistent action and determined struggle under the leadership of American finance, which consolidated its pre-eminence on this occasion. Popular struggles were defeated amid the ebbing of the international Soviet and Communist threat.[5]

---

[4] Thus comprising the management of production, as well as electronic trade and the new techniques that govern financial operations. These new techniques are especially characteristic of multinationals, major funds, and markets – institutions that all now possess a planetary, *global* dimension.

[5] Just as, for example, the 1970s policy of credits for the Third World at negative real interest rates had been dictated by the anti-communist struggle, so the 1979 decision to increase them to levels that were intolerable for these countries was made possible by the ebbing of this threat (see Toussaint 1998).

To measure the consequences of these drastic changes in terms of income and property, it is necessary to enter into the labyrinth of the statistical series.[6] The financial income of the dominant classes had been very significantly reduced during the 1970s (negative real interest rates, weak distribution of dividends, flagging stock markets). The situation was abruptly reversed. At a time when the crisis had still not come to an end, and workers' purchasing power was stagnating (or, in the case of some categories, falling), neoliberalism engineered a prodigious enrichment of the dominant classes. Previous inequalities were restored and even accentuated.

A feature of the neoliberal period is the major development of financial activities, or *financialisation*: an explosion in financial operations, in the financial sector, and in firms' financial activities. We are familiar with the impact on prices in different stock markets, which took off in concert in the developed countries at the beginning of the 1980s. Obviously, this edifice posed risks for the capitalist economies that are reminiscent of the 1929 crash.

In the course of these events, the internationalisation of capital continued. Neoliberalism, shattering the arrangements set up at Bretton Woods at the end of the Second World War or hijacking the international institutions established at the time (IMF, World Bank) to its advantage, gave this internationalisation a financial dimension, whose main feature is the free circulation of capital (the globalisation of markets). This freedom of manoeuvre for capital sowed the seeds of the financial instability with which we are familiar. A more in-depth study of these developments reveals the driving role and hegemonic position of American finance. Whether as regards financial, trade, currency, or industrial mechanisms, we can speak of new forms of imperialism, of a new hegemony.[7]

This is not the first time that finance has been hegemonic. The emergence of modern finance at the beginning of the twentieth century was accompanied by a similar process, which was interrupted by the 1929 crisis. Thus, history is in very large measure repeating itself: a new favourable course of technical

---

[6] See Duménil and Lévy 1999b.

[7] See the contributions by François Chesnais, Odile Castel and Bernard Gerbier to Duménil and Lévy (eds.) 1999a, as well as those of Gilbert Achcar, Noam Chomsky, Larry Portis, Giovanni Arrighi, Peter Gowan, Fredric Jameson, James Cohen, and Jacques Bidet to *Actuel Marx*, no. 27, 2000. See also Amin 1996 and Chesnais 1997.

change (governed by a revolution in management in the broad sense); an explosion in financial activity; and financial instability. Thus, the present period combines two features, which should not be deemed contradictory *but complementary*: a revival of growth and dangerous financial instability.

If neoliberalism is indeed the expression of finance's restored hegemony, and hence the reassertion of major features of capitalism (the prerogatives and profits of property owners), these transformations are nonetheless fraught with ambiguity. The current revolution in management, in stimulating an expansion in managers and employees, is once again blurring the boundaries of the division between *capitalists* and *proletarians*. New property forms at the beginning of the twentieth century had created a distance between share-holders and firms, distorting the notion of ownership of the means of production. Contemporary capitalism, which some characterise as *institutional*, witnesses the concentration of capital in gigantic funds (pension and investment funds) managed by specialists. The position of the capitalist property-owner has survived and is reasserting its pre-eminence, but through institutional transformations that increase the many delegations from it, and hence dissolve it in a certain way.

The tools

The relevance of a Marxist toolkit in explaining these phenomena can be demonstrated in many respects. It goes without saying that we cannot pretend to any exhaustiveness here and the exercise encounters many other difficulties. The main one is linked to the fact that the different analyses are mutually related. The meaning of a theory like that of value, for example, can only be grasped at the end of long detours through other theoretical fields. We have selected ten themes: (1) the theory of value; (2) competition and concentration; (3) historical tendencies – in particular, the tendency for the rate of profit to fall; (4) the structural crises and phases of capitalism; (5) the conjunctural cycle (the sequence of overheating and recessions); (6) the law of capitalist accumulation and unemployment; (7) capitalist anarchy; (8) finance and its relations with the real economy; (9) classes and class struggle; (10) the mutation in the relations of production and the possible supersession of the explanatory power of traditional concepts. All these themes are related to the analysis of the tendencies and transformations of contemporary capitalism referred to above – relations that are more or less strong, direct or indirect, justifying the unequal treatment of them that we propose to suggest.

Here we shall confine ourselves to bringing out the explanatory power of Marxist concepts with respect to the contemporary world, while restricting critical remarks about other theories, especially the dominant neoclassical economics, to a minimum. Moreover, we shall set aside any analysis of socialism.

The theory of value

If Marx's labour theory of value derived directly from the dominant thought of his time – that of his classical predecessors (Smith and Ricardo) – in our day it seems highly singular. Following an interminable historical controversy over the *transformation of values into prices of production*,[8] many Marxists have rejected it, troubled as they often are by the narrow notion of productive labour associated with it (and which is opposed to a broader view of exploitation in contemporary capitalism). The stumbling block is thus twofold: intellectual and political.

This is, in fact, a very particular point of Marxist theory: a theory of value, distinct from that of prices, which leads to a theory of exploitation of the productive worker (the extortion of surplus-value). Marx draws a very strict distinction between two types of labour: productive labour, which creates the value from which surplus-value is extracted; and work of a different kind – likewise justified by the employment of capital (value captured in a movement of self-expansion) – which is dubbed *unproductive*. He devotes considerable attention to unproductive labour, such as the circulating costs of capital (for instance, the wage of an employee in sales), but it cannot be denied that he allots such labour a peripheral position – one further from the core of his system than productive labour. The function of unproductive labour is the *maximisation of the profit rate*. Schematically, this involves conceiving, organising, and supervising the labour process (productive) and making capital circulate (buying, selling, minimising stocks, managing accounts).[9] These

---

[8] See Duménil 1980; Foley 1982; Lipietz 1982; Dostaler 1985; Ehrbar and Glick 1986; and Freeman 1996. See also the picture of the controversy sketched in Jorland 1995.

[9] We can distinguish between tasks concerned with the maximisation of the profit rate in a given state of technique and organisation, and innovatory tasks aimed at

unproductive jobs, which can be those of the *active capitalist* or delegated to wage-earners, correspond to what is now called *management*: management in the broad sense, *à la* Marx.

Is this distinction between productive and managerial forms of relevance to the analysis of present-day capitalism? Enormously relevant, on condition that we recognise the quantitative expansion and qualitative transformation of managerial tasks (their constantly renewed forms, their effects, and so on). If, in the mid-nineteenth century, Marx could assign them a subaltern position, this is no longer possible at the end of the twentieth century. But it is not a question of everything merging and becoming confused, or of abandoning a theoretical corpus with undue haste. Without a shadow of a doubt, the theory of capitalist exploitation refers to the appropriation of the surplus-labour of the productive worker (an exploitation that is now planetary). But new social categories have emerged and it is up to us to develop the already very substantial elements with which Marx supplied us for analysing them.

Is it important? What is at stake is nothing less than our understanding of the new forms of exploitation, the mutation in the relations of production, tendencies and counter-tendencies, income creation in present-day capitalism – particularly finance income – and so on. We shall return to this.

Competition and concentration

Marx also took from the classics an analysis of competitive processes – the so-called *theory of the formation of production prices in competition*. This analysis must be related to Marx's theses on the concentration and centralisation of capital. Unquestionably better than anyone else, Marx had perceived the tendency of capitalism to concentration; and the relationship of this to contemporary capitalism and the globalisation of capital is obvious. While encompassing these tendencies, Marx never called into question his highly classical analysis of competitive processes.[10] Firms that are heterogeneous in terms of size and performance confront one another in markets, entering into competition as soon as their products, goods or services can lay claim to

---

obtaining new products and enhanced efficiency (whose criterion is always profitability), for which the acquisition of knowledge is vital.

[10] Cf. Marx 1981, Chapter 10. For the contemporary reformulation of these mechanisms, see the special issue of *Political Economy* 1990, as well as Bidard 1984.

similar uses (defining branches). Capitalists invest their capitals in these firms to various degrees, and hence in these branches, comparing the profit rates obtained (what is referred to as the *inter-branch mobility of capital*). This search for maximum profitability creates a tendency to the equalisation of profit rates between branches, while maintaining the differences between firms, and adjusts the proportions of supply to those of demand. Competitive struggle stimulates the process of concentration and elimination of the less successful.

This theory's alleged loss of the explanatory value fascinated Marxists from the time of the crisis of competition at the end of the nineteenth century, resulting in the theory of monopoly capitalism. Numerous versions of this exist, from Hilferding and Lenin onwards. How does this relate to contemporary capitalism? In our view, it is vital to understand that this tendency to the equalisation of profit rates is still operative, despite the increased size of firms.[11] Financial institutions and mechanisms likewise grow in size and efficiency, facilitating the inter-branch mobility of capital; opportunities for profit are exploited at great speed. We must therefore look elsewhere for an explanation of the dynamics of late twentieth-century capitalism and treat theses that focus either the attenuation of competition, or on its exacerbation, with caution. Monopolistic trends have not transformed the tendency for the rate of profit to fall into a tendency for the rate of surplus-value to rise;[12] excess competition does not explain falling profit rates.[13]

The decline in the rate of profit, the other tendencies, and counter-tendencies

No economic theorist has placed the profitability of capital (the profit rate) at the centre of his interpretation of the dynamic of capitalism in the same way that Marx did, in neither the neoclassical nor the Keynesian traditions. When this variable is taken into account, particularly in empirical work, it is assigned a secondary role. However, we are dealing with a key point when it comes to understanding the long-term dynamics of capitalism and its structural crises – particularly the reversal in trends between the 1970s and the 1980s. Two types of question are involved: *tendencies and counter-tendencies,*

---

[11] Cf. Duménil and Lévy 2002a.
[12] Cf. Baran and Sweezy 1966.
[13] Contrary to the thesis defended in Brenner 1998.

which are dealt with in this section, and the *consequences* of the shift in the profit rate, which will be discussed in the following section.

In Volume Three of *Capital*, Marx left us with an especially sophisticated analysis of what he called the *historical tendencies* of capitalism (tendencies as regards technology, distribution, accumulation, production, and employment). As far as we know, he was the only one to conceive trajectories of *growth* in production and employment, associated with the strengthening of the capital-labour or capital-output relationship (the expression of a high degree of *mechanisation*), where the reduction in the results of technical progress translates into a fall in the rate of profit. For this reason, we refer to such trajectories as *Marxian trajectories*. Capitalism's propensity to follow such trajectories is a largely established fact. In particular, the phase of falling profit rates in the period following the Second World War has been the object of numerous investigations.[14] Marx did not bring this highly complex analysis to a conclusion and, in addition, lacked some of the empirical material required to do so.[15]

We link capitalism's tendency to follow such trajectories to certain weaknesses in the process of innovation. This difficulty without doubt testifies to the private character of research and development (costly activities) and the limits of the private appropriation of the results. Inter-firm co-operation, and especially state involvement, in research programmes and scientific training partially remedy these limitations, but only partially. However, much remains to be done to arrive at a better understanding of these mechanisms.

Marx offered important accounts of the counter-tendencies to the rate of profit to fall. They are of several kinds. Some, like the development of joint-stock companies, account for the capacity of the capitalist system to perpetuate itself despite a lower profit rate; this is more a question of a process of adaptation than of *counter-tendencies* in the strict sense. Others, like the rise in the rate of surplus-value or the fall in prices relative to capital, correspond to straightforward attenuation of the tendencies, or to their reversal. Capitalism's

---

14 See, in particular, Moseley 1992 and 1997; Shaikh 1992; Wolff 1992; Brenner 1998; and Husson 1999. We have recently devoted Duménil and Lévy 1996 and 2002b to the subject.

15 An important controversy was sparked off by Marx's description of the introduction of new techniques making it possible to obtain a surplus profit, and of the consequences for the average rate of profit of the generalisation of these techniques to the whole set of producers (see Okishio 1961).

entry into new types of trajectory during the first half of the twentieth century stems from these two sets of developments. The development of joint-stock companies (the *corporate revolution*) pertains to the former; the revolution in management (the *managerial revolution*) to the latter.

The analysis of tendencies and the analysis of counter-tendencies belong to the same theoretical corpus: the affirmation and negation of the *Marxian* character of technical change. Our interpretation of the alternation of these two types of phases refers, in what at first sight is perhaps a rather surprising manner, to the theory of value and the distinction between the two types of labour (see above). We think that the expansion of posts maximising the profit rate[16] (unproductive labour) stands out historically *as the principal counter-tendency to the falling rate of profit*, with the characteristics that have been indicated for each of the two phases of restoration: revolution through management and revolution in management.

The importance here of the articulation of two basic theories – of value and of tendencies – is therefore obvious. And this is one of the points where the need for development makes itself felt. Two types of labour co-exist: labour that produces surplus-value and labour that maximises the profit rate. The managerial revolution was the expression of the tremendous comparative development of the second type of labour during the first half of the twentieth century. But it reached its limits, in terms of quantity and efficiency alike. The new phase of declining profit rates that ensued belatedly led to a further extension of this revolution to other domains which had hitherto been less involved (like financial management – for example, in funds); and to new efficiency gains (thanks to information and communication technologies, and to the renewal of organisational practices running counter to the bureaucratic propensity of management).

Structural crises, the genesis of counter-tendencies, and phases of capitalism

The other aspect of the Marxist theory of tendencies concerns the effects of actual reductions in the profit rates. Marx is unduly brief, but categorical on

[16] This is equivalent to the minimisation of the production and circulation costs of capital, as well as to that of the sums incorporated in the various components of capital. Contrariwise, Fred Moseley regards the rise in these costs as the main factor in the falling profit rate (cf. Moseley 1992).

this point. Such falls slow down capital accumulation and provoke a proliferation of crises, as well as financial problems (hypertrophy of financial activity, speculation, etc.):

> On the other hand, however, in view of the fact that the rate at which the total capital is valorised, i.e. the rate of profit, is the spur to capitalist production (in the same way as the valorisation of capital is its sole purpose), a fall in this rate slows down the formation of new, independent capitals and thus appears as a threat to the development of the capitalist production process; it promotes overproduction, speculation and crises, and leads to the existence of excess capital alongside a surplus production.[17]

We shall call such a set of problems a *structural crisis*. The two phases of the real fall in the profit rate described above result in such periods of crisis.

In fact, in Volume Three of *Capital*, two ideas co-exist whose relationship is not wholly explicit. The first is that periods of actual decline in the rate of profit lead into structural crises; while the second is that the fall in the profit rate is counter-acted by counter-tendential developments. To maintain that structural crises play a crucial role in the emergence of counter-tendencies – at least of some of them or at the peak of their assertion – hardly goes beyond Marx's analysis. Here we return to the major Marxist theme of the obstetric violence of history. Marx sometimes refers to the powerful development of the productive forces in capitalism as its 'historical vocation', emphasising the convulsive character of the ensuing changes (obtained at the cost of repeated, profound crises).

Observation of more than a century of capitalism, for which certain systems of measurement are possible, and the numerous works of economic history suggest giving substance to these intuitions. This analytical framework is at the centre of our interpretation of the history of capitalism. Thus, we converge with perspectives that foreground the notion of long waves.[18] Such interpretations too often take a mechanistic turn. Certainly, instability is inscribed in recurrent fashion in the history of capitalism. But these phases of profound disruption and the changes that they tend to provoke can be very diverse in kind – which rules out regarding them as the expression of a cyclicality

---

[17] Marx 1981, pp. 349–50.

[18] In a Marxist framework and with respect to falling profit rates, as in Mandel 1995. See also Kleinknecht, Mandel and Wallerstein 1992.

inherent in capitalist relations. In its causes and consequences, the crisis of 1929, in particular, was profoundly different from those of the end of the nineteenth or twentieth centuries.

Having taken these methodological precautions, the analytical framework of tendencies, structural crises, counter-tendencies, and phases seems to us wholly adequate to account for the historical dynamic of capitalism and its periodisation.[19] The phase we have been in for the last fifteen years is a new expression of them.

Crises and conjunctural cycle

The relationship between a fall in the profit rate and crisis thus leads into the notion of relatively long periods of disturbance, which we have termed *structural crises*. It is necessary to distinguish these crises from the recessions of the *business cycle* that Marx also deals with, independently of the falling profit rate, which is only the factor of their proliferation during structural crises.

Since the beginning of the nineteenth century, economic activity in the capitalist countries has been subject to recurrent disruption, racing out of control – *overheating* – and contracting – *recession*. This used to be referred to as the *industrial cycle*; people now refer to the *business cycle*. Strictly speaking, these movements are more recurrent than cyclical in character. No doubt they have declined in magnitude since the nineteenth century, but the instability of the general level of activity is still a major phenomenon in the capitalism of recent decades. Their explanation is still much debated.

Marx has legitimately been criticised for never having provided a clearly articulated, coherent interpretation of them. The rich accounts of the topic that he left suggest the following observations:

(1) *Partial* crises can exist.[20] But what matters to Marx is *general* crises – the kind of crisis that affects all branches (a simultaneous decline in production in these branches). As with Keynes's, his viewpoint is macroeconomic.

---

[19] In periodising capitalism, various criteria can be privileged: tendencies, structural crises, institutional changes, relations of production, and so on. In fact, they need to be combined in a particular way (Duménil and Lévy 2001). Regulation theory offers a different combination (Aglietta 1979; Lipietz 1979; and Boyer 1986).

[20] According to the terminology of Marx 1981.

(2) Marx has no single theory of the destabilisation of the general level of activity. Various real mechanisms (a rise in wages during peaks of activity) and monetary mechanisms (a rise in interest rates or any financial fragility) are involved. Whereas Keynes endeavoured to describe *equilibria* of underemployment, Marx is much closer to a modern analysis in terms of the *stability and instability* of an equilibrium.

(3) As has been said when dealing with structural crises, the frequency and severity of these crises are reinforced by more profound developments, bound up with the major tendencies of capitalism (the falling rate of profit).

Despite the imprecision of these observations, it must be stressed that no modern theory offers a better account of the fluctuations in economic activity.

It is interesting to note that Marx combines: (1) a theory of the efficiency of the mechanisms of capital mobility and of the tendency to the equalisation of profit rates between different branches, and supplying the market with what is demanded; and (2) a theory – or elements of such a theory – of instability in the general level of economic activity. This is a strong point of Marx's analysis, on which his empirical relevance and modernity are based. It remains for economists who work in Marxian perspective to pursue the task. In the models we have constructed,[21] which correspond fairly closely to the indications left by Marx, we show that the stability of capitalism *proportionately* (concerning the allocation of capital, the formation of relative prices, and the determination of the relative quantities produced) contrasts strongly with its instability *dimensionally* – its propensity for recurrent fluctuations at the general level of activity; and that this dual property results from the same characteristics of the behaviour of firms and the mechanisms of monetary creation (whether involving control by large private banks, as in the United States in the nineteenth century, or public, centralised control, as in modern monetary policy).

The theory of disproportionalities is that of Ricardo and numerous Marxists who, on the pretext of certain of Marx's statements concerning *partial* crises (see above), have chosen to see in the reproduction schemes the theory of

---

[21] See Duménil and Lévy 1996.

capitalist crises.[22] We can be very decisive on these issues: the major recessions of the 1970s, 1980s, or 1990s did not originate in disproportionality in economic activity – an inability to inflect production in the requisite directions. Likewise, Marx's famous formula making 'poverty and restricted consumption by the masses' the 'ultimate cause [*der letzte Grund*] of crises' has led numerous Marxists to a very widely diffused interpretation of the crises of capitalism – whether structural or conjunctural-cyclical – in terms of underconsumption or, more generally, a shortage of outlets.[23] Neither the crisis of 1929, nor that of the 1970s, was caused by inadequate wages or, in more or less equivalent fashion, by excessive profits. Profits were weak in the 1920s; the crisis of the 1970s and 1980s derived from a fall in the profit rate, harboured by a long phase of decline in the performances of technical progress.

The law of capitalist accumulation, the overaccumulation of capital, and unemployment

Well before Keynes, Marx had developed an analysis of unemployment that attributed it to variations in the general level of economic activity – and not to the blockage in some adjustment of prices (of wages). Keynes articulated his analysis in term of the level of effective demand, whereas Marx stressed the *vicissitudes of capital accumulation*. But the idea is the same.

At the heart of Marx's analytical apparatus is what is called the *general law of capitalist accumulation*.[24] The study of the *overaccumulation* of capital, introduced during the treatment of historical tendencies, rounds it off.[25] It can be summarised as follows. The accumulation of capital drives up employment, to the point where it comes up against certain limits as regards the population available in the short term for work and, in this way, recurrently boosts wages. Various kinds of mechanism make it possible to overcome these tensions – recourse to more capitalistic techniques (a rise in the composition of

[22] The reproduction schemes highlight a certain number of relationships between large aggregates, such as production, consumption and investment, which are at the heart of national accounting. They do not account for the mechanisms adjusting the inter-branch proportions of supply and demand (this is the subject of *Capital*, Volume Three, Chapter 10).

[23] Marx himself refutes this thesis: 'It is a pure tautology to say that crises are provoked by a lack of effective demand or effective consumption' (Marx 1978, p. 486).

[24] Marx 1976, Chapter 25.

[25] Marx 1981, Chapter 15.

capital) and the impact of recessions, which devalue a fraction of capital and recreate a body of unemployed. This is the theory of the industrial reserve army, with its different fractions depending on the degree of their exclusion from employment (temporary or quasi-permanent), its expansion, and its phases of reduction. It shows that unemployment is not some accident of capitalism, or the result of inappropriate behaviour, but a cornerstone of the apparatus of its perpetuation, since it helps to control wages.

This framework is still perfectly adequate for analysing the conjunctural component of unemployment (responding to the fluctuations of the conjunctural cycle) in contemporary capitalism; and it has not been superseded. What is missing, however, is an explicit treatment of the other component of unemployment: so-called structural unemployment. The wave of unemployment that has arisen in the countries of the centre followed a slow-down in accumulation, which was itself caused by a fall in the profit rate. The growth in structural unemployment was a key factor in restoring control over wage costs, according to the same mechanism as conjunctural unemployment, but on a much larger scale.

Capitalist anarchy – ex-postism

In the history of Marxism and the socialist movement, the idea of the necessary supersession of capitalism has always been based on the critique of the anarchy peculiar to the system. This move already lay at the heart of the *Communist Manifesto*: capitalism brings about an unprecedented development of the productive forces, but it proves incapable of controlling the forces that it has unleashed – hence the proliferation and intensification of crises. Responsibility for this is frequently attributed to the *market*, which only planning (deliberate organisation on a societal scale) would make it possible to overcome.[26]

This type of analysis has obviously receded very considerably following the failure of the countries that claimed to be socialist. However, the persistence of unemployment and international financial crises in the recent years

[26] A *market* analysis of capitalist anarchy of this kind is foregrounded by Engels, contrasting organisation within each factory and market anarchy (see Engels 1977, Chapter 3).

has periodically led to a revival of this discourse, as a topical proposition. Here we touch on a key element in the analysis of neoliberalism.

If the characterisation of capitalism as a *market economy* is often symptomatic of narrow or simply erroneous conceptions, the debate nevertheless refers to fundamental features of capitalism. The decentralisation peculiar to it, the private character of decisions, defines one of its main properties: to a large extent, problems are resolved *a posteriori* – and these corrections can be violent. We refer in this connection to *ex-postism*. However, we must at once correct this observation, whatever its relevance, by adding that capitalism develops historically, giving rise to new *ex ante* processes of collective co-ordination (taking into account possible failures and regressions).[27]

The relations between *ex ante* and *ex post* decisions are complex. *Ex ante* organisation requires a high level of socialisation of the productive forces that capitalism first of all acquires in the firm and then at the level of society as a whole. To destroy *ex-post* adjustments in a more or less centralised or decentralised postcapitalist economy would, in every instance, be an error. The problem is to limit the scope of the dysfunctions and their consequences. But any disadjustment must give rise to correction, even in the most sophisticated society. In capitalism, too much relies on prolonged structural crises; and the costs are largely borne by the dominated classes and countries. It is the violence and unequal treatment of classes peculiar to capitalism that are at issue – not the necessity of *a posteriori* corrections.

As has been said, to refer only to the market in this connection is a very narrow conception – that of a Marxism confined to the first part of Volume One of *Capital*. Other processes must be taken into consideration:

(1) The decentralised mechanisms through which capitalism governs the allocation of capital (the inter-branch proportions of investment), and the supply of goods on the market (production), largely proceed in response to disequilibrium, that is, *ex post*. If too many goods are produced, output is reduced. From this point of view, capitalism is efficient and *ex-postism* is not synonymous with anarchy.

[27] This relationship between inter-individual and central contractuality and between organisation and market – mutual implications with many facets – is at the heart of Jacques Bidet's work (see Bidet 1999).

(2) Control of the general level of economic activity also operates *ex post*. It is the role of macro-economic policies to ensure a sufficient, but not excessive, level of demand.[28] The risks of destabilisation are large and manifest in the sequence of overheatings and recessions. What Marx called *crises* were nothing other than uncontrolled recessions. The history of the end of the nineteenth century and that of the twentieth century attests to the progress made in this area, particularly following the Keynesian revolution. Despite this progress, we can still speak of disorder, since the stability of the general level of economic activity is not fully ensured.[29] Neoliberalism has simultaneously reinforced the social procedures of stabilisation, while placing them in the service of the dominant classes (price stability rather than full employment), and revived planetary anarchy, which has now attained new degrees.

(3) The major historical tendencies and rhythms of accumulation are the main elements in this capitalist anarchy in the contemporary world. Capitalism exhibits an intrinsic difficulty in maintaining the results of technical change. Compounding this are the inhibitions bound up with preserving privileges – particularly those of property-owners (resistance to the transformation of property relations and, more generally, of production). Thus, major changes occur *ex post*, in the wake of structural crises. It is this very turbulent dynamic that becomes apparent in the successive phases of decline and recovery in the profit rate, of which the recent course of capitalism is a new expression. Accumulation is at the mercy of these movements. Moreover, it is governed by complex financial circuits and behaviour (that of the owners of capital and that of firms seeking to maximise their stock-market value).

---

[28] By means of *monetary* policy, the central bank more or less efficiently controls the mass of money and credit, and hence demand, in the economy (demand on the part of households, firms, and the state). When the supply of credit no longer finds borrowers despite a fall in interest rates, the state must borrow and spend. This is the function of budgetary policy during phases of a sharp fall in economic activity.

[29] In fact, progress in private management and financial mechanisms are vectors of new agents of instability and policies have to become historically more effective – which implies important institutional changes. We call the constant pressure of non-financial and financial private agents on macro-economic stability *tendential instability* (Duménil and Lévy 1996, Chapter 12).

Ecology is a major area where this specific dynamic of capitalism has – and could have even more – dramatic consequences and where anticipation is imperative. Analysis of it exceeds the bounds of this study.[30]

The relations between finance and the real sector

Marx's analysis of money – from the money commodity to the sign of value, from the measurement of values to money proper, as the stock of purchasing power – is remarkable.[31] It certainly helps to conceive the mechanisms peculiar to contemporary capitalism, but it fails to provide much-needed indications. In particular, the absence of any analysis of monetary creation in the modern sense of the term is sorely felt.

The relationship between financial and non-financial sectors is obviously at the heart of any analysis of neoliberalism. The Marxist theories of value and of capital have strict implications in this respect. The theory of productive labour and surplus-value leads to the characterisation of financial activities as non-productive. As with trade, the profit realised in a finance company, such as a bank, is interpreted as the realisation of a fraction of the total surplus-value appropriated elsewhere. Marx ironises about the ability of money to bear fruit, just as 'the pear tree bears pears'. Marxists are therefore particularly well shielded against the tendency to associate *financial activities* and *wealth creation* too closely. This does not mean that financial activities are useless (they possess a utility relative, obviously, to capitalist relations of production and not in general). Here we cannot go into the details of the extended accounts of finance Marx gives in Volume Three of *Capital*:

(1) Part of this analysis refers to the circuit of capital through its three forms: money-capital, commodity-capital, and productive capital. Like commercial capital, banking capital appears to have a special role in certain of the operations required by the circuit of capital. This involves the *capital of trade in money*. Its function consists in contributing to the general circuit of capital and hence, ultimately, to social (capitalist) production.

---

[30] This section does not claim to draw up a general picture of the defects of capitalism, which are much greater.

[31] See de Brunhoff 1973.

(2) Finance also contributes to making capital available to the non-financial sector, advances proper, separate from activity – another contribution to the general functioning of the system, which is likewise relative to the relations of production. This capital is *loan-capital*, which, in addition to credits proper, also comprises shares. The capital thus invested in credits and shares is the counterpart – a second expression – of the capital placed in firms in its three forms. The idea of fictitious capital results from this duplication (capital must not be counted in the real and monetary property of firms and in the title deed by securities materialising its ownership by another agent, in particular another firm);[32] or, *a fortiori*, from the existence of a title that does not represent any property of a firm, like a treasury bond.

Marx also describes the proliferation of monetary and financial mechanisms and institutions, denouncing their parasitic, speculative character, which he regards as a threat to the stability of the system.

No 'revelations' capable of making neoliberal configurations miraculously intelligible to us emerge from these hypotheses about money and finance. But this framework remains highly appropriate – overall, the most appropriate – and represents an effective barrier against various erroneous and excessive assessments. Nevertheless, it clearly needs to be supplemented.

The theory of interest rates affords an excellent example of the relevance and modernity of Marx's analysis, which are especially welcome in the analysis of neoliberalism. The following aspects might be highlighted:

(1) Marx rigorously distinguishes between rate of interest and rate of profit. No mechanism equalises them. The difference between profit rate and interest rate is symptomatic of a relation of production: the firm and the capitalist lender are two quite distinct agents (connected within certain configurations).
(2) Correlatively, Marx asserts that there is no 'law' which determines interest rates. Whereas neoclassical theory makes interest rates a price like any other, and Keynesian theory links them to the demand for liquidity, Marx regards them as the expression of a social relation – a power relation, one might say – although the conditions of general liquidity (with the course of the business cycle) affect their fluctuations. These analyses, which might

[32] In accounting terms, firms' balance-sheets must be consolidated.

be deemed vague, perfectly reflect the movement of interest rates in present-day capitalism. The rise in real interest rates experienced in 1979 – a deliberate option on the part of the political and monetary authorities – introducing neoliberalism, is a highly convincing expression of these relations.[33]

Class struggle

Marx's whole analysis reverberates with class struggle. *Capital* is shot through with the confrontation between capitalists and proletarians, to which the work supplies the keys. Taking Marx's economic and political writings together, we see the analytical framework expanding: capitalists and landowners, industrialists and financiers, small producers, as well as salaried managers. Far from being the *autonomous* agent it is often described as, the state is directly bound up with the exercise of the power of the dominant classes and its compromises.

No authentic reading of history can ignore these powers and struggles. Each of the system's transformations, be it the emergence of the institutions of modern capitalism at the beginning of the twentieth century, of private and public managerialism in the first half of the twentieth century and the concomitant development of social protection, or of the new configurations peculiar to neoliberalism, has been produced in and through struggles, taking account of the strength or weakness of the working-class movement, the combativeness of property owners (of finance), and so on. Policies are their direct expression, from Keynesianism to neoliberalism in particular.

The role allotted to technical and distributive tendencies and to structural crises in the periodisation of capitalism that we have proposed must not give the impression of *economism*. We are not caught in a hellish dilemma between two perspectives, one of which privileges tendencies while the other privileges struggles. The changes in capitalism at the beginning of the twentieth century were commanded by struggles, in which the strength of the working-class movement played a central role, combining with the internal contradictions of the ruling classes (for example, the relationship between financiers

[33] It refutes apologetic discourses – for example, those that make the rise in interest rates a consequence of public deficits, whereas the reverse can be demonstrated to be the case (see Duménil and Lévy 2004, Chapter 10).

and those in charge of the new managerial companies, on the one hand, and the old-style capitalists, on the other hand). Similarly, the reassertion of the power of property-owners in neoliberalism was the result of a prolonged confrontation, a stage in a constant battle to maintain the prerogatives of a minority. Such major historical developments can only be rendered intelligible by the combination of these various elements. Marxism is the most apt framework for such an approach – or should be.

Thinking the mutation – beyond capitalism

In the preceding sections, we have stressed the explanatory power of a set of concepts, laws or mechanisms. But there is also a lot to learn from the possible respects in which this explanatory power has been superseded. In some cases – we have given various examples – the problem is to extend the analysis and overcome some of its limitations. In others, the difficulty derives not from the imperfection of the analytical instrumentarium, but from a qualitative mutation in the phenomenon itself. This point warrants some clarification.

For example, we noted above that Marx's analysis of value and exploitation privileges a type of labour – so-called productive labour – relegating to a secondary status other kinds of labour, bound up with the maximisation of the profit rate, which we have encompassed under the term *management*. It is one thing to give these types of labour, which have become very important today, their due. It is another to ponder the possible dissolution of such distinctions – which would mean greatly distancing ourselves from the major concepts of Marxism. Must we merge working-class production tasks and the tasks of employees in commerce (salespersons, cashiers, and so on)? If we opt to do this, what position should we adopt vis-à-vis higher managerial personnel? The most economical way out in terms of theorisation is to squeeze such new complexities of our economies and societies back into old boxes – that is to say, into the traditional categories of capitalism. But is it the most appropriate? Marx had decided to base his whole system around the principal social relation: the confrontation between capitalists and proletarians, as specifically defined. We can pursue his approach, dissolving the rigour of the system, at the same time as preserving the terminology. We would thus speak of a new working or proletarian class, new capitalists, or a new petty bourgeoisie.[34] Marx's definition of productive labour and surplus-value is quietly set aside or abandoned. A more exacting approach consists in renewing the analytical framework. It is not that the concept of productive labour is to be dismissed. But we must acknowledge the gradual supersession of its explanatory power, as is normal in a changing world. It remains to reflect on what is new and to recognise the coexistence of the new and the old. The analysis of contemporary capitalism confronts us with such challenges.

Where have we got to? In our view, the process of these transformations is broader than the still partial fusion of subaltern forms of labour (those of workers and employees). The managerial tasks allocated to salaried personnel are subject to a polarisation, whose precise contours are still being defined, between tasks of execution (the *employee* component) and conception, organisation and direction (the *manager* component). This new *class* contradiction – class, because it is rooted in new relations of production – has been dialectically superimposed on the traditional contradiction between capitalists and proletarians.[35] The continuation of this development might lead to a certain fusion between employees' and workers' jobs. Until the advent of neoliberalism, the political unity of these wage groups, including managers, had been largely preserved, although this did not involve class unity. By contrast, neoliberalism, intent on maintaining the privileges of property-owners, tends to certain forms of combination of the higher fractions of these salaried personnel with capital.

Capitalist property has been subject to transformations comparable to those affecting labour; neoliberalism enormously complicates analysis of them, for it is the expression of a reassertion of certain basic capitalist characteristics of contemporary economies and societies – at least of the power of the owners of capital. The first great mutation in capitalist property (ownership of the means of production), which has already been referred to, occurred at the turning-point of the nineteenth and twentieth centuries, with the separation of ownership and management, and the concentration of ownership in finance and of management in the firm. The property relation became looser. Neoliberalism underlies a development that extends the preceding one: the concentration of capital in funds, taking account of the association of certain

---

[34] See Poulantzas 1975.

[35] See Duménil 1975 and Duménil and Lévy 1994.

salaried fractions with this capitalist power. Behind these changes some have glimpsed a supersession of the capitalist social relationship, whether invoking institutional capitalism or post-capitalism,[36] or even socialism.[37]

Our interpretation prompts us to underscore in the delegation of managerial tasks a polarisation between managers and other groups, employees and workers. We regard it as a new relation of production and a new class relation – which leads us refer to a hybrid society that we call *capitalo-cadrist*. Neoliberalism strives to preserve the pre-eminence of the traditional capitalist component, in terms of power and income, but it cannot halt the change in the relations of production, although it can possibly slow it down and certainly inflect it. To reflect on the mutation, to reflect on the balance of power – such is the analytical challenge facing us.

---

[36] See Drucker 1993.

[37] See Blackburn 1999.

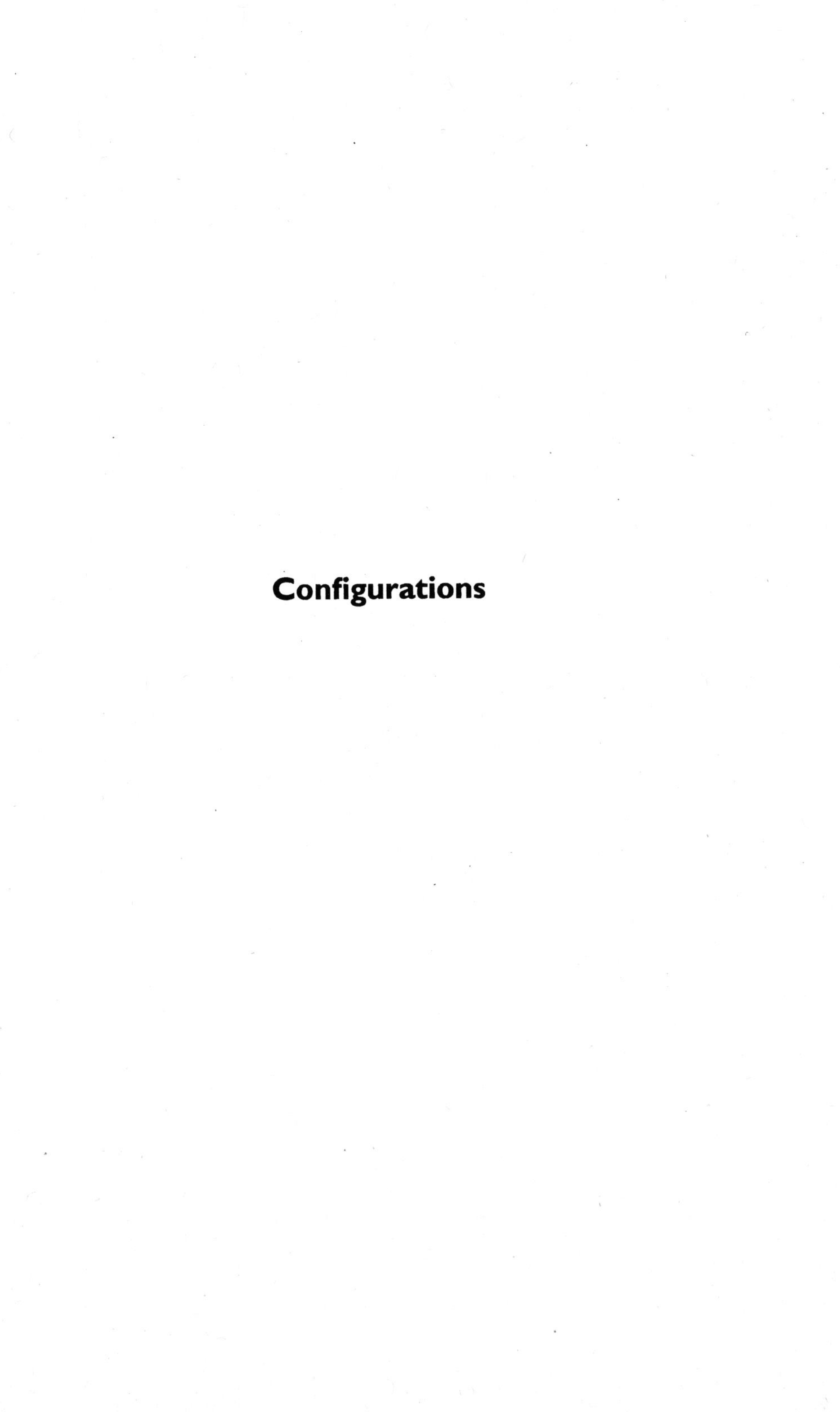

Configurations

Chapter Six

Analytical Marxism

Christopher Bertram

Analytical Marxism came into the world with the publication in 1978 of G.A. Cohen's *Karl Marx's Theory: A Defence.*[1] In that work Cohen, a Canadian from a Jewish Communist background, sought to clarify the claims of historical materialism by an application of the techniques of analytical philosophy. That endeavour must have seemed perverse to at least two sets of people. Marxists and radicals in the anglophone world may have been divided into Hegelian and Althusserian camps, but they were united in the view that analytical philosophy of the type studied at Oxford and Cambridge was both politically conservative and stultifyingly parochial in outlook. Analytical philosophers, on the other hand, had tended either to dismiss Marx as being of no properly philosophical significance or considered the central doctrines of historical materialism to be a mixture of Hegelian obscurantism and naïve philosophical mistakes. Cohen believed, however, that it was possible to use the techniques of ordinary-language philosophy to clarify and to state clearly the

[1] Cohen 1978. Henceforth, *KMTH.* It has been claimed, though, that some earlier writings should be included in the analytical-Marxist canon: notable candidates include the Polish economists Oskar Lange and Michal Kalecki and the Italian Piero Sraffa.

key claims of historical materialism as the necessary preliminary to assessing the truth or falsity of those very claims.

In carrying through his programme, Cohen was setting his face firmly against a view that most Marxists had agreed upon since Plekhanov (if not before). Namely, the view that there is a fundamental distinction in *method* between Marxism and 'bourgeois' social science. For Cohen, Marx was to be understood as making various claims about the world – about history, about social classes, about revolution – that were legitimately the object of investigation by the same methods as one might assess any other body of social theory. If Lukács had famously asserted that Marxism was to be distinguished not by its empirical claims but by its method,[2] Cohen forthrightly took the directly opposite view.

Cohen's example encouraged and brought to light an affinity with the work of other researchers, mainly (but not exclusively) in the Anglo-Saxon world: John Roemer (an American economist); Jon Elster (a Norwegian philosopher), Erik Olin Wright (an American sociologist), Philippe Van Parijs (a Belgian political philosopher), Adam Przeworski (a Polish political scientist), Robert Brenner (an American historian) and a number of others.[3] These thinkers formed a very odd school: they agreed about very little of substance and often disagreed profoundly with one another. But they at least prided themselves on the need to state arguments and positions clearly and in ways that were open to critique and debate. They self-consciously avoided indulgence in anti-falsification strategies of the sort often practised by other Marxists. For this reason, they called the group they formed (which had, by reason of the date of its annual meetings, the formal title of the 'September' group) the 'No-Bullshit Marxism' group. This group has one characteristic that is surprising in a 'Marxist' group: some of the members – most notably in this context Van Parijs – have never claimed to be Marxists at all!

---

[2] Lukács 1971.

[3] The September Group currently (2007) consists of Pranab Bardhan (Berkeley), Samuel Bowles (Amherst), Robert Brenner (Los Angeles), G.A. Cohen (Oxford), Joshua Cohen (Stanford), Stathis Kolyvas (Yale), Philippe Van Parijs (Louvain-la-Neuve), John Roemer (Davis), Seana Shiffrin (UCLA), Hillel Steiner (Manchester), Robert van der Veen (Amsterdam) and Erik Olin Wright (Madison). Jon Elster and Adam Przeworski left the group in 1993. It is important to note though that there are analytical Marxists such as Alan Carling who are not and have never been members of the group.

In what follows I shall first outline what I take to be the enduringly valuable contributions of the first phase of analytical Marxism: Cohen's work on historical materialism and John Roemer's work on class and exploitation. I shall then have something to say about the philosophy of social science associated with analytical Marxism and about whether the appellation 'rational-choice Marxism' is correct. Finally, I discuss the most recent phase of analytical Marxism, which concerns the defence of socialist values and the elaboration of institutional alternatives to capitalism in a world which is far less congenial to the Left than it was at the beginning of their project.[4]

Cohen and history

In *Karl Marx's Theory of History: A Defence*, Cohen defended a traditional and, it has to be said, unfashionable interpretation of historical materialism based on Marx's 'Preface' to *A Contribution to the Critique of Political Economy*, against philosophical criticism. Central to that defence were his attribution to Marx of a sharp distinction between the material and the social, and his insistence that historical materialism depends upon functional explanation.

At the centre of Cohen's reconstruction of historical materialism are two theses: the development thesis and the primacy thesis. The development thesis tells us that there is a tendency for the material productive forces to develop over time, where those material productive forces include not only physical means of production but also (and most importantly) technical and scientific knowledge. The primacy thesis asserts that the character of the social form of society (the social relations of production) is explained by the level of development of the material productive forces (and not vice versa). Cohen also asserts the character of political and legal institutions is to be explained by the nature of the social relations of production.

If we put the development and primacy theses together, and add the plausible thought that at different levels of development of the forces of production, different social forms are suitable for their further development, then we have

[4] There are now two book-length studies of analytical Marxism: Mayer 1994 is a sober and academic study that gives particular weight to the contributions of Roemer and Przeworski; Roberts 1996 is a somewhat intemperate polemic which concentrates on G.A. Cohen. A good selection of papers by the main protagonists is Roemer (ed.) 1986 and Carver and Thomas (eds.) 1995 contains a selection of friendly and hostile articles.

a very traditional Marxist picture of history. Forms of society act as shells for the development of the productive forces, which, at a certain point slough off those shells and replace them with new ones.

But, as Cohen was well aware, this traditional picture of history had fallen into disfavour for apparently compelling reasons, the principal one of which was the seeming inconsistency between the explanation of relations by forces (and superstructure by base) and the simultaneous insistence that the adoption of a certain set of social relations was propitious for the development of the forces (and superstructures have powerful effects on bases). Since we normally explain effects by reference to their causes (and not the other way round), it had seemed to many theorists that historical materialism was committed to incoherence or inconsistency.

Cohen' s solution to this problem was to argue that the Marxist theory of history is committed to *functional* explanations. Just as a biologist might explain the fact of a bird having hollow bones by the propensity of those bones to enable the bird to fly, Marxists can explain the character of social relations of production by reference to the propensity of those very social relations to promote the development of the material productive forces.[5]

Cohen's invocation of functional explanation in historical materialism was the occasion for one of the first major debates within analytical Marxism. Jon Elster claimed, in a series of articles, that if Marxism relied upon functional explanation, then so much the worse for Marxism. Elster accepted, in principle, three modes of explanation: causal explanation was the standard form of explanation for the physical sciences; intentional explanation, by reference to the beliefs and desires of individual persons, was the usual form of social-scientific explanation; and functional explanation was often acceptable in the biological sciences. But, in order to be acceptable, Elster claimed, a proposed functional explanation must be underpinned by a feedback loop consisting of more regular causal or intentional components. Such an elaboration is provided by Darwin's theory of natural selection (together with Mendelian genetics) for the biological sciences. But no such plausible elaboration is to

[5] See, especially, Chapters 9 and 10 of Cohen 1978.

be found for historical materialism, which – according to Elster – must be rejected (at least in the form defended by Cohen).[6]

Cohen, in turn, sought to defend his position by arguing that it can be rational to rely upon functional explanations of phenomena, even where one has no understanding of the underlying causal (or intentional) mechanisms. So, for example, it was rational to believe in the functional explanation of well-adapted features of organisms even before Darwin and Mendel had filled in the explanatory structure.[7] Other analytical Marxists have sought to defend Cohen by sketching processes which might play a role for social phenomena akin to that played by natural selection for biological phenomena. In particular Christopher Bertram and Alan Carling have both suggested that the well-adaptedness of social relations of production to the level of development of the material productive force may historically be achieved by the pressures of economic and military competition among societies.[8]

Numerous other aspects of Cohen's reconstruction have also come under attack. In particular, the development thesis has been seen by many as implausible. In *Karl Marx's Theory of History*, Cohen appeared to ground the development thesis in the rationality of individual producers faced with material scarcity. According to many, this appeared to imply a commitment to a transhistorical account of rationality, a commitment that seemed to them un-Marxist. Cohen has since clarified and developed his position: he now stresses not the technical ingenuity of individual producers faced with material scarcity, but rather the rational choice of developmentally optimal production relations. While this clarification has the merit of invoking the beneficial effects of social forms on productive development in a way consistent with Cohen's views on functional explanation, it looks deeply implausible in fact. It is highly unlikely that the more efficient character of new social relations reliably figures among the reasons for action of those making social revolutions in the way that would be necessary according to Cohen's theory.[9]

---

[6] For Elster's critique of Cohen see especially Elster 1980, Elster 1982, Elster 1986 and Elster 1985.

[7] See Cohen 1982a and Cohen 1982b. See also Cohen 1988.

[8] See Bertram 1990 and Carling 1991, Part One.

[9] See especially the critique by Levine and Wright 1980, a version of which is reprinted as Chapter 2 of Wright, Levine, Sober 1992. Cohen's reply (written with Will Kymlicka) is in Cohen and Kymlicka 1988 and Chapter 5 of Cohen 1988.

Roemer and exploitation

Central to Jon Elster's critique of Cohen's use of functional explanation was an aggressive programme in the philosophy of social science. Elster particularly commended the use of rational-choice methods and the application of the insights of game theory. Elster's own work remained at a methodological level: the principal analytical Marxist who has applied these methods to standard Marxist problems has been John Roemer. In his early *Analytical Foundations of Marxian Economic Theory,* Roemer proposed a highly mathematised neo-Ricardian reconstruction of Marx's economic theory. This was further developed in his *magnum opus*: *A General Theory of Exploitation and Class. A General Theory* really exemplifies the whole analytical-Marxist project in the way that it seeks to ground the Marxist pictures of social macrophenonena (such as class) in the micromotives of individuals. In relation to orthodox Marxism, we might say that it is simultaneously iconoclastic (in its methodology) and conservative (in its emphasis on the centrality of *class* as opposed to other dimensions of social division).[10]

Much of *A General Theory* is devoted to showing how Marxian concepts of exploitation and class can be derived from fairly standard neoclassical economic models. Roemer at first accepts a standard Marxian view of exploitation where the performance of surplus-labour indicates whether or not exploitation is going on. He demonstrates, among other things, the heretical proposition (from a Marxist standpoint) that, in an economy where all agents work for themselves and require only their subsistence requirements and where they interact only to trade their products on the market, there will be exploitation if the producers start off with differential endowments of labour-power. This is because the richer producers will have access to a wider choice of production techniques and will therefore have to work for a shorter period than is socially necessary to produce a quantity of goods that can be traded for a subsistence bundle on the market: to produce the total social product, to be divided equally, the poor work for longer than the rich.[11] In a whole series of further examples, Roemer shows that classes will emerge in an economy where there is a labour market and differential initial endowment of assets; that a credit market and a labour market achieve exactly parallel results in this

[10] Roemer 1981 and Roemer 1982a.

[11] Roemer 1982a Chapter 1. See also Roemer 1982c.

respect; and that something like a labour theory of value can be constructed but that it is logically subsequent to prices rather than being explanatory of them. The central theoretical term of this section of Roemer's book is his 'Class-Exploitation Correspondence Principle', which states that agents who optimise by selling their labour-power are exploited and that those who optimise by buying labour-power are exploiters. Whether or not agents are labour hirers or labour sellers is determined by their initial endowment of assets. Differential ownership of the means of production determines whether someone is in a labour-hiring or labour-selling class. Thus exploitation status and class position are systematically related. This relationship fails to hold, however, when agents are endowed with different quantities and qualities of labour. This is one of the reasons why Roemer seeks a theory of exploitation that is more 'general' than the labour theory.

But the difficulty of constructing a surplus-labour theory of exploitation that is well defined under all assumptions is not the only barrier to defining exploitation in terms of the transfer of surplus labour, since a neoclassical economist might agree that there is such transfer but deny that it merited the morally-charged appellation, 'exploitation'. This is because neoclassicals hold that, under competitive conditions, there is no exploitation in capitalism since everyone gains from trade. If people refused to trade and simply set up with their own assets, they would do considerably worse than they actually do. On the other hand, a neoclassical would concede that, where extra-economic coercion allows some people to live off the labour of others (as in feudal or slave society), exploitation does take place.

A further achievement of *A General Theory of Exploitation and Class* was then, to provide a general construct, of which Marxian exploitation and the sort of exploitation that the neoclassical is concerned with are special cases. If we take a society N, then a coalition S within that larger society is exploited if and only if:

(1) There is an alternative, which we may conceive of as hypothetically feasible, in which S would be better off than in its present situation.
(2) Under this alternative, the complement to S, the coalition N- S = S′ would be worse off than at present.
(3) S′ is in a relation of dominance to S.[12]

[12] Roemer 1982a, pp. 194–5.

Condition (3) is a sociological one, entailing that the coalition S′ prevents the hypothetical alternative from being realised, thus giving rise to its exploitation of S.[13] Roemer claims that he needs this condition, different in type from (1) and (2) to rule out certain bizarre examples. Roemer models (1) and (2) by specifying a game that is played by coalitions of agents in the economy. A coalition has the alternatives of participating in the economy or of withdrawing and taking its payoff under the definition of the game. If the coalition S does better for its members under the alternative of withdrawing and if its complement S′ does worse after S has withdrawn, then S is an exploited coalition under that particular version of the game.[14] It must be required that not only the allocation to a coalition be better under the hypothetical alternative, but also that the complement does worse, if the coalition is to be characterised as exploited under the rules of the game. This is because, in an economy with decreasing returns to scale, both coalitions might do better under the alternative. Conversely, if we have an economy characterised by increasing returns to scale, both coalitions might do better under present arrangements. A coalition must be exploited by someone if it is to be considered exploited at all. How is the alternative to be defined? The answer seems to depend on the level of abstraction at which Roemer is operating. In practice, the alternative is defined in terms of property relations; that is, rights to control means of production. The alternative to existing arrangements that makes clear why Marxists consider them to be exploitative is the equalisation of access to non-human means of production. At a more abstract level, this is less clear. We specify a game by stipulating *a characteristic function* v which assigns to every coalition S a payoff on withdrawal v(S). Roemer writes, 'the function v may define what some observer considers a just settlement to coalitions should be, were they to opt out of society'.[15] But he states later: 'There are, of course, both interesting and silly ways of specifying v: our task will be to specify particular functions v which capture intelligible and historically cogent types of exploitation.'[16]

Marxists have never held that a social order can be overthrown at will. On the contrary, as Marx puts it, 'No social order ever disappears before all the

---

13 Roemer 1982a, p. 195.
14 Ibid. See also Roemer 1982b.
15 Roemer 1982a, p. 196.
16 Roemer 1982a, p. 197.

productive force for which there is room in it have been developed'.[17] This is bound to pose some problems for a theory which proposes to test for exploitation in terms of feasible hypothetical alternatives. Roemer's proposal for dealing with this problem is to make the assumption that, after a coalition has withdrawn from the economy, its incentive structure remains unchanged. If the coalition then improves its position and its complement does worse, it is said to suffer 'socially-necessary' exploitation before withdrawal.

There are, according to Roemer, two distinct types of socially-necessary exploitation: dynamically socially-necessary exploitation and statically socially-necessary exploitation. If a coalition could not maintain the incentive structure of its members on withdrawal and as a consequence of that failure would immediately be worse off, then the exploitation which it suffers is socially necessary in the static sense. If such a coalition would be better off on withdrawal, but would soon fall behind the alternative because, although the coalition would work just as hard as before, it perhaps lacks incentives to technological innovation, then the exploitation it suffers is socially necessary in the dynamic sense.[18]

One of the most startling and impressive results of the first half of Roemer's investigations in *A General Theory of Exploitation and Class is* his 'Class-Exploitation Correspondence Principle'. This shows that exploitation status and class position are systematically related. This systematic relationship disappears when we talk about coalitions rather than classes. For the coalitions that have the option of withdrawing from the economy in Roemer's 'general theory' seem to have arbitrary boundaries. If we liked, we could include any selection of individuals in a coalition and test whether the coalition was exploited under the rules of a particular game. This flexibility might seem to be an advantage at first but a little reflection reveals that all sorts of problems can arise. For example, a coalition of all workers plus the richest capitalist will probably turn out to be exploited if it withdraws from the economy with its per capita share of alienable assets. By drawing boundaries in particular ways we might get the result that all agents were members of some exploiting and some exploited coalitions. Now, in fact, there are good reasons not to draw boundaries in this sort of way. The coalitions that form in games do

---

[17] Marx 1970 [1859], p. 21.

[18] Roemer 1982a, pp. 265–70.

so because it is in the interests of their members to ally in pursuit of common objectives and so it would be wise to look for some *prima facie* community of interest before including people in a coalition. The community of interest that is tacitly presupposed in Roemer's work is that possessed by classical-Marxian classes, which is in turn based on whether agents are labour hirers or sellers (a fact determined by what they own in the way of means of production). But, although the Roemerian coalitions do seem to be based on Marxian principles in practice, there does not seem to be any reason why we should seize on this type of grouping outside of the framework of a surplus-labour theory of exploitation, a framework that Roemer's analysis has supposedly transcended.

Whatever quibbles one might have with Roemer's reconceptualisation of Marxian class and exploitation theory, there is little doubt that this has been one of the most pathbreaking and fertile of the analytical-Marxist achievements.[19] The sociologist Erik Olin Wright, in his work *Classes*,[20] drew upon the Roemerian 'general theory' to propose a cross-cutting analysis of the class structure of modern societies based upon the different types of assets (labour-power, capital ownership, skills, credentials) possessed by different potential coalitions of agents. Wright's analysis had the advantage of addressing, in a new and more rigorous framework, the problem of 'contradictory class locations' that he had first explored from within an Althusserian methodology. But, like much analytical-Marxist work, the problem of its Marxist identity was once again posed. Both Roemer and Wright were focusing on a series of characteristically Marxist problems, but their methodology and solutions appeared profoundly non-Marxist. Indeed, once the analysis was translated from Roemer's formal constructs to the domain of sociology proper, it looked for all the world like a Weberian analysis based on different groups exploiting particular assets in the marketplace, rather than a Marxian one based upon conflict over surplus extraction.

If Cohen and Roemer made the most important original contributions to analytical Marxism, we should not pass over the contribution of Adam Przeworski.[21] His is the only real attempt at an analytical-Marxist political sociol-

---

[19] For some further problems with Roemer's approach, see Bertram 1988.
[20] Wright 1985.
[21] See, especially, his Przeworski 1985 but also Przeworski 1991.

ogy. His work centres on the dilemma facing socialist parties seeking political power in a parliamentary democracy. He argues that the rational pursuit of electoral majority by those parties leads them to downplay the importance of class as an axis of political organisation, this, in turn, tends to alienate their core electorate. Whatever one thinks of Przeworski's arguments, they represent an important step in Marxist political sociology. Marxist political analysis has often sought to explain the absence of political transformation in the West by reference to *ideology*: on the standard Western-Marxist view, workers are in the grip of false consciousness or dominated by ideological state apparatuses. Przeworski was able to sketch his explanations by reference to the working class's pursuit of its interests.[22]

Rational choice and methodological individualism

If there is one aspect of analytical Marxism that has provoked hostility and even incredulity among rival Marxists, it is the commitment of many analytical Marxists to methodological individualism and rational actor models of social interaction. Methodological individualism is the view that all social practices and institutions are in principle explicable in terms of the behaviour of individuals; rational-actor models use economic theory to model individual behaviour given presumed desires and beliefs. Methodological individualism is opposed to structuralism or holism which hold that the fundamental units of social explanation – pre-empting or determining individual choice – are supraindividual entities such as nations, classes or modes of production. Enthusiasm of analytical Marxists for individualistic positions and techniques has sometimes been reminiscent of the 'Robinsonades' against which Marx inveighs in the 'Introduction' to the *Grundrisse*. There are clearly a number of issues here. The first type of issue concerns the substance of whether methodological individualism is the correct position in the philosophy of social science and whether rational-actor models are an appropriate tool of analysis. The second concerns the question of whether such commitments and methods are compatible with a body of theory bearing the name 'Marxist'. Let us deal with those questions in reverse order.

---

22 For a penetrating critique of Przeworski's approach, see King and Wickham-Jones 1995.

Analytical Marxists have been able to point to a number of examples where Karl Marx himself employs what look very much like rational-actor models. For instance, the explanation given in *Capital* of the tendency of the rate of profit to fall is a classic case where the pursuit of rational self-interest by individuals brings about an outcome which is worse for all.[23] One of Marx's ways of talking about the state suggests that it plays the role of overcoming collective action problems facing the bourgeoisie: factory legislation is in the general interest of the capitalist class but the pursuit of self-interest by capitalists tends to undermine the physical health of the workers.[24] As well as examples of such analyses, analytical Marxists can point to some explicitly methodological statements by Marx which appear to support – in principle – the application of an individualistic rational-actor approach. For example, Marx says in *The Poverty of Philosophy* 'What is society, whatever its form may be? The product of men's reciprocal action'.[25] But those hostile to analytical Marxism have been quick to point out that rational-choice analyses take as given the circumstances against which choice and deliberation take place and that it is those very structural features of society that are at the centre of what Marxism takes itself to be explaining. In other words, analytical Marxism often takes as given what is most in need of explanation. Ellen Meiksins Wood has been particularly keen to press this point.[26] What analytical Marxists then take as a paradigmatic use of rational-choice explanation by Marx himself, the behaviour of capitalists, takes place in a context that is really doing all the explanatory work: it is that context – the social relations obtaining in a capitalist society – that requires explanation.

Analytical Marxists can reply to this that *both* the behaviour of individuals and the context in which they behave require explanation. Historical materialism is the theory which explains the genesis of social forms and even here some progress can be made in advancing individualistic explanations. While Cohen's reconstruction of historical materialism might be thought to be rather neutral on the questions of rational choice and methodological individual-

---

[23] See the comments by Jon Elster in Elster 1985, pp. 45–6.

[24] Ibid. Chapter 4.1.4.

[25] Cited by Przeworski 1985, p. 92. Przeworski also mentions that Engels in his letter to Bloch of September 1890 treats society as the product of strategically behaving individuals.

[26] See Wood 1995.

ism, analytical Marxists can point to Robert Brenner's work as an example of Marxist rational-choice explanation of the transition to capitalism (and Alan Carling has done some interesting work rendering the perspective of Cohen compatible with that of Brenner).[27]

But the question remains: should Marxists (or anyone) support methodological individualism and rational choice? If methodological individualism is taken to be the Hobbesian view that holds that social phenomena are explicable in terms of individual beliefs and desires that can be stated without ineliminable reference to the social, then the position is clearly absurd. But methodological individualism as defended by analytical Marxists is the much more moderate position that good social scientific explanations should show how macrophenomena issue from the action of individuals (without denying that those individuals have socially formed desires and beliefs). This position would be better characterised as an anti-holism – a denial of the autonomy of macrophenomena – rather than a genuine individualism. Many analytical Marxists have now come to see that, in any case, methodological individualism mis-states the correct view. Although it was right to insist that token social events need individualistic underpinnings, social science also investigates social *types*. Those social types can be independently realised by different combinations of individuals with very different beliefs and motives and so no individualistic-reductionist explanation may be available to account for them.[28]

The question of rational-choice theory should, in any case, be dealt with independently from that of methodological individualism. It would be possible to be a methodological individualist without being a proponent of rational-choice theory. Analytical Marxists have pursued a twin-track strategy here. Pragmatically, they have demonstrated through the successful use of rational-choice tools by Roemer and Przeworski that the key features of the Marxian programme can be illuminated by the intelligent application of neoclassical economic techniques. Philosophically, they have been 'internal' critics of rational-choice methodology: that is to say that they have not rejected it out of hand but have been concerned to point out its defects and shortcomings whilst remaining sympathetic too it. At the forefront here was Jon Elster who

[27] See Carling 1991, Chapters 1–3. Brenner 1977; Aston and Philpin (eds.) 1986.
[28] See especially Wright, Levine, Sober 1992, Chapter 6.

has combined an aggressive anti-holism with a keen awareness of the difficulties faced by rational-choice theory in the light of the psychological findings of Kahneman and Tversky and the alternative behavioural model of rationality advanced by Herbert Simon.[29]

The turn to normativity

Since the original pathbreaking contributions of Cohen, Roemer and Przeworski, analytical Marxism as a school has undergone a further loss of unity and coherence. This is despite the very interesting work that the principal members have continued to do. To take the case of Cohen first: since *Karl Marx's Theory of History*, Cohen has published two works based on numerous papers and has also begun a critical engagement with the work of John Rawls. The first of these works, *History, Labour and Freedom*, represents primarily a continuation of *Karl Marx's Theory of History* and a reply to critics of that work. Its successor,[30] *Self-Ownership, Freedom and Equality* is a work of normative political philosophy which engages first and foremost with the work of the American libertarian philosopher Robert Nozick. In his book *Anarchy, State and Utopia*,[31] Nozick had put a moral case for a minimal state and a free-market economy on the basis of premises that, in Cohen's view, were widely shared by Marxists and socialists more generally. In particular, Cohen thought that the idea of *self-ownership* lay behind many Marxist intuitions about exploitation (workers are exploited because what they have produced with the labour of *their bodies* is appropriated by the capitalist). It would therefore be a deep problem for Marxists if their most fundamental presuppositions could form the basis of an argument justifying inexorably not a communist future but a régime of market and private property.[32] Cohen was thus led to inquire more deeply into the normative foundations of property-ownership and exploitation. Cohen's investigations ultimately led to his rejection of the thesis of self-ownership and to an increased admiration for the egalitarian liberalism of John Rawls's *A Theory of Justice*. But this admiration has been heavily qualified

[29] The key texts here are his three volumes: Simon 1979; Simon 1983; and Simon 1989. Simon 1983 in particular, contains the best analytical-Marxist writing on ideology.

[30] Cohen 1995.

[31] Nozick 1974.

[32] See, especially, Chapter 6, Cohen 1995.

in recent work by an increasing dissatisfaction on Cohen's part with the way in which Rawls's theory permits incentives the play a part in determining the structure of the just society. Perhaps paradoxically, this expresses itself in a rejection of what many have seen as the most 'Marxist' aspect of Rawls's whole construction: its emphasis on the way in which the basic structure of society can be fateful for individuals' life prospects.[33]

This is not the place to examine all the details of Cohen's evolution. And it is important to stress that it is constituted mainly by a shift in philosophical attention from one set of problems to another rather than a basic change of mind concerning Marxism. What it is important to note here is that Cohen is now concerned not with specifically Marxist problems of sociology or politics, but rather with the clarification of the core values underlying socialist and communist commitment. In my view, that is not a cause for regret. It is, however, superficially problematic in Marxist terms for two reasons. First, the problems of ethics are historically a repressed aspect of Marxist thought – 'the love that dare not speak its name' – many Marxists (including Marx himself) have often denied that their commitment to the cause of revolution is based on any moral values whatsoever.[34] Second, Cohen's focus on the normative problems of political philosophy (and particularly on the problem of justice), when coupled with his rejection of any methodological barrier between Marxism and 'bourgeois' theory, means that he is now a participant in a broad field of debate that includes analytical political philosophers of all political stripes. Within that field, it is now impossible to say clearly who counts as a socialist, who is an egalitarian liberal etc. These ideological camps have fused and interpenetrated.

Further evidence for that interpenetration is found in the work of Philippe Van Parijs. Van Parijs is one of a number of September Group members who have never claimed to be Marxist. Instead, Karl Marx figures as just one of a range of influences on his work. After and early interest in the philosophy of the social sciences, a period which resulted in his *Evolutionary Explanation in the Social Sciences*,[35] Van Parijs has become renowned mainly for his pursuit

---

[33] See, for example, Cohen 1997.

[34] The question of whether Marx believed that capitalism is unjust is the subject of a voluminous literature within analytical Marxism. Norman Geras provides a helpful survey of the literature in Geras 1985.

[35] Van Parijs 1981.

of one issue: basic income. In a pathbreaking paper with the Dutch political scientist, Robert van der Veen, entitled 'A Capitalist Road to Communism',[36] he rejected the idea that the Left should pursue the goal of 'socialism', that is to say Marx's 'lower stage' of communism. Rather, the achievement of abundance, the precondition for true communism, could be best met by capitalism: a régime of market and private property. Capitalism should be conjoined, though, with a system of universal grants or 'basic income'. Everyone (or perhaps all adults) should be entitled to receive an unconditional grant independently of whether or not they participate in the labour market. This basic income would have the effect of freeing people from the obligation to have paid employment in order to satisfy their basic material needs. As well as freeing people from the obligation to work, it also responds to the demands of social justice in an age when the holding of a job has become the holding of a scarce resource by a few privileged workers to the disbenefit of the socially excluded. In a further series of papers and an important book, *Real Freedom for All*, Van Parijs has developed a number of challenging arguments in favour of universal basic income.[37]

Once again, whatever the particular merits of Van Parijs's proposals, we see that September Group members are now at a very great distance from the Marxian projects. Enthusiasm for 'basic income' is not even limited to the political Left: in one form or another, even some of the originators of the neoliberal consensus have backed related ideas. If we look, for example, at Milton Friedman's *Capitalism and Freedom* we see him advocating a 'negative income tax'. Van Parijs's proposals are, not surprisingly, more radical and redistributive than Friedman's.[38] But, in an important sense, they occupy the same ground: that of the correct social policy to be adopted by governments of liberal-democratic states. If there is to be an emancipation of the working class, it is not to be the work of the working class itself but rather of parliamentary élites and the civil service.

Rather like Van Parijs, John Roemer has now strayed a very long way from anything that looks like Marxian orthodoxy. In the 1990s, he had been strongly concerned with developing a model of a market-socialist economy.

---

[36] Van Parijs 1993.

[37] Van Parijs 1995.

[38] Friedman 1962. Van Parijs discusses the relationship between his proposal and Friedman's at p. 57 of Van Parijs 1995.

This 'socialist' economy is very different from anything that has hitherto borne the label.[39] Roemer accepts the view that an efficient and dynamic economy requires a combination of free markets and political democracy. Despite a commitment to egalitarianism, he also sees little hope in the foreseeable future for the redistribution of incomes derived from the labour market. He also rejects the idea of public ownership of industry, and is rather agnostic on the question of worker-ownership of firms. What, then, is 'socialist' about his scheme? He would focus on two things: ownership of capital and government direction of investment.

Roemer argues that there is great scope for the institutional separation of markets for stock from markets for labour and consumer goods. He envisages a scheme where capital ownership is held by all the population via coupons which they can use to buy and sell shares on the stock market. An equal number of coupons would be issued to each adult and would revert to the public treasury on the death of the holder. These coupons would be non-convertible into cash and people would be unable to give them away or trade them for any other consideration. So there would be no possibility of workers and the poor trading-in their capital assets in a way leading to a concentration of ownership in the hands of a few capitalists. All would have an equal expectation of benefiting from the profits accruing to capital. In addition to this parallel currency for stock, Roemer proposes the use by the state of differential interest rates to encourage investment in sectors where it is socially desirable that investment be increased but where normal incentives to do so are poor.

Roemer's proposals are certainly not to be dismissed out of hand. Roemer is engaging in the kind of creative thinking about the institutions of a socialist society that must be done if the project of an egalitarian and democratic society is to regain momentum. From the point of view of egalitarian justice, a proposal that permits substantial inequalities arising from the people's possession of scarce skills and abilities in the labour market, is clearly imperfect. But Roemer does, at least suggest a way beyond a society in which the means of production are in the hands of a tiny capitalist class. Nevertheless, his scheme does have many defects. First, it is far from clear how the coupon-holders are to be motivated to gather the necessary information and then

39 The proposal is advanced in Roemer 1994 and debated in the collection Roemer 1996. See also Bardhan and Roemer (eds.) 1993.

to act on it. Granted, many ordinary workers already spend a great deal of time and intellectual effort gathering and acting on information to do with horse-racing or the performance of football teams. But it seems unlikely that the performance of key stocks is going to capture the imagination of millions in quite the same way. Second, given the persistent inequalities arising from the labour market and the requirement to act as a utility-maximising agent in that market, it is probable that this market-socialist scheme would tend to promote an egoistic psychology in much the same way as capitalism. Third, it is entirely unclear how we might get from the welfare-state capitalisms of the present to such a society. It certainly seems most unlikely that the movement to create a coupon market socialism will inspire the levels of commitment and self-sacrifice that have characterised workers' movements in the past.

Conclusion

Analytical Marxism started with a group of thinkers who combined a leftist commitment to socialist goals with a willingness to expose Marxist orthodoxy to critical scrutiny using the tools of analytical philosophy and 'bourgeois social science'. In the time since the movement began, the environment in which they have conducted their enquiries has changed in far-reaching ways. First, and most dramatically, the political environment has shifted enormously: the Soviet Union and its allies have disappeared and an increasingly globalised capitalism has demonstrated both dynamism and self-confidence. The egalitarian political project has been everywhere in retreat for nearly twenty years. Second, many thinkers on the Left have over the same period been diverted away from serious reflection concerning class, inequality and political order and have, by contrast devoted their attention into the marginal and politically inconsequential agendas of literary theory, poststructuralism and deconstruction.

Whatever one thinks of the positive proposals now advanced by leading analytical Marxists, it is to their credit that they have neither lapsed into dogmatism, nor have they transmuted into apologists for the existing order. Instead, they have attempted to ally the new egalitarian political philosophy associated with John Rawls, Amartya Sen and others with the tools of 'bourgeois' social science in an attempt to devise feasible institutions to move the socialist project forward. What is clearly lacking, though, is any kind of connection between these academic theoreticians and the wide social movement of the oppressed that could force their proposal onto the political agenda.[40] But they retain a sense that the triumph of the capitalist order may be a temporary phenomenon: twenty years ago, things looked very different, and they may do so again twenty years hence.[41] For now, it is essential that those committed to an egalitarian and democratic future for humankind continue to think rigorously and creatively about the path to the future society – current setbacks notwithstanding.

In a volume devoted to post-Marxisms and neo-Marxisms, it seems appropriate to ask whether analytical Marxists are Marxists at all? Since some of them never were in the first place, it is nevertheless a slightly odd question to pose. G.A. Cohen has said that he regarded *Karl Marx's Theory of History* as a settling accounts with his Marxist upbringing and background. Once it was completed and he had done his duty by that past, he felt free to think creatively and more critically about that heritage.[42] We should see analytical Marxism as preserving the egalitarian and democratic values of Marx, but as being willing to jettison where necessary the details of Marx's analysis of capitalism, his method and his prescriptions for the future. Whether what remains should be called Marxist is a question for the historian of ideas rather than a philosophical or political one.

---

[40] This may be too strong a statement, since Philippe Van Parijs has done much to force the basic-income proposal onto the agenda of non-governmental organisations worldwide.

[41] A point powerfully made by Wright 1997, pp. 116–17.

[42] See his remarks at pp. x to xi of Cohen 1988.

Chapter Seven

The Frankfurt School's Critical Theory: From Neo-Marxism to 'Post-Marxism'

Gérard Raulet

The Institute of Social Research was founded in Frankfurt in 1924 and celebrated its 75th anniversary between the 23–5th of September 1999. Refounded by Horkheimer in 1949 on his return from exile, it was subsequently directed by Adorno until his death in 1969 and then by one of his pupils, Ludwig von Friedeburg.[1] It still expressly claims to adhere to its original conception and is committed to interdisciplinary studies of the social state, law and politics, culture and social psychology, while conceding that the general theory advocated by Horkheimer is no longer acceptable.[2]

In his inaugural lecture of 1931, Horkheimer had set out a way of organising scientific work that replaced the Marxist primacy of political economy by a 'social philosophy [*Sozialphilosophie*]'. This philosophy aimed to develop a comprehensive theory of society by integrating multidisciplinary research

---

1 By director should be understood 'executive director [*geschäftsführender Direktor*]'. In fact, the Institute had at its head a three-man directorate. In 1997, this directorate was replaced by a college which elected an executive director for five years (Ludwig von Friedeburg since 1997).

2 See Dubiel 1994, p. 12. But the 'crisis of capitalist integration' has nevertheless prompted the Institute to 'revive Horkheimer's inaugural lecture and to reorient its future research in a more general, interdisciplinary direction' (Dubiel 1994, p. 107).

(economics, sociology, psychology, philosophy), taking account of the new conditions of reproduction of advanced capitalism, namely, its ability to short-circuit the crisis mechanism by means of state intervention and the new-found weight of ideology and the cultural sphere. The principal idea was that the Marxist critique of ideology did not permit explanation of

> the relationship between the economic life of society, the psychic development of the individual and the changes within the cultural sphere in the narrower sense.[3]

Objections to the critique of ideology reached a peak in 1944 with *Dialectic of Enlightenment*, in which Adorno and Horkheimer called into question modern rationality as such. Habermas's *Theory of Communicative Action* partook of this logic, demanding a communicative regrounding of rationality. In this work from 1981, Habermas engaged in a ruthless revision of critical theory, proposing to release it from the 'ballast of historical materialism'. Once 'neo-Marxist', the Frankfurt school's critical theory was in the process of becoming 'post-Marxist'.[4]

The conjuncture of the 1980s

Following the existentialist wave, which created moderate currents of exchange between France and Germany in the 1950s and 1960s, the 1970s were marked by two distinct intellectual logics, despite the shared upheaval of 1968: the structuralist vogue in France and the revival of critical theory in Germany. These two currents – embodied in France by Althusser and in Germany by strategies for updating critical theory, on the one hand, and the rising star of Habermas, on the other – seemed impervious to one another, including (and especially) in the Marxist domain. In France, the Frankfurt school was virtually unknown; in Germany, the Althusserian approach circulated only among a limited audience in the form of pamphlets, produced outside traditional publishing, diffused by the student movement. A study of the currents responsible for this marginal diffusion and its impact on left-wing thought in

---

[3] Horkheimer 1972, p. 43.

[4] This chapter, which is restricted to the 1980s and 1990s, is extracted from an essay on the evolution and identity of critical theory.

Germany remains to be carried out. According to Wolfgang Bonss and Axel Honneth, the 'return to Marxism' in German university culture in any event undermined the impact of critical theory at the very moment when it returned to centre-stage, in the agitated context of the late 1960s.[5] According to them, in consequence it no longer appeared to be 'a continuation of Marxism but a bourgeois revision'[6] – to the extent that it may be asked whether it was critical theory which was in tune with the turn of the 1960s and 1970s, or rather a mixture in which the hopes that had been invested in it weighed more than it delivered or was in a position to offer.

In the context of a renewed interest in Marxism and rediscovery of the original critical theory, Alfred Schmidt played a significant role. He was one of the critical mediators of the reception of French structuralism.[7] He also re-edited the complete collection of the *Zeitschrift für Sozialforschung*, the essays by Horkheimer published in that journal (*Kritische Theorie*), and older texts that Horkheimer had published under the pseudonym Heinrich Regiue: *Dämmerung*. He was also responsible for the German translation of *Eclipse of Reason*. Philosopher and anglicist, Schmidt also translated a fair number of Marcuse's American works into German: *Reason and Revolution*, *One-Dimensional Man*, *Critique of Pure Tolerance*, and (jointly) *Counterrevolution and Revolt*, as well as the *Essay on Liberation*. Moreover, Schmidt did not confine himself to this decisive contribution to the turning-point of the years 1967–70. Starting with his doctoral thesis on *The Concept of Nature in Marx* (1962),[8] he also elaborated his own thoughts on historical materialism and the tradition of philosophical materialism,[9] reviving an old, aborted project of critical theory: a critical study of the materialist tradition on which Ernst Bloch had been due to collaborate (this was at the point when he was negotiating his emigration to the USA with Horkheimer).[10]

---

[5] On the development of critical theory from the return to Germany up to the 1970s, see Demirovic 1999 and Albrecht *et al.* 1999. It is also appropriate to pay tribute to the pioneering work done by Rolf Wiggershaus, who was the first person to make use of the all the available correspondence: see Wiggershaus 1994.

[6] Bonss and Honneth 1982, p. 8.

[7] See especially Schmidt 1969 and 1981.

[8] Schmidt 1971.

[9] Let us cite, *inter alia*, Schmidt 1965; Schmidt 1977a; Schmidt and Post 1975; and Schmidt 1977b. On Schmidt's *œuvre*, see Lutz-Bachmann and Schmid-Noerr 1991.

[10] In a way, Bloch carried out this project in his own right: see Bloch 1972 and Raulet 1998.

It was doubtless not fortuitous if the 1970s and the beginning of the 1980s were marked by a first wave of historical studies of critical theory/the Institute of Social Research/the Frankfurt school.[11] The three were still far from disentangled, but the Institute/school/theory had already turned a page. They could now form the subject of historical and philological studies, even as the contemporary relevance of 'critical theory' was being questioned – and often by the same figures.

In the 1980s the situation was abruptly transformed. Virtually from one day to the next, French philosophers and sociologists became an unavoidable point of reference – but it was now a question of Foucault, Baudrillard, Lyotard, Derrida and, incidentally, a few others. These are the figures characterised in the German reception as 'poststructuralists'. In its abruptness, this switch represented an ideological and political phenomenon that remains generally unexplained. We can only offer a few hypotheses. Above all, there was the exhaustion of the Marxist paradigm. Habermas's *Theory of Communicative Action* (1981) registered it and aimed to jettison the ballast represented by the Hegelian-Marxist theoretical co-ordinates of the critical theory inherited from Adorno and Horkheimer.[12] Via a different logic, French political philosophy had reached the same conclusion. One way or another, the two particularisms – French and German – were to coincide. This encounter was massively to the advantage of the French contribution (already assimilated in the USA, which doubtless rendered it all the more unavoidable for Germans). The lectures delivered at Düsseldorf and Geneva by Manfred Frank, and published under the title *What Is Neostructuralism?* in 1983, played a major role.[13] They initiated a whole generation of young, German-speaking philosophers into the new French approaches. The innovative power of French authors swept over a critical theory which, in the person of Habermas, was certainly in the process of renewing itself, but slowly. Invited to the Collège de France in 1983, he adopted the strategy of a frontal offensive against the French trends. In 1980, when he received the Adorno Prize from the city of Frankfurt, Habermas had revealed his persuasion in 'Modernity – An Incomplete Project', by character-

---

[11] See Jay 1973; Dubiel 1978; and Held 1980.

[12] See Habermas 1987.

[13] See Frank 1989.

ising the 'line lead[ing] from Georges Bataille via Michel Foucault to Jacques Derrida' as neo-conservatism:

> On the basis of modernistic attitudes they justify an irreconcilable anti-modernism. They remove into the sphere of the far-way and the archaic the spontaneous powers of imagination, self-experience, and emotion. To instrumental reason they juxtapose in Manichean fashion a principle only accessible through evocation, be it the will to power or sovereignty, Being or the Dionysiac force of the poetical.[14]

This (counter-)offensive appeared in German in 1985 under the title *Der philosophische Diskurs der Moderne*. Offered to Éditions du Seuil as early as 1983, for some inexplicable reason it was not accepted.[15] The French translation was only published in 1988 by Gallimard. In any event, its only effect was to open the floodgates to the reception of 'poststructuralism' and 'postmodern' thought in Germany. Frank had the enormous merit not only of presenting the currents under attack in the deliberately neutral form of university lectures, but also of engaging in order to create a dialogue on fundamentals with the French thinkers.[16] Although not sharing the enthusiasm of small publishers who began to publish anything hailing from France, he thereby helped to anchor reference to French 'poststructuralism' in German philosophical debates. Thereafter, alongside small publishers like Merve, major ones – Suhrkamp at their head – included French philosophers among the sure-fire assets of their publishing programmes. At the outset, there were more translations into German of texts by Derrida, Foucault, Lyotard, Baudrillard and company, than of material by Habermas and by critical theory as a whole into French.[17] One result of this Franco-German conjuncture was that, on the French side, Foucault admitted in an interview which circulated throughout the world that his positions were in no sense incompatible with those of the Frankfurt school – at least with the diagnosis of the self-destruction of Reason formulated in *Dialectic of Enlightenment* (1944).[18]

---

[14] Habermas 1985, p. 14.

[15] Here I am speaking as a witness of the affair.

[16] See Frank, Raulet and van Reijen 1988 (the fruit of two seminars, at Vienna and Amsterdam).

[17] Things were reversed only at the end of the 1980s.

[18] See Foucault 1983.

During the important Adorno conference organised for the eightieth anniversary of Adorno's birth in 1983, reference to *Dialectic of Enlightenment* formed the spinal column of the German counter-attack. In his introductory talk, Ludwig von Friedeburg gave prominence to the text jointly written by Adorno and Horkheimer, which inspired him to comment: 'Adorno's influence on critical theory is becoming perceptible today.'[19] The third generation took up battle stations. Relaying Habermas's line of argument, Helmut Dubiel declared:

> The interest of the social sciences in a continuation of the critical theory of society currently takes the form of a powerful renaissance of themes developed in *Dialectic of Enlightenment*. This renaissance feeds on a widespread cultural pessimism whose line of argument simultaneously aims at a theory of civilisation and a critique of rationality.... As for its political impact, this way of reading Adorno dramatises the crisis of Marxism to the extent that not only the current prospects for an emancipatory theory of society, but also the very meaning and possibility of a critical theoretical attitude towards the present, are put in doubt. Among experts on critical theory, this interpretation is all the more irritating in that it attempts, by means of a left-wing line of argument, to assimilate Adorno to a terrain that has always been occupied by right-wing intellectuals in the German ideological tradition.[20]

The previous year, in their preface to the proceedings of a conference that dated back to 1977, Wolfgang Bonss and Axel Honneth, colleagues of Habermas at the Max Planck Institute at Starnberg, had already adopted a defensive line of argument with respect to 'poststructuralism', while bringing out 'the unanticipated affinity between *Dialectic of Enlightenment* and French poststructuralism, from Foucault to Baudrillard'. According to them, the contemporaneity of *Dialectic of Enlightenment* and Horkheimer's *Eclipse of Reason* (translated into German in 1967) derived from a generalised scepticism about science, 'which the crisis of Marxism conceals by radicalising it'.[21] In 1983 the fallback position was *Negative Dialectics*, in line with a strategy that posited a

---

19 Friedeburg and Habermas 1983, p. 9.
20 Friedeburg and Habermas 1983, pp. 239–40.
21 Bons and Honneth 1982, p. 13.

continuity between *Dialectic of Enlightenment* and *Negative Dialectics*.[22] Anxious to stem the haemorrhage, as early as 1982 Bonss and Honneth were also foregrounding the importance 'of Adorno's aesthetics and Benjamin or Marcuse's theory of culture' for this updating of critical theory.[23] This laudable ecumenicism was at least a sign: the institutional practices of Horkheimer, who until the end of the 1960s had controlled and filtered republication of the founding texts, had been abandoned.[24] *Anything* in critical theory that could be put to contemporary use was rediscovered without any restrictions, even if this initiative was still inspired by a defensive logic: showing that there was no need for French 'poststructuralism'; demonstrating that it was the self-inflated version of a problematisation of rationality which critical theory had already conducted – even that it was ruining such work by risking fuelling metaphysical and/or right-wing excesses. However convincing, at least as a contribution to the debate, the argument suffered from a weakness: critical theory had arrived at this point under duress. Otherwise, to adopt Dubiel's words, it would not have let itself be drawn onto 'a terrain that has always been occupied by right-wing intellectuals in the German ideological tradition'. Nevertheless, without the rediscovery of *Dialectic of Enlightenment*,[25] the Franco-German dialogue over critical theory would have been largely impossible.

Habermas was not to be outdone. He too 'rediscovered' *Dialectic of Enlightenment*. In his brief introduction to Martin Jay's intervention during the 1983 Adorno conference, he suggested: 'Perhaps the discussions would have been even more gripping if the neo-structuralist interpretation of *Dialectic of Enlightenment* had been stated more clearly'.[26] He rammed home the point without further delay in Karlheinz Bohrer's collective volume, *Mythos und Moderne*.[27] Certainly, in it he does not refer to the affinities between *Dialectic of Enlightenment* and 'poststructuralism'. But following a brilliant rereading of the major themes and an interpretation of the meaning of the work in the development of critical theory, he comes to the question of total critique and affinities with Nietzsche:

---

[22] See Bonss 1983, p. 203.
[23] Bonns and Honneth (eds.) 1982, p. 15.
[24] See the edifying collective work of Albrecht *et al.* 1999.
[25] See especially Wellmer 1985 (an indispensable essay); 1988; and Honneth 1991, to which we shall return.
[26] Habermas 1983a, p. 351.
[27] Habermas 1983b.

> Nietzsche's critique of knowledge and morality anticipates an idea that Horkheimer and Adorno develop in the form of the critique of instrumental reason: behind positivism's ideals of objectivity and claims to truth, behind universalistic morality's ideals of asceticism and claims to rightness, lurk imperatives of self-preservation and domination.[28]

To understand the strategy, it is enough to consult the table of contents of *The Philosophical Discourse of Modernity* (1985), where the essay is recycled. In Chapter 4, Nietzsche is characterised as a 'turning point'. We might also speak of a bifurcation: either one pursues the line inaugurated by Horkheimer and Adorno or one engages in the 'adventures of Reason' represented by Heideggerianism and French ideologies – Derrida, Bataille, Foucault, or the neo-Nietzscheanism denounced in the Frankfurt speech in 1980. Nevertheless, a significant concession will be noted: the problematic of 'reason and self-preservation' qualifies critical theory as belonging among the 'critiques of domination'. Later on, we shall see how Habermas's pupils were subsequently to develop this opening.

But, by the same token, while mobilising its own resources, critical theory was indeed drawn onto enemy terrain – which it ultimately had to recognise as being neither Klages, nor Spengler, nor even Nietzsche. It ended up coming round to the view of Hans Robert Jauss, who, having assimilated postmodernity to the 'spectre haunting Europe' during the 1983 Adorno conference, recalled in time his own work on modernity and concluded in 1985 that one should not 'regard postmodernity as the mythologeme of a neoconservative counter-Enlightenment, but as the advent of a new epochal consciousness'.[29] As a result, the positions of the mediators prevailed – and we may count the works of Wellmer, offspring of critical theory who had ended up at Constance, among the most effective mediations.

In his small but important essay collection *On the Dialectic of Modernity and Postmodernity*, Wellmer reinterprets Adorno by looking to his deconstruction of the 'constraint of identity [*Identitätszwang*]' for the preconditions of a different form of rationality, a form of subjectivity that no longer corresponds to the

[28] Habermas 1983b, p. 421.
[29] Jauss 1988, p. 228.

> rigid unity of the bourgeois subject, but attests to a more flexible form of organisation of an ego identity 'rendered fluid by communication' (Habermas). These two aspects – the shaking of the subject and its prison of meaning in the modern world *and* the possibility of a different relationship to a world decentred by the expansion of the boundaries of the subject – were prepared well in advance in modern art. Against the excesses of a technical and bureaucratic rationality, that is to say, against the form of rationality dominant in modern society, modern art highlighted an emancipatory potential of modernity; it in fact made it possible to envisage a new type of 'synthesis' and 'unity' thanks to which what is diffuse, unintegrated, extravagant, and dissociated could find its place in a space of communication free of violence.[30]

Seemingly aligned with Habermas, this was to go beyond Habermas. Certainly, Habermas had himself claimed a role for art and mimesis as 'allusions' to a necessary paradigm change. But this mutation in rationality was ultimately to be effected by the *Theory of Communicative Action*. Wellmer too adhered to the Weberian-Habermasian conception of the inevitable separation of reason into distinct spheres – science, law and morality, art.[31] However, following Peter Bürger,[32] he was interested in the transformation of the 'art institution', in the new constellations being created between art and life-forms – that is to say, in the forms of communication that occurred in the medium of art, such as they could be observed in postmodern architecture in particular.[33] Like Bürger, Wellmer did not believe in an abolition of the distinction between expert culture and common culture, but he broke down the barrier of 'single coding' by admitting the emergence of a 'denser network of relations' between the two.[34] If he remained faithful to the idea of an 'unfinished modernity', his argument was that modernity can and must precisely discover the

---

30 Wellmer 1985, pp. 163ff. See also p. 29: 'What Adorno called "aesthetic synthesis" can be finally be related to the utopia, construed in a perfectly realistic sense, of a communication free of violence'.

31 Wellmer 1985, p. 38.

32 See Bürger 1984 and 1983.

33 Cf. Raulet 1989a; 1989b; and 1999. In the essay 'Kunst und industrielle Produktion', written for the seventy-fifth anniversary of *Werkbund*, Wellmer sought to interpret Charles Jencks's multiple coding in Habermasian fashion.

34 Wellmer 1985, p. 40.

potential for its revival in postmodernity. He did not even hesitate to query 'the desirability of a universal consensus'.[35]

Wellmer opened the Pandora's Box of new forms of social interaction, which Habermas always kept under the lid of his 'communicative reason'. If the modernity/postmodernity debate as such is exhausted, *this problem* is bound to resurface. Scarcely was the 'postmodern' chapter closed than the Frankfurt school opened another front: that of law and sociality. It certainly could and should have done so much earlier, given the extent to which the 'postmodern' context prompted such a move. But it displayed a blind spot, or rather a deliberate blindness, towards all the works that in fact fell within its field and pertained to its original vocation: 'social philosophy'. If Habermas registered in passing the mutations in social space produced by new technologies of information and communication, in *Theory of Communicative Action* they do not seem to constitute a revolution such as to demand real theoretical revision. Important in France, this line of thought was deliberately minimised. It took the debate between neo-communitarians and liberals in the United States for critical theory – Habermas and the third generation of the Frankfurt school – to emerge from the dogmatic slumber it had been lulled into by its certainty that it had hit upon an unanswerable theoretical rejoinder by ritually invoking the legacy of *Dialectic of Enlightenment*, while leaving things to 'communicative action'. Here we see that, for critical theory, what occurs in the United States is, as when Horkheimer returned to Frankfurt, more important than what happens in Europe as regards any 'social philosophy'.

The Habermas effect

Viewed from without, Habermas did not carry the day. In June 1965, the year in which Marcuse took his hat off to Horkheimer (the Horkheimer of the old Institute) in *Kultur und Gesellschaft*, Habermas too, when delivering his inaugural lecture upon taking up Horkheimer's chair in social philosophy at Frankfurt – 'Knowledge and Human Interests' – could allow himself to stress that he was adopting one of Horkheimer's 'most important lines of enquiry' in his own right.

---

[35] Wellmer 1985, p. 105.

Habermas is the only person to have completed a quasi-systematic *œuvre*, which, measured in the light of the Hegelian system, after the theory of law (*Between Facts and Norms*)[36] lacks only an 'Aesthetics' that others have produced for him or in his place, as we have just seen. In fact (and perhaps this is the reason for the absence of aesthetics), the *Theory of Communicative Action* claims to reconstruct the unity of reason separated by modernity. Therewith, it shares the diagnosis according to which instrument rationality is a 'truncated [*halbiert*]' reason. Modernisation has led to the triumph of the rationality of understanding of science and technology, or only one aspect of eighteenth-century Reason. According to Horkheimer, industrial rationality embodied this truncated reason: the aim of *Eclipse of Reason* was 'to inquire into the concept of rationality that underlies our contemporary industrial culture, in order to discover whether this concept does not contain defects that vitiate it essentially'.[37]

But Habermas's *Theory of Communicative Action* does not share the conclusions drawn in *Dialectic of Enlightenment*. Certainly, Habermas has incidentally claimed a role for art and mimesis as 'allusions' to a necessary paradigm change supposedly finally accomplished by *Theory of Communicative Action*. But, for him, it is as if the only thing at stake in 'communicative action' is to reconstruct a faltering legitimacy. Can it at the same time transform the rationality underlying this crisis of legitimacy? To what extent does *Theory of Communicative Action* overcome an ultimately rather simplistic dualism between rationality and legitimacy?

Twenty years after it was 'launched', Habermas's programme remains problematic and fragile, given the concrete forms of communication that flourished in the 1980s and 1990s as a result of the diffusion of the new technologies.[38] Notwithstanding the corrections or clarifications he has made, Habermas's position, even in *Between Facts and Norms*, remains defensive: while embellishing it with successive qualifications, he continues to invoke an ideal community of understanding. At the same time, he is certainly increasingly interested in the *reality of social interactions*, but without succeeding in really taking their measure.

---

36 See Habermas 1996.

37 Horkheimer 1947, p. v.

38 See Raulet and Hörisch 1992 and Raulet 1988.

The principle of a discursive formation of the general will remains 'counterfactual [*kontrafaktisch*]'; and the fact that Habermas has for years expressly assigned it this status in no way changes the problem. In *Legitimation Crisis* in 1973, readers were already struck by the conditionals:

> Such a counterfactually projection reconstruction...can be guided by the question (justified, in my opinion, by considerations from universal pragmatics): how would the members of a social system, at a given stage of development of productive forces, have collectively and bindingly interpreted their needs (and which norms would they have accepted as justified) if they could and would have decided on organization of social intercourse through discursive will-formation, with adequate knowledge of the limiting conditions and functional imperatives of their society?[39]

In 1979, Jean-François Lyotard had issued this warning: 'Where, after the metanarratives, can legitimacy reside?...Is legitimacy to be found in consensus obtained through discussion, as Jürgen Habermas thinks? Such consensus does violence to the heterogeneity of language games.'[40] For his part, Habermas stuck to his abstract construction of a communicative action that overcomes the fragmentation of linguistic acts and, consequently, of the general will and Reason itself. The issue of the instance that unified the different types of validity[41] was 'resolved' by invoking a rational argument, but without Habermas really asking whether the dominant language games allowed it to operate. As long as this issue is not clarified, the argument that the socialisation of individuals occurs through the internalisation of truth-dependent norms is likewise problematic. Which truth (even if purely communicative)? And what are the forms of this miraculous 'internalisation'?

This is precisely the question to which the Habermasian conception of law has attempted a response. To Luhman Habermas objects only that law represents a domain which refutes the functional differentiation between subsystems, because it is the site of awareness and rationally motivated demands

---

[39] Habermas 1976, p. 113.

[40] Lyotard 1984, pp. xxiv–v.

[41] The propositional truth of statements [*Wahrheit*]; their normative correctness [*Richtigkeit*]; their expressive veracity – in other words, the requirement of authenticity and sincerity on the part of the speaking subject [*Wahrhaftigkeit*]; the correct conformation of symbolic structures [*Regelrichtigkeit*]; the formal correctness of statements [*Wohlgeformtheit*]; and their intelligibility [*Verständlichkeit*].

and, in addition, opens up a space of deliberation and understanding for the purposes of social integration:

> [u]nder these premises, law then functions as a hinge between system and lifeworld, a function that is incompatible with the idea that the legal system, withdrawing into its own shell, autopoietically encapsulates itself.[42]

Law represents the mediating instance *par excellence* between the 'life-world' and the social systems that are independent of one another and obey particular codes. It is the transmission belt capable of checking social and political fragmentation:

> Normatively substantive messages can circulate *throughout society* only in the language of law. Without their translation into the complex legal code that is equally open to lifeworld and system, these messages would fall on deaf ears in media-steered spheres of action. Law thus functions as the 'transformer' that first guarantees that the socially integrating network of communications stretched across society as a whole holds together.[43]

Yet it is precisely at this point that the crucial problem of proceduralisation, which can be defined in Habermas's terms as 'levelling between factuality and validity', also arises. For the problem is indeed then posed on the terrain of positive law. For it to be resolved, the recipients of juridical norms must at the same time be able to construe themselves as the rational authors of these norms. This poses the issue of citizenship. The corollary of this problem is the moralisation of law: when citizens no longer regard themselves as the authors of law, not only do procedures proliferate, but they draw their inspiration from the law/morality divide. Confronted with this proceduralisation, it has to be noted that Habermas's 'D principle' (the principle of rational discussion) plays the role of a magic wand, once again elevating rational communication into mediation, but chasing its tail, because the problem posed is that of its malfunctioning! In Habermas, Law has become the stake of his whole approach, but Law resolves nothing.

It would appear that its rear normative base is now an informal 'Öffentlichkeit' – a mediocre *deus ex machina* derived from the absence of a sociological study of social interaction, but nevertheless claiming to be inspired by its

---

42 Ibid.
43 Ibid.

empirical reality. The schematisation of basic rights proposed by Habermas reflects this contradiction by adding a fifth ('contextual' and culturalist) right to the basic right to participate on equal terms in the processes of opinion and will formation, representing the framework in which citizens exercise their political autonomy and through which they establish legitimate law.

The Habermasian formulation of the four first types of basic rights itself warrants extended commentary. We shall limit ourselves to the fifth:

> basic rights to the provision of living conditions that are socially, technologically, and ecologically safeguarded, insofar as the current circumstances make this necessary if citizens are to have equal opportunities to utilise the civil rights list in (1) through (4).[44]

This 'dialectic' between the universal rights of citizens and rights to difference concretely seems to boil down to a weak version of affirmative action. Habermas concedes, moreover, that:

> Although basic rights originally consisted of negative or 'defensive' rights [*Abwehrrechten*] that grant liberties and keep an intervening administration within the bounds of law, they have now become the architectonic principles of the legal order, thus transforming the content of individual, or 'subjective' liberties [*Freiheitsrechte*] into the content of fundamental norms that penetrate and shape 'objective' law, albeit in a conceptually unclarified manner.[45]

A politics of recognition must take the form of a communicative struggle in order for identities and criteria to be defined in an authentically dialogical fashion and in the most egalitarian manner possible. The 'D principle' as magic wand! Quite clearly, it is time to assess what communicative *struggle* might consist in.

To describe the deterioration in the relationship between public opinion and politics, in *Between Facts and Norms* Habermas replaces the metaphor of siege by that of a lock: to influence political power, judicial power, and the bureaucracy that form the core of the system, 'citizens' relegated to the periphery must open the 'locks' of the democratic and juridical procedures peculiar to the *Rechtsstaat*. Law is the lock *par excellence*.[46] By reducing values to the act

---

[44] Habermas 1996, p. 123.
[45] Habermas 1996, pp. 247–8.
[46] See Habermas 1995, pp. 138ff.

of asserting them, the mediation between facts and values promised by the title *Between Facts and Norms* remains dependent on the quasi-transcendental medium of the community of understanding and, in consequence, is as unconvincing as the latter.[47]

The third generation confronted with current problematics

Today, the contours of the Frankfurt school are more fluid than ever. After the death of the two tutelary figures,[48] the legacy of critical theory was represented by Habermas and Alfred Schmidt, who both formed pupils and generated two currents, despite shared interests and some two-way traffic. The pupils of Adorno, of Horkheimer, and then of Habermas and Schmidt have scattered and in their turn created new poles of critical theory: Oskar Negt (whom the student movement wished to nominate as Adorno's successor) in Hanover in the 1970s;[49] Clause Offe at Bielefeld;[50] Albrecht Wellmer in Constance in the 1980s and then in Berlin after German reunification.

---

[47] See Raulet 1999.

[48] Adorno in August 1969 and Horkheimer – who officially retired in 1964 but remained active in the Institute – in 1973. The third historical witness – Pollock – died in 1970.

[49] Negt was one of the brains of the SDS [*Sozialistischer Deutscher Studentenbund*] excluded from the SPD during the Godesberg congress in 1960 and whose organ was the journal *Neue Kritik*. It is striking that in this journal we find practically no mention of Horkheimer and Adorno, but instead Marx himself, Lukács, Baran and Sweezy, Joan Robinson, and Wolfgang Abendroth, with whom Habermas had taken refuge after his departure from Frankfurt (when Horkheimer had opposed his *Habilitation*). In his 1962 doctoral thesis (on Comte and Hegel), experts calculate Negt's references to critical theory at 0.5 per cent (Behrmann 1999, p. 385). Negt has pursued a career in constant tension between the academy and trade unionism and was particularly active in the permanent formation of the DGB [*Deutscher Gewerkschaftsbund*]. In 1969, he created the 'Socialist Bureau [*Sozialistisches Büro*]', an unorthodox political organisation. If there is a base line in his theoretical output and political engagement, it consists in the notion of political culture and, in particular, the formation of the political consciousness of workers. With respect to the Habermasian 'public sphere [*Öffenlichkeit*]' – he was Habermas's assistant at Heidelburg from 1962–4 and followed the latter to Frankfurt in 1964 when he succeeded Horkheimer – he adopted a radical position: the public sphere only serves the self-representation of the dominant class (see Negt and Kluge 1993). This approach contains aspects worth taking into consideration again today: in particular, the dialectic of organisation and spontaneity that Negt articulated at the time with reference to Rosa Luxemburg. This continues to be a stumbling block for 'communicative action', since it must (or should) start out from real forms of interaction. In Negt and Kluge 1981, Negt attempts to implement, in what is in a sense a 'Benjaminian' fashion, an apprehension of 'expressive' forms of experience that is precisely supposed to correct the rigidity of the Habermasian model.

[50] See Offe 1984.

Succeeding the second generation today is the third, composed of pupils of Habermas (Axel Honneth), of Schmidt (Matthias Lutz-Bachmann and Gunzelin Schmid-Noerr),[51] and of Wellmer (Martin Seel).[52] It began its career with the debates of the 1980s. For example, Honneth stepped into the 'opening' in the form of the concession finally made by Habermas in his polemic against poststructuralism in the early 1980s. His first major work – *The Critique of Power* (1985) – is the very image, the archetype, of the strategy for rendering critical theory contemporary that we have described. In its first part, it acknowledges the lacunae, even aporiae, of critical theory as regards social analysis. It goes back to 'Horkheimer's original idea' (this is the first, philological move); notes its 'defects' and seeks its salvation in 'the turning-point in philosophy of history' represented by *Dialectic of Enlightenment*; and then turns, in a third, equally expected move, towards Adorno. Nevertheless, the thesis is not wanting in vigour: critical theory failed to apprehend an integral part of its definition – the social. Whence a dramatic turn (part two): this 'rediscovery of the social' is to be sought in…Foucault and Habermas. The argument is not particular about details: it aims at nothing less than reintegrating into the intellectual horizon of critical theory (such as it has been codified since the beginning of the 1960s) anything that might contradict it:

> Both the theory of power, which Foucault has grounded in historical investigation, and the theory of society, which Habermas has developed on the basis of a theory of communicative action, can be viewed as attempts to interpret in a new way the process of a dialectic of enlightenment analyzed by Horkheimer and Adorno. If the history of critical social theory is reconstruction from this point of view, then Foucault's theory of power proves to be a systems-theoretic and Habermas' social theory a communication-theoretical solution to the aporias encountered by Adorno and Horkheimer in their philosophical-historical analysis of the process of civilization.[53]

While the trick is unsubtle, the tactics are clever. In sum, they consist in saying: we are not going to revert to the Habermas-Luhmann controversy. This major

---

[51] See Lutz-Bachmann 1991 and 1997; and Schmid-Noerr 1988.
[52] See Seel 1996a; 1996b; and 1997.
[53] Honneth 1991, p. xi.

debate of the 1970s[54] is kept on the sidelines because, as everyone observed, it ended in a peace of the brave. Critical theory cut its losses and since then it has not been rare to find references to both – the theory of communicative action and systems theory – combined in research. But systems theory is indirectly condemned, since the French – Foucault – can be regarded as one of its manifestations (they were previously characterised as Nietzscheans, but no matter: the main thing is to label them and thereby keep them at a distance). After the Pyrrhic victory over systems theory, it is necessary to win a victory of at least equal (if not greater) magnitude over the Gallic theory of power. Eureka: to demonstrate that it is a theory of the social (which it unquestionably is and the argument is in fact unimpeachable) and thus render it 'acceptable [*salonfähig*]' to critical theory. Consequently, the problems are dismissed, if not resolved: let us embrace, Luhmann, Foucault, Habermas – unite and fight! Except, obviously, that it still has to be demonstrated that critical theory, accused in part one of having neglected the social, has finally discovered it in Habermas. In this strategico-tactical night in which all cats are grey, a few glimmers of critique emerge – reflections that take their distance from Habermas and venture towards Wellmer, even towards Lyotard (who, naturally, is not cited):

> If... linguistic understanding represents the particular form of a coordination of goal-directed actions that comes about by virtue of the mutual accomplishments of interpretation, it may be asked how all the processes of coordinating action that exist in the physical or psychological, moral or cognitive relations between a subject and its object are to be characterized. To be sure, in the section of his work on speech-act theory Habermas attempts to demarcate forms of strategic action oriented to understanding, but the former do not systematically appear in his argument as ways for coordinating actions.... Habermas loses... the communication-theoretic approach he had initially opened up: the potential for an understanding of the social order as an institutionally mediated communicative relation between culturally integrated groups that, so long as the exercise of power is asymmetrically distributed, takes place through the medium of social struggle. Only a consistent elaboration of this alternative vision would make it possible to understand the social organizations that Adorno and

[54] Habermas and Luhmann 1971; 1973; and 1974.

> Foucault mistook as power complexes functioning in a totalitarian manner as fragile constructions that remain dependent for their existence on the moral consensus of all participants.[55]

Obviously, one cannot but subscribe to this diagnosis. Today, as a result of the attenuation or disconnection of a shared normative instance, everything hinges on the level of the capacity of social agents to asset their 'difference of opinion' and thereby influence the 'consensus'. In other words, the articulation of the expressive and the normative must be rethought. In this respect, according to Honneth, it appears that

> The communicative model of action that lies at the basis of Habermas's social theory has changed considerably in comparison with his previous approaches... the dimensions of communicative and instrumental rationality, which Habermas had previously distinguished, are extended by the third dimension of aesthetic-expressive rationality, which is supposed to be set forth in the authentic relationship of the subject to the world of his internal perceptions and experiences. From this Habermas derives a view of aesthetics that, in problematic ways, attempts to connect the rationality of a work of art to the truthfulness of expressions formed within it.[56]

We indicated our opinion of this above. At least in 1985 this was a lucid diagnosis. And we can only rejoice to note that it has entered into the programme of the Institute of Social Research, albeit in Habermasian fashion – that is to say, using the metaphor of the siege of institutions by civil society. The Institute's current thinking on civil society is in fact described thus:

> Civil society refers to the sphere of the public arena in which individuals who are victims of discrimination begin to act in communicative fashion and to demand rights. They aim to besiege, check and civilise the power of the state and market, not to abolish it.[57]

---

[55] Honneth 1991, pp. 287 and 303.

[56] Honneth 1991, pp. 286–7.

[57] Institut für Sozialforschung an der J.W. Goethe-Universität Frankfurt am Main, *Mitteilungen*, no. 10, 1999, p. 117. The following works by Honneth are also to be referred to: Honneth 1995 and 1999.

Hauke Brunkhorst, whilst enormously involved in reflecting on the new political and social challenges,[58] has opted for a route that is just as difficult, and whose co-ordinates are not unprecedented either: on the one hand, likewise preserving the strained arc between the programme of the 1930s and its Habermasian revision; and on the other, calling a halt to the 1970s debate between Habermas and Luhmann and, in his own right and without preconceptions, accepting theoretical stimulus from both camps. The issue that he pursues is likewise not unprecedented, quite simply because it involves *the issue* of contemporary political philosophy. He merely formulates it in more radical fashion. It is in fact clear that the desire to render critical theory contemporary can only take the form of a *theory of democracy*. But, whereas Honneth has recently drawn his main theoretical inspiration from American communitarianism, including the 'civil-society approach', Brunkhorst proves more inflexible when it comes to the question of sovereignty as the core of the problem of the transformation of (post)modern democracy. At the same time – and this is what distinguishes him from Habermas and prompts his publicity and activity – he attaches less value to the constitution of norms than to their effective operation. Here, evidently, lies the 'defect' (to use Honneth's term) of critical theory as a 'social philosophy'. It keeps turning it over, as indicated by the September 1999 edition of its bulletin. It is perfectly obvious that it has not overcome it.

[58] See Brumlik and Brunkhorst 1993, 1994 and 1998.

Chapter Eight

The Late Lukács and the Budapest School

André Tosel

Up until approximately the late 1970s, Marxism remained an explicit reference point in major social and intellectual debates. This was the period when from within international Communism the great heretics of Marxism, whose thinking had been formed from the 1920s onwards and who had experienced the vicissitudes of Stalinism and post-Stalinism, made their final contributions and won a certain audience. This was the case with Gyorgy Lukács and Ernst Bloch, who died in 1971 and 1977 respectively, after having published their last great books: *On the Ontology of Social Being* (1971) and *Experimentum Mundi* (1977). In a way, this was also true of Antonio Gramsci's major work: the *Prison Notebooks* were published in 1975 in their original version by Valentino Gerratana (replacing the old thematic edition organised by Palmiro Togliatti, which had formed a whole generation of Italian Marxists from the 1950s) and imparted a final radiance to the philosophy of *praxis*. All these works sought to subject the worn-out orthodoxy of Marxism-Leninism-Stalinism to a critique of its presuppositions and to challenge its claim to represent the one and only truth. A survivor of the Soviet repression of the 1956 Hungarian uprising, Lukács explicitly made his ontology of social being a new theoretical basis for a democratic revival of real socialism.

These years also witnessed a multiplicity of programmes for an intellectual and moral reform of Marxism, united in their rejection of Soviet diamat and histomat and their concern to give a second lease of life to a revolutionary movement confronted with its own involution and impasses. These full-scale endeavours accept theoretical pluralism as a fact, but do not renounce a new unity of theory and practice whose vehicle is to be a communist party that has certainly been democratised, but nevertheless maintained in its revolutionary unicity. Over and above their shared anticapitalist passion, it is doubtless this political and organisational assumption that profoundly unites them. Each seeks to rediscover a unity of theory and practice; and the theory is always identified with historical materialism as a system of knowledge of capitalist development, its contradictions and its possible transformation, just as the practice is identified with the historical action of the masses guided by Communist parties. Finally, all of them are convinced of the necessity of a distinctively philosophical or meta-theoretical clarification of Marx's theory as a condition of its revival and of its heuristic capacity for analysing changes in capitalism and socialist society.

These points of agreement soon give way to substantial disagreements, which demonstrate both the fertility and the ambiguity of Marx's legacy; to notable differences in theoretical references, with the crucial problem of assessing Hegel and interpreting the dialectic; and to significant divergences on the politics to be pursued (in particular, as regards the role of the state, law, ethics, ideologies, and culture). In the guise of a return to Marx, each constructs its own Marx – a Marx who is, above all, meta-theoretical.

The late Lukács and the ontology of social being

Reverting at the end of his enterprise to the themes of *History and Class Consciousness* (1923), the late Lukács criticises the Weberianism of his leftist youth – a romantic Weberianism, focused on the denunciation of capitalist rationalisation-alienation. He abandons the subject-object dialectic embodied in the class consciousness of the proletariat, charged with overcoming the bourgeois separation between subject and object via the teleology of history. He stops exalting the revolutionary subjectivity of a class that is the only one capable of putting an end to the abstractional effects of commodities and exchange-value, of surmounting the catastrophic crisis of capitalist rationalisation identified with a socio-economic mechanism of reification. He once and for all criticises what he had himself imposed on Western Marxism, with a work that was as dazzling as it was over-simplistic: the theme of the consciousness of an exceptional class that had become totalising knowledge of social existence beyond the limited perspectives of the bourgeois sciences, and which was adequately represented by its party. Haunted by the failure of the socialist bureaucracy to realise the radical-democratic content of this imputed class consciousness, and conscious of the fact that this speculative rehabilitation of party organisation had proved capable of unwisely sanctioning the twists and turns of Stalinist policy, Lukács proposed an ontological reconstruction of theory with the ultimate aim of constituting a materialist and dialectical ethics furnishing norms for the democratic action of the communist state.

Lukács starts out from the priority of being and its independence from thought. Philosophically, Marx's *œuvre* pertains to an ontological approach that enables it to form an alternative to the specular couple of the Heideggerian ontology of *Dasein*, which negates any scientific objectivity (accused of inauthenticity), and of neo-positivism, which only acknowledges the scientificity of those sciences that analyse the physical or biological levels of being. Social being constitutes a level of objectivity – the level conceptualised by Marx. The essential fact in social being is labour, which both presupposes and, in recurrent fashion, clarifies the other levels of objectivity, which are subject either to causality or to a causality woven out of an immanent quasi-teleology. Labour is a causal activity establishing teleological sequences producing intentional objects – that is to say, objectifications which in the capitalist mode of production can generate specific forms of estrangement under the pressure of the search for relative surplus-value, of the real submission of labour to capital. Neo-capitalist manipulation succeeds the open violence of the formal submission of labour to capital. But, for its part, socialist society is based on specific objectifications that do not realise the freedom of a *praxis* combining objectification of the capacities of labour and a connection with the forms of social being in its various levels. Ontology dissolves the deleterious economism of Stalinist historical materialism by returning to Marx and making critical use of Hegelian categories or 'reflexive determinations', which constitute human *praxis* as a self-realisation of human capacities in the unity of the industrious appropriation of nature and of objectification in social relations.

Lukács in fact distinguishes between objectification, alienation, and estrangement. Objectification is the teleologically adequate transformation through which a natural object is worked on so as to endow it with social utility; it is posited by the 'ideal' moment that determines the goals of labour. As such, it is the framework for any scientific knowledge, which presupposes a minimum of exploration of means, an identification of independent causal chains, and a knowledge of certain natural relations and laws. If science as adequate reflection becomes autonomous of this objectification, in that it acquires a capacity for de-anthropomorphisation, it cannot be severed from industrious objectification. But there is no objectification without alienation, without this objectification rebounding on individuals, without a necessary separation between things and the personality of individuals. Alienation combines with objectification in that it designates the appearance of new needs and new goals by virtue of the retroactive effect of objectifying *praxis* itself on individuals. Alienation is therefore positive, but it can be transformed into estrangement with relations of exploitation and domination. Individuals are in fact posited as instruments of execution of a teleological social situation, such as capitalist valorisation. In this way, systems of finalisation become autonomous; and their effect is to influence individuals to perform the directly teleological roles required for the realisation of a dominant, indirect teleological phenomenon – valorisation – which contradicts the possibilities for creating the rich social individuality that such valorisation simultaneously facilitates and frustrates.

The human race arrives at the threshold of an ontological alternative, beyond classes and nations: either it remains a species in itself – mute, subject to manipulation by the estrangement that separates individuals from any subjective appropriation of accumulated capacities, or it becomes species for itself – allowing human beings to realise themselves as beings capable of responding to the challenge of their modern ontological situation and to produce the teleological projects that derive from their personality. Accordingly, ontology is not an abstract metaphysical translation of Marx, but the most powerful expression of his potential – one equal to our age, which obliges us to ask ourselves the ontological question: to be or not to be. To be for the general manipulation that negates the possibilities of the species for itself, or to be for a 'capacity to be' by realising the determinate alternative, which is to treat the humanity in each and every one of us as an end. The horizon of ontology is an ethics in which what should be introduces no rupture in that which is, but is determined as a what-could-be liberated in being itself: 'You can, therefore you must.' The struggle against radical ontological manipulation thus combines a critique of neo-capitalism extended to the sphere of the reproduction of subjectivity and a fight against the degenerated forms of socialism. And it still has confidence in the capacity of the party-state to reform itself.

The Budapest school: between an ethical-anthropological exit from Marxism and the pursuit of a critique of globalised capital

With this we must compare the trajectory of the members of what was once called the Budapest school, and which belongs by its culture to the German zone. Pupils, disciples, and colleagues of the old Lukács in Hungary, they followed the project of the ontology of social being with interest. Critics of the Communist régime, Ferenc Fehér (b. 1933), Agnes Heller (b. 1929), György Màrkus (b. 1934), and István Mészáros (b. 1930) became dissidents to one degree or another and were excluded from the University of Budapest. The first to follow this path was Mészáros, who participated in the activities of the Petöfi Circle in 1956 and who became a professor in England (at Sussex University). Heller and Markus followed suit after the repression of the Prague Spring in 1968 and in the 1970s moved to Australia, where they taught and worked.

These philosophers have taken different theoretical paths. They have been united above all by a common desire to participate in what was to be a self-criticism of Marxist orthodoxy, and which proved a fruitless attempt at reform. Their activity unfolded in two phases: a reform of Marxism by way of a social anthropology integrating numerous aspects of political liberalism; and a deeper disaffection which led them, with the notable exception of Mészáros, to situate themselves outside Marxism.

The first phase involved exploiting the standpoint of the ontology of social being against Marxist-Leninist dialectical materialism and rethinking Marx's contribution, without inscribing it in a socio-cosmic conception of the universe charged with defending and illustrating a sociopolitical order dominated by a party-state that was unshakeable in its claim to perform a leading role, and yet increasingly incapable of analysing the social and economic reality which it determined. The road initially taken consisted in an anthropological inflection of the Lukácsian perspective, centred on the notion of radical needs of individuals as expressed in everyday life. With *The Theory of Need in Marx* (1973), translated into numerous languages, Heller began a series of works receptive to contemporary research, which took their distance from Lukácsian ontology, deemed to be still too dominated by a paradigm of production incapable of integrating the diversity of human *poeisis-praxis*. The importance of everyday life as the life-world where human enterprises are tested was maintained. These works, following one another with great rapidity, were *Soziologie des Alltagsleben* (1974), then *Instinkt, Agression, Charakter. Einleitung zu einer marxistischen Sozialanthropologie* (1977) and *Theorie der Gefühle* (1978), and *A Theory of History* (1981). For his part, Markus carried out the most scathing critique of the production paradigm with *Language and Production* (1981). He examined the emergence of the linguistic turn in philosophy already signalled by Jürgen Habermas's research, in its confrontation with Hannah Arendt, and hermeneutics. He showed how the linguistic paradigm paid for its undoubted relevance by idealising the virtues of discussion and consensus and neglecting the antagonistic objectivity of social relations. Meanwhile, the production paradigm peculiar to Marx left the construction of communist forms exposed, because it radicalised production for production's sake by separating it from all forms of domination (relations of class exploitation, state domination, subjection to ideological fetishisms). In any event, for Heller and Markus alike, Marx remained relevant in so far as he undertook to combine a theory of alienation radicalising the theme of the human right to dignity with a social phenomenology.

At the same time, the Budapest theoreticians sought to analyse the 'socialist' societies and criticised orthodox historical materialism for its inability to account for the reality that it intended to govern in the name of science. With Ferenc Fehér, Heller and Markus published *Dictatorship over Needs* in 1982. This work may be regarded as the culmination of the critique of the irremediably blocked 'socialist' societies. It radicalised earlier works by the economist Andras Hegedus. Contrary to what Lukács had thought, 'real socialism' could not be reformed. The suppression of the market coincided with the suppression of civil society in favour of the state, and a single plan for production and distribution, regarded by Marxist-Leninist orthodoxy as the economic basis of 'socialism', was intrinsically incompatible with pluralism, democracy, and liberties. The replacement of private property by state property could only result in the dictatorship over needs that represented the anthropological originality of the 'socialist' societies. Producers are subjected by the mechanisms of this dictatorship to a new class: the bureaucracy of the party-state. This critique thus adopted elements of the liberal critique in its own right, and it is only natural that it should conclude with a defence of the market and the spontaneity of civil society. But it would be unfair to forget that, for Heller, the imperative of a radical democratisation of civil society represents the other logic operative in modernity, and that the categorical-utopian imperative of satisfying the needs of the destitute of all countries, as a matter of priority, was on the agenda.

This synthesis combines Marx's conception of the human essence, a Marxist version of the thesis of totalitarianism, and a Weberian theory of rationality. The self-realisation of human essence remains the basis, but it requires a resolutely pluralistic interpretation of life forms against any reduction to the all-encompassing unity of the party-state. Dictatorship over needs is an unprecedented, total system of social domination, wherein a new corporative apparatus appropriates the social surplus-product. This apparatus is the sole material foundation and decisive economic-political component of a mechanism that carries out the expropriation of social agents, whose individual right to chose their work and to consume it recognises, while crushing them by means of a centralised administrative system. The subject of this mechanism is the apparatus, which goes beyond the mere logic of a new dominant class. The goal is neither production for production's sake, nor consumption, but a functional equivalent of ownership: the corporative ownership exercised by the apparatus in a command economy. The pretension to transcend the market results in liquidating civil society, substituting non-quantifiable markets. The result is the coexistence of two complementary economies: the planned set of public enterprises and activities and a set of private activities where services are exchanged according to informal relations of assistance within the apparatus itself. Ideological totalitarianism is the condition for the operation of this system, generating a permanent elimination of civil society, incorporated into the party-state, and a constant restriction of needs. It excludes visible struggle between opposed interests and, while seeking the re-politicisation of society, excludes it.

The second phase of the activity of the Budapest school thinkers initiates a chapter of post-Marxism. Heller has produced a multi-faceted, original *œuvre*, close to Habermas, focused on the urgency of developing a theory of modernity. Gone are the days when it was necessary to test the value of the Marxist tradition via a comparison with the experience of historical Communism, to stress the centrality of the individual, and to reformulate the concept of *praxis* defined either as social activity, directed towards a goal where human beings realise the potentialities of their being, which is to be an end in itself, or as a complex unity of the three dimensions represented by the creation of a specifically human world, the constitution of freedom through struggle, and a connection with humanised nature. Henceforth the Lukácsian theory of objectification must be transformed into a systematic theory of modes of objectification. From *The Power of Shame: Essays on Rationality* (1983) up to *A Theory of Modernity* (1999), Heller has developed a theory of rationality based on a distinction between three spheres of objectification: objectification in itself as an *a priori* of human experience (shared language, objects produced for human use, customs); objectification for itself – an anthropological translation of the Hegelian absolute spirit (religion, art, science, philosophy); and objectification in and for itself (the system of political and economic institutions). This theory becomes a kind of grammar of modernity in that a logic of social organisation based on the market and the social division of labour constantly limits a logic of justice and freedom inherited from socialism, and the three spheres of objectification are shot through with this conflict. The untenable promises of a socialism built on the idea of an unlimited self-realisation, which underestimates the constraints of the logic of organisation, must be abandoned. But the fight for a modernity that maintains the perspective of a just polity in globalisation cannot be eliminated. In particular, it is important to develop a form of ethical thinking beyond political cynicism, in order to nourish an ethico-politics in tune with the materialisation of social rules and human capacities in their economic context. Twentieth-century 'socialism' was a form of modernity that sought to take account of one logic while underestimating the other (*A Philosophy of Morals*, published in 1990, and *An Ethics of Personality*, in 1996). This ethics discloses that there is a world beyond justice in the freedom of each and every one person to fulfil themselves.

It is precisely this disengagement from the specifically Marxian instance of the critique of political economy, in favour of a normative theory of the axiological logics of modernity, that is rejected by the other major thinker of the Budapest school, whom we have hitherto left to one side. The figure in question is István Mészáros, who, having been the first to embark on dissidence, is also the only one to have maintained a direct link with Lukács and Marx, avoiding the temptation of social-liberal reformism and a radically reformist ethics. Mészáros won renown in 1970 with *Marx's Theory of Alienation*, a study that was humanist in inspiration. Following various essays, in 1990 he published a comprehensive survey, *Beyond Capital*, which fused several lines of research. It was not so much a question of exploring a post-Marxist path as of defining a Marxism for the third era in the West. The first Marxism was that of the original Lukács in *History and Class Consciousness*, which explored the tragic tension between the universal perspectives of socialism and the immediate limit of historical actuality (the failure of the revolution in the West and of socialism in one country). The second Marxism was Marxism-Leninism, with its dissident currents (Bloch, Gramsci, the second Lukács). It was based on the form of the separate party-state that blocked the materially based self-activity of the workers. It criticised capitalism without going beyond the empire of capital. It could only effect a critique of its aporias by appealing to reserves of practical energy and to the *Prinzip Hoffnung*. If, with Gramsci, it reflected on the transition from capital to a form of intensive totality, it was incapable of constructing any alternative. The Marxism of the third epoch involves taking the measure of the process through which capitalism, as the most recent form of the production of capital (production based on exchange-value and separation from the means of production), becomes global integration and takes capital as a mode of control regulating the totality of social relations to its limit.

Mészáros pursues his line of reasoning within Marxist theory and historicises it by showing that Soviet socialism was based on a novel form of personification of capital. By personification is to be understood a form of imposition of objective imperatives on the real subject of production as commands. Capital is a system without a subject that includes a personification of subjects, who are called upon to translate the imperatives in a practical direction on pain of exclusion. It is personified in labour-power destined to enter into a contractual relationship of politically regulated economic dependence. The USSR had realised a new form of personification of capital, while asserting as its political objective the negation of capitalism. It had invented a new type of control whose aim was an accelerated rate of extraction of surplus-labour by the party, which justified itself on the grounds of catching up with the capitalist countries. The limited objective of negating capitalism involved a refusal to go beyond capital. The social-democratic experience was based on state control of the economy, forgetting that the social state itself functions as a political structure ensuring the transformation of capital into a coherent system. It too did not succeed in breaking capital, a self-referential system in which the presupposition is also the goal. Ongoing globalisation poses the question of the saturation of mechanism of self-reproduction, which has hitherto been capable of transcending the internal obstacles to its own expansion. Against Heller and Markus, who consider the critical capacity of Marxism exhausted, Mészáros reopens the question of the transition to a different mode of control of the metabolism, based on the invention of a process of decision-making derived from the base, leading capital to come up against its absolute limits. Globalisation poses the issue using processes of malfunctioning at the level of basic functions (production/consumption, circulation/distribution), right up to the jamming of the mechanisms of the displacement of contradictions. Mészáros analyses the structural crisis signified by the saturation of capital in connection with the emergence of three problems: (a) a decreasing rate of utilisation in the lifetime of goods and services; (b) accelerating speeds of circulation of capital and under-utilisation of structures and equipment-machinery, with an artificial reduction in their cycle of depreciation; and (c) a growing gap between the mass consumption required by capital and the decreasing need for living labour. The quest for global regulation, even global governance, indicates the novelty of the crisis. Theories of modernity are invited to make way for a critique of globalisation as a contradictory scenario, which is not predetermined. In surprising fashion, Lukácsian ontology has thus supplied itself with a critical organon in the powerful work of this stubborn pupil.

In any event, the level of the world economy is indeed the pertinent one today. Any theory is faced with the challenge of analysing it in its relationship with the real submission of labour taken as a guiding thread, and to develop the skein of this thread. The crisis of the neoliberal order has always been the negative precondition for a revival of Marxism. If the twentieth century was the short century that ran from capitalism to capitalism; if it opened with a catastrophic crisis that revealed the fragility and potential inhumanity of the liberal-national order; if it had at its centre the failure of the first attempt at communism, it did not only close with the crisis of Marxisms. It also ended with the onset of a new crisis bound up with the barbarism of the liberal new order. This is where the neo- or post-Marxisms can find a new historical justification, the object of their analyses, and the occasion for their radical self-criticism, which is also the critique of the neoliberal order by itself. This is the terrain for a reconstruction of their positive condition: the emergence of new social movements and new practices, beyond the monstrous impasses of organisation as a state-party. This is where the possibility of weaving a new link between theory and practice, whose forms neither can nor should be prejudged, will be played out.

Chapter Nine

The Regulation School: A One-Way Ticket from Marx to Social Liberalism?

Michel Husson

Michel Aglietta's book, *A Theory of Capitalist Regulation*, dates from 1976 and may be regarded as the founding act of regulation theory. Its republication in 1997 and the accompanying afterword doubtless mark the end point of a trajectory that has led this school some considerable way from the Marxism from which it partially derived.

Genesis of a school

On publication, Aglietta's work provoked a debate to which it is appropriate to return today. Did it represent a reformulation/revision of Marxism or a completely new theoretical approach? At the time, the regulationists (with the notable exception of Boyer) situated themselves within the field of Marxism. Aglietta came from the PCF, Lipietz from Maoism, Billaudot directed the economic committee of the PSU, in which Bertrand was likewise active. For the most part, the founding members were former students of the École polytechnique and worked as economists in the 'ideological state apparatuses' (to adopt Althusser's category), rather than in the academy. They were therefore marked, on the one hand, by a Colbertian or Saint-Simonian tradition and, on the other, by a certain – likewise very French – version of Marxism. Lipietz was not wrong when he cast them as the 'rebel sons of Massé and Althusser',[1] for their project can be analysed as a dialectical rupture with this dual filiation.

The crisis afforded them their opportunity. The project in fact emerged in a very precise conjuncture. On the political level, this was the period of the debate on the Common Programme, which was to conclude with the rupture of the Union of the Left in 1977. On the economic level, the generalised recession of 1974–5 signalled the onset of 'crisis'. In some respects, this vindicated the PCF's theoreticians, who for two decades had forecast that 'State Monopoly Capitalism' would ultimately become bogged down. But above all it revealed the dogmatism of a pessimistic theorisation of postwar capitalism. The regulationists' intuition was that the key to the crisis lay in understanding the *trente glorieuses* which had just ended, without the fact having been fully registered. Two founding texts resulted: Aglietta's book in 1976 and then the 1977 report by Boyer, Lipietz et al. on inflation (*Approches de l'inflation*).

Rereading them today confirms the impression at the time that they offered a reformulation of Marxism whose principal novelty resided in casting off its Stalinist rags. In the main, Aglietta's book is a rather classical account of the laws of capitalist accumulation as applied to the United States. The novelty, which, to my mind, was relative, consisted in referring to intensive accumulation, defined as based on the production of relative surplus-value. Various of Marx's concepts were confronted with national accounting macro-economic data and Aglietta proposed some pseudo-concepts, forgotten today, such as 'real social wage cost', which is nothing other than the share of wages in value added. Empirical analysis led him to venture that the best statistical indicator 'for representing the evolution of the rate of surplus-value is the evolution of real wage costs'. This was scarcely an amazing discovery.

However, the regulationists had a sense that they were making radical innovations at a methodological level, simply by virtue of the fact that they tested their concepts against empirical reality. Here again, the break with 'Marxist' structuralism, combined with their integration into the economic bureaucracy, inclined them to pursue an empirical quantification of their analyses. But they marvelled at this epistemological break with the ardour of neophytes:

[1] Lipietz 1994.

> this return to empirical assessment, even when difficult and invariably unsatisfying given the precise origin of the statistics used, introduces the possibility of refuting the initial theoretical framework, however satisfying it might be from a strictly logical standpoint.[2]

This was the least they could do! The naïve discovery of the autonomy of concrete reality with respect to theoretical logic cannot seriously claim to supersede the Marxist method and remains far inferior, for example, to Karel Kosik's extremely rich and subtle contribution, *Dialectics of the Concrete* (1970). It can certainly be regarded as progress by comparison with dogmatism, but it is also a banality for any living Marxism. In this respect, it was Phéline who was to claim the title of precursor for the 1975 article in which he analysed the evolution of surplus-value (without naming it!) in a Finance Ministry journal. But the continuing hesitation about using statistics of dubious 'origin' (bourgeois?) will provoke a smile in readers of Marx and Lenin – or, nearer in time to us, Baran, Sweezy, or Mandel – who know very well that these Marxist critics of *Capital* spent their lives amassing statistics. That the need to rub shoulders with the statistics could seem such a daring idea speaks volumes on the regression represented by the particular resonance of Stalinism in France.

The rupture with Althusser was described at length in 1979 by Lipietz, who principally criticised him for

> denying that on the material basis of social relations something could constitute itself which can say 'it's us' and change the system of relations. For us, this something was the revolutionary movement of the masses.[3]

This quotation is entertaining, first of all because of the development of the 'prospective concepts' used by a Lipietz who is today promoter of mutual insurance companies as the depository of wage-earners' savings. But, above all, it is extraordinary to present the intervention of the revolutionary movement of the masses as 'something' that has to be rediscovered in order to revive Marxism, when it is obviously one of its constitutive elements! This ability to break down open doors attests to the Stalino-Maoist lead weight that the inventors of regulation theory had to lift in order to find themselves in the open air once again. This trajectory is not irrelevant, for it kept them

---

[2] See Bertrand et al. 1980.
[3] See Lipietz 1979.

estranged from the living tradition of Marxism, which they practised only by way of Althusser, Mao, or Boccara. There is therefore nothing surprising about the fact that they were wonderfully ignorant of fertile currents in Marxism (particularly Anglophone ones), like the one embodied by Ernest Mandel, whose fundamental work *Late Capitalism* appeared in France in 1976. But all this does not mean that at the time the regulationists were not fairly consistent critics of capitalism.

When regulationism was not (yet) a harmonicism

We owe Lipietz the following eloquent definition of the regulationist approach:

> one is a regulationist as soon as one asks why there are relatively stable structures when, given that they are contradictory, logically they should disintegrate from the outset...whereas a structuralist finds it abnormal that they should enter into crisis.[4]

But if Marxism is not reduced to structuralism, study of the modalities of the reproduction of capital naturally forms an integral part of its critique, which has no need for a kind of theorem of constant collapse.

However that might be, Aglietta's initial reflections on neo-Fordism indicate that at the time he situated himself squarely within the field of Marxism and that, on one key point, he was possibly not wholly regulationist in the sense that we understand it today. In fact, Aglietta envisaged the possibility of a resolution of the crisis based on a 'neo-Fordism' that he defined thus:

> A new regime of accumulation, Neo-Fordism, would arise from the crisis, articulating the progress of capitalist accumulation to the transformation of the totality of conditions of existence of the wage-earning class – whereas Fordism was geared simply to the private consumption norm, the social costs of mass consumption continuing to be met on the margins of the capitalist mode of production.[5]

---

[4] Lipietz 1994.

[5] Aglietta 1979, p. 168.

In other words, the crisis might be resolved by extending to collective consumption (health, education, transport, etc.) what Fordism had realised in the case of private consumption (housing and household appliances, private cars). This theme is also to found in Attali, who wrote for example:

> Post-industrial society will probably be hyper-industrial. But production in it is geared to new sectors, substitutes for the collective services that generate demand, for schools, for hospitals. It is based on a new technological and social network, generating demand for these market items.[6]

However, Aglietta introduced a decisive qualification by immediately stressing that '[t]he fact that this transformation of the foundations of the regime of intensive accumulation is the sole durable solution to the crisis does not in itself mean that it is possible under capitalism'.[7] This qualification indicates that the regulationist approach was at the time free of harmonicist temptations and could thus be absorbed into the Marxist corpus without difficulty.

The wage relation: a key concept

In another founding text, Boyer introduced a distinction between 'major crises' and 'minor crises',[8] without adding much by comparison with the formulation of the theory of long waves,[9] which he has always managed to confuse with a resurgence of Kondratiev. Instead, it was around the notion of wage relation that the originality of the postwar period was established. Boyer notes in the first instance a 'rise of monopolistic structures' – a common place of the heterodox thinkers of the period. But in order to establish a 'monopolistic' regulation, which replaces 'competitive' regulation, an additional ingredient is required, namely, the establishment of an adequate 'wage relation'.

This new wage relation was institutionalised after 1945 with the establishment of a minimum wage, collective agreements, and the extension of the indirect wage. As a result, wages growth was no longer governed by the pressure of unemployment. It depended

[6] Attali 1978.
[7] Aglietta 1979, p. 168.
[8] See Boyer 1979.
[9] See Mandel.

> on the one hand, upon a quasi-automatic adjustment to the development of the cost of living and, on the other, upon implicitly or explicitly taking account of the productivity increases expected or registered at the level of firms, sectors, or even the economy as a whole.[10]

Capitalist contradictions had not disappeared, but they had been displaced: 'the reduction in the tensions bound up with non-realisation eventually comes up against the stumbling block of the problems of capital valorisation'.[11] To all this must be added the extension and transformation of the role of the state.

The real novelty is basically to be found in this analysis of the Fordist wage relation. Boyer makes it a key indicator of the specificities of monopolistic regulation: cyclical adjustment no longer operates through prices;[12] institutions help to align the average increase in wages with industrial productivity.[13] For his part, Aglietta introduced the key notion of 'consumption norm' and clearly showed how Fordism precisely marked the entry of goods produced with significant productivity gains into wage-earners' consumption.[14] Finally, Bertrand confirmed this hypothesis by means of a 'sectional' analysis of the French economy that adopted *Capital*'s reproduction schemas.[15]

Once again, from a theoretical standpoint, what was involved was a redeployment of debates and schemata already available elsewhere, although we do not know whether the regulationists, who appeared to be ignorant of Marxism after Marx, were conscious of these filiations. To take one example, to my knowledge a link was never established with the prolonged debate involving Marxist economists in the years before and after the First World War: its protagonists were called Kautsky, Bernstein, Lenin, Bukharin, Luxemburg, Bauer, and Tugan-Baranovsky. The latter, for example, proposed reproduction schemata in which a decline in production is compensated for by accumulation, and for this reason rejected the thesis of ultimate capitalist collapse. Bauer arrived at a similar result and concluded that capital accumulation was valid within certain limits governed by productivity and population. His polemic with Luxemburg revolved around an issue which is precisely the

---

10 Boyer 1979.
11 Boyer 1979.
12 See Boyer 1978.
13 See Boyer and Mistral 1978.
14 See Aglietta 1979.
15 See Bertrand 1979.

question of regulation: why does capitalism not collapse? These references are never cited and this often imparts a certain naïveté to the regulationists, as if tackling such themes betokened a major impertinence to Marxism, which is assimilated to the official manuals published in Moscow, Peking or Paris.

A different source of inspiration, by contrast, is very clearly affirmed in the case of Boyer: the Cambridge school. The basic intuitions of the model developed in the forecasting department of the Finance Ministry[16] – in particular, the profit-growth relationship – are directly drawn from Kalecki's or Joan Robinson's conceptualisations. In *The Accumulation of Capital*, Robinson proposed, for example, a definition of the 'golden age' which very closely resembles Fordist regulation.[17] This acknowledged filiation is perfectly legitimate and is only mentioned here to highlight the extent to which regulation theory is a fruitful synthesis of Marxism and Cambridge post-Keynesianism.

Rather than representing some supersession of Marxism, regulation theory thus seems to be the updating or reappropriation of it required to take account of the historical specificities of postwar capitalism and to escape dogmatism. In my view, the work that in this respect represents the veritable synthesis of the regulationist contribution is Dockès and Rosier's book, published in 1983, which also deserves to be reprinted. The analysis of the wage relation and the consumption norm can readily be assimilated by a living Marxism, on condition that we abandon the implicit hypothesis of a constant real wage – something that does not problematise the general analytical framework.[18] Finally, there is no reason why a study of 'institutional forms' should be incompatible with highlighting the contradictions of the capitalist mode of production. But there is something more in the regulationist approach that constitutes its real specificity, but also its principal limit: harmonicism.

The harmonicist turn

From the correct thesis that capitalism can function, the regulationists imperceptibly proceed to a different position, which is not a necessary deduction from it, but a possible extension of their analysis: that, in the end, capitalism

[16] See Boullé et al. 1974.
[17] Robinson 1956.
[18] See Dockès and Bernard 1983; and see Husson 1999.

can always function in a relatively harmonious fashion. As Lipietz clearly puts the point: 'if we understand how it has worked, we will also understand how to make a different model work'.[19]

This slide was all the more tempting in that the arrival of the Left in power in 1981 afforded the regulationists an opportunity to quit the position of enlightened critics and become advisers to the prince. Their position in the apparatus of the economic bureaucracy and their formation as economic experts naturally prompted them to wish to 'act' – in other words, to influence the establishment of a new mode of regulation making it possible to resolve the crisis from above.

At a theoretical level, the turn was effected around the notion of consumption norm. It can be precisely dated from the contribution by Aglietta and Boyer to a conference organised in 1982. On the basis of a typically regulationist analysis, their text issued in an initial recommendation: it was necessary to

> maintain a certain increase in consumption, so far as is compatible with the recovery of industrial investment and the balance of external payments

and to seek to identify the new demand 'whose emergence and development are being curbed today by the instability and uncertainty brought about by the crisis'.[20] This analysis approximated to a more 'technologistic' version of the regulation school, which cast the electronics sector as the natural site for the emergence of solution to the crisis, as a result of a line of reasoning that logically followed from the analysis of Fordism:

> Our perception of a resolution of the crisis corresponds to our explanation of it. The new sites of accumulation must therefore generally respect the set of constraints set out in our representation – i.e. simultaneously allow for productivity increases and for a new consumption norm – and transform a proportion of unproductive labour into productive labour.[21]

The regulationist work programme was then refocused on the invention of a post-Fordism. This involved imagining a new, positive social compromise, based on 'new productivity' and a new 'social model'. Ten years after the first report for CEPREMAP, in 1987 Boyer co-ordinated a massive study entitled

---

[19] Lipietz 1994.
[20] Aglietta and Boyer 1982.
[21] Lorenzi, Pastré and Toledano 1980.

Aspects de la crise, whose concluding volume was entitled *Economies in the Process of Fording the River*. In it, we discover a logic, typical of French-style planning (Massé!), that consists in presenting three scenarii, which might be dubbed the good, the bad, and the lazy. The last is a rather lacklustre continuation of current trends; the second corresponds to a switch to a socially regressive model; and the first represents the positive option. These scenarios outline 'three main perspectives, defined by developments that are fairly coherent and plausible from a socio-political standpoint'.[22] This coherence is defined around the differential combination of five basic elements: technical system, forms of competition, wage relation, public intervention, international régime. The type of picture formed by this combinatory, constantly used thereafter by Boyer, irresistibly evokes the famous matrices of the Boston Consulting Group, and, basically, it is indeed a question of social management tools. The regulationists address themselves to decision-makers, indicating the options available and assessing their respective advantages: regulation theory has become a regulatory technique.

The option of doing nothing is always available; and this is the scenario dubbed 'going with the stream' to serve as a foil. Obviously, it is also possible to opt to implement a 'voluntarist programme of returning to the market', neoliberal in inspiration. But naturally the positive scenario is the third option. It is equally voluntarist, but it aims to establish 'collective forms of adaptation' to the changes and assumes 'negotiation of a new configuration of the wage relation', based on an 'original principle for distributing productivity gains between wage increases, a reduction in working hours, and job creation at the level of society as a whole'.[23] The regulationist touch is evident here: there was once a good Fordist wage relation, but it has served its time and we must all of us therefore hit upon an alternative.

This project has the effect of pointing up several gaps in the theory, once faced with what is for it the unprecedented question of the conditions of emergence of a new mode of regulation. Will the best one necessarily win out? And what happens in the interim? The latter question is especially tricky for the regulationists. On the one hand, their main problematic consists in studying how capitalism works, given that it does not collapse. On the other hand,

---

[22] Boyer et al. 1987.
[23] Boyer et al. 1987.

however, they show that there is a choice between several ways in which capitalism might function. In these circumstances, one of the major problems with the regulationists is that, twenty years after the crisis, they are forever elaborating different possible scenarii, as opposed to studying the really existing neoliberal model.

This shift was accompanied by a theoretical reorganisation. Where the founding texts integrated institutional forms into the framework defined by capitalist invariants, the plasticity of modes of regulation now comes to be regarded as virtually boundless. It was Coriat who formulated this analytical slide with the greatest lucidity:

> In regulation theory, these structural forms have gradually acquired the status of genuinely intermediate categories in the following sense: as between pure theory and invariants on the one hand, and observed and modelled facts on the other, they provide the indispensable tools we were searching for in order to be able to conceive changes and their specificities, over and above constants.[24]

The door was now open to an infinite combinatory.

Consequently, the central theoretical question shifts and becomes that of the genesis of modes of regulation. This led to a temporary alliance with conventions theory, which was no doubt a serious tactical error. The rather distressing article by Boyer and Orléan illustrates the dead end involved in this manner of subscribing to a fundamentally individualist methodology and neglecting any social dynamic.[25] As a result, regulation theory is torn between two symmetrical positions: sometimes saying that 'the bad capitalism is prevailing over the good one'; and sometimes showing that there only exist concrete capitalisms, which are constructed from a combinatory that can be drawn on at will. As between analysis and norms, the message is definitively scrambled, or reduced to a few worthy commonplaces: competitiveness does not depend exclusively on labour costs; the market cannot be wholly efficient in the absence of institutions; unbridled capitalism is not necessarily the most legitimate form of capitalism; and the Japanese model has been affected, but is nevertheless resistant.

---

[24] Coriat 1994.

[25] See Boyer and Orléan 1991.

This trajectory has just led the regulationists to a new change of direction. The post-Fordist horizon (reduction in working hours in return for wage-earner involvement) is definitively abandoned for that of patrimonial capitalism (increased work and a wage freeze in return for stock options). This is a point that must be firmly underscored and which the regulationists carefully avoid assessing in their collection:[26] capitalist reality has inflicted a stinging refutation of this prospectus, since what has actually been installed is a neoliberal model. And what they are suggesting today is utterly different what they were proposing ten years ago, without the implications of this turn having been truly drawn.

The new mode of regulation of capitalism

If Fordism is at an end and capitalism has not collapsed, it is because it has been able to invent something new and a new mode of regulation has been instituted. Basically, the regulationists have forgotten to be regulationist, because they have spent twenty years explaining that we are 'at a crossroads', rather than studying the mode of regulation being established before our very eyes. Or, taking the drift towards harmonicism to its ultimate conclusion, we should reserve the label for good, stable, coherent and legitimate forms of regulation. But what is going on during periods of unstable coherence and, in particular, during this recessive phase of the postwar long wave?

In contrast, it seems to me that it is perfectly possible to set out, from a Marxist-regulationist standpoint if one wishes, the co-ordinates of a model for the functioning of capitalism based on a conjoint increase in the rate of exploitation, the rate of unemployment, and the share of national income going to rentiers. Rather than invoking neo-Fordism, we should be speaking of neo-Malthusianism. Alongside his famous demographic law, Malthus was also the inventor of an interesting theory demonstrating the need for a class of unproductive consumers 'as a means of increasing the exchangeable value of the total sum of products'. Certainly, Malthus would have liked to think that 'the happiness of the great mass of society' was possible. But an excessive increase in wages 'is bound to increase production costs; it is also bound to reduce profits and diminish or destroy the motives underlying accumulation'.

---

[26] See Boyer and Saillard 1995.

On the other hand, Malthus was aware that consumption by the productive classes would tend to be inferior to the supply of material products; it was therefore fairly logical for him to conclude that a 'body of consumers who are not directly involved in production' was required. These are old regulationist issues and it seems to me that this is precisely how contemporary capitalism operates.[27]

In these circumstances, where a high unemployment rate entails constant pressure on wages and where alternative outlets to wage-earner demand exist, it is rational to freeze wages. All the arguments about a new productivity underpinning a new social consensus fade before an observation[28] that can be summarised thus: the employers can have their cake (wage-earner involvement) and eat it (wage freeze). This constitutes the revenge of capitalist invariants and, in pride of place, of competition between private capitalists.

The theory of patrimonial capitalism, or the involution

But this involves a highly regressive regulation; and the regulationists believe that capitalism can do better. Via circuitous routes, they are in the process of reconstructing a unified position around a proposal for wage-earners' shareholding appropriate to 'patrimonial capitalism'. To reach this point, it has been necessary to effect a new switch and to make the relations between finance and industry a basic relationship overdetermining the wage relation. The operation has been conducted by Aglietta, who suggests a new principle of periodisation of capitalism based exclusively on the way in which accumulation is financed:

> over a very long period, finance guides the development of capitalism. It determines the conditions of financing which, in turn, bring about long phases in which growth is first encouraged and then discouraged.[29]

The history of capitalism is thus supposedly punctuated by the succession of two major modes of financing. Financial systems 'with administered structures' have the advantage of 'safeguarding investment projects', such that

---

[27] See Husson 1996.
[28] See Coutrot 1998.
[29] Aglietta 1995.

'capital accumulation is maintained but inflation can fluctuate'. Liberalised finance possesses the converse properties: it 'encourages stable, low inflation, but fetters accumulation'. Aglietta thus summons us to an original reading of the long history of capitalism and its crises. Twenty years after proposing an analysis of capitalism based on notions such as the consumption norm of wage-earners, Aglietta reconsiders this understanding of the necessary articulation between the different domains of the reproduction of capital, reducing the whole dynamic of capitalism to a single dimension: finance. A cycle is thereby definitely closed, bringing the regulationists back to one of their starting points: in other words, Keynesianism.

In a text written for the Saint-Simon Foundation, Boyer and Jean-Louis Beffa conclude that 'the creation of wages funds at the instigation of firms and unions, and their management in accordance with jointly decided objectives, even if entrusted to professionals, could mark an advance in terms of new social rights'.[30] Aglietta justifies new forms of remuneration through changes in work:

> With current technologies, what is prized is initiative and adaptation... you no longer have a guaranteed job, but you do receive a share of the profits in the form of an interest, profit-sharing, or stock options for senior managers: the distribution of responsibilities is accompanied by a distribution of profits.[31]

As for Lipietz, he has discovered the new institutional form for the twenty-first century in mutual insurance companies:

> Even if one remains convinced of the robustness of contributory pension schemes amid financial and demographic instability, one can no longer exclude the contribution of a complementary component by capitalization.... This development corresponds to two social demands: the desire for a certain flexibility and a certain diversification...a desire to put the capitalization of French firms on a financial basis that is concerned with employment in France.[32]

---

30 Beffa Boyer and Touffut 1999.
31 Aglietta 1998.
32 Lipietz 1999.

Thus, the cycle is complete. The regulationists have opted to become apologists for wage-earners' shareholding and, in passing, have abandoned all scientific rigour. The way in which Aglietta praises democracy in America is in fact a veritable travesty of something based on an unprecedented concentration of income (and possession of shares). Moreover, in suggesting that this model can be transferred, the regulationists quite simply forget the advantages derived from the USA's position as dominant power, thereby confirming their inability to integrate the concept of the global economy. Elements of analysis and useful literature surveys can still be found in regulationist texts, but they contain few developed suggestions for those who want to understand the world and change it. This is a pity, because this trajectory was doubtless not the only possible one: regulation theory could have done more enduring work, rather than breaking with the critical tradition of Marxism in order to become a sort of think tank for human resources directors.

Chapter Ten

Ecological Marxism or Marxian Political Ecology?

Jean-Marie Harribey

The twentieth century ended against a backdrop of global general crisis. The capitalist mode of production was extended to the ends of the Earth and gradually subjected all human activities to the reign of the commodity. However, for the first time in its history no doubt, it produced two simultaneous, major regressions. The first was social, for, despite a significant increase in the amount of wealth being created, poverty and misery are not on the decrease: 1.3 billion human beings dispose of the equivalent of less than a dollar a day; as many have no access to drinking water or the most elementary health care; 850 million are illiterate; 800 million are undernourished; at least 100 million children are exploited at work; and, during the last four decades, the inequalities between the richest twenty per cent and the poorest twenty per cent have progressed from 30 to 1 to 80 to 1. This social disaster affects even the richest countries, since the United States contains 34.5 million people living beneath the poverty line and the OECD countries include 34 million people suffering from hunger, 36 million reduced to unemployment, and many more whose situation is becoming insecure.

The second major regression involved nature and eco-systems, which were seriously affected or threatened by the exhaustion of certain non-renewable resources and pollution of every sort. Moreover, the bulk of scientific opinion concurred in taking fright at the risk of global warming bound up with the emission of greenhouse gases. The origin of this ecological crisis is unquestionably the industrial mode of development pursued without any other evaluative criterion than the maximum profitability of the capital employed, but whose legitimacy is ensured by the ideology according to which increased production and consumption are synonymous with an improvement in well-being from which all the planet's inhabitants will sooner or later benefit.

If it can be established that the simultaneous advent of these two types of disaster, social and ecological, is not fortuitous – or that they are the result of the economic development stimulated by capital accumulation on a planetary scale and, worse still, if they are its inevitable outcome – then the question of an encounter between the Marxist critique of capitalism and the critique of productivism dear to ecologists is posed. Now, not only were these two critiques born separately, but they have largely developed in opposition one another in so far as the first was identified throughout their existence with the experience of the so-called 'socialist' countries, whose ecological depredations – like their social depredations – were equivalent to that of the capitalist countries, while the second critique long hesitated to resituate humanity's relationship with nature in the framework of social relations.

However, the conjunction of three events has created the conditions for a rapprochement between the two approaches. First of all, there is the disappearance of the 'socialist' (anti-)models that handicapped the use of Marx's theory for the purposes of a radical critique of capitalism. The second is the complete liberalisation of capitalism, under the supervision of globalised financial markets, which ended in a reversal in the balance of forces to the advantage of capital and the detriment of labour. The third event is the convergence of popular mobilisations and social struggles against the ravages of capitalist globalisation, particularly by clearly identifying what is at stake in negotiations within the World Trade Organisation. Rejection of the commodification of the world and of the privatisation of living beings in itself contains a challenge to the two terms of the crisis – social and ecological – striking the worst-off populations with especial severity.

The last element – social struggle – is not the least. Of itself, it grounds the possibility of developing a general theoretical critique of a crisis that is global. Of itself, it justifies theoretical research to overcome a sterile, paralysing opposition between a traditional Marxist critique of social relations severed from human relations with nature and a simplistic ecological critique of human relations with nature that makes no reference to the social relations within which humanity pursues its project of domesticating nature.

Consequently, the material conditions seem to have been created for a *materialist* theorisation of the knowledge and transformation of human relations with nature – and this in two directions: the formulation of a naturalistic materialism and the reintegration of political ecology into a comprehensive analysis of capitalism, in a sort of cross-fertilisation of two paradigms. However, a sizeable obstacle confronts this alliance: a new paradigm only prevails by replacing another one. The most plausible wager is therefore that the necessary condition for the birth of a Marxian political ecology or an ecological Marxism is a complete, definitive supersession of the form taken by traditional Marxism as an intellectual and practical movement bound up with a given historical period – a movement, roughly speaking, encapsulated in, and reduced to, the collectivisation of the means of production without any alteration in social relations. Conversely, the thinking of political ecology will not be able to lay claim to the title of new paradigm if it does not manage to integrate itself into a much larger corpus aiming at social transformation. Today, although this dual enterprise is far from being completed, we can report an important number of contributions in an innovative direction. Some of them indicate that materialism can, under certain conditions, constitute the conceptual matrix for due consideration of ecology by society; while others define the bases for an ecology rid of the illusion of a clean capitalism.

Materialism as the conceptual matrix of ecology

Marx's *œuvre* proposes a conceptual framework which, firstly, locates human beings' social activity within a natural material environment and, secondly, makes a radical distinction between the labour process in general and the process of capitalist production. However, several problems remain, whose resolution is indispensable if we are to be able to integrate the ecological problematic into it.

Society in nature

An initial consensus exists among authors who identify with Marx today and who are concerned with ecology: natural material conditions exist that are indispensable to human activity, whatever the mode of production. 'Nature is man's *inorganic body*' or '[m]an lives from nature', Marx wrote in his 1844 *Manuscripts*.[1] Consequently, according to Ted Benton,[2] Marx and Engels's philosophical positions pertain at once to naturalism and materialism. At first sight, this vision of nature as 'man's inorganic body' could be interpreted as purely utilitarian. Alfred Schmidt challenges this interpretation of Marx, for Marx distances himself from such a conception inherited from the Enlightenment and adopts a dialectical position: 'Nature attains self-consciousness in men, and amalgamates with itself by virtue of their theoretical-practical activity'.[3] For John Bellamy Foster, 'this ecological perspective derived from his materialism'[4] and Paul Burkett has demonstrated Marx's ecological consciousness.[5]

James O'Connor, founder of the American socialist ecological journal *Capitalism, Nature, Socialism*, pursues the point, indicating that the fundamental difference between the natural conditions of production and the productive forces usually considered by Marxism, as well as the superstructural conditions for employing them, is based on the fact that the former are not produced.[6] The fact that these objective natural conditions are not produced, and that their existence is posited *ex ante*, grounds a materialist approach to ecology and establishes a first point of convergence with the principles of thermodynamics, whose implications for the economy Nicholas Georgescu-Roegen was one of the first to draw: 'the entropy of a *closed* system increases continually (and irrevocably) towards a maximum. In other words, usable energy is continually transformed into unusable energy, up to the point where it dissipates completely'.[7] For economic development is based on the reckless utilisation of the terrestrial stock of energy accumulated over time. This is

---

1 Marx 1975, p. 328.
2 See Benton 1989.
3 Schmidt 1971, p. 79.
4 Foster 2000, p. viii.
5 Burkett 1999.
6 See O'Connor 1992.
7 Georgescu-Roegen 1995, pp. 81–2. See also Georgescu-Roegen 1971.

a point of convergence but not identity, because, as René Passet suggests,[8] Marx and Engels are doubtless closer to the idea of a 'creative destruction' *à la* Ilya Prigogine than an inexorable decline of the universe.[9] However, Juan Martinez-Alier recalls that, for Georgescu-Roegen as for Vladimir Vernadsky, the Earth is an open system, because it receives external energy from the Sun. Thus, processes of growth and complexification can unfold on it over time.[10] But the process of the structuring of life takes place over a timescale that has nothing in common with the human timescale which thus has to deal with the problem of resource scarcity.

The fact that human activity unfolds within a natural envelope legitimates the 'normative management with constraints' advocated by Passet. Authors like Georgescu-Roegen and Passet, although not identifying with Marxism, approximate to it when they challenge the reduction of the social to the economic and a conception of the economy solely in terms of equilibria.

The distinction between the labour process in general and the process of capitalist production

From the outset in *Capital*, Marx distinguishes between the labour process in general, which is an anthropological characteristic whose goal is the production of use-values that can satisfy human needs, and the labour process peculiar to the capitalist mode of production, which only represents a phase in human history and whose goal is the production of surplus-value making the valorisation of capital possible. In the latter case, the production of use-values ceases to be an end and is merely a means for value, of which the commodity is the support. Henceforth, as Jacques Bidet explains,[11] the possibility exists that real social needs will not be satisfied and, on the contrary, that externalities and social 'counter-utilities' will be generated by a mode of production 'focused on profit'.[12] Thus, according to Benton and Bidet, the principle of the

---

[8] Passet 1996, p. xvii.
[9] See Prigogine 1979.
[10] See Martinez-Alier 1992a, p. 21 and 1992b, pp. 183–4. On Vernadsky 1924, see Deléage 1992.
[11] See Bidet 1992 and 1999.
[12] Bidet 1992, p. 103.

ecological critique is already – at least implicitly – contained in the distinction made by Marx.

However, Marx devoted the bulk of his work to analysing the contradiction resulting from the exploitation of labour-power, which in his view was fundamental: capital's difficulty in securing the production and then the realisation of surplus-value. And, although conscious of them, he arguably in part neglected the ecological consequences of the development of capitalism. To explain this, Benton advances the hypothesis that he underestimated the 'non-manipulable natural conditions' of the labour process and overestimated the role and technical capacities of human beings.[13] Marx was thus unable to detach himself from the Promethean standpoint that marked the nineteenth century and was guilty of complacency or, at any rate, of a lack of vigilance as regards what ecologists today call productivism. This criticism is challenged by Reiner Grundman,[14] who believes that the desire to utilise nature with a view to satisfying human needs cannot be assimilated to a project of the automatic, deliberate destruction of nature. The reason for this is that to destroy nature would backfire on the satisfaction of these needs. It seems to me that this argument can only be advanced if the practices destructive of nature are intentional, determined in accordance with a destructive goal. If capital accumulation derived from a conscious collective project, there would be no logical reason why the imperative of saving nature should not be substituted for that of maltreating it. And this would mean that the precautionary principle could potentially be enshrined in capitalist activity. The least one can say is that this appears unlikely and we cannot therefore totally exonerate Marx from the charge of having been a – willing? – victim of the myth of progress.

The preceding discussion has introduced the idea that the development of capitalism generates two contradictions. The first is the one Marx devoted his whole life to. By fashioning the concepts of labour-power and surplus-value, and making the theory of value a critical theory of capitalist social relations, Marx laid bare the basic antagonism between capital and labour, which could only be superseded in communism. And he allegedly neglected on the theoretical level a 'second contradiction' of capitalism.

---

[13] Benton 1989, p. 64.

[14] See Grundman 1991.

This idea has been advanced by O'Connor and several other authors in *Capitalism, Nature, Socialism*, like Enrique Leff, Paul Burkett, Stuart Rosewarne, and Tim Stroshane, and is adopted by Bidet.[15] The definition of the second contradiction is wanting in precision and varies somewhat from author to author. For O'Connor, it involves the costs pertaining to 'sociological or political categories'.[16] Whereas the first contradiction manifests itself more in the difficulty in realising surplus-value than in producing it, the reverse is true of the second. This comprises two aspects. According to Bidet, the first is the fact that members of society are dispossessed 'of the ability to confer meaning on their existence'; the second is connected, in both O'Connor and Bidet, with 'the externalisation of a certain number of costs of social production'.[17]

Several remarks are in order here. First, the contradiction between capital and labour – what is here called the first contradiction – combines the two problems of producing and realising surplus-value. It is false to counter-pose overaccumulation of capital and underconsumption, for they are indissociable, corollaries of one another. Secondly, authors who analyse what is called the second contradiction slide from the notion of externalisation to that of exteriorisation. What justifies characterising the ecological contradiction of capitalism as an 'external' contradiction, while reserving characterisation as a contradiction 'internal' to the capitalist production process for the exploitation of labour-power?[18] This seems to me to constitute a retreat from the materialist postulate of the necessary integration of capitalist production into the natural environment. Consequently, both the first and the second contradictions are internal to the capitalist mode of production and hence cannot be separated. Without the exploitation of nature, exploitation of labour would have no material support; and without the exploitation of labour, exploitation of nature could not have been extended and generalised. It follows that the social crisis and the ecological crisis are two aspects of one and the same reality.[19] Moreover, Bidet, joined by Daniel Bensaïd, agrees with André Gorz when he establishes a link between the intensification of the ecological crisis

---

[15] See Leff 1986; Burkett 1996; Rosewarne 1997 and Stoshane 1997; and Bidet 1992 and 1999.

[16] O'Connor 1992.

[17] Bidet 1992, pp. 104–5.

[18] See Bidet 1999, p. 296.

[19] See Rousset 1994 and Harribey 1997. I stress a logical point: capitalism develops the two contradictions conjointly; they are therefore internal to it – which does not

and a fall in the profit rate.[20] And O'Connor confirms this link when he says that capital reduces its possibilities for profitability as it subjects the natural conditions of production to its law. Thirdly, and finally, the loss of the capacity to endow existence with meaning is nothing other than the alienation already analysed by Marx and is wholly bound up with exploitation. It is true that the destruction of nature produced by capitalist activity involves a loss of meaning, but if ecological disasters were conveyed by the single philosophical concept of alienation, what need would there be for a science called *ecology* to arrive at a knowledge of them?

The remaining theoretical difficulties

The issues raised above indicate the persistence of theoretical difficulties, which remain an obstacle to a genuine symbiosis within current Marxist research on ecology. They essentially bear on the hypotheses and purposes of Marx's model.

In the first place, is the distinction between the various forms of labour process adequate for analysing the relations between human beings and nature? In other words, is the process of capitalist production the sole culprit in the destruction or undermining of ecosystems? Were human activity to be restricted to producing use-values, would any contradiction between this activity and the set of biological equilibria disappear? This is not certain, and we know that some societies which are scarcely technologically developed, and not subject to the law of profit, can find themselves compelled to engage in agricultural practices that result in rapid soil exhaustion. Conversely, within technologically advanced societies the disappearance of capitalism is a necessary but insufficient condition for a balanced co-development of living systems. This is what emerges from an observation registered by Martinez-Alier: planning is no better than the market at resolving the problem of the lack of a common yardstick between present and future.[21] Can the fundamen-

---

mean that it is the only mode of production that has to confront the contradiction vis-à-vis nature, as we shall see later.

[20] See Gorz 1978 and 1992; and See Bidet 1992 and Bensaïd 1993.

[21] See Martinez-Alier 1987. Elsewhere, in 1992a, Martinez-Alier also stresses the fact that the debate between Hayek and Lange in the 1930s did not pose the problem of the inter-generational allocation of non-renewable resources.

tal origin of Marxism's belated acknowledgement of the ecological question be located in the 'meta-structural insufficiency' of Marx's approach – that is to say, in the fact that he established an identity between capitalism and the market, making it impossible really to think the liberty-equality pair through, with the result as regards ecology of making it impossible to reflect on the use of the world? Such is Bidet's thesis,[22] which has the advantage of connecting property, power and ethics.

In order to appreciate the significance of this problematic, it is appropriate first to reopen the discussion about the existence of natural limits. The violence with which Marx and Engels opposed Malthus's theses on population has profoundly marked the history of Marxism. Although starting out from a basically correct criticism, their desire to construct a socio-historical theory of capitalism doubtless had unintended consequences. Engels rejected the principle of entropy and unequivocally condemned the attempt by Sergei Podolinsky to combine a labour theory of value with an energy theory of value.[23] While it is true that it is impossible to reduce all the aspects of human activity to an expenditure of energy measured in calories, and that it is pointless searching for a universal equivalent, Podolinksy's thesis cannot be reduced to this. It maintains that, if techniques allow them to, human beings can produce more calories than they expend, thus removing the prospect of thermic death.[24] Podolinsky paved the way for the subsequent analyses by Howard Odum,[25] measuring the efficiency of a living system by its capacity to maximise its incorporated energy, which he calls *emergy*. The development and outcome of human activities does not mechanically depend on natural conditions, but on the social and technical conditions of the utilisation of natural conditions. Contrary to Engels's unduly hasty conclusion, Podolinsky was therefore perfectly aligned with a materialist viewpoint – one, moreover, that was Marxism – and does not merit the treatment still meted out to him today by some Marxist authors.[26]

In reality, the reticence of Marx and Engels, and then of Marxists in general until recently, is largely explained by the fear that, hidden behind the

---

[22] Bidet 1999, p. 297.
[23] See Engels 1976 and See Podolinsky 1880a, 1880b and 1880c.
[24] See Vivien 1994 and 1996.
[25] See Odum 1971.
[26] For example, in Husson 2000, p. 141.

argument of natural limits to human activity, was a conservatism unwilling to speak its name. However, according to Benton, the issue of natural limits does not come into conflict with emancipatory projects as long as the elements of the labour process that are 'impervious to intentional manipulation'[27] are identified – for example, photosynthesis, repeated or accumulated human interventions that create unwanted and undesirable effects, like the greenhouse effect, and interventions that have obscured or altered certain limits, such as genetic manipulations.

Ultimately, the problem can be summarised thus: natural 'limits' are not fixed, but shift in time and place according to the socio-technical organisation of society; and yet that displacement itself is certainly not infinite. Must we not therefore bid farewell to boundless economic growth which, according to Herman Daly,[28] cannot be durable? And begin to think 'beyond development', which is an 'ideology in ruins', as invited to by Wolfgang Sachs and Gustavo Esteva, as well as Serge Latouche?[29]

> [A]n ecosystem is invariably a totality which is only reproduced within certain limits and which imposes on humanity several series of specific material constraints

writes Maurice Godelier.[30] As a result, another problem emerges, raised by Hans Jonas, who is regarded as the founder of a philosophy of respect for life and the conditions of life that he calls the *responsibility principle*.[31] Jonas is not a Marxist philosopher, but his interrogation of Marxism bears precisely on one of the latter's most important philosophical foundations. For him, the ethic of responsibility cannot be reconciled with the notion of utopia and, in particular, the utopia of abundance. Given the limits of nature's tolerance, the promise of abundance must be abandoned, especially because it will be impossible to bring the underdeveloped countries up to the level of the developed countries without yet more recourse to technological progress – which serves to exacerbate the contradiction with respect to the principle of responsibility. Like those of liberal ideology, the material bases of the Marxist utopia, which

---

[27] Benton 1989, p. 68.
[28] See Daly 1992.
[29] See Sachs and Esteva 1996; Latouche 1986.
[30] Godelier 1986, p. 28.
[31] See Jonas 1984.

would have made it possible to make the transition from the 'realm of necessity' to the 'realm of freedom',[32] will never be created. Even an author who has endeavoured to rehabilitate the Marxian utopia, Henri Maler, is categorical about the productive forces inherited from capitalism that are supposedly vehicles of emancipation: this involves 'lethal illusions'.[33] For all that, must we take no interest in improving the material conditions of existence? No, replies Jonas, '[b]ut as regards the much-needed improvement of *conditions* for much or all of mankind, it is vitally necessary to *unhook the demands of justice, charity, and reason from the bait of utopia.*'[34] For Jonas, the principle of responsibility is not compatible with Ernst Bloch's hope principle.[35] The renunciation of abundance in Jonas can be compared with the notion of 'sufficiency' in Gorz:

> The establishment of a norm of sufficiency is incompatible – by virtue of the self-limitation of needs and the agreed effort that it involves – with the pursuit of maximum output, which constitutes the essence of economic rationality and rationalisation.[36]

However, the abandonment of the illusion of abundance does not imply that Marxism should give up the development of humanity, especially for its poorest fraction. As John Bellamy Foster says: '[e]conomic development is still needed in the poorest regions of the world'.[37]

In a way, Jonas anticipates the rejection of the primacy of the productive forces formulated by Alain Lipietz, an ecological economists and theorist issued from Marxism. According to him, by reducing the history of the human race to its transformative activity, Marxism is 'at odds with human ecology' and 'nature is not man's inorganic body, but equally the inorganic body of the bee or royal eagle':[38] respect for biological diversity is a principle of existence,

---

32 Marx 1981, pp. 958–9.
33 Maler 1995, p. 245.
34 Jonas 1984, p. 201.
35 See Bloch 1986.
36 Gorz 1992, p. 22. See also Gorz 1990.
37 Foster 2002, p. 80.
38 Lipietz 1996, pp. 186–7. Here we are far from the provocation of Husson 2000, p. 72: 'Humanity can live without whales or tortoises, as it has learnt to live without dinosaurs'. The argument of this Marxist economist is that biodiversity should be defended not for utilitarian reasons, but in the name of ethical or aesthetic values. Since this is precisely the position of most ecologists, Husson's condemnation of the latter invalidates itself. But it is more important to observe that there is a fine line between

which must take precedence over all others. Lipietz's first criticism is excessive, if Marx had reduced the history of humankind to its productive history, labour would have contained its own end in itself – *praxis* as opposed to *poiesis*. On the other hand, Marx was doubtless wrong to regard productive history as human prehistory – the condition of access to true history. The second criticism is more legitimate. Paradoxically, however, it implicitly posits the radical incompleteness of an ecology that is not integrated into a perspective of social transformation.

Ecology integrated into social relations

The theoretical difficulties Marxist thought experiences in grasping the ecological question are the mirror image of those that still constitute an obstacle to integrating ecological struggles into a general struggle against capitalism. The latter issue inevitably brings to mind Karl Polanyi's concepts of disembedding/re-embedding, to which O'Connor explicitly refers in order to theorise a socialist ecology.[39]

Political ecology finds it difficult to go beyond a limited critique of productivism, regarding it as simply the pursuit of 'production for its own sake', as Jean-Paul Deléage defines it.[40] However, what is required is a critique of production whose sole purpose is commodity value for the profit that it contains, heedless as it is of all the values of justice and of respect for life.

Ecology and value

Awareness of ecological disruption has obliged neoclassical economic theory to integrate into its models negative externalities attributable to the economic development of modern societies. Environmental economics has thus become a rapidly expanding discipline that seeks to reintroduce the social costs gener-

---

the opinion expressed by Lipietz and that of the extreme current of deep ecology. Hence the difficulty of conceiving a humanism conscious of the need to respect all life forms, as far removed from a utilitarian anthropocentrism with respect to other living species as it is from a 'non-humanist, even anti-humanist normative ethic' which, according to J.P. Maréchal (Maréchal 1997, p. 176), would be 'self-contradictory'.

[39] See O'Connor 199?, pp. ?; see also Polanyi 1944.

[40] Deléage 1993, p. 12.

ated by environmental degradation into traditional economic calculation. By internalising its externalities through the market, via taxes or negotiable pollution permits,[41] the dominant economics aims to promote the 'valorisation' of natural goods, or to determine and take account of the supposedly intrinsic economic value of nature, which has hitherto (so we are told) been ignored.

But this approach – characterised as weak sustainability, because it banks on the possibility of replacing exhausted natural elements by manufactured products – threatens to pervert political ecology, which would allow itself to misled by the mirage of internalisation, whose problematic contains several insurmountable theoretical contradictions.

The first is this: of the social costs generated by polluting productive activities, only the monetary costs detrimental to other activities can be taken into account. Furthermore, this limited measure is itself impossible to implement: first of all, as Elmar Altvater explains,[42] because the exploitation of natural resources by capitalism establishes a rhythm of utilisation superior to that of natural cycles; second, following Passet,[43] because it involves reducing biological time to an economic time through the intermediary of a rate of actualisation; and finally because, as David Pearce has demonstrated,[44] it only involves a monetary penalty for pollution when the threshold of the self-purification of ecosystems has been crossed, thus inexorably lowering that threshold.

The impossibility of evaluating unproduced natural elements in monetary terms, other than by calculating the production cost of their economic exploitation or the production cost of repairing the damage inflicted on them, is in truth attributable to nature possessing no intrinsic economic value, contrary to what is claimed by neoclassical economists who affect disapproval of political economy's traditional neglect of the 'value' of nature. Today, several ecological theoreticians – in particular, Gunnar Skirbekk, Martinez-Alier, Altvater,

[41] The eco-tax derives from an idea advanced in Pigou 1920; and negotiable pollution permits have been theorised by Coase 1980, who claims that the internalisation of external effects can be achieved without any state intervention other than the establishment of property rights, and solely through market negotiation between polluters and polluted, whatever the initial distribution of rights between them.

[42] See Altvater 1991 and 1992.

[43] See Passet 1996.

[44] See Pearce 1974 and, for an introduction, Harribey 1998.

Leff, and Harribey[45] – who situate themselves in the framework of a renewal of Marxism, have demonstrated that this assertion is utter nonsense. If the light of the Sun, pure air, and water, or any other resource, condition life, and if one starts out from the idea that these elements possess an intrinsic economic value, then it can only be infinite. Yet an infinite economic value or price for available goods or services is a nonsense. A logical error of this kind can be committed because the old Aristotelian distinction between use-value and exchange-value is rejected by neoclassical economists, who identify the two notions without realising that use-value is a necessary condition of exchange-value, but that the converse is not true. By arbitrarily positing an identity between use-value and exchange-value, one can persuade citizens that the maximum satisfaction obtained through the use of goods and services takes the form, and can only take the form, of maximising exchange-value – that is to say, the commodification of the world. But a single counter-example is sufficient to demonstrate the inanity of the thesis that use-value and exchange-value are identical. The Sun's light is necessary to make wheat grow and yet the price of wheat does not contain the 'value' of solar light, which has no meaning. The milk drunk by the baby at its mother's breast has a use-value but no exchange-value, whereas powdered milk in a feeding bottle has a use-value – the same as the mother's milk – and an exchange-value. Thus, not all wealth is value – something that Aristotle, Smith and Ricardo had clearly sensed, and which Marx repeated tirelessly. Contrariwise, what is distinctive about a negative externality is that it in no way constitutes wealth, whether individual or collective, and yet it sometimes possesses an exchange-value: radioactive waste can be an object market exchange for thousands of years without possessing any utility – other than that of making money. As a result, a possible price for the right to pollute must not be regarded as an economic price. It is necessarily a sociopolitical price, deriving directly from the permissible level of pollution determined by society; and this norm itself reflects the balance of forces in society.

Two options are then open to ecologists. Either they leave it up to the market to achieve a better allocation of resources by establishing eco-taxes or the sale of pollution permits – but, in that case, they are led to extend the range

---

[45] See Skirbekk 1974; Martinez-Alier 1992a; Altvater 1997; Leff 1999; and Harribey 1997 and 1999.

of market accounting, which has precisely demonstrated its inability to take account of biological phenomena, time, and uncertainty. Or, following José Manuel Naredo,[46] they recognise the futility of seeking to objectify natural things in prices and pursue a different path – establishing measures for natural resources, and ways of accounting for energy expenditure, on condition that these are not converted either into a labour-equivalent or into money; and developing functions of social objectives outside any criterion of profit maximisation.[47]

The incommensurability of natural elements and ordinary commodities therefore precludes applying the labour theory of value to the former.[48] The 'value' of nature is different in kind from economic value and refers to values of an ethical order. But this does not discredit the labour theory of value, whose field of application has always been – and can only be – that of the commodity. Unfortunately, ecological literature is full of writings that betray a misunderstanding of the theory of value of commodities as a theory of the capitalist social relations governing the production of these commodities. Yet the labour theory of value contains two points that are fundamental for an ecological problematic: on the one hand, *'it is the law of the least effort for producing a use-value'*;[49] and, on the other, it is the critique of production for profit at

---

46 See Naredo 1999. In the current of 'ecological economics', and from a post-classical perspective, see also M. O'Connor 1996.

47 After the French government had rallied to the proposal to create a market in pollution permits, the opposition hardened between those, like Lipietz (1998 and 1999), who were favourable to it, and those, like Husson (2000), who firmly rejected the idea. Is this opposition insurmountable, in so far as it would seem that the use of economic instruments remains a possibility once it is subordinated to political decision-making? An eco-tax or the price of the right to pollute cannot be market prices because nature cannot be evaluated. Lipietz is therefore wrong when he asserts that a market in pollution permits is the best system 'in theory', because neoclassical *theory* is wrong from beginning to end: it reduces all human behaviour to the rationality of *homo oeconomicus*; it proceeds as if the difficulty in constructing functions for individual and collective preferences had been overcome; it ignores the interdependence between the decisions of agents; it is silent about the fact that it has now been demonstrated that the existence of externalities prevents the competitive system being Pareto optimal and that the impossibility of assigning a monetary price to nature precludes the re-establishment of such an optimum by means of a simple eco-tax or a market pollution permit; it regards the factors of production – including natural factors – as permanently replaceable; and it conflates use-value and exchange-value.

48 We make no reference, obviously, to the so-called utility theory of value advocated by neoclassical economics, since it is not even a theory of the value of commodities, but simply a legitimation of the latter's appropriation.

49 Bidet 1999, p. 295.

the expense of human needs, a reasonable use of nature and, more generally, social justice. Value theory is therefore at the heart of a general theory integrating ecology and social organisation. Ecological Marxism thus fixes itself the aim of subordinating social activity to use-value.[50] This is also the sense of ecosocialism as defined in the International Ecosocialist Manifesto[51] which was inspired by the proposals of, among others, James O'Connor and Joel Kovel.[52]

Ecology and justice

In so far as it clearly identifies action to preserve natural equilibria as a component of anticapitalist activity, ecology brings to Marxism something that it had hitherto not taken into account: inter-generational fairness. Social justice can therefore now be envisaged on two levels: in the present – within contemporary societies marked by profound inequalities in terms of power, income, living and working conditions, access to natural resources, to health care, to education, to culture; and in time – between different generations, in terms of access to natural resources.

Lying at the junction between ethics and politics, the relationship between ecology and social justice contains at least three basic requirements, which are theoretical and practical in kind.

The first requirement is to develop a theory of justice that integrates three dimensions: a critical theory of injustice in the here and now; a theory of a just society; and a theory for being just in a society that is still unjust. John Rawls's theory[53] does not satisfy these conditions, because it starts out from an individualistic conception of the social contract and the co-operation that is to derive from it. It excludes any idea of regulation other than that performed by the market order, which is supposed to be efficient. Bidet has shown that this construct assigns no place to a collective project and, above all, represents a regression with respect to the Kantian categorical imperative by not formulating a principle of action in favour of immediate greater justice.[54] Moreover,

---

[50] Harribey 1997.
[51] See Löwy (ed.) 2005.
[52] J. O'Connor 1998 and Kovel 2002.
[53] See Rawls 1971.
[54] See Bidet 1995, pp. 130–5.

as I have argued elsewhere,[55] the Rawlsian notion of primary social goods focusing on right and liberties guaranteed for all should, if it is to have genuine significance, be extended to the right of access to natural resources and the right of access to employment, which conditions access to the resources that are produced.

The second requirement bears on the definition of collective ownership rights, which is today sorely lacking in a reconstruction of a socialist project, in the emergence of an ecological project, and, obviously, in an eco-socialist project. The failure of the state collectivisms – or capitalisms – on the one hand, and the attribution of the degradation of nature to the absence of private ownership of it, on the other, fetter reflection on the forms that could be taken by collective ownership of goods belonging to humanity as a whole – for example, air, water, and any resource conditioning life. Analyses of private property rights in nature by the neoclassical economist Ronald Coase, and of enclosures by the biologist Garret Hardin, proceed to an illegitimate assimilation of collective property to non-property.[56] In the opposite camp, proposals to establish new collective rights in the present and future still remain at the level of a statement of principles. Thus, Leff refers to collective property rights in nature that make it possible to reconstruct processes of communal production, established while respecting cultural autonomy, in the framework of social movements.[57]

If the development of a theory of justice and a theory of collective property rights is proving difficult, there is one point whose theorisation is easier, even if its application is tricky. This involves the third requirement for connecting ecology and social justice: sharing productivity gains and allocating them in the first instance to a reduction in working hours, so as to improve the quality of life, rather than to a constant increase in production, once essential material needs have been satisfied. It will be observed that here we are once again dealing with a collective reappropriation – this time, of the wealth created – by wresting back the time that capitalism seized hold of at the dawn of the industrial revolution. Control of their living time by all human beings and respect for the time that has led to the flourishing and complexification

55 See Harribey 1997.
56 See Coase 1960 and Hardin 1968.
57 See Leff 1999, pp. 99–100.

of living systems – such are the two inseparable terms of a Marxian political ecology.[58]

Just as the ecological crisis has not replaced the 'social question', given that they are linked, political ecology has not supplanted Marxism as an instrument for analysing capitalism and as a political project. Political ecology was not born *ex nihilo* and it inherits nearly two centuries of social struggle against exploitation and alienation. As Gorz has shown,[59] ecology forms an integral part of working-class history at two levels: the demand for social justice and the opposition to capitalist economic rationality. But it diverges from it when it comes to the myth of infinite material progress. That is why, conversely, traditional Marxism does not exhaust the issues posed by the development of modern societies.

Epistemologically, the encounter between Marx's materialist theory and political ecology is based on a rejection of methodological individualism. 'Methodological individualism comes up against the insurmountable ontological difficulty of taking future generations into consideration', writes Martinez-Alier.[60] The socio-historical approach to human existence is holist and the concept of the biosphere is likewise holist. Social relations as interactions in the biosphere are viewed in dialectical fashion. A Marxian political ecology or an ecological Marxism will only be constructed if we manage to overcome the fetishisation of human relations with nature severed from social relations. Two traps, mirror-images of one another, are therefore to be avoided: on the one hand, what Jean-Pierre Garnier calls the 'naturalisation of social contradictions'[61] (a version of an emollient ecologism that denies the logic of capital accumulation and its consequences for the way in which human beings appropriate nature); on the other hand, the socialisation of the contradictions of the destruction of nature (a version of a trivial Marxism that persists with the notion that the relations of production alone pervert the use of technology and nature).

---

[58] Numerous theoreticians have explored this path. Readers are referred to Lipietz 1993 and Harribey 1997. Becker and Raza 2000 seeks to integrate regulation theory and political ecology.

[59] See Gorz 1994.

[60] Martinez-Alier 1992a, pp. 23–4.

[61] Garnier 1994, p. 300.

In negative terms, we can even say that Marxism and political ecology present twin defects: for example, Marxism's propensity for a centralised management of society is echoed in Jonas's belief in the capacity of an authoritarian government to adopt and impose safety measures; or, to take another example, both Marxism and ecology contain numerous currents and have their respective fundamentalists.

Finally, a major difficulty remains to be resolved if a Marxian ecological paradigm is to progress: which social forces are capable of embodying a democratic, majoritarian project for the transformation of society, acting in the direction of greater justice for the worst-off classes and future generations? Martinez-Alier cautiously suggests that the social movements are the vectors of ecological aspirations, because the concentration of wealth increases pressures on natural resources and social demands aimed at improving working conditions, health, and security oblige capitalists to integrate certain social costs.[62] Moreover, the international dimension of anticapitalist struggle finds a – natural – extension in the universal demand for a habitable planet for all living beings. This can only become a reality by establishing a freely agreed global right, which would be a 'right to equal use' in Bidet's formula.[63]

It is customarily said that humans are the only living beings to reflect on nature. They are also the only ones to reflect on their social organisation and inflect its evolution. For these two reasons, a great responsibility falls to them, which can form the basis for a new, universalistic humanism.

---

[62] See Martinez-Alier 1992a, pp. 25–6.
[63] Bidet 1999, p. 305.

Chapter Eleven

Theories of the Capitalist World-System

Rémy Herrera

The national structures of capitalism operate and are reproduced locally in the first instance, through a combination of a domestic market, where commodities, capital and labour are mobile, and a corresponding set of state apparatuses. By contrast, what defines the *capitalist world-system* is the dichotomy between the existence of a world market, integrated in all aspects except for labour (which is forced into an international quasi-immobility), and the absence of a single political order at a global level that is more than a multiplicity of state bodies governed by public international law and/or the violence of the balance of forces. It is the causes, mechanisms, and consequences of this asymmetry at work in the accumulation of capital, in terms of unequal relations of domination between nations and of exploitation between classes in particular, that the theoreticians of this capitalist world-system endeavour to conceptualise. The latter have in fact produced a comprehensive theory whose object and concept is the modern *world* as a concrete socio-historical entity forming a *system* – that is to say, an assemblage (Greek *systema*), structured by complex relations of interdependence, of several elements of reality into a coherent, autonomous totality that situates them and gives them meaning.

Among the representatives of this intellectual current, I shall (to restrict myself to the essentials) select four major authors: Samir Amin, Immanuel Wallerstein, Giovanni Arrighi and André Gunder Frank. There seems to be no point in trying to extract a unitary position from their works, so vast are their fields of investigation and distinct their sources of inspiration – even if the impetus given by the *Monthly Review* team had a very marked influence on all of them. It should nevertheless be noted that their scientific approaches intersect, without ever fully coinciding, in their recourse to a common stock of theoretical references (basic Marxist concepts, but also the Braudelian one of *world-economy*, or the structural-CEPALian or "ECLACian"[1] one of *centre/periphery*, etc.); methodological premises (a holist explanatory model, a structural analysis, a combination of history and theory, and so on); intellectual ambitions (a comprehensive representation of phenomena, an attempt to combine the economic, the social, and the political, etc.); and political aims (a radical critique of the planetary ravages of capitalism and US hegemony, a 'worldist' bias, the perspective of a postcapitalist society, etc.).

In these conditions, situating these theoreticians, who are unclassifiable in as much as each seems to constitute a *sui generis* category, vis-à-vis Marxism is far from easy. Amin has always said that he is a Marxist; and still does. But his *œuvre*, which has not uncritically drawn upon theories of imperialism and pioneering works on under-development like those of Raúl Prebisch or, more marginally, François Perroux, distances itself very clearly from the 'orthodox corpus' of Marxism. For his part, Wallerstein, who is in the tradition of Fernand Braudel and the *Annales* school, while also drawing some of his resources from Ilya Prigogine's theory of so-called 'dissipative structures', proposes a free reading of Marxism which is so heretical that he seems to leave it behind. Accordingly, he may appropriately be regarded instead as a 'systemsist'. As for Giovanni Arrighi, he belongs to the Marxist school of historical sociology of the world system. Meanwhile, André Gunder Frank – close to the writings of Paul Baran on the political economy of growth and certain Latin-American structuralists – is often ranged among radical 'dependency theorists', while the trajectory of his research, strongly but not exclusively influenced by Marxism, soon led him to analyses of the world-system.

---

[1] "ECLACian", from ECLAC, or the Commission for Latin America and the Caribbean (CEPAL in Spanish).

Marx's legacy

It remains the case that, among all the intellectual legacies invoked by theoreticians of the capitalist world-system, whether neo-Marxist or not, the first and foremost source of inspiration is to be found in the work of Marx. Marx cannot be credited with a finished *theory* of the world-system, on the general model of the theory of structure and dynamic of capitalism he furnished us with. However, by virtue of the richness of the problematics he invites us to reflect on, and the multiplicity of the analytical implications he draws, Marx made a powerful contribution to laying the theoretical foundations for this current and stimulating its contemporary reflection. In my view, it is therefore necessary and productive to make a detour via Marx in order subsequently to return better equipped to a presentation of the main theorisations of the capitalist world-system.

For it is indeed Marx who paved the way for them. He did so in two ways. First of all, he criticised the myth of the infallibility of a different *system* – Hegelian philosophy – which, excepting the efficacy of the dialectic, he shattered in the prolonged labour of constructing historical materialism (the first break with Hegel, at the dawn of his reflections, can be dated to 1843–5). Next, he abandoned the vision of the unfolding of history in accordance with a universal line proceeding from the Eastern world to Western civilisation, which he called into question in an attempt to preserve Marxism from any economistic-evolutionist-determinist temptation (the second break with Hegel in Marx's final research of 1877–81).

Marx's analysis of the accumulation of capital and the proletarianisation of labour-power makes capitalism the first *globalised* mode of production, contrasting, on account of its *globalisation*, with all precapitalist modes of production: *the tendency to create a world market is included in the concept of capital itself.*[2] The starting point of capitalism is in fact the *world market*, which is established with the generalisation of commodities and the confrontation between money-capital and forms of production other than industrial capitalism. By means of primitive accumulation and colonial expansion, the genesis of capitalism, although geographically situated in Western Europe and historically located in the sixteenth century, no longer pertains exclusively to Europe. For, if the

[2] Marx 1973, p. 408.

space of reproduction of the capital-labour relationship is identified as global, and not simply national, societies outside Europe find themselves inserted into the contemporaneity of the time of capitalism – and violently so.

To my mind, Marx's theoretical contribution cannot therefore be reduced to the assertion of the driving force: firstly, of the Western industrial proletariat in capitalist processes (through the production of surplus-value in the M-C-M schema and expanded reproduction); secondly, of the advanced countries in the future triumph of the revolution and construction of communism (which leads to assimilating capitalism to 'progress', certainly dragging individuals and peoples through blood and dirt, misery and degradation, but ultimately a 'progress of bourgeois civilization', painfully but surely carrying the contradictions of capitalism to a conclusion);[3] and thirdly, of industrial capital and the sphere of production, as compared with commercial capital and the sphere of circulation, in identifying the site of exploitation and 'genuine capitalism'.

For, in writings that straddle his central work, preceding or following the publication of Volume One of *Capital*, Marx also provides not (let me repeat) a theorisation, but an outline of constitutive elements of a social theory of the world-system. Among these, which sometimes take the form of cautious nuances qualifying propositions that are liable to generate confusion (the *de te fabula narratur!*, for example), and sometimes that of unresolved uncertainties in fields which had scarcely been explored by the social sciences of the time (particularly as regards the evolution of the Russian *obschina*), I shall select the following five elements, all of which are articulated around the axis of the 'world market'.

Element 1. Marx registers a superimposition of relations of domination between nations onto relations of exploitation between classes (the speech on the 1830 Polish uprising in 1847 and the 1848 speech on free trade). This complicates class struggle, internationalist in essence but national in form, by a proletariat structurally divided by a criterion of nationality (letters to Kugelmann and Engels in 1869). Marx would go so far as to maintain that the revolution in Ireland, where the colonial and national questions fused, constituted 'the precondition for any social change' in England (letters to Meyer and Vogt in 1870; letter from Engels to Kautsky in 1882). However, this assertion

[3] Marx 1976.

would not be transposed beyond the Irish case, either by Marx (to Algeria: 'Bugeaud' in *The New American Encyclopedia*, of 1857), or by Engels (to Egypt: letter to Bernstein in 1882).

Element 2. Marx stresses and repeats the determination of 'the whole internal organisation of populations' by the world market, its division of labour, and its 'inter-state system' (letter to Annenkov of 1846 and *Critique of the Gotha Programme* of 1875), constraining according to laws which govern them together[4] the productive structures of 'oppressed nations' destroyed by colonisation to be regenerated by specialisation in strict conformity with dominant metropolitan interests ('The British Rule in India' in the *New York Daily Tribune* of 1853). These nations thus end up suffering both from the development, and from the lack of development, of capitalism. But Marx was never really to relinquish the idea of 'progress' via capitalism (The *Communist Manifesto*, in 1848; articles on the US in the *Neue Rhenische Zeitung* in 1850 and *Die Presse* in 1861).

Element 3. Marx explains that in England the state is firmly in the service of the interests of the industrial bourgeoisie, because this country, 'demiurge of the bourgeois cosmos', has succeeded in its 'conquest of the world market' and is identified with the capitalist 'core', exporting its recurrent crises to the rest of the world and, as a result, cushioning it against the revolutions breaking out on the European continent (*Class Struggles in France*, appeared in 1849). But if he establishes the connection between the national social structure and the international dimension in the abstract-concrete shape of the 'world market' and 'state system' (1853 article on revolution in China and Europe in the *New York Daily Tribune*), as Jacques Bidet has put it, 'Marx fails to produce the concepts of the immediate contemporaneity of the national and the international, or the concepts of the system'.[5]

Element 4. Marx also recognises a similarity between certain modes of exploitation – of the small peasantry, in particular – and that of the industrial proletariat (*The Eighteenth Brumaire of Louis Bonaparte*, in 1852). He acknowledges that surplus-value can be extracted even in the absence of a formal subsumption of labour to capital ('Results of the Immediate Process of Production', between 1861 and 1863); and that 'the plantation system, working

[4] Marx and Engels 1978, pp. 35–41.
[5] Bidet 1999, p. 233ff.

for the world market' in the United States must be considered a necessary condition for modern industry[6] and productive of surplus-value from its integration into the process of circulation of industrial capital, as a result of 'the existence of the market as a world market'. The same is true, moreover, of other forms of non-wage relation – those to which Chinese coolies or Indian *ryots*, for example, are subjected.

Element 5. Finally, in his letter of 1877 to Mikhailovsky, Marx expressly and categorically rejects any 'historico-philosophical theory of the general path of development prescribed by fate to all nations, whatever the historical circumstances in which they find themselves'. And he shows himself capable of manifestly, albeit gropingly, apprehending 'singular historicities' (to employ Étienne Balibar's term) – that is to say, the non-linear, non-mechanistic development of social formations, which are to be conceived as combinations of modes of production and differentiated according to their 'historical environments' (*Grundrisse*, in 1857–9 and *Contribution to the Critique of Political Economy*, in 1859). Marx is thus ultimately open to envisaging transitions to socialism different from the 'long, bloody calvary' of the capitalist path – albeit, in the Russian case, under strict conditions, including that of incorporating the positive contributions of the capitalist system in the West (draft letters and letter to Vera Zasulich of 1881).[7]

These clarifications, prompted by Marx's caution and attention to complexity, have all too frequently plunged Marxists into confusion (when they have not simply 'forgotten' them). They should instead be regarded, in and through the very indeterminacy of successive comparisons, as an opportunity for reflection capable of profoundly renewing Marxism so that it can remain a way of conceiving the real development of the world and priming its revolutionary transformation.

Samir Amin

The core of Samir Amin's scholarly contribution consists in his demonstration that capitalism as a really existing *world-system* is different from the capitalist

[6] Marx 1981, p. 940.
[7] Godelier (ed.) 1978, pp. 318–42.

mode of production on a world scale. The central question behind all his work is why the history of capitalist expansion is identified with a global *polarisation* between central and peripheral social formations. The goal of his answer is to grasp the reality of this polarisation, immanent in capitalism and conceived as the modern product of the law of accumulation on a world scale, in its *totality* – the requisite analytical unit being the world-system – so as to integrate the study of its laws into historical materialism.

However, while identifying with the methodological perspective of Marxism, Amin sharply distances himself from various interpretations that have long been dominant within this intellectual current. His originality consists, in the first instance, in his rejection of an interpretation of Marx which suggests that capitalist expansion homogenises the world; projecting a global market integrated in its three dimensions (commodities-capital-labour). Since imperialism induces commodities and capital to transcend the space of the nation in order to conquer the world, but immobilises labour-power by enclosing it in a national framework, the problem posed is the global distribution of surplus-value. The operation of the law of accumulation (or of immiseration) is to be found not in each national sub-system, but at the level of the world-system. Hostile to any evolutionism, Amin also rejects an economistic interpretation of Leninism which, underestimating the gravity of the implications of polarisation, poses the question of transition in inadequate terms. If the capitalist centres do not project the image of what the peripheries will one day be, and can only be understood in their relationship to the system as a whole, the problem for the periphery is no longer to 'catch up', but to build 'a different society'.

Underdevelopment is therefore regarded as a product of the polarising logic of the world-system, forming the centre/periphery contrast through a constant *structural adjustment* of the latter to the dictates of the capital expansion of the former. It is this very logic which, in the peripheral economies, has from the outset prevented the qualitative leap represented by the constitution of auto-centred, industrial, national capitalist productive systems, constructed by the active intervention of the national bourgeois state. In this optic, the economies appear not as local segments of the world-system, albeit underdeveloped (and still less as backward societies), but rather as overseas projections of the central economies – heteronomous, dislocated branches of the capitalist economy. In the organisation of their production, the peripheries have been fashioned to serve the accumulation of metropolitan capital, in the context of a productive system that has become genuinely global and which expresses the global character of the genesis of surplus-value.

The world-system is in fact based on the capitalist mode of production, whose nature is expressed in commodity alienation, or the pre-eminence of generalised value, which subjugates the whole of the economy and of social, political and ideological existence. The essential contradiction of this mode of production, opposing capital and labour, makes capitalism a system that creates a constant tendency to overproduction. In the framework of a model of expanded reproduction with two departments, Amin shows that the realisation of surplus-value requires an increase in real wages proportional to the growth in labour productivity, which assumes abandoning the law of the tendency for the rate of profit to fall. Whence a version of the theory of unequal exchange – distinct from that proposed by Arghiri Emmanuel – as a transfer of value on a world scale through a deterioration in two factorial terms of exchange: at the centre, wages increase with productivity; at the periphery, they do not.

Polarisation, indissociable from the operation of a system based on an integrated world market of commodities and capital, but excluding labour mobility, is thus defined by a differential in the remuneration of labour – inferior in the periphery to what it is in the centre – of equal productivity. On a world scale, Fordist regulation in the centre, conducted by a state enjoying real autonomy (not so much a social-democratic as a 'social-imperialist' regulation, given that 75 per cent of the world's population resides in the periphery), involves the reproduction of the unequal relationship between centre and periphery. The absence of any regulation of the world-system thus translates into the unfolding of the effects of the law of accumulation, with the centre-periphery opposition being organised around the articulation between production of means of production/production of consumer goods (which defines the auto-centred capitalist economies) and between export of primary goods/luxury consumption (which characterises the peripheral social formations).

Given this, polarisation cannot be abolished in the framework of the logic of really existing capitalism. Amin regards the attempts at development implemented in the periphery, in the variant forms of neocolonial liberalism (opening up to the world market), and radical nationalism (modernisation in the spirit of Bandung), as well as Sovietism (priority for industrialising industry over agriculture), not as a challenge to globalisation, but as its continuation.[8] Such experiments can only lead to the general 'failure' of development – the 'success' of a few newly industrialised countries should be interpreted as a new, deeper form of polarisation. Amin's critique of the concepts and practices of development is accompanied by an alternative: *delinking*. The latter is defined as subjecting external relations to the logic of internal development, via state action to select positions in the international division of labour that are not unfavourable. What then needs to be developed is systematic action to construct a *polycentric world* – the only one capable of opening up autonomous space for the advance of a popular internationalism and making it possible to effect a transition 'beyond capitalism' and to construct world socialism.

The construction of a theory of accumulation on a world scale, reintegrating the law of value at the heart of historical materialism, also calls for a history of social formations. Rejecting the thesis of the 'five stages' and the multiplication of modes of production, Amin identifies only two successive stages: *communal* and *tributary* – the different 'modes of production' finding a place as a variant of these categories. The social systems preceding capitalism all evince relations that are the inverse of those which characterise capitalism (with society dominated by the instance of power; with economic laws and exploitation of labour that are not obscured by commodity alienation; and with ideology necessary for the reproduction of the system that is metaphysical in character, etc.). The internal contradictions of the communal mode of production were resolved in the transition to the tributary mode. In tributary societies, with a differentiated degree of organisation of power (whereby surplus extraction was centralised by the exploiting ruling class), the same basic contradictions were operative, preparing the transition to capitalism as the objectively necessary solution. But in the peripheral forms, which are more flexible, as was the case with feudalism in Europe, the obstacles to any transition to capitalism offered less resistance. Hence the evolution towards a central form in the mercantilist era by putting the political instance in the service of capital – and hence the 'European miracle'. Amin's *œuvre* thus invites historical materialism to make a self-criticism of its own Eurocentrism and to fulfil its 'Afro-Asian vocation'.

---

8 Amin and Herrera 2000, 2005.

Immanuel Wallerstein

Immanuel Wallerstein likewise seeks to understand the reality of this historical system that is capitalism so as to conceptualise it globally, as a whole. Whereas Amin's approach is explicitly an interpretation of the world-system in terms of historical materialism, Wallerstein's ambition is seemingly the reverse: elements of Marxist analysis are to be integrated into a systems approach. In reality, as Wallerstein makes clear, '[o]nce they are taken to be ideas about a historical world-system, whose development itself involves "underdevelopment," indeed is based on it, they [Marx's theses] are not only valid, but they are revolutionary as well.'[9] The world-system perspective is explained by three principles. The first is spatial – 'the space of a world': the unit of analysis to be adopted in order to study social behaviour is the world-system. The second is temporal – 'the time of the *longue durée*': world-systems are historical, in the form of integrated, autonomous networks of internal economic and political processes, whose sum total ensures unity and whose structures, while continuing to develop, basically remain the same. The third and final principle is analytical, in the framework of a coherent, articulated vision: 'a way of describing the capitalist world-economy', a singular world-system, as a systemic economic entity organising a *division of labour*, but without any overarching single political structure. This is the system that Wallerstein intends to explain not only in order to provide a structural analysis of it, but also in order to anticipate its transformation. As Étienne Balibar notes, its whole force consists in its capacity 'to conceive the overall structure of the system as one of generalized economy and to conceive the processes of state formation and the policies of hegemony and class alliances as forming the texture of that economy.[10]

For Wallerstein, the capitalist world-economy displays certain distinctive features. The first peculiarity of this social system, based on generalised value, is its incessant, self-maintained dynamic of capital accumulation on an ever greater scale, propelled by those who possess the means of production. Contrary to Braudel, for whom the world since antiquity has been divided into several co-existing world-economies, 'worlds for themselves' and 'matrices of

[9] Wallerstein 1991, p. 161.
[10] Balibar and Wallerstein 1991, p. 3.

European and then global capitalism'[11] according to Wallerstein, the European is the only world-economy, constructed from the sixteenth century onwards: around 1500, a particular world-economy, which at that time occupied a large part of Europe, could provide a framework for the full development of the capitalist mode of production, which requires the form of a world-economy in order to be established. Once consolidated, and according to its own internal logic, this world-economy extended in space, integrating the surrounding world-empires as well as the neighbouring mini-systems. At the end of the nineteenth century, the capitalist world-economy ended up extending over the whole planet. Thus, for the very first time in history, there was one single historical system.[12]

Explaining the division of labour within the capitalist world-system between centre and periphery makes it possible to account for the mechanisms of surplus appropriation on a world scale by the bourgeois class, through unequal exchange realised by multiple market chains ensuring control of workers and monopolisation of production. In this framework, the existence of a semi-periphery is inherent in the system, whose economic-political hierarchy is constantly being altered. The inter-state system that duplicates the capitalist world-economy is, however, always led by a hegemonic state, whose domination, temporary and contested, has historically been imposed by means of 'thirty-year wars'. Like those that it succeeded (the United Provinces in the seventeenth century and England in the nineteenth century), the US hegemony established since 1945 will come to an end – Japan and Europe are already asserting themselves, with more or less success, as the claimants to the next global hegemonic cycle. Wallerstein pays minute attention both to the cyclical rhythms (the 'microstructure') and the secular trends (the 'macrostructure') operative in historical capitalism, which stamp it with alternating periods of expansion and stagnation and, above all, to recurrent major crises: historically, capitalism entered a structural crisis in the first years of the twentieth century, and will probably experience its end as a historical system during the next century.[13]

---

[11] Braudel 1985.
[12] Wallerstein 1974.
[13] Wallerstein 1983.

Giovanni Arrighi

Giovanni Arrighi's contributions to the theories of the capitalist world-system concern, among other things, reflections on the origins of capitalism, on its articulation with precapitalist modes of production, on its tight relation with imperialism, as well as on its present crisis. Arrighi considers that capitalism's formation process as modern system of the world totality does not originate in the predominent socio-economic relations within the great European national powers (in agriculture in particular), but rather in the interstices that connected them to one another and to other 'worlds', thanks to the late-thirteenth-century Eurasian trade. Interstitial organisations have initially taken the forms of city-states and extra- or non-territorial business networks, where huge profits from long-distance trade and finance were realised. 'World-capitalism did not originate within, but in-between and on the outer-rim of these states [of Europe]'.[14] It is here that began the 'endless' accumulation of capital.

Most of the studies Arrighi devoted to colonial primitive accumulation relate to capitalism's penetration in Africa and to its articulation with communal modes of production. He specifically analysed the effects on class structures of capitalist forms which appeared there and differentiated their paths according to the various opportunities encountered by capital, in particular in its demand for labour (local and migrant, unskilled or semi-skilled workers), but also as a function of the patterns taken by this penetration (more or less competitive, capitalistic...) – quite differently from what happened in Latin America for example. Whereas, in tropical Africa, capitalism imposed itself without formation of a proletarian class, nor even of a bourgeoisie, on the contrary, South-African workers have been transformed into a proletariat, by the concentration of lands and mines in the hands of European capitalist settlers, and by expulsion of African peasants, impoverished in the very process of their integration into the monetary, market economy.[15] In both cases, this capitalism is characterised by a 'development of underdevelopment'.

Arrighi also directed his efforts towards the reformulation of a theory of imperialism, to be adapted to present trends of capitalism.[16] By resorting to the concept of 'hegemony' in a long-run perspective, he proposes a periodisation

---

14 Arrighi 1994.

15 For example: Arrighi 1966, 1970.

16 Arrighi 1978.

of history with two criteria: that of hegemonic power and that of the specific feature of imperialism this power tends to organise. After having achieved its national construction and tried to dominate a space from Canada to Panama, under the unifying principle of market, the United States have progressively reached to organise a 'formal imperialism', which secured, within the framework of the hierarchical order it imposed on the world-system, peace between capitalist countries and their unity against the Soviet Union. Revealed by the structural accumulation crisis at the beginning of the 1970s, the decline of US hegemony has to be understood as a transitional process towards the emergence of a new hegemonic power. In this way, the present period of chaos could be interpreted as the conclusion of a systemic cycle of capitalist accumulation, or the end of a fourth 'long century'[17] – after those of Genoa, the United Provinces and England –, presenting, in spite of an increase in complexity, similarities with the past cycles, such as the resurgence of finance or a proliferation of social conflicts, but also some singularities. Among the latter, Arrighi underlines the rise of transnational firms – financial capital, no more identified to a single national interest, becomes *transnational*, emancipating itself from both productive apparatuses and state powers –, as well as a shift of accumulation energies away from Europe. From this context, new East-Asian candidates to the hegemony over capitalist world-system, especially Japan, start to emerge. The neoliberal step of globalisation tends to bring the social formations of the centres and the peripheries closer together, connecting active and reserve armies by exacerbating competition and reducing labour remunerations. Therefore, workers' movements have a future, even if their composition and struggles have significantly changed over the last decades. It is thus no surprise in these conditions to see Arrighi's powerful analytical constructions usefully and efficectively mobilised against some of the 'intellectual fashions' of the neoliberal era (Negri's *Empire* among others).

André Gunder Frank

Paul Baran concentrated most of the empirical applications of his challenge to the progressive role of capitalist expansion (with the stress on extracting an economic surplus) on the Asian continent. Working in this theoretical

[17] Arrighi 1994.

tradition, André Gunder Frank for his part has devoted most of his reflections to Latin America, whose reality (according to him) can only be understood by going back to its fundamental determinant, the result of the historical development of the contemporary structure of global capitalism: *dependency*. Once the spheres of production and exchange are regarded as closely imbricated for the valorisation and reproduction of capital in the context of a single world process of accumulation and a single capitalist system undergoing transformation, dependency is no longer perceived simply as an external – 'imperialist' – relationship between the capitalist centres and their subordinate peripheries. It also becomes an internal – and, *de facto*, an 'integral' – phenomenon of the dependent society itself.

The underdevelopment of the peripheral countries is therefore to be interpreted as an outcome inherent in the global expansion of capitalism, characterised by monopolistic structures in exchange and mechanisms of exploitation in production. Frank's position is that since the European conquests of the sixteenth century, integration into the capitalist world-system has transformed initially '*un*developed' Latin American colonies into '*under*-developed' social formations, which are fundamentally capitalist because their productive and commercial structures are tied into the logic of the world market and subordinated to the pursuit of profit. The 'development of underdevelopment' has its origin in the very structure of the capitalist world-system, constructed as a hierarchical 'chain' of expropriation/appropriation of the economic surpluses linking

> 'the capitalist world and national metropolises to the regional centres... and from these to local centres and so on to large landholders or merchants who expropriate surplus from small peasants or tenants, and sometimes even from these latter to landless labourers exploited by them in turn'.[18]

Thus, at each point in this chain, which stamps the forms of exploitation and domination between 'metropolises and satellites' with a strange 'continuity in change', the international, national and local capitalist world-system has, since the sixteenth century, simultaneously issued in the development of certain zones 'for the minority' and underdevelopment elsewhere, 'for the major-

[18] Frank 1969, pp. 7–8.

ity' – in those peripheral margins of which Braudel remarked that 'human existence there often conjures up Purgatory or even Hell'.[19]

The ruling classes of the satellite countries thus strive to maintain these bonds of dependency on the capitalist metropolises, which install them in a dominant position locally while giving them status of a 'lumpen-bourgeoisie', by means of voluntary state policies 'of underdevelopment in the economic, social and political life of the "nation" and the people of Latin America.'[20] To illustrate his thesis, Frank looks to the economic history of Latin America, which forms an arresting contrast with that of North America, a 'sub-metropole' controlling a triangular flow of trade from its modern origins. Neither industrialisation via import substitution (embarked on after the crisis of 1929), nor the promotion of export industries (reactivated after the Second World War), and still less strategies for opening up to free trade (after independence in the nineteenth century or, more recently, at the end of the twentieth century) have enabled the Latin American countries to break the chain of surplus extraction, effected by unequal exchange, direct foreign investment, and international aid. For Frank, in these circumstances the only solution to the 'development of under-development' for the periphery of the capitalist world-system is socialist revolution, which is at once 'necessary and possible'.[21]

Theories of the capitalist world-system form one of the richest, most dynamic, and most stimulating fields of research that Marxism has engaged in in recent decades. By strengthening both the interactive links between the economic and the political and the relations between the *intra*-national and the *inter*-national; by reformulating the problems of the periodisation and articulation of modes of production and of the combination of relations of exploitation and domination, these modern analyses of capitalism have made it possible to clarify certain theoretically and politically crucial categories, which have long been examined within the Marxist tradition – for example, those of class, nation, state, market, or globalisation. Marxism has manifestly been considerably enriched in the process, renewing and establishing itself on

---

19 Braudel 1985.
20 Frank 1972, p. 13.
21 Frank 1981.

more solid theoretical and empirical foundations, which are at once broader and deeper, non-historicist and non-economistic.

The significance of these advances, which have been made in a confrontation with critical Marxist economists (like Charles Bettelheim, Paul Boccara, Robert Brenner, Maurice Dobb, Ernest Mandel, Ernesto Laclau, Paul Sweezy, and many more), and other intellectual 'movements' (structuralism in particular), must be measured by the real, multifarious influence exercised today by the theoreticians of the capitalist world-system. It is evident in the case of 'neo'- or 'post'-Marxists in various domains of social science (among others, Giovanni Arrighi or Harry Magdoff in economics, Étienne Balibar or Jacques Bidet in philosophy, Pablo Gonzales Casanova in political science, Pierre-Philippe Rey in anthropology, etc.), or of reformist authors (such as Osvaldo Sukel, or Celso Furtado, in particular).

Borne along by the ground swell of national popular liberation movements in the Third World, these theorisations, going beyond theses on imperialism while retaining them, can ultimately only find a favourable echo in the Latin-American, Africa, Arab and Asian countries, which Western neo-Marxist researchers would gain from working with, at a time when the dominant neoclassical discourse functions like some new idealist system as a machine for absorbing heterodox theses and subjecting reality to the necessity of the established order.

Chapter Twelve

Liberation-Theology Marxism

Michael Löwy

In the first instance, liberation theology is a set of writings produced since 1971 by figures like Gustavo Gutiérrez (Peru), Rubem Alves, Hugo Assman, Carlos Mesters, Leonardo and Clodovis Boff (Brazil), Jon Sobrino and Ignacio Ellacuría (El Salvador), Segundo Galilea and Ronaldo Muñoz (Chile), Pablo Richard (Chile and Costa Rica), José Miguel Bonino and Juan Carlos Scannone (Argentina), Enrique Dussel (Argentina and Mexico), and Juan-Luis Segundo (Uruguay) – to name only some of the best known.

But this corpus of texts is the expression of a vast *social movement*, which emerged at the beginning of the 1960s, well before the new works of theology. This movement involved considerable sectors of the Church (priests, religious orders, bishops), lay religious movements (Catholic Action, the Christian student movement, Christian young workers), pastoral committees with a popular base, labour, land and urban pastoral committees, and ecclesiastical base communities. Without the *practice* of this social movement, which might be called a *Christianity of liberation*, one cannot understand such important social and historical phenomena in Latin America over the last thirty years as the rise of revolution in Central America – Nicaragua and El Salvador – or the emergence of a new working-class and peasant movement in Brazil (the Workers' Party, the Landless Peasants' Movement, etc.).[1]

The discovery of Marxism by progressive Christians and liberation theology was not a purely intellectual or academic process. Its starting point was an unavoidable social fact, a massive, brutal reality in Latin America: poverty. A number of believers opted for Marxism because it seem to offer the most systematic, coherent and comprehensive explanation of the causes of this poverty, and because it ventured the only proposal sufficiently radical to abolish it. In order to struggle effectively against poverty, it is necessary to understand its causes. As the Brazilian cardinal Dom Helder Câmara puts it:

> As long as I was asking people to help the poor, I was called a saint. But when I asked: why is there so much poverty?, I was treated as a communist.

It is not easy to present an overview of liberation theology's stance towards Marxism. On the one hand, we find a very great diversity of attitudes within it, ranging from the prudent employment of a few elements to a complete synthesis (for instance, in the 'Christians for Socialism' tendency). On the other, a certain change has occurred between the positions of the years 1968–80, which were more radical, and those of today, which are more reserved, following criticisms from Rome, but also developments in Eastern Europe since 1989. However, on the basis of the works of the most representative theologians and certain episcopal documents, we can identify various common reference points.[2]

Some Latin-American theologians (influenced by Althusser) refer to Marxism simply as a (or *the*) *social science*, to be used in strictly instrumental fashion in order to arrive at a more profound knowledge of Latin-American reality. Such a definition is at once too broad and too narrow. Too broad, because Marxism is not the only social science; and too narrow, because Marxism is not only a science: it rests upon a practical option that aims not only to understand, but also to transform, the world.

In reality, the interest in Marxism displayed by liberation theologians – many authors speak of 'fascination' – is wider and deeper than borrowing a

[1] See Löwy 1996.
[2] See Dussel 1982 and Petitdemange 1985.

few concepts for scientific purposes might lead one to believe. It also involves the *values* of Marxism, its ethico-political options, and its anticipation of a future *utopia*. Gustavo Gutiérrez offers the most penetrating observations, stressing that Marxism does not confine itself to proposing a scientific analysis, but is also a utopian aspiration to social change. He criticises the scientistic vision of Althusser, who

> obscures the profound unity of Marx's oeuvre and, as a result, prevents a proper understanding of its capacity for inspiring a revolutionary, radical and constant *praxis*.[3]

From which Marxist sources do the liberation theologians derive inspiration? Their knowledge of Marx's writings varies greatly. Enrique Dussel is unquestionably the figure who has taken the study of Marx's *œuvre* furthest, publishing a series of works on it of impressive erudition and originality.[4] But we also find direct references to Marx in Gutiérrez, the Boff brothers, Hugo Assmann, and several others.

On the other hand, they show little interest in the Marxism of Soviet manuals of 'diamat' or of the Latin-American Communist parties. What attracts them is rather 'Western Marxism' – sometimes referred to as 'neo-Marxism' in their documents. Ernst Bloch is the most frequently cited Marxist author in *Liberation Theology: Perspectives* – Gutiérrez's major inaugural work of 1971. In it we also find references to Althusser, Marcuse, Lukács, Henri Lefebvre, Lucien Goldmann, and Ernest Mandel.[5]

But these European references are less important than Latin-American reference points: the Peruvian thinker José Carlos Mariátegui, source of an original Marxism that was Indo-American in inspiration; the Cuban Revolution – a key turning-point in the history of Latin America; and, finally, the dependency theory – a critique of dependent capitalism – proposed by Fernando

---

[3] Gutierrez 1972, p. 244. It is true that since 1984, following the Vatican's criticisms, Gutierrez appears to have retreated to less exposed positions, reducing the relationship to Marxism to an encounter between theology and the social sciences: see Gutiérrez 1985.

[4] See Dussel 1985, 1990 and 2001.

[5] In the remarkable work that he has devoted to revolutionary Christianity in Latin America, Samuel Silva Gotay lists the following Marxist authors among the references of liberation theology: Goldmann, Garaudy, Schaff, Kolakowski, Lukács, Gramsci, Lombardo-Radice, Luporini, Sanchez Vasquez, Mandel, Fanon, and *Monthly Review*: see Silva Gotay 1985.

Henrique Cardoso, André Gunder Frank, Theotonio dos Santos, and Anibal Quijano (all mentioned on several occasions in Gutiérrez's book).[6]

Liberation theologians – and 'liberation Christians' in the broad sense – do not limit themselves to using existing Marxist sources. In the light of their religious culture, but also their social experience, they break new ground and reformulate certain basic themes of Marxism. In this sense, they may be regarded as 'neo-Marxists' – that is to say, as innovators who offer Marxism a new inflection or novel perspectives, or make original contributions to it.

A striking example is their use, alongside the 'classic' terms workers or proletarians, of the concept of *the poor*. Concern for the poor is an ancient tradition of the Church, going back to the evangelical sources of Christianity. The Latin-American theologians identify with this tradition, which serves as a constant reference and inspiration. But they are profoundly at odds with the past on a crucial point: for them, the poor are no longer essentially objects of charity, but subjects of their own liberation. Paternalist help or aid gives way to an attitude of solidarity with the struggle of the poor for their self-emancipation. This is where the junction with the truly fundamental principle of Marxism, namely, that 'the emancipation of the working classes must be conquered by the working classes themselves' – is effected. This switch is perhaps the most important political innovation, full of implications, made by the liberation theologians with respect to the Church's social teaching. It will also have the greatest consequences in the domain of social *praxis*.

No doubt some Marxists will criticise this way of substituting a vague, emotional and imprecise category ('the poor') for the 'materialist' concept of the proletariat. In reality, the term corresponds to the Latin-American situation, where one finds, both in the towns and the countryside, an enormous mass of poor people – the unemployed, the semi-unemployed, seasonal workers, itinerant sellers, the marginalised, prostitutes, and so on – all of them excluded from the 'formal' system of production. The Marxist-Christian trade unionists of El Salvador have invented a term, which combines the components of the oppressed and exploited population: the *pobretariado* ('pooretariat'). It should be stressed that the majority of these poor people – like, moreover, the majority of the members of church base communities – are *women*.

---

[6] On the use of dependency theory by the liberation theologians, See Bordini 1987, Chapter 6 and Silva Gotay 1985, pp. 192–7.

Another distinctive aspect of liberation theology Marxism is a *moral critique of capitalism*. Liberation Christianity, whose inspiration is in the first instance religious and ethical, displays a much more radical, intransigent and categorical anticapitalism – because charged with moral repulsion – than the continent's Communist parties, issued from the Stalinist mould, which believe in the progressive virtues of the industrial bourgeoisie and the 'anti-feudal' historical role of industrial (capitalist) development. An example will suffice to illustrate this paradox. The Brazilian Communist Party explained in the resolutions of its sixth congress (1967) that 'the socialisation of the means of production does not correspond to the current level of the contradiction between the productive forces and the relations of production'. In other words, industrial capitalism must develop the economy and modernise the country before there can be any question of socialism. In 1973 the bishops and senior clergy of the centre-west region of Brazil published a document entitled *The Cry of the Church*, which concluded as follows:

> Capitalism must be overcome. It is the greatest evil, accumulated sin, the rotten root, the tree that produces all the fruits that we know so well: poverty, hunger, illness, death. To this end, private ownership of the means of production (factories, land, trade, banks) must be superseded.[7]

As we can see with this document – and many more issued from the emancipatory Christian tendency – solidarity with the poor leads to a condemnation of capitalism and therewith to the desire for socialism.

As a result of the ethical radicalism of their anticapitalism, Christian socialists have often proved more sensitive to the social catastrophes created by 'really existing modernity' in Latin America and by the logic of the 'development of underdevelopment' (to use André Gunder Frank's well-known expression) than many Marxists, enmeshed in a purely economic 'developmentalist' logic. For example, the 'orthodox' Marxist ethnologist Otavio Guilherme Velho has severely criticised the Brazilian progressivist Church for 'regarding capitalism as an absolute evil' and opposing the capitalist transformation of agriculture, which is a vector of progress, in the name of the precapitalist traditions and ideologies of the peasantry.[8]

---

[7] *Obispos Latinamericanos* 1978, p. 71.
[8] See Velho 1982, pp. 125–6.

Since the end of the 1970s, another theme has played an increasing role in the Marxist reflection of some Christian thinkers: the *elective affinity between the Biblical struggle against idols and the Marxist critique of commodity fetishism.* The articulation of the two in liberation theology has been facilitated by the fact that Marx himself often use Biblical images and concepts in his critique of capitalism.

Baal, the *Golden Calf, Mammon, Moloch* – these are some of the 'theological metaphors' of which Marx makes ample use in *Capital* and other economic writings, in order to denounce the spirit of capitalism as an idolatry of money, commodities, profit, the market or capital itself, in a language directly inspired by the Old-Testament prophets. The stock exchange is often referred to as the 'Temple of Baal' or 'Mammon'. The most important concept of the Marxist critique of capitalism is itself a 'theological metaphor', referring to idolatry: *fetishism*.

These 'theologico-metaphorical' moments – and other similar ones – in the Marxist critique of capitalism are familiar to several liberation theologians, who do not hesitate to refer to them in their writings. Detailed analysis of such 'metaphors' can be found in Enrique Dussel's 1993 book – a detailed philosophical study of the Marxist theory of fetishism from the standpoint of liberation Christianity.[9]

The critique of the system of economic and social domination in Latin America as a form of idolatry was sketched for the first time in a collection of texts by the Departamento Ecumenico de Investigaciones (DEI) of San José in Costa Rica, published under the title *The War of Gods: The Idols of Oppression and the Search for the Liberating God*, which had considerable resonance. Published in 1980, it was translated into seven languages. The viewpoint common to the five authors – H. Assmann, F. Hinkelammert, J. Pixley, P. Richard and J. Sobrino – is set out in an introduction. It involves a decisive break with the conservative, retrograde tradition of the Church, which for two centuries presented 'atheism' – of which Marxism was the modern form – as Christianity's arch-enemy:

> The key question today in Latin America is not atheism, the ontological problem of the existence of God.... The key question is idolatry, the adulation

[9] See Dussel 1993.

> of the false gods of the system of domination.... Each system of domination is characterized precisely by the fact that it creates gods and idols who sanctify oppression and hostility to life.... The search for the true God in this war of gods leads us to a vision of things directed against idolatry, rejecting the false divinities, the fetishes that kill and their religious weapons of death. Faith in the liberating God, the one who unveils his face and secret in the struggle of the poor against oppression, is necessarily fulfilled in the negation of false divinities.... Faith is turning against idolatry.[10]

This problematic was the subject of a profound and innovative analysis in the remarkable co-authored book by Hugo Assmann and Franz Hinkelammert, *Market Idolatry: An Essay on Economics and Theology* (1989). This important contribution is the first in the history of liberation theology explicitly dedicated to the struggle against the capitalist system defined as idolatry. The Church's social teaching had invariably only practiced an ethical critique of 'liberal' (or capitalist) economics. As Assmann stresses, a specifically theological critique is also required – one that reveals capitalism to be a false religion. What does the essence of market idolatry consist in? According to Assmann, the capitalist 'economic religion' manifests itself in the implicit theology of the economic paradigm itself and in everyday fetishistic devotional practice. The explicitly religious concepts to be found in the literature of 'market Christianity' – for example, in the speeches of Ronald Reagan, the writings of neoconservative religious currents, or the works of 'enterprise theologians' such as Michael Novack – do not merely possess a complementary function. Market theology, from Malthus to the latest document from the World Bank, is a ferocious sacrificial theology: it requires the poor to offer up their lives on the altar of economic idols.

For his part, Hinkelammert analises the new theology of the American Empire of the 1970s and 1980s, strongly permeated by religious fundamentalism. Its god is nothing other than the 'transcendentalized personification of the laws of the market' and worship of him replaces compassion by sacrifice. The deification of the market creates a god of money, whose sacred motto is inscribed on every dollar bill: In God We Trust.[11]

---

10 Assmann et al. 1980, p. 9.

11 See Assmann and Hinkelammert 1989, pp. 105, 254, 321.

The research of Costa Rica's DEI has influenced socially engaged Christians and inspired a new generation of liberation theologians. For example, the young Brazilian (Korean in origin) Jung Mo Sung, who in his book *The Idolatry of Capital and the Death of the Poor* (1980), develops a penetrating ethico-religious critique of the international capitalist system, whose institutions – like the IMF or World Bank – condemn millions of poor people in the Third World to sacrifice their lives on the altar of the 'global market' god through the implacable logic of external debt. Obviously, as Sung stresses in his latest book *Theology and Economics* (1994), in contrast to ancient idolatry, we are dealing not with a visible altar, but with a system that demands human sacrifices in the name of seemingly non-religious, profane, 'scientific', 'objective' imperatives.

What do the Marxist critique and the liberation-Christian critique of market idolatry have in common and where do they differ? In my view, we cannot find an atheism in Christianity (contrary to what Ernst Bloch thought), or an implicit theology in Marx, contrary to what is suggested by the brilliant theologian and Marxologist Enrique Dussel.[12] Theological metaphors, like the concept of 'fetishism', are used by Marx as instruments for a scientific analysis, whereas, in liberation Christianity, they have a properly religious significance. What the two share is a moral ethos, a prophetic revolt, humanist indignation against the idolatry of the market and – even more important – solidarity with its victims.

For Marx, critique of the fetishistic worship of commodities was a critique of capitalist alienation from the standpoint of the proletariat and the exploited – but also revolutionary – classes. For liberation theology, it involves a struggle between the true God of Life and the false idols of death. But both take a stand for living labour against reification; for the life of the poor and the oppressed against the alienated power of dead things. And above all, Marxist non-believers and committed Christians alike wager on the social self-emancipation of the exploited.

[12] See Bloch 1978 and Dussel 1993, p. 153.

Chapter Thirteen

Market Socialism: Problems and Models

Tony Andréani

Are socialism and the market incompatible?

Market socialism has long been regarded as a contradiction in terms. If, so as to avoid getting involved in a theoretical debate about the concept of socialism, we accept with Weisskopf[1] that a socialist society is characterised by an impulse towards social equality, genuine democracy, communal ties, and greater social rationality, then the market seems of necessity to foil it. It creates inequalities, makes economic democracy difficult, even impracticable (especially when private property becomes capitalist), secretes individualistic behaviour, and renders production 'opaque' (through the price 'mechanism') and 'anarchic' (by virtue of its decentralised structure). Despite the failure, and then collapse, of the Soviet system and 'real socialism', which intended – at least in principle – to meet these objectives, there are still authors today who maintain that socialism and the market are incompatible, whether they completely reject the market and propose to replace it by radical democratisation and the planning of needs,[2] or accept it in a very partial and temporary fashion,

[1] See Weisskopf 1993, p. 121.
[2] See Ticktin 1998.

while emphasising its corrosive aspects. Contrariwise, some supporters of market socialism regard the market as an irreplaceable and probably untranscendable structure. And, while they acknowledge its defects, they think that it can be reconciled with public or social-property forms conducive to equality and democracy, and with regulation that makes it possible to at least limit its most harmful and perverse effects.

I do not intend here to go into the details of this vast debate, which would take up all the space allotted to me, but will instead briefly refer to the historical experiences that can be categorised under the rubric of 'market socialism', and then focus on a few models, which will give an idea of the problems that arise and of attempted solutions to them. I shall merely indicate that, to my mind, socialism needs to be distinguished from a certain utopian vision of communism as a society of abundance where work has disappeared; a society of individuals in perfect solidarity; a society in which calculation is carried out exclusively in terms of use-values; a society that evaluates and plan needs *a priori*; a society with a planned distribution of products, with an imperative planning of output, and with a 'fully developed democracy' at the central level; and, finally, a vision of revolution that can only be global in scope. But this in no way precludes reflecting on a feasible communism, resting on different bases (decentralisation *and* incentive planning; producer autonomy *and* the realisation of common objectives; competition *and* co-operation; individual freedom *and* community; private goods *and* social goods; evaluation in value terms *and* price movements; economic democracy *and* central democracy – in short, a reconciliation of opposites), which remains the end goal of socialism. I will add that reading Marx in no way contradicts the idea that market socialism is a necessary transition.[3]

I hope readers will forgive me for skipping this vast debate. I believe that at present the only real alternative to the new capitalism consists in some form of market socialism; and that the main thing is to find answers to the internal obstacles which the historical experience of socialism has revealed and to assess the responses to them which the 'models' seek to provide. In fact, there exists a considerable literature, Anglo-American for the most part, which is ignored or unknown in France, of which this text aims to provide at least a brief survey.

[3] See the, to my mind, largely convincing Lawler 1998.

The theoretical framework

On a theoretical level, market socialism goes back a long way, since its two main founders offered suggestive sketches of it in 1938 (Lange) and 1946 (Lerner). Their work has given rise to a very important academic debate, which liberals did not disdain to participate in at the time, particularly Hayek. There is a paradox here, because these original models of market socialism, constructed on the basis of neoclassical theory, provided the best possible illustration of a system capable of realising Walrasian equilibrium and, later, the famous Arrow-Debreu model of general equilibrium. State committees were, in effect, best placed to realise supply and demand equilibria, through price determinations.[4] Neoclassical economists have, in fact, had to demonstrate that it was precisely market imperfections which accounted for the superiority of the system of private ownership and price determination by a multiplicity of mechanisms that socialism was ill-placed to employ. Thus, Stiglitz (subsequently chief economist at the World Bank) explained that, in the absence of futures markets, incentives are required to pursue the reliable information which permits risk-taking (bound up in particular with innovation); that the necessary separation between ownership and management (in place of the single figure of the entrepreneur) dictates control over managers to prevent them abusing their power over information; and that mechanisms other than price movements exist to inform agents, such as 'reputation', 'contracts', or 'negotiation'.[5] Private ownership is superior because it supplies proper incentives, proper means of control, and proper procedures for organising exchange. Private owners of capital in fact only pursue profitability for their capital and, to that end, are determined to control managers, to

---

[4] In Lange's model, the central planning office announces, as Walrasian auctioneer, a set of prices for production goods. As in the model of perfect competition, the managers of public enterprises regard these prices as givens and take their decisions in such a way as to maximise their profit rate (equalisation of the price to the marginal cost), while consumers seek to maximise their utility and workers the income from their labour. On the basis of the information supplied by entrepreneurs about the variations in their stock, reflecting the relations between supply and demand, the office announces a new series of prices for production goods and the process continues until equilibrium is achieved for all goods. Lange maintained that this procedure of trial and error would function much better than the competitive market, because the planning office would have a broader knowledge of what occurs in the economy as a whole than private entrepreneurs. Profits are then distributed by the state to workers in accordance with democratically determined criteria.

[5] See Stiglitz 1993.

incentivise them effectively, and to look out for all opportunities for profit, whereas the state is more indulgent towards its agents, has preoccupations other than maximising the profit rate, and is always ready to moderate competition that ultimately obtains only between firms. More generally, neo-institutionalist theories of the firm,[6] which all stress market weaknesses and costs, likewise attempt to demonstrate the superiority of capitalism; and they will be closely attended to by theoreticians of market socialism. As we can see, the debate on market socialism has assumed a new dimension since the initial works. But it has not enclosed itself in the conceptual framework inherited from the neoclassical approach.

Without neglecting the contributions of the latter, other currents have worked in the framework of the Marxist paradigm, while borrowing from Keynesianism. For some authors, this involves adopting the Langian idea of *ex ante* planning, making it possible to carry out a more rational calculation than the market and to achieve mastery of the economic and social process, in contrast to the anarchy and crises bound up with the commodity economy. But the price mechanism would be preserved as an indicator of supply and demand relations, while planning would be conducted democratically, from the bottom up: a dual difference with the Soviet system. Albert and Hahnel thus propose a highly decentralised form of planning, resting on forms of democracy at the base, with workers' councils and consumers' councils realising equilibrium via a mechanism of price signals.[7] Devine, in his model of participatory planning, where firms are owned by their workers, but also by their clients, suppliers and representatives of local communities and of the planning committee, likewise proposes a form of calculation based on physical measurements (workforce, stock inventory) and market indicators (orders, profitability).[8] Cockshott and Cottrell go further: they believe that thanks to second-generation computers, it is possible to calculate the labour value of products and to adjust prices to them over the long term.[9] I shall not go into the details of these models, which open up some interesting paths. But I will

---

[6] This mainly involves the theory of transaction costs (Williamson), the theory of property rights (Alchian and Demetz), and the theory of agency (Jensen and Meckling).

[7] See Albert and Hahnel 1991.

[8] See Devine 1988.

[9] See Cockshott and Cottrell 1993.

say that, in my view, they encounter some very strong objections as to their feasibility. The first is that the democratic procedures they suggest would be very costly socially and too burdensome for individuals, who would rapidly become abstentionists. The second is that calculation of the labour values in the model of Cockshott and Cottrell still appears unobtainable, when one considers the complexity of products. The third is that even this calculation necessarily diverges from prices as long as interest is paid on the capital made available. It seems extremely difficult to dispense with credit at interest if one wishes to encourage producers to economise resources and make efficient use of investment (the Soviet system offers *a contrario* proof of this). Consequently, it is labour values that can serve as indicators, signalling to the planning bodies what it costs society in terms of labour expenditure to produce some particular good. That is why, along with most authors, I think that planning can only take the form of incentive planning, guiding price formation more than it anticipates it. I shall return to this.

As we shall see, different approaches have led to very different models. In addition, treatment of the problems is uneven. Thus, some models remain centred on the most efficient allocation of resources and the motivation of agents, neglecting (as Devine emphasises),[10] another dimension of economic efficiency: the discovery of opportunities and the mobilisation of 'tacit' knowledge.

A glance at history

Historically, market socialism made some timid appearances in the Soviet system, mainly in the form of a revaluation of the criterion for profit rates – something that did not have much sense in an economy that was only minimally a market one and which was non-competitive.[11] It was then experimented with more systematically in certain of the Eastern-bloc countries, especially Hungary and Poland from the 1970s onwards, and then – very briefly – in the USSR during the Gorbachev period. Now, it must be said that none of these experiments was successful. By reintroducing market relations between firms

[10] See Devine 1988.

[11] There did indeed exist a kind of informal 'administrative' competition, but it prevented any true prices.

as well a degree of competition, they reduced some shortages, especially in the consumer-goods sector. But they did not check the decline of the 'socialist' economies and even generated new problems at the macro-economic level (inflation, public deficits, trade or balance of payments deficits). It might be thought that this failure can be explained by the problems arising from the transition from a command economy to a market economy; by the fact that the reforms were carried out too hesitantly and did not go far enough; by the fact that the party-state in power was utterly unwilling to let go of the levers of control; by the absence, if not of a multi-party system, then at least of a genuine public debate on these issues; and, finally, by the fact that the reforms came too late, at a time when the régime was discredited and the population, tired of experiments, preferred to resort to the alluring recipes of a capitalism that it imagined differently. All these reasons must certainly be taken into account, but they are insufficient to explain the failure. A different historical experiment in market socialism was conducted in Yugoslavia. It was very distinct, because it was based on self-management principles and gave full rein to the market, except as regards the capital market. It yielded excellent results, but it too ended in failure, the reasons for which were not exclusively extra-economic. The only exception is China, followed by Vietnam, although it is too soon to be sure, since the transition to a market socialism is underway there. It is nevertheless important to examine how this relative success is bound up with the fact that the Chinese way differs significantly from what was done, for example, in Hungary.

The other experiment in market socialism – but was it not in many respect a state capitalism? – took place very partially in some Western countries, including France. And in a way it confirms, at least in part, the negative or pessimistic diagnosis that has been made – sometimes in good faith – of state-market socialism. If we set aside the particular case of public enterprises delivering public services, such enterprises in the competitive sector have frequently been less dynamic than those in the private sector, in strictly economic terms.

I shall not dwell here on the positive aspects of these socialisms. Such aspects should not be forgotten and they explain the regret, even nostalgia, felt by large sections of the populations of the ex-socialist countries which, without understanding what was happening to them, were cast – sometimes with extreme brutality – into the transition to a capitalist market economy. They also explain the attachment to their public services often displayed by citizens in the Western countries. It is more important to investigate the reasons for these failures. Thus, we can summarise some of the main problems, and main defects, experienced by state socialism, setting aside the diversity of the countries and historical circumstances.

The problems to be resolved

The first problem is the *allocation of capital*. The initial difficulty here is that the state, sole owner of enterprises and sole shareholder in each enterprise, does not always allocate capital according to a criterion of 'economic' profitability. It is thus often criticised for being lax, or sometimes for being too stringent, as regards financial profitability (return on capital). Whereas, on capital markets, private shareholders penalise low profitability by selling their shares, and respond to good prospects for profitability by buying them, the state does not sell itself its own property titles. So this is to criticise it for not behaving like a capitalist. But economic profitability could only consist in claiming a remuneration for its own capital similar to that of borrowed capital (determined by the market in loan capital, just like the remuneration of social shares in co-operatives, which cannot exceed the average yield of bonds), in which case the state would behave as a simple lender, taking only a fixed share of profits (in the form of dividends and capital increases). Why is this not most commonly the case? And why does it not allocate capital between its enterprises by itself proceeding to a valuation? Why does it not punish them directly, without taking the detour of the market and share prices on the stock market?

We thus come to a broader difficulty: rather than behaving as an economic agent, as a real owner (in the name of society), the state plays a multiplicity of roles. (1) It uses a percentage of the profits of enterprises (dividends) for general policy ends – covering deficits, administrative expenses, military expenditure, and so on – rather than simply subjecting its enterprises to taxes like all other enterprises. (2) It assigns its enterprises 'social' objectives from without, which can come into conflict with their pursuit of profitability (financial or simply 'economic'): for example, job protection or increased wages. (3) It favours a public enterprise with cheap credit and by rescheduling or postponing debt, via public banks, if it considers the enterprise to have a strategic function – and this at the expense of other public or private enterprises. It thereby deprives itself of the means with which to assess their competitive position. (4) It intervenes in the last resort, when the enterprise is loss-making, with aid, grants, or recapitalisation, at the expense of other public enterprises, which also need capital. (5) It is more sensitive to the pressure exercised by the wage-earners in a public enterprise than in private enterprises. These arguments are among those invoked in favour of privatisation.[12]

A second problem concerns the *motivation of agents*. Analysis has above all focused on the relationship between the state and managers. In fact, the state has an ambiguous relationship with the directors of public enterprises, because they are civil servants assigned to these duties, and not specialists recruited on the labour market in managers. This problem has been studied at length in the economic literature under the rubric of the principal/agent relationship, borrowed from the theory of 'agency'. The core of this theory consists in the notion of an asymmetry of information. An owner who appoints an agent to take care of her interests is faced with someone who possesses information and is concerned in the first instance with her own interests (remuneration, reputation, good relations with subordinates, etc.). She must therefore keep a constant eye on her and, in order to do this, regularly demand accounts (above all, his financial results). At the same time, she must motivate her by means of powerful incentives (good treatment, distribution of stock options). Now, the state (so it is said) is a bad supervisor, because it cannot fire one of its servants like any other wage-earner; and a bad incentiviser, because it cannot reward her too highly, since that would risk upsetting its other senior servants, not to mention ordinary wage-earners. For her part, the state manager is aware that she runs no great personal risk, is above all concerned to earn his minister's high opinion by meeting her objectives, rather than those of the enterprise, and knows that, in the event of poor management, the state will be held responsible and will come to the rescue. How are managers to be disciplined? This is the question that obsesses the theoreticians of state market socialism. And the collusion noted between the political authorities and the directors of state enterprises, both during the reforms carried out in the ex-socialist countries and in the public sector in Western countries, tends to vindicate them.

---

[12] Although capitalist enterprise do not forego recourse to state aid!

This set of problems has been referred to by the Hungarian economist Janos Kornai in a phrase that has been very widely remarked – 'soft budgetary constraints'.[13] These are supposedly inevitable when the state is investor, insurer, and creditor of last resort. The same economist has concluded that private ownership alone is capable of exercising hard budgetary constraints, ensuring success in economic competition and stimulating the economy, without yielding when faced with the imperatives of 'creative destruction'. Market socialism was manifestly condemned to relative inefficiency, dooming it to extinction in the natural selection of economic systems.

But the problem of motivation cannot be restricted to the issue of budgetary constraints. It is also necessary for workers to find meaning and interest in their work and to be rewarded for their efforts. This is a crucial question. For, as supporters of industrial democracy (from various forms of participation to self-management) stress, this is where the main source of socialism's superiority, including as regards efficiency, might lie.

The third problem involves *entrepreneurial spirit and the active pursuit of innovation*. Here again, historical market socialism has proven highly flawed. The state as owner (1) is reluctant to take risks, even though it has all the necessary resources for taking them, in particular because it fears not being able to halt a project if it turns out to be a bad one; (2) does not encourage innovation, because it is insufficiently motivated by financial gain and takes too long to make decisions; (3) does not encourage enterprise creation, so as not to create problems for those enterprises that already exist. These are so many arguments that once again militate in favour of private ownership and even capitalist ownership (for, as we shall see, co-operatives are bad at resolving the problems).

The fourth problem is that of *planning*: how can it be combined with an economy in which enterprises are autonomous and concerned with their own interests? How can material shape be given to something that remains a basic ambition of socialism, and which is opposed to the blind operation of capitalism, even to the social absurdities to which the latter leads today?

---

[13] See Kornai 1980.

Models geared towards the maximisation and egalitarian distribution of profit

I shall first of all examine a set of models that attempt to respond to these questions, but, in my view, incompletely and in accordance with a logic that remains close to that of capitalism – while presenting, in appearance at least, the advantage of greater historical feasibility.

Just as Oskar Lange proposed that the plan imitate the market, for these authors the task is to hit upon institutions that imitate private property, the capital market, and the market in managers, while maintaining state or at least 'public' ownership of state assets (through a system of 'coupons'), in such a way as to ensure more equality than in the capitalist system and to deal with a certain number of ills of capitalism at the macro-economic level (unemployment, recurrent crises, 'public harms', etc.), by ensuring public control over investment – which is where the market proves defective (for want of future markets).

The main problem with which these authors are concerned, in the light of the defects of the Soviet system, is therefore efficiency in allocating 'factors of production'. The maximisation of the profit rate seems to them the means *par excellence* of optimisation. As for incentives for agents, they are highly sceptical about the virtues of self-management: in addition to problems with decision-making, they criticise the laxity of the associated workers as regards investment and restructuring. This is why the traditional hierarchical system, with some amendments, seems to them to represent a better guarantee of efficiency. It remains to motivate and supervise managers. As in the capitalist economy, this is the role of the owners, but the ownership is to be social. Two main routes have been explored. The first consists in public ownership. However, since such ownership is to be released from political intervention by the state, it is the public enterprises that supervise themselves, by means of a mechanism of interlocking interests, with each enterprise finding it beneficial to watch over the profitability of the other's capital (here, inspiration is derived from the Japanese and German models, which have proved themselves, albeit in the context of a private capitalism). The second route is ownership by the public, the idea for which derives both from the distribution of coupons in the ex-socialist countries during denationalisation and the distribution of shares to wage-earners in contemporary capitalism or of 'popular' share-owning by means of investment funds and pension funds.

I shall first of all present the model that Pranab Bardhan has proposed, taking the first route.[14] John Roemer offers the following summary of it:

> ...firms belong to groups, each associated with a main bank, whose job is to monitor the firms in its group and arrange loan consortia for them. There would be a very limited stock market. Banks would own shares of firms, and each firm in a group would own some shares of the other firms in its group as well. The board of directors of a firm would consist of representatives of the main bank and of the other firms who hold its shares. The bank's profits (including its share of firms' profits in its group) would return in large part to the government, to be spent on public goods, health services, education, and so on: this would constitute one part of a citizen's consumption of social profits. In addition, each firm would receive dividends from its shares of other firms in its group, and these would be distributed to its workers, constituting the second part of the social dividend. Because a citizen's income would come in part from the profits of other firms in her *keiretsu*, she would have an interest in requiring those firms to maximize profits, an interest that would be looked after by her firm's representatives on the boards of directors of the other firms.... If [firms] started performing badly, [the other firms] would be able to sell their stock...to the main bank, who would have an obligation to buy it. This would put pressure on the bank to discipline [the firm's] management.[15]

I shall next set out in summary form the model that Roemer has presented, pursuing the second route, in an article and then in a book entitled *A Future for Socialism*.[16] Enterprises would be nationalised. 'Clamshells' would be distributed in equal quantities to all citizens, who would convert them into shares in the enterprises of their choice and would receive the dividends until their death, when they would revert to the state. However, in order to prevent the least well-off among them selling their shares to other people, who would thereby become large property-owners – this is what happened in the ex-USSR and the other Eastern countries – individuals could only exchange their shares (at the price of the clamshells) for different shares, not for money. This would impel them to keep an eye on the yield of their shares, if not doing

[14] See Bardhan 1993.
[15] Roemer 1992, p. 269.
[16] See Roemer 1992 and 1994.

it themselves, then at least entrusting the task to managers, even by changing managers. Since shares would not be a way of raising capital, financing would derive from credit. It would be provided by public banks that could not transform themselves into merchant banks – that is to say, acquire an interest in the capital of non-financial or financial institutions. Institutional arrangements would make the public banks independent of the state, but their profits would largely flow to the Treasury. The banks would oversee the enterprises, the movement of the clamshells providing them with information about the quality of their management. As for the management of the enterprises, it would be appointed by their boards of directors, which would include representatives of fund managers, of enterprises supplying credit, and of employees. This would ensure good incentives. Moreover, capitalist enterprises would be authorised, in order to encourage the entrepreneurial spirit. However, when they reached a certain size, they would be nationalised and their shares distributed to the public. Finally, the plan would act on investment by indirect means – mainly by manipulating interest rates.

There is no doubt that these models, supposing they were viable and met with the popular support required for their implementation, would differ appreciably from contemporary capitalism. But can we speak of socialism? Are we not instead dealing with a state capitalism or a 'popular' capitalism? Many arguments lead in this direction.

Marx's whole endeavour was to show that capital is a social relation, the figure of the capitalist playing a comparatively secondary role. The purpose of capitalism is to valorise a money-capital involved in a process of production, marketing, or credit (today, we would have to say more broadly: finance), by employing all possible means to obtain the optimal return. In terms of modern accountancy, this means ensuring the financial profitability of one's own capital (as opposed to borrowed capital which, once lent, no longer disposes of means of action). In the models that I have just considered, it is indeed the principle of shareholder value that prevails.

In contrast, I would argue that the purpose of socialism is to maximise the income not of capital, but of labour, once not only the costs of exploitation but also financial (and exceptional) costs have been deducted. In this light, it is clear that the models of market socialism rest on a capitalist foundation. However, what the market socialists would doubtless reply is that this is of little importance once the income derived from capital reverts to the workers either via the state that represents them all, or through the more or less equal distribution of these incomes. Workers, it will be said, cannot exploit themselves. For several reasons, this is false.

This accounting vision, centred on distribution, misunderstands what the relations of production in the strict sense are (within what Marx calls the immediate process of production). Maximising capital revenues comes down to always increasing their share with respect to that of the direct income of labour or, if one wishes, their share in value added. Workers in the work collective then always work for someone other than themselves, be it the state, or other wage-earners, or the population as a whole, of which they certainly form part, but in an abstract and remote fashion (as when they pay taxes). They only really wear two hats – as workers and property-owners – in co-operatives. Consequently, it is the whole set of capitalist relations of production that is set in motion.

In order to increase capital incomes, workers must be compelled to produce by all the means that capitalism has employed: the prolongation and intensification of work; the use of methods directed more towards intensity than productivity (in Marx's sense); performance-related or merit pay; creating internal competition; and so on. Even if the workers elected their own directors, they could only give those directors their mandate to satisfy share-holders, who never coincide with them. Otherwise, they would run the risk of seeing the share-holders withdraw their capital and put their enterprise in danger. They would thus become heteronomous workers, not having the choice, for example, of foregoing additional pay in order to increase their free time or improve their working conditions.

Naturally, the situation is worse if they do not choose their directors, but have them imposed by the proprietor-state, or by other public firms, or by the managers of 'popular' assets. They find themselves wholly subject to the exigencies of exploitation, counter-balanced only by possible counter-powers (workforce representatives, trade unions, works councils).

In addition, it is clear that the intermediaries between the citizen-owners and the workers are going to profit from the power they possess to appropriate the largest possible share of the surplus-value that has been produced, either in the form of high salaries, even of bloated personnel, for the political authorities and public administrators – without even counting the possible diversion of a percentage of the dividends to the state budget – or in the form of high salaries for the managers of the wage-earners' assets. Here, extortion turns into literal exploitation.

Finally, the whole system remains dominated at the level of representations by what Marx calls the 'capital form' and its double, the 'wage form'. In the eyes of the actors, capital is the vector of value, money naturally and spontaneously makes more money, and wages are nothing more than the price of the factor of labour, a commodity like any other. The whole economy is immersed in the 'enchanted world' of these representations. Here, I pass over the work of legitimation that will inevitably come (in the name of efficiency) to reinforce this spontaneous ideology and obscure what it might still allow to emerge.

This is why, to go to the heart of the matter, these models of 'market' socialism pertain more to a popular capitalism than to socialism. But, in addition, they make far too many allowances for the market. If (as I believe to be the case) certain market mechanisms must be allowed to operate for a long time, and possibly forever, it is also necessary to reduce their field of operation and counter their negative effects by contrary mechanisms.

I am not going to examine these models, from which there are certainly ideas to be drawn, any further. I shall therefore simply say that, constructed in accordance with the same criteria and the same instruments of efficiency as those of the capitalist system, they run the risk of not matching it, for a benefit that remains decidedly limited (a little more distributive equality), but not more democracy or community of enterprise. As regards hard budgetary constraints, nothing will replace the ferocious competition that private capitals in pursuit of the highest gains can engage in.

In addition, these models leave the problems of motivating workers in the performance of their tasks and mobilising collective knowledge virtually untouched.

Self-management models

Socialisms of the self-management variety represent a much more profound break with the capitalist system, for two basic reasons: they no longer aim at capital profitability, but at maximising labour incomes (or per capita income); and they are based on industrial democracy.

The objection often directed against self-management is that it leads workers to look after their 'own interests' in the first instance. This cannot be denied, but we need to look at all its positive aspects, which seem to me undeniable. A collective of workers must 'see the point of its acts' and, in particular, know if it is performing socially useful work (which is not a particularly selfish, material motivation). Very often, people only see the negative side of market sanctions, which (it is true) are very useful (they penalise wasted effort, poorly directed effort, bad management, etc.). But market sanctions also rewards work that is well done, inventive, well-organised, carried out at the lowest cost for the consumer (whether a firm or private individual). Now, self-management is the only system in a position to make workers fully responsible in this respect. In the second place, it is good that workers should also receive material compensation for their work, for they would find it completely unjust if they did not (we remember, for example, the complaints of Soviet workers on this score). Certainly, there are all sorts of other reasons for the success of an enterprise apart from the effort of its members. But it is impossible to see how material incentives could be wholly dispensed with.

Self-management models offer a solution to some of the problems encountered by models of state socialism. To the extent that enterprises are autonomous from the state, they are no longer subject to its multiple interference, which disrupts economic calculation and distorts the competitive mechanism. And, as the directors are elected, they find themselves under the supervision of workers, which *a priori* resolves the problem of the principal/agent, although in practice thing are much more complicated (all concrete experience indicates that democracy can remain largely formal). The involvement of workers also encourages the mobilisation of knowledge. On the other hand, the problem of capital allocation once again raises major difficulties, which the model seek to resolve in various ways.

These difficulties are highlighted by co-operatives and suggest going beyond a socialism based (to be brief) on a co-operative system combined with central planning – the direction in which Marx set out. Co-operatives represent a decentralised mode of allocating capital. But historical experience shows that they are bad at resolving the problem of their financing. They cannot call upon external capital, because they would have to share control over management with it, which would be contrary to the self-management principle. Not being able to apply to financial markets, they must resort either to self-financing or credit. Now, self-financing presents a certain number of drawbacks, because workers are hesitant to invest in their own enterprise, not so much as a result of a lack of foresight that leads them to privilege their immediate income, as because their contributions in capital are necessary unequal (they do not stay in the enterprise for the same amount of time), badly remunerated (on account of the existence of reserves that cannot be shared out), and risky. This often entails a tendency to under-investment, confirmed by empirical studies, which might go further in explaining the stagnation of the sector than the existence of an unfavourable capitalist environment. As for credit, it is difficult to obtain, in particular because of limited funds and their non-liquid character.

Self-management socialisms are also threatened by other sources of inefficiency, such as a tendency to guarantee job stability more than job mobility (reluctance to hire, since it is necessary to expand the distribution of income, and reluctance to fire, when it is necessary to part company with associates); or slow decision-making. But it is easy to show that these drawbacks have their compensations and it must be reiterated that self-management ('working for oneself', sharing in decisions) brings with it powerful motivations that are well-nigh absent from capitalism and other forms of socialism. The problem of financing and capital allocation remains its Achilles heel.

Finally, self-management socialism, while it encourages equality and community within the enterprise, can generate significant inequalities on account of the difference in results between enterprises. These are not necessarily bound up with the labour performed or the effort at internal savings, and in the absence of a centralised form of profit distribution can only be corrected by regulating the labour market and by traditional forms of redistribution.

The different models are so many attempts to face up to these problems – primarily that of financing. We may roughly distinguish between two types of model: those that resort to a market in property titles and those that only resort to a credit market.

Thus, in the first category, Sertel proposes to introduce a market in partnership rights.[17] For his part, Estrin imagines an economy in which co-operatives would rent capital to competitive holding societies, whose shares would be

[17] See Sertel 1982.

held by the government and by the self-managed firms themselves, and which would take responsibility for innovation, research and development, and exploring the market.[18] Here we shall dwell on Weisskopf's model, because it seeks to respond in the broadest fashion to the problems raised.[19]

In order to resolve the key issue of the financing of assets, Weisskopf has proposed to combine several sources: credits (loans from banks that are themselves self-managed or from other intermediaries); share issues to mutual insurance funds or foreign investors (who, as in capitalism, would expect dividends and capital gains when they are transferred), but without these shares conferring any right to vote; and, finally, investment from workers themselves, in the form of shares, but likewise without the right to vote and only transferable to other members of the enterprise when people leave it. The mutual funds would collect 'coupons', allocated to each citizen and only exchangeable for different coupons – an idea adopted from Roemer. They would be self-managed and competitive.

As can be seen, this model ingeniously combines two capital markets – even three when we count foreign share-holders, no doubt introduced in order to facilitate the economy's openness to the outside world – which are highly restrictive and cut off from one another, with the self-management principle, whereby only labour possesses voting rights. It thus seems to combine all the advantages. The external share-holders have a power of sanction over the management of enterprises and, more widely, over the work collectives. But this power is indirect (sale or purchase of titles depending on firms' results); and the system of coupons prevents the concentration of wealth in a few hands. In the enterprise, the function of worker and the function of share-holder are distinct and the second cannot encroach on the first. In addition, the existence of worker-share-holders prevents hostile takeover bids. The differences with capitalism are striking and Weisskopf can affirm that the main problems of market socialism have been overcome (the problem of supervising managers is resolved by the activity of workers and the operation of the market in coupons; that of financing by multiplying the sources of capital, which also makes it possible to ward off the risk of under-investment; the

[18] See Estrin 1989.
[19] See Weisskopf 1993.

problem of capital allocation between enterprises by decentralisation, etc.), while all its advantages are exploited (worker motivation, relations of trust between workers and directors, etc.).

However, it is not clear that this combination of a socialism of the 'public' and partners – for assigning rights over capital income – with a socialism of self-management – for determining rights of control – does not operate to the detriment of the latter. For the logic of share-ownership, even when that of 'citizens' and partners, remains financial profitability; and it necessarily comes into contradiction with the logic of the workers, centred on maximising labour income. Certainly, the mutual funds cannot exercise control over firms with the same stringency as in capitalism (cf. the rules of 'corporate governance'). But their power remains considerable and operates in the direction of profit maximisation. As for the self-management of these funds, it does not make much difference: the owners of shares will have no more power than, for example, in a pension fund and the staff in these funds will naturally seek to maximise their financial yield. The very principle of share-holding, unlike credit or even bonds, is that the financial return of capital is *variable* and, in a competitive situation, it is inevitably the highest returns that will attract investors. The model cannot therefore genuinely overcome the contradiction between a kind of popular capitalism, whose power is simply limited, and a socialism whose goal is to valorise labour. However, it must be acknowledged that such a model possesses a certain advantage: it ensures more equality in the distribution of profits than purely self-managerial models, if they are not complemented by devices for reducing inequalities.

A second category of model rests, at the level of financing, on some form of credit market. The divergence from preceding models is not insignificant. In fact, there are no investors here (whether external or even internal) seeking to maximise the return on their capital. The supplier of capital certainly claims an interest for the credit extended, but the amount of interest is fixed during the transaction and the provider can exercise no control other than agreeing and renewing the credit or not. In addition, he does not himself seek to realise a capitalist profit. Thus, the spirit of these models can be summarised as follows: labour rents capital and is subject to no other constraint than reimbursing the capital and/or paying interest on it. Moreover, it maximises its own income.

The model advanced by Schweickart is of this kind.[20] Enterprises are endowed with a social capital, whose value they are obliged to maintain. They pay a tax on this capital – the equivalent of an interest payment – to a national investment fund, which serves to finance enterprises and public services at a national level and to create a fund for the regions (on a per capita basis), which will do the same at their level. These various investment funds finance new investments (during enterprise creation) and the net investment of enterprises already created via banks, which are like second-degree co-operatives (directed by representatives of their workforces, of the funds, and of the client enterprises). In the last instance, it is these banks that allocate capital to enterprises, in accordance not only with a criterion of profitability, but also with social criteria, such as job creation. However, the banks are not themselves guided by the criterion of profitability: they are public institutions, financed out of taxes, whose members are civil servants, interested only in the benefits.

Remarkable for the simplicity of its operating principle, this model nevertheless meets with various objections. We shall mention two. In so far as the financing depends on bodies of an administrative type, allocation by banks runs a high risk of being distorted by collusion between the management of firms and bank personnel and by pressure on the political authorities (as was noted in Yugoslavia). In the second place, the planning of investment runs into the following dilemma: raising taxes on capital to increase the investment fund discourages enterprises from investing (since economic profitability is more difficult to achieve with a higher tax on capital); reducing them does indeed encourage investment, but dries up the source of enterprises' financing.

A second model has been proposed by Marc Fleurbaey.[21] Here, the suppliers of capital are households. But they do not do it directly. They make deposits and loans with banks (which excludes the possession of shares and bonds), which themselves open up credit lines to enterprises. The novelty of this model is that, on the basis of all the arguments put forward by Vanek in favour of

[20] See Schweickart 1992 and 1993.
[21] See Fleurbaey 1993.

external financing in order to remedy the defects of the co-operative system,[22] it abolishes self-financing: enterprises no longer have their own funds and finance themselves exclusively out of credit. As for the banks, they are self-managed, operating like other enterprises (maximising labour income). The relationship between enterprises and banks must also be much closer. Since they take more risks, in that they have no guarantees in the shape of capital within enterprises, they must exercise much stronger 'supervision'. The relationship between banks and households takes the form of a market in loan capital. This market must adjust spontaneously, by the operation of different interest rates, household savings and the financing requirements of enterprises. Fleurbaey's model also comprises indirect planning, like all the other models, and original procedures for reducing inequalities: not an inheritance tax, but a restriction on the size of legacies to children and, as regards wages, a mechanism of mandatory insurance included in the contracts signed with banks.

I have proposed a model that is likewise based on financing enterprises exclusively through credit, by way of competing, self-managed banks, but placed under the control of a central fund. There are various forms of the model, but here is one.[23] Household savings are likewise put to use in the form of savings coupons (alongside the interest payments paid by enterprises and a stabilisation fund derived from taxes). But they only pass in transit through banks to supply a national financing fund, which allocates sums of credit to banks depending on the quality of their management (management whose yardstick is always the maximisation of labour incomes). On the other hand, interest rates are administered (as today with popular savings accounts in France), whereas credit rates are free. This form therefore rests on a public bedrock: all loan capital is ultimately centralised and allocated by the fund. Moreover, the model comprises supervision of the labour market, so as to limit inequalities in the remuneration of work, and public information networks – a proposal adopted from Diane Elson[24] – in order to reduce market opacity. Finally, planning is indirect (essentially using differential interest rates and

[22] See Vanek 1977.
[23] See Andréani 1993, 2004b, and 2005.
[24] See Elson 1988.

taxation), but omnipresent. Coupled with an economic policy that is all the more efficient in as much as the economy functions entirely by credit, planning allows for some control over spontaneous trends and for more coherent, harmonious and sustainable development. It is also the privileged site of democratic decisions – the site where the major social choices about working time, the balance between consumption and investment, income bands, priority programmes, and so on, are made and implemented.

This survey of the various models of socialism could convey an impression of 'laboratory' research that is far removed from the real movement of history; and remote, indeed, from the ideas circulating in the social movements and debated in political parties. They inspire many reservations, attributable not only to the fact that they break with traditional ideas about socialism, but also to the fact that they are the work of intellectuals prone to 'constructivism' and oblivious of the complexity of the real world. In contrast, I think that they are of the greatest interest, because they outline possible alternatives, without which any critique of the existing system is condemned to archaism, utopianism, or impotence. It remains the case that, in the current situation, they often skip over the problem of historical feasibility, of the social forces capable of embodying them, and of the possible forms of transition, especially in an open economy. A major opportunity was missed during the crisis of the historical socialist systems, for reasons that it would take too long to explain here, but which do not only stem from the feeble imagination of theoreticians or the sabotage organised by the masters of a triumphant capitalism. And the predictable crisis of the new capitalism dominated by finance, which is forecast even by numerous analysts who in no way identify with socialism, will not necessarily afford a new historical opportunity. So it seems to me to be indispensable that work on the models of socialism should result in concrete proposals, capable of being realised in the impending conjuncture.

It is obviously possible to conceive the lessons that might be derived from such modelling in the case of countries where the public sector remains predominant (at least in industry and services), such as China or Vietnam. But it also contains suggestions, which are different, for overhauling the public sector in Western countries (wherever it still retains some significance), at the level of both management autonomy and its democratisation and guiding principles, on the one hand in public services (where profitability, even when it has some meaning, should never be financial profitability), and on the other in public enterprises in what is called the 'competitive sector' (where financial profitability, if it is to be imposed for various reasons, should be tempered). One might thus explore the idea of a 'third sector' of a self-managed variety. But all that would exceed the bounds of this contribution.

Chapter Fourteen

The American Radicals: A Subversive Current at the Heart of the Empire

Thomas Coutrot

At the end of the 1960s, the influence of critical and/or Marxist currents in social science grew. But even economics, spontaneously allied with the forces of money as it is, was not spared. Within prestigious academic institutions, famous theoreticians challenged the very foundations of the Western bourgeois and imperialist societies. In the United States – worse still, at Harvard – a group of left-wing economists, combining undisputed technical competence and a constant concern for links with social movements, formed itself into an explicitly subversive intellectual current, claiming the title of 'radical'. Since then, the 'American radicals' have achieved the remarkable feat of creating a critical current at the very heart of the citadel of triumphant neoliberalism. The durability and fertility of this current cannot be understood unless we recognise that it is the vector both of a theoretical-scientific project and a political-organisational project. The latter has no doubt altered over time, but remains explicit in the approach of its authors – contrary to orthodox economists, who the deck themselves out in the attire of pure science in order to justify the existing order and proclaim it the best possible world.

A political-organisational project

It was in 1968 – the date is scarcely a coincidence – that the 'American radicals' founded the Union for Radical Political Economics (URPE), an 'interdisciplinary association devoted to the study, development, and application of radical political economic analysis to social problems'. The group asserted that it

> presents a continuing left critique of the capitalist system and all forms of exploitation and oppression while helping to construct a progressive social policy and create socialist alternatives.[1]

The anchorage of the radical current in the social movements and the critique of the capitalist system is not only a historical fact: it is also a wholly deliberate theoretical orientation. As three of the current's distinguished figures explain:

> Our approach...differs fundamentally from that of many American Keynesians and European right social democrats who are inclined to provide advice to progressive governments on reforming their capitalist economies. In contrast to such a 'top-down' approach to social change, we are advocating a strategy that is designed to serve as an *instrument for mobilization* – to promote the formation of a popular coalition upon which any program for progressive change must stand for a serious chance of realization.... In this task a coherent alternative economic program is an indispensable tool. If this kind of organizing begins to take root, we further believe that a unified democratic movement pursuing and advancing an egalitarian and democratic growth strategy would eventually begin to challenge the rules of the capitalist game.[2]

Even if (as we shall see) the political perspectives have changed, we can characterise this type of relationship between intellectuals and social movements as 'organic' in the Gramscian sense of the term. The *Review of Radical Political Economics* continues to publish regular articles on gender issues and discrimination of every variety, on the trade-union movement and the class struggle in the United States and elsewhere, on the political economy of imperialism.

---

[1] This quotation is drawn from the text introducing the URPE, which still features in the issues of the association's quarterly journal, the *Review of Radical Political Economics* (RRPE).

[2] Bowles, Gordon and Weisskopf 1984, pp. 282–3.

Every August, the URPE holds a four-day summer university, which members attend with their families, engaging in intellectual and sporting activities. Every January, during the annual meeting of the Association of Applied Social Science, URPE holds a symposium comprising thirty debates, each of which involves between one and two hundred participants. In short, the radicals form an intellectual and political current in a class of its own, which keeps the flame of critical, alternative thought alight in the belly of the beast.

And a theoretical project

According to Rebitzer, '[t]hree fundamental ideas distinguish radical political economy from other approaches in modern economics': i) '[k]ey economic processes are fundamentally' political 'in the sense that they depend, even at the most abstract level of analysis, on institutional arrangements that enforce the power and authority of a dominant group vis-à-vis a subordinate group'; ii) '[t]he institutional arrangements that enforce the authority of dominant groups are less efficient (and/or less just) than some feasible alternative arrangement'; iii) '[e]xisting economic structures are the contingent result of particular historical developments and threfore have no a priori claim to optimality or efficiency'[3] – the role of politics in the economy, the desirable nature of institutional change, and the historically contingent character of economic structures, these three propositions define a research paradigm that is utterly distinct from the dominant paradigm in economics.

Nevertheless, the clear, self-proclaimed Marxist inspiration behind the radical approach does not prevent it distinguishing itself from the orthodox-Marxist tradition, in particular by 'the formal theoretical structure of Marxist political economy…mainly to the analytics of the labor theory of value and the falling rate of profit'.[4] One of the radicals' main sources of inspiration is the heterodox-Marxist current of Baran, Sweezy and *Monthly Review* – particularly Harry Braverman's work *Labor and Monopoly Capital* (1974), which describes and theorises capitalism's constant tendency to 'deskill' work and expropriate workers' knowledge. Since the 1940s, *Monthly Review* has preserved a living tradition of independent Marxist analysis in the USA, which

3 Rebitzer 1993, p. 1395.
4 Reich 1993, p. 44.

the radicals have drawn on abundantly. Here, we shall only mention three of the main fields of their theoretical intervention, which might be said to represent the current's theoretical identity card: the segmentation of the labour market; the social structures of accumulation; and economic democracy.

The segmentation of the labour market: a fertile paradigm

The first major contribution of the radical North-American current was the revelation and theorisation of 'labour-market segmentation'. Following in the tradition of black and feminist movements fighting discrimination, the radical economists sought to explain how, contrary to the predictions of mainstream economics, 'non-compensatory' differences (those unexplained by disparities in productivity, working conditions, and the like) could be maintained in the long term, rather than being spontaneously absorbed by the laws of the market. Thus, neoclassical economists (like Gary Becker) can only explain why entire categories of worker simultaneously endure hard work, job instability, and low wages, whereas others (generally white and male) enjoy stable, protected, and well-paid employment, by resorting to the pretty grotesque artifice of 'employers' taste for discrimination'. The founding text of the theory of segmentation is Doeringer and Piore's *Internal Labor Markets and Manpower Analysis* (1970), which attempted to explain the existence of 'internal markets' – protected spaces within major firms where wage-earners benefited from automatic careers and regular wage increases. However, Doeringer and Piore retained their links with mainstream economics. For an explanation, they looked to the 'specificity' of labour processes, which dictated a long apprenticeship on the job for workers to be efficient. Accordingly, it was in the interest of the rational entrepreneur to secure this costly manpower by establishing wage and career rules that were more generous than those of the external labour market.

It was three of Doeringer and Piore's students at MIT – Richard Edwards, David Gordon and Michael Reich – who really launched the radical theory of segmentation, in an article published in 1975 by the prestigious and highly academic *American Economic Review*. Combining their respective work on racial discrimination, hierarchical control of work in the firm, and the dual labour market, they defined labour market segmentation as 'the historical process whereby political-economic forces encourage the division of the labor market into separate submarkets, or segments, distinguished by different labor market characteristics and behavioral rules'.[5] The 'dualism' theorised by Doeringer and Piore became the more complex 'segmentation' in Edwards and the rest, comprising at least three segments: a 'primary' segment, comprising stable, well-paid jobs, which was itself divided into a 'primary independent' segment containing highly skilled and/or supervisory jobs with good career prospects, and a 'primary subordinate' segment composed of low-skilled, repetitive jobs; and a 'secondary' segment of insecure, badly paid jobs. The intellectual success of this analysis was such that it rapidly came to represent a 'challenge to orthodox theory',[6] which a number of neoclassical economists were to work on in subsequent years.

Edwards's group showed how this segmentation was inextricably economic and political in character. It accompanied and facilitated the differentiation of the economy into a monopoly sector, comprising large firms in a dominant position, and a competitive sector of small and medium-sized enterprises that were dominated and weak. It derived from capitalist political strategies of 'divide and rule', which cultivated and exacerbated ethnic and gender divisions between categories of wage-earner in order to prevent their constitution as a collective agent capable of challenging the dominant order. This socio-economic-historical analysis culminated in what doubtless today remains the major work of the North American radical school: Edwards, Gordon and Reich's *Segmented Work, Divided Workers* (1982). In this work, basing themselves on an in-depth historical analysis, the group indicated the succession of three modes of operation and organisation of the labour market in the US: initial 'proletarianisation' (1820–80); the 'homogenisation' of work (1880–1920); and the 'segmentation' of work (1920–75). The book concluded with a more ambitious theoretical construction than simply analysis of the labour market, since it proposed a view of 'long swings' of capitalist growth and a conceptualisation in terms of 'social structures of accumulation'.

---

5 Edwards, Gordon and Reich 1975, p. 359.
6 See Cain 1976.

The social structures of accumulation: what about the present?

For Edwards and the others, ample empirical proof – in the tradition of Kondratiev and relayed to Marxist economists by Mandel – demonstrated the existence of 'long waves' in capitalist development lasting several decades. An expansionary phase, during which conjunctural recessions are brief and not deep and booms durable, is succeeded by a phase of very slow growth, with the converse characteristics. However, unlike authors such as Kondratiev and Schumpeter, who assigned technical factors the main role in explaining the development and decline of a long wave, Edwards's group explain these long-term trends by the development and decline of a set of institutions that organise and channel class conflict in firms and on the labour market, but also the competition between capitals, the monetary sphere, and so on. Following Edwards's works, the co-authors based their analysis on the modes of managing labour-power in the enterprise. For them, the capital-labour relationship is the basic social relation and plays a key role in the overall dynamic of capitalism. But they expand the field of their analysis to take account of the international division of labour, the organisation of the monetary and financial system, and North-American domination of the rest of the world (and particularly of countries producing raw materials) – the 'Pax Americana'. They also included in the 'social structures of accumulation' the institutions of social security and the counter-cyclical public policies implemented under the influence of the post-war 'Keynesian consensus'. These policies and institutions ensured citizens a certain protection from the pure logic of capitalist profit (what they call the 'capital-citizens agreement'). The erosion of the 'corporate system'[7] derives at once from the decline of the USA's international domination and the collapse of the 'capital-labour pact' as a result of the slowdown in productivity gains, which were themselves caused by social resistance to Taylorism and increasing assignment of the social and ecological costs of the drive for profit to large firms.

According to the American radicals, anti-imperialist, social, ecological and consumer struggles play a central role in explaining the activation of the 1970s crisis. The affinity with the French regulation school is clear, but the American radicals pay greater attention to the concrete forms of the organisation and

---

[7] See Bowles, Gordon and Weisskopf 1984, Chapter 4.

control of work, to the heterogeneity and segmentation of the labour market, to employer strategies for dividing the working class, and to social and political struggles. In short, their approach is more directly historicist and clearly 'engaged'. Nevertheless, like the French regulationists, the radicals considerably underestimated the coherence and effectiveness of the Reagan counter-revolution. It took them a long time to understand that neoliberalism could generate new social structures of capitalist accumulation, which were certainly less homogenising and less egalitarian than those of the postwar period, but nevertheless capable of restoring the profitability of investments on an enduring basis. In the 1980s they consistently denounced Reaganite policies for their ineffectiveness – doubtless not the main criticism that might be directed at them. Thus, according to Bowles, Gordon and Weisskopf, monetarism would not restore the high, stable profits so essential to long-term capitalist growth, at least for years to come'.[8] And, in 1990, they were still claiming that the programme for restoring 'business' domination would not result in a viable social structure of accumulation.[9] Right up until his sudden death in 1996, Gordon basically maintained this analysis.[10]

Only David Houston, in an article of 1992, diagnosed the emergence of a new social structure of accumulation, resting on the following pillars: (1) an 'agreement' between capital and labour that had switched from 'negotiation' to 'domination', with anti-union attacks and a considerable reduction in wage costs, accompanied, for certain wage-earners, by greater autonomy at work and a stake in the capital of firms; (2) an 'agreement' between capital and citizens based on anti-statist and populist propaganda, chauvinism, and the extolling of profit at any price; (3) a restructuring of capital by the closure and relocation of most traditional industries, a switch of accumulation to services, particularly financial ones, and through the privatisation of public services (education, police, prisons); (4) a defence of the threatened hegemony of the USA by means of the World Bank, the IMF, and its exclusive position as sole super-power, in order to impose its law on recalcitrant rivals. Houston concluded his short article with this warning: 'we should not forget

[8] Bowles, Gordon and Weisskopf 1984, p. 206.
[9] See Bowles, Gordon and Weisskopf 1990.
[10] See Gordon 1996 and Bowles and Weisskopf 1999.

or underestimate the formidable strength of this SSA', even if the latter was 'fraught with contradictions'.[11]

More recently, the radicals have acknowledged the assertion of a new social structure of accumulation, but without really producing a detailed analysis of it.[12] It is striking that no article published in the *Review of Radical Political Economics* offers an analysis of the emergence of institutional investors (pension funds and mutual insurance funds), or of their role in what we now call in France the financial or neoliberal régime of accumulation. Reich certainly cites the works of Ghilarducci, Hawley and Williams, or of Lazonick and O'Sullivan on the impact of 'corporate governance' on wage-earners, but without dwelling on it. The main works of the radical economists seem in fact to have shifted both the axis of their alternative proposals and the way in which they argue for them. The works of the 1980s denounced Reaganism for its brutality and injustice and called for the formulation of radical social-democratic policies, advocating not only neo-Keynesian public regulation, but above all a revival of accumulation based on an increase in wages, productivity, and union power. In the 1990s, registering the retreat of egalitarian and democratic ideals, as well as the collapse of the Berlin Wall, Bowles, Gintis and Weisskopf recast their line of argument. Thus, Weisskopf rallied to the theses of the supporters of 'market socialism', rather than the 'social-democratic approach', to achieve socialist objectives.[13] More astonishing still is the evolution of Bowles and Gintis.[14]

Economic democracy: self-management socialism or productivist egalitarianism?

The radical economists, in general supporters of a democratic, self-managerial socialism, were nevertheless barely active in the theoretical debates on the 'pro-market' reforms that have followed one another in Eastern Europe since the 1960s. With collapse of the Wall, a crop of articles appeared in the *Review of Radical Political Economics* (as in other Anglo-American Marxist jour-

---

[11] Houston 1992, p. 67.
[12] See Reich 1997 and Lippit 1997.
[13] See Weisskopf 1992.
[14] See Bowles and Gintis 1998.

nals) on the need to reconstruct a model of viable socialism.[15] In the current North-American context, a certain consensus seems to be emerging among the radicals. Given the hegemony of anti-state ideologies, the social-democratic road (a classical capitalist accumulation moderated by social policies and redistributive taxation) and the path of planning, even of a democratic variety, are unfeasible at the political level. It is therefore necessary to redefine an emancipatory project that totally and unreservedly accepts the role of market, but on the basis of a radical redistribution of ownership rights: self-management market socialism. Thus, in a collective work published in the 'Real Utopias' project co-ordinated by Erik Olin Wright, Bowles and Gintis abandon the term 'socialism' and formulate what they call an 'asset-based egalitarianism', which assumes complete deconcentration of ownership of the means of production and the free operation of initiative and the markets. To conservative supporters of laissez-faire, they object that

> there are compelling economic arguments and ample empirical support for the proposition that there exist changes in the rules of the economic game which foster both greater economic equality and improved economic performance. Indeed...inequality is often an impediment to productivity [and] impedes economic performance

– and this for three reasons. In the first place, 'institutional structures supporting high levels of inequality are often costly to maintain', for 'states in highly unequal societies are often obliged to commit a large fraction of the economy's productive potential to enforcing the rules of the game from which the inequalities flow.

For their part, firms incur

> high levels of expenditure on work supervision and security personnel. Indeed, one might count high levels of unemployment itself as one of the enforcement costs of inequality, to the extent that the threat of job loss contributes to employers' labor discipline strategies: in less conflictual conditions, unutilized labor might be allocated to productive activities.[16]

The second reason for this link between efficiency and equality is that

---

[15] See, for example, Weisskopf 1992 and Schweickart 1992.
[16] Bowles and Gintis 1998, pp. 4–6.

> More equal societies may be capable of supporting levels of cooperation and trust unavailable in more economically divided societies. Yet both cooperation and trust are essential to economic performance, particularly where information relevant to exchanges is incomplete and unequally distributed in the population.

And Bowles and Gintis proceed to quote Kenneth Arrow, the major neoclassical economist, who highlights the 'norms of social behavior, including ethical and moral codes, [which may be] reactions of society to compensate for market failure' (*sic*).[17]

Finally, a third factor in favour of greater equality is that, if workers become the owners of the firm's capital, this will make it possible to enhance their incentives to work, and to reduce supervision and maintenance costs, thus authorising 'general improvements in well-being (including possible compensation for the former owner)'.[18] Faced with such an economistic plea for a democratic market and a wage-earner capitalism, the philosopher Daniel Hausman dryly replies that not only is it pointless trying to convince conservatives of the productivist merits of egalitarianism, 'it is also dangerous, because it obscures the grounds for egalitarianism and thereby undermines the real case for egalitarian policies'. For '[e]quality is of intrinsic moral importance because of its link to fairness, self-respect, equal respect, and fraternity'. To construct an alternative societal project on the ideal of greater productivity is to forget that a good society is 'not about Nintendo games in every home and more trips to the Mall'.[19] The sociologist Olin Wright goes much further: 'certain features of the Bowles and Gintis model may have the unintended effect of themselves systematically eroding community', on account of the decisive role allotted to the operation of free competition: 'Markets may have certain virtues, but... in general they are the enemy of community'.[20] No radically egalitarian reform is politically viable in the end without the endogenous assertion of community norms, vectors of empathy, mutual trust, and the gradual disappearance of market opportunism.

---

17 Bowles and Gintis 1998, p. 6.
18 Bowles and Gintis 1998, pp. 7–8.
19 Hausman 1998, pp. 80, 83, 84.
20 Wright 1998, p. 96.

Conclusion

In his historical retrospect of 1993, Michel Reich highlights the radicals' delay in understanding the Reagan turn: 'many of us assumed that reducing government's role in the economy was contrary to capitalism's true interest and that the apparent turn toward laissez-faire would not last long'.[21] The defeat of North-American 'liberals' (or, Keynesian centrists), widening the gulf between centrists and Reaganite ultra-liberals, considerably reduced the one separating radicals and neo-institutional 'liberals'. Whereas the latter (Stiglitz, Solow, Williamson) were developing analyses that explained market inefficiencies (incomplete information, efficiency wages, transaction costs) and which responded, with neoclassical tools, to the 'challenge' of theories of segmentation, the radicals strove to develop micro-analytical tools and the use of game theory to formalise their reasoning. The American radicals have always been empiricists, carefully testing their analyses against the available historical and statistical data. But, under the pressure of neoclassical academic circles, and conducing to their rapprochement with the centrist 'liberals', they have gradually tended to reconcile their conceptual tools with those of the mainstream.

The political switch and theoretical switch have occurred in tandem. As the radicals came to realise that 'not all capitalist economies were alike',[22] and that social-democratic reforms in Europe had constructed models of capitalism which were more acceptable than the US model, they evolved towards 'a broader acceptance of the role of markets',[23] and increasingly situated themselves in the amended neoclassical paradigm. The actual outcome of this move is the endeavour by Bowles and Gintis to demonstrate the economic superiority of a wage-earner capitalism over patrimonial capitalism, by using only standard theoretical tools. Abandoning their tradition of empirical analysis and original critique of the realities of contemporary capitalism, the main radical authors seems to have taken refuge in an attempt at a 'progressivist' subversion of the standard micro-economic theory as amended by neo-institutionalism. The 'great wall'[24] that separated radicals from 'liberals' in

[21] Reich 1993, p. 46.
[22] Reich 1993, p. 48.
[23] Reich 1993, pp. 48–9.
[24] See Reich 1993.

the 1960s has collapsed with the Berlin Wall – to the extent that it is no longer clear that deep theoretical differences exist between the most distinguished radical authors and neo-institutionalists. Were this development to be confirmed, the main victim of the rapprochement would doubtless be the radical current's capacity for critical and historical analysis, which has today largely run out of steam. However, given its historical anchorage, we may still hope that it will be able to take advantage of the new social movements that are emerging at the beginning of the new century and help to propose new strategic perspectives.

Chapter Fifteen

Political Marxism

Paul Blackledge

Over the last three decades, Robert Brenner and Ellen Meiksins Wood have attempted to develop and defend a revolutionary interpretation of historical materialism which avoids the pitfalls associated with both orthodox historical materialism and post-Marxist idealism. They have done so through a series of brilliant interventions in historical, cultural, political, social and economic theory that are breathtaking in both their sweep and originality. As part of this project they have produced, or have influenced those who have produced, new, exciting and thought-provoking contributions to many fundamentally important historical and political debates. Above all, Brenner's analysis of the transition from feudalism to capitalism has influenced all subsequent intelligent interpretations of that process.[1] Important work has also been carried out into areas as diverse as classical political theory,[2] the emergence of the modern United States,[3] the histories of India, China, and South Africa,[4] the birth of political economy,[5] the

---

[1] Aston and Philpin (eds.) 1985; Brenner, 1985a, 1993, 2001.

[2] Wood, 1988; Wood and Wood, 1978.

[3] Post 1982, 1995, 1997.

[4] Huang 1985 and 1990; Kaiwar 1992 and 1993; Murray and Post 1983; Brenner and Isett 2002.

[5] McNally 1988.

politics of the New Left,[6] the nature of the English Revolution,[7] the rise of bourgeois Europe,[8] the trajectory of the postwar world economy,[9] the nature of the 'new imperialism';[10] and the nature of the Westphalian state system.[11] Commenting on just two of these achievements, Perry Anderson has described the historical element of Brenner's *œuvre* as 'magisterial', while suggesting that through Brenner's analysis of the postwar world economy, 'Marx's enterprise has certainly found its successor'.[12] Whether or not we accept Anderson's appreciation of their importance, Brenner and Wood deserves serious consideration.[13]

Political Marxism

The term 'political Marxism' was coined by the French Marxist Guy Bois, who, in a critical response to Brenner's analysis of the transition from feudalism to capitalism, argued that Brenner's thesis

> amounts to a voluntarist vision of history in which the class struggle is divorced from all other objective contingencies and, in the first place, from such laws of development as may be peculiar to a specific mode of production.[14]

Despite this deprecatory pedigree, Ellen Wood enthusiastically embraced the term political Marxism as a reasonable description of both hers and Brenner's work, but denies that the term implies a voluntarist interpretation of history.[15] Rather, she insists, political Marxism overcomes the weaknesses of previous

---

[6] Wood 1986 and 1995.

[7] Wood 1991; Wood and Wood 1997; Brenner 1993.

[8] Mooers 1991.

[9] Brenner 1998, 2002, 2004.

[10] Wood 2003.

[11] Teschke 2003

[12] Anderson 1992, p. 58 and 1998, p. v.

[13] For some critical commentaries on political Marxism see the essays collected in Aston and Philpin (eds.) 1985, two special issues of *Historical Materialism* 4 and 5, devoted to Brenner's economics, the articles collected in *Comparative Studies of South Asia, Africa and the Middle East* Vol XIX, No. 2, 1999, and Anderson 1993; Barker 1997; Callinicos 1995, pp. 122–37; Dumenil et al. 2001; Fine et al. 1999; Foster 1999; Harman 1998, pp. 55–112; Manning 1994; McNally 1999; and Blackledge 2002/3, upon which this chapter is based.

[14] Bois 1985, p. 115.

[15] Wood 1995, p. 23.

mechanical versions of Marxism by 'simply [taking] seriously the principle that a mode of production is a *social* phenomenon'.[16]

Political Marxism delineates itself from traditional interpretations of Marxism in two fundamental ways. First it rejects the classical-Marxist model of historical change as outlined in Marx's preface to *A Contribution to the Critique of Political Economy*. Secondly, and in place of this model, Brenner and Wood maintain that explanatory primacy in history should be accorded to changes in the relations of production. Political Marxism, Wood suggests, combines an application of Edward Thompson's critique of the crude utilisation of the base/superstructure metaphor, with Brenner's alternative account of capitalist development. It synthesises these two elements so as to re-establish a firmer grounding for a non-teleological account of history.[17]

Wood is keen to reaffirm an anti-teleological reading of Marx, and she offers two reasons for doing so: one scholarly, the other political. The orthodox-Marxist case, which ascribes explanatory primacy in history to the development of the productive forces, assumes, she claims, that a peculiar rationality, characteristic only of the capitalist mode of production, is a constituent element of human nature. Consequentially, in the orthodox model, capitalist rationality is naturalised in a fashion that both acts as an impediment to our cognition of the past, and as an obstacle to our realisation of socialist hopes for the future. Thus, if human history is read as a process leading to the unleashing of capitalist rationality then scholars will fail to grasp the specificity of capitalist rationality, and politicians will fail to grasp the possibility of its transcendence.[18]

Wood also argues that many orthodox Marxists, in applying the base/superstructure metaphor, collapse historical materialism into

> a rigid determinism...in the realm of social structure,...while the real, empirical world remains effectively contingent and irreducibly particular.[19]

Edward Thompson, in *The Making of the English Working Class*, avoids this unpalatable dichotomy, through his insistence that 'we should not assume any automatic, or over-direct, correspondence between the dynamic of economic

---

[16] Wood 1995, p. 25.
[17] Wood 1999a, p. 59.
[18] Wood 1999a, p. 7.
[19] Wood 1995, p. 50.

growth and the dynamic of social or cultural life'.[20] Indeed, with respect to the cultural processes operating in England at the turn of the nineteenth century, he suggests,

> it is the political context as much as the steam engine, which had the most influence upon the shaping consciousness and institutions of the working class.[21]

Elsewhere, Thompson argues that because historical materialism attempts to study the social process as a totality then it must reject reified conceptualisations of the 'economic' and the 'political' etc.[22] Wood suggests that Thompson's theoretical framework requires

> a conception of the 'economic', not as a 'regionally' separate sphere which is somehow 'material' as opposed to 'social', but rather as itself irreducibly social – indeed, a conception of the 'material' as constituted by social relations and practices. Furthermore, the 'base'... is not just 'economic' but also entails, and is embodied in, judicial-political and ideological forms and relations that cannot be relegated to a spatially separate superstructure.[23]

Thus the base/superstructure metaphor will not do as an adequate framework for interpreting history. Instead, particular social formations must be analysed historically as evolving totalities.

So, in answer to Perry Anderson's question regarding the underlying rationality of Thompson's decision, after writing *The Making of the English Working Class*, to focus his research on the eighteenth century rather than looking forward towards the twentieth, Wood answers that Thompson was attempting to 'explain the establishment of capitalism as a social form', a task to which Brenner has so forcefully applied himself. By breaking with a crude application of the base/superstructure metaphor, Wood believes that political Marxism is true to Marx's own anti-teleological approach to historical methodology. She argues that it is Weber's work, not Marx's, that can be characterised by its teleological theory of history, since Weber

---

[20] Thompson 1980, p. 211.
[21] Thompson 1980, p. 216.
[22] Thompson 1978, pp. 70–8.
[23] Wood 1995, p. 61.

> looked at the world through the prism of a unilinear, teleological and Eurocentric conception of history, which Marx had done more than any other Western thinker to dislodge.[24]

Indeed, Weber's concept of the Protestant ethic 'cannot account for the "spirit of capitalism" without already assuming its existence'.[25]

In this sense, Weber's approach is, Wood argues, a variation of the 'commercial model' of capitalist development; according to which capitalism is associated with towns and cities, and the triumph of capitalism is associated with the triumph of the town and city dwellers, the bourgeoisie, over the precapitalist country folk.[26] In contrast to this model, Wood defends Brenner's reading of capitalist development as originating in England as a form of agrarian capitalism: only on the basis of capitalist development in the countryside was it possible that the towns could take on a capitalist, as opposed to a merely bourgeois, character. Thus, for the political Marxists, the key task facing those of us who would desire to develop a clear understanding of the contemporary world does not lie in a search to discover the basis for the unleashing of the creativity of the bourgeoisie under feudalism, but rather lies in explaining the growth of capitalist social relations in the (English) countryside.

From feudalism to capitalism

In a review of Maurice Dobb's analysis of the transition from feudalism to capitalism, Brenner argued that Dobb's thesis 'continues to be a starting point for discussion of European economic development'.[27] Whatever the veracity of this claim, it is certainly true that Brenner's own analysis of the transition was written, in part, as an attempt to overcome some weaknesses in Dobb's argument.[28]

Brenner opened his review of Dobb's *Studies in the Development of Capitalism* by commending Dobb's break with the 'transhistoric' musings of the classical and neoclassical economists. To them, the peculiar ethos of modern capitalism

---

[24] Wood 1995, p. 146.
[25] Wood 1995, p. 164; 1999a, p. 17.
[26] Wood 1999a, p. 13.
[27] Brenner 1978, p. 121.
[28] Wood 1999a, p. 44; Harman 1998, p. 65.

is naturalised as a fundamental attribute of human nature.[29] However, while Dobb insisted that the necessary prerequisites for the transition to capitalism included an increase in the productivity of labour such that the change from serfdom to wage-labour would became economically viable, he did not explain how such a productivity increase could develop systematically within feudalism.[30] Similarly, he argued that the story of the destructive influence of commerce on feudal society 'can largely be identified with the rise of towns', but went on to suggest that 'it would be wrong to regard [towns] as being, at this stage, microcosms of capitalism'.[31] Furthermore, he failed to integrate his analysis of the rise of towns in the medieval world into a model of the internal dynamic of feudalism. He noted several explanations for the rise of towns but did not attempt to integrate these insights into a rounded theory.[32]

Moreover, as Brenner argued, because Dobb both equated feudalism with serfdom whilst simultaneously arguing that serfdom had been superseded from around the fifteenth century, then on his reckoning feudalism should have been 'dead' long before the upheavals of the 1640s. As a consequence of this, the viability of the concept of a bourgeois revolution in the seventeenth century was thrown into question.[33]

In his alternative account of the transition from feudalism to capitalism, Brenner argues that capitalism originated not as a result of a victory of the peasantry over the feudal nobility in the class struggle, and still less the product of a rising bourgeoisie, but as an unintended consequence of the class struggle under feudalism.[34]

This is not to suggest that Brenner ignores the role of towns in the transition. For, on the one hand, he argues that his model of the transition from feudalism to capitalism is premised upon the 'necessary precondition' of the prior development of merchant capitalism in the medieval period,[35] and on the other hand, he placed London's merchant community at the centre of his

[29] Brenner 1978, p. 121; compare to Dobb 1963, pp. 7–8.
[30] Dobb 1963, p. 55.
[31] Dobb 1963, pp. 70–1.
[32] Dobb 1963, pp. 72–5.
[33] Brenner 1978, p. 132.
[34] Brenner 1985a, p. 30.
[35] Brenner 2001, pp. 276 and 289.

analysis of the English Revolution. Nevertheless, Brenner argues that the 'traditional social interpretation' of the transition is untenable,[36] because

> by the era of the Civil War, it is very difficult to specify anything amounting to a class distinction of any sort within the category of large holders of land, since most were of the same class.[37]

In his essay 'Agrarian Class Structure and Economic Development in Pre-Industrial Europe', Brenner argues that

> the breakthrough from 'traditional economy' to relative self-sustaining economic development was predicated upon the emergence of a specific set of class or social-property relations in the countryside – that is, capitalist class relations. This outcome depended, in turn, upon the previous success of a two-sided process of class development and class conflict: on the one hand, the destruction of serfdom; on the other, the short-circuiting of the emerging predominance of small peasant propert.

In France, serfdom was destroyed by the class struggle between peasants and lords, but the process went beyond that needed for the development of capitalism, leading instead to the establishment of widespread small peasant property. In Eastern Europe the peasants were defeated, leading to the reintroduction of serfdom. Only in England did conditions evolve that were optimal for the evolution of agrarian capitalism.[38] Thus capitalist development in England, and as a corollary in Europe and the world, was not a consequence of a victory of the peasantry over the feudal nobility in the class struggle, and still less the product of a rising bourgeoisie. Rather, capitalism evolved as an unintended outcome to the class struggle in the English countryside.

In the debate that followed upon the publication of his paper, Brenner was widely criticised for his deviation from Marxist orthodoxy. However, in defence of his revisionism, Brenner argues, in 'Bourgeois Revolution and the Transition to Capitalism', that Marx's works of the 1840s, particularly *The Communist Manifesto, The German Ideology*, and *The Poverty of Philosophy*, have at their heart a defective model of the transition from feudalism to capitalism that was borrowed from Adam Smith. Brenner suggests that Marxists should

[36] Brenner 1993, p. 638.
[37] Brenner 1993, p. 641.
[38] Brenner 1985a, p. 30.

begin to remodel their account of the transition, not from these early works, but from Marx's later works, particularly *Capital* and *Grundrisse*: for while Adam Smith developed a powerful account of the nature of capitalism, he premised this account upon a highly questionable thesis as to capitalism's origins.[39] In effect, Smith assumed the universality of capitalist rationality, and therefore in his analysis of the transition from feudalism to capitalism Smith looked for fetters to capitalist development within feudalism, rather than to forces that could facilitate the evolution of rational capitalist individuals. Brenner quite rightly argues that this is an unsustainable position given the lack of historical evidence for capitalist behavioural patterns in premodern societies.

Brenner suggests that the model of the transition offered in Marx's earlier writings parallel Smith's approach. One key effect of this methodology is that the young Marx, like Smith, does not in fact develop a theory of societal transformation; his model of the transition

> appears peculiar, for in neither town nor country is anything amounting to a transformation from one type of society to another actually envisaged. As for the urban economy, it is, from its origin, entirely bourgeois.... As to rural development, feudalism...has no positive role.... Finally...the bourgeoisie's rise to power is quasi-automatic.[40]

Brenner argues that

> if England was, in fact, essentially a feudal society...it was necessary to explain why the rise of trade should have led to capitalist development rather than the reproduction of the old feudal order.... On the other hand, if English feudalism was on its way to dissolution...rural society was already well on its way to capitalism, and it was necessary to explain why its landlords were anything but capitalist.[41]

Brenner concludes this exploratory essay with the argument that a social interpretation of the transition was still necessary, but that, and this position

[39] Brenner 1989, p. 272.
[40] Brenner 1989, p. 279.
[41] Brenner 1989, p. 296.

is merely implied, the old Marxist concept of a bourgeois revolution should be rejected.[42]

Thus, Brenner's historical methodology is framed around a polemic against that which he considers to be an ahistoric approach to the issue of the development of capitalist rationality. Conversely, he attempts to uncover an explanation for the development of capitalist relations of production, and hence the evolution of capitalist rationality, rather than assume the universality of this type of behaviour:

> The prevalence of certain quite specific, historically-developed property relations...provides the fundamental condition under which individual economic actors will find it rational and possible to follow patterns of economic action supportive of modern economic growth.[43]

Therefore

> it is only given the prevalence of certain quite specific, historically developed property relations...that the individual economic actors will find it rational and possible to follow the patterns of economic actions supportive of modern economic growth outlined by Adam Smith.[44]

With respect to English history, Brenner argues that the pattern of class struggle up to and after the period of the Black Death, around 1350, created exceptional conditions whereby

> the English lords' inability either to re-enserf the peasants or to move in the direction of absolutism...forced them in the long run to seek what turned out to be novel ways out of their revenue crisis.[45]

This new path led towards agrarian capitalism. In this system, large landowners rented out their land to tenant farmers, and this social relationship underpinned the move towards a self-expanding economy: only in these exceptional conditions could 'Smithian 'normal' development take place'.[46]

In developing his thesis, Brenner outlines a devastating critique of Malthusian explanations of the transition. He does this, not by contradicting the

---

42 Brenner 1989, pp. 303 and 295.
43 Brenner 1986, p. 25.
44 Brenner 1985b, p. 18.
45 Brenner 1985b, p. 48.
46 Brenner 1985b, p. 50.

evidence presented by the Malthusians, but by showing that, in different parts of Europe, similar demographic trends led in differing directions.[47] Moreover, Brenner argues that these consequences of the various class struggles across Europe were independent of the economic growth of towns.[48] It is in this sense that Brenner most clearly distinguishes himself from both Smith and Marx.

In France, Brenner argues, the class struggle culminated in the evolution of small peasant property. Furthermore, French absolutism was closely connected to this type of proprietorship and was a 'class-like phenomenon'.[49] Wood elaborates this point. Absolutism, she argues, represented a 'centralisation upwards of feudal exploitation'.[50] In contrast, the fact that the English state 'was not itself the direct instrument of surplus extraction' set it radically apart from the non-capitalist absolutist states.[51] Moreover, the mercantilist policies of absolutism could foster the growth of towns and yet have no relation to capitalism. As she argues,

> we may be utterly convinced that, say, the French Revolution was thoroughly bourgeois... without coming a flea-hop closer to determining whether it was also capitalist. As long as we accept that there is no necessary identification of bourgeois (or burger or city) with capitalist.[52]

Developing this mode of reasoning, one of Wood's former PhD students, George Comninel, argued, 'it may be better simply to drop the idea of bourgeois revolution'.[53]

As if in response to this *reductio ad absurdum* of his thought, Brenner replied in 1993 with a 700-page monograph, *Merchants and Revolution*, on the English Revolution.[54] Moreover, as the title suggests, he put London's merchant community at the centre of his analysis of the revolution. As I note above, in an 80-page 'postscript' to this book Brenner argues that the 'traditional social interpretation' of the transition was untenable as the available evidence could

[47] Brenner 1985a, p. 34.
[48] Brenner 1985a, p. 38.
[49] Brenner 1985a, p. 55.
[50] Wood 1988, p. 23.
[51] Ibid.
[52] Wood 1999a, p. 56.
[53] Comninel 1987, p. 205.
[54] The main body of Brenner's monograph was based upon his PhD research of the 1960s.

not sustain the idea of a rising bourgeoisie confronting a feudal aristocracy.[55] However, he was convinced that the revisionist challenge to the old social interpretation was even less compelling, for the revisionists had reduced the Civil War to a conflict over particular individual and group interests within a general ideological consensus. Against this position, Brenner pointed out that 'analogous political conflicts over essentially similar constitutional and religious issues broke out on a whole series of occasions in the pre-Civil War period'.[56] Thus Brenner maintains that a social account of the Civil War is indispensable, while insisting that the traditional Marxist account of the revolution is indefensible. Brenner suggests that, while the landowners as a whole had been transformed into a capitalist class in the previous centuries, the monarchy maintained its position at the head of the state via a medieval legacy: monarchs, he argued, 'were no mere executives, but were great patrimonial lords'.[57] Moreover, 'the king was largely politically isolated from the landed class as a whole until the autumn of 1641'.[58] Therefore, the fundamental conflict at the heart of the English revolution was between this 'patrimonial group', who derived their wealth from politically constituted property rights, and the rest of the landowning class.

At the heart of this divide was a conflict over the nature and role of the state. Because the landlords had moved towards the production of a social surplus through capitalist exploitation they no longer required extra-economic forms of surplus extraction. Rather, they required a state with a minimal, but national role to protect absolute private property.[59] The aristocracy was therefore more than happy to see the centralisation of state power in the hands of the monarchy, while the monarchy was happy to begin the movement towards absolutism, based upon politically constituted property.[60] These differing bases for the evolving consensus on the direction of the development of state power could only act along the same vector up to a point: specifically the

[55] Brenner plays something of a slight of hand here by creating a straw man from what he labels as an 'amalgamation' of ideas taken from the work of Hill, Tawney and Stone. Unfortunately, while he acknowledges that neither Hill nor Stone would adhere to this model today, he does not attempt to address their mature theses. Brenner 1993, p. 638.

[56] Brenner 1993, p. 648.

[57] Brenner 1993, p. 653.

[58] Brenner 1993, p. 643.

[59] Brenner 1993, p. 652.

[60] Brenner 1993, p. 653.

> monarchs tended to undertake specific wars – and pursue particular foreign policies – of which the parliamentary classes could not approve.[61]

Brenner argues that

> whereas capitalism and landlordism developed more or less symbiotically, capitalist development helped precipitate the emergence of a new form of state, to which the relationship of capitalist landlords and of the patrimonial monarchy were essentially ambiguous and ambivalent and ultimately the source of immanent fundamental conflict.[62]

In effect Brenner's narrative of the Revolution is the story of how a certain group of 'new merchants' came into conflict with the monarchy to the point of igniting open conflict. Traditionally, Brenner argues, England's merchants shared 'a profound dependence on the Crown-sanctioned commercial corporations that provided the foundation for their protected trade'.[63] Despite the arbitrary taxes imposed on this group by the Crown in the 1620s, this relationship ensured that these merchants played a conservative role in the Revolution.[64] However, from the early seventeenth century a new group of merchants arose that had a much more contradictory relationship with the Crown. These 'new merchants' were not 'mere merchants', as were their traditional counterparts, but were also actively involved in the process of production itself.[65] They were so involved because as poorer types, relative to the mere merchants, they could not enter into the enclosed world of the chartered merchant associations. This new group in effect could only thrive where the traditional merchants had failed, for it was here that markets were open. As members of London's burgeoning capitalist community they had the experience to apply themselves practically to the production process in situations where the traditional merchants, who were merely interested in buying cheap and selling dear, could not exploit existing producers.[66] This new merchant group did not benefit from the élite merchants' relationship with the Crown. Moreover, the 'new merchants' not only did not share in any of the protec-

[61] Brenner 1993, p. 648.
[62] Brenner 1993, p. 651.
[63] Brenner 1993, p. 83.
[64] Brenner 1993, pp. 225 and 91.
[65] Brenner 1993, p. 160.
[66] Brenner 1993, pp. 160 and 54.

tionist benefits of the traditional merchant groups, but they did feel all of the burdens of arbitrary taxation. It was in response to the arbitrary actions of the Crown that, in the period 1640–2, this group took up leading positions within the Revolutionary ferment.[67]

Contemporary politics

The problem of the transition from feudalism to capitalism was not simply of an academic interest to Brenner. He operates within a heterodox variant of the Trotskyist tradition, and is an editor of the radical journal, *Against the Current*. As such he is directly involved within the socialist movement at a political level.[68] Furthermore, his historical work contains a direct political message which is perhaps most apparent in his paper, 'The Origins of Capitalist Development: A Critique of Neo-Smithian Marxism'. In this essay, Brenner deployed his model of the origins of capitalism to advance a critique of the displacement of class struggle from the analyses of capitalist development and underdevelopment associated with Frank, Wallerstein and Sweezy.[69] Concluding his evaluation of their histories of capitalism with a critique of their political conclusions, he argues that their analyses led to 'Third-Worldist' conclusions, which in turn led to an underestimation of the potential for socialist transformation in the West.

> This perspective must also minimize the extent to which capitalism's post-war success in developing the productive forces specific to the metropolis provided the material basis for... the decline of radical working-class movements and consciousness in the post-war period. It must consequently minimize the potentialities opened up by the current economic impasse of capitalism for working-class political action in the advanced industrial countries.[70]

In emphasising the class relations at the heart of capitalism, Brenner restates the classical-Marxist case for proletarian revolution in the West. Indeed in his internationalist attack on the aims of the USA in the first Gulf War he

67 Brenner 1993, p. 317.
68 Brenner 1985c; 1991c.
69 Brenner 1977, p. 27.
70 Brenner 1977, p. 92; Brenner 1991c, p. 137.

concluded with the classical-Marxist call for the American Left to 'rid itself once and for all of its lingering elitism – the belief that ordinary people are incapable of discovering and acting in their own interests'.[71] And, as any Marxist theory of revolution must be rooted within an analysis of the economic laws of motion of capitalism, of fundamental importance to his Marxism was the desire to understand the nature of postwar capitalism.

In a series of extended essays, he sought to develop a theory of the postwar boom and crisis. In the first of these essays, 'The Regulation Approach: Theory and History', written with Mark Glick, he took issue with the French regulation school's approach to the cognition of the world economy. Brenner and Glick criticise both the methodology of the regulationists, and their reformist political conclusions. Methodologically, Brenner and Glick argue that because the regulationists' starting point is the national economy, they are unable to explain the 'simultaneous and general character of the crisis on an international scale'.[72] Politically, Brenner and Glick argue,

> since the Regulationists find the ultimate source of the current crisis in the crisis of 'informal involvement' of workers' participation...it follows that Lipietz should propose an anti-Taylorian revolution as the way out. This would bring into being a new class compromise.[73]

However, since

> the source of the current crisis is not a problem of productivity growth,... so an improved rate of productivity increase cannot restore aggregate profitability and prosperity.[74]

Moreover,

> in this situation of ongoing economic crisis, for workers to involve themselves in 'team concepts'...will destroy their own ability to defend their conditions.[75]

In the second of his major interventions into economic theory Brenner went beyond a critique of the ideas of others to formulate his own analysis of the

[71] Brenner 1977, p. 137.
[72] Brenner and Glick 1991, p. 102.
[73] Brenner and Glick 1991, p. 115.
[74] Brenner and Glick 1991, p. 116.
[75] Brenner and Glick 1991, p. 119.

world economy. He begins his 1998 essay 'The Economics of Global Turbulence' with a decisive refutation of the dominant supply-side explanation for the onset of economic crisis. However, it is only when he outlines his own theory of the crisis that the contradictions of his thought become apparent. Idiosyncratically, he suggested that an implicit Malthusianism marred Marx's theory of crisis.[76] In its place, he develops what Perry Anderson succinctly terms a theory of crisis born of 'over-competition':

> I offer an alternative approach which takes as its point of departure the unplanned, uncoordinated, and competitive nature of capitalist production.[77]

Thus, Brenner rejects the traditional Marxist account of economic crisis, which locates capital's crisis prone tendencies within the production process itself. In turn, he replaces this account with a model within which capital's problems are understood to lie within the realisation process.

Brenner argues that the specificity of capitalism lies in the way that it systematically encourages the growth of the forces of production. However, 'given capitalism's unplanned, competitive nature, realization problems cannot be assumed away'.[78] Further, if capitalists had a perfect knowledge of their competitors' actions, and could adjust to the developing situation, then 'cost cutting technical change poses no problem'.[79] However, in the real world of capitalism, 'individual capitalist producers can neither control nor predict the market for their goods'.[80] Capitalism is thus characterised not by planning, but by risk taking and a process of what Schumpeter called 'creative destruction'. However, Brenner suggests, 'Schumpeter may...have underestimated the potentially destructive side of creative destruction'.[81]

Unfortunately, in neither 'The Economics of Global Turbulence' nor his more recent *The Boom and the Bubble*, does Brenner move to develop explicit strategic political conclusion from his economic analysis of contemporary capitalism. Rather, his analysis concludes with a strong critique of optimistic analyses of the prospects for the US economy: he casts doubts on the possibilities of a

[76] Brenner 1998, p. 11.
[77] Anderson 1998, p. iv. Brenner 1998, p. 8.
[78] Brenner 1998, p. 24.
[79] Ibid.
[80] Brenner 1998, p. 25.
[81] Brenner 1998, p. 26.

continued US expansion, and suggests that the USA today is in an ominous position, similar to that of Japan in the late 1980s just before its bubble burst, and from which a serious risk of a descent into recession is likely; a development that would, in all likelihood, set off an international recession.[82]

Wood has added some political meat to the bones of Brenner's economic analysis of modern capitalism. Whereas Perry Anderson and Tom Nairn had argued on the pages of *New Left Review* that Britain's economic woes could be overcome if her state could be modernised,[83] Wood countered with the argument that it is precisely the 'pristine' capitalist nature of the British state that best explains its economic decline: 'It is not... the gentility of British capitalism that has hindered its development but, on the contrary, its unbridled rapacity'.[84] Thus, for Wood, the fight, in England at least, is not against any elements of the *ancien régime*, but against capitalism pure and simple.[85]

In her book *The Retreat from Class* she argues that, while capitalism is characterised by the separation of the economic from the political, this separation could be overcome in periods of crisis. Published in 1986, the most obvious contemporary example of political class struggle in the West was the British Miners' Strike of 1984–5. Wood argues that this conflict

> demonstrated how 'merely economic' class struggles, even when their objectives are limited, have a unique capacity to alter the political terrain and to unmask and confront the structures of capitalist power, the state, the law, the police, as no other social force can do.[86]

Thus, Wood defended the socialist project in the aftermath of one of the biggest defeats in British working-class history. Indeed the thesis of her book was a critique of those post-Althusserian socialists who had rejected the working class as the potential agency of socialist transformation. Wood, recalling a phrase from *The German Ideology*, describes these thinkers as the 'New True Socialists (NTS)'.[87] She argues that NTS was characterised by its 'autonomization of ideology and politics from any social basis, and more specifically,

---

[82] Brenner 2002, pp. 276, 278, and 2004, p. 100.
[83] Anderson 1992, p. 47.
[84] Wood 1988, p. 167.
[85] Wood 1988, p. 18.
[86] Wood, 1986, p. 183. On the forces that mediate against the generalisation of economic into political conflicts see Wood 1995, pp. 44–8.
[87] Wood 1986, p. 1.

from any class foundation'. Moreover, she insists that, politically, NTS was characterised by the 'repetition of banal and hoary right-wing social democratic nostrums'.[88] In contrast to these arguments, Wood maintains that the working-class

> can uniquely advance the cause of socialism (though not completely achieve it) even without conceiving socialism as their class objective, by pursuing their material class interests, because these interests are by-nature essentially opposed to capitalist class exploitation and to a class-dominated organization of production.[89]

Wood ends this book with a discussion of the practical implications of her criticisms of NTS. One key programmatic policy that she rejects is dogmatic electoralism: a strategy that is blind to the processes that have over the last century or so robbed democracy of its social content.[90] For, under capitalism, where the economic and the political are separate, the self-limitation of socialist politics to the electoral arena would ensure that socialists would remain excluded from the real locus of decision making. A socialist strategic perspective based upon the struggles of the working class could, in comparison, hope to overcome the dualism between economics and politics.

Wood also rejects the idea of market socialism; for this ideology, she insists, ignores the fact that capitalist social relations are based upon compulsion rather than opportunity.[91] She believes that this criticism is securely underpinned by Brenner's economic analysis of capitalist crises which both undercuts political reformism, and strengthens the case for working-class industrial militancy; if the crisis of capitalism is a direct consequence of the operation of market relations then theorists of a 'third way' have their regulated market exposed as a utopia. Furthermore, if crises are not the consequence of the squeeze of wages upon profits then arguments for the cessation of militant working class struggles, so as to ameliorate crisis tendencies, are also undermined. In contrast to these reformist perspectives, Wood insists that socialists should foster the fights for reform within capitalism and attempt to link them

88 Wood 1986, pp. 2, 7.
89 Wood 1986, p. 189.
90 Wood 1986, p. 198; compare to Wood and Wood 1997, p. 136.
91 Wood 1999a, p. 119.

to a broader, if more difficult, struggle against capitalism.[92] More generally she notes, first, that while socialists should recognise the resilience of working-class reformism, they should be wary of retreating from revolutionary politics before its seeming omnipotence;[93] while, second, she insists that socialism can only be achieved, as Marx pointed out, through the self-emancipation of the working class.[94]

This model of socialism as the self-emancipation of the proletariat informs Brenner's rejection of Stalinism. In 'The Soviet Union and Eastern Europe', he argues that

> the bureaucracy has constituted and reproduced itself as a ruling class by virtue of its ability to take a surplus *directly by force* from the collectivity of the direct producers, the working class.[95]

Thus, he argues, as Stalinism negated the socialist hopes of 1917, its demise should fill socialists with hope rather than despair.

Conclusion

Political Marxism aims to be more than another academic sub-discipline by continuing the classical-Marxist tradition of developing theory that might act as a guide to socialist practice. Whether or not it has succeeded in this aim, and I have argued elsewhere that the jury is still out on this question,[96] it is surely true that it has proved to be of enormous analytical power, informing a series of sophisticated historical and political analyses of the modern world.

---

92 Wood 1999b.
93 Wood 1995, p. 107.
94 Wood 1987, p. 138.
95 Brenner 1991a, p. 27.
96 Blackledge 2002/3.

Chapter Sixteen

From 'Mass Worker' to 'Empire': The Disconcerting Trajectory of Italian *Operaismo*

Maria Turchetto

It is not difficult, in Italy at any rate, to reach linguistic agreement on the term *operaismo*. There is no doubt about the main journals around which this current of thought was formed in the 1960s and 1970s (*Quaderni Rossi, Classe Operaia, Potere Operaio*); or about the authors who are its principal representatives (Raniero Panzieri, Mario Tronti, and Antonio Negri unquestionably hold a privileged position with respect to many other exponents, even when latter have made very important contributions).[1] Today, however, *operaismo* is more than a school: it is above all a readily identifiable 'mentality', an attitude, and a lexicon. At a distance of some forty years (it would be legitimate to date the birth of the movement from the publication of the first issue of *Quaderni Rossi*, in June 1961), a number of basic theses, the use of certain passages from Marx (the well-known fragment on machines in the *Grundrisse*), and some keywords (general intellect, class composition, autonomy) still function as a powerful apparatus of

[1] In this sense, I am in agreement with Damiano Palano's 'Cercare un centro di gravità permanente? Fabbrica, Società, Antagonismo', in *Intermarx* <http/www.intermarx.com/>. The author reconstructs the the history of *operaismo*, of which he offers a good synthesis, as well as an interesting 'reckoning' from within.

recognition. Without a doubt, this is more linguistic than theoretical, and evocative as opposed to genuinely propositional. But it nevertheless serves as a reference for the various branches of what used to be the 'movement' (another keyword) in the 1970s.

In fact, Italian *operaismo* primarily consists today in this impoverished reference, in this collection of words standing in for theory, which confers an *apparent* unity and identity on confused positions that have gradually become hostage to cultural fashions or nostalgia. However, this resistance, this capacity to survive and at least suggest a different line of thinking in these dark times of *la pensée unique*, attest to an original strength that must be taken seriously.

The 1960s: the 'mass worker [*operaio massa*]'

Let us therefore start at the beginning in the 1960s, with the experience of the *Quaderni Rossi* and the group of young theoreticians who ran this journal (Panzieri, Tronti, Alquati).

In the 1960s, the historical organisations of the working class remained loyal to the orthodox idea of the 'progressive development of the productive forces', motor of humanity's march towards communism – a march temporarily checked by 'the anarchy of the market' and deflected by another characteristic of capitalism: the iniquitous distribution of social wealth. This 'productivist' conception, which construes capitalism as private property plus the market, counter-posing to it socialism understood as public property and planning, implies that the capitalist organisation of production is accepted in the main. By seriously challenging the apologetic vision of scientific and technological progress that characterised the Marxist tradition, Panzieri's account introduced some decisive theoretical premises for a radical critique of this position. In 'Plusvalore e pianificazione' (1964), he wrote:

> Faced with the capitalist imbrication of technology and power, the perspective of an alternative (working-class) use of machinery obviously cannot be based on a pure and simple reversal of the relations of production (of property), conceived as an envelope which at a certain level of growth of the productive forces is supposedly destined to fall away, simply because

> it has become too narrow. The relations of production are internal to the forces of production and the latter are 'fashioned' by capital.[2]

From this viewpoint, science, technology, and the organisation of labour are released from the limbo of some rational and neutral 'development of the productive forces' in itself. They emerge, instead, as the fundamental site of the 'despotic' domination of capital.

Panzieri's turn – a veritable 'Copernican revolution' against the Marxism derived from the Third International – led to a reassessment of aspects of Marx's analysis that the Marxist tradition had largely abandoned: not only the passage from the *Grundrisse* on machines mentioned above,[3] but also (especially in this phase) the themes of part four of Volume One of *Capital*, as well as the unpublished chapter on the 'Results of the Immediate Process of Production'. Basic categories used by Marx in his analyses of mechanised industry (the concepts of the formal and real subsumption of labour to capital, the idea of the 'subjective' expropriation of the producers as regards the 'mental powers of production', etc.)[4] were adopted and applied to the study of 'neo-capitalism' and the Fordist factory. The idea took root that the concrete modalities of the distribution of labour within an organisation whose goal is the extraction of surplus-value constituted the real heart of the problem. Hence capitalism was not equivalent to private property plus the market, but was above all a form of organising labour that found consummate expression in the norms of Taylorism and Fordism.

It was not only a question of a 'return to Marx'. The analytical instruments rediscovered in Marx's texts served primarily to interpret the processes underway in Italy – the effects of the accelerated economic development of the postwar period and migration from the South to the metropolises of the North – and to develop new and original interpretative categories. Thus were

---

[2] Panzieri 1994, pp. 54–5.

[3] The fragment was cited for the first time by Panzieri in 'Plusvalore e pianificazione' and was likewise published in the fourth number of *Quaderni Rossi* in 1964. Perhaps it should be observed that Panzieri signals in a note how 'the model of a *direct* transition from capitalism to communism' sketched in the fragment is contradicted by 'numerous passages in *Capital*' (Panzieri 1994, p. 68).

[4] See Panzieri 1994, pp. 47–54.

born the concepts of 'class composition' and 'mass worker', introduced for the first time by Romano Alquati in an article devoted to the Olivetti labour force at Ivrea.[5] The 'mass worker' was the new productive subject of 'neo-capitalism', technically deskilled by comparison with the preceding figure of the 'craft worker'. He was therefore 'subjectively expropriated' and 'really subordinated' to capital and, in addition, socially rootless and politically without traditions. But the 'mass worker' was regarded as the bearer of a very powerful potential for conflict. 'Class composition'[6] was intended to express the bond between the objective *technical* characteristics evinced by labour-power at a given historical moment, as a result of its position within the capitalist organisation of the production process, and its subjective, *political* characteristics. It is precisely the synthesis of these two aspects that determines the class's potential for struggle.

This theoretical account found a specific reference in the factory struggles of the 1960s. This period witnessed the emergence of strong opposition to the official trade-union line, centred on the defence of working-class 'professionalism' – a line that corresponded in the 1950s to an attempt to defend the bargaining power achieved during the struggles of the immediate post-war period. The limits of this defensive struggle, based on an unquestioned identification between 'professionalism' and the 'skills' dictated by the capitalist organisation of labour, emerged precisely when the latter underwent profound alteration as a result of the large-scale introduction of Taylorist methods and the assembly line. In the face of these changes, accompanied by the arrival in the large northern factories of thousands of young southerners recruited as unskilled labourers, the slogan of professionalism turned into an instrument that weakened and divided the working class.

Accordingly, the demystification of the slogan of professionalism, the resumption of the themes of the alienation and deskilling of labour, and the identification of a levelling down of working-class strata implied by these phenomena, possessed an obvious practical import during this phase. The recourse to the *inquiry*, in which the *Quaderni Rossi* group placed much faith,

[5] See Alquati 1962. In attributing paternity of these expressions to Alquati, I rely on what Palano says in 'Cercare un centro di gravità permanente?'.

[6] The concept mimics the Marxist concept of the 'organic composition of capital', understood as a synthesis of 'technical composition' and 'value composition'.

helped to further this line of thought and to marry theoretical elaboration with research on the ground.

This original *operaismo* – roughly speaking, that developed in the first numbers of *Quaderni Rossi* – seems to possess everything required to be a *good theory*: a theory that has great critical value, produces analytical tools, and guides *praxis*.

Factory and society

The wave of working-class struggles that peaked during the 'hot autumn' of 1969 seemed to offer an extraordinary confirmation of the theoretical premises of *operaismo*. The 'mass worker' not only furnished evidence of his *existence*, but also confirmed all the hopes that had been lodged in his *conflictual potential*. Here was a social figure of substance and a politically strong figure, which could serve as a reference-point for the other movements that emerged at the time. The mass worker could form the vanguard of an Italian revolutionary movement.

In truth, divisions had already appeared within *Quaderni Rossi* over the link between factory struggles and the revolutionary project. In July 1963, Tronti, Negri, Alquati and others resigned from the editorial board of *Quaderni Rossi* in order to set up the journal *Classe operaia* the following year. Here is what Panzieri wrote in this connection, with critical reference to Tronti's texts:

> An important aspect of the current situation is the danger of simply taking the 'savage' critique of organisations that is implicit, and often explicit, in workers' behaviour...for the immediate possibility of developing a comprehensive revolutionary strategy, ignoring the problem of the specific content and instruments required to construct such a strategy.[7]

The continuity between workers' struggles and revolution established by Tronti, and challenged by Panzieri, rested on two pillars. The first was the particular theory of the link between factory and society that the former had already set out in the article 'La fabbrica e la società'[8] – a theory that represents

---

[7] Panzieri 1994, pp. xivii–iii.

[8] Originally published in *Quaderni Rossi*, no. 2, 1962, the article was reprinted in Tronti 1971.

the central kernel of his whole argument. The second was the idea that the logic of the factory is progressively extended to the whole society – an idea likewise found, in part at least, in Panzieri, and which was to be variously shared by all subsequent elaborations of *operaismo*.

According to Tronti, the relationship between factory and society was above all one of *opposition*. For him, the real contradiction of capitalism was not that between the 'productive forces' and 'relations of production' theorised by orthodox Marxism, but the contradiction opposing the 'process of production', which unfolds in the factory, to the 'valorisation process', which unfolds in society.[9] In society, labour-power presents itself as *exchange-value*. In this role, the worker is a slave to the market, an atomised, defenceless, passive consumer incapable of developing the least resistance to capitalism. In the factory, by contrast, labour-power is *use-value*. Although purchased by the capitalist, it continues to belong as such to the worker, who thus retains his antagonistic capacity and, when inserted into the mechanism of co-operative production, can develop it in the form of collective action.

Accordingly, it is the factory – and it alone – that generates antagonism. But, if this is the case, a problem is posed comparable to that envisaged by Panzieri in the passage above: the problem of a revolutionary strategy that is more complex than spontaneous factory struggles. Or rather, the problem is resolved automatically. Capitalist development in fact gradually extends the factory to society; and thus the initial opposition between factory and society is itself destined to be resolved by the supremacy of the former over the latter. As Panzieri had already put it, 'the more capitalism develops, the more the organisation of production is extended to the organisation of the whole society'.[10] For his part, Tronti wrote:

> At the highest level of capitalist development, the social relation becomes a *moment* of the relation of production, the whole society becomes an *articulation* of production. In other words, society as a whole lives according to the factory and the factory extends its exclusive domination over society as a whole.[11]

---

[9] In a rather debatable use of Marxian terminology, Tronti construed the 'production process' as the sphere of production and the 'valorisation process' as the sphere of circulation of commodities and money.

[10] Panzieri 1994, p. 68.

[11] Tronti 1971, p. 51.

The similarity of the two formulae in fact conceals significant differences. For Panzieri, the extension of the logic of the factory to society basically consists in an increase in the aspects of economic *planning* characteristic of 'neo-capitalism'. In this respect, Panzieri proves to be rather in tune with orthodox Marxism, which interpreted the historical development of capitalism as a succession of 'stages', wherein the initial stage, corresponding to competitive capitalism, was followed by increasingly 'regulated' forms: first of all, the monopoloy-oligopolistic capitalism of the era when Lenin and Kautsky fashioned a theory of it and then the 'planned capitalism' of the present (a concept that differs not at all from that of 'state monopoly capitalism' as employed by official Marxism). The only criticism of the traditional position, pretty much taken for granted at the time, consisted in denying that a 'final stage' could be identified in this development by stages.[12]

In Tronti's formulation, the idea of a 'gradual transformation of society into a factory', when closely examined, possesses a different meaning. It designates not so much greater recourse to forms of regulation and planning, as the growing subordination to production itself of spheres of social action that are distinct from production. In seemingly similar formulations, the two authors were in reality referring to different *phenomenologies*. In Panzieri, the idea of a 'plan' that extends from factory to society essentially refers to the phenomenon of growing capitalist *concentration* and its effects. In Tronti, by contrast, the idea of the extension of the factory above all refers to the phenomenon of the *expansion of the service sector* in the economy. Against the moderate interpretation of the time, which regarded growth in the employee and service sector as an expansion of middle strata and thus a diminution of the working class, Tronti regarded these processes as 'the reduction of all labour to industrial labour'[13] – and hence the generalisation of the wage-labour relation, the proletarianisation of vast swathes of the population, and the direct subjection of sectors traditionally regarded as unproductive to the imperatives of production.

It was Tronti's interpretation that was going to prevail in the subsequent development of *operaismo*, where it played a crucial role. These premises in fact gave rise to the idea of the 'social worker' – a powerful intuition, but also

12 Panzieri 1994, p. 70n.
13 Tronti 1971, p. 53.

a source of ambiguities and, above all, a means of escaping reality to take refuge in extremism. If the factory encompasses society and extends its logic ubiquitously, and if the whole social process is now integrated into a single organic process of production-reproduction, then all the subordinate members of society form part of a total 'social worker', opposed to a capital that for its part embodies the whole of 'direction'.

The 1970s: the 'social worker'

In the event, it was not Tronti who drew these conclusions. The category of 'social worker' took shape in the 1970s, the dark years of the crisis and political repression, and formed the core of Antonio Negri's theoretical elaboration above all.

Let us first consider the new context. After 1973, the cycle of working-class struggle entered into a descending phase. The spectre of economic recession, rendered obvious by the oil crisis, functioned as a powerful weapon with which to impose a restructuring of production. The new computer and electronic technologies were only just emerging and reference was not yet made to the virtues of the 'Japanese model'. What was on the agenda was a restructuring primarily conceived as a rationalisation and reorganisation of existing productive structures, entailing a very heavy price for the working class in terms of wages and employment. In particular, the system of jobs and skills was redefined, wrong-footing the egalitarianism of the 1960s struggles and giving a new lease of life to the old trade-union line of defending 'professionalism'. This now assumed an openly reactionary significance, since it became the vehicle for imposing a new division within the working class and, above all, for securing labour mobility. The restructuring effected what might be defined as a conscious 'class decomposition': the *technical* dismantling of the former organisation of production was at the same time a *political* dismantling of the working-class strength achieved during the earlier cycle of struggles.

On a more general political level, the historical organisations of the Left remained loyal to the old 'productivist' idea. Thus, the proletariat was one again summoned to raise the banner of 'productivity' cast aside by an increasingly 'parasitic' bourgeoisie. The PCI of the period extended this ideology to complete acceptance of capitalist compromises, to the slogan of a 'producers' alliance' (the working class and 'productive capital' against the parasitic plundering of capitalism), to 'austerity' and the 'line of sacrifices' that weighed so heavily in the major working-class defeat of the 1980s. More serious still was the PCI's complicity in the project of criminalising dissent, which took a decisive step at the end of the 1970s with the special laws enacted following the Moro affair. *Potere Operaio*, and other movements that identified with the positions of *operaismo*, figured among the indicated victims.

In this climate, the *operaista* group divided along two main lines which, from attempts to respond to the crisis, gradually turned into veritable lines of flight: initially, a flight towards other realities, different from the factory; but ultimately, a flight from reality itself, towards ever more utopian and imaginary dimensions.

The first line was the one adopted by Tronti: 'the autonomy of the political'. Faced with the increasing difficulty faced by working-class struggles and their tendency to fade – let us recall that, according to this author, they were the only *possible* ones – Tronti severed the Gordian knot of the factory-society relationship, attributing to the state an unexpected 'autonomy' from society. It was therefore a question of reassessing *political* action as compared with to workers' demands and reconquering the terrain of the state, where the 'workers' party' (itself 'relatively' autonomous of the corresponding class) could ratify the conquests of factory struggles at an institutional level. The line of the 'autonomy of the political' was to be rather short-lived, serving above all to transport a percentage of *operaista* militants and theoreticians onto the tranquil shores of parliamentary politics. The upshot of this fairly massive *trahison des clercs* was to put paid to revolutionary velleities, but also to any theoretical originality.

The route taken by Negri – that of the 'social worker' – seemed more viable, at least at the outset. The emergence of this new category, intended to replace that of 'mass worker', is generally dated back to the 1971 article 'Crisi dello Stato-piano'. But it was certainly in the second half of the 1970s that the idea was clarified. Although the term 'state-plan' evokes Panzieri's 'planned capitalism', Negri's account was in fact much closer to Tronti's. His analyses centred above all on the phenomenon of *tertiarisation*:

> Faced with the imposing alterations brought about – or in the process of being brought about – by restructuring, the body of the working class becomes distended and [is articulated as a body of social class...]. In the past, the proletariat became workers. At present, we are witnessing the

> converse process: the worker is becoming a tertiary worker, a social worker, a proletarian worker, a proletarian.[14]

In addition to the Trontian influence, other sources soon converged in the thematic of the 'social worker'. On the one hand, there was Alquati's research, which used the term to refer to a new, highly educated political subject – and hence very different from the unqualified 'mass worker', fruit of the processes of proletarianisation and massification of intellectual labour.[15] On the other, there were the historical studies conducted by the political sciences collective at Padua University (to which, besides Negri himself, Sergio Bologna, Luciano Ferrari Bravo and Ferrucio Gambino belonged) – sources of a new vision of capitalist development and its 'stages', which was to become one of the axes of *operaista* thinking.

What emerges from these studies is a notion of capitalist development whose motor is not so much the logic of profit as workers' struggles. In this optic, Taylorism and Fordism correspond to capital's need to liberate itself from the 'craft worker', whose professionalism served as a lever for developing a powerful potential for struggle.[16] On the other hand, the 'mass worker' who replaced the 'craft worker' certainly seemed at the outset to be one of the solutions to the problem (the absence of qualifications and the rootlessness, political and social, characteristic of the 'mass worker' prevented him conducting and developing struggle in the organisational forms of the previous cycle of struggles). Subsequently, however, he would prove capable of expressing a distinctive capacity for resistance, attuned to the new organisation of labour, which was more collective and egalitarian, and hence even more dangerous for capital. Thus, the restructuring of the 1970s was interpreted as bound up with capital's need to free itself of the 'mass worker': a change that had succeeded temporarily, given the interruption of factory conflicts, but which in no way precluded hopes that the new organisation of production would give rise to a new antagonistic subject – the 'social worker'. Having theoretically deduced his existence, and abstractly outlined his features, it only remained to await, in messianic fashion, the concrete appearance of the 'social worker'.

---

14 Negri 1976, p. 9.

15 See Alquati 1976.

16 Sergio Bologna, for example, linked the council movement of the immediate post-First World War period, which was especially strong in Germany, with the figure of the craft worker. See Bologna 1972, p. 15.

Negri took the implicit determinism concealed in this inverted sequence of 'stages', where it is the working class that pressures capitalism into the development of technology, to its extreme conclusion. He adds to it a *final* stage: the one prophesied in the celebrated fragment on machines (since Negri, the citation has become ritual). With enormous technological and scientific development,

> [t]he *theft of alien labour time, on which the present wealth is based,* appears a miserable foundation in face of this new one, created by large-scale industry itself.... With that, production based on exchange value breaks down.[17]

Negri is convinced that Marx's prophecy has already been realised: it is no longer labour that creates wealth, but science and technology – the general intellect – whose site is not the factory, but society. Capitalism is already dead, superseded by its own development, economically useless. It survives as a sheer will to power, as mere 'political' coercion, now disconnected from the objective of valorisation.

The result is paradoxical, in as much as it leads to a complete reversal of *operaismo*'s original positions. On the one hand, the old orthodoxy which formed the main target of the critiques developed in *Quaderni Rossi* – the 'development of the productive forces' propelling history towards communism – is revived, with the sole difference that in Negri's position it is workers' struggles (not the 'law of surplus-value', as Panzieri had it)[18] which compel capital to take the path of technological innovation. On the other hand, the resistance to capital, originally situated in the sphere of production and regarded as impracticable in the sphere of commodity circulation and consumption, is now located in 'the practices of the reproduction of labour-power' – a category that comprises the totality of workers' behaviour *outside* the factory (from consumption to education and the organisation of leisure),[19]

[17] Marx 1973, p. 705.

[18] Panzieri 1994, pp. 51ff.

[19] See Negri 1977, pp. 310ff. In this text, Negri theorises 'the autonomy of the reproduction of labour-power', arguing that 'minor circulation' (the portion of capital advanced, indicated by L, with which the worker acquires his means of subsistence) is alien to capitalist valorisation: 'the alien character of L and working-class consumption...assumes not only the possibility of the relative independence of the consumption, the needs, the use-value of the working class from capitalist development, but also the form of an (antagonistic) dialectic on this whole terrain': Negri 1977, p. 314.

considered to be endowed with autonomy and invested with an immediate anticapitalist value.

The 1980s: technological utopias

The rehabilitation of technological determinism, as the well as the flight from the factory defined by the line of 'the autonomy of reproduction', were fertile soil for the reception of the huge advertising hype that accompanied the first major wave of diffusion of technologies based on computers and electronics in the 1980s. The new technologies were approved, with the whole accompanying propaganda apparatus, which was not that difficult to unmask.

The literature that accompanied the advent of the new technologies in the 1980s was in fact blatantly apologetic: optimistic, full of wonderful promises, directed, like all self-respecting publicity, to the collective imaginary rather than the production of knowledge. The science concerned with these problems has rarely approximated so closely to science fiction. People competed in the production of fantastic futurologies and sociologies that ultimately converged in presenting an *omnipotent* technology confronting a completely malleable society. Omnipotent and *good*, technology would do what the major social movements had proved incapable of doing: it would take charge of redressing all capitalism's wrongs, or at least the most grave of those of which it was guilty with respect to humanity and nature. Two myths took shape: the myth of the future postindustrial society, which took the notion that 'small is beautiful' as far as the dream of a totally atomised society where towns have disappeared and individuals live in an unpolluted Arcadia, connected by terminals that allow them to communicate, work, educate themselves, and do their shopping – an idea that links up with that of 'immaterial production'; and the old myth of the 'end of work', which generalised the phenomena of automation and the expulsion of manpower – phenomena that always accompany phases of restructuring – seeing them as the of sign of an imminent, even current, end to the *need* to work.

The *operaisti* like these myths. They like the idea of the 'postindustrial society', which seems to confirm the old idea of the factory diffused and diluted in society to the point where it disappears. Naturally, they like the myth of the 'end of work': the idea of the *pointlessness* of capitalist direction – in the sense envisaged above – happily marries up with that of complete automation, regarded as already feasible and delayed only by a perverse desire to prolong the existing power structure beyond its historically necessary term. In this optic, capitalist direction is increasingly *symbolic*, ever more disconnected from material production and the factory. Ultimately, it is merely a *way of thinking*, of representing reality, of generating meaning and linguistic rules, diffused *everywhere* and internalised by *everyone*: 'intelligent' workers in the integrated factory, electronic engineers, managers, intellectuals. All of them, by the same token, are the 'cognitive labour-power' of this system and, at the same time, 'a mass intellectuality' capable of extricating themselves from it, thanks to exodus of which Paolo Virno, for example, speaks.[20] In general, the *operaisti* like the terms that fuel the new myths and which they employ in order to imagine the future antagonistic subjects who will succeed the 'craft worker', the 'mass worker', and even the 'social worker', who – alas – never materialised.

With this exercise of the imagination, with this attempt to conjure up by the power of words the new redemptive subjects who never have the good grace to exist, the trajectory of *operaismo* ended in the 1990s. From the 'mass intellectual', who briefly flourished during the ephemeral student movement of 1990,[21] to the 'immaterial worker',[22] and the 'Immaterial Workers of the World', who were due to found a new 'revolutionary unionism' and transform the 'social centres' into 'post-Fordist trades councils',[23] *operaismo* founders in this frantic search for new terms and new slogans: a slave of cultural fashions and, consequently, of the worst neoliberal politics. In this headlong flight, Negri is once again in the van: he embraces globalisation, Europe, federalism, with ever more delirious formulations ('nomadic federalism' as a 'programme of European proletarians' for the 'proletarian reappropriation of administrative space');[24] he even speaks, in connection with the Veneto, of a 'communal entrepreneurship':

[20] See Virno 1990.

[21] The daily paper *Il Manifesto* the same year launched an 'Appeal to Mass Intellectuality'. See *Il Manifesto*, 27 February 1990 (reprinted in *Banlieus*, no. 1 1997, which assembles what survives of the *operaista* camp).

[22] See Lazzarato and Negri 1992.

[23] See 'Che te lo dico a fare?', under the signature 'Immaterial Workers of the World', in *DeriveApprodi*, no. 18, 1999, pp. 31–9.

[24] Negri 1999, p. 45.

> Our country, the Veneto, is wealthy and its wealth has been produced by a communal entrepreneurship. The heroes of this productive transformation are certainly not only the employers and small employers who sing its praises today. It is the workers of the Veneto, who have put their effort and intellect, labour-power and creative power, at the service of all. They have invested and accumulated professionalism in communal networks, through which the entire existence of the population has become productive.[25]

A new 'producers' alliance' comparable to that preached by the PCI during the 'years of lead'? Or are we instead to believe that the 'mass entrepreneur' is going to be the new revolutionary subject of the third millennium?

En route, *operaismo* has become a *bad theory*: a blocked form of thinking, which neither produces any critique, nor casts any light on the facts; a consolatory ideology, even a veritable hallucination, which makes it impossible to perceive anything that does not correspond to its desires.

Empire, a postmodern book

There is no doubt that the extraordinary impact of Hardt's and Negri's book *Empire* opened a new phase in the trajectory of 'operaismo'. The French edition opens with the statement that this book is 'an attempt to write a new "Communist Manifesto" for our times'. The same claim is repeated in the *feature* dedicated to the subject of the 'Political Manifesto'.[26] However, it is not totally clear as to why *Empire* should aspire to belong to the genre of the 'manifesto' when, as a matter of fact, it takes the form of a new literary genre – one which is much more in tune with our times. A 'manifesto' – be it political, artistic or philosophical – is, by definition, brief, original and radical. *Empire* is something quite different; in fact it is the opposite of a manifesto.

To start with, it is certainly not brief; it is a 'mammoth' of a book, almost 500 pages long. *Absit iniuria verbis*: to be fair, Marx's *Capital* is a 'mammoth' work too, in fact much more so; a work which has shaped history (and not only the history of thought), perhaps even to a greater extent than *The Communist*

[25] Negri 1997.

[26] Hardt and Negri 2000, pp. 63–6. I call 'features' those short chapters appearing in italics throughout the book.

Manifesto ever did. But *Capital* is a rich and systematic work, and as such it must be read from start to finish, and only in this order, if one is to understand correctly its structure of argument (it was no accident that Marx gave such a lot of thought to the issue of *presentation*, that is, to the difficulties of translating into a sequential discourse a conceptual construction articulated in such a complex way). *Empire* bears no resemblance to *Capital*: leaving aside its size, it is a lightweight cultural production, inside which readers can 'navigate' with a certain degree of freedom.

What *Empire* resembles more closely are other, more recent 'mammoths' coming in the main from the United States, such as *The End of Work* by Jeremy Rifkin, or *The End of History and The Last Man* by Francis Fukuyama. *Empire* shares with such books a strong argument (a clearly *exaggerated* argument, it has to be said), a wide-ranging but lightweight narrative, a popularising tone, numerous but rarely explored references and, above all, the quality of functioning almost as a *hypertext*. Indeed, here the strong argument almost becomes a mantra, so as to function as an easily identifiable (and easily expendable) slogan while, at the same time, becoming a link for accessing the various sets of arguments in the book that remain relatively independent from one another. The whole structure of *Empire* lends itself well to a reading in chunks and in any order whatsoever, without its fundamental meaning being affected in any considerable way.

However, the approach I have chosen to take what follows is that of a *systematic reading*: in other words from the beginning to the end, in this order. Given the disturbing contradictions that emerge, it appears that the postmodern genre of the 'American-style mammoth' does not lend itself well to this reading.

A modern grand narrative (or two, or three)

The first contradiction is the contradiction between the *style* of this book, which is clearly postmodern, and its *conception of history*, which could not be more *modern*. *Empire*'s history is *teleological*, with a clearly identifiable direction (so much so, that it even allows for predictions) and a dialectical movement in the most Hegelian sense of the word: a history that marches on through its beloved Theses, Antitheses and Syntheses, toward its (happy) End. A history working for good people (that is, for the liberation of the 'multitude'), in which in the end the last shall come first and the 'poor'[27] shall inherit the Earth. A history in which 'we are History', 'a product of human action'[28] (driven by a powerful and conscious Subjectivity).[29] Althusser would have called it the little drama of the Subject, the Origin and the End, Lyotard a 'grand narrative', to all intents and purposes a secularised religion (and not that all secularised either).[30] In a nutshell: everything that postmodernist thought has ever criticised, denied, prohibited.

It should be said that Hardt and Negri do not feel themselves part of postmodernity but are already well past it; they are, so to speak, post-postmodernists. It is for this reason that they find 'postmodernist critiques of modernity' (under which they group postmodern theorists in the strict sense of the word, from Lyotard to Harvey; postcolonialist theories like that of Bhabha; religious fundamentalists and the neoliberal ideology of the world market)[31] to be inadequate and ultimately useless, since they 'find themselves pushing against an open door'.[32] This is so because they attack a logic of power that has already declined. At any rate, while the most outspoken modern authors are still look-

---

[27] Indeed, from the *feature* entitled 'The Poor', we learn that the 'multitude' is made up of 'the poor' – 'every poor person, the multitude of poor people' (p. 158).

[28] Hardt and Negri 2000, p. 237.

[29] This claim as to the character of history is contained in the *feature* called 'Cycles', Hardt and Negri 2000, pp. 237–9.

[30] Despite the value attributed to 'immanence', religious inspiration is quite visible, in the frequent references to *Exodus*, to Saint Augustine's *Celestial City*, to gnostic suggestions (a symptom of which is the very word multitude – *multitudo* is the Latin translation of *pleroma*). It is also thanks to this point that *Empire* can be seen as a widely usable multicultural product. It is good for atheists (thanks to the ambiguity of the word 'humanism', which, in American culture, means in the first instance 'a system of belief and standards concerned with the needs of people, and not with religious ideas', and only as a secondary meaning does it denote 'the study in the Renaissance of the ideas of the ancient Greeks and Romans', see Longman, *Dictionary of English Language and Culture*). It is good for believers of various creeds (who, according to their religion, will be able to interpret the epic of the multitude as a journey of the chosen people to the promised land, as an episode of salvation, or as a celestial city for pilgrimage on Earth, or alternatively as the *pleroma-multitudo* re-ascending to a divine whole, etc). The Catholic world is well taken care of, since the hero eponymous with the multitude, the prototype and universal militant, is none other than St. Francis of Assisi, to whom the final *feature* of *Empire*, 'Militant' (Hardt and Negri 2000, pp. 411–13.) is devoted. But Islamists should not lose heart: they too have a small place, representatives as they are of *postmodernity* – see Hardt and Negri 2000, pp. 146–50).

[31] See Chapter 2.4 'Symptoms of Passage'.

[32] Hardt and Negri 2000, p. 138.

ing for signs of a decline of the nation-state, Hardt and Negri are already talking about the decline and fall of that very same Empire,[33] which according to their analysis is about to replace the nation-state (or has it in fact already replaced it? It is hard to keep one's bearings in these fast incursions into the future). Perhaps the dialectics is not postmodern, but, for all we know, it could well be post-postmodern. Whatever the case, the two authors use it in large doses.

The history of Western thought presented in Part 2 is all along the lines of a Hegelian-style dialectics. It is almost a *Philosophy of Spirit* for North American consumption, since it is here that the Spirit reaches its apex: not in the Prussian state, but in the Constitution of the United States. This story could be summed up in the following way.

Thesis: Humanism and the Renaissance. This was a 'revolution' in 'Europe, between 1200 and 1600, across distances that only merchants and armies could travel and only the invention of the printing press would later bring together'.[34] The readers should leave aside the question of the dates and all those encyclopaedias that date the Renaissance in Italy only at the end of 1400. The 'humanism' described here is rather odd, a 'hybridity' to use the authors' language – something that does not quite tally with what we were taught at school. Looking closer, this Thesis is in turn an Overturning: the overturning of Transcendence into Immanence, of the creator divinity into productive humanity.[35] According to this, 'humanism' was not a handful of men of letters, of scholars of Greek and Latin classics, but rather a 'multitude' of genius atheists like Pico della Mirandola, innovators like Schumpeter's entrepreneurs and productive men like Stakhanov. This 'multitude' had an incredible potential, so it goes without saying that someone would want to profit from it in the end.

Antithesis: The Enlightenment. From Descartes to Hobbes, Rousseau, Kant and Hegel…Once again, one should not care too much about dates and

33 See Part 4, 'The Decline and Fall of Empire', Hardt and Negri 2000, p. 351.

34 Hardt and Negri 2000, p. 70.

35 The greatest champion of this overturning was Spinoza, whose philosophy 'renewed the splendors of revolutionary humanism, putting humanity and nature in the position of God, transforming the world into a territory of practice, and affirming the democracy of the multitude as the absolute form of politics' (Hardt and Negri 2000, p. 77). To my taste, this is a Spinoza a bit too similar to Feuerbach, but let us try not to be picky.

definitions. The Illuminists (Descartes, Hobbes, Rousseau, Kant, Hegel) appear as a group of thinkers scheming to create a mundane transcendence, to keep under control and – if possible – exploit, the industrious multitude who discovered immanence. The result of their efforts is the modern sovereign state, the 'transcendent apparatus' *par excellence* – 'God on Earth' in Hobbes' definition.[36]

From the history of philosophy we now have to jump to that of political institution, following the evolution of the *European states* and the creation of that *modernity* which identifies itself with this history: from the great monarchies of the eighteenth century, through the nineteenth-century invention of the 'people', up to the nation-state which purports to rely on consensus but ultimately degenerates in the totalitarian régimes of the twentieth century. This goes to show how the Antithesis of power is not sufficient to contain the Thesis of the multitude.

As we all know, Reason (especially reason of the dialectical kind) is astute and, in fact, across the ocean it has already succeeded in creating a negation of the negation or, to be more precise, an *Alternative to the Antithesis: Empire*. The exodus of settlers toward the Americas – of a multitude fleeing modernity – 'rediscovers the revolutionary humanism of the Renaissance and perfects it as a political and constitutional science',[37] laying the foundations for a kind of sovereignty totally different from that which established itself in Europe. The American Revolution is a true revolution (unlike its French counterpart) and the United States (who, lest we forget it, are a federation) are from the outset – i.e. from the Declaration of Independence – an Empire, not a nation-state. Moreover, they are an Empire of the Good, or at least of the Lesser Evil.

At any rate, the modes with which power is exercised in the States are different from Europe. For example, let us look at the way Europeans relate to the natives in the colonies. Theirs is a mode based on cultural dualisms, on antagonism between Inside/Outside, Self/Other).[38] These are the very sources of

---

[36] Hardt and Negri 2000, see pp. 77–83.

[37] Hardt and Negri 2000, p. 162.

[38] See Hardt and Negri 2000, Chapter 2.3, 'The Dialectics of Colonial Sovereignty' p. 114 onwards. It should be noted that, in this chapter, the use of dialectics is so extensive (the authors employ it to explain both the modes of colonial rule and the fooling of the multitude by colonialists), that it results in statements such as: '*reality is not dialectical, but colonialism is*' (Hardt and Negri 2000, p. 128). A case of overdosing, perhaps?

modern racism – the ferocity of which we know only too well. But let us look instead at the way in which American settlers related to Native Americans: they did not regard them as a cultural Other, but as a mere natural obstacle to overcome, just like when you fell a tree or remove rocks from the ground to make room for cultivation:

> Just as the land must be cleared of trees and rocks in order to farm it, so too the terrain must be cleared of native inhabitants. Just as the frontier people must gird themselves against the severe winters, so too they must arm themselves against the indigenous populations. Native Americans were regarded as merely a particularly thorny element of nature.[39]

Then there is the issue of black people, altogether not such an edifying affair; not to speak of certain relations with Latin America, so aggressive as to seem 'imperialist' rather than 'imperial' in the strict sense of the word. And then came the Vietnam War.... It appears then that even our Alternative to the Antithesis on the other side of the Pond is deeply antithetical – it is dialectical: it has a good and an evil soul. Its evil soul tends to emulate European imperialist nation-states. This was, for example, the temptation for Theodore Roosevelt, who 'exercised a completely traditional European-style imperialist ideology'.[40] The good soul is Woodrow Wilson, who instead 'adopted an internationalist ideology of peace'.[41] What matters is that the good soul, the truly democratic soul, has prevailed (in the past, it was Tocqueville who grasped this; now it is Hannah Arendt who recognises it).[42] It is the embodiment of a sovereignty that does not consist 'in the regulation of the multitude' by transcendence, but rather it arises 'as the result of the productive synergies of the multitude'.[43] Control, if it exists at all, does not follow the principle of repression, but a 'principle of expansion' not dissimilar to that practised in Imperial Rome. Faced with conflicts, the European nation-states react by strengthening their borders, exasperating the distinction between Inside/Outside, between Self/Other; the American Empire moves these borders further, turning the outside into its inside, including the other into the self.[44]

---

39 Hardt and Negri 2000, p. 170.
40 Hardt and Negri 2000, p. 174.
41 Ibid.
42 See Hardt and Negri 2000, p. 164.
43 Ibid.
44 See Hardt and Negri 2000, pp. 166–72.

We now come to the *Synthesis:* the modern *global Empire*, which 'is materializing before our very eyes'.[45] With no more barriers to economic and cultural exchange, with no more distinctions between inside and outside, with no more spatial restrictions thanks to information technology and internet communications, Empire is now a *non-place*.[46] The United States *does not form its centre*,[47] for the very simple reason that a non-place cannot have a centre. Moreover, the US is not a *world leader* either, *'and indeed no nation-state can today'*.[48] The United States have indeed inspired the birth of Empire, 'born through the global expansion of the internal US constitutional project'[49] and, for this reason, let us admit it, they do enjoy a 'privileged position'.[50] But the US too are themselves absorbed and subsumed – and in the end extinguished – within a wider logic. Empire is the accomplishment of Wilson's internationalist and pacifist project – the crowning and the ultimate Aim of history. It is where the long journey (lasting nearly a millennium, if you choose to anticipate humanism by just a tiny bit) through the Thesis (*Humanism*), the Antithesis (the European *Nation-State*) and the Alternative to the Antithesis (the American *Empire*), up to the supreme Synthesis of the *Empire sans phrase*, in which – true to the rules of dialectics – we shall find once again the Thesis, by now finally liberated and living happily ever after.

Capitalism and Empire

A reader with an old-fashioned Marxist background may now wonder where *capitalism* is to be found in this history. Well, actually, it is nowhere to be found in the first sequence, save for a pithy statement: 'European modernity is inseparable from capitalism'.[51] Capitalism is the subject of a different story.

The history of capitalism, too, is a history with a capital 'H', a 'grand narrative'. Here it is not so much Hegelian dialectics that is at work, but rather the 'dialectics between productive forces and relations of productions' on which Marxist tradition has fed for so long. As is well known, on the basis of such

[45] Hardt and Negri 2000, p. xi.
[46] See Hardt and Negri 2000, p. 190.
[47] Hardt and Negri 2000, p. xiv.
[48] Ibid.
[49] Hardt and Negri 2000, p. 182.
[50] Ibid.
[51] Hardt and Negri 2000, p. 86.

dialectics, an evolutionary model of stages of development was built. This is true both for humankind in its entirety (through an actual *evolution*, from that elusive 'primitive communism' to the ancient mode of production, and then from the feudal to the capitalist mode of production, until the future realisation of communism in its true sense, when in the End we shall find the Origin, by now in its unfolded form), and for the capitalist mode of production considered separately (where a *biological order* is actually at work, in which the various stages resemble closely the birth, growth, maturity, old age and death of living organisms). In Part 3 of *Empire*, we find ourselves in this second dimension and we now begin to follow not so much the history of humanity, but the various stages in the development of capitalism.

Empire does not throw anything away (or very little anyway),[52] so, to begin with, it is a matter of recuperating all that Marxists have already analysed. We are told that, from its *competition stage*, capitalism enters into a *monopoly stage* (a tendency which Marx had already predicted) and, with it, to *imperialism*. As Lenin said, following Hilferding's analysis but discarding some notions that foreshadowed Empire – the idea of a world bank – as well as Kautsky's 'ultra-imperialism': 'If it were necessary to give the briefest possible definition of imperialism we should have to say that imperialism is the monopoly stage of capitalism'.[53]

Among the theorists of imperialism, Hardt and Negri favour Rosa Luxemburg, whose well-known underconsumption theory is here cut back to the bone (low wages equal low consumption; the growth of organic composition, with the ensuing reduction in variable capital – 'that is, the wage paid the workers'[54] – equals even lower consumption, therefore 'the realization of capital is thus blocked by the problem of the "narrow basis" of the powers of

[52] With a reconstruction that welcomes and appreciates practically all contributions to Marxist theory, disregarding any difference of interpretation (here there is room for orthodox Marxism as well as heterodox Marxism, both for Lenin and Kautsky, for Gramsci, the Frankfurt school, Althusser, for the regulation school). The only clear ostracism is reserved for the so-called world-system school, and particularly Giovanni Arrighi, to whom *Empire* devotes an outraged *feature* (Hardt and Negri 2000, pp. 237–9). It is not surprising that our two authors should find hard to swallow the idea of the cyclical nature and the recursiveness of capitalist dynamics proposed by this author, for it actually clashes rather violently with the 'grand narratives' used by Hardt and Negri, not to mention the strong subjectivism that has always characterised the workerist approach.

[53] Lenin 1996, p. 89.

[54] Hardt and Negri 2000, p. 223.

consumption')[55] and now becomes the main contradiction of capitalism. It is in this problem that an explanation for all other 'limitations' and 'barriers' of capital can be found.[56] Anyhow, Luxemburg's approach lends itself well to an account of the tendency of capitalism to expand, to the '*capitalization* of the noncapitalist environment itself'[57] and also to an explanation of how, 'in the process of capitalization *the outside is internalized*'.[58] (But was not this 'internalization from outside' a feature peculiar to the *American Empire*, nay, the very thing that distinguished it from *European imperialism*? This story may well be not even coherent with the previous one.)

According to Hardt and Negri: 'Capitalist crisis is not simply a function of capital's own dynamics but is caused directly by proletarian conflict'.[59] Whatever pushes capitalism forward, eventually the imperialist stage is passed and a new stage of development begins. Its model is Roosevelt's *New Deal*, born in the US and later exported to all Western countries after the Second World War. Its features are the economic regulation carried out by the state, as well as Keynesian policies and the welfare state. And what is this new stage of development of capitalism called? 'State monopoly capitalism?'. 'Fordism?' Wrong. It is called *Empire*. All roads lead to Empire, just like once upon a time all roads led to Rome.

So, we discover that Lenin fooled us when he called imperialism the 'highest stage' (that is, the *last* stage) of capitalism. He fooled us knowingly, as he knew well (after all, did he not know all those ultra-imperialist theses?) that – faced with the very deep crisis culminating in the First World War – history could have taken two different paths: *Revolution* or *Empire*. He then prevented the outcome of Empire, so dead set was he on making the Revolution. He

---

[55] See Hardt and Negri 2000, p. 223. It should be said that to attribute to Marx any reading of the crisis along the lines of underconsumption is – to use a euphemism – rather reductive.

[56] In so doing, *Empire* puts forward a drastic simplification of workerist lucubrations on the famous passages in *Grundrisse*, which this school of thought sees as fundamental and which it subjects to endless as well as obscure exegeses. Dialectical contradictions, intrinsic barriers, negations of negations: all is reduced to a problem of underconsumption: 'all these barriers flow from a single barrier defined by the unequal relationship between the worker as producer and the worker as consumer' (Hardt and Negri 2000, p. 222). This is a really bold enterprise and, to me, it deserves applause (before blurting out 'but why didn't you say so before?').

[57] Hardt and Negri 2000, p. 226.

[58] Ibid.

[59] Hardt and Negri 2000, p. 261.

wanted to make it immediately, before capitalism reached its full maturity.[60] Once the Revolution failed, we found ourselves with Empire, with the true 'highest stage', for two reasons. Firstly, because in this stage factory discipline was imposed on the whole of society (good, I see you have spotted the good old workerist thesis): 'The New Deal produced the highest form of *disciplinary* government',[61] '*a disciplinary society is thus a factory society*'.[62] Secondly, because, after the process of decolonisation, we went from the *formal subsumption* of the world to capital – a feature of the 'extensive expansion' of old-style imperialism – to the *real subsumption* of the world to capital, as capital today practices an 'intensive expansion'.[63]

The end of History?

The end of this story (which is really also the end of all stories or of History *tout court*) is that it was really a good thing that Lenin's plans failed and that, in the end, Empire was able to develop and expand without any more boundaries on the planet. As Hölderlin's poem goes: 'Where danger is, grows also that which saves'.

First of all, Empire shall save us from environmental catastrophe: the 'real subsumption' of the world, i.e. its intensive exploitation actually coincides with the age of the *postindustrial*, which as we well know is clean, small and beautiful. This seems to be the real capitalist response to the threat of 'ecological disaster', a response that looks to the future'.[64]

And, above all, Empire has created the antagonistic Subject *par excellence*, the most powerful, creative and incredible Militant the world has ever seen: the *social worker*, who now replaces the professional worker and the mass worker of the past. Whereas the professional worker (corresponding to the 'phase of industrial production that preceded the full deployment of Fordist and Taylorist régimes')[65] was engaged in *reappropriating* his own productive labour; and the mass worker (who 'corresponded to the deployment of

[60] See Hardt and Negri 2000, pp. 233 onwards.
[61] Hardt and Negri 2000, p. 242.
[62] Hardt and Negri 2000, p. 243.
[63] See Hardt and Negri 2000, p. 271.
[64] Hardt and Negri 2000, p. 272.
[65] Hardt and Negri 2000, p. 409.

Fordist and Taylorist regimes'[66] even dared to create 'a real *alternative* to the system of capitalist power',[67] the social worker (corresponding to the phase of 'immaterial labor') can finally express himself 'as self-valorization of the human', realising 'an organization of productive and political power as a biopolitical unit managed by the multitude, organized by the multitude, directed by the multitude – absolute democracy in action'.[68]

Empire shall fall, is about to fall, it is falling, has already fallen! What is the problem, after all? Deep down it is just a matter of mental attitude: all you have to do is oppose (as Francis of Assisi – the subject of the last *feature* in *Empire*, 'Militant'[69] was already doing all that time ago) your *joie de vivre* to the misery caused by power. Beware, all ye powerful: a smirk will be the death of you. And you, multitudes, go in peace: the 'mammoth' has ended.

[66] Ibid.
[67] Ibid.
[68] Hardt and Negri 2000, p. 410.
[69] Hardt and Negri 2000, pp. 411–13.

Chapter Seventeen

Marxism and Postcolonial Studies

Neil Lazarus and Rashmi Varma

It is no easy matter to speak about Marxism *and* postcolonial studies, because as a field of academic enquiry postcolonial studies has, in general, been characterised from the outset by a constitutive anti-Marxism. The supplementarity of the field to post-structuralism has often been registered; and internal 'dissidents' have identified some of the defining theoretical and ideological dispositions in the field – the repudiation, not only of Marxism, but of any struggle-based model of politics; the hostility towards totality and the aversion to dialectics; the disavowal of all forms of nationalism, and the corresponding exaltation of migrancy, liminality and hybridity, for example – precisely by referring them to poststructuralist theory. Poststructuralism might indeed be *part* of the story here: but the dominant conceptual horizon of postcolonial studies needs to be grasped more decisively than this. This essay traces the career of post-colonial studies as an academic field of enquiry and examines its founding principles by periodising it within the key global economic and social transformations since 1945. It looks at and assesses some of the central debates within postcolonial studies – the critique of Eurocentrism; nationalism; subalternity; the positing of an alternative modernity; and the retreat from politics to ethics.

Periodising postcolonial studies

Postcolonial studies needs to be situated in relation to the 1970s global economic and political crisis that signalled the demise of the social order that had structured developments worldwide since 1945. Thirty years of explosive economic growth, marked by significant gains and the unprecedented dispersal of social and political benefits to wider populations all over the world came to an abrupt halt at this moment, as the world system stumbled into economic recession amidst a general crisis of capitalist accumulation. What has followed has been a further thirty years marked by the global assertion of US political hegemony and what Amin has tersely called 'the logic of unilateral capital'.

The 'boom' period (roughly, 1945 to 1975) was marked in the 'West' by the historic achievement of the 'welfare state' and a measure of social democracy; but there were also substantial social, political and economic gains in the 'East' and the 'South'. It is important to register some of the successes enjoyed by newly independent states and peoples in the era immediately following decolonisation. The achievement and maintenance of secular democracy in India; Nasser's stand on Suez in 1956; the popular platforms established by Castro in Cuba and Nkrumah in Ghana – these were all developments which fired the imaginations of millions of people, placing on to the world stage, perhaps for the first time, the principled and resolute figure of 'Third World' self-determination. Domestically, many of the newly inaugurated postcolonial regimes undertook ambitious projects intended to improve the livelihood and welfare of their citizenry.

Yet this advance of social democracy in the formerly colonial world was extraordinarily tenuous and fragile. The neo-imperial world order that replaced the older colonial régimes was structured in such a way that the new régimes in postcolonial states proved unable in general to consolidate the momentous social advance represented by decolonisation or to sustain the postcolonial project of democratisation. After 1975 there was not only insufficient development; growth itself stopped or went into reverse. A savage restructuring of class relations worldwide was set in train, under the sign of 'neoliberalism'. In the 'West', the practical effects of this restructuring have been to privatise social provision, dismantle the welfare state, force millions of people into *structural* unemployment, and break the back of militant trade unionism. In the 'Third World', the effects have been analogous, but deeper and worse. Throughout the postcolonial world over the course of the final quarter of the twentieth century, Structural Adjustment Programmes became the favoured means of disciplining postcolonial states, domesticating them and rendering them subservient to the needs of the global market. They also became a means of ensuring that postcolonial states retained their peripheral status, neither attempting to de-link themselves from the world system nor ever imagining themselves capable of participating in it from any position of parity, let alone power.[1]

The two-phased historical schema laid out here (1945 to 1975; 1975 to the present) provides a necessary sociological preamble to any consideration of postcolonial studies as an academic field. This is because the *emergence* of postcolonial studies towards the end of the 1970s coincided with the puncturing of the postwar 'boom' and – one consequence of this puncturing – the decisive defeat of anticapitalist or liberationist ideologies within the Western (or, increasingly, Western-based) intelligentsia, including its radical elements. The *consolidation* of the field in the 1980s and 1990s can then be seen, at least in part, as a function of its articulation of a complex intellectual response to this decisive defeat. On the one hand, as an initiative in tune with the spirit of the age, postcolonial studies breathed the air of the general anti-liberationism then rising to hegemony in the wider society. The field not only emerged in close chronological proximity to the end of the 'Bandung era' and the collapse of insurgent 'Third Worldism'. It has also always characteristically offered, in the scholarship that it has fostered and produced, something approximating a monumentalisation of this moment – a rationalisation of and pragmatic adjustment to, if by no means uncomplicatedly a celebration of, the downturn in the fortunes and influence of insurgent national-liberation movements and anticapitalist ideologies in the early 1970s. On the other hand, as a self-consciously *progressive* or *radical* initiative, postcolonial studies was, and has remained, opposed to the dominant forms assumed by anti-liberationist policy and discourse in the dark years since then – years of neoliberal 'austerity and 'structural adjustment', political 'rollback', and a triumphalist new imperialist rhetoric. Postcolonial studies entered into strategic alliance with the new social movements that swept across university campuses in the US and elsewhere, articulating a politics of identity – with reference to race, ethnicity,

[1] Larrain 2000; Gwynne and Kay 1999.

sex, and gender – as against class struggle, and privileging a rhetoric of recognition over one of redistribution even as universities were being brought systematically within the purview of neoliberal calculation and instrumentalism. The intersections of postcolonial studies and multicultural politics provided a domain in which radicalism could be espoused within the constraints of a seemingly undefeatable global order.

The Janus face of postcolonial studies

There are, then, two aspects to postcolonial studies as an academic enterprise, one accommodationist, the other subversive. In the former guise, the field has been governed at a very deep level by the supposition that the decline of 'Third-World' insurgency in the late 1960s and early 1970s was part of a wider – epochal – shift, heralding, as has often been claimed (and not only within postcolonial studies itself, of course), the demise of the 'modern' forms of political struggle and identification – liberalism, socialism, secularism, nationalism, internationalism, etc. – and of the grand sociological categories associated with them: revolution, unevenness, the nation-state, modernity, even imperialism. With the collapse of historical Communism and the fall of the Berlin Wall in 1989, Marxism itself was pronounced finally dead and buried.

It is partly due to this apocalyptic understanding of contemporary history, no doubt, that most scholars in the postcolonial studies field should have been so remarkably little interested in work done prior to the emergence of the field itself on the very questions that they themselves ostensibly investigate. Why pay attention to work published before 1975 when all of this work had been premised on assumptions that had, quite simply, been rendered obsolete by the 'epochal' developments of the late-1960s and early 1970s? The 'post-' of postcolonial studies has in this sense been emphatically the 'post-' of postmodernism: between the new initiative and earlier scholarship there is taken to have been a clean epistemological break.

In reckoning with postcolonial studies' image of itself in these terms as radically new, we must not discount disciplinary explanations. Postcolonial studies is very much a creature of literature (typically English) and cultural studies departments, even if it has subsequently found fertile soil to grow in some other beds of the Humanities garden (history, anthropology, geography) and even, much more limitedly, in the social sciences. (We should go further still: the initiative that would come to be known as postcolonial studies initially assumed critical mass not in literary critical circles abstractly conceived, but specifically in departments of literature in *élite* universities. Postcolonial studies was not a 'bottom-up' but a 'top-down' intervention.) The troping of power in semiological terms clearly (also) registers a *disciplinary* disposition.

This has constituted a particular problem for Marxists within postcolonial studies, since the long history of Marxist or neo-Marxist engagements with questions relating to colonialism and 'postcolonialism', imperialism and anti-imperialism, racism and nationalism, has been a dead letter for mainstream postcolonialists. A short list of the kind of work that might be referenced here would include:

1) early Marxist accounts of 'non-Western' or 'precapitalist' societies, colonialism and anticolonial revolt (not least, and certainly controversially, Marx himself on India);
2) classical-Marxist accounts of imperialism (Lenin, Bukharin, Luxemburg, Hilferding, etc.);
3) later accounts of imperialism in the contexts of world-systems theory, development and underdevelopment, and 'dependency' (Baran, Cox, Frank, Furtado, Wallerstein, Arrighi, Amin, etc.);
4) writings by Marxist politico-intellectuals active in anti-imperialist, anticolonialist and/or national-liberation struggles (Ben Barka, Cabral, Castro, Fanon, Guevara, C.L.R. James, Li Ta-Chao, Lin Piao, Sison, Mao, Mariátegui, E.M.S. Namboodripad, Jayaprakash Narayan, Neto, Nkrumah, Padmore, Rodney, M.N. Roy, Truong Chinh, etc.);
5) writings by Marxist or socialist scholars, wherever located (Abdel-Malek, Eqbal Ahmad, Alavi, Chandra, Davidson, Galeano, Habib, Hodgkin, Kosambi, Rodinson, Sarkar, Worsley, etc.).

A Marxist appraisal of postcolonial studies would therefore need to register the debilitating loss incurred by the field in its neglect and ignorance of the resources suggested in and by this list. It would then also need to challenge the tendentious and selective reading of Marxism itself that surfaces in so much postcolonialist scholarship, including in writings by some of the most influential theorists.[2]

The fact that postcolonial studies should have been constituted as an arena of scholarly production within which the specific investments and stockpiles of knowledge of Marxist scholars tend to remain unrecognised and undervalued has led some Marxists to repudiate the field *tout court*, to insist upon its fundamental irrelevance. But other Marxists have opted for a different strategy. Positioning themselves actively in the field, they have called for a body of scholarship capable of registering the actuality of the world system and the structuring effects of this system (upon consciousness, culture and experience as well as upon material conditions of existence), by way of opposing and criticising it. Part of their work in this respect, as Bartolovich has argued, has involved reactivating the very Marxist heritage that has been actively disavowed in mainstream postcolonial studies, identifying its theoretical achievements and pointing to the resources available in its long-term engagement with many of the dilemmas that postcolonialists have raised, invariably without any reference to Marxism. In this capacity, Marxist scholars have contributed importantly to the elaboration of the progressive or subversive aspect of postcolonial studies. Conceding to the field the authentic insights and advances generated within it, and committing themselves never to fall behind these, they have succeeded – to some degree, at least – in ensuring that 'specifically Marxist interests and tendencies' have been given an airing in the postcolonial discussion.[3]

Critique of Eurocentrism

The essential gesture of postcolonial studies in its progressive aspect might be said to consist in the *critique of Eurocentrism*. At a fundamental level, this has involved the sustained critique of a *specific* set of representations – those famously addressed by Said under the rubric of 'Orientalism'. Building upon Said's canonical formulation of Orientalism as 'the enormously systematic dis-

---

[2] E.g., Chakrabarty 2000, Lowe and Lloyd 1997, Miller 1990, Prakash 1990, Serequeberhan 1997, Young 1990.

[3] Bartolovich 2002, pp. 3–4.

cipline by which European culture was able to manage – and even produce – the Orient politically, sociologically, militarily, ideologically, scientifically, and imaginatively during the post-Enlightenment period',[4] postcolonial scholars have done a lot of enormously valuable work on 'Western' conceptions of the 'non-West', in which they have been concerned to demonstrate not only the falsity or inaccuracy of these conceptions but also their systematicity, their symptomaticity, and their capacity to ground, engender, or constitute social practices, policies and institutions.

Yet if the attempt to 'unthink Eurocentrism'[5] has been lodged as a foundational aspiration of postcolonialist scholarship, there has been wide disagreement as to what is entailed in and by such 'unthinking'. A predominant tendency in the field has been to situate Eurocentrism less as an *ideological* formation (selective, interested, partial, and partisan) than as an *episteme* (a trans-ideologically dispersed field of vision, or conceptual 'atmosphere'). If we understand Eurocentrism as an *ideology*, then it can become subject to critique. One's general methodological assumption would be that it is always in principle (and indeed in practice) possible to stand outside any given problematic in order to subject its claims to scrutiny. This, of course, is the classical notion of critique as encountered in Kant and exemplified most significantly for radical scholarship in Marx's various critiques of bourgeois political economy and idealist philosophy. It is ideology-critique on this model that had been activated in anti-colonialist writing and scholarship prior to the advent of postcolonial studies: in Aime Césaire's *Discourse on Colonialism*, for instance, but also in the publications of such politico-intellectuals as C.L.R. James, Frantz Fanon and Walter Rodney (to draw examples only from the Caribbean), and in the many critiques of anthropology or modernisation theory or development studies (not least by practising anthropologists, sociologists and political scientists themselves) published during the 1960s and 1970s.

Scholars in postcolonial studies, however, have tended to address Eurocentrism less in terms of ideology and more as an *episteme* or intellectual atmosphere – as, so to speak, the very air that must be breathed by anybody engaging in questions relating to 'Europe and its Others'. Eurocentrism

[4] Said 1979, p. 3.
[5] Shohat and Stam 1994.

emerges on this conceptualisation as an untranscendable horizon governing thought – its forms, contents, modalities, and presuppositions so deeply and insidiously layered and patterned that they cannot be circumvented, only deconstructed. Eurocentrism is in these terms not susceptible to critique, since it is entailed in the very fabric of disciplinarity, institutionalised knowledge production, and even 'reason' itself, as that concept has come to be understood in the philosophical discourse of modernity. In postcolonial theory, this way of seeing things has tended to give way almost inevitably to a further proposition, concerning the constitutive Eurocentrism of all intellectual practice that stakes a claim to representation. The signature critique of Orientalist (mis-)representation in postcolonial studies has thus increasingly tended to broaden and flatten out into a critique of representation as such. Perhaps this latter impetus was already latent – even if coincidentally so – in Said's *Orientalism*, with its unstable concatenation of Foucault and ideology critique. Arguments about the provenance, thrust and implications of Said's method in *Orientalism* continue to rage. Nevertheless it is clear that in the consolidation and institutionalisation of postcolonial studies during the 1980s and 1990s, the putative ambivalence of *Orientalism* in this respect was progressively 'ironed out' as scholars in the field, in step with their colleagues elsewhere in the circuits of poststructuralist theory, moved to junk the concepts of truth and thence, by negative association, of ideology too, as so much metaphysical or essentialist baggage. In the process, *the critique of Eurocentric representation was increasingly subsumed by a critique of representation itself as Eurocentric*. The suggestion is that the desire to speak *for*, *of*, or even *about* others is always shadowed – and perhaps even overdetermined – by a secretly authoritarian aspiration.

Nationalism

This suggestion has framed – or indeed dominated – the way in which the subject of nationalism has tended to be raised within postcolonial studies, for example. There have been two main lines of argument. The first is associated most prominently with Homi Bhabha, who focuses on the propensity of nationalist discourse to produce and institutionalise a 'unisonant' narrative of the nation. Bhabha himself draws centrally on Benedict Anderson's seminal argument[6] concerning the virtual imagination of community in nationalist discourse. Anderson had proposed that nation-ness is never a given, historically fixed instance (actuality or value), but one ceaselessly in the process of being made and remade. Bhabha builds upon this idea: in his work, nationalist discourse is both unstable and volatile; in the context of anti-colonialism, moreover, it is mimetic, enacting an ambivalent reiteration of metropolitan nationalist discourse from which it subtly articulates a difference within the semiotic space of the same. Bhabha claims to find in Fanon's writing a prefiguring of these themes, but this claim is unconvincing. For, far from representing an abstract critique of nationalism as such, Fanon's celebrated treatment of 'The Pitfalls of National Consciousness' in *The Wretched of the Earth* was delivered from an *alternative nationalist standpoint*. Since Bhabha mistrusts what he rather dismissively calls 'naively liberatory' conceptions of freedom, he is obliged to misread Fanon on this score: he argues, thus, that Fanon's political vision does 'not allow any national or cultural "unisonance" in the imagined community of the future'.[7] In truth, however, Fanon had committed himself to precisely such a 'unisonant' view of the decolonised nation in distinguishing categorically between bourgeois nationalism and another would-be hegemonic form of national consciousness – a liberationist, anti-imperialist, nationalist internationalism, represented in the Algerian arena by the anticolonial resistance movement, the Front de Libération Nationale, to whose cause he devoted himself actively between 1956 and 1961, the year of his death.

The second line of argument concerning nationalism in postcolonial studies is associated pre-eminently with Gayatri Spivak, who argues that, no matter how or where it is raised, or by whom, the claim to speak for 'the nation' always entails the simultaneous bracketing and marginalising or silencing of a variety of popular forms of self-understanding, social practice and struggle – forms that do not articulate themselves in the language and syntax of national consciousness. The burden of Spivak's argument is to suggest that anticolonial nationalism is in all instances an élite configuration. In claiming to represent the aspirations of 'the people', anticolonial nationalists of all

---

6 Anderson 1983.
7 Bhabha 1991, p. 102; see also Bhabha 1994.

stripes posit the nation as an 'imagined community' to which all classes and groups in the society have equal access and to which they all share the same allegiance. Spivak is perfectly willing to concede that, ideologically speaking, she finds some of these competing imaginings of the nation vastly more attractive than others. She insists, however, that the competition between them is, and remains, fundamentally a competition between élites. Authority in the representation of 'the people' is for her more a function of the relative social power of the nationalist spokesperson than of any putative 'identity' between nationalist discourse and popular consciousness.

Subalternity

It is on the basis of this general argument that Spivak moves in her work to offer a theory of *subalternity*. The work that had initially appeared under the historiographical imprimatur of the India-based 'Subaltern Studies' collective in the early 1980s had still been committed to the enterprise of recovering or uncovering the contents and forms of consciousness of 'the people', those spoken of and for in élite representations, but never afforded sanctioned or public space to speak of and for themselves: the 'wretched of the earth', in Fanon's famous formula; the 'people without history', in Eric Wolf's. Spivak's theory deviates sharply from this project. She defines 'subalternity' very austerely as a structured inarticulacy at the élite levels of state and civil society – such that to be positioned as 'subaltern' in any discursive context is to be incapable of representing oneself within that context. The subaltern is the *object* of discourse, never the subject. Subaltern practice, on Spivak's construction, cannot signify 'as itself' across the divide that separates social élites from those who are not élite. Within the élite spheres, including that of progressive anti-colonial nationalism, '[t]he subaltern cannot speak'.[8] On Spivak's reading, the actual contents of the social practice of 'the people' are always, indeed definitionally, unrepresentable, whether by artists, intellectuals or political spokespeople. Whatever is read (that is, represented) as 'subaltern' within élite discourse has for her always-already been made over, appropriated, traduced. It is precisely the irreducible gap between popular practice and its

---

[8] Spivak 1988, p. 308.

(misrecognising) construal in élite discourse that the term 'subalternity' designates on her usage of it.

In an important challenge to Spivak's theorisation, Benita Parry has argued that it 'gives no speaking part to the colonized, effectively writing out the evidence of native agency recorded in India's 200-year struggle against British conquest and the Raj'.[9] It might be suggested on Spivak's behalf, perhaps, that her theory of subalternity is not really a theory of 'native agency' at all, but of the ways in which the social and symbolic practice of disenfranchised elements of the 'native' population are represented in colonialist-élitist discourse. The subaltern is for Spivak not a person but a discursive figure in a battery of more or less integrated dominant social and cultural 'texts'. Intellectual and political practice – no matter what their ideological character – are, by virtue of their social conditions of possibility, ineluctably dependent upon these dominant 'texts'. To speak of 'the people' is therefore inevitably to speak instead of 'them', that is, to silence 'them' in the act of speaking of 'them' – even where such speech is intended as an intervention on 'their' behalf.

In *Representations of the Intellectual*, Said speaks of the intellectual as 'an individual endowed with a faculty for representing, embodying, articulating a message, a view, an attitude, philosophy or opinion to, as well as for, a public', adding that the fundamental responsibility here is always to 'represent all those people and issues that are routinely forgotten or swept under the rug'.[10] Spivak's standpoint does not allow for a practice of representation conceived in these terms. On her understanding, as Larsen has pointed out, even the development and articulation of anti-imperialist discourses 'only make room within the "Subject" for a third world intellectual, or class (or gender) élite, still banishing the "subaltern" to the far side of Spivak's epistemologically constructed "international division of labor"'.[11]

The thesis of incommensurability

In postcolonial studies, intellectual representation has, following Spivak, been taken to be a game of high stakes. The danger has been thought to rest in the

---

[9] Parry 1987, p. 35.
[10] Said 1994, pp. 11–12.
[11] Larsen 2005, p. 47.

fact that in speaking of or for others (and it is of course the élite spokesperson's own relative privilege – schooling, among other things – that has put him or her in a position to do so and even or especially to *think* of doing so), one might unintentionally and unwittingly find oneself both objectifying 'them' and superimposing one's own élite cognitive maps on 'them' as one does so. The resort, therefore, has been to a consideration of difference under the rubric of *incommensurability*. Critics have supposed that if they work on the strategic assumption that what is 'other' to the representing subject is radically and categorically so, they might be able to put a spoke in the wheel of any *unselfconscious* project of representation, at least. Thus O'Hanlon, in her contribution to the debate on subaltern studies, has suggested that, despite itself, the progressive attempt to recover popular consciousness has invariably ended up misrepresenting 'the people' by transforming them 'into autonomous subject-agents, unitary consciousnesses possessed of their own originary essence, in the manner which we now understand to be the creation, very largely, of Enlightenment humanism's reconstruction of Man'. O'Hanlon speaks of the fundamental 'alienness' of the subaltern from the representing subject.[12] This is a *definitional* 'otherness' or incommensurability, of course, intended strategically to prevent those who take up the burden of representation from assuming – from their own positions of relative power, relatively untheorised by themselves – that 'the people' are, as it were, 'just like them', only contingently poorer or more disempowered, and that, if these 'people' were to be given the opportunity to do so, they would make the same choices and think the same sorts of thoughts as those doing the representing.

The thesis of incommensurability has been put forward in postcolonial studies as both philosophically radical and ethically sensitive. But a Marxist critique of it might proceed on either philosophical or political grounds. *Philosophically*, it might be argued that the anti-humanism upon which it rests has thrown the baby out with the bathwater. Following Said's general example, one could propose that, while it makes for a salutary methodological caution, the thesis of incommensurability – the idea that there is a fundamental 'alienness' between the representing subject and the 'subject' being represented – is no more intellectually defensible than the contrary idea of

[12] O'Hanlon 2000, p. 96.

ideologically-secured affinity and communality across and athwart the social division of labour. *Contra* Spivak and O'Hanlon, Said insists on the category of *universalism*, which betokens for him the suggestions both that 'certain democratic freedoms, certain freedoms from domination of one kind or another, freedom from various kinds of exploitations, and so on, are the rights of every human being',[13] and also, reciprocally, that every human being has an *interest* – in principle, articulable – in these freedoms. Between representing subject and the 'subject' being represented there is for Said, therefore, no necessary or unforgoable 'gap'. On the contrary, the whole purpose of political representation is to forge an identity between the subject and the object of discourse.

The thesis of incommensurability is susceptible to *political* critique on the grounds that it is reductionist. The arguments, a) that there is an unforgoable 'gap' between subject and object of representation; and b) that this 'gap' is identifiable in terms of a power differential, can readily be conceded. But it is then surely incumbent upon the theorist to specify the precise form(s) of power involved? Yet postcolonialists arguing for incommensurability have tended to conceptualise representational power summarily and without formal justification on the model of (colonial) domination. To speak of or on behalf of another is, in their eyes, to subject that other to one's authority. In arguing thus they conflate authority and authoritarianism, casting the former as merely an instance of the latter and promoting an active disregard of the contents of different (and competing) representations. (If all 'translations' violate the integrity of what is translated, then we need not waste much time arguing over the respective merits and demerits of different translations?) This is both counter-intuitive and unhelpful. While it is true, for instance, that Nelson Mandela's discourse and Hendrik Verwoerd's are 'alike' in figuring 'the South-African people' as their object and in claiming to speak for them, this is scarcely the most important point to make about their competing representations. To privilege the abstract question of the conditions of possibility of the generation of 'truth-effects' over the concrete question of representational adequacy is politically disenabling.

---

[13] Said 2004, p. 197.

The turn to ethics

If 'unthinking Eurocentrism' has constituted one of the essential gestures of postcolonial studies, a key modality of that gesture has been the transmutation of the *political* project of anticolonial struggle and decolonisation into an *ethical* one. Bhabha's recent writing on Fanon, especially, is exemplary of this process. Since the early 1990s, a number of sharp materialist critiques of Bhabha's 'postcolonialist' appropriation of Fanon have been advanced, to cumulating influence and effect. Macey's massive biography of Fanon is perhaps the most decisive of these.[14] It demonstrates conclusively that Bhabha's construction of Fanon cannot be squared either with Fanon's actual writings or with the trajectory of Fanon's own career, and proposes therefore that there is no future for the illusion that has been the 'postcolonial' Fanon.

In this context, the 'Foreword' that Bhabha was commissioned to write in 2005 for a new English translation of *Les Damnés de la terre* is of interest, since one looks for some new thoughts about Fanon. At one level, the 'Foreword' merely restates Bhabha's preference for a Fanon who speaks to the psychic-affective dimensions of anticolonialism as opposed to a Fanon for whom the anticolonial struggle constituted the means not only to repossess abjected identity, but to accede to revolutionary subjectivity, and, through resistance, reclaim land and sovereignty. Bhabha consigns Fanon's project of revolutionary anticolonialism to the dustbin of history. At another level, however, the Foreword does contain some new ideas, although these are scarcely unproblematical. '[W]hat might be saved from Fanon's ethics and politics of decolonization to help us reflect on globalization in our sense of the term?' Bhabha asks.[15] He evokes Fanon's commentary on the subjectivity of the colonised man and woman: these provide us with 'figures of instruction for our global century'.[16] These figures need not be situated precisely or historicised, evidently: in their universalism they are assimilable to a 'project of futurity'. The 'people' who Fanon himself had represented quite specifically as acceding to revolutionary consciousness in the course of the national-liberation struggle – he had spoken of the 'awakening of the people's intelligence and the onward

14 Macey 2000.
15 Bhabha 2005, p. xi.
16 Ibid.

progress of their consciousness'[17]– are transformed in Bhabha's reading into abstractions that can endlessly and indeed constitutionally signify the condition of 'wretchedness'.

In Bhabha's 'Foreword', we can identify a privileging of ethics over politics. This move is significant: as the centre of gravity of postcolonial studies has shifted in recent years, there has been a pronounced turn to ethics. The disavowal of struggles based on class is continued, with emphasis being placed on the *effects* of globalisation (more typically upon culture or consciousness than upon, say, employment) rather than on its determinants or structures. In concluding his 'Foreword', Bhabha proposes what is essentially an abstract humanism as an alternative third term between socialism and capitalism: he proposes a global culture of humanitarianism in which the right to equitable development would be made universal. However, the questions of how this right might be bestowed or imposed, and by whom, are left unanswered; and while the evocation of 'debt relief and forgiveness' answers to a politics of *recognition*, no consideration is given to the mechanisms of *redistribution*. In short, as the terms of materialist analysis and critique are transformed into an ethical, liberal-humanist project, the idea of a critical anti-globalism that would also be anti-imperialist is eviscerated.

Modernity and 'alternative modernity'

However politically questionable the shift to ethics might be, Bhabha's surprising endorsement of human rights and universalism seems to signal a departure from the earlier discussion of these issues in postcolonial studies, where they had typically been understood as the products of a blighted colonial modernity. An important debate in postcolonial studies has indeed centred on the category of modernity. Marxists in the field have sought to link this category to capitalism and capitalist development (what, following Jameson's usage, might be termed 'modernisation'). Harootunian, for instance, has proposed that as long as it remains sensitive to the 'differing inflections of the modern', the Marxist concept of modernity is capable of '[providing] a framework of temporal imminence in which to locate all societies'.[18] Harootunian

[17] Fanon 1968, p. 188.
[18] Harootunian 2000, pp. 62–3.

speaks in this context of 'peripheral modernities' – a term that he prefers to 'alternative modernities' – as designating a world order 'in which all societies share…a common reference provided by global capital and its requirements'. What is at issue here is an attempt to pluralise modernity – to argue that because there are multiple determinate experiences of modernity, there is a need, correspondingly, to produce 'site-based readings of modernity'.[19] The call to pluralise modernity – which has sometimes gone under the rubric of 'alternative *modernities*' – does not entail the evocation of another 'time' or 'history' radically different from, or outside, the history of capitalism. It concedes the idea of a *singular* modernity[20] that is uneven and global even as it derides the ethnocentrism of the dominant philosophical discourse of modernity. It is constituted by an attempt to register the multiple ways in which the non-West produces its own practices and philosophies of modernity, sometimes though not exclusively in response to the sense of modernity as part of the colonial (and now neocolonial) logic of rule. If modernisation is understood under the rubric of 'Westernisation', then are all 'non-Western' forms of modernity alternative to 'Western modernity' in the same ways? If not, then on what grounds do we compare 'Nigerian' modernity, say, with 'Chinese' modernity? And where, in terms of the articulation of multiple and proliferating regional, national and local forms of modernity, does the culture of indigenous peoples fit? These are the sorts of question raised within the conceptual framing of the problematic of 'alternative modernities'. Ultimately, the question is raised of the very nature of 'modernity' itself – is it a project, an epoch, a discourse, an attitude, a condition, a critique, an abstraction, or all of the above?

The idea of an 'alternative modernity' (in the singular), by contrast, has emerged as a project of establishing radical alterity through a commitment to historical difference. What is looked for is an alternative not only to the Eurocentric supposition that the form(s) assumed by modernity in the 'West' are paradigmatic of 'modernity' as such, but to the very notion of modernity itself as that notion has been elaborated in the development of the discipline of history (in the 'West'). In the project of 'alternative modernity', the terms 'West', 'Europe', 'history', 'Enlightenment' and 'modernity' are conflated and

[19] Gaonkar 1999, p. 14.
[20] Cf. Jameson 2002.

flattened. This conflation is best illustrated in the critique of colonial 'governmentality', in which, as in Chakrabarty,[21] an attempt is made to deconstruct the purported universalism of Enlightenment concepts as part of the project of 'provincialising Europe'.

This project involves the necessary disavowal of the Enlightenment concepts of reason, progress, democracy, and secularism, viewed as categories external to the 'non-West'. And if colonialism itself cannot be thought of outside an intrinsically and unforgoably Eurocentric 'modernity', neither can *anticolonialism* or struggles for democracy in the *postcolonial* era. Chakrabarty writes:

> Concepts such as citizenship, the state, civil society, public sphere, human rights, equality before the law, the individual, distinctions between public and private, the idea of the subject, democracy, popular sovereignty, social justice, scientific rationality, and so on all bear the burden of European thought and history.[22]

Formulations like this represent a stunning concession to 'Europe' of some of the great achievements of *humanity*, ironically lending intellectual credibility both to right-wing fundamentalist movements in the 'Third World' and to neo-conservative accounts[23] of 'the world revolution of Westernization' in the 'West'.[24] Scott goes so far as to argue against the idea that concepts such as 'democracy (even a purportedly radical one) should have any particular privilege among ways of organising the political forms of our collective lives'.[25] While the relationship between intellectual positions and political practice can be subjected to debate, there can be no doubting the profoundly anti-materialist orientation in such work. In effect, the postcolonialist investment in articulating an 'alternative modernity' seeks to place 'non-Western' cultures outside the history of capitalism – the latter is viewed generically as part of an instrumentalising, rationalising modernity. By extension, the Marxist critique of capitalism is also consigned to the dustbin of an oppressive 'European' modernity.

---

[21] Chakrabarty 2000.
[22] Chakrabarty 2000, p. 4.
[23] E.g., von Laue 1987, Huntington 1998.
[24] See the critical discussion in Lazarus 2002.
[25] Scott 1999, p. 156.

The distinction drawn earlier between concepts of Eurocentrism as ideology and episteme is again relevant here. The theory of 'alternative modernity' involves the repudiation of modernity as episteme. What is emphasised, as Cooper has argued, is the 'critical examination of the subject position of the scholar and political advocate' rather than modernity as an historical concept that might explain how 'the trajectories of a colonizing Europe and a colonized Africa and Asia shaped each other over time'. Cooper maintains that what he calls the 'stance' approach works not merely to 'obscure the details of colonial history and the experience of people in the colonies, but the aspirations and challenges posed by political movements in the colonies over the course of history disappear beneath the ironic gaze that critics have directed towards claims for progress and democracy'.[26]

Mainstream postcolonial theory reduces modernity to its Euro-modernist formulations, reason to rationalism, and democracy to imperialism and colonial dictatorship – and then, understandably if prematurely, disavows modernity, reason and democracy. The critics implicated fail to think through the fact that claims to freedom from slavery and colonialism were levelled historically on grounds that may have had fundamental features in common with those that produced pro-slavery and colonialist discourse but also dissented sharply from them. From the Haitian Revolution of the late eighteenth century to the Indian freedom struggle of the mid-twentieth, from Toussaint L'Ouverture's challenge to French ideas of citizenship to Gandhi's strategic ironisation of 'Western civilisation' as a 'good idea' (his tongue-in-cheek suggestion, of course, was that it would be a good idea if the West *were to become* civilised!), the history of anticolonial struggle is replete with instances not of 'alternative modernity' but of claims made to civic rights, freedom and citizenship on the ground of modernity. To state it more boldly, Enlightenment values such as freedom and human and individual rights are not transformed into universally accepted/recognised values only through domination and imposition (although *la mission civilisatrice* is inextinguishably part of the story); instead it is precisely through the agency of the anticolonial struggles that concepts falsely promoted as 'European' are actually demonstrated to be a common human inheritance. One of the unintended consequences of the project of 'alternative modernity' has been to flatten out the history of Europe

[26] Cooper 2005, pp. 3–4.

itself – where ideas of secularism and reason were never singularly construed, or resolute, or, indeed, universally accepted.

Assigning 'ownership' of modernity to Europe is a theoretical move that has debilitating effects on a range of progressive political projects, including those of 'Third-World' or 'trans-national' feminism. The dichotomy typically posed by postcolonial feminist studies – between a dominating 'universalism' (feminism as articulated to the paradigms of freedom, emancipation and autonomy designated as 'Western') and 'alternative modernity' – makes it impossible to understand the development of feminist consciousness. Postcolonial feminists who conceptualise feminism binaristically, either as always already imported and thus inauthentic, or as embedded in native and traditional practice (an 'alternative modernity'), in fact obscure the politicised relationship between oppression and consciousness.

The repudiation of modernity *per se* as oppressive and as essentially external to 'non-Western' cultures has led to the production of an avant-gardist historiography that questions history itself. The entire discipline – indeed, disciplinarity itself – is condemned as oppressive. The paradoxical commitment to a 'different' historical time has led historians like Chakrabarty to reject what he terms the 'totalizing thrusts' or the 'historicism' of Marxist historiography, which on his reading entails a 'stageist' view of history and of capitalist modernity (as that which constantly overcomes difference). This totalising historiographic initiative Chakrabarty names 'History 1'; and he counter-poses to it a 'History 2'.[27] The latter stands outside the process of capitalist development, interrupting it from time to time. The problem with this elaboration of 'two kinds of histories' is not that its critique of 'History 1' is without substance (although the inferences that Chakrabarty himself draws from this critique are in excess of what the critique actually demonstrates), but that its presentation of 'History 2' is unhistorical! Chakrabarty himself observes that while 'History 1' is analytical, 'History 2' 'beckons us to more affective narratives of human belonging', providing us with 'our grounds for claiming historical difference'.[28] Rather than opening up the Marxist theory of history to critique as promised, Chakrabarty's account turns to 'Heideggerian ruminations on the

[27] Chakrabarty 2000, p. 66.
[28] Chakrabarty 2000, p. 71.

politics of diversity'.[29] How these ruminations might be thought to substitute for an 'analytical' history – or indeed to accomplish anything that is not plausibly within the compass of 'analytical' history – is left unexplained.

'Alternative modernity' implicates space as well as time. It claims a space radically exterior to the spaces of capitalism. As such, it has affinities with various forms of nativist discourse. In its more progressive versions it lays claim to the politics of indigenous knowledge and 'women's ways of knowing', pitted against 'modernity' and its handmaiden, science – the latter seen to enact an epistemic violence on the life-worlds of native peoples who live harmoniously outside the grasp of capitalism. The work of intellectuals such as Ashis Nandy, Gustavo Esteva, Cheikh Anta Diop, Walter Mignolo, and Vandana Shiva draws upon the politically resonant ideas of 'difference' and 'cultural authenticity' to construct a thesis of 'alternative modernity' whose own political implications remain uninterrogated. The idea of 'alternative modernity' selectively employs the idiom of progressive utopian thought for nativist purposes. The necessary critique is supplied by Ferguson, among others, in his work on Africa in the neoliberal world order. He writes:

> the application of a language of alternative [modernity] to the most impoverished regions of the globe risks becoming a way of avoiding talking about...and thus evading the question of a rapidly worsening global equality and its consequences. Forcing the question of Africa's political-economic crisis to the center of the contemporary discussion of modernity is a way of insisting on shifting the topic toward...the enduring axis of hierarchy, exclusion, and abjection, and the pressing political struggle for recognition and membership in the emerging social reality we call 'the global'.[30]

Empire and imperialism

Parry has recently noted 'the many signs of Marxism's return to intellectual life'.[31] Her cautious optimism stems in part from the robust debate on Marxism and the contemporary conjuncture generated by the publication in 2000 of Hardt and Negri's *Empire*, a book that fired and captured the imagina-

---

[29] Chakrabarty 2000, p. 50.
[30] Ferguson 2006, pp. 192–3.
[31] Parry 2004, p. 93.

tion and the mood of a global anticapitalist movement on the rise, seeking to invent a new global commons, as exemplified in the space of the World Social Forums, the first of which was held in 2000 in Porto Alegre, Brazil. In the years since the publication of *Empire*, however, global capitalism has continued its onward march, and attention has been drawn to the catastrophic and reactionary event of '9/11' and, more catastrophic still and just as reactionary, the ensuing developments in Afghanistan and Iraq. In these contexts, and in the absence of a serious commitment to international solidarity along class lines and a coherent analysis of what exactly is being opposed, Hardt and Negri's optimistic declarations seem wildly and implausibly overstated. Their thesis runs counter to the work of theorists of uneven development in the 'Third World', who point to the rapidly escalating *inequalities* in the 'globalised' world order. There is in *Empire*, as Parry has pointed out, a 'spectacular failure to address the substantive and experiential situations of the settled populations of the nation-states of Asia, Africa and Latin America'.[32] In what has come to be known as the 'War on Terror', moreover, we are patently witnessing, *pace* Hardt and Negri, a contradictory and powerful recuperation of *imperialism* as a mode of organising global politics, a vehicle to re-assert the superiority of 'Western' values and material interests. In a strange reversal, while 'liberation' in the age of decolonisation had meant liberation *from* imperialism, contemporary discourses on democracy, women's rights, and human rights posit imperialism *as a precondition for* liberation, a position captured most clearly in the coupling of occupation/liberation with respect to Iraq.

Empire has elicited considerable enthusiasm in postcolonial studies, too, although it is not for the most part its equivocal allegiance to Marxism that has been the focus of attention, but rather its preoccupation with deterritorialisation and border crossings in the presumed aftermath of the nation-state. These have been taken to confirm and reinvigorate long-standing investments in the field. Although a special issue of the flagship journal, *Interventions*, devoted to *Empire*, gave central space, under Abu-Manneh's guest editorship, to Marxist and materialist criticisms of the book, the fact remains that, for many in postcolonial studies, *Empire* has been viewed (and welcomed) as signalling the obsolescence of imperialism as a cardinal category for understanding capitalist development, above all in the contemporary era of 'globalisation'.

[32] Parry 2004, p. 100.

Ironically, it is within the contexts of nation-states and regional entities that the most serious challenges to imperialist globalisation are taking place. Throughout Latin America, for example, and above all in the countries implicated in Tariq Ali's suggestively titled *Pirates of the Caribbean: Axis of Hope* (2006), we are witnessing a renewed resistance to neoliberalism and to the United States, clearly identified as the imperialist adversary. To refer to these examples is not to propose a 'theoretical' privileging of the nation-state but to emphasise the attention to historical specificity and geographical unevenness that are necessary for any adequate accounting of contemporary realities and possibilities. Ahmad had made just this point in criticising the undifferentiating disavowal of nationalism in postcolonial studies as long ago as 1992:

> For human collectivities in the backward zones of capital…all relationships with imperialism pass through their own nation-states, and there is simply no way of breaking out of that imperial dominance without struggling for different kinds of national projects and for a revolutionary restructuring of one's own nation-state. So one struggles not against nations and states as such but for different articulations of class, nation and state.[33]

More recently, Marxist theorists have sought to reinvigorate the debate on world systems, focusing on the primitive accumulation of capital as an ongoing process – what Harvey calls 'accumulation by dispossession' – and, in literary studies, on the questions of 'world literature' and 'Third-World' aesthetics. These debates might well come to strengthen the Marxist hand within postcolonial studies although there is clearly a danger that, inasmuch as 'world literature' is fast becoming another academic buzzword, its potential to open up new ways of thinking the relationship between capitalism, modernity and aesthetic form will be dissipated. The debate on primitive accumulation speaks of struggle in a more urgent register, referencing the continuing expropriation of the global (and local) commons by national and transnational capitalists hoping to pre-empt future crises of capitalist accumulation. The choice between industrial growth or economic impoverishment, land for poor farmers and jobs for a surplus urban labour force can perhaps be grasped within the context of ongoing debates within Marxist theory and postcolonial studies.

---

[33] Ahmad 1992, p. 11.

We began by sketching the contours of the global economic and social set-up around the crisis of 1973. Bello suggests that a new crisis of capitalism is already with us, combining subsidiary crises of legitimacy, neoliberal ideology and overextension.[34] The anticapitalist movements are confronted today by the renewed growth of the Right. The list of the different sites of capitalist collapse – Mexico, Argentina, Brazil, Russia, the Asian Tigers and the debt-ridden African countries – is a sobering one. Even within the heart of global capitalism, the United States and Europe, there is a deepening recession marked by over-speculation and overcapacity. The World Bank and the IMF have been severely discredited. If the previous crisis provided the context in which postcolonial studies was established as a field of academic inquiry whose constitutive elements were anti-Marxist, the present conjuncture might just, and however belatedly, open up space for speaking of Marxism *and* postcolonial studies.

---

[34] Bello 2004.

Chapter Eighteen

British Marxist History

Paul Blackledge

In a recent defence of the relevance of Marxism to the study of history, Eric Hobsbawm has reminded us that Marx aimed to provide a basis for understanding history as a totality.[1]

> [T]he new perspectives on history should also return us to that essential, if never quite realisable, objective of those who study the past: 'total history'. Not a 'history of everything', but history as an indivisible web in which all human activities are interconnected.[2]

Similarly, Brian Kelly, in his Isaac and Tamara Deutscher Memorial Prize-winning study *Race, Class and Power in the Alabama Coalfields, 1908–21* (2001), followed John Saville, Alex Callinicos, Elisabeth Fox-Genovese and Eugene Genovese in extolling the totalising ambitions of history from below, and criticising those of its practitioners who have embraced historical relativism.[3] On a related note, Perry Anderson suggested that because Trotsky was the first to succeed in writing total history, he could lay claim to being the first 'great Marxist historian'.

---

1 Thanks to Kristyn Gorton for her help with this essay.
2 Hobsbawm 2004.
3 Kelly 2001, pp. 5–6.

> No other classical Marxist had so profound a sense of the changing tempers and creative capacities of the masses of working men and women, pushing at the foundations of an archaic social order 'from below' – while at the same time pre-eminently able to chart the complex shifts and organised political forces 'from above'.[4]

Alex Callinicos has argued that the necessity of totalisation in the study of history and society does not arise, as postmodernists would have it, 'from some totalitarian urge to dominate and control'. Rather, it emerges

> from the fact that... the capitalist mode of production... operates according to a logic that is in the most literal sense global, incorporating and subordinating every aspect of social life everywhere to the drive to accumulate.[5]

Nonetheless, Marx and Engels were adamant that, while the capital accumulation process provided the basis from which the totality could be understood, it would be a grave mistake, as Engels famously insisted in a letter to Joseph Bloch – 21 September 1890, to mechanically reduce processes in the legal and political superstructure to epiphenomena of developments in the base.

Fortunately, the Stalinist attempt to reduce historical materialism to just such a form of crude economic reductionism did not become absolutely hegemonic within the Communist movement. Historians of France and England especially were blessed with Marx's historical analyses of these countries which provided a rich legacy informing the research of a string of later historians. This was nowhere truer than in Britain, were in the 1950s the Communist Party Historians' Group (CPHG) brought together a number of Marxists who later made their names as amongst the most important historians of the twentieth century. Interestingly, while this group originally convened to inform the publication of a second edition of a Communist-Party book on English history, from the earliest moment their work transcended this narrow basis, and informed all subsequent Marxist historiography. Indeed, in 1986 Edward Thompson suggested that historians are still 'exploiting the terrain' opened by the 'breakthrough in British radical history' associated with the early work of the historians who came to found this group.[6] Two decades later, Thompson's

---

[4] Anderson 1980, p. 154. Compare to Callinicos 1998, p. 37. See also Blackledge 2005c.

[5] Callinicos 1998 p. 36.

[6] Thompson 1994, p. 361.

point retains all of its pertinence. A trajectory can be traced from the works of these writers to the joint winners of the 2004 Isaac and Tamara Deutscher Memorial Prize: Benno Teschke and Neil Davidson. Teschke's work is deeply informed by 'political Marxism', which developed as a synthesis of the work of Robert Brenner and Edward Thompson. If Davidson's Marxism is of a more classical bent, like Teschke it is informed by Thompson's thought, but as critically developed by Alasdair MacIntyre. Given the undoubted importance of Thompson's contribution to radical history, this paper will concentrate on surveying the debates occasioned by his work. If it concludes with a discussion of Davidson's work rather than Teschke's, this reflects the fact that I have discussed political Marxism at length elsewhere in this volume.

People's history

In 1935, Comintern General Secretary George Dimitrov noted that across Europe fascists were writing national historical myths through which they hoped to justify their contemporary political project. In response to this development, he argued, it was imperative that Communists should challenge those myths with their own histories of the progressive struggle for democracy experienced within each national state: 'to link up the present struggle with the people's revolutionary traditions and past'.[7]

Irrespective of the political merits of this programme, historiographically it opened the door to a series of studies of movements which had sought to create and deepen democracy. 'We became', wrote CPGB historian James Klugmann,

> the inheritors of the Peasant's revolt, of the left of the English revolution, of the pre-Chartist movement, of the women's suffrage movement from the 1790s to today.[8]

Nevertheless, while this innovation appealed to the CPGB's historians, the novelty of the imputation of the decidedly non-Marxist concept 'the people'[9] into the Marxist lexicon cannot be overstated. Marx's claim that 'the history

7 Dimitrov 1935.
8 Schwarz 1982, p. 56.
9 Hill 2000, p. 89.

of all hitherto existing society is the history of class struggles...oppressor and oppressed, stood in constant opposition to one another' would imply, even to the most cursory reader, that an undifferentiated conception of 'the people' was a concept about which Marxists would have traditionally been very critical.

While this is true, Raphael Samuel has argued that Communist 'people's history' provided 'the groundwork on which Marxist historians have built' monumental structures.[10] From Maurice Dobb's *Studies in the Development of Capitalism*, Leslie Morton's *A People's History of England* and Dona Torr's *Tom Mann and His Times*, to the mature works of Christopher Hill, Rodney Hilton, Eric Hobsbawm, Victor Kiernan, George Rudé, John Saville, and Edward Thompson et al., the achievements of this group have been praised across the historical profession. For, despite starting from political decisions originating in Moscow, it would be wrong to reduce the Marxism of this group to Stalin's vulgarisation of the same.[11] Indeed, despite the sectarianism of the Communist Party, CPHG members read and were inspired by, amongst others, C.L.R. James's magnificent *The Black Jacobins* (1938).[12] James was a Trotskyist, whose Marxism was, according to Robin Blackburn, 'alive to the ways in which the explosion of political and social contradictions allows the masses to emerge as makers of history'.[13]

If James's, and through him Trotsky's influence can felt in the histories produced by members of the CPHG, it was Maurice Dobb's *Studies in the Development of Capitalism* (1946), which, in the words of Eric Hobsbawm, 'formulated our main and central problem'.[14] The CPHG began to meet formally in 1946 with a view to aiding the production of a second edition of Morton's *A People's History of England*. Morton's book was among the most significant intellectual products of the Popular-Front period. In many ways, this book was also a model of radical historical popularisation. It was written in beautiful prose with a keen eye for detailed micro-narratives which illuminated the grand narrative of the people's struggle for freedom. From the earliest settlers through the revolts against feudalism and the English Revolution to the

10 Schwarz 1982, p. 71; Samuel 1980, p. 37.
11 Samuel 1980, p. 64.
12 Hobsbawm 1978, p. 23.
13 Blackburn 1995, p. 82.
14 Hobsbawm 1978, p. 23.

modern struggles of the industrial age, Morton wove a compelling synthetic 'history from below' of England.

Unfortunately, despite the many strengths of this book, it received very little attention within academia. The same cannot be said of the Hill's 'The Norman Yoke' (1954), which became, according to Schwarz, the 'central text' of the Historians' Group. In this essay, Hill traced the notion of the Norman yoke from the seventeenth century – though he suggests that the concept may have had roots going back to 1066 – through to the birth of the modern socialist movement. Interestingly, while Hill argued that Norman-yoke theory – the idea that the oppressive institutions of the English state were imported at the time of the Conquest, prior to which 'the Anglo-Saxon inhabitants of this country lived as free and equal citizens, governing themselves through representative institutions'[15] – became 'subsumed by theories of socialism',[16] he did not, as Schwarz implies, suggest a simple continuity between early popular struggles against absolutism and the contemporary socialist movement.[17] Rather, alongside his narrative of radical continuity, Hill stressed important moments of change:

> after 1832 (as after 1660) the theory of continuity became an anti-revolutionary theory... Paeans in praise of the ancient constitution suited those who wished to preserve the status quo.[18]

Therefore, while Hill undoubtedly traced a continuous trajectory of democratic struggle associated with the Norman-yoke theory between the seventeenth and the nineteenth centuries, his was no simple model of upward evolutionary progress. For Hill was keen to stress the novel role played by the proletariat in the democratic struggle that developed from the nineteenth century onwards.

If Hill was the first to publish a powerful historical justification for this position, the inspirational Dona Torr outlined the fullest version of this perspective. In her *Tom Mann and His Times* (1956), Torr argued that Mann was a representative of the 'newfangled'[19] working class of the industrial age, a class

15 Hill 1958, p. 64.
16 Hill 1958, p. 119.
17 Schwarz 1982, p. 70.
18 Hill 2000, pp. 117–19.
19 Torr borrowed this phrase from Marx 1973, p. 300.

that had inherited half a millennium of struggles for freedom.[20] For Torr, the hopes of the nation had come to be embodied in the democratic struggles of the workers – the class which inherited the mantle and the struggles of 'the people' for the realisation of full democracy.

Socialist humanism and structuralism

Torr's torch was taken up by members of the CPHG generally, and specifically by her 'protégé'[21] Edward Thompson. In his 'Socialist Humanism: An Epistle to the Philistines' (1957), written after his break with the Communist Party, Thompson outlined a brilliant and original contribution not just to the analysis of Stalinism specifically, but also to historical materialism more generally. Thompson characterised his Marxism as a version of socialist humanism because it placed 'real men and women at the centre of socialist theory and aspiration', whilst simultaneously reaffirming 'the revolutionary perspectives of Communism'.[22] The essay opened with the claim that 'a quarter of the earth's surface is a new society, with a new economic structure, new social relations, and new political institutions'.[23] However, despite the novelty of these social relations, oppression in many varied forms continued as a reality of life in those states: the persistence of oppression, despite the suppression of private property, convinced Thompson of the falsity of the traditional Marxist view that all forms of oppression were rooted in economic exploitation. Against such 'economistic' models of historical materialism, Thompson sought to re-emphasise human agency at the heart of his Marxism, and in particular to reaffirm the importance of ideas as the basis for action. This reinterpretation of Marxism allowed him to conceptualise both the rise of Stalinism and the revolt against it in 1956. He explained the anti-Stalinist revolt as the rebellion of the human spirit against the deadening grip of authoritarianism, while Stalinism itself had arisen as a reaction against malign ideas within the Marxist canon.

---

[20] Torr 1956, p. 98.
[21] Renton 2004, p. 105.
[22] Thompson 1957, pp. 107–9.
[23] Thompson 1957, p. 105.

> Stalinism did not develop just because certain economic and social conditions existed, but because these conditions provided a fertile climate within which false ideas took root, and these false ideas became in their turn part of the social conditions.

Those false ideas were rooted in the classical-Marxist tradition which occasionally tended 'to derive all analysis of political manifestations directly and in an over-simplified manner from economic causations'.[24] This mistake linked Stalinism to crude Marxism, as, in their cruder moments, Marx and Engels understood revolutions as mechanical consequences of the clash between forces and relations of production, rather than as products of the actions of real men and women. This weakness in their *œuvre* was most apparent when Marx and Engels used the metaphor of base and superstructure to aid their conceptualisation of reality. Thompson insisted that this was a

> bad and dangerous model, since Stalin used it not as an image of men changing in society but as a mechanical model, operating semi-automatically and independently of human agency.[25]

This 'denial of the creative agency of human labour', when combined with working-class 'anti-intellectualism' and 'moral nihilism', acted to rob Marxism of its human element and to freeze it into the dogma of Stalinism, which was itself 'embodied in institutional form in the rigid forms of democratic centralism'.[26] Developing this point, Harvey Kaye suggests, following Eugene Genovese, that the British Marxist historians have, collectively, sought to transcend the limitations of both the traditional interpretation of the base/superstructure model and the crude economistic model of social class.[27]

According to Thompson, the Stalinist distortion of Marxism could be explained, in part, as a consequence of the application of the more mechanical side of Marx's legacy. However, while Thompson was critical of Stalinism in practice as well as in theory, he insisted that the Stalinist states were socialist structures, albeit distorted:

---

[24] Thompson 1957, pp. 106–8.
[25] Thompson 1957, p. 113.
[26] Thompson 1957, pp. 132 and 121.
[27] Kaye 1995, pp. 3–4.

> the fact that British socialists do not like all the features of this society has no bearing upon the fact of its existence. It was obviously only short-sightedness which ever led socialists to conceive of the new society stepping, pure and enlightened, out of the fires of the old.[28]

To help explain this contradictory phenomenon, Thompson wanted to reclaim Marx's dialectical interpretation of progress – 'that hideous pagan idol, who would not drink the nectar but from the skulls of the slain' – and apply it to the interpretation of Stalinism, such that he explained it as a system that was simultaneously economically progressive and morally reactionary.[29]

While the power of Thompson's interpretation of historical materialism was realised in his magnificent *The Making of the English Working Class* (1963), his political perspectives in the period of the New Left were much less successful. Indeed, in 1966, Perry Anderson suggested that that all of Edward Thompson's strategic and tactical essays for New-Left publications in the late 1950s and early 1960s could be characterised by

> their uniform abstraction, their wandering subjectivism, their inflated rhetoric, their utter renunciation of any attempt to analyse rather than merely invoke present realities. Socialism, in them, gives way to a maundering populism. The categories of this thought are so vacuous and simplistic that it is difficult to credit that they are those of the same man who could write such overpoweringly concrete history.[30]

Fourteen years later, and in a somewhat less polemical register, Anderson suggested that the 'remarkably vague' nature of Thompson's conceptualisation of socialist revolution after 1956 was best understood in relation to the limitations of his break with Stalinism. While the authenticity of Thompson's moral critique of capitalism was not in question, his strategic perspective was inherited almost complete from 1950s' Communism.[31]

In an attempt to overcome the strategic limitations of the first New Left's socialism, Anderson penned his own schematic history of England, which he intended as a historical basis for a more robust English socialist strategy. His 'Origins of the Present Crisis' (1964) included a history of the failure of

---

[28] Thompson 1957, p. 106.
[29] Thompson 1958, pp. 98–100.
[30] Anderson 1966, p. 34.
[31] Anderson 1980, pp. 190–1.

the British bourgeoisie fully to modernise the British state, and, as a corollary of this, it was a history of the aristocracy's successful struggle to maintain its control over the levers of state power.[32]

Thompson produced a spirited polemical assault on Anderson's interpretation of English history in 'The Peculiarities of the English' (1965). A central criticism Thompson made of 'Origins of the Present Crisis' was of its normative structure:

> There is, indeed, throughout their analysis an undisclosed model of Other Countries, whose typological symmetry offers a reproach to British exceptionalism.

In contrast to this methodology, Thompson insisted that capitalist development 'happened in one way in France, in another way in England'.[33]

However, it was Anderson's conceptualisation of class that more than any other element of his thesis outraged Thompson: Anderson, he wrote, tended to clothe classes 'throughout in anthropomorphic imagery'.[34] He flattened the struggles for hegemony that had occurred within the proletariat into an overarching unity, within which Labourism was never seriously challenged. Class, perceived as a unified *it*, had two immediate consequences for Anderson's work: first, it enabled him to ignore the real struggles for hegemony that had taken place between reformists and revolutionaries within the British labour movement over the preceding century; second, it permitted him to read-off the attitudes of the mass of workers from the ideologies of their leaders in the Labour Party and trade-union movement.[35] Consequently, 'history is flattened, stretched, condensed; awkward facts are not mentioned; awkward decades are simply elided', in the pursuit of an untenable argument. While Thompson did not deny that Labourism was hegemonic within the English working class, he did deny that this hegemony was written in stone. In particular, he took offence at Anderson's dismissal of the existence of minority socialist traditions within the English proletariat.[36] In contrast to Anderson's schematic history, which had the effect of misrepresenting

---

[32] Blackledge 2004, pp. 18ff; Anderson 1992a, pp. 17–19.
[33] Thompson 1978, pp. 247 and 257.
[34] Thompson 1978, p. 279.
[35] Thompson 1978, p. 176.
[36] Thompson 1978, pp. 275–6.

crucial periods of struggle, Thompson maintained that 'we can only describe the social process...by writing history'.[37] From that standpoint, Anderson's schema was particularly debilitating because he did not investigate any of the periods of working-class resistance that he briefly mentioned. For Thompson, the schematic structure of Anderson's history, by focusing on overarching themes, tended to act as an objectivist apologia for the status quo. The schematic structure of his thesis was therefore not a forgivable vice, given the overall nature of his work; rather it masked a further shift towards an idealism in which the past was not simply viewed through the lens of the present, but was constructed from the ideologies of the present with scant regard for accuracy. Anderson's method therefore led to 'reductionism' whereby there occurred a 'lapse in historical logic by which political or cultural events are "explained" in terms of the class affiliation of the actors'.[38]

Anderson's reply to Thompson, 'Socialism and Pseudo-Empiricism' (1966), was ostensibly an aggressive defence of his own model of English social development against Thompson's criticisms. However, in the text, he both acknowledged the implicit idealism to be found in 'Origins of the Present Crisis', and noted that there were signs of 'a counter idealistic trend within European Marxism of a potentially comparable strength and sophistication' to the earlier tradition on which he had drawn: 'Althusser's work has this promise'. Nevertheless, by 1972 at the latest, Anderson had been convinced of Althusser's idealism, and it is apparent that by the 1970s *NLR* was no longer an Althusserian journal.[39] Irrespective of this development, Thompson's growing anger at the influence of Althusser on the British Left generally, and within Anglophone historiography more specifically, led him to extend his earlier polemic against Anderson's historiography to a general critique of Althusserian Marxism, within which category he subsumed Anderson and the *NLR*.[40] The result was Thompson's passionate defence of the historian's craft against any reductionist methodology: *The Poverty of Theory* (1978).

---

[37] Thompson 1978, p. 289.

[38] Thompson 1978, pp. 275 and 290.

[39] Anderson 1972.

[40] That Thompson was right to detect this influence is evidenced by the critique of his and Eugene Genevese's work made by Richard Johnson (Johnson 1978; compare with Johnson 1980). The next issues of *HWJ* carried a stimulating debate centred on Johnson's argument with contributions from Keith McClelland, Gavin Williams, Simon

Thompson argued that Althusser came 'not to offer to modify [Marxism] but to displace it'.[41] Althusser's epistemology, he argued, 'consists of an idealist mode of theoretical construction' that created a

> self-generating conceptual universe which imposes its own ideality upon the phenomena of material and social existence, rather than engaging in a continual dialogue with these.[42]

Althusser confused 'empirical procedures, empirical controls, with something he calls empiricism'.[43] By contrast, historical materialism, Thompson observed,

> differs from other interpretive orderings of historical evidence not (or not necessarily) in any epistemological premises, but in its categories, its characteristic hypotheses and attendant procedures.[44]

Thompson contended that Althusserianism built on the weaker elements of Marx's thought: in *Capital*, Marx deployed historical concepts to explain capitalism, while, in the *Grundrisse*, his thought remained trapped within the static structure of political economy.[45] It was from within this second tradition that Althusser arose: 'Althusser and his colleagues seek to thrust historical materialism back into the prison of the categories of Political Economy'.[46] Thompson saw an ancestor of Althusser's structuralism in Stalin's *Marxism and Linguistics*, and Althusserianism was, like Stalin's Marxism, a static system which could not begin to understand history as a process: it was, he argued with characteristic directness, 'unhistorical shit'.[47] Against this form of structuralism, Thompson remarked, 'I feel myself revert to the poetry of voluntarism'.[48] Thompson argued that Marxists should move from the scientific and static analysis of capital to the historical analysis of capitalism.[49] To make this leap,

---

Clarke, Tim Mason, Gregor McLennan, David Selbourne and Raphael Samuel. See also Johnson 1981 and Thompson 1981.

[41] Thompson 1978, p. 4.
[42] Thompson 1978, p. 13.
[43] Thompson 1978, p. 32.
[44] Thompson 1978, pp. 44 and 57.
[45] Thompson 1978, p. 61.
[46] Thompson 1978, p. 68.
[47] Thompson 1978, p. 108.
[48] Thompson 1978, p. 72.
[49] Thompson 1978, p. 154.

the historical-materialist method ought to have at its heart the aim of analysing the intentions of actors in real historical time. Additionally, as individuals understand their experiences through culture – the middle term between capitalism and the individual – Marxists were asked to prioritise the analysis of this sphere in their theoretical work.[50]

Thompson's reinsertion of human agency into the centre of Marxist theory was nowhere clearer than in *The Making of the English Working Class*. In the Preface to this masterpiece, he defended his book's 'clumsy title' with the claim that through it he was seeking to convey the sense of class formation as 'an active process, which owes as much to agency as to conditioning'. He noted that his title referred to the working class rather than to the more 'descriptive term' working *classes*, because the analytical power of the former term would allow him to explain history as a process. However, in contrast to Stalinist Marxism, he defined class

> not as a 'structure', nor even as a 'category', but as something which in fact happens (and can be shown to have happened) in human relationships.

While

> class experience is largely determined by the productive relations into which men are born...[c]lass consciousness is the way in which these experiences are handled in cultural terms'.

Where class experience is 'determined', class consciousness is not. This humanist framework allowed Thompson, first, to reject wooden Stalinist deductions of class consciousness from class location; and, second, to examine human action in its own terms, with the hope that the participants even in failed struggles will help teach us something of the 'social evils which we have yet to cure'. This latter point is used to justify the memorable passage in which he notes his aim of rescuing

> the poor stockinger, the Luddite cropper, the 'obsolete' handloom weaver, the 'utopian' artisan, and even the deluded follower of Joanna Southcott, from the enormous condescension of posterity.[51]

---

[50] Thompson 1978, p. 171.
[51] Thompson 1980, pp. 8–13.

In contrast to many of the 'historians from below' who have followed his lead, Thompson's democratic methodology had nothing in common with academic specialisation.[52] Rather, he aimed to unearth the stories of human struggles for freedom with the goal of informing contemporary socialist practice.[53]

In *Arguments within English Marxism* (1980), Anderson responded to Thompson's challenge through a threefold critique of *The Making of the English Working Class*. First, he argued that it was marred by the idealistic thesis of 'co-determination', by which Thompson argued that the working class 'made itself as much as it was made'; second, Thompson mistakenly had equated class 'in and through' class consciousness; and, third, Thompson had implied that the process of working-class formation had, essentially, been 'completed by the early 1830s'.[54]

Anderson's critique of Thompson's theory of co-determination is perhaps the most persuasive of the three points. For, despite Thompson's claim that class formation was an equal product of both objective and subjective circumstances, in practice he left largely unexamined the structural side of the structure-agency couplet and hence proposed a thesis that could not be 'adjudicated' on given the evidence cited in his book. Anderson noted several contextual elements that Thompson had left largely unexplored, including the impact of the French and American Revolutions, the commercial nature of London and the 'spearhead sectors of the industrial revolution'.

Anderson's criticism of Thompson's equation of class with class consciousness, centred on the claim that Thompson had made abusive generalisation from a peculiar history that could lead to voluntarist and subjectivist deviations from materialism.[55] Against Thompson's model of class, Anderson cited Gerry Cohen's 'fundamental work', which was 'unlikely to need further restatement'.[56] Third, in contrast to Thompson's implied claim that the making of the English working class had been closed in 1832 Anderson called for an analysis of the re-making of that class.[57]

---

52 Palmer 1990; Thompson 2000. For Marxist criticisms of some of the malign consequences of 'history from below' see Saville 1977; Saville 2003, p. 180; Kelly 2001, pp. 3–15; Callinicos 1998, pp. 37–9.

53 Thompson 1980, pp. 11–12; Anderson 1980, p. 2.

54 Anderson 1980, pp. 31–2.

55 See Ste. Croix 1983, pp. 62ff, and 1984.

56 Ste. Croix 1983, pp. 38–40.

57 Ste. Croix 1983, p. 45.

Whatever the undoubted merits of Anderson's critique of Thompson's voluntarism, his own analysis of the remaking of the English working class after 1848 smacked of the opposite error of reductionism. In 'The Figures of Descent' (1987), as in 'Origins of the Present Crisis', Anderson maintained that the British working class had experienced a 'deep caesura' between Chartism and the emergence of the Labour Party. He explained the shift from the two types of politics as a reflection of the changing structure of the English working class. The specificity of the new English working class lay in the contrast between its high degree of 'industrial organisation' compared with its exceptionally weak 'political project'. Politically,

> British labour as an organized force was a captive client of the Liberal party down to the end of the century after which the Labour Party grew as part of the liberal revival.[58]

Subsequently, Labour's path to power was no road of its own making: the First World War destroyed the Liberal Party, while the Second World War created the conditions for massive state intervention. The smooth transfer of power to the Conservatives in 1951 showed just how little the Labour Party had affected the 'structures of Britain's imperial economy'.[59]

Bob Looker has suggested that 'read as an account of the Labour Party there is little new or original here – Miliband's *Parliamentary Socialism* mapped this terrain decades ago'. However, Anderson went beyond Miliband in assuming that Labourism set the 'structural limits to working-class consciousness and activity'.[60] Whereas previous Marxist analyses of the English working class had shown the impossibility of the Labour Party seriously challenging the status quo, Anderson deepened this thesis, to dismiss the potential of English working-class anticapitalism. This dismissal rested on the claim that 'the English 1848 closed a history'.[61] By this he meant to suggest that the political and organisational legacy of Chartism was almost nil: the new factory proletariat had no use for the old ideology. What is striking, therefore, about Anderson's analysis of Labourism is the way that it is, first, founded on a mechanical model of the relationship of consciousness to industrial structure, while, sec-

[58] Anderson 1992b, pp. 157–60.
[59] Anderson 1992b, p. 164.
[60] Looker 1988, p. 17.
[61] Anderson 1992b, p. 157.

ond, it is equated, anthropomorphically, with the politics of the working class itself. Consequently, in 'The Figures of Descent', Anderson appears to reduce the consciousness of England's proletariat to the objective co-ordinates of England's social structure[62] As Bob Looker argued, Anderson

> has failed to grasp what Thompson's analysis of the English working class clearly demonstrated; the issue isn't a matter of conceptual distinctions but of real movements rising through class practice.[63]

Beyond the linguistic turn

However, if Anderson's conceptualisation of the relationship between class consciousness and class structure seemed too reductive, he was right to recognise idealistic tendencies inherent in Thompson's model. As Bryan Palmer suggested in a generally appreciative discussion of Thompson's work; 'the theoretical claims of Thompson and [Raymond] Williams were all too easily incorporated into the emerging orthodoxy' of the linguistic turn in the 1970s and 1980s.[64]

The idea that the social world is irredeemably discursive such that there can be no privileged vantage point from which we might grasp 'real' underlying relations was forcefully argued in Britain by the historian and ex-Marxist Gareth Stedman Jones in *Languages of Class* (1983). Stedman Jones suggested that historical enquiry should begin from a realisation that language is not to be understood simply as 'referring' back to some 'primal anterior reality'. Following the logic of this suggestion, he argued, rather than attempt to look through language to underlying real interests, historians must 'study the production of interest, identification, grievance and aspiration within political language themselves':

> language disrupts any simple notion of the determination of consciousness by social being because it is itself part of social being. We cannot therefore decode political language to reach a primal and material expression of

[62] Anderson 1992b, p. 168.
[63] Looker 1988, p. 27.
[64] Palmer 1990, p. 210.

> interest since it is the discursive structure of political language which conceives and defines interest in the first place.[65]

The Marxist historian Neville Kirk responded to this challenge to historical materialism by pointing out that Stedman Jones's method was 'idealistic' because it 'effectively dissolves reality back into language'.[66] Similarly, Samuel insisted, 'the historical record cannot be read only as a system of signs', for historians must look beyond language if they are to measure 'words against deeds'.[67] Commenting on Stedman Jones's reading of Chartism, Dorothy Thompson argued that

> I find it difficult to believe that anyone who has worked in the archives and has studied the published and unpublished language of the Chartists can fail to see that the idea that above all united them into a nation-wide movement was the belief that there was a profound unity of interest between working people of all kinds.[68]

Likewise, in his *1848: The British State and the Chartist Movement* (1987), John Saville found that he could only make sense of Chartism by going beyond those interpretations, such as that made by Stedman Jones, which concentrated on its, formally, moderate political demands. Saville argues that it was precisely because the demands for the People's Charter were rooted in an underlying class struggle at the point of production that Chartism both had a mass working-class base, and also generated such a popular and reactionary middle-class response:

> the outstanding feature of 1848 was the mass response to the call for special constables to assist the professional forces of state security. This was the significance of 1848: the closing of ranks among all those with a property stake in the country, however small the stake was.[69]

In reasserting the concept of material interest, Saville et al. re-engaged with the problem of how to relate ideas to social structures without succumb-

---

[65] Stedman Jones 1983, pp 20–2.

[66] Kirk 1997, p. 333. For other Marxist criticisms of Stedman Jones see Kirk 1996; Foster 1985; Callinicos 2004, pp. 143ff.

[67] Samuel 1992, pp. 245–6.

[68] Thompson 1993, p. 36.

[69] Saville 1987, pp. 224–7.

ing to reductionism. The answer articulated by political Marxism, as I have suggested elsewhere in this volume, is that properly understood, and when synthesised with the work of Robert Brenner, Thompson's approach offers a powerful basis both from which to comprehend the past and upon which to found a contemporary revolutionary politics. Conversely, Alex Callinicos, Neil Davidson, Chris Harman and Brian Manning[70] have recently argued that attempts by political Marxists to conceptualise the English Revolution specifically, and the transition from feudalism to capitalism more generally, without reference to changes in the forces of production has resulted in an inadequate model of the formation of the modern world. For example, Manning criticised Neal and Ellen Wood's study of political ideas in the seventeenth century thus:

> Viewing the aristocracy as already a capitalist class before the revolution is too simple. It diverts attention from where capitalism was actually developing among large farmers and elements in manufacturing and how that relates to the revolution. And it leaves little room for assessing the ways in which the revolution actually did facilitate the development of capitalism.[71]

Similarly, he criticised Brenner's account of the Revolution both for ignoring the growth of industry in the decades that led up to 1640, and for overemphasising the growth of capitalist farming amongst the aristocracy before in the same period. Interestingly, Manning did write that Brenner's empirical findings, relating to the role of merchants within the revolution, cohered with his own much more classical thesis that it was the 'middling-sort' who drove the revolution. He suggested that the growing importance of this group should be related to the development of industry; and because Dobb stressed this development, his model was better able than Brenner's to explain why 'industrial districts – not all of them – provided a main base for the parliamentarian and revolutionary parties'.[72] Following Dobb, therefore, Manning argued that

70 Harman 1998; Callinicos 1995; Davidson 2005; Manning 1994.
71 Manning 1997, p. 29.
72 Manning 1994, pp. 84–6; Manning 1999, p. 50.

the English Revolution could best be understood as a bourgeois revolution located within a framework dominated by 'the rise of capitalism'.[73]

Neil Davidson has similarly insisted that the development of the productive forces must be at the centre of any adequate Marxist account of the transition from feudalism to capitalism.[74] With regard to the concrete case of the Scottish bourgeois revolution, Davidson has convincingly shown, in his *Discovering the Scottish Revolution* (2003), that it is possible to conceptualise a sophisticated political narrative of events within a complex rendering of the base/superstructure model. Davidson's understanding of Marxism is indebted to Alasdair MacIntyre's early Marxist writings, which Thompson described being 'of the first importance' to historians.[75] Interestingly, the essay to which Thompson referred, MacIntyre's 'Notes from the Moral Wilderness', was intended as a rectification of some of the limitations of Thompson's 'Socialist Humanism' in the wake of criticisms by other members of the New Left in the 1950s.

In this essay, MacIntyre aimed at deepening Thompson's humanism through the medium of a reinterpretation of Marxism. The Stalinist insistence that history's general course was predictable rested, or so MacIntyre insisted, on a misconception of the role of the base/superstructure metaphor in Marxist theory. What Marx suggested when he deployed this metaphor was neither a mechanical nor a causal relationship. Rather, he utilised Hegelian concepts to denote the process through which the economic base of a society provides 'a framework within which superstructures arise, a set off relations around which the human relations can entwine themselves, a kernel of human relationships from which all else grows'. Indeed, MacIntyre wrote that in 'creating the basis, you create the superstructure. These are not two activities but one'.

Thus, the Stalinist model of historical progress, according to which political developments were understood to follow automatically from economic causes, could not be further from Marx's model. For, in Marx's view, 'the crucial character of the transition to socialism is not that it is a change in the

---

73 Manning 1999, pp. 45; 51. For a general overview of Manning's contribution to a Marxist understanding of the English Revolution and the transition from feudalism to capitalism see Blackledge 2005.

74 Davidson 2005.

75 Thompson 1978, p. 401.

economic base but that it is a revolutionary change in the relation of base to superstructure'.[76]

Whether or not one accepts something like MacIntyre's reinterpretation of the base/superstructure metaphor or Thompson's alternative, Davidson's and Teschke's works, alongside many others, are testament to the continued power and vitality Marxist historiography in the Anglophone world.

---

[76] MacIntyre 1998, p. 39. For more on MacIntyre's early Marxism see Blackledge 2005b. For sophisticated defences of the base/superstructure metaphor see Harman 1998 and Callinicos 2004.

Chapter Nineteen

Developments in Marxist Class Analysis

Vivek Chibber

Introduction

During the efflorescence of Marxist theory during the 1960s and 1970s, class analysis emerged as one of the central objects of debate and discussion. Those years were among the most fecund in the twentieth century for the development of scholarship around class issues. It was certainly the only time in Western academia that the concept came to occupy a central place across the disciplinary divide. This was a direct expression of the growth of interest in Marxism among a new generation of students coming out of the many social movements of the 1960s. As student interest in exploring Marxism exploded across the academic spectrum, so did an interest in the concept most centrally associated with that tradition. By the 1990s, this interest had either ebbed significantly, or had transmuted into a shift away from the Marxist variant of class analysis, toward more fashionable avatars steeped in cultural and discursive commitments. To the extent that an interest in class analysis, of a recognisably Marxist kind, can be found in Anglo-American academia, it exists in somewhat small and isolated pockets. Perhaps the one discipline where scholarship concerned with class has maintained a significant foothold is in Sociology, though here too, it is nowhere near as popular as it was a generation ago.

We will examine developments in class analysis along three dimensions central to its deployment as an analytical and political category: class structure, the labour process, and class formation/class struggle. *Class structure* refers to the location of social agents in the basic property relations, or production relations of an economic system. The *labour process* refers to the organisation of production, in which is produced the surplus that the dominant class appropriates from the direct producers. *Class formation* refers to the process through which agents located in differed classes organised around their interests. *Class struggle* is what happens when agents engage in the contentious pursuit of their interests.

Class structure

The concept of class structure has always been at the very heart of Marxist theory. Even though Marx was not alone in seeing class as critical to the basic dynamic of capitalism, he is the only modern thinker to build his social theory around the concept. It is therefore somewhat surprising that careful interrogations of its basic properties and its internal coherence as a concept were hard to find among twentieth-century Marxists before the New Left. Debates at the time of the Second and Third Internationals revolved far more tightly around empirical and political issues. The concern with unpacking what class denotes, at a fairly high level of generality, was simply not very visible among Lenin's contemporaries. Its prominence among late twentieth-century theorists is undoubtedly a product of their environment: the fact that they were typically housed in universities, where the mainstream opinion regarding class concepts ranged from scepticism to outright hostility. The development of class theory in this setting required a simultaneous clarification and defense of the concept against its critics.

In this newer generation of theorists, there is little doubt that the most significant stream of work has been produced by the American sociologist, Erik Olin Wright. Starting with the publication of *Class, Crisis, and the State* in 1978, Wright has produced a steady outpouring of scholarship on the logic of class as a concept, as well as an extremely ambitious cross-national survey of class structure. The project has been remarkable not only for its ambition, but for the stamina with which Wright has stuck to a consistent research agenda. The central elements of this project have been two closely related questions: first, what the properties of class structure are at the highest level of abstraction, and second, how it can be concretised in a fashion that is both empirically adequate – so it captures the most important observable tendencies in the contemporary setting – and theoretically consistent – so theoretical adjustments to empirical findings are not in tension with the abstract definitions of the concept.

The basic class concept

At the highest level of abstraction, class structures are defined by the distribution of the means of production – the productive assets – in a society. The degree of control that agents exercise over the means of production determines the range of strategies they available to reproduce themselves. Consider the difference between the following scenarii: one in which an agent has no productive assets at all, leaving him with just his physical powers, and another in which the agent owns a plot of land, or directly produces some commodities that can be sold on the market. The first case will have little choice but to find some way of earning money, typically by offering to work for someone else; the second, because of his ownership of productive property, has the option of escaping the burden of working for someone else. Different ownership situations bring about quite dissimilar sets of choices. As Wright summarises this principle, 'what you *have* determines what you *have to do*' to make a living.

It is important to note that property relations do not automatically generate class relations. They do so only when they assign power over assets *unequally*, so that one group of agents can enforce claims on the productive activities of another. When the former group can actually live on the claims it makes on the labour of the latter, Marxists regard it as a relation of exploitation, and hence, a class relation. The *fact* that productive assets are distributed unequally means that one class *can* exploit another; the precise *enumeration* of those rights will determine *how* the one class exploits the other. So, for example, the fact that rural landlords under feudalism enjoy superior but not absolute rights over land means that they can claim some of their tenants labour as rent; but because their claims are not absolute, and peasants also have partial rights to the land through custom, lords must wield the threat of physical force to realise their claims. In capitalism, by contrast, the exploiting class does not have to rely centrally on a direct use of coercion to extract labour. The fact that one group has no direct access to productive assets means that the only reasonable option open to them for survival is to hire themselves out to others for work, in exchange for money; for this, they actively seek out those in society who do possess productive assets. Thus, there is an extraction of labour effort in both feudalism and capitalism. But whereas in feudalism, it is the exploiter who must seek out the exploited, in capitalism it is the other way around. And whereas in feudalism, the exploiter must rely on the use of force – or the threat of force – in capitalism, the labouring class has no choice but to offer itself up for exploiting. As Marx observed, the 'dull compulsion of economic relations' replaces the interpersonal coercion of feudal times.

The preceding discussion carries two central implications. The first comes from exploitation being central to class. Exploitation occurs when one group lives of the labour of another, by either directly forcing work out of them, or by forcing them into a *situation* where they have to offer their work to the potential exploiters. The process of exploitation thus creates an interdependence between the two groups; but this interdependence is, at its very core, an antagonistic one. The fact that there is some measure of coercion involved in the process means that the exploited always resent their situation – hence the antagonism. But the dominant group must not only exercise power over the labouring group, it must also take some responsibility for the latter's well-being. Exploiters *need* the exploited. Class thus generates an antagonism, but it is one that must be contained so it can be reproduced. Classes constantly struggle against each other, but they also reproduce each other.

A second implication of the concept is that, since class structures set the strategies that agents must follow to reproduce themselves, qualitatively different class structures will generate very distinct patterns of social reproduction. This leads to a foundational principle for Marxist theory: societies with qualitatively different class structures ought to be seen as entirely different *social systems*, with entirely different logics of economic reproduction, different mechanisms for income distribution, and quite distinct aggregate development patterns. This is true at any given point in time: at any moment in history, regions with different basic class structures should be expected to exhibit very distinct systemic properties. But it is even more potent as an axis for historical periodisation. In different historical epochs, social reproduction has been governed by very distinct class structures – different modes of production – which have generated recognisably different 'laws of motion', to use a favorite phrase of Marx. Hence, human history can be divided into distinct epochs, each characterised by its own basic class structure, and its own laws of motion. Class thus becomes not only a principle of differentiating between agents, or groups of agents, but also a means of differentiating historical epochs.

The past two decades or so have witnessed some very ambitious efforts to cash out this claim for class structures as markers of epochal breaks. In the classical schema proposed by Marx, Eurasian history could be broken into at least three distinct social formations, three epochs distinguished by their modes of production – classical antiquity, feudalism, and capitalism. Marx suggested that each of these had its own laws of motion, but, famously, he only made progress on elucidating the laws of capitalism. The older forms were left largely untouched, but for some very provocative observations. The most ambitious attempts by twentieth-century Marxists on this score came during the 1980s. For antiquity, we have Geoffrey de. Ste Croix's monumental *The Class Struggle in the Ancient Greek World*, which, despite its title, ranged all the way to the fall of Rome.[1] Ste. Croix's work was not only recognised as an instant classic as a purely historical account; it was also hailed as one of the most theoretically sophisticated works of Marxist sociology, as it carefully showed just how the class relations of antiquity generated a particular development logic – distinct from the social systems that followed it historically. And around the same time, American historian Robert Brenner developed a highly influential analysis of medieval feudalism, showing with exemplary clarity just what the 'laws of motion' of the feudal economy were.[2] And, more importantly, he showed more clearly than any other Marxist before him, how feudalism exhibited entirely different economic dynamics than capitalism, based on the way that its class structure generated a distinct micro-logic for economic actors.[3] By the 1990s, Marxist theory could justly claim to have come

[1] Ste Croix, 1981.
[2] Brenner 1976; Brenner 1982.
[3] Brenner 1985.

some distance toward demonstrating Marx's basic intuition about relation between class and historical differentiation.

Dealing with Complexity

On the basic concept of class, as defined above, there was and remains a wide-ranging consensus among Marxists. Problems begin when we confront the reality of occupational structures in capitalism, which do not reflect the simple two-class schema laid out in the abstract conceptualisation. Most pointedly, there is a thick layer of positions which seem to fall somewhere in between the position of worker and capitalist. Developing a conceptual apparatus that incorporates this reality, in a way that is consistent with the more general criteria for class laid out above, has been an overriding concern of contemporary Marxists. If class is defined by coercive appropriation of labour effort, what is the class position of actors who are in the middle strata?

There have been two general responses to this challenge. One is to make the argument that many of the positions in the middle class are really just more complex forms of the basic class relations of exploiter and exploited. Hence, though these positions may seem to be neither capitalist nor worker, this is misleading. On closer inspection, they can be assimilated into this more basic structure, so that, for the most part, the basic two-class schema does end up mapping on to the empirical realities of capitalism.[4] Another, more common response, has been to recognise that middle strata are irreducible to one of the two fundamental class positions. This is the approach favoured by Nicos Poulantzas, Guglielmo Carchedi, and Erik Olin Wright.[5]

Wright's arguments on this score have been the most influential, and are worth examining in more detail, since they have evolved over time. The basic idea to which he has remained committed is that occupations in the middle class are so defined because they simultaneously embody elements of both the workers and capitalists. So, whereas one solution is to insist that positions in between capitalist and worker are actually more complex forms of either one *or* the other, Wright proposes that they are simultaneously one *and* the other. Middle-class occupations thus combine aspects of the worker with aspects of

[4] Loren 1978; Fredman 1973.
[5] Poulantzas 1978; Carchedi 1977; Wright 1978.

being a capitalist. The most obvious example is the 'owner-operator' in agriculture – the independent farmer – or the independent artisan in urban sectors. In both cases, the actor possesses the means of production like a capitalist does, but also has to directly put these implements to work as wage-labourers do. Hence, she has a managerial position, but she manages – herself. She works for a living, but she 'is her own boss', as the saying goes. More complex forms are supervisory positions within a firm, such as middle managers. In this case too, they embody aspects of the fundamental class positions. Managers directly control the labour of others in their supervisory capacity, as do capitalists; yet, they do not own the means of production. They are employed by capitalists, sometimes for a wage, and are working only at their employer's pleasure. In this respect, they are like workers. In both cases, the owner-operator and the middle manager, the class position has been described in a manner that is consistent with the more abstract definition – they are in the middle because they embody those elements that define a worker and a capitalist. Finally, because they objectively share in the properties of both classes, they have interests that are also pulled in both directions. Hence, Wright refers to them as 'contradictory class locations'. This is meant to capture the dictum that the middle class does not generate a political programme of its own, that its politics cannot be predicted outside of the political conjuncture. Since it is pulled both toward the proletariat and the bourgeoisie, which way it leans will depend on facts about the political scene.[6]

The labour process

The labour process occupies a central place in Marxist class theory, because of the underlying centrality of exploitation. This link is not a conceptual one: there is nothing in the concept of exploitation that necessarily leads to an examination of the labour process. The connection is based on an empirical fact about capitalism – that the pressure on capitalists to increase the rate of surplus extraction leads to an intensification of control and domination within the firm, at the level of the shop floor. In order to drive down costs to meet

6 Wright 1978, 1985, 1989, 1995. The broader conceptual apparatus in which this insight has been located has shifted over time for Wright, But the commitment to seeing the middle class as *sui generis*, and as comprised of conflicting elements, has remained steady.

competitive pressures, capital is forced to constantly reorganise the internal division of labour, as it brings in new technology and new work relations. This is because, in capitalism, the labour process is actually organised by capital itself. Feudal class relations, in contrast, left the labour process largely in the hands of peasants. The intensity and the quality of work therefore remained out of the hands of the lordly surplus extractors. To secure an increase in the rate of surplus extraction, lords did not have the option of manipulating the actual organisation of work. They had to renegotiate the terms on which peasants handed them their seasonal harvest, or their labour services – which typically required threats and force. Thus, in the two systems, the use of interpersonal coercion occupies a very different place. Capitalists can rely on the worker's own circumstances to get her to commit to work; but once she comes to work, the pitch, intensity, and care of her work is undetermined. To affect these, managers take direct control over the labour process and exert control over its details – through dominating the worker. In feudalism, lords cannot rely on the peasants' circumstances to get them to work for the lord. Coercion is required for this very fact. Once they consent to give some of their labour to the lord, the actual process of work is left in their hands. The place of coercion is thus neatly reversed in feudalism and capitalism – located within the labour process in one, and outside it in the other.

Precisely because production is organised by capitalists and their lieutenants, they are forced to devise ways to better extract labour effort from their employees. And this, in turn, involves a reduction of the employees' autonomy on the shop floor, their subordination to ever-increasing and changing demands. The result is that the class antagonism at the macro level within capitalism is reproduced at the micro level, within the workplace, as employers and employees lock horns around the organisation of work. Class struggle within capitalism thus extends from the detailed organisation of work to the distribution of resources at the level of the social system as such.

The work that made this point most dramatically, showing with great drama and flair how capital extended its control over the labour process over the twentieth century, was Harry *Braverman's Labor and Monopoly Capital*, perhaps the most widely-read Marxist work of the 1970s.[7] It had always been a staple of radical theory – Marxist as well as non-Marxist – that the employ-

[7] Braverman 1974.

ment relationship was a conflictual one. Braverman made this argument much more specific by zeroing in on the central instrument through which managers ensured their domination over labour: the drive to reduce worker's control over the labour process by deepening the division between mental and manual labour. This in turn was secured by an ongoing effort to reduce the level of skill associated with any particular job classification. The progressive deskilling of labour has two critical consequences favorable to capital: it removes the only leverage that workers possess as atomised sellers of labour-power – their possession of scarce skills; and it also reduces their ability to hinder management's dictation of the pace and intensity of work. Whereas craft production rests on the worker's possession of significant autonomy to set the pace of her own work, the usurpation of her knowledge of the production process makes possible the shift to industrial production – and the reduction of the worker to a mere appendage of the machines she is operating.

In Braverman's argument, management's drive to dominate workers on the shopfloor was built into capitalist production. Starting in the late 1980s, however, a stream of literature appeared that argued against any such determinism. Perhaps the most heralded of such work came from an MIT project to study the effect of changing technologies on industrial relations. In *The Machine that Changed the World*, James Womack, Daniel Jones and Daniel Roos suggested that new production designs and the increasing skill requirements in manufacturing had made possible a new era in industrial relations.[8] In this new régime, shopfloor despotism was not only unnecessary, but counter-productive. In order to take advantage of the possibilities created by new technology, managers had to elicit the creative abilities of their employees and enter into a co-operative relation with them. Instead of the old, rigid system of production-line work associated with Fordism and Taylorism, you would now have groups of workers collected into small teams, which handled multiple tasks and poured their creative energies into solving problems – a system that became known as 'lean production'. The lines between managers and production line workers would have to be obliterated, and co-operation would replace conflict as the organising principle for production. The authors took their inspiration from a particular understanding of Japanese industrial

---

[8] Womack et al. 1990.

relations, and predicted that this nimble, synergistic approach would soon become the standard practice in American industrial production

By the early 1990s, this line of research had produced a flood of literature expressing enthusiasm about the possibilities offered by this new approach, and recommending that the old industrial relations apparatus built up in the US over the past half-century – based on collective bargaining, union representation, and an assumption that the employment relation was an adversarial one – be dismantled and replaced by a new system premised on a mutuality of interests between labour and capital. It was especially popular among progressive scholars of labour and industrial relations. Apart from its empirical base, it drew upon a powerful sentiment among progressive intellectuals, to the effect that traditional Marxist approaches were too rigid in their understanding of capitalism, and too 'objectivist' about interests – there were no objective interests 'out there', to which politics had to be adjusted. Rather, interests were endogenous to institutional and organisational settings. It was thus mistaken to assume that the labour-capital conflict was built into the system because of their objective interests. There was every possibility, the argument went, that the two actors could coalesce around a joint project, which was positive-sum with regard the outcome.

This line of analysis seemed to spell the death of Braverman's influence. But almost immediately, a response was offered by some labour intellectuals that undercut the argument's main elements. Interestingly, the first response did not come from within academia. It came from labour strategists and journalists, most notably Kim Moody, Mike Parker and Jane Slaughter. Associated with the Detroit-based labour publication *Labor Notes*, they showed in great detail that, far from opening a new era of industrial relations, lean production actually intensified the deskilling and the speed-up associated with Taylorism.[9] Lean production was not much different from Taylorism in its aims, but it was much more skilled in its propaganda. Though it took academia some time to catch on, Parker and Slaughter were eventually followed by a rapid-fire release of critiques of lean production, buttressed with more evidence of the gap between rhetoric and reality. It was found that the new techniques, where employed, resulted more often than not in more speed-up, more stress, less autonomy, and more 'bench-marking' – pitting employees against one

[9] Parker and Slaughter 1988.

another so that the fastest times became the norm to which all workers had to perform.[10]

In 1997, Ruth Milkman published one of the most detailed studies of lean production in *Farewell to the Factory: Auto Workers in the Late Twentieth Century*, and Kim Moody released his *Workers in Lean World*. While these books further undermined the case for jointness and the promise of the new work relations, they also marked, in retrospect, a surprisingly quick end to the debate. Whereas the scholarly enthusiasm for post-Fordism and lean production had been at an extraordinary high in the early nineties, it had largely dissipated by the end of the decade, perhaps under the weight of the mounting evidence complied by its critics. This did not signal by any means a resurgence in Marxist approaches to industrial relations or a rejuvenation of Braverman's line. The general turn away from traditional class analysis continued largely unabated, and has since. What it did signal was that, at least for the time being, one very ambitious challenge to Braverman's conceptualisation of the labour process had lost steam. The fundamental conclusion of his work – that the relation between capital and labour is intrinsically antagonistic, and this antagonism is reproduced on the shopfloor – seems to still have traction.

Class formation and class struggle

The final aspect of class analysis to consider is the problem of class formation and class struggle. This is perhaps where there has been the greatest turn within radical scholarship. During the 1970s, and even into the '80s, there was a concerted effort at recovering the conflictual history of labour-capital relations. These were the years when, under the influence of E.P. Thompson, Herbert Guttman, and David Montgomery, labour history experienced a veritable explosion of interest in Anglo-American academia. But for the most part, there was a lack of connection between those Marxists working on political economy and the labour process on one side, and those working on labour history on the other. Among the latter group, there was, from the start, a much greater valence given to culture and ideology – reflected in the fact that among social historians, the influence of Thompson and Guttman continued to grow through the eighties, even as the stature of Marxism was declining. This no

10 Grenier 1988; Babson 1995; Berggren 1993; Graham 1995.

doubt reflected the enormous weight the two pioneering historians placed on cultural mediation, and even on cultural construction. Hence, while someone like Braverman stressed capital's built-in drive to deskill labour, and labour's ubiquitous resistance to it, the influence of this approach never extended very deeply into social history – where contingency, context, and malleability were stressed much more than the unrelenting pressures of capital accumulation.

Labour history did not take long to start expressing an impatience for the Marxist insistence of a connection between class structure and class formation. If class formation depended critically on workers' consciousness of their situation, and if this consciousness was mediated by the discourses in which workers were steeped, then surely an interest in class formation had to concentrate first and foremost on the problem of culture, ideology, etc.? If workers organised against capital only if they perceived their commonality with others, then surely a focus on identity was of the first order – what were its roots, whence did it emerge? Not surprisingly, the conclusion of much of this research was that there was no necessary relation between occupying the position of a worker in the class structure, and internalising it as ones primary identity. Why, then, privilege class as an identity? This line of argument generated a subtle shift in radical analysis from looking at class as a something that structures the actual range of strategies that actors can pursue, to a focus on it as a kind of identity. Naturally, once it is re-conceptualised in this way, there is no reason to give it any more prominence as a structuring principle than any other identity.

The notion that class depended on identity, and that such identities were hard to come by, made for a general disillusionment about the whole Marxist programme. The unease was given plenty of succour by the fact that, as the worries about class formation were setting in, the political power of labour organisations was beginning to ebb across much of the capitalist world. It seemed to offer proof that Marxists vastly overestimated the importance of class as a critical factor in political life.

The noteworthy aspect of this whole line of reasoning was that it concentrated its focus, almost without exception, on *one* class – workers. But all the while that this class was being declared unfit for travel, the other end of the class divide, capital was reconstituting itself as a political actor in the most spectacular fashion; even more, it was using its organisational muscle to wage one of the most intensive attacks on labour that had been witnessed in the twentieth century. Hence, in the very years when social history was writing an obituary for Marxist class analysis, a class war of remarkable proportions was being waged in the Atlantic world.

The political constitution of capital during these years did not go entirely unnoticed among radical scholars. It was captured and studied with great care, mostly by American sociologists. Starting in the mid-1980s, several scholars produced a stream of analysis on the New Right, which showed its base in the American corporate class. There were two aspects to this work. First, it examined the organisational basis for capitalist political action. The core political actor was taken to be financial firms, which were able to act as co-ordinators because of their wide connections to the entire corporate structure. But added to this was the presence of a small group of CEOs and managers, who sat on several corporate boards and served as an interlocking directorate, straddling several sectors, and hence organisationally able to rise beyond the narrow interests of one firm or one sector.[11] The second dimension studied was the means by which these power centres mobilised their resources to shift the balance of power. Here, the key mechanism was financial donations to political candidates, funnelled through Political Action Committees (PACs).[12] The peculiarity of the American electoral system is that it is overwhelmingly run on private funds. This made it relatively easy for a highly mobilised capitalist class to channel its influence to the political arena, as its financial prowess simply overwhelmed that of labour. This scholarship continues to grow and deepen, and has provided a rich analysis of how capital has organised around its interests, and then stamped them on the political scene.

The most important consequence of the business offensive, at least with regard to the issue of class formation, was a massive decline in the level of unionisation within American labour. From a high of about 36% after the Second World War, union density declined to just over 10% by the middle of the 1980s – basically as a result of intensified resistance by employers.[13] Underlying this shift in class strategy was a precipitous decline in the economy-wide rate of return on investment, which set in during the late 1960s. As businesses across the country found their profit rates declining, they set about

[11] See Mizruchi 1996 and Burris 2005 for surveys.
[12] Burris 1987; Salt 1989; Akard 1992; Jenkins and Eckert 2000.
[13] Goldfield 1987.

dismantling many of the postwar institutional supports for labour that, in happier times, they had learned to live with. In part this was accomplished by shifting location, from the traditional heartland of manufacturing in the Midwest, to the non-unionised South. But, even more importantly, they dug in their heels in the daily struggle on the shopfloor – resisting new unionisation drives and breaking some of the key strikes of the decade.[14] By the late 1990s, workers in the US were so demoralised that, even as unemployment dropped to its lowest levels in two decades, wages hardly recovered at all – a sign that workers were too cowed to demand raises, even in tight labour markets.

Conclusion

Despite the general turn away from class analysis in radical circles, there has been much work done in the are over the past two decades, and it still continues to progress. There is no denying that Marxist theorisation of class is richer and more sound today than it was at the start of the Reagan-Thatcher era. Still, if we look to the future, there is some reason to worry. There is a clear generational gap in the enthusiasm for Marxist theory among intellectuals, with much of the most interesting work still being done by stalwarts of the New Left. Younger scholars have neither shown as much interest, nor produced as much. This will most likely show up as a noticeable decline in the quantity and quality of theorising by the second decade of the millennium.

There is also a conspicuous unevenness in production along the disciplinary frontier. Class theory has, for the time being, established a toe-hold in American sociology, and also geography, but has been retreating along much of the remaining intellectual landscape. Perhaps most conspicuous has been its decline among historians. Much of the most innovative work on class was produced, understandably, by a new generation of labour historians during the 1970s and '80s. But labour history has, like much of social history more generally, lost its enthusiasm for studying the themes central to Marxist theory. To the extent that it still soldiers on, the field is largely dominated by the study of discourse and identity formation. One consequence of this, which seems to have gone unnoticed by practitioners, is that there has been very little progress on the themes opened up by Robert Brenner and G.E.M. de

[14] Moody 1988.

Ste. Croix – the study of the internal dynamics of precapitalist formations and long-term change more generally. Indeed, the most heralded work on these themes in recent years has been by non-Marxist theorists, and offered as an explicit critique of the Marxist framework.[15] Apart from the work of Brenner and de Ste. Croix, one cannot point to much original scholarship produced by Marxists on feudalism, or on antiquity, in the past two decades.

In the study of politics, there has also been a similar retreat. To take but one example, there are still very few studies of the rightward shift of the Democratic Party since the 1970s, despite the general recognition that this shift was a critical component of the assault on labour and the welfare state. The analysis of how the New-Deal era came to an end is thus woefully incomplete. While there are a large number of studies on how the Democrats were forced to accommodate labour and other oppressed groups in the 1930s, there is no parallel study of how and why it came to attack them after the 1970s. Every four years there is a vigorous debate among American progressives on how to orient to the Democrats – but still no detailed study of their transformation after the Carter presidency.

Hence, while progress in class analysis has been significant, the momentum behind it is weaker now than at any time in recent memory. The balance-sheet is therefore somewhat mixed. Whether, and to what extent, there is surge of interest in it again will depend on broader social and political conditions. But in the event that such an interest should re-emerge, it will have a sold foundation of research and theory to build upon.

---

15 Bin Wong 1997 Pomeranz 2000.

Chapter Twenty

New Interpretations of *Capital*

Jacques Bidet

Capital proposes an 'economic' theory. Yet the reinterpretations I shall be referring to derive from the work of philosophers. The reason for this paradox is that Marx treats economics not as an abstract, ahistorical discipline, but as a social science grasping economic phenomena in their imbrication with the social, technological, juridical and political system as a whole. As well as Marxian economics, these reinterpretations therefore also involve the social theory it presupposes, in all its epistemological and philosophical implications.

They are motivated by the major political and social movements, cultural changes and theoretical innovations of recent decades. They represent reactions on the part of intellectuals against the readings that used to be considered orthodox in the 'working-class movement'. They operate in their own particular way, by testing and re-translating the Marxist theoretical legacy into contemporary philosophical forms.

We can distinguish three main orientations. First, the continuation of the *Hegelian tradition*, especially around the Frankfurt school, in Germany, but also in Italy, France, Central Europe, Japan, and elsewhere. Second, a current I shall refer to as that of *historical materialism*, which is particularly active in France, especially via the Althusserian school. Finally, and most recently, the group of *analytical Marxism*, which attests to the influence of Marxism in Anglo-American culture.

Work in the human sciences on the concepts of *Capital*

Philosophers do not broach *Capital* (or at least they should not) without also having in mind the work of Marxist economists, sociologists and historians. In these new contexts, the latter, each in their own domain, have also reinterpreted this theory by applying it to new situations, reworking its concepts, or taking up its classical problems.

In economics mention must be made of a wide variety of works on monopoly capitalism (Baran and Sweezy, Boccara, Mandel);[1] on the world system and unequal exchange (Emmanuel, Amin, Gunder Frank, Wallerstein, Arrighi);[2] on imperialism (Chesnais, Harvey);[3] the solutions offered by Gérard Duménil and Duncan Foley to the problem of the 'transformation of value into production prices';[4] works geared towards political ecology (O'Connor, Altvater, Martinez-Alier, Harribey),[5] an alternative economics (Gorz),[6] self-management (Schweickart, Andréani),[7] or different 'models of socialism' (Elson, Blackburn).[8] In research involving *Capital* there have also been interventions by the regulation school (Aglietta, Lipietz, Boyer);[9] American radical economics (Bowles and Gintis);[10] and the neo-Ricardianism derived from Sraffa (Benetti and Cartelier).[11] Also worthy of note is the concept of 'cognitive capitalism' recently proposed by followers of Toni Negri.

The Frankfurt school, involving a close combination of Marxism and sociology, has prompted re-examination of the question of labour starting from *Capital*, as has Italian *operaismo*. Marxian class analysis has been revived by

---

[1] Baran and Sweezy 1966; Boccara 1973; Mandel 1976.
[2] Emmanuel 1972; Amin 1970; Frank 1970; Wallerstein 1980; Arrighi 1990.
[3] Chesnais 1997; Harvey 2001.
[4] Duménil 1980; Foley 1986.
[5] O'Connor 1993; Altvater 1992; Martinez-Alier 1987; Harribey 1998.
[6] Gorz 1991.
[7] Schweickart 1993; Andréani 2001.
[8] Elson 1993; Blackburn 2004.
[9] Aglietta 1979; Lipietz 1983; Boyer 1986 and 1995.
[10] Bowles and Gintis 1988 and 1998.
[11] Sraffa 1960; Benetti and Cartelier 1975. See also Dostaler 1985.

Bourdieu, who expands the Marxian concept of reproduction; by Erik Olin Wright in the context of analytical Marxism;[12] and by the pursuit of work on the working class (Bottomore and Brym, Pialoux and Beaud),[13] divisions among wage-earners (Bihr, Duménil and Lévy),[14] the commodification and subjection of labour (Burawoy, Lebowitz),[15] domestic labour and sexual social relations, and the evolution from Taylorism to Fordism and post-Fordism (Coriat, Coutrot, Linhart),[16] up to the age of generalised computerisation (Lojkine) and 'flexibilisation' (Vakaloulis).[17]

And we should also take into consideration the immense labour of historians, from *Annales* to works on the working class (Thompson),[18] the origins of capitalism (Bois, Wood),[19] the history of the family (Seccombe),[20] and so on. There are also anthropological analyses of the theory of modes of production, of which *Capital* furnishes the paradigm, by Emmanuel Terray, Maurice Godelier and Claude Meillassoux.[21] Not to mention the reflection of jurists on the foundations of the theory of law (an issue posed, from Pashukanis onwards, on the basis of *Capital*), and, recently, on the juridical nature of the wage-earning class (including, outside Marxist ranks, by Supiot).[22]

A philosophical interpretation should be capable of revealing why Marx's theory is capable of generating such a profusion of work.

Dialectical interpretations

The MEGA – the complete edition of Marx and Engels's works begun in 1927 – furnished the indispensable instrument for the study of the genesis and overall interpretation of *Capital* (Rubin, Rosdolsky, Il'enkov, Vygotsky).[23] The publication of the *Grundrisse* (in 1939–41) was to play a significant role in

12 Olin Wright 1985 and 1997.
13 Bottomore and Brym 1990; Pialoux and Beaud 1999.
14 Bihr 1989; Duménil and Lévy 1994 and 2003.
15 Burawoy 1985; Lebowitz 1992.
16 Coriat 1990; Coutrot 1999; Linhart 1991.
17 Lojkine 1992; Vakaloulis 2001.
18 Thompson 1963.
19 Bois 2000; Wood 1999.
20 Seccombe 1992 and 1993.
21 Terray 1972; Godelier 1970; Meillassoux 1975 and 2002.
22 Supiot 1994.
23 Rubin 1972; Rosdolsky 1977; Il'enkov 1982; Vygodskij 1973 and 1976.

the specifically philosophical interpretation. In this initial outline, written in 1857–8, Marx develops his programme of a 'critique of political economy' by constant recourse to the categories of Hegel's logic. However, in the course of various successive drafts, up to the publication of the first edition of Volume One in 1867, a second edition in 1873, and a French edition between 1872 and 1875, this philosophical conceptual system was progressively marginalised. An enormous labour of exegesis will tend to restore it, to comment on *Capital* and explain it on the basis of this original approach and in the light of the philosophy of the young Marx.

The philosophical exegesis of *Capital* was revived in the West in the intellectual and political context of the late 1960s, particularly by disciples of Adorno: Alfred Schmidt, Hans-Georg Backhaus, and Helmut Reichelt.[24] Various study groups and works devoted to *Capital* then appeared (Haug, Göhler).[25] A vast field of research, dialectical in spirit, also opened up in Italy and is still active today, combining, in accordance with the Gramscian tradition, philosophy and politics and often marked by the influence of Lukács: Claudio Napoleoni, Mario Dal Pra, Alberto Gajano, Enrico Grassi, Roberto Finelli, Stefano Garroni, Alessandro Mazzone, Roberto Fineschi.[26] Likewise in France, in a similar spirit, there is the work of Jacques D'Hondt, Solange Mercier-Josa, Lucien Sève, Ruy Fausto, Emmanuel Renault and Jean-Marie Vincent.[27] A current more explicitly inspired by Lukács developed in Central Europe with Karel Kosik, István Mészáros and Agnes Heller.[28] Other works, particularly South-American ones inspired in part by liberation philosophies, like those of Enrique Dussel, can also be related to this context.[29] In addition, there is an important Japanese school (from Kôzô Uno, who used the dialectic in an original way, to Hiromatsu, Uchida, etc.), bound up with an interest in Marxism dating back to the 1930s and the influence of German philosophy.[30] Several studies make it possible today to understand these works as a whole – in par-

---

[24] Schmidt 1971; Backhaus 1997; Reichelt 1970.

[25] Haug 1974; Göhler 1980.

[26] Napoleoni 1973; Dal Pra 1977; Gajano 1979; Grassi 1979; Finelli 1987; Garroni 1997; Mazzone 2001; Fineschi 2001.

[27] D'Hondt 1972; Mercier-Josa 1980 and 1999; Sève 1980; Fausto 1986; Renault 1995; Vincent 1973 and 1991.

[28] Kosik 1976; Mészáros 1970; Heller 1976.

[29] Dussel 2001.

[30] Uno 1980; Hiromatsu 1974; Uchida 1988.

ticular, those by Michael Heinrich[31] and, above all, Roberto Fineschi, as well as the monumental dictionary published by Wolfgang Fritz Haug since 1994.

These authors react on the one hand against the logico-historical reading that was prevalent, in the context of a certain (triumphalist) philosophy of history, within political Marxisms endowed with authority; and, on the other, against the often rather pragmatic reading of economists. They had the merit of foregrounding the exigency of a 'logical' – that is, theoretical – interpretation of *Capital*, as did the Althusserians in the same period, albeit with different philosophical references.

This reading, notably in Hans-Georg Backhaus and Helmut Reichelt, prioritised the text of the first edition of 1867 over that of the second (1873), sometimes presented as the result of a 'popularisation' by Marx. The first, 'esoteric', more philosophical exposition was then opposed to the 'exoteric' exposition of the later version, which alone supposedly corresponded to Marx's 'dialectical method'. The model taken as a reference-point for interpreting *Capital* was thus to be found in the *Grundrisse*. The starting-point was what is referred to as the 'contradiction' – *Widerspruch* – between use-value and exchange-value in the 1867 version. It was stressed that the intention of Marx's exposition was to demonstrate that the market, far from being what it presents itself as – a space of interaction between rational individuals – constitutes an alienated social relationship, where use-value is imprisoned in the abstract objectivity of value, with labour becoming indifferent to its content. At the centre of analysis is the 'reduction of concrete labour to abstract labour' generated by the market. In this optic, it is the examination of 'simple circulation' that constitutes the starting-point for the logical exposition of capital, the object of Part One: one starts from the market understood as a general system of *exchange*, with the monetary expression that involves, abstracting from the specifically capitalist relation of *production*, which will be the object of Part Three. And this starting-point, as we shall see, is what gives impetus to the interpretation as a whole.

Thus, emphasis is laid on the fact that Marx's theory is a 'theory of the value-form', of value as a social form – a thesis sometimes turned against the 'labour theory of value', which is allegedly substantialist. Advanced by Alfred Sohn-Rethel, the notion of 'real abstraction', which refers to the fact

31 Heinrich 1990.

that it is not only a question here of abstract forms of thought, but that these define the reality of the social relation, is adopted to impart full significance to this 'reduction of concrete labour to abstract labour', which thus refers to the real domination of concrete labour by abstract labour. This approach prompts consideration of money, in its abstraction, as a social relation constitutive of capitalist society. It endows commodity fetishism with a potent realistic meaning: what is involved is not merely an intellectual phenomenon, but the very condition of modern humanity, in the circumstances of capitalism as a society governed outside its control by the market. And this theme is pursued in the analysis of the specifically capitalist social relation, as Marx sets it out in Part Three, making it possible move beyond a reading in terms of the quantitative extraction of a surplus. In effect, it makes it possible to understand that exploitation is also a relation of domination, but with this peculiarity when compared with previous class systems that it is geared to the accumulation not of use-values, but of *abstract* wealth – surplus-value – regardless of its concrete content. This reveals that capitalism is not only contrary to the interest of the workers whom it exploits, but heedless of the effects of material production on the population as a whole and on nature.

If the general orientation of readings that highlight the dialectical element might legitimately be summarised thus, we can understand why they have been able to play a stimulating philosophical role in the Marxist critique of capitalism, helping it to supersede incomplete representations of the capitalist relation – both its quantitative reduction to the simple *extraction* of a surplus and its formal, qualitative representation in terms of *domination*. It foregrounds a problematic of *abstraction*, which demonstrates the full potential radicalism of Marx's critique of commodity and capitalist *alienation*, its singular contemporaneity at a time when capitalism is revealing its power by producing needs themselves and capturing desires – that is, demonstrating its capacity to appropriate the very definition of use-values, in accordance with a logic that imperils the elementary conditions of humanity's prudent conduct of itself in its relationship with 'nature', with production ultimately turning into destruction.

This brief, ideal-typical summary does not refer to an established 'doctrine' common to the 'Hegelian' orientation, whether inspired by the Frankfurt school or based on autonomous relays. It simply seems to me that these are the terms in which, over and above the contribution of any particular author, we can represent the general spirit informing it and account in principle for the subversive stimulus it continues to have among new generations, ensuring communication between the Marxist tradition and contemporary currents challenging consumption and production, from situationism to the critique of work, everyday life, culture and ecology. It is a precious heritage, nothing of which must be lost.

Such work on the Marx-Hegel relationship is also to be found in a number of Anglo-American authors. In particular, we can mention the works of Thomas Sekine, Bertell Ollman, Fred Moseley (with contributions by Smith, Murray and Reuten), Chris Arthur, and Mark Meaney.[32] Several of them have adopted the title of a 'new Hegelian Marxism'. Some, like Arthur, have assigned themselves a more specific project, under the rubric of the new dialectic. They propose to base themselves on the 'systematic' dialectic of the *Logic* for interpreting *Capital*, understood as a theory of the capitalist 'system' (see the chapter devoted to them by Jim Kincaid in the present work). This hypothesis is fairly old (cf. the work of Fineschi), but here it is the object of a systematic development to the point of perfect virtuosity (see Sekine). It is true that dialectical forms, whether explicit or underlying, are omni-present in *Capital*. Such philosophical exegesis therefore illuminates a number of facets of Marx's theorisation. What remains problematic is the idea that the general matrix of a 'science of logic' is to be discovered at the same time in a 'theory of the capitalist mode of production'. And this is so even if certain analogies are clear. The counter-proof is furnished by the fact that the correspondence between the respective concepts of the *Logic* and those of *Capital* are, depending on the author, the object of utterly divergent, mutually exclusive interpretations – something that tends to render the project as such problematic.

In the Hegelian register we should also mention other research, like that of Colletti, who nevertheless ended up coinciding with the positions of Popper;[33] or of Denis, who rejects the theory of *Capital*, preferring the dialectic of the *Grundrisse*.[34] But other philosophies are also called upon – for example, phenomenology, notably in the work of Henry, who offers a reading of *Capital* firmly anchored in the preparatory texts and those of the young Marx, and

32 Sekine 1984–6; Ollman 1992 and 2005; Moseley 1993; Arthur 2002; Meaney 2002.
33 Colletti 1973 and 1980.
34 Denis 1980.

centred on the opposition between abstract labour and the organic subjectivity of individual praxis.[35] As for Derrida's intervention, with the figure of the 'spectre' it makes Marx's text pass the test of its deconstructive critique.[36] Referring to Spinoza and Deleuze, Negri has proposed a stimulating problematic in terms of the 'power of the multitude' that nevertheless marks a considerable distance from the concepts constitutive of Marxian analysis, beginning with those of value and production, which Negri believes to be called into question by the generalisation of intellectual, supposedly 'immaterial' labour.[37]

Problems with a *Grundrisse*-style interpretation

A certain number of problems attach to the Hegelianising approach in so far, at any rate, as it draws its inspiration for the interpretation of *Capital* from the *Grundrisse*. First of all, there are grounds for doubting that the best way to explain the final text is take the initial 'rough draft', however brilliant, as the key. When one proceeds thus, one tends to explain the result by its supposed 'sources'. One ignores the fact that when Marx wrote a new version on the same subject, it was in order to *correct* the previous one. One also tends to neglect the fact that what occurs in his case is what happens to every genuine researcher: he discovers something other than what he was looking for. In his process of development, in reality Marx proceeds like any other inventor: faced with problems he still only vaguely understands, he strives with the formal resources of his culture. Thus, both for his general plans and his particular analyses, he draws at each step on the Hegelian instrumentarium, with a view to recognising the new theoretical spaces it glimpses and formulating the theoretical questions that gradually appear to him. Such is the role of experimentation in theoretical research. Thus, when, as is regularly apparent from one draft to the next, Marx abandons a certain number of concepts, distinctions and sequences inspired by Hegelian logic, we must always ask whether he did not have good grounds for so doing. This does not mean that Marx turned his back on Hegel. Every page of *Capital* contains a wealth of precious philosophical determinations, which refer to classical German phi-

---

[35] Henry 1976.
[36] Derrida 1994.
[37] Negri 1991; Hardt and Negri 2000 and 2004.

losophy, modern political philosophy, even to Aristotle. But the dialectical performance evident in the research texts does not authorise regarding them as theoretically superior. On the contrary, we must ask why, in the gradual course of his research, Marx abandoned a certain number of dialectical resorts and whether his reasons were sound.

In particular, a decisive alteration in the exposition occurs between the *Grundrisse* and *Capital*. The draft – *Rohentwurf*, as German commentators gladly say – is divided into two parts: the 'chapter on money', which deals with 'simple circulation', and the 'chapter on capital', which deals with capitalist production. An analogous division is found in the final work, between Part One of Volume One ('Commodities and Money') and the rest of Volume One. But this resemblance conceals a major innovation: Part One of *Capital* no longer deals with *simple circulation* (or 'simple' – i.e. precapitalist – production), but with *commodity production* as such (according to its concept), or the 'market', but defined in abstraction as a commodity system of *production*-circulation. There thus emerges a new problem – the relationship between *commodity production*, with its juridico-political conditions, and specifically *capitalist* production, which is defined by Part Three. In other words, a double thesis: the capitalist economy cannot be defined as a 'market economy'; the concept of commodity economy is distinguished from that of capitalist economy. From this initial result of Marx's analysis we cannot draw any direct conclusions about the possible place of the market in a postcapitalist economy. The question is simply posed, rendering the prospect of basing socialism on the abolition of the market less self-evident.

Because they do not take account of this decisive advance in Marx's theoretical elaborations, interpretations of *Capital* based on the *Grundrisse* generally tend to impute *immediately* to the market what pertains to capital, to the *capitalist* market. Part of the critique in the name of 'abstraction' thus misses its true target, which is capitalism, where the process of production has as its object (as Marx explains) abstract wealth as such – something that cannot be said of commodity production according to its concept, expounded in Part One. Moreover, in its final draft, the latter in fact excludes the notion of 'contradiction between use-value and value' at this level and integrates the concept of abstract labour into a rational representation.

Finally, it is very difficult for purely dialectical interpretations to escape the charge of a 'dialectic of history'. This tendency, it is true, can be observed in the very text of *Capital*, which begins with the figure of the *market* – inter-individual rationality – to end with that of socialism, understood as socio-central rationality, based on devised *organisation*.

The tradition of historical materialism

It was precisely an 'anti-Hegelian' reaction in this sense which, from the 1960s onwards, provoked the emergence of a new current in France around Althusser and his followers – in particular, Étienne Balibar and Pierre Macherey.[38] The most significant subsequent works in this optic are doubtless those of Balibar on historical materialism and Marx's philosophy. Throughout the world, researchers were to some extent to identify with this new reading of Marx in philosophy and the human sciences. It should be noted that at the same time there was developing in Italy, with della Volpe, an attitude similarly occupied with the scientific character of Marx's *œuvre*; and an epistemological current, made famous by Ludovico Geymonat, persists today with Mario Cingoli or Franco Soldani.[39]

The emergence of the Althusserian current attested to a similar distancing from the more or less official Marxism of the period and its philosophy of history. It seems to me correct to refer to it as the 'current of historical materialism', rather than confine it to the epithet of 'structuralist'. It was in fact the inheritor of a whole context connecting part of the French philosophy of the period to materialist traditions dating back to the Enlightenment and Spinoza, which are expressed in a variety of different forms in the epistemology of Bachelard and Canguilhem and the parallel research of Lévi-Strauss, Bourdieu, Foucault or Lacan. In particular, it helped to put Marxism and the themes of these authors (epistemological break, structure, reproduction, unconscious, etc.) in league with each other and thereby establish new, fertile philosophical links between Marxism and the social sciences. What Althusser challenged was the representation of a society as a totality expressive of itself in each of its moments, which is realised in a fantastical dialectic of history. He thus guided research towards more prudent strategies, which consider

---

[38] Althusser 1965; Althusser et al. 1996; Althuser and Balibar 1970; Balibar 1974 and 1995; Macherey 1979. See also Duménil 1978.

[39] Cingoli 1996; Soldani 1992 and 2002.

particularities, overdeterminations, discrepancies, and conjunctures in their own right.

The work of the Althusserian tradition often tends to disturb economists rather than inspire them with confidence (that is why, despite the distance, they often prefer to turn towards Hegelianising interpretations, thinking it possible to discover a 'bit of soul' in them, as we say in France). As regards *Capital*, Althusser in fact inaugurated a more distanced way of posing questions about this work, privileging discontinuities, trial and error, ruptures. He encouraged people to register the difference between philosophical categories and 'scientific' categories – a necessary condition for the analysis of the relationship between these modes of rationality. More generally, the leitmotif of an 'epistemological break' between the young Marx and the mature Marx is in stark contrast to the very widespread tendency to believe that there is such a thing as 'Marx's thought', present in all of his writings, such that one text can always be explained, clarified or commented on by means of another; and also to the tendency to be concerned exclusively with the issue of the 'progressive construction' of his system. In short, Althusser encouraged a transition from the 'interpretation' of *Capital* to the question of the requisite revisions of it.

The intervention of analytical Marxism

Anglo-American analytical Marxism emerged in the 1980s out of a political impulse from the previous decade, as is explained by its founder G.A. Cohen, who felt compelled to account for Marxism in terms of analytical philosophy – in his view, the only legitimate kind of philosophy.[40] It focuses on the problem of the variety of forms of explanation (functional, causal, intentional) proposed by Marx and the necessity of analysis in terms of rational individualism. It prioritises two 'theses'. The first is the 'primacy of the productive forces': at each level of their development, their specific nature is said to explain which relations of production are required for their employment. The second thesis is the 'correspondence' between these two terms: the relations of production that are established are those which function positively for the development of the productive forces. The ensuing debate, marked by the intervention of

[40] Cohen 1978.

Jon Elster,[41] focused in particular on the grounding of the first thesis, which Cohen linked to the rationality of human beings in social relations in general; and on the meaning to be given in the second thesis to the notion of functionality, which cannot be defined in socially neutral fashion: the individuals or groups that launch themselves into the most appropriate type of domination prevail over the others in as much as they succeed in both *stimulating* the development of production and *appropriating* the social power inherent in it. This analytical research is conducive to clarifying debates on the explanation of major epochal changes, like that of the ongoing globalisation, and more broadly on the relations between the intentional and the unintentional, on the share of human initiative in historical processes.

The economist John Roemer has advanced a 'general' theory of exploitation and class, which furnishes elements for a reworking of *Capital*.[42] He generalises the approach on two levels: on the one hand by drawing a parallel between exploitation through unequal exchange and through the wage relation, and on the other by comparing 'capitalism', based on property differentials, and 'socialism', marked by skills differentials. His approach has inspired the sociologist Erik Olin Wright, who analyses these two types of class relations within capitalism.[43] In the context of analytical philosophy, Marx's theory of exploitation has also been examined as a 'theory of justice' and highlighted as such.[44]

Despite the problems that prevent this form of non-dialectical thinking from embracing Marx's programme, particularly as a result of the resonance of methodological individualism, it has helped to clarify and put back on the intellectual agenda a set of questions, especially concerning exploitation and class theory.

General perspective: the meta/structural interpretation

We can, it seems to me, link up these various lines of research. At least, this is the project I have developed in the spirit of historical materialism.[45]

---

[41] Elster 1985.
[42] Roemer 1982.
[43] Wright 1985 and 1997.
[44] Cohen 1995.
[45] Bidet 1999, 2004 and 2007.

The concept of 'epistemological break' must be applied to the relationship between the *Grundrisse* and *Capital*. This results in reading Part One of *Capital* Volume One with all the rigour of analytical Marxism and construing it (as do consistent Marxist economists) as the exposition of the abstract model of *rational production* in a market – on the basis of private property, hence in conditions of competition. These are the conditions in which concrete labour is 'reduced' to abstract labour, meaning in the first place, at this level of analysis, that 'socially-necessary labour-time' determines exchange-value in the last instance. But what is involved is not merely a figure of rational social understanding [*Verstand*]. For Marx stresses that what is presupposed here is the liberty-equality-rationality of exchanging producers: in other words, a presupposition of (juridico-political) reason – *Vernunft* – as much as of (economic) understanding. But it seems to me that such a figure is coherent only if dialectically developed. For such partners cannot be considered free-equal-rational if they acknowledge themselves to be subject to a natural common law – that of the market. They can only mutually posit themselves as such on condition that they define themselves as those who together develop the law to which they submit. And this social centrality concerns both political reason, in accordance with the tradition of democratic political philosophy, and economic understanding, in accordance with the institutionalist, realist position that opposes to the neoclassical dogma of the market the complementary character of two primary, antagonistic forms of social co-ordination: market and organisation.

Thus is realised Marx's basic theoretical thesis, according to which the peculiarity of the modern form of class consists in the fact that it is founded on a *rational-reasonable* social relationship – the market – by turning it into its opposite sense: the exploited and oppressed worker being declared to be inscribed in a relationship of free, equal and rational exchange; being 'posited' as such. But it is only realised only by being sublated [*aufgehoben*]. This supposition, this 'position', can in fact only be coherently formulated in accordance with the complex figure (irreducible exclusively to the market, as Marx would have it), which constitutes the genuine modern *fiction* on whose basis we must begin the exposition of the modern form of production and society. It contains the two 'poles' of the inter-individual and the social-central, according to the two 'faces' of the economic and the juridico-political. Thus, Marx's theory is fully embraced, but adopted on a 'broader', more realistic and more dialectical basis.

This initial fiction – the 'Eden of the rights of man and the citizen' referred to by Marx in Part One – possesses a merely ambiguous form of existence, an ontological status that only a dialectical analysis makes it possible to conceive, being contradictorily posited by the dominant as what *is* and by the dominated as what *should be*. Like the juridico-political relationship of production for exchange that is Marx's starting point, it is only ever posited as the universal social form by being transformed into its opposite, in a situation where property, which governs the market, and competence, which governs the organisation, are always already unequally distributed – and this in conditions that reproduce the asymmetry between those who posses nothing but their labour-power and those who share in property and the employment of capital. Such is the dialectical relationship that obtains between the structure of capitalism, understood as a class structure, and its *presupposition*. Analysis must begin with it, with this abstract moment that merits the name of 'metastructure'. (And Marx, in his 'narrow' framework, had already demonstrated that the theory of exploitation cannot be expounded without having constructed the theory of value – that is, the theory of the logic of commodity production.) But this *presupposition* is only *posited* by the development of capitalism.

The logic of capital is the logic of the accumulation of abstract wealth; the logic of the working population is that of concrete wealth, of forms of free and equal existence, collectively devised. The inherently revolutionary character of the modern form of society stems from the fact that exploitation and domination can only be exercised in the regime of modernity – that is, the official, common declaration of liberty-equality-rationality, which is such as to provoke constant class struggle over the control and purpose of production.

The metastructure is therefore only ever posited in the structure. Yet this dialectical circularity is not to be construed as a structural phenomenon, as if the practices of agents merely corresponded to a position in a social structure. Social practices and social struggles, which alone ultimately impart determinate content to this situation of modernity, to this contradictorily invoked liberty-equality-rationality, always intervene through events, with the tendencies of this structure, in the uncertain conditions of conjunctures. If the global concept contains a dialectical circularity, which stems from the fact that the positions of liberty-equality-rationality are historically renewed in the class struggle, the historical tendencies wherein practices are asserted cannot be the object of some dialectical deduction from the capitalist structure: they unfold in line with the course of technological changes which, following the unintentional accumulation and conjunction of intentional actions, arrive at intervals to call into question the relations of production. The dialectical element is therefore to be understood in the non-dialectical context of a history in which we can intervene, even though it remains, beyond our projects, a natural history that escapes the grasp of any dialectic. Contrary to the dialectical materialism of the old orthodoxy, the dialectical element is subordinated to the regime of historical materialism.

This realist perspective corrects the logico-historical, teleological bias that mars the exposition of *Capital*. The writing strategy of Volume One in effect locates *the market at the logical commencement* of the exposition and culminates in *the organisation as its historical result*, fruit of the gradual concentration of capital, leading to great oligopolies which, with a working class educated and organised by the very process of production, form the prelude to the revolutionary transition to the universally devised organisation. This perspective, which presses the democratic *organisation* of the whole of social existence against the multiform domination of the capitalist *market*, is a strong point in the Marxian legacy. Yet it must not lead us to forget that market and organisation, which are the two complementary forms of the rational co-ordination of social production, constitute – converted into their opposites – the two interconnected factors of class in the modern form of society. This forms the basis for more productive relations with the work of Marxist economists, with contemporary political philosophies and sociologies (by way of examples, readers are referred to the articles on Habermas and Bourdieu in this work), and with the whole of the movement that seeks the revolutionary transformation of modern society (and here readers can refer to the 'Keys' proposed in the introduction).

Chapter Twenty-One

The New Dialectic

Jim Kincaid

In recent years, the logical construction of Marx's *Capital* has been the focus of much new research and controversy in the anglophone world.[1] In this work, a leading role has been played by a group of European and American scholars whose distinctive approach to the reading of *Capital* is widely referred to as the *new dialectics* or the *new dialectic*. As we shall see, the individuals involved vary greatly in the ways in which they read Marx and the new dialectic is not a unified theoretical tendency. What its exponents have had in common since they began collaborative work in 1991, has been a shared belief that in understanding the organisation and movement of the argument of *Capital*, Marx's use of elements drawn from Hegel's two books on *Logic* should be a central focus of attention. In addition, as Fred Moseley explained in the 'Introduction' to the first of a series of volumes of essays by new dialectic scholars, the contributors agreed that Engels's logical-historical interpretation of *Capital* needed to be rejected. Moseley writes that according to Engels,

[1] My thanks to Pete Green for many discussions, and to Terry Dawson for skillful guidance in the reading of Hegel.

> Marx's logical categories in *Capital* correspond to an idealised periodisation of the actual process of history. The clearest and most influential aspect of this interpretation is its assumption that the subject of Part 1 of Volume 1 is not capitalism but rather a precapitalist 'simple commodity production', in which producers own their own means of production and there is no wage labour.[2]

Thus, the new-dialectic programme began with the rather bold claim that Engels had misunderstood *Capital*.[3] Though Marxism is widely seen as essentially a theory about history and historical change, the new-dialectic approach insists that *Capital* itself is not organised as an historical work. In this the new-dialectic scholars were guided by Marx's own account. Marx records that during the winter of 1857–8, when he was writing the first draft of *Capital* (the *Grundrisse*), it was a rereading of Hegel's *Science of Logic* which helped him to make a decisive breakthrough both in his analysis of capitalism and in the method he would use to present his argument.[4] On 16 January 1858, in a letter to Engels, Marx announced that, after 'overdoing very much my nocturnal labours', (fuelled by, 'nothing stronger than lemonade...but an immense deal of tobacco'),

> I am discovering some nice arguments [*hübsche Entwicklungen*]. E.g. I have completely demolished the theory of profit as hitherto propounded. What was of great use to me as regards *method* of treatment [*Methode des Bearbeiters*] was Hegel's *Logic*.... If ever the time comes when such work

[2] Moseley (ed.) 1993, p. 1. The other new-dialectic collections so far published are: Moseley and Campbell (eds.) 1997, Arthur and Reuten (eds.) 1998, Campbell and Reuten (eds.) 2001, Bellofiore and Taylor (eds.) and Moseley (ed.) 2005.

[3] Also rejected was Engels's interpretation of dialectic as a general vision of the nature of the real world, stressing changes of quantity into quality. The new dialectic is not interested in what happens when kettles boil, nor in other ontological features of the dialectical-materialist tradition, such as that reality is a unity of inherent contradictions, or that change takes place via negation of the negation. See Bottomore 1992, pp. 142–3, for a useful short summary of the theory of dialectical materialism. Rees 1998 offers a modern defence of the 'old' dialectic – the dialectic of nature and of history in a tradition derived from Engels. Rees, however, disassociates his position from Soviet variants and favours a Lukácsian inflection.

[4] Hegel wrote two versions of his *Science of Logic* – the longer version first published in 1812–16 and a shorter version in 1831. It was the longer version which Marx reread in 1858, but he also used the shorter logic in the 1860–3 period during which he was writing the second draft of *Capital*.

> is again possible, I should very much like to write 2 or 3 printers sheets making accessible to the common reader the *rational* aspect of the method [*das Rationelle an der Methode*] which Hegel not only discovered but also mystified [*mystificirt hat*].[5]

The time never did come when Marx was able to write a sustained account of the rational dialectic. But it is of great significance that he mentions Hegel's *Logic* in direct connection with one of the central and fundamental new insights of *Capital* – Marx's revolutionary theory that the source of profit was unpaid labour-time. This letter was written just at the moment, early in 1858, that, in the final section of the last *Grundrisse* notebook, Marx wrote down the sentence which later was to become the starting-point of *Capital*, Volume 1: 'The first category in which bourgeois wealth presents itself is that of the *commodity*'.[6] As is made clear in the Introduction (written the previous year) to the *Grundrisse* manuscript, he had originally intended to start *Capital* with a general review of processes of production, consumption, distribution and exchange in human societies. But, after looking again at Hegel's *Logic*, the decision was taken to start the work by assuming the capitalist mode of production in full operation, and then to move immediately to examine the category of *commodity* as a form of appearance which encapsulated the essential nature of capitalism. Thus the first sentence of *Capital*,

> The wealth of societies in which the capitalist mode of production prevails appears [*erscheint*] as an immense collection of commodities: the individual commodity appears as its elementary form. Our investigation therefore begins with the analysis of the commodity.[7]

Thus, the capitalist mode of production is introduced at the very start of *Capital*, but Marx does not, as the reader might expect, then move directly

---

[5] Marx and Engels 1983, p. 249. A printers sheet would contain sixteen book-size pages. The new-dialectic approach was also influenced by Marx's statement in the first draft of *Capital* that, 'it would therefore be unfeasible and wrong to let the economic categories follow one another in the same sequence as that in which they were historically decisive. Their sequence is determined, rather, by their relation to one another in modern bourgeois society, which is precisely the opposite of that which seems to be their natural order or which corresponds to historical development'. Marx 1973, p. 107.

[6] Marx 1973, p. 881.

[7] Marx 1976, p. 125.

into an explanation of how capitalism works. Instead, he slowly and painstakingly explores a series of more elementary categories – commodity, use-value, exchange-value, money and labour. All of these feature in many types of precapitalist society, which is why Engels was misled into thinking that the early sections of *Capital* deal with societies which predate industrial capitalism. Why is it that the category of *productive capital* is itself subject to a laborious and indirect process of *theoretical production* taking more than a hundred pages of *Capital*?

In *Capital*, there *are* phases of historical narrative – for example the section at the end of Volume 1 on the primitive accumulation of capital. There is also on occasion, massive use of empirical evidence, such as on the working day. However, these are strictly subordinate to an account of capitalism as a self-sustaining system of interdependent elements. What the new-dialectic group of scholars have argued is that Hegel's *Logic* was a vital influence in *Capital* because Marx learned from it a method of developing an argument in which the essential mechanisms of capitalism as a system could be explained in terms of *interdependence* and *dialectical necessity*.

Scientific categories in Hegel's *Logic*

From Marx's student days, the period of his first deep immersion in Hegel's work, he saw the latter as essentially a theological writer. The central concern of Hegel's philosophy is a cosmic 'superspirit' which he calls *Geist*: 'the reality which we perceive as finite subjects is the embodiment of *Geist* or infinite subject'.[8] But Hegel's *Geist* is not a Very Big Divine Person who has created the world *from outside*. *Geist* is rational thought in action, not some kind of spooky figure. As Marx puts it,

> for Hegel, the process of thinking [*Denkprozess*], which he even transforms into an independent subject [i.e. active agent], under the name of 'the Idea', is the creator of the real world [*der Demiurg des Wirklichen*] and the real world is only the external appearance of the Idea.[9]

---

[8] Taylor 1975, p. 225.
[9] Marx 1976, p. 102.

Thus, Hegel is a pantheist, and both the natural world and the course of human history are portrayed by him as an expression of the creativity of *Geist*. *Geist* is not a static, transcendental figure, externally organising the development of the universe – but a Spirit which immanently develops itself in and though the historical evolution of the natural world and of human history. Hegel is an idealist, but he is not a mystic. He is scornful of people who try to connect to and understand the Divine Spirit via mystical contemplation. Since *Geist* is the spirit of *rational* thought, what is needed is the scientific study of the natural and the social worlds – to explain their structures, the way these develop over time, and the meaning of that development. Hegel also insists that the sort of science needed is *dialectical*. He studied intensively and wrote much about the natural sciences of his period – especially physics.[10] But he condemned much contemporary scientific work as the mere collection of empirical facts. He rejected such 'knowledge' as abstract and lifeless. Only a science which itself develops as a theoretically integrated body of knowledge is capable of articulating truths about a world which develops historically, through time, and in all its manifestations, is an expression of divine rationality.[11]

A number of aspects of dialectical science, as practised by Hegel, are especially relevant to Marx's *Capital*. Marx saw capitalism as a system of interdependent elements and processes:

> in the completed bourgeois system every economic relation presupposes every other in its bourgeois economic form, and everything posited is thus also a presupposition, this is the case with every organic system.[12]

Certainly, Hegel is fundamentally a theological thinker, but in his *Logic* comments about God are very sparse. There is however a great deal about mathematical questions such as the nature of the calculus, and about concepts such

---

[10] See Hegel 1970, a three-volume work on the natural sciences which Marx studied when writing his dissertation, the topic of which was a comparison of the physics of Epicurus and Democritus and the philosophical implications of their theoretical differences.

[11] Recent developments in the natural sciences put into question the received wisdom which counterposes Hegelianism and scientificity in Marx's political economy. The trajectory of physics since Einstein, and the development of non-linearity, complexity and emergence as major paradigms in the natural sciences, have encouraged a more sympathetic reappraisal of the scientific character of Hegel's dialectics. See Houlgate 1998, and Cohen and Wartofsky 1984. For a brief but favourable comment on Hegel's critique of Newtonian science, see Prigogine and Stengers 1984, pp. 89–91.

[12] Marx 1973, p. 278.

as system and causality as these are used in physics and biology. In research published in the late 1960s and 1970s, a number of West-German philosophers challenged the traditional view of Hegel's *Logic* as a theological work, and elaborated, what one of them, Klaus Hartmann, called a non-metaphysical reading of the work.[13] This approach was further developed by David Kolb, Terry Pinkard and other scholars.[14] What they identify in Hegel's work on *Logic* are attempts to establish the way in which thought must work if it is to produce an intelligible reconstruction of the real world. Hegel's *Logic* is a systematic examination of the categories which science and philosophy need to understand the universe in a rational and scientific way. Hegel's logic, 'is not a collection of metaphysical claims. It is a study of the categories that must be used in thinking'.[15]

> Hegel is not simply some 19th century romantic listening to his own incantations of the World Spirit but a philosopher concerned with working out the logical relations between all the different ways in which we experience things and talk about that experience.[16]

In his two works on *Logic*, Hegel lays great stress on the order in which categories are introduced. The principle he adopts is to deal first with simple, general and abstract categories. As these are shown to be inadequate to understand the world (because too abstract and insufficiently precise) more complex and more concrete categories are derived and clarified. Hegel's *Science of Logic* is divided into three main sections. Book 1 is called *Being* and deals with the concepts which thought uses in providing a descriptive account of what is immediately *there* in the world. When we talk about things we can state how big they are, or how many of them there are. Here, Hegel says, we are using the category of *quantity*. Or we can ask what are the specific characteristics of things. The general category being used here is that of *quality*. Or we can think about the limits of things or processes – whether things have definite bound-

---

[13] See Hartmann 1972. Also often called an *ontological* reading of Hegel's *Logic*. Other major West-German discussions of Marx's *Capital* in relation to Hegel's account of the logic of categories included Backhaus 1969 and Reichelt 1970. Heinrich 2001 is a later, and notably innovative work, within the same tradition.

[14] There are outstanding commentaries on Hegel's *Logic* in Pinkard 1985, pp. 85–109, and in Kolb 1986, pp. 38–95.

[15] Kolb 1986, p. 43.

[16] Pinkard 1985, p. 109.

aries, a beginning and an end, or whether they are continuous and ongoing processes. Here, thought uses categories of the finite or the infinite. Later, the categories of unity and plurality (the *one* and the *many*) are covered, and also those of attraction and repulsion as these figure in Newtonian physics. Thus, in the book of *Being*, Hegel is examining categories which are used simply to *describe* the world. Moreover, although the categories discussed come in contrasting pairs, there is no intrinsic interconnection between the two members of each pair. There is either *one* of something or *many* of it – similarly *quantity* is quite different from *quality*. These categories have a large presence in *Capital*. Marx counterposes exchange-value as sheer quantity to use-value as the qualitative dimension of commodities. In the overall architecture of *Capital* Marx deals first with capital as *one*, i.e. capital-in-general and exploitation of labour. In the second half of the work he deals with capital as *many* – i.e. with competition and profitability.

Book II is called *Essence*, and deals with more complex ways of reconstructing the world in thought. It also examines concepts which come in pairs, but here each term is interlinked with its partner. There is a interdependence between the concepts of cause and effect, and between form and content. Hegel gives a great deal of attention to the couplet, essence and appearance, and essence is considered so important that it is used as the title of Book II. *Essence* is the basic nature of something. This is different from the way a thing appears in its everyday empirical existence. Caterpillars look different from butterflies – the essence here is a creature which develops from one into the other, and can be thought of as expressing its inner essential nature in and through its successive forms of appearance. To explain and make sense of the world, thought must find ways of getting beyond appearances to underlying reality, that is, to essence. But Hegel is no Platonist, and does not consider that appearances are simply forms of illusion or contingency which must be unveiled in order to arrive at essence. There is no mystical direct route to essence in Hegel. What is required, he says, is the careful empirical study of phenomena, and hard rigorous thinking which reconstructs what must underlie appearances. And, since appearances are often at variance with essence, the essential nature of an object can only be established by a chain of necessary argument. But, to achieve this, thought must move restlessly between essence and appearance, trying to interlink the two dimensions of reality with arguments which identify necessary connections.

The other oppositions which Hegel deals with in the *Essence* section are similarly interdependent – *determinations of reflection*, Hegel calls them – instances in which the meaning of each category is reflected in that of its partner. Other binaries which are discussed are: form/matter; form/content; whole/parts; inner/outer. There is also a sequence which covers the series: contingency, possibility, necessity and actuality. All of these categories figure in various ways as important elements in the conceptual narrative which Marx develops in *Capital*.

Book III of Hegel's *Logic* is called *Begriff* [conceptuality], the capacity of thought to grasp the most complex forms of organisation in the world. Here, for example, Hegel examines ways of explaining the mechanical cause and effect sequences identified by physics, the patterns of reaction studied in chemistry, and the concept of life as used in biology. He discusses the concepts we use to describe living subjects, individuals who are capable of self-conscious and self-managed development – concepts such as need, self, feeling, and pain.

In the *Begriff* section of Hegel's *Logic*, there is heavy emphasis on systems which are characterised by integrated organic structures.[17] To explain these Hegel gives much attention to the syllogism. In this figure there is an amalgamation of three elements. The opposition between *Universal*, and the *Particular* which was one of the binary oppositions which Hegel deals with in the Book of Essence, is overcome, in a new more complex structure in which the two are retained, but blended into a higher and more complex whole which includes a new dimension – *Individuality*. The term *syllogism* names this integrated blend of these three dimensions and I will say more about this later. The process of 'overcoming' which leads to the new higher order structure Hegel calls *Aufhebung*.

The new-dialectic reading of the Hegel-Marx connection

There is general agreement among the new-dialectic group of scholars that, in Marx's analysis of capitalism as a system, he made large use of elements drawn from Hegel's systematic-logical account of scientific categories. There

[17] Hegel does not have the modern conceptualisation of *system* at his disposal, and much of the difficulty of this section of his text arises as he struggles to find a language to describe processes such as feed-back or homeostasis.

is in *Capital* a sequence of argument which moves from a general and abstract summary of the essence of the system – that is, the commodity as a contradictory combination of use-value and exchange-value – to a fully developed and concrete description of capitalism as driven by competition and profitability, fuelled by surplus-value extracted from labour, equipped with financial markets, organised internationally, subject to the ups and downs of the business cycle, and to stresses which arise from tendencies for the rate of profit to decline.[18]

Capital is presented by Marx both as a process and a social relation. It is a process in which sums of money capital are changed into means of production and wages. Then commodities are produced and surplus-value created by the hours of labour for which no wages are paid. As the commodities are sold, capital is transformed back into money form, enlarged by surplus-value if things have gone according to plan. Capital is also seen as a relation between its owners and labour, both directly as a source of surplus-value, and indirectly in that the machines and raw material used in production are stored-up labour.

It is common ground in the new-dialectic reading of *Capital* that Marx enlists the help of Hegel's *Logic* to organise his argument as a series of moves involving some kind of *necessity*. Just as capitalism is being portrayed as a system of interdependent and necessary processes, so an explanatory and critical account of such a system must itself be developed as a chain of necessary dialectical arguments. But the question of what sort of necessity is one which divides the new-dialectic scholars themselves. It is also a point on which critics of their approach have fastened. The complaint has been widely expressed that the new critics are saying that Marx used a chain of necessary derivations to lead to conclusions which are then mechanically and externally projected onto the real operation of capitalism. For example Alex Callinicos attacks, 'ultra-Hegelian Marxists who argue that Marx derived the concrete structure of the capitalist mode of production from the concept of capital itself'.[19] The

[18] These themes in *Capital* are examined in two of the most useful contributions which the new dialectic scholars have made, namely the collections of essays on *Capital*, Volume II (Arthur and Reuten (eds.) 1998) and on *Capital*, Volume III (Campbell and Reuten (eds.) 2001). On the latter work, see Green 2005 for some important points of criticism.

[19] Callinicos 1998, p. 98.

new-dialectic emphasis on conceptual derivation is severely condemned by Callinicos:

> At worst this substitutes dialectical wordplay and scholastic commentary for the analysis of concrete social formations; at best it has a tendency to reduce Marx's method to a purely conceptual dialectic.[20]

What sort of necessity drives Marx's dialectical argument?

Against such criticism, the new-dialectic work of Patrick Murray offers a lucid defence. What the critics fail to appreciate is that if political economy is to be both scientific and critical, it requires the deployment of arguments based on dialectical necessity. Murray examines with meticulous care the ways in which Marx drew on the discussion of essence and appearance in Book II of Hegel's *Logic*. The key difficulty in science, as Marx saw it, was that only the empirical surface appearances of phenomena are available for scrutiny. From these, underlying and hidden relationships and forces must be inferred. Thus, as noted earlier, arguments based on some kind of necessity must be developed to explain the nature of underlying determinants which are operative. But, for Marx, the validity of such arguments about essence is always subject to empirical confirmation. This means a fully developed scientific account must include explanations of why appearances are as they are, and why they can be deceptive. Marx writes that, 'all science would be superfluous if the form of appearance of things directly coincided with their essence'.[21] The rate of profit, for example, is the, 'visible surface phenomenon', but underlying profit is surplus-value, and this is, 'the invisible essence to be investigated'.[22] Another example: on the surface, it seems that the value of commodities is determined by the combined contribution made to production by the three factors of capital, labour, and land. The empiricism of mainstream economics takes such a proposition to be self-evident. As I noted above, it was the Hegelian logic of categories which in the winter of 1857–8 helped Marx to construct the sequence of argument in support of the labour theory of value – one of the

---

[20] Callinicos 1998, p. 98. Here Callinicos is endorsing the critique of new dialectic in Rees 1998, pp. 108–18.
[21] Marx 1981, p. 956.
[22] Marx 1981, p. 134.

decisive scientific and political paradigm shifts of *Capital*. Marx himself at one point suggests the Copernican revolution as a model for political economy.

> A scientific analysis of competition is possible only if we can grasp the inner nature of capital, just as the apparent motions of the heavenly bodies are not intelligible to any but him who is acquainted with their real motions, motions which are not perceptible to the senses.[23]

In *Capital*, Marx interweaves two strands of argument – the book is both a critique of the categories of classical political economy, and a critical account of how capitalism works. The two strands are deeply interconnected. The essential inner nature of capitalism is such that it generates appearances which are misleading and at variance with underlying reality.

Even the work of the greatest of the classical political economists, Ricardo, is ideological because it does not trace out the mediations which link essence to surface appearances. Ricardo is attacked by Marx because he does not use a correct scientific method to establish underlying essential structures and relationships, and the reasons why these create a misleading surface appearance. The difficulty here is not simply one of penetrating through illusions to underlying reality. What appears on the surface may be an illusion, but it need not be. Price is a category of the surface, and there is nothing unreal or illusory about prices. To establish a chain of connection between the prices at which commodities are sold and an underlying essence of labour-time requires a process of abstracting from a large number of complicating influences to establish what is fundamental. The underlying determinants of value cannot be arrived at by simple empirical procedures. It is not possible to move by empirical, factually based arguments from rates of profit to the rates of surplus-value which underlie them. Marx noted the difficulty which political economy faced in comparison with chemistry, 'in the analysis of economic forms neither microscopes nor chemical reagents are of assistance. The power of abstraction [*die Abstractionskrafte*] must replace both'.[24]

New-dialectic scholars stress that the category of money is introduced by Marx in a way which is quite different from the usual explanations in mainstream economics textbooks which start with the function of money as

---

[23] Marx 1976, p. 433.
[24] Marx 1976, p. 90.

a convenient means of exchange. Marx's argument is, rather, that it is the contradiction between the use-value and exchange-value of the commodity which gives rise to the category of money. Use-value is linked to the natural sensory qualities of the commodity, but value is a *social* property of commodities and can only appear in the relationship of commodities to each other. Money develops as a necessary form which allows the contradiction between the natural form of the individual commodities and their form as values to be overcome – though the contradiction is not got rid of, but merely displaced to other ontological levels.[25]

The scientific deployment of categories interconnects with the politics of Marx's text. Arguments based on necessity are used by Marx to challenge the way in which bourgeois economics projects the categories of capitalist society as natural and universal. By tracing the patterns of interdependence of the particular elements and processes of capitalism as a system, Marx is establishing the historical specificity of those components. Marx is challenging the ideological use of general definitions which allow economists to say, for example, that capital is universal in human societies. He notes, for example, the argument in classical political economy that that, even in the earliest human societies, means of production were used – the stone to throw at the animal being hunted, the stick to reach fruit in trees.[26]

Arthur has emphasised the importance of negation in shaping the sort of necessity which propels Marx's dialectical argument forward. Here, Arthur acknowledges the important work of Roy Bhaskar. In a powerful critique of empiricism and positivism, Bhaskar attacks what he calls their *ontological monovalence*. In contrast, Bhaskar advocates ontological stratification as a paradigm which allows for what he calls *real negation*. 'It connotes, inter alia, the hidden,

[25] 'The further development of the commodity does not abolish these contradictions, but rather provides the form in which they have room to move'. Marx 1976, p. 198. See Kincaid 2005 pp. 95–8 for a discussion of Marx's thesis that exchange-value is represented (and necessarily so) in money as a *use-value*. This gives rise, in turn, to a contradiction between capitalism's drive to increase profitability by evolving cheap forms of money, such as cheques or electronic transfers, and the need of capital for a stable monetary medium in which value can be preserved, passed to other owners, or used as a measure of value in contracts. There is a perceptive account of Marx's treatment of money by Martha Campbell in Campbell (ed.) 1997, pp. 89–120.

[26] The point is made in Marx 1976, p. 291. See Murray 1988, especially pp. 121–9 and 228–32, for a searching exploration of Marx's attacks on dehistoricisation in economics.

the empty, the outside, desire, lack, need...It is real negation which drives the Hegelian dialectic on'.[27] Thus Marxism contains, as part of its scientific character, a critique of capitalism and the basis of a practice of transformative negation. The ontology in terms of which Bhaskar theorises the Marxist project is complex and contains three interrelated dimensions: the real, the actual and the empirical. As implemented by Marx in political economy, the real is the concrete, an account which interlinks essence and appearance, and treats appearances as real, even if often illusory. Marx does not confine his science to what is empirically and immediately actual and present. His attention is constantly focused on change and on emergent forces. The rational dialectic, Marx writes,

> includes in its positive understanding of what exists a simultaneous recognition of its negation, its inevitable destruction; because it regards every highest developed form as being in a fluid state, in motion, and therefore grasps its transient aspect as well.[28]

Pinkard, Kolb and others have traced the presence in Hegel's text of two interlinked patterns of argument.[29] Firstly, a progressive dialectic, which is the forward movement from abstract to more concrete concepts. Hegel's claim is that the principle of advance is dialectical necessity. Progression is driven by thought's dissatisfaction with the contradictions which abstractions give rise to, or with the emptiness and poverty of detail when things are specified abstractly. Abstract concepts when looked at critically, are revealed as contradictory. For Hegel, contradictions are a source of movement and change. Bhaskar explains the forms of necessity which are employed, as follows:

---

[27] Bhaskar 1993, p. 5. It is one of the merits of Bhaskar's work that he argues cogently for a vision of the social sciences in which they incorporate a practical dimension aiming to abolish social ills. His argument is that, as medical science is organised round a conception of health, or engineering aims to build structures which do not fall down unexpectedly, so a social science like political economy should be committed to the creation of just, democratic and sustainable societies.

[28] Marx 1976, p. 103. For an outstanding brief introduction to the many forms of dialectic within the theoretical tradition of Marxism, see Bhaskar 1992, pp. 143–50. As well as the methodological (epistemological) dialectic which I have been discussing here, Bhaskar also reviews the ontological dialectic and the dialectic of history.

[29] These scholars also identify in Hegel a third pattern, the architectonic. This specifies determinate negation as controlling the moves which categories make vis-à-vis each other. So far as I am aware, no one has yet suggested that Marx uses any similar architectonic.

> For Hegel truth is the whole and error lies in onesidedness, incompleteness and abstraction; it [error] can be recognised by the contradictions it generates, and remedied through their incorporation in fuller richer, more concrete conceptual forms.... The Hegelian dialectic progresses in two basic ways: by bringing out what is implicit, but not sufficiently articulated, in some notion, or by repairing some want, lack or inadequacy in it.[30]

Contradictions can arise either in reality or in thought, but, contrary to a scurrilous rumour (promulgated, for example, by Karl Popper) for Hegel, neither thought or the material world are inherently contradictory. In both, contradictions arise, but are experienced as intolerable, and generate pressures to find ways of resolving contradictions. Here, for example, is the process which Hegel calls *Aufhebung* – the emergence of higher forms in which contradictions are attenuated by being reconstructed as part of a more complex whole. For Hegel, wherever contradictions arise, they are a source of instability and change whether in the material world or in thought.

The sort of necessity that gives direction to a new dialectic type of argument is not the sort to be found in formal logic: if A = B, and B = C, then A = C etc. It is probabilistic in character. It is akin to *natural necessity*, a term employed within the realist tradition in philosophy of science to refer to processes occuring in the natural or social world which have a high degree of probability of producing a given outcome.[31] There is a deep, though usually indirect linkage, in Marx between the necessary progression of a dialectical argument and the processes which he sees as operating with natural necessity in the capitalist system. Here, there are two main types of situation. Firstly, where action is subject to what Marx calls 'the silent compulsion of economic relations'.[32] Secondly, where there is greater scope for alternative strategies but where the economic action of agents is subject to laws of selection, for

---

[30] Bhaskar 1992, p. 143.

[31] See Harré and Madden 1975 for a critique of Hume on causality, and the lucid development of a theory of natural necessity and causal powers. For a remarkable Marxist development of this approach, see Bhaskar 1993, Chapter 2.

[32] The use of direct extra-economic force to ensure labour supply becomes exceptional once capitalism is fully developed – i.e. after peasants have been made dependent on wage-work by being deprived of their land. There are then, 'masses of men who have nothing to sell but their labour-power...the silent compulsion of economic relations sets the seal on the domination of the capitalist over the worker'. Marx 1976, p. 899.

instance, capitalists are free to operate their businesses with any sort of efficiency or inefficiency they choose – but, if the latter, they then risk being put out of business.

Marx's argument is *Capital* is often said to move from abstract to concrete. In fact, the pattern is more complex. The narrative of *Capital* is not a continuous unilinear journey from an abstract to a concrete account of capitalism, but more like a *spiral*, in which there is a repeated return to an underlying level of abstraction, though one which is specified in increasingly complex ways. Thus, for example, *Capital* starts with the commodity as a general and abstract category – defined simply as goods and services produced for sale. But Marx ends Volume I with a chapter in which the commodity is presented as not only the product of capital, but as one of the forms taken by capital in its productive circuit. In addition, *necessity* has entered the analysis. The capitalist is under pressure to sell commodities produced because there is a wage bill to meet, and inputs to buy in order to continue in business.[33]

As Rosdolsky stresses in his great commentary on Marx's political economy, fundamental to the architecture of *Capital*, is the distinction between capital-in-general and many capitals.[34] Throughout Volume I and most of Volume II of *Capital*, Marx makes the enormous abstraction of leaving aside the division of capital into individual competing firms. This allows him to focus on the relation between capital and labour, and to clarify the origin of profit in surplus-value, or the value created by workers during the proportion of their working time which is unpaid. When, towards the end of Volume II, Marx turns to examine capital as many capitals in competition, this is not a move which follows on from the capital-in-general abstraction, but represents a return to a new abstract starting-point. The two great oppositions on which the argument of *Capital* is founded – capital versus labour, and capital versus capital – are depicted as interlinked, but also as both constitutive of the capitalist mode of production, and thus as requiring separate levels of analysis. Callinicos argues correctly that

[33] For reasons which are still not clear, this important chapter (known as the *Resultate*) was not published by Marx himself in any of the three editions of Volume I which appeared before his death. This major text is to be found in Marx 1976, pp. 943–1084.

[34] Rosdolsky 1977, especially pp. 41–50.

> *Capital* does not trace the manner in which a simple essence (value) is both manifested and concealed, but uncovers a complex structure involving levels which are both interdependent and irreducible to each other.[35]

Begriff logic in Hegel

In Hegel's *Logic*, the sphere of *Essence*, with its unresolved binary oppositions is the terrain of the negative dialectic. But, for Hegel, the negativity of *Essence* is only a way-station on the road to the culmination of his logic, the fundamental shift from *Essence* into the sphere of *Begriff* logic. Here, the tensions and oppositions of *Essence* logic find reconciliation in higher, more complex, and harmonised structures. Thus, the second stage of negative dialectic (unassimilated otherness) is overcome in a third stage of organic integration. In *Begriff* logic, the conceptual structures of subjectivity and agency are defined and explored. And in a final move, Hegel ends his *Logic* with a discussion of conceptuality itself, as having the capacity to grasp and comprehend the organic forms of self-conscious life. One of the major debates in the new dialectic group has been about the role of Hegel's *Begriff* logic in Marx. A brief review of the radically opposed views of Tony Smith, Patrick Murray and Christopher Arthur on this question will make clear some of the broader theoretical differences which divide the exponents of the new dialectic.

Marx and the syllogism

Tony Smith considers that Marx was profoundly influenced by the syllogistic patterns which inform and organise the *Begriff* section of Hegel's logic. Indeed the whole tenor of Smith's widely discussed book on *The Logic of Marx's 'Capital'*, published in 1990, is a relentless quest for syllogistic arguments in Marx's political economy. Smith is an unusual figure, who holds an unfashionable belief that the continuing power and relevance of Marx's thought arises *directly* from the Hegelian elements in Marx's work. He is strongly opposed

---

35 Callinicos 1982, p. 129. In a important paper Fine, Lapavitsas and Milonakis 2000 argue correctly, against Tony Smith, that Marx does not treat capital-in-general as *abstract*, and contrast it with a *concrete* of many capitals. Rather, a fully concretised account of the system must trace the interrelations between these two dimensions of capital.

to the view, advanced by Althusser and by the school of analytical Marxism, that *Capital* marks a radical rejection of Hegel's influence. Smith identifies Hegel as himself a strong critic of the nascent capitalism of his time, though one who sees his own work as a contribution to moral and intellectual regeneration. Smith depicts Marx as developing a deeply Hegelian version of a materialist critique of capitalism. What Smith aims to prove is that Marx's *Capital,* in its method of argument, was essentially faithful to Hegel – and, in particular, that the critical power and the scientific coherence of *Capital* derives from repeated use of the *syllogism* which traces the active processes in the social world through which organic entities construct themselves, by combining dimensions of universality, particularity and individuality.

Smith's starting-point is that 'dialectical logic is nothing more than the set of rules which operate when transitions from simple and abstract categories to complex and concrete ones are made'.[36] In Smith's explanation, there are three stages in a dialectical sequence. First, we begin a with category which emphasises what objects or processes have in common, a stage of simple unity. It is simple because differences within the object which the category refers to are, for the time being, ignored and abstracted from. For example, in all societies there has to be a mechanism for allocating labour. Marx once noted that this was something obvious even to a child.[37] In Stage 2, the category is modified to emphasis differences in whatever is covered by the initial category. For instance, there are a variety of ways in which the allocation of social labour can be carried out. By communal tradition, by having a state which directs labour, or, as in a capitalist economy, by firms making independent decisions about what their workers will produce, and then finding out in the marketplace whether or not they have made profitable use of the labour they employ.

Stage 3 of a dialectic – *Begriff* logic – combines the two previous stages of unity and difference into a new higher-order category. Marx notes near the start of *Capital* the possibility of a form of society in which a free association of producers could determine the allocation of their labour in production for need, not profit. In a socialist society, labour would be allocated to production

36 Smith 1993, p. 97.
37 Marx letter to Kugelmann, 11 July 1868.

on the basis of a democratically agreed plan to use production to meet collectively identified needs.

It is Smith's claim that the essential structure of the argument of *Capital* is formed by varaints of such syllogistic patterns. For example he argues that the first major section of *Capital* concentrates on *capital in production*, and to the relation between capital as a simple abstract (capital in general), and the labour it exploits. The second section, which starts near the end of Volume 2, deals with capital in the form of many capitals and the competition between them. And, in the final section, Marx moves on to explain the distribution of surplus-value – this being, in Smith's view, a third stage, combining the first two stages into a more complex syllogistic structure.

Murray and the wooden sword of Hegel

As against Smith, Patrick Murray insists that, in analysing capitalism, Marx does not make use of a third-stage logic of reconciled opposites. He argues that in Hegel the completion of the syllogism by the use of a *Begriff* logic is indissolubly linked to Hegel's project of social reform and class reconciliation.[38] Marx is out to abolish, not preserve in a higher form, the oppositions and contradictions of capitalist society. Murray finds in *Capital* the same sort of intransigence which characterised Marx's early critique of Hegel's political philosophy.[39] In an argument which, as Murray points out, is central in Hegel's *Philosophy of Right*, Marx notes that the law-making power of state is seen by Hegel as the syllogistic mediator between the empirical singularity (civil society) and the empirical universal (sovereign principle). Murray quotes Marx's summary of the way in which Hegel uses the syllogism to reconcile social oppositions:

> one can say that in Hegel's development of the rational syllogism the whole transcendence and mystical dualism of his system comes to the surface.

---

[38] See also Pinkard 2000, an outstanding biography of Hegel which has, as one of its main themes, the close relation between Hegel's philosophy and his commitment to social reform.

[39] The *Contribution to the Critique of Hegel's Philosophy of Right*, in Marx and Engels 1976.

> The middle term is the wooden sword, the concealed opposition between universality and singularity.[40]

Hegel's attempted reconciliation is based on verbal trickery, and is no more than an empty boast – *a wooden sword*. The truth is that Hegel's state transcends civil society without transforming its logical atom, the abstract egoistic individual. Murray is quietly scathing about the supposed reconciliation effected in the syllogism: in Marx,

> the logic of essence poses irreconcilable conflicts rather than a necessity differentiation that pushes on to higher unity. Third parties, such as heaven, the state, or money, signal submerged conflict, not achieved harmony.[41]

Murray's argument is that, throughout *Capital*, Marx remains on the terrain of the oppositions and tensions of *Essence* logic. Contradictions may be displaced from one form to another, but they are not subject to any sort of *Aufhebung*, or reconciled assimilation into a higher organic totality. Capitalism is to be abolished by social action, not verbal manoeuvres – real swords, not wooden ones. And, since *Capital* is a scientific text, Murray insists, as I have noted earlier, that the crucial opposition which structures its narrative is that of surface appearances versus underlying processes.

The term *negative dialectic* is now indelibly associated with the name and work of Adorno. And with good reason. Deeply influenced by his friend Walter Benjamin, Adorno powerfully explored the problems posed by a thought which explores oppositions and contradictions, but which refuses to attempt any kind of reconciliation. To do this, they considered, was to produce an implicit endorsement of the injustices of the capitalist system. 'Dialectics is the ontology of the wrong state of things', Adorno writes.[42] Adorno believed that there was a deep interconnection between: (1) the claim of abstract concepts to cover the concrete particularity of the objects they refer to; (2) the domination of abstract exchange-value over the use-values of commodities; and (3) the domination of the individual citizen by the abstract capitalist state.[43] Although Adorno is an adherent of the commodity-fetishism school and his

---

40 Murray 1993, p. 41, Marx and Engels 1975, p. 84.
41 Murray 1993, p. 41.
42 Adorno 1973, p. 11.
43 There are valuable accounts of these themes in Jameson 1990, and Jarvis 1998.

critique of capitalism is focused on exchange, rather than on capital, political economy has still much to learn from his theorisation and mode of presentation of negative dialectic.

Christopher Arthur and capital as dominating automaton

There is, however, a third perspective on Marx's use of *Begriff* logic, that of Christopher Arthur. His position is that Marx uses Hegel's reconciled Absolute Idea as a figure which expresses precisely the reified nature of a system dominated by capital. Arthur points out that there are two views of Hegel to be found in Marx. His exoteric view is the one I discussed earlier, Hegel as an onto-theologist, 'conceiving the real as the product of thought'.[44] But Marx's esoteric view is that Hegel is a secret empiricist. Hegel's dialectic is an upsidedown alienated mode of thought, in which abstractions lord it over their empirical instances.[45] Capitalism is also a topsy-turvy system, one in which products are dominative over the workers who made them. Arthur writes that, both in Hegel's *Begriff* and Marx's concept of capital, we encounter,

> alien pseudosubjects that subjugate real individuals. From this perspective, dialectical logic is a perversion of thought, but this is exactly what makes it a suitable method for understanding the perverted reality that is capitalism.[46]

Arthur is a distinguished representative of the value-form tradition in Marxist scholarship.[47] In a crucial passage early in *Capital*, Marx noted that his political economy was fundamentally different from that of Adam Smith or David Ricardo because it did not 'treat the form of value as something of indifference, something external to the nature of the commodity itself'.[48] For Arthur, the crucial moment at the start of *Capital* is Marx's assertion that in capitalist exchange, the use-value of commodities is set aside and commodities count only as so much exchange-value. Arthur takes this to mean that, at

---

[44] Marx 1976, p. 101.

[45] Hegel seems to argue, in effect, that the concept 'lion' takes precedence over actual particular lions.

[46] Arthur 1993, p. 29.

[47] Also exemplified in the new-dialectic group by Geert Reuten. See Reuten 1989.

[48] Marx 1976, p. 174.

this stage in the argument, commodities exist only as the mere empty form of exchangeability. As Marx develops the concept of money, the formal emptiness of the exchange relation is redefined as a relation in which commodities exchange for amounts of the abstract substance of money. Thus the emptiness of exchange now finds expression in the pure blank abstraction of money as incarnation of value. The next stage, as Arthur reads *Capital*, is the build-up of sums of money-capital which are then transformed into means of production and wage-labour. In the processes of industrial production and the extraction of surplus-value from labour, capital finds a source of self-expansion and power which enables it in time to establish dominance over the world economy. Thus, starting as pure form, value transforms itself into the material reality of a self-perpetuating system of exploitation, but one which remains essentially determined by the initial emptiness of the value-form. For Arthur, the value-form expresses an ontological emptiness which lies at the heart of capitalism. Value as capital becomes

> an unnatural form that clings vampire-like to labour and feeds off it.... an ontological vampire that bloats its hollow frame at our expense.[49]

This is the basis of the homology which Arthur traces between Hegel's *Logic* and Marx's *Capital*. Hegel's *Logic* starts with the emptiest possible abstractions – *Being* (simple *is-ness*) and *Nothing* (*is-not-ness*). The *Logic* ends, as I have noted, by constructing, in its final sections, the systematically interrelated concepts required to comprehend the most complex realities which both scientific thought and everyday thinking have to deal with. For example, what is covered by terms like 'life' or 'person'. Thought also has attained the self-sufficiency of being able to think about thinking. Thus, the homology with capital which Arthur identifies. The impersonal abstractions of Hegel's logic, and the patterns of necessity which define it, can express and explain the domination of humanity by an economic system which is driven by the imperative of profitability and sheer accumulation.

Arthur's homology thesis has proved highly controversial, but he has developed and defended it with clarity and considerable scholarly authority. Many of his critics concede that his account articulates a set of themes which have

[49] Arthur 2002, pp. 157 and 167.

a strong presence in *Capital*.[50] Marx does at times use metaphysical language to suggest how capitalism operates as a reified system, and how capital is a thing-like automaton whose domination creates inverted and dehumanised forms of society which logic can help grasp and explicate. However Arthur's vision of capital as Hegelian *Idea* has been widely attacked and on many grounds. For example, critics have questioned the way in which the value-form approach marginalises the category of use-value. The effect is to soften the use-value versus exchange-value contradiction and make it external to the commodity. There is too strong a focus on value-form as it is established in *exchange* rather than in *production*, and the material realities of labour process and exploitation are given insufficient weight. There has been a widespread rejection of Arthur's contention that Marx was wrong to introduce the category of labour right at the start of *Capital* as determinant of the value of commodities. Arthur believes that the category of labour should not have been introduced until much later on, and as the only logically possible answer to the problem of where surplus-value comes from. However Arthur's critics hold that in asserting labour as an initiating category, Marx's is making a move which exactly defines the line of difference between him materialism and the idealism of Hegel. Politically, Arthur is uncompromising, and follows Marx in portraying capital as a vampire feeding of surplus-value. But, in *Capital*, enormous attention is also given to the competition between capitals. By focusing too much on capital in general and its relationship with labour, Arthur gives too little attention to competition (or capital as many vampires) and thus to Marx's consequent analysis of profitability, accumulation and the laws of motion of capitalism.[51]

---

[50] For critiques of Arthur's value-form Marxism, see Smith 2003, and the symposium by a number of scholars, and including a reply by Arthur in *Historical Materialism*, 13, 2, pp. 27ff. The value-form approach is a major variant of the broader commodity-fetishism reading of Marx, which derives from two classic works, Lukács 1971 and Rubin 1973. The commodity fetishism interpretation of *Capital* has been extended and developed in innovative ways in the work of Moishe Postone. See Postone 1996, and also the thorough critical examination of this remarkable work from a wide range of differing theoretical viewpoints in *Historical Materialism*, 12, 3, pp. 43–283, published in 2004.

[51] See Kincaid 2005 for a more detailed discussion of these criticisms.

Tony Smith and historical agency

One of the questionable aspects of Arthur's work is the way in which social agency is monopolised by the dominating power of capital-in-general.[52] This issue is explored in much more scientifically promising ways by Tony Smith. This is somewhat paradoxical, given that, of new-dialectic philosophers under discussion here, it is Smith who is most deeply imbued with Hegelianism. But Smith has a clear vision of social action which is guided by constraints – logics which select and shape action in patterned ways. For example, Smith interprets Hegel's *Philosophy of Right* as arguing that,

> given the social form defined by the category 'property', it is necessarily the case that social agents acting within this social form will tend to act in such a way that the social form defined by the category 'contract' would come about'.[53]

Thus, for Smith, 'the key element in a transition from one categorial level to the next involves the behaviour of social agents'.[54] If a given social form, 'necessarily generates structural tendencies leading social agents to institute a different social form', then this is the sort of necessity which dialectical logic claims to identify and to track, since then, 'the necessity of the derivation is materially grounded in the practice of social agents'.[55] Smith insists that, 'transitions in dialectical social theory demand microfoundations', a point which he says is missed by the school of analytical Marxists when they criticise dialectical logic as lacking an account of *individual* motivation.[56] In Arthur's account, dialectical progression can be read off from the manoeuvres of the Hegelian dialectic which mimes the development of capitalism as a reified system. Smith insists, however, that we need a theory based on material practices, not automatic logic.

---

52 Though Arthur does also recognise long-term limits to the viability of capitalism, which he sees as depending on working-class willingness to continue supplying surplus-value, as well as on ecological conditions which capitalism is undermining.

53 Smith 1993, p. 19.

54 Smith 1993, p. 25.

55 Smith 1993, p. 20 and 25.

56 Smith 1993, p. 34.

> Hegel did not deduce the nature of capitalism from his logic of the concept, but rather his studies of capitalism led him to assert that the logic of the concept is exemplified in the capitalist order.[57]

Smith worries that any reading of *Capital* based only on capital as agent will produces a reified depiction of the system. He points out that commodities do not beget money of their own accord:

> 'commodity', 'money' and 'capital' have then indeed become alien forces dominating the human community. But they are not things. They are constituted in and through social relations, however alien from social control these social relations have become. In themselves they lack both independent metaphysical status and any causal powers.[58]

Moreover, at a concrete level of analysis, the agency of capital is implemented by individual firms and owners of capital. It is towards the end of Volume II of *Capital* and throughout Volume III that Marx deals with many capitals and the patterns of competition. Smith's concern for micro-agency has led him to produce valuable work on recent developments in the capitalist world economy. For example on the intensification of international competition in the industrial sector of capitalism in the latter part of the twentieth century and consequent patterns of deskilling and speed-up in the major industrial countries, and the rapid growth of industrial production in large parts of the developing world.[59] More recently, Smith has written a powerfully argued book which uses Hegelian-Marxist frameworks of dialectical logic to analyse a range of explanatory models of the structure and workings of the international economy. He examines, in turn, neoliberal, democratic cosmopolitan, and Marxian models. The book ends by sketching out a possible structure for a socialist world economy.[60]

[57] Smith 1993, p. 29.
[58] Smith 1993, p. 27.
[59] Smith 2000.
[60] Smith 2006.

Evaluating the new-dialectic approach

The new-dialectic approach to Marx's *Capital* has produced a remarkable literature of creative scholarship and lively controversy. But it has a number of limitations which it is hoped will be addressed in future research. It is, for example, surprisingly parochial. So far, no one has produced a sustained examination of the powerful tradition of German work on the logical construction of *Capital*, and compared it systematically with the themes explored in the anglophone new dialectic literature.[61] There has been a similar neglect of the large and complex body of work on the Hegel-Marx connection which has been produced by Japanese scholars.[62]

The most frequently expressed criticism of new-dialectic explorations of the Hegel-Marx connection is that they substitute conceptual derivation for historically based empirical research. In a well-argued variant of this line of criticism, Alfredo Saad-Filho concludes that,

> new dialectic is insufficient and potentially misleading because it aspires to reconstruct the reality purely through concepts, even though the concrete is historically grounded and, therefore, irreducibly contingent. The concrete can be analysed theoretically only if historical analysis belongs *within* the method of exposition.[63]

Only a few brief comments are possible here about the large questions raised in Saad-Filho's criticism. In fact, in their best work, the new-dialectic scholars spend little time on the exploration of *pure* concepts. As I have tried to show, concepts are scrutinised for their clarity and precision in grasping the essential nature of capitalism and in allowing its dynamics to be scientifically reconstructed in ways which reflect the necessary logics of the operation of the system. The objectives of the new-dialectic writers are generally limited and precise, and no claim is made to offer accounts of the detailed historical evolution of capitalist society. They have tried to clarify how and why Marx organised the argument of *Capital* in the strange way that he did. They

---

[61] See especially Backhaus 1997, Reichelt 2001, Heinrich 2001.

[62] The leading influence in Japan Marxist scholarship has been the work of Kozo Uno (1897–1977). For useful surveys of Japanese interpretations of Capital, see Sekine 1997 and Albritton and Sekine 1995.

[63] Saad-Filho 2002, p. 19. See also Callinicos 1998, and the denunciation of new dialectic in Rosenthal 1998.

have taken seriously Marx's thesis that the topsy-turvy reality of capitalism requires a distinctive set of categories, linked by a logic involving dialectical necessity. Where they do make bold claims is in arguing that such categorial logics can be used to model the patterns of constraint and pressures in the operation of capitalism as a system.

Certainly there are questions to be raised about the concept of *system* as it figures in new-dialectic literature. In focusing on synchronous analysis rather than historical narrative, the new dialecticians have been able to explore the imperatives and dynamics of capitalism as a system while making no claims about the operation of necessity in historical change. They are thus able to avoid confident assertions and predictions about future developments in the history of capitalism. Their approach explicitly rejects the kind of teleology which has done so much to discredit the received tradition of orthodox Marxism as a serious science.

Nevertheless it is true, I believe, that the new-dialectic scholars have not sufficiently defined the relationship of their project to approaches focusing on historical narrative and empirical contingency.[64] Even when clarifying the structure of systems, and the conditions for their scientific analysis, historical narrative is necessary. Systems are subject to processes of formation and disintegration. Their structure evolves in response to internal and external threats to their viability. Marx himself endorsed a definition of dialectical method as analogous to the methods of dealing with system and change in evolutionary biology:

> most important all is the precise analysis of the series of successions, of the sequences and links within which the different states of development present themselves...every historical period possesses its own laws.... In short economic life offers us a phenomenon analogous to the history of evolution in other branches of biology.[65]

We can accept that Engels was wrong to claim that the crucial early chapters of *Capital*, Volume I are organised round a historical sequence in which simple commodity production is replaced by the capitalist mode of production. But Engels was right to hold that a fully developed Marxist political

---

[64] Though see Reuten 2000.
[65] Marx 1976, p. 102.

economy is historical in its essence. As I have noted, new-dialectic work has been limited by insufficient attention to the logics of capitalist *competition*.[66] In the general body of new-dialectic work, attention is concentrated on the fundamentals of value theory. The laws of motion of the system are not a central concern. There is little exploration of the *law of value* – the concrete logics of competition and selection (operating with particular severity in crises) which shape the widely varying institutional structures of industrial and financial capitalism and set the conditions for class struggle, state formation, and the organisation of the world market.

[66] A partial exception is Tony Smith. But his work, though outstanding, remains rather constricted by the syllogistic frameworks he so frequently employs. These are inadequate to grasp the many displaced forms of the law of value – e.g. as implemented by allocation of capital by the banking and financial systems, or by agencies such as the IMF and World Bank. For further discussion of competition and the law of value as allowing integration of systemic and historical logics in political economy, see Kincaid 2005.

Chapter Twenty-Two

States, State Power, and State Theory

Bob Jessop

There has been a major renewal of Marxist work on state theory in the last thirty years. This has been prompted by the crisis of the national state and its typical forms of intervention in the 1970s; the challenge to Eurocentric theorising caused by the economic success of Japan and other Asian powers; liberation from the deadening effect of official Marxist-Leninist doctrines after the Soviet Union collapsed; the emergence of new forms of government, governance, and governmentality; the reciprocal interaction of 'globalisation' and the restructuring and recalibration of state apparatuses; and new sources, stakes, and forms of social resistance to the logic of accumulation on a world scale. Thus contemporary Marxist analyses not only explore conventional themes and approaches in state theory but are also addressing many new issues, developing new theoretical and political arguments, and critically re-evaluating classic texts and approaches.

Re-reading the Marxist classics

Marx's and Engels's work on the state comprises diverse philosophical, theoretical, journalistic, partisan, *ad hominem*, or purely *ad hoc* comments. The changed political conjuncture and the continuing (but still incomplete) publication of the *Marx-Engels Gesamtausgabe* have prompted critical re-evaluation of Marx's theoretical and political analyses and Engels's own contribution to their development. While this has transformed our understanding of Marx's critique of political economy and revealed his concern with political ecology, it has also prompted new interpretations of his critique of the state and politics.[1]

The same sort of re-reading can be seen in traditional Marxist approaches to the state, which have generally been organised around four main axes. First, economic reductionist analyses sought to explain state forms and functions in terms of more fundamental economic structures, interests, and struggles – thereby ignoring the specifically political dimensions of the state and their implications for state power. Contemporary Marxism generally eschews crude economic reductionism, but there is still much interest in the path-dependent co-evolution of different forms of state and 'varieties of capitalism' – at the risk of reifying national capitalisms as so many independent forms of capitalist organisation rather than locating them within a broader, 'variegated' world market.[2]

Second, a certain 'historicist' voluntarism emphasised the transformative potential of autonomous political class struggle without paying due regard to the strategically selective institutional legacies of political structures. While there is now more appreciation of how forms and institutions 'make a difference', celebration continues of mass movements, the 'multitude', and autonomous, self-organising, and decentred collective wills as key forces in political revolution and the dismantling of the official state apparatus. Two influential works in this vein were Hardt and Negri's post-operaist identification of the 'multitude' as the new revolutionary subject operating inside the heart of the new imperial beast (see below) and Holloway's 'open-Marxist' argument that it would be possible for autonomous, self-organising groups to assume control of social life without reconstituting the state machine and state power.[3]

---

[1] Artous 1999; Cowling and Martin 2002; Draper 1977–1986; Fineschi 2006; MacGregor 1996; Panitch and Leys 1998; Teeple 1983; Texier 1998; Thomas 1994; Wells 1982.

[2] Albritton et al., 2001; Bischoff 2003; Candeias and Deppe 2001; Hoffman 2006; Nitzan and Bichler 2002.

[3] Hardt and Negri 2000, 2004; Holloway 2002.

Third, inspired particularly by Marxist-Leninist doctrine but drawing on detailed empirical research, there were many interesting 'state monopoly capitalism' analyses of how the ties between monopoly capital and the state exclude other capitalist groups and the subordinate classes and of how imperialist rivalries and world-market integration were promoting the development of international state monopoly capitalism. While such analyses are less prominent at the national level (despite the rise of blatant neoliberal and neoconservative attempts to deploy state power in an open class war in favour of capitalist interests), research has expanded massively on the internationalisation of the state, the development of a transnational class, and the expansion of various types of international apparatus and international régime tied to transnational capital.[4]

Fourth, following the end of nineteenth-century liberal capitalism and the rise of mass politics, there has been increasing interest – associated especially with Western Marxism and critical cultural studies – in the development of authoritarian statism, whether normal or exceptional in character, and the increased importance of the mass media in the organisation of economic, political, and ideological class domination. This theme has also been taken up and explored in an increasingly sophisticated body of Marxist and *marxisant* work on authoritarian mass parties, plebiscitary democracy, the mediatisation of politics, the importance of 'soft power' in the overall exercise of state power, and the increasing tendency towards new forms of exceptional state.[5]

Key insights of Marxist revival

Turning from thematic to more theoretical issues, the best work in the 1970s and 1980s, especially in the German-speaking world, formulated three key insights into the state that have continued to influence contemporary Marxist work. First, against the usual functionalist and reductionist temptations, some West-German Marxists explored how the typical form of the capitalist state actually caused problems for capital accumulation and political domination rather than securing its overall functionality in these respects. For the

---

[4] Altvater and Mahnkopf 1999; Bonefeld and Holloway 1996; Hirsch 1995; Jessop 2002; Panitch 1994; Poulantzas 1975; Robinson 2004; Wissel 2007.

[5] For example Poulantzas 1978; Scheuerman 2004.

state's institutional separation from the market economy, a separation that was regarded as a necessary and defining feature of capitalist societies, results in the dominance of different (and potentially contradictory) institutional logics and modes of calculation in state and economy. There is no certainty that political outcomes will serve the needs of capital – even if (and, indeed, precisely because) the state is operationally autonomous. For it then becomes subject to politically-mediated constraints.[6] This conclusion undermined previous concerns with the 'relative autonomy' of the capitalist state in the sense that the state would (or should) have precisely that degree of autonomy necessary to secure the needs of capital and pointed instead towards the importance of the structural contradictions and strategic dilemmas and, hence, of competing economic and political imaginaries and continuing struggles over accumulation strategies, state projects, and hegemonic visions that continually shape (and reshape) the state apparatus, views about the nature and purposes of government, and state power. In short, it highlighted the importance of the complex, contingent interplay of social struggles and institutions, marking a return to the work of the founding fathers.

Second, Marxist theorists began to analyse state power as a complex social relation. This involved studies of different states' structural selectivity and the factors that shaped their strategic capacities. Attention was paid to the variability of these capacities, their organisation, and exercise and their differential impact on state power and states' capacities to project power into social realms well beyond their own institutional boundaries. As with the first set of insights, this also led to more complex studies of struggles, institutions, and political capacities.[7] Discussion went beyond the stale issue of 'relative autonomy' to include variable state capacities and the modalities of exercise of state power. A key figure in this regard was Poulantzas, who claimed to have completed the unfinished Marxist theory of the state in proposing that the state, like capital, is a social relation.[8] But the same insight, even if not formulated so explicitly, can be found in many other postwar studies as well as in the work of the classical-Marxist thinkers, such as Marx, Engels, Lenin, Bauer, and Gramsci.

---

[6] Artous 1999; Hirsch 2005; Wood 1981b.
[7] Barrow 1993; Jessop 1990.
[8] Poulantzas 1978.

And, third, abandoning base-superstructure arguments, Marxists discovered the specificity and effectivity of semiosis, discourse, language (and mass media) in shaping the political imaginaries at the heart of the state and political struggle. As subject positions, identities, and interests are no longer regarded as self-evident but are held to depend on specific practices of subjectivation [*assujetissement*] and particular conjunctural horizons of action, there has also been increasing interest in specific narrative, rhetorical, or argumentative features of state power as well as of class relations and identity politics.[9] Thus case studies of policy-making suggest that state policies are discursively-mediated, if not wholly discursively-constituted, products of struggles to define and narrate 'problems' that can be addressed in and through state action. The impact of policy-making and implementation is therefore closely tied to their rhetorical and argumentative framing and this is a crucial area for the exercise of soft power through struggles for hegemony mediated through the mass media, mass organisations, and, increasingly, new networked forms of communication.

Formal vs functional adequacy

Building on the revival of Marxist form-analysis in the critique of political economy, there has been a growing interest in state forms and functions, especially given the crisis of the national state-form in the last thirty years. Marx had argued that the modern (capitalist) state was distinguished by the institutional separation of the political sphere from the profit-oriented, market-mediated economy. He particularly highlighted the formal adequacy of the modern representative state based on rational bureaucracy and universal suffrage for consolidated capitalist social formations. Thus economic agents' freedom to engage in exchange (belied by the factory despotism within the labour process) is matched by the freedom of individual citizens to determine public policy (belied by the state's subordination to the logic of capital).[10] Marx had also identified the basic contradiction at the heart of this formally adequate type of capitalist state, namely, that it relied on the continued willingness of the property-owning minority to accept the political rule of the

---

9 Jessop 2002; Müller et al. 1994; Neocleous 2003.

10 Marx 1975, 1978; cf. Artous 1999; Hirsch 2005; Jessop 1990, 2002.

majority on the condition that the propertyless majority continued to accept the economic rule of the property-owning minority. This contradiction could be managed, as Gramsci among others noted, insofar as the state apparatus in its broadest sense operated to organise a capitalist power bloc and to disorganise subordinate classes and other subaltern forces.[11] Only in this way could the normal (or bourgeois-democratic) form of capitalist state serve to promote the interests of capital and, at the same time, to disguise this, rendering capitalist political domination relatively opaque due to the complex mediations involved in the exercise of state power. When a normal type of capitalist state is established, political class domination is secured through the dull routines of democratic politics as the state acts on behalf of capital, but not at its direct behest. Unsurprisingly, given the contradiction at the heart of the democratic constitution, this is also a fragile political régime. For its stability depends on the continued willingness of the dominated classes to accept only political emancipation rather than press for social emancipation and/or on the willingness of the dominant class(es) to be satisfied with social domination (i.e., with the *de facto* subordination of the exercise of state power to the imperatives of capital accumulation) rather than press for the restoration of their earlier monopoly of political power.

The mere presence of the constitutional state and representative democracy does not secure the expanded economic and extra-economic reproduction of capital. Because forms are the strategically selective medium through which the contradictions and dilemmas of the capital relation develop, there is a permanent tension between form and content. Continuing action is required to ensure that form and content complement each other and prove functional for capital accumulation and political class domination. This problem may be overcome in the short term through trial-and-error experimentation; and it may be solved in the medium- to long-term through the mutual selection and retention of complementary forms and contents. Those policies get selected that correspond best to the dominant forms; and forms will be selected that are most adequate to the overall logic of capital accumulation. In short, content is selected by form, form is selected by content.

Other work has been more concerned with the functional adequacy of prevailing state institutions, regardless of their form. This concerns the capacity of

[11] Gramsci 1971b.

a state in capitalist society to secure the economic and extra-economic conditions for accumulation in a given conjuncture. It focuses on how policies come to acquire a particular content, mission, aims, and objectives that are more-or-less adequate to expanded reproduction in specific conjunctures through specific strategies and policies pursued by particular social forces. This does not mean that the state form is irrelevant but, rather, that its strategic selectivities do not directly serve to realise the interests of capital in general. More attention goes to the open struggle among political forces to shape the political process in ways that privilege accumulation over other modes of societalisation and to the changing balance of forces in order to show how political class struggles and their outcomes are mediated and condensed through specific institutional forms in particular periods, stages, and conjunctures regardless of whether these forms corresponded to the capitalist type of state.

Territoriality and historical constitution

A revival of interest in the historical constitution of the modern state and inter-state system has seen detailed studies of the classical polity, feudal states, absolutism, early-modern state formation, and the development of the Westphalian system (allegedly set up by the Treaty of Westphalia in 1648 but realised only stepwise during the nineteenth and twentieth centuries). Of crucial significance here is the question of changing forms of the territorialisation of political authority and their role in facilitating the development of the capitalist world market and an inter-state system favourable to capital in the context of pre-existing forms of state organisation. The development of the capitalist form of state in Europe and its gradual displacement of dynastic state forms involved the intersection of politically organised coercive and symbolic power, a clearly demarcated core territory governed by a state based on the rule of law, and a fixed population on which political decisions were deemed to be collectively binding.[12] Thus the key feature of the modern state is the historically variable ensemble of technologies and practices that produce, naturalise, and manage territorial space as a bounded container within which political power is then exercised to achieve various, more or less well

---

[12] Teschke 2003.

integrated, and changing policy objectives.[13] Nonetheless the Westphalian system, which is so often taken-for-granted and involves formally sovereign, mutually recognising, mutually legitimating national states exercising sovereign control over large and exclusive territorial areas, is only a relatively recent institutional expression of state power. Other modes of territorialising political power have existed, some still co-exist with the Westphalian system, new expressions are emerging, and yet others can be imagined.[14]

A provocative thesis in recent work on the historical constitution of the modern state is the argument that the state is polymorphous[15] or polycontextural.[16] Criticising the view that states in capitalist societies are necessarily capitalist in form and function, Mann argued that the state's organisation and capacities may be primarily capitalist, military, theocratic, or democratic in nature according to the balance of forces, especially as these affect the state ensemble and its exercise of power. Its dominant crystallisation as one or other of these four forms is contestable and varies conjuncturally. Much the same point is made when Taylor distinguishes between the state as a capitalist state ('wealth container'), a military-political apparatus ('power container'), a nation-state ('cultural container'), and a welfare state ('social container').[17] To this, we could add the state as a patriarchal state ('the patriarch general'). In short, there is no guarantee that the modern state will always (or ever) be essentially capitalist and, even when accumulation is deeply embedded in their organisational matrix, modern states typically consider other functional demands and pressures from civil society when promoting institutional integration and social cohesion. Whether it succeeds in this regard is another matter. Adopting this approach entails looking at actually existing state formations as polyvalent, polymorphous crystallisations of different principles of societal organisation that can crystallise in different ways according to the dominant issues in a given period or conjuncture, with general crystallisations dominating long periods and specific crystallisations marking particular situations.

---

13 Escolar 1997; Foucault 2004; Scott 1998.

14 For example, Beck and Grande 2007; Friedrichs 2001; Segesvary 2004; Shaw 2000; Voigt 2000; Ziltener 2001.

15 Mann 1986.

16 Willke 1992.

17 Taylor 1994.

The scope for alternative crystallisations also highlights the importance of the historical semantics of state formation and the variability of political imaginaries. Indeed, whatever the precise origins of the different components of the modern state (such as the army, bureaucracy, taxation, legal system, legislative assemblies), their organisation as a relatively coherent institutional ensemble depends crucially on the emergence of the state idea. Thus state discourses have played a key role in the separation of the political sphere from other institutional orders and, whether as mystification, self-motivation, or self-description, continue to shape the state as a complex ensemble of political relations linked to their respective social formations. The discursive as well as material constitution of the boundary between state and civil society enables state managers to deploy that movable boundary in the exercise of state power. It also shapes the ways in which other political actors on the political scene orient their actions towards the 'state', acting *as if* it existed; and struggles over dominant or hegemonic political and state imaginaries have a crucial role in shaping the nature, purposes, and stakes of government.[18]

New forms of political domination

Given the crisis of the national state-form that had become naturalised through the Atlantic-Fordist-Keynesian welfare states, export-oriented developmental states, import-substitution industrialisation strategies in Latin America and Africa, and the more general desire for national self-determination in the wake of decolonisation and the decomposition of the Soviet Bloc, interest has grown in the implications of globalisation for the national territorial state. Theory and research have moved well beyond the initial views that globalisation would fatally weaken the national state or leave it largely unchanged and have generated various accounts of the rescaling, recalibration, and reorientation of the state apparatus. There is still no consensus within, let alone beyond, Marxist scholarship on what, if anything, is replacing national states.

Hardt and Negri[19] achieved short-lived fame for their claim that a new but still precarious postnational, postimperialist, postmodern state form was emerging. This was a global 'Empire' based on self-organising, networked

[18] Cf. Bartelson 1995, 2001; Mitchell 1991.

[19] Hardt and Negri 2000, 2004.

forms of power premised on a conception of 'imperial right' and liberal interventionism oriented to universal human values, permanent peace, and social justice. This imperial network was taking the form of a three-tiered pyramid of power dominated by the United States, with a series of middle-ranking national states occupying the middle layer, and other states below it. The obvious tension between the unicity of Empire and the plurality of actually existing national states is resolved through the exercise of its hegemonic power by the USA over other states in the interests of maintaining Empire as a whole rather than in pursuit of its immediate, economic-corporate, imperialist interests. America's capacity to fill this role derives from its unique historical development and its association with capital's immanent drive to expand and to internalise every 'outside' so that collective biopolitical body of world society is subsumed under its logic. Hardt and Negri also argued that, with the increasing importance of an immaterial bio-economy and the general intellect, the industrial proletariat, to the extent that it still exists, has lost its hegemony in the class struggle to the multitudinous masses of an expanded proletariat and the 'poor'. As this Empire gets formed, the prospects for revolution are enhanced. The multitude has nowhere to hide because economic power is now exercised by the global monetary system, political power is exercised through police actions and imperial control oriented to local effectiveness, and cultural power is mediated through global networks of communication that integrate the symbolic with the biopolitical in the service of imperial power. But a multitude of acts of resistance against economic globalisation and Empire will trigger shock waves throughout the system and lead to the emergence of counter-globalisation, counter-Empire strategies. This prediction was challenged historically by the re-assertion of American imperialism shortly after the book's publication but there were also many logical and theoretical objections to Hardt and Negri's grand narrative despite its obvious appeal in identifying the totality of the dispossessed (the 'multitude') as the self-organising force of revolutionary transformation deep within the emerging empire. In particular, Hardt and Negri overlooked the continuing significance of major conflicts between different fractions of capital, between different regions and scales of capital accumulation, and different strategies (including their quite different implications for the differential integration-exclusion of sections of the proletariat, however defined).

Shaw has argued that we are witnessing the tendential emergence of a global state, i.e., a multi-tiered global political organisation that is seeking to reorder the global world around issues of security as well as accumulation.[20] On closer inspection, this global state is actually a 'Western Conglomerate State' organised in the Western hemisphere under US domination and seeking to order the rest of the world; and its major institutions (such as the World Bank, International Monetary Fund, G-8, and United Nations) are not neutral bodies but heavily implicated in the contested exercise of transnational class powers.

Various scholars have argued that the principal change that is occurring is the transnationalisation of the state apparatus as one or both of two processes occur. First, the institutional and strategic distinctions between national states and transnational state apparatuses are disappearing as each national state (a) aims to integrate its economic space and capitals operating within it into the world market on the most favourable conditions possible and (b) is persuaded, induced, or coerced by the dominant neoliberal forces to secure the conditions for neoliberal accumulation on a global scale.[21] Second, just as the exercise of state power in national states reflects an institutionally-mediated condensation of social forces, so the exercise of power in transnational apparatuses reflects a second-order condensation of power among national states and the respective balances of power.[22] More generally, Jessop, following Poulantzas,[23] suggests that the restructuring of the state is characterised by three trends and associated counter-trends which, together, imply that the national state remains an important political force in a changing world order.[24] The three trends comprise: the de-nationalisation of statehood, the de-statisation of politics, and the internationalisation of policy-making; and the three counter-trends comprise: the enhanced role of the state in interscalar articulation, the shift from government to meta-governance to continually reorder the relationship among different forms of governance, and the increased struggle for hegemony and dominance over international policy régimes and policy implementation.[25]

---

[20] Shaw 2000.

[21] Gowan 2000; Overbeek 1993; Panitch 1994; Robinson 2004; *Science & Society* 2001–2.

[22] Altvater and Mahnkopf 1997; Brand and Goerg 2003; Hirsch 2005.

[23] Jessop 2002, 2007, following Poulantzas 1975, 1978.

[24] For a good overview, see Nordhaug 2002.

[25] Jessop 2002.

An interesting real-time experiment for testing different arguments about the transformation of the state is provided by the European Union as a state-in-the-process-of-becoming. There are at least five different accounts of its character as an emerging form of state: liberal intergovernmentalism – the EU is an important site for traditional international conflicts between national states; supranationalism – it is a potential rescaled national state that is gradually gaining the same capacities and competences as a traditional national state; a network state – powers are being redistributed among diverse official, economic, and civilian actors that must co-operate to produce effective policies; multi-level governance – a multi-tiered, multi-stakeholder political arrangement has developed with a tangled hierarchy of powers; and multi-scalar meta-governance in the shadow of postnational statehood.[26]

Some new themes

Notwithstanding declining interest in the more esoteric and abstract modes of state theorising that dominated the 1970s and early 1980s, substantive critical research on states and state power exploded from the 1990s onwards. The crisis of the national state form in advanced capitalist social formations has led to new theoretical concerns that are growing more urgent. These include: the historical variability of statehood (or stateness); the relative strength or weakness of states; the changing forms and functions of the state; issues of scale, space, territoriality, and the state; the future of the national state in an era of globalisation (see above); and the rise of governance and its articulation with government.

There has been growing interest in factors that make for state strength. Internally, this refers to a state's capacities to exercise authority over events and social forces in the wider society; externally, it refers to the state's power in the inter-state system. This concern is especially marked in recent theoretical and empirical work on predatory and/or developmental states. The former are essentially parasitic upon their economy and civil society, exercise largely the despotic power of command, and may eventually undermine the economy, society, and the state itself. Developmental states also have infrastructural and network power and deploy it to in allegedly market-conforming ways.

[26] For a critique of these views, see Jessop 2007.

Unfortunately, the wide variety of interpretations of strength (and weakness) threatens coherent analysis. States have been described as strong because they have a large public sector, authoritarian rule, strong societal support, a weak and gelatinous civil society, cohesive bureaucracies, an interventionist policy, or the power to limit external interference. In addition, some studies run the risk of tautology insofar as strength is defined purely in terms of outcomes. A possible theoretical solution is to investigate the scope for variability in state capacities by policy area, over time, and in specific conjunctures.

The restructuring of the state has prompted growing interest in the forms and functions of the capitalist type of state and of states more generally. This can be studied in terms of the state's role in: (a) securing conditions for private profit – the field of economic policy; (b) reproducing wage-labour on a daily, lifetime, and intergenerational basis – the field of social policy broadly considered; (c) managing the scalar division of labour; and (d) compensating for market failure. On this basis, Jessop[27] characterises the typical state form of the postwar advanced capitalism as a Keynesian welfare national state. Its distinctive features were an economic policy oriented to securing the conditions for full employment in a relatively closed economy, generalising norms of mass consumption through the welfare state, the primacy of the national scale of policy-making, and the primacy of state intervention to compensate for market failure. He also describes the emerging state-form in the 1980s and 1990s as a Schumpeterian workfare postnational régime. Its distinctive features are an economic policy oriented to innovation and competitiveness in relatively open economies, the subordination of social policy to economic demands, the relativisation of scale with the movement of state powers downwards, upwards, and sideways, and the increased importance of governance mechanisms in compensating for market failure. Other types of state, including developmental states, have been discussed in the same terms.

Recent work on globalisation casts fresh doubt on the future of national territorial states in general and nation-states in particular (see above). This issue is also raised by scholars interested in the proliferation of scales on which significant state activities occur, from the local through the urban and regional to cross-border and continental co-operation and a range of supranational entities. Nonetheless initial predictions of the imminent demise of the national

[27] Jessop 2002.

territorial state and/or the nation-state have been proved wrong. This reflects the adaptability of state managers and state apparatuses, the continued importance of national states in securing conditions for economic competitiveness, political legitimacy, social cohesion, and so on, and the role of national states in co-ordinating the state activities on other scales from the local to the triad to the international and global levels.

The increased significance of governance, that is, networked forms of self-organisation rather than hierarchical forms of command and control, as opposed to government; and their role within the overall exercise of class and state powers. States have generally relied in varying degree on market mechanisms, planning and command, networks, and solidarity to pursue state projects and at stake in this debate is the changing weight of these different mechanisms and their forms of co-ordination. Governance operates on different scales of organisation (ranging from the expansion of international and supra-national régimes through national and regional public-private partnerships to more localised networks of power and decision-making). Although this trend is often taken to imply a diminution in state capacities, it could well enhance its power to secure its interests and, indeed, provide states with a new (or expanded) role in the meta-governance (or overall co-ordination) of different governance régimes and mechanisms.[28]

Interest in governance is sometimes linked to the question of 'failed' and 'rogue' states. All states fail in certain respects and normal politics is an important mechanism for learning from, and adapting to, failure. In contrast, 'failed states' lack the capacity to reinvent or reorient their activities in the face of recurrent state failure in order to maintain 'normal political service' in domestic policies. The discourse of 'failed states' is often used to stigmatise some régimes as part of inter-state as well as domestic politics. Similarly, 'rogue state' serves to denigrate states whose actions are considered by hegemonic or dominant states to threaten the prevailing international order. Moreover, according to some radical critics, the USA itself has been the worst rogue state for many years.[29]

Closely linked to this interest in government, governance, and meta-governance is a tendency for a Marxist rapprochement with Foucauldian work on

[28] Messner 1998; Slaughter 2004; Zeitlin and Pochet 2005.

[29] For example Blum 2001; Chomsky 2001.

governmentality – prompted in part by the later Foucault's growing interest in the role of the state as a site for the strategic codification of power relations and his work on governmentality as a distinctive type of statecraft that complements more micro- and meso-level forms of disciplinary power. In contrast to his earlier hostility to theorising the state and his emphasis on the micro-physics of power, Foucault turned to *raison d'état*, statecraft, and state projects. Combined with his heuristically powerful analytics of power, this has provided the basis for research that synthesises in different ways Marxist and Foucauldian themes.

There is also interest in the changing scales of politics. While some theorists are inclined to see the crisis of the national state as displacing the primary scale of political organisation and action to either the global or the regional scale, others suggest that there has been a relativisation of scale. For, whereas the national state provided the primary scale of political organisation in the Fordist period of postwar European and North-American boom, the current after-Fordist period is marked by the dispersion of political and policy issues across different scales of organisation, with none of them clearly primary. This in turn poses problems about securing the coherence of action across different scales. This has prompted interest in the novelty of the European Union as a new state form, the re-emergence of empire as an organising principle, the prospects for a global state.[30]

The state as a social relation and the 'strategic-relational approach'

An innovative approach to the state and state-building has been developed by Jessop and others in an attempt to overcome various forms of one-sidedness in the Marxist and state-centred traditions. His 'strategic-relational approach' builds on Poulantzas's claim that the state is a social relation. For, 'like "capital", *it is . . . a relationship of forces, or more precisely the material condensation of such a relationship among classes and class fractions, such as this is expressed within the State in a necessarily specific form*').[31] Jessop suggested that this claim can be reformulated as follows: the state is not a thing but a social relation between

[30] See, for example, Beck and Grande 2005; Brenner 2004; Shaw 2000.
[31] Poulantzas 1978, pp. 128–9, italics in original.

people mediated through their relation to things;[32] or, again, the state is not a subject but a social relation between subjects mediated through their relation to state capacities. More precisely, this approach interprets and explains *state power* (not the state apparatus) as a *form-determined* condensation of the changing balance of forces in political and politically-relevant struggle. It follows that the exercise and effectiveness of state power is a contingent product of a changing balance of political forces located within and beyond the state and that this balance is conditioned by the specific institutional structures and procedures of the state apparatus as embedded in the wider political system and environing societal relations.

Thus a strategic-relational analysis would examine how a given state apparatus may privilege some actors, some identities, some strategies, some spatial and temporal horizons, and some actions over others; and the ways, if any, in which political actors (individual and/or collective) take account of this differential privileging by engaging in 'strategic-context' analysis when choosing a course of action. This approach also introduces a distinctive *evolutionary* perspective into the analysis of the state and state power in order to discover how the generic evolutionary mechanisms of selection, variation, and retention may operate in specific conditions to produce relatively coherent and durable structures and strategies. This implies that opportunities for re-organising specific structures and for strategic reorientation are themselves subject to structurally-inscribed strategic selectivities and therefore have path-dependent as well as path-shaping aspects. For example, it may be necessary to pursue strategies over several spatial and temporal horizons of action and to mobilise different sets of social forces in different contexts to eliminate or modify specific constraints and opportunities linked to particular state structures. Moreover, as such strategies are pursued, political forces will be more or less well-equipped to learn from their experiences and to adapt their conduct to changing conjunctures. However, because subjects are never unitary, never fully aware of the conditions of strategic action, never fully equipped to realise their preferred strategies, and may always meet opposition from actors pursuing other strategies or tactics, failure is an ever-present possibility. This approach is intended as a heuristic and many analyses of the state

32 Cf. Marx 1976, Chapter 23.

can be easily re-interpreted in strategic-relational terms even if they do not explicitly adopt them or equivalent terms.[33]

To translate this account into concrete-complex analyses of specific political periods, stages, or conjunctures requires the study of three interrelated moments: (1) the state's historical and/or formal constitution as a complex institutional ensemble with a spatio-temporally specific pattern of 'structurally-inscribed strategic selectivity'; (2) the historical and substantive organisation and configuration of political forces in specific conjunctures and their strategies, including their capacity to reflect on and respond to the strategic selectivities inscribed in the state apparatus as a whole; and (3) the interaction of these forces on this strategically-selective terrain and/or at a distance therefrom as they pursue immediate goals or seek to alter the balance of forces and/or to transform the state and its basic strategic selectivities.

---

[33] Jessop 2002, 2007.

Chapter Twenty-Three

Marxism and Theories of Racism

Robert Carter

It is a commonplace now to observe the declining influence of Marxism on the social sciences in Europe and America, its armies in dismal retreat before the advancing forces of postmodernism and relativism, its Enlightenment weaponry – the belief in the application of reason to human affairs and in the pursuit of objective knowledge, the commitment to social transformation – scattered and blunted. In the local disciplinary battlefield constituted by the sociological analysis of racism and ethnicity, casualties have been particularly high: a cursory internet search reveals the extent to which Marxist analyses of racism have fallen into desuetude, a striking contrast to the situation of twenty years ago. I shall suggest that there are three principal reasons for the waning interest within Western universities over the past decade or so in Marxist accounts of racism and ethnicity. Firstly, Marxist theories have rarely challenged the notion of race itself and, in so far as they have failed to do so, they have reproduced many of the shortcomings associated with its use in orthodox social science. Marxists have largely failed to identify a distinctively Marxian view of the phenomena of race and ethnicity. This is ironic in view of the second reason, namely the advance of postmodernism. Whilst it can be acknowledged that the term postmodernism covers a wide range of sympathies, in the social sciences its most far-reaching effect has been seen in the rise of a species of relativism and a corresponding 'loss of nerve', to use Goldthorpe's expression,[1] in the epistemic claims of social research. Marxism, with its concern with social transformation and its commitment to scientific, materialist theory, has thus found itself increasingly peripheral to the academic social sciences, which in turn often regard Marxism as discredited or anachronistic. Finally, political developments, particularly the global pre-eminence of US interests since 9/11, the 'War on Terror', and the response to these developments by those who are the targets of US policy, have shifted the interest of sociologists to issues of identity politics, multiculturalism and religion, topics for which many consider Marxism to be ill-suited because of its putative unconcern with matters of politics, subjectivity and ideology. I shall deal with each of these reasons in turn before concluding with an assessment of Marxism's resources for responding to them.

I. Marxism and concepts of race

Classical figures in Marxism such as Marx and Engels, Kautsky, Luxemburg, and Trotsky unsurprisingly wrote little that addressed specifically the issue of racism (although they had a good deal to say about imperialism, colonialism and nationalism and the ways in which these relations affected the views held by the working classes of the imperial states of the colonised; Marx and Engels's discussion of British rule in India and Ireland are two cases in point). The interest of Marxists in the analysis of racism only emerges as significant in the 1930s and 1940s and principally in response to the efforts of black Americans to challenge racism and discrimination in the USA. W.E.B. DuBois (1868–1963) and O.C. Cox (1901–74) were key contributors to the development of a distinctively Marxian view of racism. An early anti-racist activist and co-founder of the NAACP, DuBois's views were decisively shifted towards Marxism by the Bolshevik revolution in 1917 and his subsequent visit to the USSR in 1927 (although he did not join the US Communist Party until 1961, at the age of 93). He became a powerful critic of imperialism, arguing that a necessary condition for proletarian revolution was the uprising of the exploited

[1] Goldthorpe 2000.

classes in Africa, South America and the Far East. For DuBois, the problem of what he called the 'color line' remained the greatest obstacle facing the world Communist movement; indeed, the failure to transcend this line would be catastrophic for the future of humankind:

> The proletariat of the world consists not simply of white European and American workers but overwhelmingly of the dark workers of Asia, Africa, the islands of the sea, and South and Central America. These are the ones who are supporting a superstructure of wealth, luxury and extravagance. It is the rise of these people that is the rise of the world.[2]

Unlike DuBois, Cox never became a member of the Communist Party, but his work on capitalism and racism, particularly *Caste, Class and Race* first published in 1948, was highly influential. For Cox, racism functions as the rationalisation or ideology of capitalist exploitation, with the capitalist using racism to keep labour freely exploitable. Racism and colour prejudice, for Cox, is not simply an antipathy towards others based on somatic features, but 'rests basically upon a calculated and concerted determination of a white ruling class to keep peoples of color and their resources exploitable'.[3] Significantly, the function of racism in constraining the conditions under which the exploited class labours also imparts to it a certain autonomy since racism becomes an emergent cultural resource such that 'both exploiters and exploited for the most part are born heirs to it.' Cox's model is therefore *not* an example of a Marxism in which superstructural forms (such as racism) are merely epiphenomenal reflections of the economic base. The starting point for an understanding of racism remains the class relations of capitalism, but *only* the starting point, since racism once established becomes a contextual condition of action for subsequent social actors, shaping their plans, alignments and ambitions and thus influencing class formation.

Nevertheless, Cox's model is not without difficulties. To begin with it assumes that the capitalist class *as a whole* benefit from racism, a claim that might be queried not only for its assumption of a unitary class with a homogeneous (and identifiable) set of interests, but also for the presumption that racism *necessarily* benefits this class. Partly as a consequence of this view, Cox

[2] DuBois 1939, p. 54.
[3] Cox 1972, p. 214

argued that the ruling class was the *only* beneficiary of racism; the working class had no investment in racism as an ideology since it divided them against themselves and fissured their unity in the face of ruling class oppression. However, working-class racism remained an indubitable fact of US political life and so Cox found himself compelled to adopt a 'false-consciousness' approach as a means of explaining the presence of something which, at least in Cox's terms, operated clearly against the interests of the working class. Racism was seen as inauthentic to the working class, something externally imposed by the ideological dominance of the ruling class. This was not only sociologically unpersuasive, but it discouraged serious consideration of racism within the working class, since the real sources of such racism were held to be the ruling class and its functional need to manage the conditions of labour exploitation.

Although I have argued against regarding Cox's analysis as crudely reductionist, it does illustrate some of the shortcomings of Marxist approaches to racism. Moreover, his analysis, with its concentration on the social relations of the workplace, offers little scope for exploring racism in other contexts or considering its connections with other forms of social division, such as gender and religion, which may not be primarily workplace-based. Despite the recognition of racism as an emergent cultural form, Cox himself only intermittently pursued its implications. Others have been more consistent.

2. Gramsci, hegemony and the politics of racism

In developing his notion of hegemony, Gramsci recognised the critical role of ideas in social action. He insisted that the dominant class in modern capitalist societies ruled as much by consent as it did by coercion and that this was in significant measure attributable to the limited ideational resources available to the dominated. These limits were secured through obvious means such as widespread censorship and restricted access to education, but also indirectly through the persistence of 'common sense' as a source of meaning in everyday life. In seeking to account for their experience of the social world, people routinely drew on a reservoir of traditional ideas that directly or indirectly reaffirmed the class hierarchies and other social divisions of capitalist society and served to secure the ideological hegemony of the ruling class.

Nevertheless, there were, for Gramsci, important practical limits to the dominance, or hegemony, of ruling-class ideas. Firstly, such hegemony is in a significant sense the product of a cultural and political effort on the part of the ruling class and its intellectuals – hegemony has to be brought about and, once brought about, it has to be maintained against, for instance, radical critics and oppositional ideas generally. Secondly, the limits to any hegemonic project are set by the systemic imperative to reproduce the conditions of capital accumulation. So although hegemony is primarily cultural and political, it nevertheless has to sustain the legitimacy of a particular set of capitalist economic relations; these relations have to carry a practical legitimacy in everyday terms for both the rulers and the ruled (both of whom, but for different reasons, need to be assured that exploitation and inequality are the necessary basis of economic growth and expansion).

Gramsci's notion of hegemony introduces a more dynamic view of the relation between capitalism and ideas, one in which the realms of culture and politics are more loosely connected to economic relations than in the work of the classical Marxists and of DuBois and Cox. Hegemony is not secured in an automatic sense by the social relations of production; instead it is the outcome of political and ideological struggles between dominant and subordinate groups. Not only does this imply that hegemony is unstable, but also that, in so far as cultural and political struggles are discursively construed, social groups and collectivities may understand their political interests in a variety of ways. The older notion of a homogeneous bourgeoisie confronting an equally homogeneous working class is undermined; indeed, the need for hegemony itself arises precisely from the inability of the social relations of production to generate a coherent and unifying understanding of class interests and a corresponding basis for group unity.

By stressing the cultural and ideological basis of collective organisation and mobilisation, Gramsci initiates an important shift of emphasis in Marxist theory. The concern with the *functional* role of ideas in the maintenance of capitalism (through the misrepresentation of class inequalities as 'race inequalities', for example) moves aside in favour of an interest in how people make sense of the social world at the level of lived experience and how their resources for doing so may be organised by the politically powerful.

It was the Centre for Contemporary Cultural Studies (CCCS) under Stuart Hall that began systematically to apply Gramsci's insights to the analysis of racism. However, these insights were powerfully mediated in the UK by the work of the French Marxist, Louis Althusser. Althusser's own reading of Gramsci's work was influenced by the structuralism in vogue in the 1960s and early 1970s.[4] Deriving from the work on language carried out by the Swiss linguist Ferdinand de Saussure, structuralism's central principle was that cultural forms, belief systems and ideologies can best be understood as systemic wholes, whose meaning was generated by their immanent structural relations. This led Althusser to insist on a fundamental distinction between science and ideology; Marxism itself becomes a scientific analysis of capitalism *as a system*. One consequence of this is the diminished role of social agency, exemplified in Althusser's stiffening of Gramsci's ideas about hegemony into the more deterministic notion of 'ideological interpellation'. In this process of interpellation, individuals are transformed into particular sorts of human subjects (for example, as 'men' or 'women', as parents, as consumers or as 'part of the community') through recognising themselves in forms of ideological representation (rather in the way that adverts for cars appeal to us as a particular type of consumer or ideas about nationhood appeal to us as a certain type of person). For Althusser, the reproduction of society is as much about ideology as it is about economics,[5] and this was to be a central element in the approach developed by Stuart Hall and his colleagues.

3. Hall, Gilroy and the poststructuralists

Policing the Crisis, which was published in 1978, sought to develop an account of the rise of an authoritarian politics of immigration and 'race'. Hall and his colleagues at CCCS argued that a 'moral panic' about the crime of 'mugging' was being used to secure a new form of political hegemony in 1970s Britain, one in which ideas about race were a central feature. The crisis of hegemony, in the CCCS view, had been brought about by the social dislocations generated by the efforts of post war British capitalism to adjust to a post-Fordist reorganisation of the global economy. The CCCS approach represented a significant advance on earlier Marxist formulations of the relationship between class relations and racism: not only did it retain the customary strengths of Marxist analyses – the emphasis on the systemic, international character of capitalism and on the political consequences of class conflict – but it also

4 Dews 1987; Benton 1977.
5 Joseph 2006.

recognised the key role played by ideational resources in shaping forms of hegemony. Thus the key reworking of what was a systemic crisis of British capitalism, primarily arising from adjustment in the context of decolonisation to a new global order, into a political and moral crisis about 'race' was in considerable measure facilitated by an antecedent body of ideas about race, colour and colonialism which were a legacy of British imperial rule.

Here then was a Marxist account in which ideology was accorded a key role. Moreover, following Gramsci, the emphasis was on the effects of ideology not just at the level of social classes and the state, but at the level of popular consciousness. The powerful signifier 'race' was able to gather together a bundle of ill-formed and inconsistent notions about somatics and nationhood and fashion them into a powerful political commitment to a 'white Britain'. Margaret Thatcher's 'populist authoritarianism' exploited this to widen her appeal to working-class voters in the face of her advocacy of neo-liberal economic policy likely to have a severe impact on working-class living standards. Yet this account still left unspecified the processes and mechanisms by means of which a 'crisis of capitalism' (and it was not obvious in what sense capitalism was in a 'crisis', or even what sort of crisis this might be) came to be necessarily expressed in terms of 'race'.

Unsurprisingly in view of this, *Policing the Crisis* left an ambiguous legacy. On the one hand, it gave rise to a view of the concept 'race' as expressive of all those forms of politics that were organised or construed around notions of race. Paul Gilroy's work[6] is probably the most well-known using this view of race. One of the chief defects of Gilroy's approach has been to further the use of race as an analytical category within social research (although his more recent work has indicated his own unease with concepts of race as analytical categories); this in turn has inhibited the thoroughgoing critique of it that has hampered the development of a compelling Marxist account of the relationship between racism and capitalism. On the other hand, *Policing the Crisis* encouraged a concern with the ideological, but one strongly influenced by Althusser's notion of interpellation. Interestingly, this led to a disregard for the specificity of notions of race similar to that of the Gilroy position: the historical content of race ideas was less important than the power of

[6] Gilroy 1987, 1993, 2001.

such ideas to create particular types of human subject. More significantly, it encouraged an exiguous view of human subjectivity which was to leave Marxism ill-equipped to respond to the concerns about identities that emerged in the late 1990s.

These and other points were raised by a consistent Marxist critic of the CCCS, Robert Miles. In a series of writings during the late 1970s and the 1980s, Miles[7] uncompromisingly insisted that the concept of race was an ideological, not an analytical category, and that its use in social research and in Marxism ensured its social reproduction whilst generating obfuscatory theory. In any case, argued Miles, Marxism (or political analysis more generally) did not need a notion of race; the object of analysis should be racism. Against the CCCS, Miles argued for a restricted concept of racism – as an ideology deploying a concept of race – and insisted that the relationship between racist ideologies and social action was not straightforward. So, for instance, empirically demonstrable inequality of outcome, in say, housing allocation or levels of unemployment, could not be interpreted as necessarily being the result of racism. Miles also favoured the use of the term racialisation to refer to the process 'by which meaning is attributed to particular biological features of human beings, as a result of which individuals may be assigned to a general category of persons which reproduces itself biologically'.[8] Thus, black workers in the 1980s were characterised by Miles as a racialised fraction of the working class, an indication of the extent to which Miles himself had been influenced by the same structuralist tradition as the CCCS, albeit by the work of Poulantzas rather than Althusser.

The Miles-CCCS debate dominated academic discussion of these topics during the 1980s in the UK, (the extent of its impact elsewhere is less certain). The axial principle of the discussion was the relationship between class relations and racism and it held great interest to Marxists because of this. The work of Balibar and Wallerstein represented another approach to this relationship. The influence of Althusser is evident in the move away from considering the development of capitalism within a mode of production to considering it in the context of a social formation. An important consequence of doing this is

[7] Miles 1982, 1987, 1989, 1993.
[8] Banton 1998, p. 184

that *all* aspects of class struggle, including those previously seen as 'merely' superstructural, must be regarded as playing a determining role in the configuration of the relations of production. For Balibar and Wallerstein, this entails attention not only to the organisation of the labour process and the reproduction of labour-power itself broadly understood, but also the cultural formation of the labouring classes. And here, under the influence of Foucault, they move beyond notions of ideology as understood in earlier Marxist work to insist that

> The very identity of the actors depends upon the process of formation and maintenance of hegemony.... The universalism of the dominant ideology is therefore rooted at a much deeper level than the world expansion of capital and even than the need to procure common rules of action for all those who manage that expansion. It is rooted in the need to construct, in spite of the antagonism between them, an ideological 'world' shared by exploiters and exploited alike.[9]

Racism is a central element of this ideological world.

Viewing racism in this way enables Balibar and Wallerstein to loosen productively the relationship between politics and economics. 'For my part', notes Balibar, 'I do not believe that racism is the expression of class structure; rather, it is a typical form of political alienation inherent in class struggles in the field of nationalism, in particularly ambivalent forms'.[10] So this is to be a particular form of loosening, an extending of the leash; the leash itself is kept firmly in place by two other claims which place Balibar and Wallerstein's approach firmly in the camp of structuralist Marxism. Firstly, racism (along with sexism) retains its functional role within capitalism:

> if one wants to maximize the accumulation of capital, it is necessary simultaneously to minimize the costs of production (hence the costs of labour power) and minimize the costs of political disruption (hence minimize – not eliminate, because one cannot eliminate – the protests of the labour force). Racism is the magic formula that reconciles these objectives.[11]

---

9 Balibar and Wallerstein 1991, p. 2.
10 Balibar and Wallerstein 1991, p. 12.
11 Balibar and Wallerstein 1991, p. 33.

Implicit in this formulation is a second claim, characteristic of many structuralist-Marxist analyses of racism, that racism has an agency of its own: it '*inscribes itself* in practices…in discourses and representations',[12] 'racism *sees itself*…',[13] and 'racism constantly *induces*…'[14] (emphases added). However, the notion that racism magically works to minimise the costs of production and of political disruption is undermined by these authors' own subtle accounts of the tensions between racism and nationalism, and of the ways in which these are shaped by people's historical experiences and by developments within global capitalism.

Within the space of five years or so, this concern with class relations in debates about racism and ethnicity had receded, erased by the rise of postmodernist and poststructuralist concerns with identity, subjectivity and discourse. One effect of the Miles-CCCS debate lingered: the hesitancy about using the term *race*, expressed in the collar of scare quotes which usually accompanied its appearance in texts.

4. Postmodernism and poststructuralism: race triumphant

The concerns with ideology and hegemony that characterised the work of the CCCS were taken up in a political context that saw a growing disillusionment amongst academics and researchers with Marxism. In the study of racism this disillusionment took the form of a closer concern with social and personal identity and the effort to understand the apparent continuing appeal of ideas about race, ethnicity, nationalism and so on. Added force was given to this concern by a series of political conflicts – in many of the states of the former Soviet Union, Rwanda, the former Yugoslavia, Somalia and elsewhere – which were represented by many Western commentators as ethnic conflicts. Consequently, Marxism found itself sidelined as academic interest shifted to the question of racial and ethnic identities and cognate themes such as multiculturalism, religion and democracy.

---

[12] Balibar and Wallerstein 1991, p. 18.
[13] Balibar and Wallerstein 1991, p. 59.
[14] Ibid.

A key feature of this shift was the unwillingness of many Marxists to examine critically notions of race and ethnicity, which made it difficult to develop a distinctively Marxist position on these matters. For example, Callinicos's 1993 account of the relationship between 'race and class' does not go beyond a reworking of Cox with the addition of the more recent view that races are 'invented' or constructed. Yet this latter insight is not incorporated theoretically into an analysis of racism. Instead, racism is

> not a matter of the ideas in people's heads, but of *oppression*, of systematic inequalities in power and life chances stemming from an exploitive [sic] social structure.... Revolutionary Marxists...regard racism as a product of capitalism which serves to reproduce this social system by dividing the working class.[15]

This usefully outlines the core elements of what we might term the orthodox-Marxist theory of racism and class relations: racism is not simply an ideological phenomenon but refers also to structural inequalities; it is a product of capitalism and therefore its removal is dependent on the removal of capitalism; and its chief function is to divide the working class. Ethnicity only figures here as a modern mutation of racism, employing a 'rhetoric of cultural difference' to the same ends of justifying discrimination on the basis of characteristics held to be inherent in the oppressed group.[16]

This is also the case with the work of Sivanandan. In several books,[17] but more significantly in the journal *Race and Class*, he has elaborated a distinctive neo-Marxist position that has consistently sought to link racism with globalisation and contemporary politics[18] whilst trying to explore the ideological and political tensions to which racism gives rise. Sivanandan thus provides a more nuanced political account of contemporary forms of racism than is sometimes found in Marxism, but his use of concepts such as race and ethnicity remains indistinguishable from that of Callinicos.

One consequence of this inattention to concepts of race and ethnicity in the orthodox-Marxist approach is that it has allowed the emergence of a radical race perspective to go unchallenged. There are several aspects to this new

---

[15] Callinicos 1993, p. 11.
[16] Callinicos 1993, p. 33.
[17] Sivanandan 1991, 1981.
[18] Sivanandan 2006.

politics of race, but its general position is to emphasise the social reality of beliefs about race and ethnicity, and on the basis that therefore 'race matters', to defend forms of group politics based on notions of racial or ethnic identity. There is a serious danger here that notions of race come to be entwined with notions of culture and the unalterability of race comes to be the unalterability of cultures too. Since cultures (and races), in this view, exist more or less independently of politics, a robust notion of social agency is no longer possible. Theorists influenced by postmodernist and poststructuralist ideas have added to this extinction of agency through the notion of racism as a discourse. Let me illustrate these claims with some examples.

The work of Goldberg[19] exploits the idea, shared with Callinicos, in which racism refers both to an ideology and to social practices, but exploits it in a distinctly un-Marxist direction by identifying what he terms 'the racial state'. In Goldberg's account, race is a product of modernity and its need to account for, to know and to control 'Otherness'; in modernity 'what is invested with racial meaning, what becomes increasingly racially conceived, is the threat, the external, the unknown, the outside'.[20] Race is also a form of crisis management, a means of containing the threat of the diverse and the different:

> The racial state, the state's definition in racial terms, thus becomes the racial characterization of the apparatus, the projects, the institutions for managing this threat, for keeping it out or ultimately containing it...[21]

This depiction rests on a commonsense understanding of race, and as such reproduces it as a reified form, but it also conceives of race as a practice, as something done to some people by others. (It is always possible to do this with race precisely because the meaning of the term is so indeterminate). The racial state becomes a behemoth stubbornly resistant to political intervention and change:

> In states that are racially conceived, ordered, administered, and regulated, the racial state could be said to be everywhere. And simultaneously seen nowhere. It (invisibly) defines almost every relation, contours virtually all intercourse. It fashions not just the said and the sayable, the done and

19 Goldberg 2002.
20 Goldberg 2002, p. 23.
21 Goldberg 2002, p. 34

> doable, possibilities and impermissibilities, but penetrates equally the scope and quality, content and character of social silences and presumptions. The state in its racial reach and expression is thus at once super-visible, in form and force and thoroughly invisible in its osmotic infusion into the everyday, its penetration into common sense, its pervasion (not to mention perversion) of the warp and weave of the social fabric.[22]

On this view, as Goldberg acknowledges, the racial state is as much 'a state or condition of being as it is a state of governance'. Such a state is the normal form of the modern state, according to Goldberg, and leads him to identify current global arrangements as a 'racist world order'.[23] Here, the term race (and its cognates racial, racism) has lost specific meaning; once race is everywhere (with the racial state) it is, of course, nowhere since it is impossible to identify. The political consequences of this position are dire: should anyone be foolhardy enough to challenge this 'super-visible...and thoroughly invisible' mammoth, their chances of succeeding must be accounted meagre.

There are less malign analyses drawing on unreflective, commonsense meanings of race, particularly in the USA. Three perspectives have dominated recent work: Critical Race Theory (CRT), intersectionality and whiteness studies. Each in their different ways rests on an uncritical use of the concept of race.

CRT emerged in the 1990s from a critique of legal theory in the US, which, it was claimed, had neglected questions of race. Using the concept in much the same fashion as Callinicos, it drew the opposite conclusion to him, uncompromisingly insisting that race should be at the fore of legal and social analysis and that racial liberation should be the most significant objective of emancipatory struggle.[24]

To some extent, the epistemology of CRT drew upon another theoretical development, that of intersectionality. The notion of intersectionalty had its origins in feminist responses to the assumption often made, in politics as well as social science, that the subject of history was the white male. This conceptualisation of human experience, feminists argued, was one which did not recognise or acknowledge the distinctiveness of women's experiences, and

---

[22] Goldberg 2002, p. 98.
[23] Goldberg 2002, p. 104.
[24] Delgado & Stefancic 1999.

especially the ways in which gender differences powerfully shaped these experiences. This positing of a distinctively women's experience created the opportunity for further reflection on the particularity of people's experience and the consequences of this for their self-understanding or identity. In particular, writers such as DuBois[25] and Zora Neale Hurston[26] identified and deliberated upon the impact of racism on one's sense of self.

In the 1990s, a number of feminist writers developed these insights,[27] arguing that theories of racial inequality that fail to incorporate gender into their frameworks were insufficient for understanding the lives of women who suffer from racism (just as for CRT theories of legal inequality that fail to incorporate race are insufficient). However, the emphasis on the intersection of race, class, and gender moves beyond simply including race in research on gender or including gender in studies of race. Intersectional approaches maintain that gender and race are not independent analytical categories that can simply be added together.[28] Rather, intersectionality theorists argue that 'race is "gendered" and gender is "racialized", so that race and gender fuse to create unique experiences and opportunities for all groups – not just women of color'.[29] Class, in this perspective, is similarly 'raced' and 'gendered'.

The emphasis on identity and self-understanding central to both CRT and to intersectionality theorists is shared by those who have advocated the study of whiteness. An early influence was the work of Kovel,[30] but the most well-known contribution has been Roediger's *Wages of Whiteness*, originally published in 1991 and republished as a revised edition in 1999. Roediger explicitly considers the relationship of Marxism and racism, arguing that Marxist historians have been seriously neglectful of: 'the role of race in defining how white workers look not only at Blacks but at themselves';[31] 'the pervasiveness of race'; and 'the relationship between race and ethnicity'.[32] Marxists, in short, have largely ignored the 'white problem', namely 'why so many workers define themselves as white'.

---

[25] DuBois 1973.
[26] Neale Hurston 1991.
[27] See, for example Collins 1999, Essed 1991, Glenn 1999.
[28] King 1989, Weber 2001.
[29] Browne and Misra 2003, p. 488.
[30] Kovel 1984.
[31] Roediger 1991, p. 5.
[32] Roediger 1991, p. 6.

Roediger's work raises some interesting and difficult questions for Marxists,[33] but, as I have already indicated, Marxist interpretations of race, racism and ethnicity have made themselves vulnerable to these charges partly because of their foot-shooting reluctance to critically engage with the concept of race. Predictably perhaps, Roediger describes some recent Marxist efforts to rethink the commitment to the notion of race as a 'retreat from race and class'.[34]

5. Can Marxism explain racism?

Despite the neglect into which Marxist analyses have slipped, in this concluding section I want to argue that Marxism has the resources for a plausible account of racism and ethnicity. However, in order to realise these, it would need to resolve a number of key questions. For expository purposes, these may be loosely grouped under three headings: the concepts of race and ethnicity; the relationship between racism, ethnicity and class relations; and the role of social agency.

a) *The concepts of race and ethnicity*

Whilst Marxists continue to use these terms, they will find if difficult to escape the theoretical muddles characteristic of much analysis of racism and ethnicity and will fail to exploit the distinctiveness of Marxist theory. The case against the use of the concept race in social science is well established[35] and it need only be summarised briefly here.

The central difficulty with the term *race* as a social-science concept is that its referent is indeterminate. This does not imply that that all social-scientific concepts must have a referent that is objective, in the sense that there is no dispute about what is meant when the term is used; after all, terms such as social class, bureaucracy, rationalisation or globalisation are used in a variety of ways by social scientists. Rather, to become part of the conceptual repertoire

[33] For an excellent discussion of, and response to, these see Allen 2002

[34] Roediger 2006.

[35] See, for example, Miles 1989, 1993; Banton 1998, Carter 2000, Darder and Torres 2004, Hirschman 2004.

of social science, a term must have, to use Desrosières's phrase,[36] a 'meaning that holds', that is to say, a meaning defensible within the vocabulary of social science itself (does this concept improve upon existing ones by, for instance, formulating problems in a new way or by exposing other concepts as partial?) *and* one that refers to a feature, or features, of the social world that cannot be grasped other than through this concept. The concept of race fails on both counts: its origins in eighteenth- and nineteenth-century science to refer to biologically distinguishable human groupings renders it unsuited to the language of social science, whilst the discrediting of its ontological referent – races of human beings – leaves it without an object. The case of ethnicity as a concept is perhaps less straightforward. Nevertheless, writers such as Banton, Fenton and Brubaker[37] are surely right to argue that, like the concept of race, it has no consistent referent and serves only to obscure sociological explanation.

The difficulty of employing a concept of race in social research is that it is impossible to formulate a research question using it that is capable of being answered. No one, as Michael Banton[38] has remarked, has ever seen another person's race (just as no one has seen another person's ethnicity), yet research is routinely formulated on the basis that race or ethnicity are social variables whose meaning is sufficiently stable for them to be investigated.

Against this, I want to suggest that race and ethnicity be regarded as concepts used in the description of human social differences; both are constituents of various propositions or claims about the world made by lay persons and sociologists. Whether the concepts are a significant constituent of such propositions or claims, and whether they are explicitly formulated, will often be matters for empirical judgement. Such judgements are difficult, for a variety of reasons: people frequently disguise their motives, mostly intentionally but sometimes not; they may not be able to formulate their ideas in a readily accessible way; and the relation between behavioural outcome and motivational intent is commonly opaque.

These empirical difficulties notwithstanding, race and ethnicity are forms of social description; they are, if you like, social constructions, in the sense

---

36 Desrosières 1998.

37 Banton 1998, 2000; Fenton 2003; Brubaker 2004.

38 Banton 1988.

that they are the products of human efforts to describe the world. Like all such products, ideas about race and ethnicity have the potential to become an ideational resource: once they become a part of society's circuits of communication (as ideas of race did during the eighteenth and nineteenth centuries) they become available to social actors with access to those circuits, who may deploy them in pursuit of a range of vested interests. In the course of doing this, people may work such ideas up to become elements of formal propositions ('black people are inferior to white people', 'foreigners should not have jobs in our country'); these, in turn, may be elaborated into world views such as Nazism or ethno-nationalism (and world views themselves afford all sorts of ideational opportunities); and once discursively established in this way, such ideas may become powerful ways of 'making up people'.[39] In this way, racism, ethnicism, culturalism may all have material effects, becoming, for example, the basis of institutional arrangements, of legal enactments, of rules for hiring and firing employees and so forth. Racism may here develop into an axis of social differentiation (but note: one that requires racists to ensure its maintenance and reproduction).

None of the above claims, it seems to me, are incompatible with a Marxist view of ideology and consciousness that stresses the central role of human agency and which regards such agency as the crucial mediator of structural forms and forces. However, they do insist upon a particular view of social description and especially the role of such descriptions in the vocabularies of social science (and Marxism, in so far as it makes claims to be a scientific account of the social world). This means abandoning the concepts of race and ethnicity *as sociological concepts*.[40] Doing so allows a reformulation of the relationship between racism and class relations.

b) *The relationship between racism, ethnicity and class relations*

Marxism possesses a distinctive resource for challenging conventional sociological accounts of 'race and class', namely the analytical dualism of structure and agency present in its more dynamic versions. Briefly, Marxism, in arguing that human beings make history but not in circumstances of their own

39 Hacking 2002.

40 This is emphatically not to dismiss their centrality to many lay accounts, although see Fenton 2006 for a sceptical view.

choosing, acknowledges a distinction between the contexts in which people find themselves and the efforts of those people to change or reproduce those contexts. The forces shaping these contexts are the social relations of production; these are emergent from human social practice but are irreducible to individuals and subject to only partial discursive penetration (as Marx himself noted, if the world were transparent there would be no need for science). On this account, the social relations of production are antecedent to particular historical individuals and define the context within which all forms of social inequality are generated. Here, 'race', or, more properly, racism, cannot have an equivalence: the social relations of production refers to emergent, and relatively enduring forms of social relation; racism to ideas and ideology, to the forms of thought developed in response to, and in the effort to manage, these social relations. Class relations and racism refer to different types of social object.

Ironically, the commitment of some Marxists to the notion of race has muted the force of these insights and has encouraged the use of reified categories such as 'ethnic group' and 'race'. Yet the insights are a powerful source for a post-race social science. Let me give one example, using the work of Sayer,[41] to illustrate the point.

Distinguishing analytically between structure and agency allows each to be considered as abstractions. Considering capitalism as an abstraction in this way enables one to identify what is essential or necessary to capitalism for it to be described as such, what minimal conditions need to be fulfilled for an empirical case to be classified as capitalism (as opposed to, say, feudalism). Conversely, this process also allows identification of those features that are historically contingent to actually existing capitalism rather than a structural necessity for it; they do not define capitalism *qua* capitalism but are contingently co-present for various reasons (such as pre-existing capitalist social relations of production in the case of certain types of gender relations).

Sayer develops this distinction between necessary and contingent elements to propose a further analytical distinction between what he terms 'identity-neutral' and 'identity-sensitive' mechanisms. Identity-neutral mechanisms, in Sayer's terms, are those mechanisms whose operation is not necessarily dependent upon any aspect of the identity of social actors. To be a police

[41] Sayer 2005.

officer merely requires you to be over five feet eight inches, it does not require that you see yourself first and foremost as a tall person; to labour in a factory requires only that you have the necessary dexterity or experience to operate the machinery, it does not require that you be a woman or white or see yourself as in the vanguard of the proletariat. Many forms of capitalist social relations are indifferent to whatever identities individuals may cherish for themselves. They are structural determinants in the sense that they are not reducible to the wills of individual agents.

Identity-sensitive mechanisms, on the other hand, rest upon the identification of relevant identity attributes, excluding those who do not possess them. Most forms of racist and sexist discrimination are identity-sensitive mechanisms, where gender or colour (or language, religion, place of origin and so on) either facilitate or disqualify one's participation in certain types of social relations or access to resources. Identity-neutral and identity-sensitive mechanisms are everywhere in interaction, but their interdependence is only contingent, a feature often overlooked in both class reductionist accounts of inequality and in postmodern, identitarian ones. This 'contingent co-presence of identity-neutral and identity-sensitive mechanisms in determining inequalities' suggests that the causes of class and gender differences are radically different, and that, though 'economic relations are always socially embedded – which in our society inevitably means in ways that are gendered, 'raced', etc. – it does not follow that identity-neutral dimensions are not also present, any more than the fact that birds can fly means that gravity is suspended'.[42]

The distinction between identity-neutral and identity-sensitive mechanisms is an important one for disentangling the confusion about 'race and class'. Let me draw out two pertinent implications.

Firstly, and importantly, the distinction strongly suggests that '...progress in eliminating these cultural, identity-sensitive forms of domination and exclusion need not wait upon finding a successor for capitalism'.[43] Secondly, whilst the subjective experience of class is not a necessary condition of the (re)production of economic class in capitalism (though it contingently affects its course), the subjective experiences of, and identification with, 'being black' or 'being a woman' are necessarily constitutive of 'racial' or gender differences

[42] Sayer 2005, p. 87.
[43] Sayer 2005, p. 89.

because such differences are ascriptive in character: 'racism is a necessary condition for the reproduction of 'race', but class-ism is not a necessary condition for the reproduction of class'.[44] Racism requires racists; class relations do not require class-ists.

Again, none of this is incompatible with Marxism, but such a nuanced account is difficult once conventional notions of race or ethnicity are invoked. As I have already argued, one of the major consequences of invoking these categories is that race and ethnic groups come to be regarded as cultural pre-givens, existing outside of politics. Instead of conceding this point, Marxists should be advancing a political account of group formation, that is, an account which sees groups as the products of the pursuit of interests within social contexts. This is not instrumentalism, since interests here have a moral or normative dimension – they have agential force only when they come to be valued by people. In other words, to understand inequalities, domination, competition and resistance we need to examine why they should *matter* to people.

c) *The question of agency*

The questions of what matters to people and why are empirical ones, yet often they are overlooked or assumed once terms such as race or ethnicity are employed. Or rather, what matters to people is inferred from their race or ethnic grouping or from their 'whiteness'. Archer has referred to this strategy as 'the myth of cultural integration',[45] whereby culture is defined as a community of shared meanings, thus eliding the 'community' with the 'meanings'; to belong to this ethnic group or that racial group by definition meant sharing certain meanings about what mattered, about how the world was to be understood and so on. Culture and community are here regarded as mutually constitutive and this makes it exceedingly difficult to develop a political account of group formation, let alone one that is sensitive to the complexities of human commitments and social action. Seeking a historical-materialist understanding of human life entails rejecting the 'myth of cultural integration' and the assumptions associated with it. In particular, the notion that

44 Sayer 2005, p. 94.
45 Archer 1988, p. 99.

cultures exist more-or-less independently of what states and politics do because they are in some sense prior to politics lends itself readily to the treatment of groups as units in a world of their own making, not as actors *doing* things to reproduce or modify social contexts. Such a view is inimical to a radical or Marxist analysis of racism.

Conclusion

I have argued that the quiescence of Marxism within current debates in Europe and the USA about racism, ethnicity, multiculturalism and identity is due in some measure to its complicity with a sociological vocabulary of race. This has not been a good deal for Marxism: on the one hand, it has seen race concepts flourish within the ambit of various forms of postmodernism and poststructuralism, encouraging ever denser forms of theoretical and political mystification; and on the other, Marxism itself has frequently found itself at odds with the sorts of dominant analyses which rely centrally on concepts of race and ethnicity. As with class collaboration, so with conceptual collaboration: the powerful always come out on top. In refusing to challenge concepts of race and ethnicity, by taking them at their everyday, common-sensical, face-value meaning, Marxists have forfeited one of their traditional strengths: the development of a critical analysis of racism and ethnicity that encompasses both the world of empirical appearances and the generative relations responsible for these. There are signs that the process of developing forms of Marxism able to do this is under way,[46] but it requires a critique of Marxism's use of concepts of race and ethnicity as much as a critique of sociology's use of them. And that is a tall order.

[46] See, for example, work by Meyerson 2001, Virdee (forthcoming) and Darder and Torres 2004.

Chapter Twenty-Four

Historical Materialism and International Relations

Frédérick Guillaume Dufour

Researchers from the historical-materialist tradition made major contributions to the field of international relations during the last two decades. Among other things, they contested the American field of international relations' theoretical and historical account of the concepts of *balance of power*, the *sovereign state*, *hegemony* and the *international division of labour*. With respect to the Marxist tradition, contemporary historical materialism seeks to come to terms with the problematic character of techno-deterministic explanations, of teleological conceptions of history and of functionalist economism. Meanwhile, strategies to address these issues are not consensual. My survey of these contributions and achievements will focus on the influence and legacy of two theoretical trends in international relations theory: *neo-Gramscianism* and *political Marxism*. In each case, I will minimise the intra-paradigmatic differences for the purpose of the overview. They are, nonetheless, significant on questions of theoretical priorities and empirical emphases.

1. Neo-Gramscianism

It is more suitable to designate a Gramscian-inspired *group* of scholars in international relations, than a neo-Gramscian *theory*. This group evolves around the groundbreaking work of Robert W. Cox. It embraces contributions from Stephen Gill and the Amsterdam school (Kees van der Pijl, Otto Holman and Henk Overbeek) and other scholars such as Mark Rupert, Adam David Morton, Andreas Bieler, Isabella Bakker, Craig N. Murphy, André Drainville and Matt Davies. Aside from Antonio Gramsci, it has been influenced by a variety of figures from Fernand Braudel, Nicos Poulantzas and Giovanni Arrighi to Suzanne Strange and the *École de la régulation*. The coherence of the Gramscian-inspired constellation is found in the application of Gramsci's theory and concepts to the analysis of global politics. The concepts of hegemony, historical bloc, passive revolution, organic intellectual, and civil society include some of the ideas used by these scholars.

1.1. *The critique of positivism and neorealism*

During the beginning of the 1970s, Robert W. Cox sought to identify the limitations of mainstream accounts of international organisations and international politics. In the late 1970s and during the beginning of the 1980s, he offered a major epistemological, ontological and normative critique of the mainstream schools of international relations.[1]

At the ontological level, Cox and the Gramscian-inspired literature condemn neorealism's reification of structures and processes of international relations. Neorealism marginalises the *problématique* of social change and historical transformations in favour of an emphasis on predictability, stability and reproduction of existing world orders. Neo-Gramscianism makes a sharp break away from this ontological tradition. Neo-Gramscians argue that specific processes and issues of global politics must be analysed in relation to *historical structures*: particular configurations of a *world order, social relations of production* and *forms of states*. The global political economy is a totality characterised by profound open-ended processes of structural transformations. Thus, its ontology needs to be constantly recaptured and revisited.[2] In the Gramscian-inspired literature, Mark Rupert has probably been the first to

[1] Cox 1976; 1981.

[2] Cox 1976, 1987; Gill 1990; Murphy 1994; Overbeek 1990; Overbeek (ed.) 1993; Rupert 1995; van der Pijl 1984, 1999.

emphasise the importance of grounding the analysis of the state-society complex and the inter-states system on a historical ontology informed by a Marxist critique of alienation and fetishism.[3] In their recent work, Isabella Bakker and Stephen Gill have reformulated the Coxian ontology in an attempt to ground it on a historical dialectic: 'We see these [world orders, forms of states and production] not as levels as such, but as different moments in the constitution of a contradictory totality of world order'.[4] This reformulation testifies as to the attempt to move away from a mechanistic interpretation of the Coxian ontology which would reduce it to a web of mechanically interacting ideal-types. Also significant in the latest work of Bakker and Gill is the effort to incorporate a broadly defined dimension of *social reproduction* in the Gramscian ontology.

At the epistemological and normative levels, neo-Gramscianism defends a conception of the relation between theory and practice anchored in Antonio Gramsci's conception of the *organic intellectual*. Academics are influenced by their social location in the labour process of a *historical structure* and they contribute to its reproduction or transformation by the formulation of hegemonic or counter-hegemonic *ideas*. They participate in the construction of the intersubjective structures of ideas of a world order. Cox denounces the mainstream accounts of international relations' self-portrayal as value-neutral. His reflexive stance toward theoretical activity is crystallised in the distinction he makes between *problem-solving theory* and *critical theory*. Whereas the first limits itself to solving problems in a given world order, the second is concerned with understanding the historical origins of a world order. This enables critical theoreticians to provide emancipatory alternatives to the world order anchored in the everyday practices of resistance. Since, 'theory is always for someone and for some purposes', the role of critical theory and *organic intellectuals* is to highlight these purposes and unmask the structures of power that theory consolidates, reproduces and reifies. This critique of problem-solving theory proposes an historical approach to the transformation of world orders, and it aims to demystify institutions that traditional approaches take for granted. This project of demystification starts with the *problématique* of hegemony.

[3] See Rupert in Gill 1993; 1995, pp. 14–38.

[4] Bakker and Gill 2003, p. 25.

1.2. *Hegemony and comprehensive concepts of control*

Gramsci argued that in states with an important state-society complex, the terrain of revolutionary struggle had to be civil society, the vast range of cultural, educational and religious institutions, which participated in the everyday life production and reproduction of common sense. Civil society is the terrain where a long-term war of position has to be fought by the working class in alliance with progressive social forces in order to form a counter-hegemonic bloc. Cox adapts this argument to the analysis of world orders. He conceives the development of capitalist international relations as the succession of different *historical structures* where *hegemony* is reproduced or transformed through the interactions of *ideas, institutions* and *material capabilities*.[5] National and transnational *social forces* emerge from and are transformed by social relations of production. Their actions can transform both the forms of states and world orders. Hegemony depends on the capacity to articulate and orient common sense at the national and global levels through powerful international *institutions*[6] and *material capabilities* such as the mass media.[7] Hegemony relies both on coercion and consent. A coherent *historical bloc*, clarifies Gill, cannot emerge in the absence of 'a large degree of political congruence between "sets of relations of force"'.[8] Likewise, *world hegemony* 'has for its origin the outward expansion of the internal or national hegemony, established by the dominant or ruling class within the most powerful state'.[9] The concept of hegemony, nonetheless, has been addressed in uneven ways by the Gramscian literature.

The Amsterdam school, in particular Kees van der Pijl, addresses hegemony through the notion of *comprehensive concepts of control*. Before entering in contact with the work of Cox and Gill, the Amsterdam school was already concerned with the analysis of the internationalisation of capital, the labour process and the fractioning of the ruling class. The notion of *comprehensive concepts of control*, notes van der Pijl, 'seeks to capture the unity (again, a broader, meditated historical/transformational rather than immediate unity) of the

---

[5] Cox 1981; 1987.
[6] Gill 1990; Murphy 1994.
[7] Davies 1999.
[8] Gill 1990, p. 44.
[9] Gill 1990, p. 47.

interests of fractions of capital and the need to impose the discipline of capital on society at large'. In the analysis of hegemony, the notion refers to:

> the projects of rival political alliances which on account of their appropriateness to deal with current contradictions in the labour, intersectoral/competition, and profit distribution processes, as well as with broader social and political issues, at some point become *comprehensive*, crowding out of others by their greater adequacy to a historically specific situation – until they themselves unravel in the course of further development and struggle.[10]

The concept seeks to bring to light the *political articulation*, rather than the mechanical connection, of a hegemonic project and a strategy of accumulation. Another distinctive feature of this school's examination of processes of hegemonic formation is its emphasis on the role of the *managerial class*.[11]

In a different vein, Stephen Gill presents a study of the transformation of hegemony since the 1970s in *American Hegemony and the Trilateral Commission*. According to Gill, the widely held argument that the United States entered a phase of hegemonic decline during the 1980s was misplaced. He describes this period as a 'crisis of hegemony' characterised by 'a struggle over the definition of "national interests" and the conduct of American Foreign Policy in the 1970s and 1980s'.[12] The crisis led to a restructuring of American power orchestrated through international social forces such as the Trilateral Commission, rather than its decline:

> What has been developing in the 1970s and 1980s is a shift away from an international economic order of economically sovereign states and national political economies, linked together primarily by trade flows, towards what I call a transnational liberal economic order. In this ascending order, capital flows and interpenetrating investments are fusing the world economy into a more integrated whole.[13]

It resulted in a *transnationalisation* of American hegemony channelled through the *structural power of capital* at the international level.[14] These processes led

[10] van der Pijl 1998, p. 4.
[11] See for instance, van der Pijl 2005.
[12] Gill 1990, p. 7.
[13] Gill 1990, p. 88.
[14] Gill 2003, pp. 102–15.

to the consolidation of an austere state-society complex during the 1980s and favoured the imposition of a *new constitutionalism*: a political and legal framework exposing states to the increasing pressures of *disciplinary neoliberalism, panopticism* and *market civilisation*.[15] In the last decades, Gill's work has emphasised the ways in which the constitutional embedding of the neoliberal agenda made it possible for new dimensions of social reproduction and social life to be commodified.[16]

Rupert presents a third contribution to the analysis of hegemony during the postwar period, which emphasises the role of class relations in the internationalisation of the state. In *Producing Hegemony*, he criticises the Gramscian-inspired literature for neglecting the role and form of domestic production in the making of world hegemony, that is the historically specific form of class compromise emerging in the US with Fordism. Rupert notes:

> the exercise of US global power was shaped by the historically specific ways in which mass production was institutionalized, and by the political, cultural, and ideological aspects of this process at home and abroad.[17]

His recent work offers an examination of the diverse and contradictory social forces opposing globalisation in the US during the 1990s. He presents a nuanced picture of this opposition, highlighting proximities between the far Right and segments of the Left, and thus, the need to develop a progressive common sense that is sensitive to the politics of class, gender and race.[18]

With respect to their analysis of transformative agencies, these contributions are distinct from Gramsci's in one respect. Gramsci identified the *party* as the modern Prince that is able to organise and channel transformative practices in a progressive direction. However, contemporary Gramscian-inspired scholars seek transformative agency in transnational social forces such as the antiglobalisation movements, global unions and the World Social Forum.[19] Progressive transformative agencies need to connect local resistance to global politics.

---

[15] Gill 1995a.
[16] Bakker and Gill 2003.
[17] Rupert 1995, p. 2.
[18] Rupert 2000.
[19] Cox and Schechter 2002; Gill 2000; Harrod and O'Brien 2002; Drainville 2002; Rupert 2000; 2003.

1.3. *Globalisation and the new constitutionalism*

Robert W. Cox did not present an historical revision of the relation between capitalism and the inter-state system; this task has been tackled in the recent work of van der Pijl. Pijl argues that capital found a proper space for expansion in the *Lockean Heartland* of capitalism, the English state, where fractions of capital are organised along a *transcendent comprehensive concept of control* and under a *self-regulating market*. The *Lockean Heartland* exercised geopolitical pressures on the contending Hobbesian *states* which recourse to state led strategies of development and formulate national interest along the lines of their ruling class.[20] Contrary to the *Lockean heartland* whose mode of expansion is transnational, the mode of extension of the Hobbesian states is international.[21]

With regards to the analysis of recent developments in the global political economy, most neo-Gramscians locate a structural change in the *historical structure* of the postwar *world order* during the 1970s and 1980s. Cox refers to this shift, occurring during the 1970s with the increasing transnationalisation of production and capital circuit, as a transition from Fordism to post-Fordism.[22] With this transition, states increasingly served as a 'transmission belt' for transnational social forces in the process of forging a *world order*. All the while, Cox argues, most national and local social forces lost in part their agential power to the benefit of transnational capitalist forces. According to Cox, the internationalisation of the state at the centre of the process of globalisation of production and finance brought about a spatial reconfiguration of capitalism. This entailed that categorical distinctions between centre, periphery and semi-periphery ceased to refer to geographical locations and tended to transcend societies.[23] Some argue that the inherent logic of this process of globalisation should lead to the consolidation of transnational classes and eventually to a global state.[24] Others interpret the necessity of a 'double movement', *à la* Polanyi, similar to the 'self-defence of national societies against the market', but at the global level.[25]

---

[20] van der Pijl 1998, pp. 64–88.
[21] For a periodisation of this dynamic see van der Pijl 1998, p. 85.
[22] Cox 1987; van der Pijl 1998.
[23] Cox 1992.
[24] Burbach and Robinson 1999.
[25] See Cox 2001; Gill 1995b.

During the last decades, neo-Gramscian researchers have built on, developed and expanded Cox's work in different directions. They have incorporated elements of feminism,[26] of the analysis of civilisations,[27] and of ecological studies.[28] They have provided critical analysis of international law,[29] of the role of international organisations in industrial changes,[30] of struggle between fractions of capital,[31] regionalisation,[32] global governance,[33] immigration policies,[34] (in)security,[35] the mass media[36] and political resistance.[37]

Meanwhile, this literature has been challenged. Critiques of Gramscian-inspired international theory developed both inside and outside this group of scholars. Major disagreements came from 'open Marxism' – Peter Burnham and Simon Clarke. Burnham argued that both Cox's articulation of the concepts of relations of production, forms of states and world orders, and his articulation of the relations between institutions, ideas and material capabilities are problematic. He contends that the relations between these elements are presented in a multi-directional and reciprocal fashion that fails to develop anything beyond a 'version of Weberian pluralism oriented to the study of the international order'.[38] Other critics argue that the Coxian-inspired presentation of the contemporary state as a 'transmission belt' of the neoliberal agenda of transnational social forces underplays the states' role in the production of this world order.[39] It overestimates the role of ideology and ideas in social changes[40] and does not recognise the fractured nature of the neoliberal project.[41] Likewise, it fails to acknowledge the role of social forces

---

[26] Peterson 2003; Bakker and Gill 2003.
[27] Cox and Schechter 2002; Gill 1995a.
[28] Cox and Schechter 2002.
[29] Gill and Law 1988; Cutler 1997.
[30] Murphy 1994.
[31] van der Pijl 1984, 1998; Overbeek 1990, 1993.
[32] Bieler and Morton 2001.
[33] Egan 2001; Rupert 2003.
[34] Pellerin 2003; Overbeek and Pellerin 2001.
[35] Cox 1993b; Bakker and Gill 2003, Chapters 3 and 8–11.
[36] Davies 1999.
[37] Gill 2000; Drainville 2002.
[38] Burnham 1991, p. 77.
[39] Burnham 1991, p. 86; Panitch 1994, 1996.
[40] Burnham 1991, pp. 79–80; see also Shilliam 2004.
[41] Drainville 1994.

resisting the imposition of this agenda and the unevenness of the process of internationalisation of the state.[42]

2. Political Marxism

The development of political Marxism and the theory of social-property relations stem from the work of historian Robert Brenner on the transition to capitalism. Ellen M. Wood and George C. Comninel further developed the theoretical foundations laid out by Brenner both empirically and theoretically. Since the 1990s, Justin Rosenberg, Benno Teschke and Hannes Lacher drew upon Wood and Brenner's arguments to revisit central *problématiques* of international-relations theory such as the social and geopolitical dynamics of capitalism, and the genesis of modern sovereignty, globalisation and uneven and combined development.

2.1. *Brenner and Wood*

The work of Brenner emerges as strikingly different in the heterodox group of *analytical Marxists*. It is empirical, historical, and comparative all at once. Brenner's work proceeds from an analysis of social-property relations in order to understand comparative social developments, forms of states, demographic trends and relations of power. In this respect, he breaks with approaches that focus on productive forces or individual choices. Contributions of political Marxists to international-relations theory have extended this theory to the study of geopolitics, sovereignty and territoriality.

Brenner's articles on the social origins of agrarian capitalism in pre-industrial Europe emphasise how the balance of class forces and social-property relations led to the development of significantly different social trends in precapitalist and capitalist Europe.[43] Once more, the focus on social-property relations and balance of class forces breaks away from approaches that overplay the importance of the world system, world order or productive forces. Brenner reconstructs the following causal chain. Specific social-property relations and balance of class forces bring about different antagonistic rules and strategies

[42] Egan 2001.
[43] Brenner 1976, 1982, 1985a, 1990b, 1991.

of social reproduction. In turn, the interaction of these different antagonisms lead to often unintentional trajectories of social development. Different social-property relations, he emphasises, evolve neither systematically nor in a linear way from one to another. They are not a *structure* from which another structural outcome can be derived by conceptual necessity. A given social-property régime, capitalist or precapitalist, is characterised by specific social contradictions, but the ultimate outcome of these contradictions is a matter of historically specific balance of class power. Brenner's argument challenges three influential views. First, he breaks away from the Malthusian explanation of development through an emphasis on demographic trends (Le Roy Ladurie). Second, he challenges Wallerstein's explanation of the emergence of capitalism through an emphasis on the modern world-system. Finally, Brenner questions the economistic account of the transition from feudalism to capitalism which emphasises the removal of the 'obstacles' to capitalist development in precapitalist Europe (Guy Bois).

Reconstructing the comparative developments of social-property régimes in Europe, Brenner, and later on Ellen M. Wood, George C. Comninel and Colin Mooers, highlight the regional and national specificities of these developments. They focus on how different rules of reproduction of power develop in England, France and the Holy Roman Empire after the breakdown of feudalism. These scholars note that while manorialism continues to structure life in England, seigneurialism emerges in other regions of the continent. Finally, they underscore the different strategies of reproduction of social power that arise in different parts of Europe. Whereas capitalist reproductive strategies emerge in England, France and Prussia become enmeshed in absolutist strategies of social power reproduction.[44] This research programme clarifies important paradoxes in Marxist social theory. The latter, for instance, struggles to account for the fact that both Spain and Portugal, though sometimes considered to be the first imperialist and capitalist states, were far behind in processes of industrialisation and urbanisation during the nineteenth century. However, the theory of social-property relations arrives at the conclusion that these states were not capitalist during the fifteenth century. Marxist social theory also had difficulty explaining why despite its 'bourgeois' revolution, capitalist development in France lagged far behind that of England during the

[44] Brenner 1995b; Comninel 1990, 2000; Wood 1991; Mooers 1991.

nineteenth century. Here, the theory of social-property relations concludes that the revolution was bourgeois, but not capitalist.[45] While all these cases pose problems to classical-Marxist historiography, Brenner, Comninel and Wood argue that they need not if one begins by distinguishing between pre-capitalist and capitalist rules of social reproduction. In the first case, exploitation is directly anchored in political domination, while in the second, even though processes of exploitation and domination are politically constituted, the moment of exploitation becomes indirect. This distinction brings about a critique of the commercial model of capitalism and of the conceptual association of the capitalist class with the bourgeoisie.

2.2. *The critique of the commercial model of capitalism*

The critique of the commercial model of capitalism was formulated in the work of Robert Brenner and developed by Wood in *The Origins of Capitalism*. According to Brenner and Wood, many theories of the development of capitalism, from Paul Sweezy's to Immanuel Wallerstein's, shared a Smithian *commercial* model of capitalist development. According to this model, the take-off of modern economic growth was made possible by the growth of commerce. Indeed, the growth in commercial activity pushed individual economic actors to adopt capitalist strategies of reproduction and increased the division and specialisation of labour.

Three critiques are addressed to this model. First, it takes for granted that sooner or later the development of capitalism is *inevitable*. Its development is the necessary outcome of a *teleological* process, insofar as capitalist development had to 'wait' for several obstacles to be removed in order for it to finally come to, or achieve, its complete maturity.[46] Therefore, Wood clarifies, what needs to be explained: the emergence of capitalism is already presupposed in some embryonic or proto-form. Hence, the model is circular, and it tends to conflate cause and effect. Second, because it emphasises the development of commerce rather than the emergence of a distinct social relation, the model reconstructs the emergence of capitalism as a quantitative rather than qualitative process. Thereafter, it locates the development of capitalism essentially in the sphere of circulation at the international level rather

45 Comninel 1990; Teschke 2005.
46 Wood 2002; Teschke 2005, p. 10.

than at the level of social relations. Braudel, for instance, identifies a series of mechanisms of sophistication of capitalism from the Italian city-states to the American superpower. However, none of these mechanisms of sophistication introduce a qualitative shift at the level of social relations.[47] Third, in its neo-Weberian and neorealist variances, the model considers capitalism as a purely economic category. Political Marxism argues precisely the opposite: capital is a social relation and its emergence has profound implications on a broad range of social processes – including processes of state formation and geopolitical dynamics.

2.3. *The separation of the economic and the political in capitalism*

According to Wood, the distinctiveness of capital as a social relation is that it is the first social relation of domination which can potentially operate entirely through the mediation of the market. While former relations of domination linked *necessarily* the economic moment of surplus extraction and the political moment of domination, capital does not. Slavery, serfdom, absolutism and other precapitalist social-property régimes implied the fusion of the economic power of exploitation and the political power of domination. Absolutist politics and mercantilist economic doctrines worked hand in hand while monopolistic strategies of accumulation were granted by the state and secured through military force. Capital as a social relation differs from the previous strategy of geopolitical accumulation:

> Capitalism is a social relation between persons in which all 'factors of production,' including labour-power, have become commoditised and where production of goods for exchange has become market-dependent and market-regulated. On this basis, capitalism does not mean simply production for the market, but competitive reproduction in the market based on a social-property regime in which property less direct producers are forced to sell their labour-power to property-owners. This separation of direct producers from their means of reproduction and their subjection to the capital relation entails the compulsion of reproduction in the market

[47] For this critique see Rosenberg 1994, p. 40; Teschke 2003, pp. 129–50; Wood 1984, 2002.

> by selling labour-power in return for wages. This social system is uniquely dynamic, driven by competition, exploitation and accumulation.[48]

The capitalist state enforces the separation of the economic power of exploitation and the political power of domination. This does not imply that the state is entirely autonomous. What it does imply, clarifies Lacher, is that the state is autonomous enough to reproduce this institutional separation.[49] A state's capacity to impose this institutional separation in order to pursue its own interests at the international level follows a capitalist rationality.

A major geopolitical implication of the emergence of this social relation in rural England is that precapitalist strategies of political accumulation, including the compulsive force of political accumulation through territorial expansion, were slowly replaced by the emergence of a new form of hegemonic reproduction. In theory, the latter is not incompatible with political coups orchestrated from outside in the name of the *sovereignty of the people* and war in the name of liberating a people from tyranny.[50] Therefore, the implication of the argument on the separation of the economic and political powers is not that capitalist firms are not in principle close to the political power; they are, and obviously they weigh on the elaboration of foreign policy. The point is that with the development of capitalism, strategies of geopolitical accumulation ceased to be the states' *prima ratio*; first, because they became too costly; second, because they were no longer intrinsically linked to a strategy of accumulation of surplus.[51]

2.4. *Modern sovereignty*

In *The Empire of Civil Society*, Justin Rosenberg introduced Wood's work in the field of international relations. Here, Rosenberg reconstructed the relation between different social relations of production and geopolitical strategies of reproduction of power. He criticised the neorealist and neo-Weberian separation of the economic and the political in international-relations theory. Yet, he did not explicitly endorse Brenner's conception of capitalism. Rosenberg builds on the work of Wood, Simon Bromley, Eric Hobsbawm, Eric Wolf

---

48 Teschke 2005, p. 11.

49 Lacher 2005, p. 41. See also Wood 1981b.

50 Wood 2003.

51 This argument is developed at length in Teschke 2003.

and Trotsky in order to challenge a-historical *lieux communs* of international-relations theory and history. He questions and rejects the so-called modernity of the Treaties of Westphalia and Utrecht. Rather, he argues that the political context of both treaties was still characterised by premodern strategies of political accumulation having little or nothing to do with the modern anonymous and impersonal strategies of the 'balance of power'. Hence, it was neither Westphalia nor Utrecht that brought about the modernity of international relations, but the development of capitalism toward the end of the nineteenth century. It was capitalism, he argues in *The Empire of Civil Society*, that created the separation of the political and the economic. In turn, it was this separation that enabled liberalism, as the purely economic fiction of inter-state reconciliation through commerce, and *realism*, as the purely political form of mediation of relations between states through the mechanisms of balance of power, to emerge simultaneously, thus embodying the Janus' faces of modern international relations.[52]

After *The Empire of Civil Society*, Rosenberg has consistently argued that the ahistorical theory of the balance of power must be abandoned in favour of Trotsky's theory of uneven and combined development. The first task of such a theory would be to explore the consequences of the fact that 'the development of backward societies took place under the pressure of an already existing world market, dominated by more advanced capitalist powers'.[53] This peculiar dynamic should lead one to abandon a unitary conception of the sovereign state as the central unit of analysis of international relations. Rosenberg notes with respect to this that:

> we cannot begin with a logical model of homogeneous states: the variety of political forms is simply too great. We would have to begin instead with a historical analysis which reconstructs the uneven and combined development of capitalism which has produced such a variegated world of states.[54]

Moreover, Rosenberg presents the theory of uneven and combined development as a challenge to the sociological tradition's lack of theorising the international and its privileging of ahistorical forms of static analyses.[55]

52 Rosenberg 1994, p. 150; 1996, p. 14.
53 Rosenberg 1996, p. 7.
54 Rosenberg 1996, p. 8.
55 For these recent developments see Rosenberg 2005, 2006.

It was Benno Teschke who introduced the theory of social-property relations in the field of international relations.[56] His work was the first to systematically explore the implications of Brenner's theory for international-relations theory since Brenner's critique of neo-Smithian Marxism in 1977. Teschke proposes an analysis of pre-1648 geopolitics that comes to terms with the mainstream theorisation both of medieval geopolitics and of the meaning of 1648. Extending the work of Brenner, he employs a diachronic and synchronic comparative strategy to reconstruct the historically specific relations between social-property régimes and their attendant strategies of reproduction that governed different geopolitical dynamics. Teschke aims to remedy two limitations that he identifies in Rosenberg's work. First, he questions Rosenberg's inclination to identify structurally determined links between social-property régimes and geopolitical dynamics, rather than identifying phases of transition between both. Second, he challenges the argument that the international system had achieved a mature capitalist form during the nineteenth century. Adopting an explanatory strategy that stresses periods of transition, Teschke grounds the qualitative shift to the first modern and capitalist state in England between the Revolution of 1688 and 1713. Meanwhile, the emergence of English capitalism slowly imposed its geopolitical pressures and dynamics onto the Continental, absolutist states. It co-existed with precapitalist states and precapitalist geopolitical dynamics slowly forcing them to stretch or adapt their capacities of geopolitical accumulation in order to withstand the competitive pressures of the first capitalist state. Teschke's explanatory strategy seeks to reconstruct the national, international and global historical processes through which specific capitalist property relations that emerged in England slowly imposed their rhythm on other states.

In a series of recent contributions, Hannes Lacher develops the *problématique* of the social origins of modern territoriality.[57] He sees limitations in *The Empire of Civil Society* insofar as it offers no systematic explanation of why the modern state system *only* became possible with the emergence of capitalism. Hence, Lacher contends that Rosenberg underestimates the depth of the system of sovereign territorial states to the territorial dynamics of the

[56] Teschke 1998; 2002; 2003.

[57] Lacher 2002; 2003; 2005.

absolutist era.[58] Lacher and Teschke argue that there are no intrinsic reasons why capital as a social relation would systematically generate and contribute to the reproduction of a system of sovereign nation-states. The modern state system inherited a territorial dynamic from the absolutist era, but nothing guarantees that it will survive. Lacher argues that *capital* as a social relation encourages the systematic development of the commodity-form, which *in principle*, tends toward the global. However, he notes, precisely because the emergence of capital imposed from the start a globalising social dynamic on modern geopolitics, the framing of the debate between realists and globalists in international relations is misleading. According to Lacher, modern international relations contained international and global dynamics from the start. The co-existence of these simultaneous dynamics and strategies of reproduction of power is obscured by teleological attempts to explain the transition from a Golden Age of sovereign states to an emerging Global Age.

Rosenberg and Teschke's contributions draw our attention to the premodern nature of the 1648 geopolitical context. Teschke and Lacher's work offer an important analysis of the legacy of absolutist geopolitics on the historical formation of modern geopolitics. They question the conceptual necessity of a relation between the expansion of capital as a social relation and the reproduction of the modern state system.

2.5. *Capitalism, globalisation and uneven and combined development*

Historical understanding of the changing dynamics of geopolitical régimes benefited from the work of political Marxists in comparative history. Over the last decades, however, the contributions of Rosenberg, Teschke and Lacher – though distinct – share the aim of developing an historical account of geopolitics in the compared histories of social-property régimes. There is an underlying preoccupation in Rosenberg's ambition to explore the potential of Trotsky's theory of uneven and combined development; in Teschke's endeavour to develop accounts of social revolutions and transitions to capitalism in different social, historical and geopolitical contexts; and in Lacher's project of revising the intertwined relations between the national, the international and

[58] Lacher 2005, pp. 28, 30.

the global since the beginning of the modern era. All of these research projects are preoccupied with the need to enrich the comparative historical agenda of political Marxism with an historically informed and socially differentiated theory of geopolitical or international relations.

Teschke contends that most Marxian-inspired models of social history lack a systematic theorisation of international relations.[59] The price to pay for the absence of such theory is significant:

> this theoretical fixation on exclusively national dynamics and its concomitant invocation of comparative history fundamentally fails to problematize the fact that these plural roads towards capitalism do not run in parallel and mutual isolation, neither chronologically, nor socio-politically, nor geographically. In fact, they constantly, to stretch the metaphor, 'cross each other' in the wider force field of the international.[60]

Teschke argues that political Marxism lacks a theoretical account that comes to terms with the 'geopolitically mediated development of Europe as a whole – a perspective that is fully alive to the constitutive role of the international in historical development'.[61] Ultimately, he sums up:

> we need to come to terms with the nationally specific and diachronic, yet cumulatively connected and internationally mediated nature of 'capitalist transitions' within the framework of socially uneven and geopolitically combined development.[62]

An important question for the future of international relations is whether the expansion of capital as a social relation will bring about the end of the sovereign state system or whether both will reinforce each other? Teschke and Lacher have both argued that the system of territorial states did not emerge with capital as a social relation, but rather that it is a remnant of European absolutism. Both argue that there is no conceptual reason why the expansion of capital would not sooner or later bring about the formation of a global state: 'Indeed, I have argued that the form of statehood that corresponds to the

[59] Teschke 2005, p. 4.
[60] Teschke 2005, p. 7.
[61] Teschke 2005, p. 4.
[62] Teschke 2005, p. 13.

concept of capital is the global state'.[63] Such a process should not be equated with the current phase of 'globalisation', however. Lacher notes:

> while a global state is an essential requirement for the successful continuation of capitalist globalization, it cannot be presumed that such a process will indeed take place. While there are, indeed, discernible movements towards global state-formation, there are equally strong movements towards political fragmentation.[64]

Criticisms of *The Empire of Civil Society* have evolved around three issues. I will conclude by noting how political Marxists have addressed these criticisms since then. First is the argument, here reformulated by a critique of Rosenberg, that 'the underlying constituents of sovereignty, of raison d'État and ultimately of the modern state lay in capitalism'.[65] Teschke and Lacher have systematically dealt with this issue by stressing the imprint of absolutism on the territoriality of the modern state-system.[66] Second is the argument that the system of states was capitalist as a whole in the nineteenth century.[67] Rosenberg distanced himself from this argument and his reorientation toward the theory of uneven and combined development seeks to come to terms with this issue.[68] The third is that *The Empire of Civil Society* lacks an emphasis on agency of international relations.[69] This emphasis on agency was deployed in *The Myth of 1648*.[70] Tensions between the research projects of those who try to internationalise political Marxism are important. Yet, judging from the proliferation of recent work in this tradition, it should lead to lively debates over the next decades.

---

[63] Lacher 2005, p. 45.

[64] Lacher 2005, p. 46; for a similar analysis see Teschke 2003, pp. 262–8; see also Wood 2003.

[65] Ariffin 1996, p. 130.

[66] Teschke 2003; Lacher 2003; 2005.

[67] Ariffin 1996, p. 131; Teschke 2003.

[68] See the recent debate between Rosenberg and Callinicos, Rosenberg 2007.

[69] Ariffin 1996, p. 132–3.

[70] Teschke 2003, pp. 57–60.

Chapter Twenty-Five

Marxism and Language

Jean-Jacques Lecercle

I. Paradox

1.1. The question of Marxism and language is the site of a paradox, with important, and mostly negative, theoretical and political consequences. On the one hand there no theory of language to speak of within Marxism; even more regrettable (for it could be argued that language, being the object of an independent science, the science of linguistics, lies outside the scope of Marxism), there has not been an ongoing debate within Marxism about questions of language, as there has been, for instance, about aesthetics. Whereas the bourgeoisie has always been aware of the importance of the question of language, has always employed armies of specialists, deployed specialist discourses (for instance about the importance of 'communication'), and has always made sure that it dominated key institutions, such as the school or the media, in which the dominant ideology in the matter of language reigned, if not unopposed, at least with assured success. On the other hand, however, we do find within Marxism what almost amounts to a tradition of thinking about language: a number of Marxists have broached the question of a Marxist philosophy of language, not always directly and explicitly (Vološinov is an exception), but more often *en passant* – the revolutionary struggle imposes its priorities, and unfortunately language is never one of them. The result is the bare outline of a tradition, which remains mostly submerged.

1.2. There are historical reasons for such a situation. The founding fathers have left us only a few hints, and they belong either to the young Marx, in the *1844 Manuscripts* or in *The German Ideology*, where language is famously defined as 'practical consciousness', not to mention the cryptic marginal comment, 'language is the language of reality', or to the aging Engels: there is a celebrated passage in the *Dialectics of Nature*, where the myth of the origin of language in collective work is formulated. Not to speak of the marginal comment in Lenin's *Philosophical Notebooks*, where the formula, 'history of thought = history of language' is surrounded by a square surrounded by a circle.

But the main reason for this sad state of affairs is Stalin's intervention, *On Marxism in Linguistics*, a series of articles in *Pravda*, later issued as a pamphlet with a number of letters to inquiring comrades. Stalin's objective was to put an end to the domination in Soviet linguistics of the school of Nikolai Marr. Marr, a late convert to Marxism, had produced a number of theories, of a highly fantastic nature, about the origin and development of language. Having converted to Marxism, he sought to prove that language was a superstructure, to be revolutionised with the political revolution. Stalin's pamphlet is characterised by a form of common sense (he pointed out that in the USSR the revolution had been victorious for more than thirty years, but that the Russian language had not been significantly affected), which, with hindsight, can be read as a capitulation to the dominant bourgeois ideas about language. The following four theses are central to his argument: 1) Language is not a superstructure. 2) Language is an instrument of communication that benefits the whole people. 3) Language is directly linked to production. 4) Language is not a class phenomenon. The first thesis pre-empts any serious Marxist discussion of language; the second reproduces the main thesis of the dominant ideology about language, the addition of 'which benefits the whole people' only adding a populist flavour; the third thesis seeks to take us back within the orbit of Marxism; whereas the fourth develops the first, with the same consequence. The effect of this intervention, in the conjuncture in which it occurred, was twofold: it was greeted with a sigh of relief by the academic linguists who happened to be also members of the CP (for instance M. Cohen in France) – it came to them as a breath of fresh air after the leftist errors of the 'proletarian versus bourgeois science' debate and the disaster of the Lysenko affair; but it also stifled any independent thinking about language in Marxist circles for at least a decade. And it is not certain that, even in the case of Marr and his slightly mad ideas about language, Stalin's commonsensical strictures were entirely apposite: Marr's disciples played a leading role in the description and salvage of minority languages in the Soviet republics, and Vološinov's appreciation of Marr appears to have been sincere. The net result, however, was that a specific Marxist elaboration of the question of language was avoided.

1.3. One can take the work of Althusser as an example of this, as an embodiment of the paradox. Apart from a few elements on the use of language in Lacan, his intervention on the question of language is limited to a footnote in the 'Ideological State Apparatuses' essay, in which he notes the errors of linguists, who tend to treat language as transparent because they ignore the effects of ideology. In fact the criticism could almost apply to Althusser himself, although in an inverted form: the limits of his concept of ideology are due to his neglect of the role of language, whose ghost haunts his texts, in the two stages of the development of the concept. In the first stage, the essay of humanism in *Pour Marx*, ideology is already defined as necessity as much as error – allusion as much as illusion. But the sign, or symptom, that we are dealing with an ideological proposition is linguistic: ideology reveals itself in the practice of *punning* [*jeu de mots*]. Thus, the bourgeoisie celebrates freedom in two senses: the real sense of the freedom of enterprise on which the capitalist system is based, and the imaginary sense in which every human being is free – a claim immediately denied by the existence of exploitation and its consequent oppression. So that, in the second stage of the theory, the 'Ideological State Apparatuses' essay, although language is never mentioned, it can be usefully reintroduced in the system of concepts, in so far as speech-acts are excellent candidates for insertion into the chain of interpellation that goes from institution (apparatus) to ritual, from ritual to practice, and the result of which is the transformation of the individual into a subject:

apparatus → ritual → practice → speech-act → subject

And it soon becomes clear that interpellation, which in the famous primal scene of interpellation occurs through linguistic hailing, involves a language component at all its stages, that the process is in fact pervaded by language, so that the proposition that *ideology is language* need not be restricted to the work of Barthes (it is explicitly stated in the Collège de France lectures on 'le neutre'): discourses are constituent parts of institutions (a university does not consist only in buildings and students), rituals have a strong discursive component, practices are always-also linguistic practices. This aspect of the theory, which was developed in the work of Judith Butler, allows for a concept of counter-interpellation: the subject, through her own speech acts (for instance, by returning to the sender the hate speech that aggresses her) counter-interpellates the language that interpellates her.

1.4. The question of language, however, was not always ignored or avoided by Marxists. We can briefly sketch the lineaments of a tradition. This would start with the Bakhtin circle and the seminal work of Vološinov, and would include Vygotsky on language and thought, the work of Gramsci, who was a philologist by training and whose notebook n° 29 is devoted to the question of grammar, Tran Duc Thao on the origin of language, the Marxist semiotics of language as labour and as market in Rossi-Landi, Sohn-Rethel's critique of epistemology and the division between intellectual and manual labour, Pêcheux's semantics and theory of discourse, J.J. Goux's numismatics, R. Lafont's praxematics, R. Balibar on French as a national language and the treatment of language in the school apparatus, Henri Lefebvre's book on language and even Bourdieu, in spite of his earnest claim not to be a Marxist. And I would like to single out the chapter on language in Raymond Williams's *Marxism and Literature*, much influenced by both Vološinov and Gramsci, and an essay by Pasolini, devoted to 'a poetical approach to the question of Marxism in linguistics', an obvious answer to Stalin's commonsense view of language, inspired by the historicism of the Italian tradition, and especially by Gramsci's concept of language as conception of the world and practical philosophy.

2. Marxism and the critique of the philosophy of language

The first interest of a Marxist positioning the field of language is not, as the title of Stalin's pamphlet suggests, that it allows an intervention in the field of linguistics (there is a science of linguistics that should be left alone by Marxists) but that it provides a critique of the dominant ideas about language, in other words that it gives us a Marxist philosophy of language both in its critical and its constructive aspects. And the dominant ideology about language can be formulated in one proposition: 'language is an instrument of communication'. This, in turn can be spelt out in the six following principles. The first is the *principle of immanence,* which is central to the structuralist versions of linguistics: it states that the explanation of the workings of language must be sought in language itself, and not outside it – thus deliberately ignoring both the speaker and the context. The second is the *principle of functionality*. It states that language has functions, and that its main function is communication, that is the exchange of information. The third is the *principle of transparency*. It is a consequence of the second principle and states that language, being a mere instrument, must make itself forgotten, must not obtrude. The fourth is the *principle of ideality*. Language is divided between an abstract ideal system and its actualisation inspeech of writing (you have recognised Saussure's dichotomy of *langue* and *parole,* or Chomsky's dichotomy of competence and performance): the consequence is that, as a system, as *langue,* language has no material existence and belongs to Popper's third world of ideas. The fifth is the *principle of systematicity*. It states that the study of language is the study of a system: *parole* is too idiosyncratic and messy to provide an object of study – which, of course, reinforces the principle of immanence. The sixth and last principle is the *principle of synchronicity*: the system is a synchronic entity, it is not subject to history and time, or rather, since it is only too obvious that language is a historical phenomenon, the history of language is deemed irrelevant or marginalised under the name of 'diachrony'.

2.2. It is clear that my six principles that support the main research programmes in linguistics are far more complex and explicit that the simple statement that language is an instrument of communication. But dominant ideology is an articulated structure that operates at three distinct levels. It operates at the elementary level of *common sense,* where its strength is due to the fact that it states the obvious, what goes without saying, and need not therefore be explicitly formulated and defended. It is only when we try another formulation, such as 'language is a weapon', or 'language is an expression of affect', that we realise that there is a philosophical position behind the obvious. But our six principles show that dominant ideology also operates at the level of what Althusser, in his course of lectures for scientists, calls a *spontaneous philosophy for scientists,* the set of beliefs that scientists hold unquestioningly, because they are deemed too general or too vague to be the object of an explicit exposition: my six principles belong to that category. And they support a third mode of operation of the dominant ideology, in the explicit philosophy of language that spells out and consciously supports the dominant ideas about language. A Marxist position in the field of language must engage the dominant ideology at all three levels: it must, in the manner of Barthes, expose the mythical nature of linguistic common sense; it must provide alternative principles and determinations for a concept of language; and it must provide a critique of the explicit philosophies of language that dominate the field.

2.3. Thus, while supporting Chomsky's political positions in their strong opposition to imperialism, a Marxist will criticise his research programme, which is by far the most influential worldwide. She will resist the *methodological individualism* that the programme involves (grammatical competence is situated in the mind/brain of the individual speaker). She will denounce the *reification* that reduces a practice, the practice of language in interlocution to a series of 'things', a 'Universal Grammar', a 'Language Acquisition Device', inscribed in the neurone circuits or the genetic programme of the speaker. She will therefore oppose the *naturalism* that reduces a social practice to its material basis in the human brain, and the *ahistoricism* that, by making language a natural endowment of the species, reintroduces the quasi-eternity of human nature (the only time involved is the time of the evolution of the species) and explicitly denies any relevance to historical time in the field of language. Whereby it appears that such a programme combines a form of reductive materialism (what the Marxist tradition calls 'vulgar', or 'mechanical' materialism) and rank idealism (language is a faculty of the human mind/brain, and it is innate: this combines the theory of knowledge of Plato's *Meno* with a form of Leibnizian monadology) – the dominant aspect of the contradiction is, of course, idealism.

2.4. We find a second example of the dominant ideology in the field of language in Habermas's philosophy of communicative action and general pragmatics. This research programme is of immediate interest for a Marxist, as it is presented as a critique and reconstruction of historical materialism, which seeks to preserve its emancipatory impulse, by moving from work to communication as foundation of human societies. The advantage of such a position over Chomsky's methodological individualism (for methodological individualism may be defended in some fields, but certainly not in the field of language: there is no way I can treat language as the composition of the rational decisions of individual speakers) is that it starts from the social: the very structure of language, according to Habermas, presupposes agreement, or at least a tendency towards it. The disadvantage is that the social so conceived becomes irenic, a site for polite debate and unselfish agreement (Habermas, of course, does not deny the phenomena, and is fully aware that not all social or linguistic encounters are *eirenic* in such a way: his propositions, he claims, are transcendental, even if 'weakly' so). Against this, a Marxist, for whom all history is the history of class struggle, will maintain that language, like society, is *agonistic*. What Habermas describes is in fact a form of linguistic communism: his structural tendency towards agreement through debate is a situation devoutly to be wished, except of course that it has nothing structural about it, and all the characteristics of a Kantian idea of reason, what we should struggle for as a long-term objective. In fact, a Marxist will tend to historicise Habermas's philosophy of language, show that there is a 'Habermas conjuncture', which is the conjuncture of post-Nazism and post-Communism, the climax of which occurred with the fall of the Berlin Wall, but which in the present period of a return to blatant imperialism is no longer relevant. Habermas himself, a strong believer in international institutions, had to recognise that the sequence of events that led to the war in Iraq had little to do with a structural tendency towards agreement through discussion.

2.5. A Marxist position in the field of language must therefore operate a systematic change of point of view. It is not sufficient, for instance, simply to invert the six principles that support the dominant philosophy of language, and suggest a *principle of non-immanence* (language is *of* the world and *in* the world), or a *principle of opacity* (language never lets itself be forgotten, it obtrudes): inversion does not allow us to leave the field. I suggest that this change in point of view should take the following five forms. First, a Marxist position in the field of language will adopt the point of view of *process*, not 'things' or 'facts': avoiding the fetishism that characterises the dominant philosophy of language involves, for instance, treating language not as a system but as a system of variations. Second, it will adopt the point of view of the *collective*, as opposed to the individual speaker: the speaker is spoken by her language at the very moment when she believes she speaks it, she must learn to inhabit a language that is exterior and anterior to her. Our point of view, therefore, must be the point of view of social interaction, as in Habermas. Thirdly, it will adopt the point of view of *historicity*: the time of language is not the eternity of human nature, or the arrested time of evolution, but the time of human history. A language is a monument of the life of a society, it inscribes it in its words, phrases and grammatical markers, it is the repository, as Gramsci claims, of conceptions of the world. Fourth, it will adopt the point of view of *totality*. This, as Lukács has taught us, is the best protection we have against the operation of fetishism. We must therefore substitute the dialectics of *parole* and *langue* (if we keep those terms, which will soon prove to be inadequate) for their separation and the consequent reification of both object (language as system and structure) and subject (the speaker as owner of her language, which she uses as an instrument). Lastly, a Marxist position will adopt the point of view of *rapport de forces*, the point of view of *agon* as opposed to *eirene*. Rather than co-operative interaction, the origin, or main function, of language will be seen as the establishment of a system of places, contemporary with the emergence of the division of labour, the result of which is the interpellation of individual into subjects and the distribution of hierarchical social positions. Such a change in point of view has actually occurred in Marxists theories of language, for instance in the work of Vološinov.

3. Marxism and the philosophy of language: Vološinov

3.1. Since Volosinov's work, *Marxism and the Philosophy of Language* (1929), is the only full-fledged exposition of a Marxist position in the field of language that the tradition has given us,we must expect to find in it the two moments of the Marxist approach, the critical and the reconstructive moments. And we do find a critique of linguistics and the philosophy of language, under the two headings of subjective idealism (Humboldt is the main object of the critique) and abstract objectivism (associated with the name of Saussure): language as *energeia* rather than *ergon* insists of the processual aspect of linguistic interaction, but it ends up treating language as an aesthetic object, with the methodological individualism that such a romantic notion of creativeness implies; whereas the positivist reduction of *langue* to a fixed code, to a system, precludes any conception of language as practice and ignores the active creation of meanings which is at the heart of such practice.

3.2. The constructive aspect of Vološinov's work involves the reinterpretation of a number of familiar concepts, such as the concept of sign (conceived as the site of the process of meaning in the course of social *agon*), of ideology (the Russian term denotes not a system of ideas but a social and cultural activity), of word (which is the name for the sign in so far as it takes part in a process of meaning, and inscribes a social practice) and of consciousness. The last concept is the most important, as it involves a critique not only of Saussure but also of Freud (made explicit in Vološinov's essays on Freudianism): for him, consciousness is not the source of language and action that it is in the idealist tradition, but the interiorisation of the exterior, that is of linguistic interaction. The centre of consciousness is inner speech, the private is an effect of the public, and the individual is always preceded by the collectivity of speakers engaged in interlocution.

But the development of an original Marxist position also needs the creation of new concepts, for instance the concept of the *pluri-accented sign* (every sign is the site of a multiplicity of virtualities of meanings, and it sediments the history of their actualisation in various interlocutions), of *refraction* (a concept familiar to readers of Bakhtin, which stresses the grounding of language in the social context, yet seeks to avoid the reductionism of the classical-Marxist concept of reflection) and of inner speech, or *interior monologue*. The last concept is perhaps the most interesting, and the least expected in a Marxist text (the Greek and scholastic tradition of *logos endiathetos* has petered out, and contemporary cognitivists prefer to talk in terms of *mentalese*): it seems to belong rather to literary theory than to linguistics or Marxism. But it is, as we have seen, the result of the inscription of the inversion of the inner and the outer, and the monologue consists in fact in a plurality of competing voices.

3.3. The result is a Marxist philosophy of language which can be briefly summed up in the five following theses. 1) Language cannot be restricted to *langue* as system, which is merely an abstraction and an instance of fetishism. 2) If language is not an abstract system, it is because language is a concrete human practice, a continuous process actualised in verbal interaction. 3) As a result, the laws of language development and evolution are social rather than psychological. This excludes any form of methodological individualism or intentionalism (the theory that ascribes the meaning of the utterance to the intentions of meaning of the individual speaker). 4) Language creativeness is not 'rule-governed', as in Chomsky. The constraints on the production of utterances are ideological: they concern the interpellation of individuals into subjects and the consequent counter-interpellation (here I am aware that I translate Vološinov in a later theoretical language). 5) This last thesis sums up the first four: the structure of the utterance is social, and actualised only in the social interactions of the community of speakers: any form of immanent, or 'internal' linguistics is rejected, and the core of the study of language is a form of what we now call pragmatics.

4. Post-Marxism and language: the case of Deleuze and Guattari

4.1. The relationship between Deleuze and Guattari and Marxism is questionable, at best indirect and certainly complex. Yet it can be argued that they operate a systematic shift of a number of key Marxist concepts (from modes of production and productive force to régimes of signs and flows of libidinal energy; from history to geography, from work to desire, from ideology to assemblage – machinic assemblages of desire and collective assemblages of enunciation; from party, *qua* 'subjected group' to the 'subject group' one finds in more open movements; from molar to molecular analysis of social phenomena). And they explicitly engage with Marxism in the fourth plateau of *Mille Plateaus*, where they read Lenin's pamphlet on slogans and derive from it a critique of the 'four postulates ' of linguistics that *a contrario* contains the elements of a new philosophy of language which cannot leave Marxists indifferent.

4.2. In July 1917, Lenin, who is hiding from arrest in the country, found the time to write not a treatise on language but a pamphlet on slogans. His aim was to persuade his comrades that the conjuncture of the slogan 'All Power to the Soviets' was now exhausted, and that the most urgent task was to prepare from the violent overthrow of the provisional government. But the pamphlet's interest goes beyond the conjuncture, important as that conjuncture turned out to have been. It sketches a theory of slogans and of their performative nature, of the force (in pragmatics it is known as the 'illocutionary' force of an utterance) that they exert. And it does so by noting three aspects of the illocutionary force of the right slogan: it identifies the *moment of the conjuncture* (on 4 July 1917, the first, peaceful, stage of the revolution is finished); it names the political objective that corresponds to the moment and it condenses and embodies the concrete analysis of the concrete situation: without the right slogan the revolution must fail. The consequences of this analysis go far beyond the question of the revolution: they concern a theory of meaning and a philosophy of language. For Lenin implicitly uses a concept of meaning as linked to a *rapport de forces* in a determinate conjuncture (meaning is the result not of co-operation but of struggle); as a result, an utterance is not a description of a situation but an intervention within it (it can modify the said *rapport de forces*); the right slogan is not true but just, that is adapted to the conjuncture in which it intervenes; yet Lenin does use the word 'truth': the revolutionary activist must tell the truth to the people: but such truth is an effect of the just slogan, of its adjustment: in pragmatic terms, the illocutionary force of the right slogan exerts a perlocutionary effect of truth in the conjuncture; lastly, the concept of meaning implicitly used here is a *political* concept and language becomes a political phenomenon.

My reading of the Lenin pamphlet anticipates Deleuze and Guattari's reading: they interpret the effect of the new slogan in terms of incorporeal transformation (a term Deleuze derived from his reading of the Stoics). And they add that the slogan does not only exert a performative effect in the situation, but contributes to the constitution of the class that, as a result of its adoption, will seize power. This enables them to introduce the concept of collective assemblage of enunciation as an ontological mixture of bodies, institutions and discourses.

4.3. And they draw the consequences of this analysis that Lenin, who had other cares, was not able to draw: they proceed to a systematic critique of linguistics, according to what they call its 'four postulates': (1) 'Language is informational and communicational'; (2) 'There is an abstract machine of language that does not appeal to any extrinsic factor; (3) There are constants or universals of language that enable us to define it as a homogeneous system; (4) Language can be scientifically studied only under the conditions of a standard or major language. One can recognise in those postulates the explicit version of the dominant ideology of language. And the negative formulation of the postulates (which is clearer in French as the sentences are in the conditional mood: 'le langage serait informative et communicatif') conceals positive theses that make up a full-fledged philosophy of language. It can be summed up in the following theses. (1) The basic form of the linguistic utterance is not he declarative sentence but the *slogan*; (2) The basic type of discourse is not direct speech, which is supposed to refer to the outside world and transmit information about it, but *indirect speech*; (3) The basic field for the study of language is not phonology (as in the structural school of linguistics) or syntax (as in Chomsky), but *pragmatics*; (4) Speech-acts in so far as they are slogans, exert a *force*, and enjoy a specific *efficacy*, which takes the form of *incorporeal transformations*. (5) The source of utterances does not lie in individual speakers but in *collective assemblages of enunciation*; (6) Language is not a homogeneous system because it is riddled with contradictions. The main contradiction opposes the *major* dialect or use of language and a host of *minor* dialects or usages.

4.5. It is clear that we are very close to a Marxist philosophy of language: their insistence on the slogan as the original form of utterance is inspired by their reading of Lenin; their version of pragmatics is political; they insist on the material efficacy of the speech-acts that constitute language (the concept of 'incorporeal transformation' does not deny the materiality of the speech-act, at least not for the Marxist who is familiar with the thought that ideas have material efficacy when they move the masses); and their insistence on the contradictions within language turns language into a collection of social, historical and political phenomena. In the field of language, the post-Marxism of Deleuze and Guattari turns out to be very close to classical Marxism.

5. Theses for a Marxist philosophy of language

5.1. It now appears that the body of Marxist thought about language is considerable. It does not amount to a coherent and explicit tradition, but it enables us to suggest the first elements of a Marxist philosophy of language. The political urgency of such a philosophy has already been noted: the political centrality of the ideology of communication in the political life of contemporary bourgeois democracies, with its directors of communication, unashamed spin and blatant manipulation of media hypes, need hardly be stressed. And merely inverting the main tenets of this dominant ideology is not enough. We need a number of positive theses for a Marxist philosophy of language.

5.2. The most general, foundational thesis is that we must treat language as a form of *praxis*. The return to such a term, systematically used by Gramsci, but abandoned by Althusser for the concept of 'practice' must be justified. Language as we conceive it can hardly count as an example of practice (unless we treat it as an instrument of communication, we can hardly claim that in speaking we transform the raw material of ideas into the finished product of the utterance, using words and rules of grammar for our tools). So we are going back to the Aristotelian distinction between *theoria*, *poiesis* (which corresponds to our 'practice') and *praxis*, defined as the collective action of human communities. And we are indeed going back to Aristotle, to the opening section of his *Politics*, where he defines man as a political animal *in so far as he is a speaking animal*. In this original sense, language is indeed a form of *praxis*, as it is the medium in which political action takes place. But, further than this, language is also what exerts material force, allows ideas to acquire such force when they capture the masses because such ideas find their only materiality in the words that do not so much translate or express them as constitute them. It will come as no surprise that a school of post-Marxist thought, a scion of Italian *operaismo*, as exemplified in the work of Virno and Marazzi, claims that language, in what they call the post-Fordist stage of capitalism, is a direct productive force: the worker at that stage is also, *qua* worker, a speaker, and an important part of his work consists in communication (with complex machines, with the whole structure of the production process). As a result of which he is no longer a mere producer but a language *virtuoso*.

5.3. The general statement that language is a form of *praxis*, however, is not sufficient, even at the post-Fordist stage. This foundational thesis must be developed through positive theses. I borrow them from my own work, *A Marxist Philosophy of Language*. There are four of them: language is a historical phenomenon; language is a social phenomenon; language is a material phenomenon; language is a political phenomenon.

The first thesis has two aspects: language *has* a history, and language *is* history. For language, of course, has a history, which must be retrieved from structuralist neglect: there is no synchronic understanding of the value of grammatical markers without taking note of the complex history that has produced their present meanings. And it appears that the various strands or layers of language have their independent historical rhythm, as in Althusser's conception of the social structure as a whole: the lexicon changes very fast (there are generational dialects), syntax changes more slowly, but it is subject to historical change. Hence the need for the Marxist to develop a *historical semantics*, such as the one sketched in Raymond Williams's *Keywords*, or to re-read Vygotsky historical account of concept formation in the child. But language also *is* history, if we accept Gramsci's contention that every language contains a conception of the world: language is potted, or sedimented, history: Williams's *Culture and Society* is informed by such a notion of language.

The second thesis, that language is a social phenomenon seems to go without saying, except that it enables the Marxist to leave methodological individualism, and effect the reversal that makes consciousness the effect, through interiorisation, of public, social interlocution. The question, 'Who speaks?', will no longer receive the obvious answer ('why, the speaker, of course'), but a less intuitive one, such as: 'it is language that speaks the speaker who believes she speaks it', or: the sender of the utterance is not an individual subject but a collective assemblage of enunciation (slogans, if we decide after Deleuze and Guattari that they are the basic form of utterances, are never *individual* utterances). This thesis is also a means to approach the question of the relationship between language and ideology, for instance by inserting the speech-act in the Althusserian chain of interpellation (and counter-interpellation).

The third thesis stresses the material element of language. This materiality of language is already stressed in *The German Ideology*, where Marx reminds us that 'man possesses "consciousness", but not inherent, not "pure" consciousness. From the start the "spirit" is afflicted with the curse of being "burdened" with matter.' So the Marxist will pay attention to the origin of the utterance in the human body. And, in so doing, he will draw on the work of the American Marxist David McNally. But the question remains, 'which body is involved in language?', and there is more than one candidate: for Chomsky, it is the biological body; for Merleau-Ponty, or for Lakoff and Johnson, it is the phenomenological body, or a version thereof; for psychoanalysts, especially of the Lacanian persuasion, it is the erotic body; the interest of McNally is that he introduces what he calls the 'labouring' body, which is closer to the favourite themes of Marxists and feminists alike. The advantage of his position is that it grounds language in the materiality of the world, in the shape of the speaker's body, but that it also allows a wider form of materialism, with which the Marxist is familiar, the materialism of institutions, rituals and practices.

The fourth thesis has an obvious aspect that I have already dealt with: language is indeed the medium of politics, especially democratic politics (the importance of naming is stressed in the works of Balibar or Rancière). But it also has another aspect: language is the object of politics, there are politics of language and language policies, and the question of language is intimately linked with the question of nationality. There are such things as linguistic imperialism or colonialism and glottophagy (to use L.J. Calvet's concept). Not to mention linguistic sexism: Western feminists have been singularly successful in their struggle against masculinist uses of language and in favour, for instance, of the introduction of epicene pronouns (which are not marked for gender).

5.4. So a number of classical-Marxist concepts will be adapted to language: we shall talk of linguistic conjuncture, of linguistic class struggle, of linguistic imperialism. But the major concept, and this will be my concluding thesis is that of linguistic interpellation: the main function of language (if this term still applies) is not communication but subjectification/subjection, the interpellation of individuals into subjects, and the counter-interpellation by the interpellated subjects. We have come a long way from Stalin's common sense.

Chapter Twenty-Six

Adorno and Marx

Jean-Marie Vincent

Theodor W. Adorno is highly renowned. But although he is well known, it is not clear that he is genuinely recognised for what is essential about him. A stubborn legend has it that his work is primarily that of a philosopher with a passion for aesthetics and literary criticism, who turned aside from Marxism after the Second World War by abandoning any prospect of social transformation. In reality, if Adorno did indeed break with the Marxisms that emerged after Marx, he did not renounce the idea of a society freed from exploitation and oppression. It might even be said that his whole *œuvre*, even in its most aesthetic manifestations, is centred on a search for adequate means of emancipation and liberation following the historical failures of the workers' movement.

In *Dialectic of Enlightenment*, these failures are set in the more general context of the development of the culture of the bourgeois era – the self-destruction of reason with its renunciation of the project of creating meaning between, and, for human beings. For Adorno, the workers' movement and Marxists have themselves been trapped in this regressive spiral, this transformation of reason into mythology. Thus, the theory of emancipation itself needs to be resumed and rethought. In this radical reform, Marx himself must not be spared, for a 'hidden positivism' can be detected in him – positions on science and on the import of the critique of political economy that require clarification. Marx had indeed discerned a second nature in capitalist social relations, and especially in what he called 'real abstractions' (capital, value, the market). But he was unable to counter the influence of this second nature on thought processes and ways of perceiving social reality with sufficient vigilance. The critique of political economy – an enormous, unfinished labour – sometimes veers towards a positive science of the economy in search of laws of a very traditional sort.

However, these slips do not invalidate Marx's enterprise. On the contrary, it needs to be continued and taken further, by working on it and from it. In fact, the reference to Marx remains constant in Adorno, even if it is not very frequent in a whole series of his writings. It is also implicit in the sociological work carried out from the 1940s onwards and conceived as an ambitious critique of the social sciences, using analytical tools forged by Marx: market abstraction, commodity fetishism, abstract labour, and so on. Over and above any notion of a critical sociology, Adorno undertakes to deconstruct sociological theories in their blind spots and, at the same time, to deconstruct the empirical world as a social world of necessary appearances. Adorno's aim is to set fixed categories in motion, on the grounds that they fall foul of the illusion of their own immediacy, because they conceive themselves as mastering an unproblematic reality. He therefore wishes to introduce mediations where none are currently to be found, to demonstrate the distortions present in concepts, their inability to define the relations between the general and the particular; and, more precisely, to demonstrate the domination of a particularistic generality over the particular (or the singular) under the appearances of simple transitions from one to the other. The subject of capitalist society is parasitised by an abstract sociality that permeates its consciousness and unconscious alike. Human beings are socialised not only in inter-individual relations, but also by their relations to social relations that are external to them – social relations between social things (relations between capitals, commodities, and the dynamics of valorisation); and they struggle in relations of competition, in processes of evaluation-assessment, that escape them. In fact, socialisation by abstract sociality overdetermines all social bonds and forms of sociability.

According to Adorno, this antagonistic socialisation inevitably creates relations of confrontation between individuals, a constant struggle to secure an advantageous position in the fields of valorisation and power relations. There is therefore a ubiquitous violence, open or masked, in social relations and a structured symbolic universe in which others represent a permanent threat. Tendencies to aggression and self-aggression continually traverse the unconscious of individuals and cloud consciousnesses, diverting them from an accurate perception of things and social relations and, as a result, of what is really at issue in society. Already permeated by economism and thereby rendered abstract, politics risks descending into irrational and murderous conflicts at any moment. Consequently, collective action, invariably dominated by organisational bureaucrats, tends to be transferred from the usual objectives to assaults on minority, powerless sections of society. Even limited democratic debate becomes impossible and politics destroys itself by taking the form of a life-and-death struggle against a mythical enemy. Cracks open in the fragile barriers of civilisation through which modern barbarism surges, with all its unsuspected potential. As Adorno says with reference to Auschwitz, the catastrophe has occurred and humanity has since lived in a kind of barbarous normality (or ordinary barbarism) made up of brutality and incivility. It is oblivious of the fact that behind this dubious normality an even greater barbarism is only waiting to be unleashed, because the whys and wherefores of Auschwitz have not been properly understood and assimilated.

This is why Adorno cannot share a certain optimism characteristic of Marx – especially the latter's confidence in the positive import of manifestations of resistance to capitalism. At bottom, the basic antagonism between capital and labour is blind for Adorno; and the class struggle rarely takes a direction conducive to social transformation. This implies posing the issue, not posed by Marx, of the struggle against capitalist society's blinding connections or structures of blindness. It also means examining, over and above the particularistic domination of generality and real abstractions, the modalities of the intellectual division of labour, the formalism of scientific practices and, last but least, the culture industry. To link all this together, Adorno adopts an old theme of Horkheimer's: knowledge is a social relation. In other words, the production of knowledge is not a simple activity derived from the intellectual capacities of individuals: it refers to a whole social organisation of intellectual exchange and cognitive processes. Thinking is always social, employing cognitive techniques and instruments that have been produced socially in response to social imperatives. This is what is masked by the various types of scientific formalisation when they reduce the problem of producing knowledge to logical constructions, decontexualising thought processes. In this way, crucial issues can be repressed: the issue of the genesis of cognitive processes; of the social demand that lies behind the construction of objects of knowledge; of the effects on social relations; of the determination of intellectual activities (the intellectual division of labour, the divide between intellectuals and non-intellectuals, and so on). As a result, there is just as much production of ignorance as of knowledge. For Adorno, this no doubt explains many people's ambivalent reactions towards science. On the one hand, it offers security because it brings technological progress that can be invested libidinally. On the other, it is a source of anxiety on account of the dangerous nature of its applications in a capitalist context, which refers to a basic feature which is unthought: its submission to the dynamic of valorisation.

Contrary to what many have claimed, and continue to claim, Adorno did not conclude that there is no way out and that the only thing to do is to await better days. On the contrary, he thought that there was an urgency to theoretical work, an imperative to intervene radically on cognitive processes and demonstrate their one-sided, utterly erratic operation. The urgency was all the greater in that knowledge production is increasingly important in social production and social existence and because theoretico-practical, as well as technological, development take pride of place. But one must be aware that mere denunciation of the mediatisation of thinking would be impotent. In reality, it is necessary to intervene on all fronts where modes of thought and ways of apprehending society crystallise. Critique must be rendered at once internal and external. It must be immanent – i.e. not deriving from without – and embrace what it wants to subvert, so as to reveal the flaws and deadlocks of that which believes itself to be rigorous. At the same time, it must be transcendent, demonstrating the untenable character of the status quo and of the reproduction of what currently exists. The starting point of such work is necessarily subjective. More precisely, it involves subjectivities working on themselves, in order to escape paralysing cognitive apparatuses, to cast off the yoke of ready-made thought and position themselves in an external relationship to it. However, such distantiation must necessarily be followed by the development of theoretical structures of observation and elaboration that are practically opposed to mediatised thinking. This assumes collective co-operation and collaboration over and above solitary reflection. Critical theory has to struggle against the compartmentalisation and fragmentation of thought into separate domains or disciplines.

Philosophical reflection is obviously central for Adorno and he defends it against all those who proclaim its replacement by some form of linguistic analysis or some way of disposing of problems. However, like Marx, he rejects the idea that it can be self-sufficient and capable of legislating on all types of knowledge. When it conceives itself as such, and believes that it is *philosophia perennis* or *prima philosophia*, philosophy in fact contributes to the reproduction the intellectual division of labour and thus to social reproduction as a whole. However, it must not succumb to the illusion that it can immediately convert itself into *praxis*. On the contrary, as theory it must confront other theoretical practices, in order to criticise them and to problematise itself. In particular, it must confront the social sciences, which are invariably enclosed in positivism, but rich in empirical material loftily ignored by philosophers. The empire of sociology is an unproblematised empirical world – that is to say, a world taken as a set of indisputable data. Yet it is not a heteroclite, arbitrary assemblage, constructed solely by the subjectivity of researchers. In its oscillation between holism and methodological individualism, objectivism and subjectivism, structuralism and constructivism, sociology indicates the difficulty of defining social relations and the modes of individuals' incorporation into them. It does not succeed in striking a balance between the general and the particular, the static and the dynamic, the psychological and the social. In the form of unacknowledged symptoms, it reveals the disequilibria, the discontinuities that shape society, and the supremacy of uncontrolled processes that disorient individuals and social groups in their practices.

This observation is crucial: the upshot is that there can be no unity of theory and practice. The practices stuck fast in conjunctures of subjection are not readily accessible to theory and theory cannot claim to find direct material in practice. In order to theorise wisely, it is necessary to be in a state of constant tension with practices, while not rejecting them disdainfully. In fact, one must enter into their blind, groping logic in order to disrupt and disturb them. The main objective of theory cannot be to guide action. It must above all seek to rouse people, to release them from the fascination exercised by the phantasmagorias of commodities – that is to say, by the market apparel of processes of submission bound up with valorisation. Critical theory must not be a theory of practice or practices – their mere reflexive extension. In its confrontation with the empirical world and fields of activity, it must make itself a secondary reflection – that is to say, come to terms with itself as a practice to be subjected to critique, as a theoretical practice of research employing intellectual instruments. But it must also express itself as a quest for change, as an intervention on behalf of different social relations. Construed thus, critical theory cannot be uninterested in the practical construction of intellectual institutions and groupings. It is not a solitary critique, but a constant confrontation with other theoretical practices.

On the basis of such considerations, the Institute of Social Research returned to Frankfurt. Neither Horkheimer nor Adorno wanted to fashion an academic *œuvre*, still less to settle down comfortably in the academy. Adorno, in particular, was anxious to test the techniques refined in the United States for investigating the 'authoritarian personality' on a new terrain: Germany after Hitler. The main goal of their enterprise was to assess the impact of Nazism and its collapse on Germans in the West, and at the same to test the prospects for democracy. At the outset, they were not very optimistic about the likely results. For them, society's self-enclosure was virtually complete, sealed by the expansion of the culture industry, the decline in inter-capitalist competition, and the advance of state intervention. In this connection, Horkheimer tended to refer to an administered world where freedom of movement, characteristic of early capitalism (at least for certain social strata), was in the process of disappearing. He concluded that the room for manoeuvre was continuing to narrow and that it was therefore necessary to advance cautiously.

Horkheimer's pessimism was contradicted, at least in part, by events. From the outset, the Institute met with manifest success as well as avowed hostility. It destabilised the sociological profession, which was already far from self-confident, because it offered both a sociology that was highly developed empirically as well as theoretically, and a critical re-examination of the past that countered tendencies to cover it in oblivion. It practised a sociology that was utterly untraditional and disrupted many routines – those of the *Geisteswissenchaften* and of an empiricism employing old-fashioned methods. According to some observers, it created an atmosphere of civil war in the social sciences. Even if the suggestion is somewhat exaggerated, it is true that the Institute exercised ever more influence during the 1950s and 1960s, to the great annoyance of its opponents. The research it organised was varied and creative and its sociology teaching at Frankfurt University enjoyed increasing success.

In the debates in the German Sociological Association, interventions by Horkheimer, but especially by Adorno, had very considerable resonance. They began to be perceived as a sort of unclassifiable current, strongly marked by German thought of the most classical variety, but tracing strong lines of demarcation vis-à-vis it, while seeking to open up new lines of theoretical work.

It would be paradoxical if Marx had been absent from these debates and this civil war. And in fact, he was very present – less as a supplier of positive theories than as a destabiliser of the theoretical field. Despite his errors – the penetration of elements of positivism or scientism into the critique of political economy, for example – he provided key weapons for penetrating the immediate appearances and false obviousness of capitalist society, notably thanks to his accounts of the commodity as a social relation, the abstraction of exchange (its domination by value or valorisation), and the transformation of what was most important about human activities into abstract labour. These theses became all the more significant in Adorno as he gradually abandoned the theses defended by Horkheimer in 'The Authoritarian State' in 1941. For him, the false totality represented by capitalist society is neither static, nor one-dimensional. It is shot through with unforeseeable, irregular dynamics that destructure and restructure social relations and individual situations.

In a 1962 seminar, Adorno was quite explicit on his relationship to Marx: he identified him as the first great theoretician of critical theory and stressed the importance of the theory of fetishism for understanding valorisation as an abstract conceptualisation of social relations. He brought out some of Marx's uncertainties, particularly in relation to Hegel, but credited him with not falling into a problematic of the revolutionary subject and class consciousness (characteristic of Western Marxism). In conclusion, he noted that Marx had left unresolved many problems, which had not been taken up by those who claimed to be his successors. He thus implicitly accepted that the task of contemporary critical theory was to continue Marx differently, by tackling these unresolved problems. But none of this could be done from the outside. What was required was an immanent critique – that is to say, one that started out from the difficulties and impasses of Marx's theory, while trying to understand them better than Marx himself had been able to. For example, it was not possible to remain at the level of phenomena of alienation: it was necessary to penetrate the effects of the commodification of social or inter-individual relations, as well as of objectivity, much more deeply. For a left Hegelianism or a variant of ethical humanism was insufficient. As for problems of power, they must not be abstracted from the reproduction of existence, of what happens by way of bodies, in everyday relations, in relationship to objects, to time and space. The abstract conceptualisation of social relations did not only take the form of cognitive processes that escape human beings, it was also inscribed in the process of abstraction of corporeality and materiality, in their conditioning in the service of the conditioning of labour-power.

Marx's *œuvre* must therefore not be reduced to a narrow conception of the critique of political economy. It must be expanded, surmounting disciplinary compartmentalisation and cognitive barriers in order to undermine the dictatorship of real abstractions. However, to attain this objective, critical theory cannot think the negative totality directly – that is to say, think it abstractly. It must multiply partial illuminations, establish itself in the most varied domains, dismantling borders. As Adorno put it, to exhibit the truth, it must think in constellations, organise a convergence of different intellectual endeavours on developing the mediations that lead to the abstract totality. It follows that the genuinely critical thinker, while not claiming to be universal, cannot simply be a specific intellectual (in Foucault's terminology): he must explore a great deal in order to discover new paths. When Adorno engages in literary criticism, this is not the activity of an aesthete, but the meticulous, professional, strenuous labour of someone who wants to identify the impossibility of being human in an inhuman world as accurately as possible (see, for example, his commentaries on Beckett's *Endgame*). The same spirit inspires his many writings on music. Their technical difficulty can frequently prove off-putting, but it would be wrong to perceive them as the expression of a sort of élitist avant-gardism. In reality, the writings on music are an exploration of the possibilities that art contains for resisting the exhaustion of the avant-gardes and finding, even in debased forms, ways of reacting against commodification by transgressing the boundaries between genres. The fraying of forms, their contamination by forms borrowed from distant genres, furnish new means for making ways of living in society seen or heard differently; and for transcending, by way of the unexpected, the fixed intentions of those who fashion works of art.

Basically, the dispersion of Adorno's works is only apparent, for his many initiatives are coherent and complementary. Without a doubt, many of those who came into contact with him in one way or another did not always grasp the significance of his work in its full range. But many understood, at least partially, that they were in the presence of a revolutionary, utterly unconventional intellectual endeavour. The impact of this theoretical practice without any real precedent was, of necessity, ambiguous. There were misunderstandings, occasionally rash interpretations, and some uninformed enthusiasm. Nevertheless, a terrain, albeit certainly a limited one, was worked in depth; intellectual processes were set in motion, which themselves had political consequences. This is particularly clear in the student world, where a not insignificant minority recognised itself both in critical theory and in an organisation, the association of socialist students (SDS). Adorno himself was perfectly aware of this and he also knew that he was in the process of preparing a new reception of Marx's *œuvre* – one far removed from the old orthodoxies (Communist and social-democratic). The SDS's publications did indeed propagate a critical reception of Marx's work by acknowledging its unfinished character and ambiguities and by developing new examinations of it. Moreover, it was under the influence of Adorno (more indirect than direct) that the Frankfurt SDS group opposed the activism of other SDS groups (some of them influenced by orthodox Communism), while participating in campaigns against the presence of former Nazis in the state apparatus or against atomic weapons, and doing educational work in the trade unions.

The ambition of the leadership group in the SDS was limited at the outset:[1] to strengthen democracy and counter the authoritarian tendencies present in some social strata. But it was quickly outstripped by the organisation's success. For many, the SDS gradually came to embody radical opposition to the forces of the Federal Republic. Various anti-conformist currents formed around it, which were heterogeneous in their outlook and conduct. In addition, it collided head-on with the student radicalisation that followed the mass expansion of German universities. The rapid growth in members in fact destabilised the whole organisation, which was drawn into increasingly bruising confrontations with the ruling powers over anti-imperialist activities

[1] See an account of the seminar in Backhaus 1997, pp. 501–13.

(against the American intervention in Vietnam) and action against the ways in which universities were governed. The anti-authoritarian current around Rudi Dutschke, which advocated direct action (non-terrorist, illegal action), assumed greater importance and disrupted the leadership's orientation and structure. The divergences over the analysis of the situation were not insignificant. Hans-Jürgen Krahl, a student of Adorno's but close to the anti-authoritarians, believed that the authorities were adopting a harder reactionary line which would threaten democracy in the short term. Accordingly, he thought that the student movement must do everything to counter the reactionary offensive and supplant a failing, even complicit, social democracy.

Adorno's attitude during this period is often presented as fundamentally hostile to the student movement.[2] Did he not have the students who were occupying the Institute expelled by the police? In reality, his reactions were ambivalent, at once favourable to the student movement and critical of it. Adorno could not but appreciate the democratic thrust of the movement, its refusal to throw a veil over the Nazi past, its way of shaking the conventions and hypocrisy of the reigning morality. On the other hand, he was very sceptical about the movement's ability to overcome its infantile disorders, its impatience, its underestimation of the obstacles it faced, its tendency to mythologise violence, its temptation to wish to change the world without really interpreting it, and its fetishisation of subjectivity at the expense of objectivity. He glimpsed the dangers of activism – that is to say, of an atheoretical practice that was consequently blind to the pathologies of action in contemporary society. According to Adorno, part of the student movement was prey to collective hallucinations. As can be seen from his correspondence with Herbert Marcuse on the issue, for him there could be no question of subscribing to student initiatives and actions whose orientation he did not share.[3] A concern for personal comfort was certainly not absent from this remote attitude. But it would do Adorno an injustice if we forgot the fundamental, predominant reasons.

Nevertheless, Adorno's abstention was not innocent and was even paradoxical. At the very moment when critical theory was hailed as a movement

---

[2] On this period, see Demirovic 1999.

[3] See Adorno's correspondence with Horkheimer and Marcuse in Horkheimer 1996.

which, even if minoritarian, was nevertheless a mass movement with original features, it could find nothing better to do than withdraw to quarters. In a word, it did not seek to theorise the effects of its theoretical practice in the academy and the intellectual world – and this in a social context where the production of knowledge was assuming increasing importance. Adorno criticised the students' collective actions, but he did not take the trouble to attempt a determinate negation of them, by indicating the paths to be pursued. If the students' collective actions were one-sided, it was necessary to try to explain on what conditions they could become multilateral or rather multi-dimensional – that is to say, directed not only towards multiple objectives, but also towards the positioning of groups and individuals within action and towards its transcendence by employing new social logics and new social links. If the student actions were marked by many political deficiencies in their strategic and tactical approaches, it needed to be shown that different orientations were possible. Yet politics is virtually absent from Adorno's reflections. We find it, obviously, in the critique of Nazism and in texts that broach the weaknesses of democracy. But all that is far from constituting a developed theory of politics in collective action and of collective action in politics. Following in the tracks of Marx, Adorno had a firm grasp of the dependency of politics on economics and economism, but he placed it under the aegis of a sociology of domination largely adopted from Weber.

By proceeding in this fashion, he did not tackle the utterly decisive question of the articulation of politics with the organisation and circulation of power in social relations and society. Politics is not reducible to exchanges between the state and social groups, and still less to a bureaucratic administration of relations of domination and citizenship. It has something to do with what Foucault calls the micro-physics of power – that is to say, mechanisms of discipline and surveillance and the resistance they provoke. This theme of resistance (and its many forms) is obviously crucial for understanding how politics might be unlocked, how people might see through state performances and the biased representations that social groups and individuals give of themselves in political sparring. In fact, resistance to oppression and exploitation invests numerous domains – cognitive relations, relations in firms, relations between the sexes, expressive relations. On condition that they are polyphonically linked in constellations, forms of resistance are potentially levers for undermining individual and collective action, for overcoming feelings of powerlessness in face of the machine-like organisation of capital, for desiring lives different from those that are currently lived. Politics must cease to be a defence of interests (which can only operate in favour of the dominant interests of capital) and become the unveiling of abstract social relations and a struggle for their reconstruction.

However, the revival of politics and collective action will not occur from scratch. It involves a critical re-examination of the past of the workers' movement, a sort of duty to take stock, which, over and above the denunciation of crimes and errors, will endeavour to analyse the processes that led to catastrophes and to the expanded reproduction of capital. In the first instance, it is necessary to criticise the fact that the workers' movement, in its overwhelming majority, has not proved capable of breaking with the narrow and subordinate forms of politics peculiar to capitalist society. Certainly, large-scale battles have not been wanting, any more than crises with revolutionary consequences. But the political expressions given to them have remained largely prisoners of tutelary and paternalistic organisational forms. The masses have invariably been asked to rally in semi-passive fashion to orientations and apparatuses that were autonomous from them. Parties and unions were constructed in the chinks and interstices of the institutionalised world of politics. They have adopted many of its practices and failings: hierarchical systems of material and symbolic rewards and a ritualisation of collective action. To this must be added the fact that representations of the process of social emancipation have scarcely gone beyond the stage of more or less mythologised narratives – that is to say, they have not been able to trigger new cognitive processes and help create new social bonds. The degree of innovation in the politics of the workers' movement was not completely insignificant. But it was insufficient to enable it to practise politics differently, so as radically to recast it.

Adorno never tackled this complex of problems, prisoner as he was of an unduly general conception of domination. He was easily satisfied with a fluid, unexplained concept of totalitarianism to characterise the Soviet Union. This lack of analysis of the social, cognitive and symbolic processes that led to the construction of pseudo-'real socialism', and then to the submission of a large part of the workers' movement to a veritable process of social counter-emancipation, subtracted a whole dimension of social and political reality from examination. It makes it possible to understand Adorno's silence on the future to be constructed: he saw the horizon darkened by a fragile Western democracy, a possible resurgence of Nazism, and the threat of Communist totalitarianism. He did not perceive what was going on under the surface of Soviet monolithism and he therefore did not see all the indications or counter-indications that could be drawn from more developed analyses – particularly for a new conception of politics. Basically, for him, there were far too many tendencies towards a standardisation of the world and a progressive clouding of social relations. Here we find some of the ambiguities and hesitations already visible in the analysis of capitalism. Adorno knew that oppression and exploitation come from afar. But he wondered whether the catastrophic continuity of history (Benjamin) was modulated in major discontinuities. One sometimes has the impression that he construes capitalism as an essential break with many pasts and a reorganisation of part of these pasts by selection and assimilation to the present and the temporality of capital in incessant, endlessly new syntheses. The absorption of the past thus renders its reconstruction uncertain. It can now hardly be grasped other than via traces and ultimately pertains more to an archaeological endeavour than to vast historical syntheses contributing to a universal history. This is how we might interpret certain critical remarks on the philosophy of history. But, at other times, discontinuity is denied, in favour of a continuity of domination (domination over nature and humanity).

These ambiguities and oscillations obviously represent serious obstacles to any determinate negation of capitalist relations at a theoretical level. Critical theory *à la* Adorno did not link up adequately with the critique of political economy; and the abstraction of exchange [*Tauschabstraktion*] was insufficiently conjugated with the movement of abstract labour and many capitals – that is to say, with the metamorphoses of the value-form. As a result, it was not able fully to explain the mode of existence and functioning of this upside down world, which is forever prostrating itself before the new idols engendered by real abstractions. In many respects, Adorno went further than Marx and detected the economism that persisted in Marx's critique of economism. But he was unable to avoid several dead ends. He went beyond Marx, but at the same time he fell short of the founder of the critique of political economy. This is the paradox that requires reflection in order to restore vigour to critical theory.

Chapter Twenty-Seven

Louis Althusser, or the Impure Purity of the Concept

François Matheron

The fate of Louis Althusser's work today is a remarkable one. Abruptly rescued from oblivion by the publication of his autobiography *L'avenir dure longtemps* in 1992, it has since been enriched by several volumes of unpublished texts, together with the republication of texts long unavailable in the bookshops. Thus, the conditions seemingly exist for a critical re-examination of Althusser's thought, as suggested by the numerous works, articles, and conferences devoted to it. For many reasons, this is not quite what has happened. Over and above rather sterile polemics about the respective statuses of the 'acknowledged *œuvre*' and the posthumous *œuvre*; over and above the highly sensitive issue of the relations between the biographical and the conceptual; over and above disputes about inheritance and resentments towards the man and the master; over and above the excesses of a psychiatric commentary indifferent both to the texts and the 'case', an observation must be made: the field of Althusserian studies has still not been constituted. Thus, there is no detailed study of Althusser's position in the history of Marxism, in philosophy, in the history of philosophy or epistemology, even in the history of French philosophy. For this kind of approach generally assumes a comprehensive assessment,[1] at least an implicit one, which Althusser's *œuvre* precisely seems designed to discourage. How can one assess an *œuvre* that was forever destroying itself? How can one assess an *œuvre* that is so heterogeneous, where magnificent lightning flashes sit alongside shocking theoretical barbarities? How can a text as stimulating as the famous 'Ideology and Ideological State Apparatuses' be reconciled with the 'rather terrifying' 'Sur la reproduction des rapports de production', of which (minus a few details) it is nevertheless only a fragment? If retreat to the academic form of the commentary seems impossible, the same can be said of the invariably rather lazy project of separating the wheat from the chaff, of distinguishing between 'what is living and what is dead in the *œuvre* of Louis Althusser'. Difficult to inscribe in historical continuity, this *œuvre* is, in truth, irredeemably enigmatic. It is as if, behind the many proud announcements of discoveries, there is a profoundly aporetic framework that condemns all attempts at reading to generalised uncertainty. As we know, Althusser progressively destroyed the theses he had constructed. Disquieting in itself, this conceals another phenomenon, which is much more disturbing: there is not a single Althusserian concept that is not, at bottom, immediately modified by its opposite.[2] By way of a few limited examples, we shall seek to show that such is indeed Althusser's fundamental gesture; and that it is inextricably bound up with his greatness and his misery.

If Althusser's life is forever stamped by the seal of tragedy, his work is irrevocably placed under the sign of paradox. First of all, there is the paradox belatedly revealed by the tragedy itself: that of the autobiographical writing. As is well known, autobiography is, to say the least, absent from Althusserian philosophy, in which analysis of the 'interpellation of individuals as subjects' disqualifies in advance the specular illusion characteristic of the autobiographical project – such as it was practised by Althusser at least. Obviously, it can be argued in the face of all the evidence that such a paradox is unrelated to Althusser's theoretical writings. It can also be claimed, more subtly, that what is involved is striking confirmation of the Althusserian conception of ideology: no one – not even Althusser – was able to escape the trap of specu-

[1] The only attempt of this kind is that of Gregory Elliott (Elliott 1987), which predates the appearance of Althusser's unpublished texts. However, see the new edition, Elliott 2006.

[2] In a quite different language, this is one of the lessons of the magisterial study by Yoshihiko Ichida 1997.

larity.[3] But this only succeeds in displacing the paradox. The autobiographical dimension is in fact manifestly present at the heart of certain of Althusser's major theoretical texts, like 'Freud and Lacan' and especially *Machiavelli and Us*. His work on Machiavelli began in January 1962, right in the middle of a very serious depression that ended in three months' hospitalisation. Commenting on this course in a letter of 29 September 1962 to Franca Madonia,[4] Althusser stated that he was interested in Machiavelli because he identified with him, discovering in his work what he regarded as his own problem – how to begin from nothing:

> When I think about it now...in developing Machiavelli's contradictory requirement, I was actually *talking about myself*. The question I was dealing with – how *to begin from nothing* the New State that is nevertheless *absolutely indispensable* and *demanded* by a profound aspiration (which, in reality, did not have, could not *find*, did not *see* a way of being realised and satisfied) – was *mine*.

And Althusser adds:

> In developing this theoretical problem...I had an hallucinatory sense (of an irresistible force) of developing nothing other than *my own delirium*. I had the impression that the delirium of my course coincided with (and was *nothing other* than) my own *subjective* delirium...: I had the impression that the delirium of my course (objective delirium) uniquely coincided with *something in me that was delirious*.[5]

It could not be more clearly stated that Althusser's relationship to his theoretical object is here perceived in terms of identification.

Obviously, this commentary is only one commentary among others; and it would be naïve to take it for the truth of its relationship to its object: a position of principle that is especially justified in the case of Althusser, whose

[3] See Albiac 1997. For a directly opposed point of view, see in the same volume Moulier Boutang 1997.

[4] See my introduction to Althusser 1995a. The extraordinary correspondence between Althusser and Franca Madonia extends in the main from November 1961 to 1967. Whilst in no sense a theoretical correspondence, it does clearly bring out the singularity of Althusser's relationship to his theoretical objects, to the extent that much of Althusser's philosophical writing is only really intelligible in the light of this correspondence.

[5] See Althusser 1998a, pp. 221–6.

autobiography is rather disappointing in this regard. And we can also add, as he himself did in *The Future Lasts a Long Time*,[6] that the relationship of a discourse to its objects is different from the subjective relationship of the 'author' to these objects, which, moreover, are not the same. However, the reality is not so simple. For far from being restricted to a few texts that are ultimately private, this subjective dimension is paradoxically present, with a blinding presence, in Althusser's most 'theoreticist' work, *Reading 'Capital'* – especially in the theory of the 'symptomatic reading' developed in the Introduction, which is wholly devoted to the clarification of the project contained in these introductory sentences:

> We read *Capital* as philosophers, and therefore posed it a different question.... we posed it the question of its *relation to its object*, hence both the question of the specificity of its *object*, and the question of the specificity of its *relation* to that object.... To read *Capital* as philosophers is precisely to question the specific object of a specific discourse, and the specific relationship between this discourse and its object; it is therefore to put to the *discourse-object* unity the question of the epistemological status which distinguishes this particular unity from other forms of discourse-object unity.[7]

A whole generation of readers has been captivated by this virtuoso text, where Althusser simultaneously deals with Marx's reading of the classical economists, the Althusserian reading of Marx, and a reading of reality through theoretical practice in which the relation to reality becomes highly problematic. The concept of symptomatic reading is used to analyse Marx's reading of the 'text of classical economics'. At first sight, Althusser tells us, Marx made do with revealing the lacunae of Adam Smith (or of Smith-Ricardo) behind the apparent continuity of his discourse: Smith quite simply failed to see what was already there, whereas Marx saw it. Everything thus boils down to a subjective relationship of the more-or-less clear-sighted vision of an already given object. At the same time, however, Marx writes something quite different: what classical economics does not see is what it has itself produced;

---

[6] 'Only now do I think I see clearly what my relationship with Marxism was about. And once again I am not concerned with the objectivity of what I wrote, and hence of my relationship to one or more objective objects, but with how I related to an object as an "object-choice" – in other words, an internal, unconscious object' (Althusser 1993, p. 212, translation modified).

[7] Althusser and Balibar 1970, pp. 14–15.

and in the lacunae of its discourse must be seen the symptoms of a change of problematic produced without classical economics being aware of it: 'what classical political economy does not see is not what it does not see, but *what it sees*'. And if it does not see it, it is because it is attached to its old problematic, which prevents it from seeing that it has 'completely changed the terms' of the problem. As interpreted by Althusser, Marx identifies the defective use of the term 'labour' as the symptom of a different discourse, which is invisible because excluded. In the event, Smith produced a correct answer to a question (What is the value of labour-power?) that was not posed because it could not be; and Marx's whole effort consisted in re-establishing the question. In such conditions, the invisible does not depend on the greater or lesser acuteness of the knowing subject:

> The sighting is thus no longer the act of an individual subject, endowed with the faculty of 'vision' which he exercises either attentively or distractedly; the sighting is the act of its structural conditions, it is the relation of immanent reflection between the field of the problematic and *its* objects and *its* problems.[8]

And thus we arrive at that other 'reading', which is the labour of knowledge, to which Althusser devotes the bulk of his Introduction to *Reading 'Capital'*.

The explicit target is the 'empiricist conception of knowledge', construed in the broadest sense. In fact, this sense is extremely broad, since it encompasses the totality of classical theories of knowledge, including philosophies that are seemingly as non-empiricist as those of Plato, Descartes, and Hegel. In the fifth course of his philosophy course for scientists, Althusser divided theories of knowledge into two major tendencies: formalism and empiricism. However, he only gives two examples of approaches that are strongly marked by formalism: that of Kant, in whom, however, 'empiricism is ultimately dominant'; and that of Leibniz, where it is formalism that is 'dominant'.[9] But, insofar as Marx's break with the 'religious myth of reading' takes the form of a rejection of the Hegelian conception of expressive totality, which is itself connected to Leibniz's philosophy by Althusser, we are entitled to consider that, for him, empiricism predominates in classical theories of knowledge as

---

8 Althusser and Balibar 1970, p. 25.
9 Althusser 1995a, p. 279.

a whole. According to Althusser, the principal characteristic of empiricism is that it does not distinguish between the real object and the object of knowledge and conceives knowledge as an abstraction in the literal sense of the word: the object of knowledge is supposedly part of the real object – essential reality as opposed to inessential reality. Thus, there is only a single object, of which knowledge is supposedly the vision; and the sole function of the theory of knowledge is to provide a guarantee of the possibility of this vision. As is well known, Althusser's work in epistemology is wholly constructed against such an approach, in two main directions: rejection of the very idea of a guarantee, which is by its very nature ideological; and insistence on the distinction between the real object and the object of knowledge. Science does not work on real objects, but on objects constructed by it, whose relationship to the real objects is, for the time being at least, bracketed. It is therefore not a question of asking by what right science is possible, but of investigating the structure of theoretical practice, the process of production of knowledge, which occurs wholly 'in thought' (hence the term 'theoretical practice', the famous 'criterion of practice' being strictly internal to theory). Such is the Althusserian 'purity of the concept': not the product of an empirical purification, which would subsequently only demand to return to reality, but a concept situated in an adequate relationship to an object of knowledge produced by theoretical labour – a concept unfolding its specificity in order to produce what Marx called a 'concrete-in-thought'. The specificity of Marx's discourse – an epistemology of the concept conceived as a veritable weapon against any form of pragmatism – is thus that it breaks with a conception of knowledge as the transparency of a given object – that is to say, with what Althusser calls 'the yearning for a reading *at sight*', to which he counter-poses a conception of reading and knowledge as production.[10]

A relatively clear relation to an object thus seems to emerge from the analyses of *Reading 'Capital'*, which can be assessed as such quite independently of Althusser's relationship to the object Machiavelli. However, once again, the reality is much more complicated. The theory of symptomatic reading in fact acquires a strange resonance when compared with what Althusser wrote to Franca Madonia on 21 February 1964, at the very moment when he really began his reading of *Capital*:

---

[10] Althusser and Balibar 1970, pp. 16 and 34.

> There's something rather strange, when I think about it. For several months I've lived with an extraordinary capacity for live contact with some profound realities, sensing them, seeing them, reading them in beings and reality *at sight*. I've thought about this extraordinary thing, in thinking of the situation of the few rare beings whose name I revere – Spinoza, Marx, Nietzsche, Freud – and who must have possessed this contact in order to write what they left behind. Otherwise, I don't see how they could have lifted this enormous layer, this tombstone that covers reality...so as to have the direct contact with it that burns in them for all eternity.[11]

It is difficult not to be thrown by such an assertion, which is literally contradictory with the analyses of *Reading 'Capital'*, where the critique of 'reading at sight', immediately followed by a reference to Spinoza, is preceded by the following prediction with Foucauldian accents:

> However paradoxical it may seem, I venture to suggest that our age threatens one day to appear in the history of human culture as marked by the most dramatic and difficult trial of all, the discovery of and training in the meaning of the 'simplest' acts of existence: seeing, listening, speaking, reading.... And contrary to all today's reigning appearances, we do not owe these staggering knowledges to psychology, which are built on the absence of a proper concept of them, but to a few men: Marx, Nietzsche and Freud.[12]

These are the same names to whom the letter to Franca attributed the ability to read 'at sight'. How is such a contradiction to be explained? The simplest thing, obviously, would be to set it aside and foreground the distinction in principle between a theoretical text and private correspondence. But to do this would be to lose sight of the main thing.

When Althusser wrote the letter to Franca, his epistemology was, in the main, already constituted, even if the notion of 'symptomatic reading' had not yet made its appearance. And we may assume that he already had a sense of the basic difficulty that would be expounded in *Reading 'Capital'*: quite simply, the problem of the relationship between knowledge and reality with which the Introduction concludes. Advancing on highly treacherous terrain, Althusser multiplies his warnings:

---

11 Althusser 1998a, p. 524.
12 Althusser and Balibar 1970, p. 16.

> But we have gone far enough in this work for a return to the difference between the order of the object of knowledge and that of the real object to enable us to approach the problem whose *index* this difference is: the problem of the relation between these two objects (the object of knowledge and the real object), a relation which constitutes the very existence of *knowledge.* I must warn the reader that we are here entering a domain which is *very difficult* to approach....

Here we meet our greatest difficulty.

> Here we run the greatest risks. The reader will understand that I can only claim, with the most explicit reservations, to give the first arguments towards a sharpening of the question we have posed, and not an answer to it.[13]

And the text goes on shying away from the issue. It must first of all be shown that what is involved is not of a theory of knowledge, but the production of the 'knowledge effect': not by what right is knowledge possible, but by what mechanism does the labour of knowledge precisely produce knowledge, and not something else?[14] It must then be shown that it is not a question of reconstructing the effect by way of a genetic process, by reference to an original knowledge effect, to an 'original ground', to the various phenomenological representatives of the search for guarantees: the knowledge effect must derive from the actual structure of the knowledge mechanism. But Althusser, bereft, obviously, of a Spinozist theory of knowledge of the third kind, does not manage, and does not even seek, to answer his question and engages in what must be called a denegation. Each mode of appropriation of reality

> poses the problem of the mechanism of production of *its specific 'effect'*, the knowledge effect for theoretical practice, the aesthetic effect for aesthetic practice, the ethical effect for ethical practice, etc. In each of these cases we

---

[13] Althusser and Balibar 1970, pp. 51–3 and 61.

[14] See Althusser and Balibar 1970, pp. 61–2. Althusser compares this question with that of the production of the 'society effect', in an assertion whose comical tone is the most reliable index in him of a headlong flight: 'what Marx studies in *Capital* is the mechanism...which gives this product of history, that is precisely the society-product he is studying, the property of producing the "*society effect*" which makes this result exist *as a society*, and not as a heap of sand, an ant-hill, a workshop or a mere collection of men' (Althusser and Balibar 1970, p. 65).

> cannot merely substitute one word for another, as 'dormitive virtue' was substituted for opium.[15]

This is indeed a denegation, for the adequacy of knowledge to reality is manifestly unthinkable within the problematic deployed by Althusser. There then remains recourse to direct contact with reality – i.e. 'reading at sight' – for better or worse. For Althusser had precisely explored all its traps. As all his correspondence attests, he knew that that the danger was a constant headlong flight;[16] he knew that everything depended on the quality of the vision, but at the same time acknowledged himself to be incapable of writing in other conditions.[17] If a contradiction does exist between Althusser's relation to Machiavelli's text and the theory of reading expounded in *Reading 'Capital'*, it must be seen as the unsustainable tension affecting the whole Althusserian *œuvre*. And we are thus led to accord the following statements, which an uninformed reading would doubtless regard as psychologising chatter, their full significance:

> And this afternoon, precisely, thinking about some friends who possess 'genius' and who have taken on gigantic works, it appeared to me obvious how balance (or imbalance – or the more or less *artificial* balance out of which they've constructed a protection) can *impact* on their *theoretical output*, I mean on the *correctness* (or falsity) of their *theoretical inspiration*. Even in this domain, *contact* with the *reality* of the things they study is governed and determined remotely, but decisively, by their *mode of contact* with the ordinary things in life – that is to say, by their own *contact* with their own *balance*, that is to say, by the contact or lack of contact they have with *their truth*...this proves that there aren't two types of relationship with reality (rational and emotional), but *only one*.[18]

---

15 Althusser and Balibar 1970, p. 66.

16 Among dozens of possible examples, let us cite this extract from a letter to Franca of 19 January 1962, commenting on his course on Machiavelli: 'It's typical: headlong flight – promising mountains and marvels on the author – to compensate for my incredible difficulties entering into contact with my subject' (Althusser 1998a, p. 156). Jacques Rancière has justifiably stressed the 'practice of blunt statement' in Althusser which, in a different sense from that set out here, pertains less to a circumstantial expedient than the basic contradictions of his thought (see Rancière 1993).

17 Seemingly without exception, all Althusser's major texts were written very rapidly, even if they were then revised at length. As soon as the gestation period lengthened, the result was disappointing.

18 Letter to Franca of 23 October 1962, in Althusser 1998a, p. 257.

Here is perhaps to be found one of the secrets to the Introduction to *Reading 'Capital'*, written with such intensity: far from simply opposing the hallucinatory dimension evoked above, it represented something like an attempt to ward it off. And yet, in typically Althusserian fashion, this conjuration assumed precisely the form that it was intended to ward off: it would scarcely be an exaggeration to say that in Marx Althusser read on sight the rejection of any reading on sight. This is a peculiar discrepancy which perhaps lies behind a fair few Althusserian paradoxes – as if it was always a question at root of warding off demons.

In these circumstances, how do things stand with the 'purity of the concept', whose imperative in a sense encapsulates the approach of Althusser, or at least of the author of *For Marx* and *Reading 'Capital'*? If what has been said above is right, it is clear that in Althusser such purity of the concept is very precisely modified by its opposite: its modality is that of the impurity of the concept.

Let us return for a moment to Althusser's relation to Machiavelli. In a letter to Franca dated 26 January 1962, we come across the following astonishing statements:

> I even sketched a description of Machiavelli's consciousness, his will to realism in contradiction with his 'derealising' situation (to have hit upon this word was the solution: thus giving the impression that there was something there to understand which I didn't succeed in expressing in a conceptual, clear, exhaustive fashion, but saying at the same time that there was nevertheless something to sense and understand, identifying a presence that did not manage to grasp itself…), and then, thinking about this formulation again, I was extraordinarily and ironically struck by the fact that, in the guise of the supposed consciousness of Machiavelli, I'd spoken about myself…. This is perhaps why, when I celebrated the mystery of Machiavelli's consciousness with these words, something like the silence of religious revelations came over my audience.[19]

Much might be said of the vocabulary used by Althusser here. This description of a course as if it were a religious service seems, at first sight, to underscore its inadequacies: the word that supplies a presence, or allows it to be seen,

[19] Althusser 1998a, p. 163.

appears to supervene for want of the concept. Althusser insisted at length on the specificity of the concept, on the difference, for example, between the 'knowledge effect' and the 'aesthetic effect'. Thus, in his 'Letter on Art' of 1966 he writes:

> The real difference between art and science lies in the *specific form* in which they give us the same object in quite different ways: art in the form of 'seeing' and 'perceiving' or 'feeling', science in the form of *knowledge* (in the strict sense, by concepts).[20]

Given such a definition, which clearly seems to imply the superiority of the concept, whatever Althusser might say of it elsewhere, the course on Machiavelli possibly pertains more to art than to knowledge. It is, however, difficult not to note that most of the major Althusserian concepts exhibit precisely the characteristics attributed here to the inadequacies of the Machiavelli course. The concepts of theoretical practice, structural causality, overdetermination,[21] conjuncture, ideological state apparatus, when they are effective, are always handled by Althusser in such a way as to make present, as if before our eyes, the reality that is being evoked. In this respect, the central text of *For Marx* is doubtless the article on Bertolazzi and Brecht, where Althusser gives (or re-gives) us sight of what he had already seen in the production by the Piccolo Teatro.[22] This impure purity of the concept lies behind the dazzling effect produced by certain of Althusser's texts, those where the tension takes form, is embodied in a 'style' unlike any other.[23] But it is equally at the heart of an imbalance that might be called structural, producing the collapse of other texts, where the purity and the impurity of the concept serve only to neutralise one another.

As is well known, the theme of the purity of the concept is directly bound up with the sharp break established by Althusser between science and ideology, and, more generally, with the primacy of theory ceremoniously proclaimed

---

[20] Althusser 1984, p. 175.

[21] The author of these lines still recalls with emotion the extraordinary evocative power of the analysis in 'Contradiction and Overdermination' of the encounter and 'fusion' of contradictions.

[22] See also 'Cremonini, Painter of the Abstract' (Althusser 1971, pp. 209–20), where Althusser gives us sight of what he elsewhere calls the 'absent cause' or 'structural causality'.

[23] In his preface to the new edition of *Pour Marx* (Althusser 1996c), Étienne Balibar legitimately refers to 'a sort of lyricism of abstraction'.

by the whole of his *œuvre*.[24] At a time when people were often Communist and intelligent but not Marxist, or Communist and Marxist but not intelligent, or even – sometimes – Marxist and intelligent but not Communist, it was finally becoming possible to be all three at once: a Communist intellectual producing a discourse on Marx that was on a par with the theories which commanded the intellectual field at the time. The seminars organised by Althusser at the École normale supérieure on the young Marx (1961–2), on the origins of structuralism (1962–3, with two talks by Althusser on Foucault and Lévi-Strauss), on Lacan (1963–4),[25] and finally on *Capital*, played a primary role here – work behind the scenes that emerged into the full light of day with the simultaneous publication of *For Marx* and *Reading 'Capital'* during the autumn of 1965. In one gesture, Althusser dismissed the superseded figures of the philosophical field (especially Sartre) and the totality of *marxisant* discourses – or French ones at any rate – as strictly unacceptable in the new conditions (and particularly what stood in for theory in the French Communist Party). And the restrained lyricism of the Preface to *For Marx*, its rejection of the imaginary debt of not being proletarian, sounded as a veritable summons to the formation of a battalion of Marxist theoreticians. Such was the meaning explicitly assigned by Althusser to the Leninist thesis, adopted from Kautsky, of the importation of Marxist science into the workers' movement.[26] In a duplicated text dated 20 April 1965, which was widely diffused at the time, Althusser justified his project on the basis of the disastrous consequences of the period of the 'personality cult' during the Stalin era:

> The effects of dogmatic politics as far as theory is concerned can still be felt today, not only in the residues of dogmatism but also, paradoxically, in

---

[24] Althusser never really changed on this point, which he even accentuated. The primacy of science in the 1960s, which is already a primacy of philosophy, was succeeded by the absolute primacy of philosophy in the enigmatic texts of the 1980s. Thus we read in the 1985 'Thèses de juin': 'Be aware that the main task today hinges on the ideological class struggle – that is to say, in relationship with philosophy. Above all, in philosophy.... And this is why (and not for the trivial tactical reasons that were staring people in the face at the time), I have always said since 1965: "everything depends on philosophy". Which means: everything depends on the class struggle in philosophy' (IMEC archives, p. 13).

[25] See Althusser 1996a and 1996b.

[26] Subsequently, Althusser totally rejected this idea, regarding it as a kind of emblem of his 'theoreticist deviation'. See, for example, in 1978, Chapter 4 of 'Marx dans ses limites': 'Marxist theory is not external but internal to the workers' movement' (Althusser 1994b, pp. 371–87).

> the often anarchic and confused forms assumed by attempts of numerous Marxist intellectuals to regain possession of the freedom of reflection and research of which they were deprived for so long.... What is most painful – and directly expressed in these...essays – is how the period of the 'cult', far from contributing to their formation, on the contrary, prevented the theoretical formation of an entire generation of Marxist researchers, whose work we cruelly miss today.[27]

Accordingly, Althusser more or less tells us, today it is a question of doing scientific work. But, for a Marxist intellectual, this involves subscribing to the scientificity inaugurated by Marx: hence the imperative, at the same time as the Lacanian 'return to Freud', of a return to Marx over and above Marxism – that is to say, in the first instance, to the birth of Marx:[28] to the opening of the 'continent of history', otherwise referred to as 'historical materialism'. It has justifiably been said that in a sense the break represents 'Althusser's philosophical object, the one that distinguishes his philosophy' – although it must immediately be made clear that this object was reworked to such an extent that it ended up emerging from the process virtually unrecognisable.[29] Whatever Althusser's subsequent development, even in his last texts (those of 1986) he never gave up asserting a difference in kind between science and ideology – to which he never stopped adding that, however clear this opposition in principle, science is constantly menaced by its opposite, to the point of sometimes being indissociable from it in practice. If Althusser ended up accepting that elements which, to his mind, were ideological (particularly the language of alienation) were more present in *Capital* itself that he had wished to concede, he always claimed that this changed nothing when it came to the main point: historical materialism, and all science with it, is inaugurated by a rupture with its ideological prehistory and only developed by repeating this break. While history is a process without a subject, a beginning, or end(s),

27 'Theory, Theoretical Practice, and Theoretical Formation. Ideology and Ideological Struggle', in Althusser 1990, p. 21. Althusser never received a reply to his request for publication of this text in *Cahiers du communisme*. Much of Rancière 1974 consists in a violent critique of it.

28 See the letter to Franca of 13 December 1962: 'You cannot know...what an extraordinary spectacle it is to be present at the birth of Marx' (Althusser 1998a, p. 296).

29 Balibar 1993, pp. 81–116 thus distinguishes between five major moments in Althusser's elaboration: 'the break before the break'; 'the break named and identified'; 'the break generalized'; 'the break "rectified"'; and 'the break dispelled'.

science may have no subject, but it definitely does have a beginning – even an absolute beginning. However, as has been noted, the beginning formed by the break is sometimes presented in profoundly paradoxical terms.[30] If the Introduction to *Reading 'Capital'* does not explicitly deal with the break, the latter is what is involved in the notion of 'symptomatic reading'. What, according to Althusser, does Marx do when he reads the discourse of classical economics and breaks definitively with it? We have seen the answer: he produces the question that Adam Smith had already answered without knowing it. This comes down to saying that the break is affected by the modality of continuity. Jacques Rancière provides an explanation for this:

> Althusser is perhaps less interested by the break itself than by what gives rise to it – even at the price of rendering it, in the last instance, unthinkable: the closely woven fabric of good/bad answers to posed/unposed questions, which is the space of science and community – community as a site of knowledge and science as the power of a community.[31]

This is a convincing explanation. Althusser is, in fact, haunted by the fear of the letter 'without an addressee written by Marxist intellectuals to communist proletarians who do not know that they are its addressees'. In this respect, it is perfectly true that one of the keys to the Introduction to *Reading 'Capital'* is the moment when, after have set out his project of a symptomatic reading of Marx's text, Althusser shifts abruptly to a reading of what he calls the 'practical works' of Marxism, the

> still theoretically opaque works of the history of the workers' movement, such as the 'cult of personality' or the very serious conflict which is our present drama.[32]

And Rancière is not wrong to add, a little cruelly, that

> a Stalinist camp or a Vietnamese *maquis* are works awaiting the questions that will make it possible to read them, but already embedded in the common fabric of knowledge.

---

[30] See Rancière 1993. See also Matheron 1997.
[31] Rancière 1993, pp. 55–7.
[32] Althusser and Balibar 1970, p. 34. The conflict in question is the Sino-Soviet conflict.

Despite everything, the world is 'a continuum of questions and answers that give rise to antagonism and imparts meaning to it'.[33] However, the explanation is one-sided, for Althusser is just as interested by the break as by continuity: this is even one of the constitutive tensions in his work.

The concept of the break forms part of a much broader theme that runs through most of Althusser's writings: solitude and beginnings; or, more precisely, the solitude of beginnings. We find it as early as the Foreword to *Montesquieu* ('No one went before him in this adventure') and in the Conclusion ('this man who set out alone and truly discovered the new lands of history').[34] We find it in connection with Lenin, 'absolutely alone, against everyone, in an apparently lost cause'.[35] We find it *par excellence* whenever Althusser speaks of Machiavelli. We find it a hundred times in connection with Marx, particularly, with all its ambivalence, in what is virtually the final word of Althusser's contribution to *Reading 'Capital'*: 'Alone, Marx look around him for allies and supporters.... As for us, we can thank Marx for the fact that we are not alone'.[36] But it is clear that Althusser is speaking here of himself in the first instance, as someone who (if his own words are to be believed) never recognised any contemporary apart from his friend Jacques Martin. The image of solitude in Althusser must be taken seriously, for far from being reducible to a form of pathos, it belongs to a constellation that gives this conceptualisation its particular tenor. In fact, he treats solitude in the same way that he treats the beginning or the void: in and through multiple variations, we witness a perpetual inversion of the for into the against – the requisite task is simultaneously an impossible task; what is to be warded off is what is to be established. This position, which he went on fashioning and reworking, was encountered by Althusser from 1962 onwards above all in Machiavelli, with whom – to an even greater degree than in the case of Spinoza or even Marx – he never stopped identifying.

In *Machiavelli and Us*, Althusser attributes a decisive role to Chapter 9 of Book I of the *Discourses on the First Decade of Titus Livius*: 'it is necessary to be *alone* to found a new republic or completely reform it' – that is to say, the thematic of the 'New Prince in a New Principality'.

33 Rancière 1993, pp. 64, 62.
34 Althusser 1972, pp. 14 and 107.
35 Althusser 1990, p. 188.
36 Althusser and Balibar 1970, p. 193.

> In order to derive a state from nothing, the founder must be alone: that is to say, be everything: omnipotent – omnipotent before the *void* of the conjuncture and its aleatory future.[37]

For Althusser, Machiavelli's project is an absolute beginning dictated by the Italian political situation: a 'political *void* [which] is simply an immense aspiration to political *being*'.[38] An extremely rich material – Italian *virtù* – awaits a form. But this form does not arrive and its advent is unpredictable, for Machiavelli as for anyone else. It depends upon an aleatory encounter between the *fortuna* and the *virtù* of an absent subject who is to be constituted. While it is not possible to go into detail here on this interpretation of Machiavelli, and still less to try to assess its pertinence,[39] it is necessary to stress the apparatus put in place by Althusser, characteristic of the way of 'thinking in extremes' that he precisely claims to have borrowed from Machiavelli. A veritable circle of limits is in fact marked out for us: the conjuncture is purely empty, the subject who must fill this void is wholly absent. Between the two, any transition is thus, at least for now, strictly impossible. However, called for by the conjuncture, the transition is at the same time strictly necessary. Such, in Althusser's view, is 'Machiavelli's endeavour to think the conditions of possibility of an impossible task, to think the unthinkable'.[40] And, in order to dispel any ambiguity, let us make it clear that this is not a question of some dialectical synthesis: the task is indeed at once wholly imperative and utterly impossible.

We must not be misled. Althusser is not simply analysing a borderline situation characteristic only of the Italian political conjuncture and Machiavelli's thought. If he accords such importance to Machiavelli, it is because he views him as the embodiment of a problem that is above all his own. For Althusser passionately wanted to begin, and begin alone, but in such conditions that this beginning appeared impossible to him from the outset and forever thereafter. In this sense, he tells us, it is necessary to begin everything all over again: with a few rare exceptions, the Marxist tradition is, as it were, rendered void. (Aside from Marx, Engels, Lenin, Mao and – occasionally – Gramsci, Marxist references in Althusser's texts are fairly rare and most of the time pretty impre-

---

[37] Althusser 1990, p. 63.
[38] Althusser 1990, p. 54.
[39] See on this point Negri 1993.
[40] Althusser 1999, p. 52.

cise).[41] But this theoretical recommencement could not be purely speculative. Even, and perhaps especially, in his 'theoreticist' phase, Althusser sought to produce political effects. If everything needs to be recommenced theoretically, it is also – and Althusser knew it ten years before *What Must Change in the Party* (1978) – because it is necessary to recommence everything politically. Naturally, however, he did not say it, for this is precisely what was impossible for him. Althusser's attachment to a veritable ontology of the workers' movement, and even the international Communist movement, prevented him from posing head on the crucial question of the identification of political subjects. In such conditions, the 'detour of theory'[42] takes an extremely sophisticated form, closely connected to Althusser's analysis of what he calls 'Machiavelli's theoretical dispositive'.

Basically, Althusser tells us in *Machiavelli and Us*, there are two radically different kinds of 'theoretical space'. The first is that of 'pure theory': the space of any science, including political science and (we may assume) historical materialism. The other space is that of 'political practice' – by which is to be understood theory subjected to the primacy of political practice:

> the first – theoretical – space has no subject (the truth is valid for any and every subject); whereas the second possesses meaning only via its possible or requisite subject, be it Machiavelli's New Prince or Gramsci's Modern Prince.[43]

---

41 On occasion, they can be frankly fanciful – for example, the allusion to the Frankfurt school contained in the 'The Humanist Controversy' (Althusser 2003, p. 222).

42 I borrow this phrase from the sub-title of the book by Gregory Elliott cited above, without, however, sharing all its author's analyses. If it seems to me to be true that the most important political effects were produced by his 'theoreticist' writings, I certainly do not believe that the indisputable effects of closure of Althusser's public discourse at the beginning of the 1970s (philosophy as 'in the last instance, class struggle in theory') are attributable to his openness to Maoism. Or, more precisely, if they are indeed in one sense, it is in so far as Althusser decided from 1969 henceforth to situate himself strictly within the French Communist Party and to confirm his political break, which was anyway already consummated, with the Maoist groups. Such was the basic meaning of the publication in *L'Humanité* on 21 March 1969 of his article 'How to Read Marx's *Capital*', whose key is doubtless the succession in the same sentence of the names of Marx, Lenin and... Maurice Thorez (Althusser 1969, p. 304). Besides, it does not make great sense to separate Althusser's *œuvre* into chronological slices. If the beginning of the 1970s is indeed that of an extreme closure, characteristic of the *Reply to John Lewis*, it is also that of the greatest openness – of *Machiavelli and Us*. In truth, in Althusser, closure is never very far removed from freedom.

43 Althusser 1999, p. 20.

And the difference between the spaces does not coincide with that between the objects: Althusser's sole interest here is political thought and these two spaces are mutually exclusive. Machiavelli's great originality is to have deconstructed the space of pure theory. Telescoping several traditional theses that are in principle contradictory (for instance, that of the unchanging course of things and that of their constant change), he undermines the dispositive of 'political science' from within. He does not apply universal rules to the analysis of a particular case; on the contrary, he subjects the formulation of rules to the exigencies of a task to be performed. He thinks 'under the conjuncture' – which is quite different from simply analysing a particular conjuncture. Here Althusser posits a difference in kind between reflecting *on* the conjuncture and reflecting *in* the conjuncture: the different elements of the conjuncture are no longer objective data on which theory reflects, but 'become real or potential forces in the struggle for the historical objective, and their relations become *relations of force*'.[44] Such is the veritable 'concrete analysis of a concrete situation' that Althusser discovers in Machiavelli. Its major feature is that it arranges at its centre an empty place, destined to be filled by a subject, whether individual or collective. It is impossible not to realise that this 'strange vacillation of theory' is, in the first instance, Althusser's deconstruction of his own theoretical dispositive – something that he expresses in a formula full of implications: 'the space of pure theory, assuming it exists'. For this 'space of pure theory' is manifestly that of the purity of the concept developed in *Reading 'Capital'*. But it would be quite wrong to regard this as a belated category,[45] contemporaneous with the self-criticism of the 'theoreticist period'. The analyses contained in 'Contradiction and Overdetermination', written in 1962, suffice to avert such a simplistic view.

Over and above its grasp of Machiavelli's texts, the essential thing about this analysis is the radicalism of the oppositions outlined by Althusser. Between the two spaces there is in fact an absolute contradiction, with no possible resolution. It is impossible to be in both at the same time; and a third space seems inconceivable. In addition, the second dispositive is character-

[44] Althusser 1999, p. 19.

[45] It is very difficult to date the formula precisely: the manuscript is crowded with corrections at this point. Above all, Althusser's reflection on Machiavelli was a virtually uninterrupted process from 1962 and helped mould some of his analyses of the thought of Marx and Lenin – specifically those in 'Contradiction and Overdetermination'.

ised by an accentuation of the void. In Machiavelli, Althusser tells us, the place of the subjects is absolutely empty. As a result of Italian specificity, no one can predict which subject will fill this void – a negative that nevertheless has its positive counterpart. In any event, we know that it will not be any of the Italian princes currently living. But this is definitely not a question of an Italian exception. In this type of dispositive, the place of the subjects is always empty, always fashioned to be filled by future subjects, including in France in the 1960s. This is why Althusser is fascinated by Machiavelli. However, it is precisely here that things become complicated. For if everything, in a sense, prompts Althusser to think that the conjuncture is empty, and that the place of political subjects is unoccupied, a different tendency draws him in completely the opposite direction: the place of the subjects is always already occupied by a completely hypostatised working class embodied by the Communist Party.[46] This leads him to an extremely significant formula: if the space of a conjunctural analysis only makes sense if it arranges a place that is empty for the future, Althusser hastens to add: 'I say empty, though it is always occupied.'[47] In the case of Machiavelli, it is difficult to see how this place could be occupied. In contrast, however, we can see it very clearly when the formula is applied to the French situation. To adopt his own terms, Althusser too is seeking to 'think the unthinkable'. He is setting himself a task that appears to him to be as imperative as, and even more impossible than, the one Machiavelli set himself. And it is here that the 'space of pure theory' reappears, in highly paradoxical form.

In 1967 Althusser formed a politico-theoretical group around him called the 'Spinoza group',[48] which was modelled, including as regards pseudonyms, on the more-or-less clandestine organisations common at the time. If the existence of the group was contemporaneous with the initial self-criticisms of 'theoreticism', it is no less illuminating about Althusser's general relationship to his theoretical work. In a note of July 1967 'on the politico-theoretical

---

[46] As we know, for some years Althusser maintained a certain political ambiguity as to what was to be understood by the 'party': *de facto* party or *de jure* party? But over and above this ambiguity, which was rapidly dispelled, the main thing was this hypostatising of the 'working class'.

[47] Althusser 1999, p. 20.

[48] Althusser's archives contain a massive file on the 'Spinoza group', including numerous notes taken by Althusser during its meetings.

conjuncture', we thus find the language used to describe the theoretical space peculiar to Machiavelli:

> It happens that we possess a certain number of definite resources, which we alone possess. It happens that as a result of this provisional privilege we are the only ones able to occupy an *empty* place: the place of Marxist-Leninist theory and, more precisely, of Marxist-Leninist *philosophy*.

In a context where the place of political subjectivity is ontologically occupied, it is as if Althusser is proceeding here to a spectacular displacement. On the one hand, thinking in the conjuncture in the manner of Machiavelli is impossible today: such is the meaning of the comparison between Marx's *Manifesto* and that other manifesto represented by Machiavelli's *Prince*. We are today still in the horizon opened up by Marx's *Manifesto*, addressing a working class that is already ontologically constituted. There remains a typically Althusserian solution: constructing the 'space of political practice' in the form of its opposite. 'Pure theory, supposing that it exists,' would thus not be straightforwardly contradictory with 'thinking in the conjuncture'. Instead, at present it would be its only possible form, although in truth fundamentally impossible. In other words, it would be the modern form of Machiavelli's 'impossible possibility'. We can then understand the extraordinary tension affecting Althusser's 'theoreticist' texts – the tension we encountered in connection with 'reading at sight', but which is wholly absent, for example, from a work like *Reply to John Lewis*, where we can hardly hear anything but a ceaseless summons to order entirely submerged by the ontology of the proletariat. But, at the same time, we can understand the extent to which this position was difficult to maintain in the long term, as is attested by another passage in the note 'on the politico-theoretical conjuncture', where Althusser broaches the question of the relationship of members of the Spinoza group to the French Communist Party: 'in the case of those who are in it, stay in the party; in the case of those who are not, do not join it'.

We could multiply examples. Doubtless there is not a single Althusserian concept that is not, in one way or another, profoundly modified by its opposite. Unquestionably, there is no Althusserian project that could not be characterised as an attempt to think the unthinkable, to think the conditions of possibility of an impossible task. The project of a symptomatic reading of Marx's text thus wholly partakes of this dimension. On the one hand, it involves producing a Marxist philosophy that is not to be found in Marx's *œuvre* – in other words, inventing it. On the other hand, however, this philosophy is in *Capital* in the 'practical state'. Once again, symptomatic reading serves to think the beginning in the form of the non-beginning, but this time in duplicate fashion. For what is involved here is the text of *Capital*; and the symptomatic reading cannot really be the same as the one practised by Marx on Adam Smith. And if Marx's text sometimes answers questions that have not been posed, 'with a little patience and perspicacity we can find *the question* itself elsewhere [in Marx]...or, on occasion, in Engels's immediate comments on Marx'.[49] This leads us to one of the central issues confronted by Althusser: the guarantee. As we know, Althusser struggled throughout his life against the notion of the guarantee, whether epistemological or ontological, justifiably stressing the *enim* of the Spinozist statement: 'Habemus enim ideam veram'. But this struggle would never have occurred if it had not been waged against internal demons in the first instance. Precious few thinkers, to use a language that is not Althusser's, have imparted such intensity to the idea of science without a foundation; and equally few have been so surrounded by the myriad traps of the foundation and the guarantee. Althusser captures this perfectly in a letter to Merab Mamardachvili of 16 January 1978:

> I can see as clearly as daylight that what I did fifteen years ago was to fabricate a decidedly French little *justification*...for the claim of Marxism (historical materialism) to present itself as science. Ultimately, this is (was, because I've changed a bit since) in the distinguished tradition of every philosophical enterprise as guarantee and support.... I half believed in it, like any 'bold' spirit, but the portion of distrust was necessary to the other half, in order to write.[50]

Like the letters addressed to Franca, this text, in which bitterness and disillusionment predominate, cannot be taken for the truth of the *œuvre*, especially given that it is relatively late. Opting completely to overlook what was the most striking aspect of his *œuvre*, from the first line to the last, Althusser nevertheless describes the other aspect of his work with remarkable lucidity, taking the analyses developed in his *Elements of Self-Criticism*, but already

---

[49] Althusser and Balibar 1970, p. 28.
[50] Althusser 1994b, p. 527.

sketched as early as 1966, to their extreme conclusions. And nothing better expresses the painful complexity of Althusser's relation with the notion of guarantee than these lines, published in *Cahiers marxistes-léninistes* in April 1966, but naturally never reprinted in any of his books:

> Since there cannot be any other 'guide' above dialectical materialism, we can understand why Lenin attributed the character of a veritable 'political partisanship' to the adoption of a scientific position in philosophy– that is to say, recognised in it a decisive, vital importance. We can understand that, dedicated to this role, dialectical materialism demands the highest consciousness, the greatest scientific rigour, the greatest theoretical vigilance – since, in the *theoretical* domain, it is the last resort, the last possible instance, for human beings who, like Marxists, are liberated from the myths of divine omniscience or the secular form of religion: dogmatism.[51]

It is far from clear that Althusser ever entirely extricated himself from the snares of the guarantee, as indicated, for example, by a book like *Reply to John Lewis*, right up to the last texts on aleatory materialism, where the pervasive notion of the void seems to occupy the position of a paradoxical guarantee. But it is certain, on the other hand, that Althusser's most beautiful texts are precisely those where the tension between guarantee and non-guarantee takes shape in a style. In this sense, 'Lenin and Philosophy' is perhaps Althusser's most emblematic text, encapsulated in the definition of philosophy as the 'emptiness of a distance taken': a magnificent formula that is at the same time untenable. From the 'emptiness of a distance taken' to the 'class struggle in theory' is doubtless only one step. But it is a step that crosses the abyss separating Althusser from himself. For if the question of the guarantee is at the heart of Althusser's thought, it is because it is not only epistemological, but perhaps above all ontological; and because Althusser is torn between an ontology of the void and an ontology of the plenum.[52] And here we must

---

[51] Althusser 1966, p. 122. This passage is extracted from one of the versions of a kind of manual on the principles of Marxism and the 'union of theory and practice', which is itself a reworking of a duplicated text, 'Theory, Theoretical Practice and Theoretical Formation. Ideology and Ideological Struggle', dated April 1965. The 1966 version is virtually identical to that of 1965, apart from the addendum on 'political partisanship', which simultaneously changes everything and nothing.

[52] See Matheron 1997.

at least evoke one of the most disquieting aspects of Althusser's thought: his relationship to the Stalinist corpus. A simple overview of the reception of Althusser's writings immediately confronts us with a paradox. On the one hand, their publication was received as a manifesto for freedom – very precisely as what Althusser himself called a 'left critique of Stalinism'.[53] On the other hand, however, Althusser was perceived by others – and sometimes by the same people – as a restorationist. This accusation was directed at him by a few representatives of the enlightened Right, such as Raymond Aron defining the Althusserian enterprise thus: 'how to restore a *fundamentalism* after de-Stalinization and the relative success of neo-capitalism?'[54] – and, what is more, a fundamentalism for philosophy *agrégés* at the École normale supérieure. But it was mainly formulated by internal enemies. Althusser, and the Althusserians with him, were thus attacked by an increasingly important fraction of the revolutionary movement, and particularly by some of his former students who had become Maoists,[55] as an agent for the restoration of order delegated, or at least used, by the Communist Party. And he was, in addition, widely seen as a neo-Stalinist, both by the totality of anti-Stalinist revolutionary groups and by an important section of the 'international Communist movement' – the section explicitly targeted by Althusser's polemic against humanism.[56] If this criticism is disconcerting for anyone who compares the Althusserian dialectic with Stalinist 'diamat', it cannot for all that be reduced to a sheer aberration. Althusser always claimed never to have been a Stalinist. If the claim can only induce a smile today,[57] it does not thereby invalidate the idea that Althusserianism represented a 'left critique of Stalinism'.

---

[53] Even if the formula puts us rather too much in mind of the illusion, shared by many Althusserians, that Maoism represented a 'left critique' of Stalinism, it should not be situated on the same level. In the latter case, it was a question of reconciling a hypothetical practical critique of Stalinism by the Chinese Communist Party with its rejection of any theoretical critique.

[54] Aron 1969, p. 85.

[55] See, for example, Rancière 1974.

[56] It is impossible to give an account here of the precise tenor of these debates, in which the most 'humanist' were often the most virulent former Stalinists – which largely explains Althusser's characterisation of the 'Stalininian deviation' as the 'economism/humanism pair'.

[57] To be convinced, it is sufficient to read the writings of the young Althusser in Althusser 1997.

A reading of the texts published by Althusser[58] nevertheless dictates caution. In *For Marx*, he continued to offer discrete but nevertheless real praise to Stalin, who had had the great merit of eliminating the negation of the negation from the 'laws of the dialectic'. And he went much further in 1967, in a text entitled 'On Theoretical Work', which subsequently completely disappeared from view:

> A discourse like Stalin's little treatise (on dialectical and historical materialism)... treats its object by a pedagogical method. It expounds the fundamental principles of Marxism clearly, and in a generally correct manner. It offers the essential definitions, and above all makes the essential distinctions.... But it exhibits the great defect of *enumerating* the principles of Marxism, without demonstrating the necessity of their 'order of exposition' (Marx) – that is to say, without demonstrating the internal necessity that links these principles, these concepts.[59]

While we must take into account an element of coquetry here, an ambiguous wink to the French 'Marxist-Leninist' groups, and political provocation towards Communist Party leaders, it is impossible to make do with such an explanation. For this type of reference, which in Althusser always assumes the aspect of a *coup de force*, in fact functions as an ontological indicator. It abruptly asserts that, over and above all the ruptures, commencements and recommencements, the end of all guarantees, we are still, despite everything, in the horizon of the guarantee. The text that has just been quoted was initially intended to serve as a preface to a manual of Marxism-Leninism that was reworked several times, on the basis of the duplicated instalment 'Theory, Theoretical Practice and Theoretical Formation. Ideology and Ideological Practice' of April 1965. This is a fascinating work for anyone who reads it, for in it we witness the transition from one conception of philosophy to another, via the temporary notion of a philosophy 'of a scientific character': neither a science nor something different from science. A gripping work, in which the imperative of a theoretical formation, indispensable for ensuring the correctness of what the Communist tradition called 'ideological struggle', leads

[58] Not to mention an unpublished work like 'La reproduction des rapports de production', today available in Althusser 1995b.

[59] Althusser 1990, p. 53.

Althusser to produce a concept that is difficult to integrate as such into his own problematic – 'ideology of a scientific character':

> For the first time in history, we can thus be present at the birth of a radically new phenomenon: the constitution of a *transformed* ideology, because *produced by the action of scientific principles* on existing ideology: the constitution of a new ideology that is ideological in its *form* and increasingly scientific in its *content*.[60]

But a desperate work, like all the other Althusserian projects of this kind, in that it aims to compete with Stalinist 'diamat' on its own ground: that of an ontology of the working class and the party. On this ground, obviously, Althusser was defeated from the outset.

In the image of his own life, Althusser constructed his whole *œuvre* in the dimension of catastrophe. For better or worse, he always saw to it that his concepts are undermined from within by their opposites, and thus constantly threatened with immediate collapse. At the end of this trajectory, there remains something like a incredible tension of the concept, characteristic of a style unlike any other – or rather, of one of Althusser's styles. For there were in fact several styles, bound up with projects that everything in a sense separates and yet unites. If the real catastrophe supervened when the violence of the ontology of the party asserted itself, the tension of the concept is never very far off. Conversely, when the tension of the concept is asserted, the violence of the ontology is always subjacent. Althusser can at one and the same time write *Reading 'Capital'* and 'Theory, Theoretical Practice and Theoretical Formation', *Reply to John Lewis* and *Machiavelli and Us*. He can simultaneously practice symptomatic reading and reading at sight. At all events, the theoretician of the purity of the concept always wrote under the régime of the impurity of the concept.

---

60 Untitled manual on the principles of Marxism (1966–7), IMEC archives, p. 121.

Chapter Twenty-Eight

Marxism Expatriated: Alain Badiou's Turn[1]

Alberto Toscano

> If there is a crisis of Marxism, it is the crisis of a politics, of a politics for communism, what we call, strictly speaking, Marxist politics.[2]

Marxist origins and post-Marxist chimeras

Much of today's radical political theory is the offspring of a crooked dialectic of defeat and reinvention. Many of the defining traits of recent theoretical writings on the Left are obscured if we fail to address how they emerged out of a reckoning with the failure or distortion of Marxist politics, and, moreover, if we disregard the extent to which they often retain an underlying if ambiguous commitment to the Marxist impulse whence they arose. The manner of taking leave from the organisational and theoretical tenets of Marxism, in whatever guise, can speak volumes about the present resources and limitations of contributions to political thought that drew initial sustenance from it. This is certainly the case with the work of Alain Badiou, whose complex relationship

---

[1] An earlier version of this essay appeared in the Belgrade journal *Prelom*. I thank Ozren Pupovac and the editors for the initial stimulus to formulate these arguments, and for their comradeship.

[2] Sandevince 1984c, p. 10.

to his own Maoist militancy and to Marxist theory has recently become the object of rich and detailed investigations, above all in several essays by Bruno Bosteels. Bosteels's characterisation of Badiou's approach in terms of 'post-Maoism'[3] already suggests that Badiou's intellectual biography stands at a considerable remove from the entire 'post-Marxist' tendency, chiefly encapsulated in Laclau and Mouffe's *Hegemony and Socialist Strategy*, and persuasively dismantled in Ellen Meiksins Wood's *The Retreat from Class*.[4] Having said that, the effects of a common 'poststructuralist' theoretical conjuncture, along with a departure from a Hegelian-Marxist preoccupation with dialectics and social ontology, might lead one to suspect that 'the theoretical edifices of Laclau and Badiou are united by a deep homology'.[5] This 'deep homology' – which Slavoj Žižek identifies in the notion of a contingent, subjective rupture of ontological closure (or of any totality) – is nevertheless offset by a fundamental divergence, to the extent that ultimately, Badiou's

> 'post-Marxism' has nothing whatsoever to do with the fashionable deconstructionist dismissal of the alleged Marxist 'essentialism'; on the contrary, he is unique in radically rejecting the deconstructionist doxa as a new form of pseudo-thought, as a contemporary version of sophism.[6]

Rather than either homology, or frontal opposition, it might be more precise then to argue that Badiou's post-Maoism and the post-Marxism of Laclau and his ilk intersect in manners that generate a kind of 'family resemblance', but that, when push comes to shove, they are incommensurable, born of divergent assessments of the end or crisis of Marxism. Their theoretical trajectories connect many of the same dots but the resulting pictures differ radically. In order better to delineate the specific difference of Badiou's project, and of the problems that spurred it on, this chapter will examine the period between the highest speculative product of Badiou's heterodox Maoism, *Théorie du sujet* (1982), and the cornerstone of his mature work, *L'Être et l'événement* (1988), in particular the book *Peut-on penser la politique?*, published in 1985, which is to say contemporaneously with Laclau and Mouffe's *Hegemony*. I claim that

---

[3] Bosteels 2005a. Bosteels's acute analyses of Badiou's political thought will soon be brought together in the book *Badiou and Politics*. See also Badiou's comments on Maoism in a recent interview with Bosteels, Bosteels 2005c, pp. 241–6.

[4] Laclau and Mouffe 1985; Wood 1998.

[5] Žižek 1999, p. 172.

[6] Žižek 1998.

this hitherto underexamined moment in Badiou's theoretical production is rich with insights about the guiding parameters of his further work, but also contributes to a broader reflection on the fraught relationship between contemporary radical political theory and Marxism.[7]

Like many post-Marxists, and indeed anti-communists, Badiou condemns the 'metaphysics' that haunt Marxist politics. In a Heideggerian pastiche, he even describes Marxism-Leninism as the 'metaphysical epoch of Marxist political ontology'.[8] Most deconstructions of the Marxist canon have looked for such a metaphysics in Marx's supposed reductionist economism or in an imaginary constitution of the social, and of class antagonism in particular, whose correlate would lie in the putative transparency of a post-revolutionary polity.[9] While some of these points may be gleaned from Badiou's texts from the mid-1980s, the emphasis is firmly on a conceptual dyad that persists to even greater effect in more recent works like *Metapolitics*. This is the distinction between *politics* and *the political*. At the heart of Badiou's call to counter the supposed crisis of Marxist thought by its 'destruction' and 'recomposition', is the thesis that Marxism has succumbed to the homogenising *political* fiction that imagines the possibility of measuring, anticipating and representing political action. In this regard, '*the political* has never been anything but the fiction which *politics* punctures through the hole of the event'.[10] One's initial impression is of a substantial overlap with Laclau in terms of the notions of working class, proletariat or people as fictions of social cohesion, empty signifiers wherein political action would seek its guarantee. Indeed, the fundamental political fiction for Badiou is that of the 'alliance of the social relation and its measure'.[11] But Badiou does not draw from this the customary post-Marxist lessons regarding the intractable plurality of discursively generated identities and the need for hegemony. He is far from espousing the post-Marxist mix of strategic populism, sociological description, discursive ontology and *de facto* liberalism. Rather, the assault on social fictions and the

---

[7] For further thoughts on the periodisation of Badiou's work, see Toscano 2006a.

[8] Badiou 1984, p. 8; Badiou 1985, p. 61.

[9] See Laclau 1991.

[10] Badiou 1985, p. 12.

[11] As the treatment of the concept of 'state' in *Being and Event* suggests, measure is equated by Badiou to representation. I have dealt with some of the problems incumbent on Badiou's theory of the state – especially the obstacles it poses to a thinking of capital and capitalism – in Toscano 2004b.

suspension of Marxism's foundational commitment to a critique of political economy are viewed by Badiou as the occasions for a renovation, and a kind of *purification*, of the politics of emancipation.

Marxism, according to *Peut-on penser la politique?*, is unable to subject to critique its own critique of political economy,[12] thereby distorting its original political impetus, and binding it to the mediations of economy and society.[13] Marxism's retention of the categories of totality and system is accused of imprisoning the encounter and creation of a politics in the fiction of the political.[14] The political is what occludes the hiatus between state and civil society, representation and presentation. The aim of politics should not lie in the creation of a new bond; the inconsistency of the social does not open onto periodic and formally identical disputes over its content, but on the idea of an autonomy and heterogeneity of politics, which exists at a remove from any relational dialectic:

> [W]hat is dissipated is the thesis of an essence of the relations internal to the city, an essence representable in the exercise of a sovereignty, be it the dictatorship of the slaves, even if the relation is that of civil war within the class structure.[15]

Grasping this theme of detotalisation in Badiou's struggles with Marxism and its social ontology is crucial to an understanding of the development of his later work. Behind the ontology of the multiple of *Being and Event* and the attempt philosophically to establish the basis for a politics of radical equality divorced from any notion of the Whole lies Badiou's experience of, and response to, the crisis of Marxist politics in the 1980s.[16]

So, while there might appear to be a convergence or homology between Badiou and post-Marxist positions around a certain anti-essentialism, what

[12] Badiou 1985, p. 14.

[13] In this regard, Badiou's emphasis in the 1980s on retaining a commitment to 'Marxist politics' should be related to his conviction that the critique of political economy is tributary to a politics of emancipation, or to what he elsewhere calls 'communist invariants' (see Toscano 2004a). On the secondary status of the critique of political economy to Marxist politics, see Badiou 1982, p. 296.

[14] Ibid.

[15] Badiou 1985, p. 13.

[16] Besides the initial meditations on the One and the Multiple in *Being and Event*, perhaps the key text to evaluate Badiou's break with the category of totality is 'Hegel and the Whole', Badiou 2004, pp. 221–32. For a discussion of the possibility of thinking capitalism within Badiou's detotalised ontology, with specific reference to his concept of 'world' from the recent *Logiques des mondes*, see Toscano 2004b.

results from Badiou's own suspicion towards the very idea of a totality of social relations is in a link between (social) inconsistency and (political) events that still seeks to maintains an emancipatory, rationalist reference to transmissible principles and a communist reference to generic equality.[17] The 'destruction' of that political fiction that Badiou diagnoses within 'metaphysical' Marxism is not an opportunity to affirm the pluralism of political struggles, but rather a chance to argue simultaneously for their singularity (as irreducible to a dialectical totality) and their sameness (as struggles for non-domination or equality). Badiou insists, during this period, in writing of the 'recomposition' of Marxism, putting his work under the aegis of 'Marxist politics' because of what he views as the unsurpassable character of the Marxist hypothesis, the hypothesis of a politics of non-domination irreducible to the state. In *Peut-on penser la politique?* we can thus observe, in a quasi-deductive manner, the passage from an internal dislocation of Marxism to the 'metapolitical' thinking of the event that will determine Badiou's further intellectual production: 'the determination of the essence of politics, unable to find a guarantee either in structure (inconsistency of sets, unbinding), nor sense (History does not make a whole), has no other benchmark than the event'.[18]

Minimal Marxism, or, the insistence of equality

Thus, Badiou does not offer an immanent critique of Marxism as a science of capitalism and revolution, but displaces what he regards as core Marxist principles to a dissimilar practical and theoretical framework, where politics and philosophy are 'desutured'.[19] In this transitional period of his work, the aim is to bolster the retention of a minimal Marxism that conjoins the political hypothesis of non-domination with the rational identification of the sites of subversion, without thereby committing political practice to an instrumental, revolutionary or programmatic framework. Such a stress on the subjective element in Marxist politics differs markedly from the post-Marxist preoccupation with subject-positions and the hegemonic reconfigurations of identity. The anti-essentialist discursive ontology of the (empty) social is alien to Badiou,

---

[17] On Badiou's rationalism, see Ray Brassier and Alberto Toscano, 'Aleatory Rationalism', in Badiou 2004.
[18] Badiou 1985, p. 67.
[19] Badiou 1999, pp. 61–8.

whose concern, as demonstrated quite consistently even in more recent books like his *Ethics*, does not lie in the political interplay of identity and difference. Rather, Badiou's thought works at the juncture between, on the one hand, the fact of identity-and-difference as a feature of the status quo, or what he calls the encyclopaedia of knowledges,[20] and, on the other, the production of the Same.[21] Despite the deceptive resonance, this is not to be confused with the two logics of Laclau and Mouffe, differential and equivalential. Why? Because, in the latter, these two logics remain transitive to one another and map out the transcendental horizon of political contention, whilst, in Badiou, the production of sameness in the political field – the production of *equality* rather than *equivalence* – is a real production of *truth* that does not involve the strategic rearrangement and occupation of discourse (what Badiou would call 'the language of the situation'), but requires instead an organised subtraction or separation from its manner of structuring and stratifying our experience of the world.

Instead of shifting from the terrain of classical revolutionary politics, that of (the seizure of) political power, to that of discourse, Badiou's development is marked by the attempt to consolidate and purify the collective subject of politics. In a distinction that would surely strike the likes of Ellen Wood as spurious – to the degree that it circumvents class – for Badiou it is not the state but 'proletarian capacity' that lies at the heart of Marxist politics. Portraying the question of class struggle as a crucial node in the so-called crisis of Marxism, and reflecting on the possibility of a 'party of a new type', Paul Sandevince (a.k.a. Sylvain Lazarus) writes in *Le Perroquet* (the publication of Badiou's group, the UCFML, between 1981 and 1990), that: 'For Lenin, the essential is not struggle, but "antagonism against the entirety of the existent political and social order".' Lenin's declaration is then read as a warning against the logic of the absorption of the party into the state, whilst the 'other path' involves assigning 'the process of politics to the masses/State contradiction grasped in terms of consciousness [*conscience*]'.[22] This is one of the sources

[20] Badiou 2006, pp. 327–43.

[21] Badiou 2001, pp. 25–7.

[22] Sandevince 1984, p. 5. UCFML refers to the 'Groupe pour la formation d'une Union des communistes de France marxiste-leniniste'. In 1985, the UCFML disbanded and was succeeded by L'Organisation politique, a non-party organisation, whose basic theses can be accessed at L'Organisation politique 2001. See Hallward 2003 and Bosteels 2005a for detailed accounts of Badiou's militancy.

of Badiou's own continuing insistence on politics viewed not as strategy for power, or a way of ordering the social, but as an organised practice of *thought* (a 'truth procedure' in the later work). The link between the hypothesis of non-domination, the egalitarian and organised capacity for thought, and a separation from the state thus appears as one of the key tenets of this self-described 'Marxist politics'.

This gives us an inkling as to why the appellations post-Maoism or post-Leninism (the one favoured by the various authors in *Le Perroquet*)[23] are more fitting than post-Marxism. Having already stipulated that Marxist politics is not the *consequence* of a critical analysis of capitalism, but is rather the means, within capitalist conditions, for the production of communism, the direction taken in the 1980s by Badiou and his comrades is primarily born out of the crisis of the Marxist political subject (the party), and not, as with 'traditional' post-Marxism, out of a critique of the metaphysical tenets and sociological shortcomings of Marxism as a science of capitalism. If Badiou's *Théorie du sujet* had declared that the every subject is political and that subject equals party, what is at stake in this period (approximately 1982–8) which hovers between the option for a 'party of a new type' and that of 'politics without a party'?

Fredric Jameson has argued that Marxism *qua* science of capitalism gives rise to post-Marxism at moments of systemic crisis.[24] Whatever the links between such crises and the forms taken by political organisation, for Badiou it is the party *qua* subject which is the focus of the crisis, not the ability of Marxism to cope with the vicissitudes of the mode of production. Indeed, Badiou is rather sanguine about the Marxist understanding of capitalism, and does not seem to think that Marx has really been surpassed in this domain. In any instance, he is immunised against the stance according to which the failure of social ontology or economic analysis would debilitate Marxist politics. He mocks this very possibility in a vicious piece caricaturing the 'old Marxist', the one who waits for the proper study of 'social formations' before acting, who thinks that 'one of these days the "workers' movement" will give us something to talk about'.[25] To the contrary:

---

23 This is argued in particular in Sandevince 1984a.

24 Jameson 1997.

25 Peyrol 1983, p. 5. In *Peut-on penser la politique?*, Badiou puts the point as follows 'Communist politics must be wagered upon: you will never deduce it from *Capital*' (Badiou 1985, p. 87). Of course, it could be argued that far from signalling a caesura,

> Marx starts, absolutely, not from the architecture of the social...but from the interpretation-cut of a symptom of social hysteria, uprisings and workers' parties.... For the symptom that hystericises the social to be thus grasped, without pinning it to the fiction of the political, proletarian political capacity – as a radical hypothesis of truth and a reduction to fiction of every foregoing notion of the political – must be excepted from any approach via the communitarian and the social.[26]

Marxism beyond self-reference

Badiou is renowned today as a philosopher of the event, conceptualised as a drastic break with the status quo and catalyst for new truths and new subjects. But could we speak of events of closure, failure, saturation, and not just novelty and truth? Badiou grounds his treatment of the 'destruction and recomposition' of Marxism in what he calls 'the end of referents', a position presaged by an article by the same title in *Le Perroquet*, penned by Sandevince.[27] To the extent that 'Marxism alone presented itself as a revolutionary political doctrine which, if not historically confirmed...was at least historically active' it cannot evade a reckoning with its concrete incarnations.[28] These are synthesised by Badiou in terms of three primary referents: (1) *the statist referent*: the actual existence of Marxist states, as emblems of the possible victory of a Marxist politics, and of 'the domination of non-domination';[29] (2) *wars of*

this 'long wager' (p. 90) is a feature of Marx's own thinking, which never advocated such a chimerical 'deduction'. See Kouvelakis 2004. The idea of Marxism as promoting a 'deduction' of politics from the critique of *Capital* runs the risk of converging with the 'straw-Marxism' denounced by Wood. See Wood 1998, p. 187.

26 Badiou 1985, p. 20. This rethinking of the notion of capacity, it should be noted, is 'eventally' bound to the Polish workers' movement of the late 1970s and early 1980s. See the section of *Peut-on penser la politique?* precisely entitled 'Universal meaning of the Polish workers' movement', Badiou 1985, pp. 45–8, as well as Lebovici 1983.

27 There is a sense in this article, and others from *Le Perroquet*, of a political 'return to Marx', a (re)commencement of Marx that would sublate the Leninist experience. Sandevince 1984c, p. 10. But see especially UCFML 1983. The whole issue, under the heading 'Un Perroquet-Marx', marking the hundredth anniversary of Marx's death, is devoted to these questions.

28 Badiou 1985, p. 26.

29 Badiou 1985, p. 27. Post-Leninism is thus defined by the break with 'reason of state' in all its forms, a break that draws its sustenance from the founding drive of Marxism itself: 'It is not the State which is the principle of universality of Marxist politics, but rather the communist process in the deployment of class struggles and revolutions'. Sandevince 1984c, p. 10.

national liberation as another emblem of actually victorious Marxist politics, and the 'fusion of the national principle and the popular principle'[30] in the invention of new ways of linking politics and war; (3) *the workers' movement*, especially in its incarnation in 'working-class parties' with an explicit Marxist reference, 'mixed figures of a distant revolutionary Idea and the proximity of an oppositional activity'.[31]

Yet again, it is not the critical or analytical force of Marxism *qua* science of capitalism that is paramount, but the collapse of its specificity as a revolutionary thinking and politics that was historically manifest and fundamentally 'self-referential' – meaning that its manifestations were, to various degrees, homogeneous with its theory. Though Badiou will never repudiate what he calls the 'eternity of communism',[32] what is at stake here is the historicity of Marxism and the impossibility for Marxism to continue to draw any value from its actual history in the present. As Badiou puts it, 'its credit has run out'.[33]

Not only has Marxism lost its historical foothold, it no longer serves as an internal referent for nascent forms of emancipatory politics. This is what is meant by the *expatriation* of Marxism, the key aspect of a crisis which Badiou deems must be 'destructively' traversed – we should recall that for the Badiou of *Théorie du sujet*, the becoming of a subject, and of a proletarian subject especially, is intimately linked to its own destruction, so that the call to be heeded here is for Marxism to truly subjectivise itself, after having gone through the subjective destitution of its referents. In a piece from 1983, Badiou thus declares:

> Today, the referents of Marxist politics are not Marxist. There is a fundamental delocalisation of Marxism. Previously, there was a kind of self-reference, because Marxism drew its general credit from states that called themselves Marxist, from wars of national liberation under the direction of Marxist parties, from workers' movements framed by Marxist unionists. But this referential apparatus is gone. The great mass historical pulsations no longer refer to Marxism, after, at least, the end of the Cultural Revolution

30 Badiou 1985, p. 28.
31 Badiou 1985, p. 29.
32 Badiou 2003, p. 131.
33 Ibid.

> in China: see Poland, or Iran. Therefore, there is an expatriation of Marxism. Its historical territoriality is no longer transitive to it. The era of self-reference is closed. Marxism no longer has a historical home. All the political referents endowed with a worker and popular life are, with regard to Marxism, atypical, delocalised, errant. Any orthodox Marxist today will object that the Polish movement is national and religious, that the Iranian movement is religious and fanatical, that there is nothing there that fundamentally matters for Marxism. And this orthodox Marxism will be nothing but an empty object in the process of the destruction of Marxism.[34]

This theme of expatriation thus permits Badiou to maintain, albeit in a problematic register, the reference to 'worker and popular life', as well as the communist hypothesis of non-domination, in the face of some of the very events that served as grist to the post-Marxist mill.

By thinking in terms of the dislocation of Marxist politics and the tentative invention of new forms of political consciousness, Badiou can turn the political conjuncture of the 1980s – the death throes of historical Communism and the flashes of heterogeneous movements of revolt – into an opportunity for the recomposition of a politics of emancipation.[35] Crucially, this is not done in relation to a return to logics of electoral alliance or the articulation of group demands beyond the working-class referent, but in view of the possibility of a new workers' politics at a distance from the state, a non-classist, non-systemic experience of proletarian capacity. Instead of saluting the vacillation of Marxism as a chance for singing the praises of political plurality, Badiou proposes to seize it as the opportunity for a further purification and consolidation of emancipatory politics. The wager then is to look for the traits of a new politics of anti-statist emancipation in these mass symptoms, these 'hysterias' of the social. Though it transcends the limits of this chapter, it would

---

[34] Badiou 1984, p. 1. Badiou also refers to this issue in terms of the separation of Marxism from the history of the 'Marxisation' of the workers' movement, now that Marxism is no longer 'a power of structuration of real history', meaning that politics may be freed from 'the Marxified [*marxisée*] form of the political philosopheme'. Hence the radical caesura vis-à-vis the previous sequence of Marxist politics, and the proposal of the figure of (re)commencement. See Badiou 1985, pp. 5–9.

[35] Another crucial moment is of course to be registered in the death-knell of the trajectory begun in the Cultural Revolution. See Bosteels 2005a and Badiou's *Le Monde* piece on the trial of the Gang of Four, Badiou 2005a.

be fruitful to follow the attempts – ultimately frustrated by the religious and populist sclerosis of the Polish and Iranian situations – made in *Le Perroquet* to track moments of organisational invention and worker capacity in non-Marxist political scenarios. Contrary to post-Marxism, which welcomes, in the rise of 'new social movements', a radical-democratic pluralism beyond universalist[36] and communist hypotheses, Badiou's post-Leninism is committed, from the 1980s onwards, to producing a metapolitical framework for thinking the persistence of communism as a minimal, universalising hypothesis even in political scenarios where the name 'communism' is anathema.

Of liberals and renegades: between modern and contemporary politics

The requirement that the destruction and recomposition of Marxist politics be internal – dictated neither by its supposed explanatory shortcomings nor by extraneous moral or historical evaluations – is motivated by an appraisal of the subjectivity that dominates the post-revolutionary restoration of the virtues of liberalism and parliamentary democracy.[37] As Badiou provocatively suggested at a recent symposium on *Logiques des mondes*, all of his work can be placed under the sign of a confrontation with the betrayal of emancipatory politics.[38] The peculiarity of the reactive (or renegade) subjects who, from the mid-1970s onwards, publicised the return to liberty on the basis of their own failures derived from their experience of the crisis of Marxism merely as the subjective discovery of an objective fact: the fact of the impossibility of emancipation (the *nouveaux philosophes* are here emblematic). This turn is acerbically crystallised by Badiou in the typical utterances: 'we tried, it was a catastrophe' and 'I fail, therefore I am'. But, for Badiou, all that such failures and disasters prove is that resolute opposition to existent society is a 'difficult' problem. Just like a mathematician who fails in a proof does not thereby

---

36 According to Laclau and Mouffe, 'there is no radical and plural democracy without renouncing the discourse of the universal and its implicit assumption of a privileged point of access to "the truth", which can be reached only by a limited number of subjects.' Laclau and Mouffe 1985, p. 191.

37 Badiou's condemnation of the past two decades as a new post-revolutionary 'Restoration' is summed up in Badiou 2007.

38 On Badiou's understanding of non-emancipatory or anti-universal subjectivities, see Toscano 2006b.

declare as inexistent the problem that proof stemmed from, so a political militant does not make failure into either a necessity or a virtue:

> So that what is presented to us as a conjoined progress of morality (liberating us from the totalitarian phantasm) and of realism (seeing the objective virtues of the existent state of things) is in fact a confession of incapacity. The essence of reneging is incompetence.[39]

Badiou here intervenes directly in the anti-Marxist philosophy of the liberal Restoration, anchored as it is in the defence of the 'negative liberties' at the heart of parliamentary democracy (or capitalist parliamentarianism, as he will later dub it). He repeats the idea of a termination or exhaustion of the Marxist-Leninist sequence, of its specific configuration of political activity.[40] But he contends that antagonism to the status quo is still at the heart of any politics of emancipation. Moreover, a return to the Enlightenment thematic of liberty is simply insufficient, since the question of equality, which determines the '*current* stage of the political question', cannot be evaded. The issue, in wake of what Badiou dubs the Marxist-Leninist 'montage', is how to practise, under the conditions of a non-despotic state, a politics whose axiom is equality: a contemporary politics beyond the modern juxtaposition between the state of right and law (parliamentary constitutional liberal democracy) and tyranny. We cannot turn away from 'contemporary' politics, initially marked by the entrance of the signifier 'worker' into the political field, for the sake of a merely 'modern' anti-despotic politics of liberal democracy. Following Badiou's risky 'de-socialisation' of Marxism, however, equality must not be thought in terms of the equality of 'material positions' ('economistically'), but in strictly political terms. The maxim of equality becomes the following: 'what must the world be such that an inegalitarian statement is impossible within it?'

Using a common Lacanian distinction, Badiou here draws a crucial difference between the modern politics of liberty, which, ever since Saint-Just, functions in a *symbolic* register as a form of non-prohibition, and a contem-

---

[39] Badiou 1987a, p. 2. See also the section in *Peut-on penser la politique?* entitled 'The reactive meaning of contemporary anti-Marxism', Badiou 1985, pp. 48–51.

[40] 'It is certain that [the Marxist] montage is exhausted. There are no longer socio-political subjects, the revolutionary theme is desubjectivated, History has no objective meaning. All of a sudden, the antagonism of two camps is no longer the right projection for global hostility to existing society'. Badiou 1987a, p. 3.

porary politics of equality, whose aim is to engender the *real* impossibility of inegalitarian statements (this will remain the chief trait of Badiou's later concept of the generic). What is surprising here, especially in terms of the earlier commitment to a communist dialectic of destruction, is the idea of a *complementarity* between the politics of liberty and the politics of equality, along with the stipulation of the general problem of equality in 'times of peace', as detached from the revolutionary problematic of power, war and the state. As Badiou writes: 'under the general conditions of a non-despotic state, how can one think and practise a politics whose overarching philosophical category is equality?'[41] A politics of equality, in this framework, works *within* the symbolic politics of prohibition for the sake of an equality that is real but which the symbolic order relegates to impossibility (Badiou's position repeats here the Lacanian link between the Real and the impossible).

Two problematic consequences ensue from these considerations. The first is that politics cannot be primarily or directly concerned with the betterment of the polity itself, for 'politics must be thinkable as a conjoined excess over the state and civil society, even if these are good or excellent'.[42] The second lies in the implicit suggestion that the politics of emancipation, having rescinded the project of power (in short, the dictatorship of the proletariat) is externally conditioned ('in times of peace') by a kind of liberal frame. We can register here the entire ambiguity of Badiou's later conception of 'politics at a distance from the state'[43] – a position that maintains the antagonism against 'existing society' and, to an extent, the problem of how to change it, but combines this seemingly stark antagonism with the toleration of the symbolic framework provided by the very same society: 'We therefore continue to demand modern freedom (symbolic according to non-prohibition) from within which we work towards contemporary equality (real, according to the impossible)'.[44] Is this to say that Marxist politics can only persist from within a liberal envelope? Can we 'reformulate *from within politics* the synthetic vision of the backwards and nefarious character of our society and its representations' and maintain the 'difficult' problem of 'changing existing society', if we do not unequivocally pose and seek to resolve the problem of the tension between liberty

41 Ibid.
42 Badiou 1985, p. 20.
43 Badiou 2005b, pp. 150–1.
44 Badiou 1987a, p. 3. See also Badiou 1992, p. 248.

(in the state) and equality (in politics), together with their mediation by issues of power, authority and, most importantly, exploitation? To put it otherwise, can a post-Leninist radical politics of equality really afford to be post-revolutionary?

Towards a refutation of political idealism

At times, Badiou's 1980s 'expatriation' of Marxism, which already presupposes a disarticulation of Marxist politics and the Marxist critique of political economy, seems to dissolve the consistency of the Marxist project, casting doubt on the very possibility of holding onto the term 'Marxism'. After all, will not Badiou, in *Metapolitics*, peremptorily declare that *'Marxism doesn't exist'*,[45] in the sense that its political instances – its 'historical modes' to use Lazarus's terminology – are absolutely inconsistent, non-totalisable? And yet, throughout the 1980s, prior to the publication of *Being and Event*, Badiou retains the liminal validity of the notion of 'Marxist politics', at least in the sense that it is only by rigorously undergoing its destruction (and not its ironic deconstruction) that a new politics of emancipation will be 'recomposed'. What is at stake in this retention, *in extremis*, of the name of Marxism? If anything, the now moribund anglophone vogue for post-Marxism was driven by a rejection of the articulation between social class and revolutionary politics, which reduced the idea of the proletariat to a mere contested and hegemonically posited identity among others. Yet again, despite surface similarities, the move beyond class operated by Badiou and his cohorts is based on a political judgement, that is on the idea of a lost efficacy of the 'classist' mode of politics (dominated by the category of contradiction, and the transitivity between society and politics).[46] Badiou thus declares that there are more things in the crisis of Marxism than anti-Marxism can dream of – in the main because anti-Marxism merely registers an objective crisis without being able to think through its primary, subjective aspect.[47] Moreover, while Badiou is forthright about the exhaustion of the working class as a *socio-political* class (making no

[45] Badiou 2005, p. 58.
[46] See Lazarus 2005.
[47] Badiou 1985, p. 51.

such claims for the end of social class *per se*), he is equally insistent that no emancipatory politics can bypass workers.

This plea for a minimal Marxism can be observed in two steps. The first involves what Badiou, explicitly harking back to the Kant of the *Critique of Pure Reason*, calls a 'refutation of idealism'. If Marxist politics is detached from the social as the 'place of bonds [*le lieu des liens*]', what prevents the kind of idealist pluralism according to which any site and any subject, unbound from the requirements of transitivity with an ordered and ontologically grounded social structure, can be the locus or bearer of emancipation? Badiou is very aware that, having abandoned a dialectics of social latency and political subjectivation, he cannot depend on the 'substantial presupposition' of a political privilege of workers. Yet he knows that a maximal interpretation of his political axiomatic could lead to viewing the emergence of a political subject as possible at any point in the social field, as in the pluralist 'idealism' of most post-Marxist theories. To counter this prospect, Badiou proposes the minimal inscription of the egalitarian wager-intervention on an event in what he calls 'pre-political situations'.[48] Whilst this minimal, anticipatory interregnum between politics and the social does not allow a pre-emptive *construction* of political subjectivity (for instance, the party of the working class), it permits, by analogy with Kant, a merely negative *reductio ad absurdum* of the maximal claim of political contingency (namely, that any subjects can arise anywhere).

Forbidding himself any substantive resort to social ontology, Badiou nevertheless wishes to argue that to evade 'worker singularities' in the formation of a political subject would be to suppose that a politics of emancipation could deploy itself without including in its trajectory any of the places or points inhabited by the dominated. Whence the following 'theorem':

> Political intervention under current conditions ... cannot strategically avoid being faithful to events, whose site is worker or popular. Let us suppose that it can ... it would follow that this politics could deploy itself without ever including in its immediate field places where the mass (whatever its number) of the dominated ... materially exists, i.e. in factories, in the estates

---

48 'I call *pre-political situation* a complex of facts and statements in which the collective involvement of worker and popular singularities is felt, and in which the failure of the régime of the One is discernable'. Badiou 1985, p. 76.

> in the *banlieues*, in immigrant housing, in the offices of repetitive IT work. Especially if we consider factories, the exception would be radical, since we can easily establish that factories are separated from civil society and from the moderating laws that sustain its social relations. According to this supposition, the politics of non-domination would only exist, for the dominated themselves, in the form of representation, since no event giving rise to an intervention would include them in terms of its site.[49]

The point is not simply that an emancipatory politics must include the lowest rungs, the excluded, the oppressed, but that they and their 'site' must be directly involved – in other words 'presented' – by the emergent political subject. Otherwise, we remain at the level of state representation. So, this refutation of idealism does not simply attack (or literally reduce to absurdity) the 'new social movements' ideology according to which emancipation may take place anywhere, anytime, by anyone. It also undermines any notion that the dominated may be *represented* in a political *programme* without partaking of political action themselves. It is moving from this idea of a pre-political 'site', and warding off both an idealist pluralism and any kind of 'speculative leftism',[50] that Badiou will then seek to provide a metaontological solution to these problems of Marxist politics in *Being and Event*, showing the extent to which his major work remains anchored in the concepts and orientations hatched in the period of his turn away from Marxism-Leninism.

From the hidden abode of production to the factory as event-site

Starting from the refutation of anti-worker political idealism, Badiou initially develops his theory of the event-site – a crucial component of his mature philosophy – in terms of the factory and of the worker as the subjective figure of politics. This is the second step, as it were, in the argument for a Marxist politics that would be capable of surviving its own metaphysical destitution. In 'The Factory as Event-Site', a text published in *Le Perroquet* in 1987 and originally intended for inclusion in *Being and Event*, we encounter both a potent distillate of Badiou's overall doctrine and his last explicit attempt to defend

[49] Badiou 1985, pp. 81–2.
[50] See Bosteels 2005b.

a notion of Marxist politics.[51] My arguments hitherto have sought to demonstrate the internal theoretical and political necessity leading to this work on the event-site and, in so doing, to show how Badiou's intimate confrontation with Marxism is at the very foundation (albeit a vanishing one, since he eventually chose to omit this 'example' from his major work) of the project crystallised in *Being and Event*, and more recently prolonged in *Logiques des mondes*.

Far more than any of the other texts in *Le Perroquet*, this excised fragment of *Being and Event* pleads for a return to Marx (and Engels), leaving aside the matter of post-Leninism. Badiou puts his meta-ontological and metapolitical investigation under the aegis of two conceptual inheritances of the Marxian thinking of worker politics, which the attempt to 'recompose' a Marxist politics seeks to weave together. These are *the void*, which in the Marxist apparatus is connected to the specificity of the proletarian subject (having nothing to sell but his labour-power, the proletarian is the bearer of a generic capacity), and *the site*, which Badiou links to Engels's inquiries into the localised conditions according to which exploitation is organised and countered. In a pithy declaration, Badiou defines his philosophical undertaking precisely in terms of a different articulation, a different dialectic, of these two terms, one that moves beyond the 'fictions' of orthodox Marxism:

> at the very heart of the objectivist version of the necessity of a worker reference, we encounter two terms, the void and the site, which as we will see only acquire their full meaning once we decentre them toward the subjective the vision of politics.[52]

By asserting that a political event can only take place if it takes into account the factory as event-site, Badiou aims to provide a kind of minimal objectivity (that is, another refutation of idealism) *without* making the intervention of politics and of political subjectivation transitive to a socio-economic dynamic. As he puts it:

> The paradoxical statement I am defending is finally that the factory... belongs... to the socio-historical presentation (it is counted-as-one within it), but not the workers, to the extent that they belong to the factory. So that the

[51] Badiou 1987b.
[52] Ibid.

> factory – as a workers' place – is not *included* in society, and the workers (of a factory) do not form a pertinent 'part', available for State counting.[53]

This is the sense in which the factory is not the hidden abode of a production that could be reappropriated and disalienated, but a pre-political site 'at the edge of the void' (at the edge of the unpresented fact of domination), into which politics can intervene. The correlate of this notion is that the (proletarian) void itself is detached from an expressive logic of (dis)alienation and reconnected to the notion of a production of the Same, a production of communism no longer immanently bound to a communism of production.[54] It is on the basis of the speculative trajectory laid out in 'The Factory as Event-Site' that Badiou can then reassert his (contorted, heterodox, errant) fidelity to Marxism:

> Reduced to its bare bones, Marxism is jointly the hypothesis of a politics of non-domination – a politics subtracted from the statist count of the count – and the designation of the most significant event sites of modernity, those whose singularity is maximal, which are worker sites. From this twofold gesture there follows that the intervening and organised experimentation of the hypothesis must ceaselessly prepare itself for the consideration of these sites, and that the worker reference is a feature of politics, without which one has *already* given up subtracting oneself from the State count. That is the reason why it remains legitimate to call oneself a Marxist, if one maintains that politics is possible.[55]

To the extent that Badiou's subsequent work remains more or less wholly consistent with the research programme exposed in this 1987 article, we could consequently hazard to read it as an attempt to think Marxism 'reduced to its bare bones'.

By way of conclusion, I would like to touch on two problems that are especially acute in this phase of Badiou's thought and which might be seen to resonate with some of his more recent work. The first concerns the manner in which Badiou remains faithful to a certain Marxian intuition about prole-

[53] Ibid.

[54] On the question of the transitivity between society and the political, and the distinction between the communism of production and the production of sameness (or production of communism), see Toscano 2004.

[55] Badiou 1987b.

tarian subjectivity and its political vicissitudes. Badiou, after all, defines the continuity-in-separation between the legacy of Marx and his own recomposition of Marxism as follows: 'we (re)formulate the hypothesis of a proletarian political capacity'.[56] However, the refutation of idealism and maintenance of the 'worker reference' in other texts seems to demand the evacuation of any pre-political subjective privilege accorded to workers *per se* (politics must touch on their sites, but they are not latent political subjects *qua* workers). Can the void of the situation be equated with a political capacity? And if this capacity is only the retroactive effect of a post-evental intervention (the politicisation of the factory axiomatically prescribes that 'workers think') is the term 'capacity' really viable, considering its inescapable links to notions of disposition and potential and to the theory of (dis)alienation? I would suggest that Badiou's philosophical conceptualisation of the concept of the generic in *Being and Event* may be read as an attempt to transcend the tensions in his earlier 'Marxist politics' by maintaining the link between the void, equality and the subject but dispensing with any latency whatsoever.[57]

The second problem concerns the impetus behind emancipatory politics. Badiou obviously wishes to purify and politicise the concept of equality, sever its dependence on merely material criteria. But, in his allergy to the socialising fictions of orthodox Marxism, he appears to step back from contemporary criteria of politics to merely modern ones by framing his entire vision of Marxist politics in terms of the politico-philosophical concepts of exclusion, domination and representation. In a manner that is perhaps most obvious in the section on the 'ontology of the site' in 'The Factory as Event-Site', Badiou seems to deny the possibility that the concept of *exploitation* may be an uncircumventable touchstone of any contemporary politics. As I have suggested elsewhere, the difference between a politics at a distance from the state and a politics against capital might lie in the fact that the latter cannot be encompassed by the question of representation, to the extent that capitalist power, while reliant on mechanisms of representation, also works 'directly' on singularities themselves, in ways that cannot be easily mapped in terms

---

[56] Badiou 1984, p. 8.

[57] At the same time, I think that Badiou's farewell to political anthropology may be somewhat premature. For an initial statement of this problem, see Power and Toscano 2003. See also Power 2005.

of exclusion, invisibility or domination.[58] This is precisely what is at stake in the concept of value in the critique of political economy, a concept that I would suggest cannot be easily harnessed by the logic of re/presentation and whose links to subjectivity and antagonism cannot be ignored. The resulting (and rather formidable) challenge would be to combine the direct politicisation of exploitation that characterises Marx's own work,[59] with some of the meta-ontological and metapolitical guidelines provided by texts such as 'The Factory as Event-Site'. A traversal of the logic of exploitation and its effects on our thinking of political subjectivity would also allow us to ward off the possibility of an 'aristocratic' solution, distantly reminiscent of Hannah Arendt's republican and councilist advocacy of the autonomy of politics against the disastrous impingements of the 'social question'.[60] This would perforce oblige us to confront head-on one of the most arresting questions raised by Badiou's 'expatriation' of Marxism: is contemporary politics (the politics of positive equality) compatible with the continuation of modern, statist politics (the politics of negative freedom)? Or must it risk being 'anti-modern', and work on equality not just at a distance from, but *against* the state? This is not to suggest that Marx, like a political Odysseus, may soon be repatriated, and that we, faithful Penelopes warding off our post-Marxist suitors, can finally recognise him under unfamiliar garb. More modestly, let us suggest that Badiou's connection between the expatriation of Marxism and the (re)commencement of a Marxist politics under the aegis of the void and the site is a salutary alternative to the quarrels between antiquarian 'old Marxists' and treacherous new liberals, as well as a unique philosophical platform from which to (re)think Marx's politics.

[58] See Toscano 2004b. This article also seeks to delve into the tensions and contradictions in Badiou's conceptualisation of capitalism and his apparent indifference to the critique of political economy.

[59] See Kouvelakis 2004, as well as Massimiliano Tomba's 'Differentials of Surplus-Value', *Historical Materialism* (forthcoming).

[60] Arendt 1963, especially Chapter 6: 'The Revolutionary Tradition and Its Lost Treasure'.

Chapter Twenty-Nine

Revolutionary Potential and Walter Benjamin: A Postwar Reception History

Esther Leslie

Reception context: West Germany, 1968 and after

Assessments of Walter Benjamin's proximity to Marxism alter depending on the where and when of the assessor. For example, in West Germany, following 1968, there was little doubt that Benjamin's work represented a contribution to Marxist scholarship, if an unconventional one. He was also called on as a guide to political praxis. The mobilised students of the late 1960s took their lessons from him in pirate editions. The specifically 1960s' rediscovery of Benjamin by the cadres of social revolt is encapsulated in their image of him with photocopier in one hand and joint in the other. An embellishment of the image might include a Kalashnikov or bomb – Andreas Baader of the *Rote Armee Fraktion* would cite Benjamin in the coming years, for example drawing on 'On the Concept of History',[1] in his 'Letter to the Prisoners' from 1976.[2] Out of this, and sometimes in critical dialogue with it, there were significant neo-Marxist appropriations

[1] Benjamin 2003.
[2] See Markner 1994.

of him too, perhaps most notably in the work of Jürgen Habermas. Habermas's essay 'Consciousness-Raising or Redemptive Criticism', published first in German in 1972 was a keynote statement.[3] It located Benjamin as an exponent of 'redemptive criticism', in contra-distinction to 'ideology-critique' or 'consciousness-raising' criticism. Redemptive criticism had no immanent relationship to political praxis. Habermas's was an effort to wrest Benjamin away from any instrumentalist uses to which the student movement might put him.

Much of the debate of Benjamin's legacy in these years focussed on questions of art and aesthetics, with an emphasis on the relationship between technological reproduction of art (as analysed in Benjamin's 1930s essay 'The Work of Art in the Age of its Technological Reproducibility') and art's autonomy, as forwarded by Adorno in his critical engagement with Benjamin. Under examination was the interpretation of the 'politicisation of art' and the 'aestheticisation of politics', as forwarded by Benjamin in the epilogue of his 'Work of Art' essay. Key texts included Heinz Paetzold's *Neomarxistische Ästhetik* (1974) and Helmut Pfotenhauer's *Ästhetische Erfahrung und gesellschaftliches System* from 1975.[4] Through the 1970s in West Germany, Benjamin was used to establish parameters for Marxist, neo-Marxist or materialist engagement in a highly politicised scholarly field, where the legacy of communist practice and theory from the period prior to the Third Reich was re-discovered, examined and contested.

Bernd Witte's contribution in 1975 analysed Benjamin in relation to his antagonist in the field of literary studies, Georg Lukács.[5] A new 'materialist' literary theory was proposed on the basis of Benjamin's critique of Lukács. Benjamin was seen to provide writers and artists on the Left with a vocabulary for art and culture that did not share the assumptions of the socialist realism with which Lukács was associated. Socialist-realist directives ranked the intelligibility of content above form. At its most basic, socialist realism advised that the content of the picture or the story had to be clear, unambiguous, delivered through 'realist' means and present the inexorable rise of a heroic working class and peasantry. Lukács, in line with socialist realists, advocated nineteenth-

---

3 Habermas 1972.
4 Paetzold 1974; Pfotenhauer 1975.
5 Witte 1975.

century paragons of realist style such as Balzac and Walter Scott. Socialist-realist initiatives recommended the return to traditional forms of oil painting and novel writing. Walter Benjamin's analyses were directed against this course. He was a theorist of modernity. He believed that the modern age had thrown up new modes and media of representation, and, for any contemporary engagement in art, whether overtly political or not, these were forms that needed to be explored. He regretted the way that the development of socialist realism repressed a post-revolutionary wave of technological and formal experimentation in art, restoring old models of culture with their disempowering modes of reception, which expected audiences to stand in reverential awe before 'great works'. Benjamin, largely, though not without qualification, celebrated the progressive function of technical reproducibility in art. He mapped the implications of technological reproduction in art on art production more widely, pinpointing analogies between technological and technical-formal innovation. This work of Benjamin's contributed in the period following the Second World War to a burgeoning critical and media theory, as evinced the work of Hans Magnus Enzenberger with his forwarding in 1970 of the potentially liberatory uses of the photocopier within the ideologically-stultifying 'consciousness industry'.[6]

In addition, for the critical generation of intellectuals after 1968, Benjamin was a role model because of his lack of acceptance by the academic system in his lifetime. Christoph Hering, in his book from 1979, *Der Intellektuelle als Revolutionär*, presented his rendition of Benjamin's thought as written for the students in revolt who were seeking modes of revolutionary praxis, not academic sophistry.[7] Indeed, Benjamin with his paedogogical writings could serve as a guide to the critique of education, as evidenced by two 'pirate-editions' of Benjamin's 'Communist Paedogogy' in 1969 and 1974.[8] Reference was made to Benjamin's explicit attacks in the late 1920s and early 1930s on scholarly investigation as the pursuit of apparently non-committed positions, supra-political commentary and the vague class-unspecified project of freedom and a new human order.

[6] Enzensberger 1970.
[7] Hering 1979, p. 11.
[8] Benjamin 1969 and Benjamin 1974.

From 1972 to 1989, the stakes of Benjamin's legacy were debated thoroughly as volume after volume of the thirteen-part *Collected Works* appeared, replete with expansive scholarly apparatus, omissions, inclusions and editorial steerage. As the aftershock of social movements abated, so too did the use of Benjamin as model for Marxist praxis, though praxis is not necessarily the decisive factor, and Hans-Heinz Holz, who delivered a rare radio lecture on Benjamin in the GDR in the 1960s, noted that Benjamin 'was a speculative metaphysician and *as such* was a Marxist'.[9] By the end of the 1970s and into the 1980s, a strain of melancholy was identified in Benjamin's thought and work. His melancholy was seen to parallel that of a disaffected Left. The more they experienced impotence, the more Benjamin usefully articulated that impotence. Or he was castigated for it as proponent of 'radical chic' and a 'Prussian snob and Jewish melancholic', in Marx-biographer Fritz Raddatz's estimation in 1979.[10]

Through the 1980s and 1990s, Benjamin continued to be attributed to a Marxist milieu, in the main, at least one that stretched to incorporate the neo-Marxist approaches of critical theory – unsurprisingly given the situating of the editorial work on the *Collected Works* under the auspices of the T.W. Adorno archive. Rather than the question of whether Benjamin is a (neo)Marxist, the question arose of the meaning and relevance of Marxism. In 1992, former 'New Leftist' Otto Karl Werckmeister castigated Benjamin's outmodedness for pursuing an 'obsolete' Marxism. Equally, for Werckmeister in his 1997 study *Linke Ikonen. Benjamin, Eisenstein, Picasso – Nach dem Fall des Kommunismus*,[11] Benjamin, the archetypal exile, flipped into an iconic exemplar of the useless and privileged academic, remote from political action, mirroring the ways in which Marxism had accomodated itself to a purely academic stance in West Germany from the 1970s onwards. Benjamin allowed cultural-materialist analysis without real social consequences.[12] In 1992 Bernd Witte likewise distanced himself from Benjamin, under the influence of the 'present historical moment', that moment being 'the catastrophic collapse of Marxism as a factor which determines the course of history', signalling 'the disappearance of the last transcendent goal'.[13]

---

[9] His radio lectures are reworked and developed in Holz 1992.
[10] Raddatz 1979, pp. 183–213.
[11] Werkmeister 1997.
[12] Werckmeister 1992, p. 172.
[13] See Witte 1992.

Such tendencies in the interpretation of Benjamin can be related to the crisis of confidence on the Left in the aftermath of the fall of the Berlin Wall.

Reception context: France and Trotskyism

In France, in contrast, there was a significant reception of Benjamin as a productive political thinker amongst writers of a Trotskyist inflection. Daniel Bensaïd, in *Walter Benjamin: sentinelle messianique. A la gauche du possible*, from 1990, emphasised Benjamin as revolutionary thinker by focussing on the critique of progress in Benjamin's 'On the Concept of History'.[14] A similar undertaking can be found in Michael Löwy's *Walter Benjamin; Avertissement d'incendie – Une lecture des thèses 'Sur le concept d'histoire'*, from 2001.[15] Both authors foregrounded Benjamin's rejection of progress and his warnings about the dangers of barbarism, if the non-guaranteed social revolution is not forthcoming. The resultant Marxism is an 'open' or 'heterodox' Marxism, shed of any determinist elements that have attached to Marx's doctrine. Benjamin's messianism is not seen as contrary to Marxist concepts – and nor indeed is romanticism, which Löwy pinpoints as the third great influence on Benjamin's thought. All three influences offer significant impulses for criticising the present capitalist world and for allowing the imagination of absolute and potentially sudden change. Löwy's approach recombined the conspicuous project of the 'Benjaminiana' of the last quarter-century, which argued that in as much as Benjamin was a Jew, he was less a Marxist. In as much as he is drawn to Marxism he can do so only by wrestling with his Jewishness. With Löwy's analysis, no longer was Benjamin forever torn between the messianic and the materialist.[16] In the early 1990s, Löwy associated Benjamin's stance with liberation theology.[17] Löwy's reading of 'On the Concept of History' likewise built up an association between real political movements and Benjamin's thought. Revolutionary heroes of the oppressed (such as Zapata, Sandino) are discussed in the context of a Benjaminian 'history from below' and collective memory. Löwy responded to the ways in which Benjamin's history always sought the outflow of the past in the present: 'The materialist

[14] Bensaïd 1990.
[15] Löwy 2001.
[16] For one of many examples see the concluding sentiments of Gilloch 1996.
[17] See, for example, Löwy 1992.

presentation of history leads the past to bring the present into a critical state'.[18] Equally, it attempted to open up the possibilities that existed in the past but were missed.

Reception context: the anglophone world from materialism to postmodernism

In English-speaking countries, especially the US, the relationship of Benjamin to Marxism is more contested. Gershom Scholem's presentation of Benjamin in close relation to Jewish mysticism had a significant influence on the manner in which Benjamin was received, certainly in the 1980s, after the publication of Scholem's memoir, *Walter Benjamin; Story of a Friendship*, in the imprint of *New York Review of Books* in 1981.[19] Scholem castigated Benjamin's Marxism as misguided and indeed the weakness to which he ultimately lost his life: he should have chosen Zion, Hebrew and Judaism. Elsewhere, he described Benjamin as 'a theologian marooned in the realm of the profane'.[20] In addition, Scholem perceived Benjamin first and foremost as a metaphysician of language, absorbed in mystical accounts of linguistics, in the tradition of Hamann and Humboldt. Dominant streams in anglophone humanities scholarship in the 1980s and 1990s were able to find productive relationships between Benjamin's language theory and poststructuralist thought, and, subsequently, Heideggerianism. Nevertheless, in the English-speaking world, a variety of scholars have asserted an affinity between Benjamin's method and Marxist approaches in the years following 1968. Indeed Benjamin's initial introduction to a wider British public – as a theorist of mass reproduction in art – occurred through the vectors of Marxism in John Berger's mass-selling book and accompanying TV programme, *Ways of Seeing* (1972).

The match of Benjamin with Berger made sense. Like Berger, Walter Benjamin was not an academic. He tried to make a living as a critic, and, in the Weimar Republic, he broadcast lectures on the radio, frequently for children. Clearly his own life circumstances directed him into the world and questions of popular enlightenment and entertainment. Theorists and practitioners,

---

18 Benjamin 1999a, p. 471.
19 Scholem 1981.
20 Scholem 1976, p. 187.

especially those outside the university (media workers and artists) adopted Benjamin as a left mascot, and a materialist who could recommend directions for cultural production that broke with traditional 'élite' structures. This context could usefully evoke Benjamin's own concern with the changing status of the intellectual and the artist over the period of industrialisation. Several of his major studies tracked the changing fortunes of the artistic and intellectual avant-garde in nineteenth-century France. He wanted to understand the ways in which the avant-garde – originally a rebellious force – is skewered by the contradictions of capital. The failure of social revolution and the inescapable law of the market breed a hardened hoard of knowledge-workers condemned to enter the market place. This intelligentsia thought that they came only to observe it – but, in reality, it was, says Benjamin, to find a buyer.[21] This set off all manner of responses: competition, manifesto-ism, nihilistic rebellion, court jestering, hackery. The 'Work of Art' essay and 'The Author as Producer' (1934) were intended as investigations of the prospects for critical left intellectuals in the modern age, finding strategies that would avoid pressures on artists to be individualistic, competitive and promoters of art as a new religion. Critical and alternative cultural practice in the 1970s and 1980s drew fruitfully on these two texts, which were widely anthologised.

Through the 1980s and 1990s this materialist and paedogogic version of Benjamin was largely overwritten in the UK, replaced by an image of Benjamin inflected by the priorities of feminist and postmodernist scholarship as they have loomed in cultural studies, art history and sociology and visual culture. In the US, in the same period, left-wing interpretations of Benjamin placed him in the context of the Frankfurt school, most notably in the work of Susan Buck-Morss.[22] Otherwise he was and still is drawn into debates within cultural studies, which at its more Marxist articulation takes its cue from Fredric Jameson, who referred to Benjamin in his investigation of the ideological functions of art and the utopian impulses lurking in popular culture in his book *The Political Unconscious: Narrative as a Socially Symbolic Act*.[23] In both contexts, scholars turned increasingly to those aspects of Benjamin's work concerned with consumerism – and the historical home of the consumer, the city.[24] Interest

21 Benjamin 1973, pp. 170–1.
22 See Buck-Morss 1977 and Buck-Morss 1989.
23 Jameson 1981.
24 See Cohen 1993; Marcus and Nead 1999.

shifted away from cultural production and critique towards consumption and commentary. At the height of postmodernism, attempts were made to yoke Benjamin's researches into the urban scene to assaults on Marxist historical materialism via a fascination with consumption.[25] In accentuating consumption, production slid out of view, peculiarly – for Benjamin's curiosity, certainly in the last fifteen years of his life, was directed at questions of production, from questioning determinants on the production of art to the aesthetic demands raised by the Soviet avant-garde practice known as production art to reflections on modes of industrial production and the experience of labour. In his great study of shopping – the *Arcades Project* – consumption is set in relation to the totality of industrial capitalism of which it is a part, along with political movements, technologies, urbanisation and so on.

The arcades are, for Benjamin, a microcosm of historical potential and disappointment, of promise and betrayal. They encapsulate the promises of bountiful provision, of luxury for all, of international contact and exchange. The arcades were swallowed up in the Haussmannisation of Paris. Haussmannisation, a modernisation project inaugurated by Emperor Napoleon III, was the name for the construction of vast boulevards designed to confound barricade-building by rebellious workers and to enable the swift passage of state vehicles from one part of the city to another to quell rioters. Georges Haussmann, appointed as the prefect of the Seine between 1853 and the Emperor's fall in 1870, aimed in his replanning to move the working classes and the poor out of the city centre to the East and to remodel the West for the bourgeoisie. The objective was to flush out the hidden haunts of low-life where bohemia and plotters and politicos had once gathered and in which they had barricaded themselves. For Benjamin, Haussmann was a city-destroyer. Reaching between past and present, he claims: 'Haussmann's work is accomplished today, as the Spanish war makes clear by quite other means'.[26]

By his time of writing, Benjamin's object of study – the Paris arcades – had already become unfashionable, and, in part, obliterated, which makes the *Arcades Project* a piece of history writing in the sense which Benjamin loves best. The ruined hopes of the past – dimly remembered from his own childhood – loom into greater visibility in his historical construction. Benjamin, influenced

---

25 A key statement is McRobbie 1992.

26 Benjamin 1999a, p. 147.

as he was by surrealism, unearths impulses, objects, dreams, wishes and matter that has decayed. Benjamin notes:

> We can speak of two directions in this work: one which goes from the past into the present and shows the arcades, and all the rest, as precursors, and one which goes from the present into the past so as to have the revolutionary potential of these 'precursors' explode in the present.[27]

Arguably, his writings on film and technological culture are also an attempt to redeem or make explode the revolutionary potential of forms, a possibility that inhabits them but is impeded by capitalist relations of production.

In the wake of writing a blurb for the Harvard edition of the *Arcades Project*, former situationist T.J. Clark published a provocatively titled essay in 2003: 'Should Benjamin Have Read Marx?'[28] Here, he articulates the position, as he sees it, of a number of scholars and indeed acquaintances of Benjamin who saw the influence of Marxism on his work, specifically *The Arcades Project*, as detrimental. Marxism, it is said,

> muddied, multiplied, and mechanized the project's original outlines; so that finally, essentially, Marxism can only be seen as a cancer on Benjamin's work – on what should have become the last and greatest of surrealist grapplings with the nineteenth century, a settling of accounts with all the mad dreams of Grandpa and Grandville and Victor Hugo.[29]

Clark is not fully identified with this position, but finds a mode of distancing Benjamin from any close engagement with Marxism:

> No doubt the de-Marxification of Benjamin is annoying. But it would be playing into the hygienists' hands simply to reverse their emphases and exclusions, and replace one cardboard cutout with another. A 'Red Benjamin' to fight it out with 'Benjamin, Prophet of the Holocaust' or 'Benjamin, the Father of Cultural Studies'? God forbid. I believe the fairest verdict on Marxism as a mode of thought in the Paris book is that it is pervasive, vital, and superficial.[30]

---

[27] Benjamin 1999a, p. 862.
[28] Clark 2003.
[29] Clark 2003, p. 31.
[30] Clark 2003, p. 41.

Clark's evidence of this is that Benjamin's reading in Marxism came from introductions and anthologies, and that he copied out 'hoary' passages from 'Marxist scripture', and this 'like a slow learner kept after school'. His skimming was productive but remains only a surface-glance. The advantage of superficiality was, according to Clark, that he remained immune from both 'High Stalinism' and 'Frankfurt school' method. Still, Clark concedes that Benjamin's reading in Marxism deepened as the 1930s progressed and there are particular ways in which Marxism is generative. The Marxist concept of abstract labour-power comes to be crucial: the nineteenth century is presented as a society in which abstraction and the 'forced equivalence of the unequal'[31] is ever more prominent. Furthermore, Benjamin enhances Marxism by his critical intervention. Breaking towards the end of his life with a certain seduction by the commodity and the class-neutral idea of a 'collective consciousness' in which the utopian dreams of progress are embodied in the commodity-clutter of arcades and department stores, Benjamin wakes up to the negative side of historical movement and Marxism is all the better for it. Clark quotes from the *Arcades Project*:

> It may be considered one of the methodological objectives of this work to show what a historical materialism would be like which has annihilated within itself the idea of progress. Just here, historical materialism has every reason to distinguish itself from bourgeois habits of mind.[32]

One of the main impulses of Benjamin's work in his final years is to present a 'dark, inconsolable history of the proletariat',[33] which breaks with any sort of automatic idea of progress ensured by technological advance and by the diffusion of enlightenment ideals, as much as by the intervention of the Party which is to guarantee redemption.

While aspects of Clark's analysis are helpful, it does not accurately represent Benjamin's full engagement with Marxism and it operates with a peculiarly scholastic notion of what it means to understand and apply Marxist methodology. A glance at Benjamin's biography fills in some details and shifts the debate such that Marxism might be understood also as something like a field of possibility, and not simply something to be pursued academically.

---

31 Clark 2003, p. 46.
32 Benjamin 1999a, N 2:2. Cited in Clark 2003, p. 43.
33 Ibid.

The biographical context: did Benjamin read Marx?

It is certainly the case that Benjamin encountered communism before he encountered Marxism. Benjamin's first met Scholem in 1915 at a lecture by the socialist Kurt Hiller and at a subsequent meeting Scholem gave Benjamin a copy of the first issue of Rosa Luxemburg and Franz Mehring's journal *Die Internationale: Zeitschrift für Theorie und Praxis des Marxismus*, which Benjamin thought 'excellent'.[34] From this point on, Benjamin remained in contact with the theoretical field of communist ideas. Both men also had some exposure to what activism might mean, at least for others. Scholem's brother, Werner, and Benjamin's brother, Georg, were leading communists in the 1920s. Benjamin's next major encounter with communist thought aped that of a number of his generation. Escaping an expensive existence in Berlin in 1924, in Capri he read the most important book for his generation of disaffected intellectuals, Georg Lukács' *History and Class Consciousness*. He was impressed by Lukács's philosophically adroit combination of theory and practice and he was drawn to the 'political praxis of communism' as a 'binding position', though he knew that there must come tensions between Lukács' Hegelian dialectics and what he conceived as his own tendency towards nihilism.[35] On that same sojourn he met Asja Lacis. A letter to Scholem mentioning this 'most remarkable acquaintance' described her as a Bolshevik Latvian, a gentile, who acted and directed, and with whom he chatted long into the night.[36] His next letter to Scholem repeated the news – he told of meeting a Russian revolutionary from Riga, 'one of the most outstanding women' he had ever met.[37] He also noted that through her he had gained an 'intensive insight into the actuality of a radical communism', a 'vital liberation', even though it disturbed his work and his 'bourgeois rhythm of life'. In practical terms, Lacis provided a context for his developing thought. Through her, prospects opened of publication in Moscow and a dialogue with the Soviet intelligentsia.[38] From Benjamin's perspective, further engagement with Marxism and Marxist scholarly method promised a context for his work. In late May 1925 Benjamin wrote to Scholem about his miserable financial circumstances and the 'deeply

---

34 Benjamin 1995a, p. 271.
35 Benjamin 1995b, p. 83.
36 Benjamin 1995b, p. 466.
37 Benjamin 1995b, p. 473.
38 Benjamin 1995b, p. 483.

deplorable collision of literary and economic plans'. He noted that if his journalistic efforts turned sour he would 'probably accelerate' his

> involvement in Marxist politics and – with the view in the foreseeable future of going to Moscow at least temporarily – join the party.[39]

In 1926, domiciled in Paris, he continued to apprise himself of current Marxist debates. His small Paris library, he noted, was 'mainly composed of communist things'.[40] He read Trotsky's *Where Is England Going?*' He followed the controversy unleashed by Lukács's *History and Class Consciousness*, with critical contributions from Rudas and Deborin[41] and he enthused over the debates initiated by Bogdanov and Bukharin on a 'general Tectology', or the universal science of organisation, which considered the commonalities in the human, biological and physical systems. Benjamin was intrigued by this 'fragmentary first attempt at a Marxist universal history'.[42] It was at this time that he managed to get a commission to write 300 lines on Goethe 'from the standpoint of Marxist doctrine' for the New Great Russian Encyclopaedia.[43]

At the end of 1926 he went to Moscow to be by the side of an ailing Lacis. Another motive was to witness life under the Communist Party. The end of the 1920s saw ferocious struggles over official economic, social, political and cultural positions. The opposition was experiencing its final but vigorous gasps and it was clear to Benjamin that 'the restoration' had begun and 'militant communism' was being suspended.[44] Criticisms of the Soviet Union made joining the Communist Party undesirable. Benjamin continued however to engage in debate with communists and he published in communist journals such as *Das Wort*. He spent much time with Bertolt Brecht, who to an extent shared his interest in and critical stance towards Soviet Communism. Through Brecht, Benjamin met the Marxist Karl Korsch.

On various occasions Benjamin had to defend his method. For example, in a letter to the Swiss critic Max Rychner, on 7 March 1931, Benjamin agreed with Rychner that his work had nothing in common with philistine communist approaches, but he was concerned, however, to emphasise that his own

---

39 Benjamin 1995c, p. 39.
40 Benjamin 1995c, p. 133.
41 Lukács 2000.
42 Benjamin 1995c, p. 134.
43 Benjamin 1995c, p. 133.
44 Benjamin 1986, p. 53.

position also relied on materialist insight. His path to a materialist conception came not from communist brochures but rather through the best bourgeois studies in literary history and criticism of the last twenty years. Even before his closer acquaintance with Marxist method, he had worked dialectically, and cited his book on baroque tragic drama as example. But what he did not know at the time of its composition, though it became clearer soon after, was that 'from my very particular position on the philosophy of language, there exists a relay – however strained and problematic – with the viewpoint of dialectical materialism'.[45] This was because he strove to focus his thought always on those objects in which truth was most compacted, which meant 'not the 'eternal ideas', not 'timeless values', but there where historical study ushers in cotemporary revelation.[46] He disassociated his thought from 'the Heidegger School', with their 'profound circumlocutions of the realm of ideas', in order to place himself closer to the 'scandalous and coarse analyses' of the Marxist Franz Mehring, who, like him, sought in literature 'the true state of our contemporary existence'. He also conceded that he had

> never been able to research and think other than in, if I might say it in this way, a theological sense – namely in accord with the Talmudic teaching of the 49 levels of meaning in every passage of the Torah.[47]

But the recognition of the 'hierarchies of meaning' was more present in the most clichéd communist platitudes than in the apologias of bourgeois profundity.[48]

Debate on what being a Marxist might mean continued through the 1930s as he engaged in more or less defensive argument with representatives of the Institute for Social Research, in the pages of whose journal he wished to place various projects. As Clark suggests, Benjamin's self-stated aim in this time was to contribute to and enhance Marxist method, which had blind spots. He agreed, for example, at one point, with Adorno's criticism of some preparatory work on the *Arcades Project*. While the project had to be secured against Marxist objections, it had to be acknowledged that it attempted something new, namely the 'genuine abandonment of the idealist image of history with

[45] Benjamin 1995d, p. 18.
[46] Benjamin 1995d, p. 19.
[47] Benjamin 1995d, p. 20.
[48] Benjamin 1995d, pp. 19–20.

its harmonising perspective', a harmonising that Marxists too might carry out.[49] Benjamin's was a history told from the perspective of ruination, including the ruination of old models. Refinement of his Marxist understanding was a task for the summer of 1935. It was now that he informed Adorno that he had begun to read the 'alp grey' mass of Marx's *Capital*, Volume One.[50] As Clark suggests, this is late in his life and scholarly development. But it is to be understood against the backdrop of many years of more personal engagement and encounters with communism and communists, inside and outside the CP, as well as reading other relevant figures such as Trotsky, to whom he returned in 1932 and 1933.[51] Benjamin's famous 'Work of Art' essay from the mid-1930s and his proposed lecture for a communist circle 'The Author as Producer', from 1934, were investigations into the prospects for contemporary critical-left culture workers. He examined strategies that would avoid the pressures on artists to be individualistic, competitive or promoters of art as a new religion or an evasion of the 'political'. He evaluated artists' efforts to work out cultural forms that could not be recuperated by fascism. He assessed what the new mass cultural forms – radio, film, photography, photomontage, worker-correspondent newspapers – meant in the wider scheme of the social world, and how facts such as mass reproduction change humans' relationship to culture of the past and the present. Such work contributes extensively to Marxist aesthetics.

Heterodoxy in context

Benjamin's final 'testament', the theses on the concept of history, have been read as a signal of disillusion with the Left and resignation from efforts to change the world. However, others have approached these as the attempt to compose Marxist materialist theory in a tremendously violent world, during the ghastliest days of working-class defeat. Benjamin is, indeed, dispirited, for, at the moment of writing, the proletariat is not proving itself to be the struggling, conscious class. The German working class has been corrupted by the opinion, promoted by Social democracy, that it is they who were swimming with the

49 Benjamin 1995e, p. 109.
50 Benjamin 1995e, p. 111.
51 Benjamin 1995d, p. 92.

stream of technological development.[52] In fact, the world working class has been sold down the river, and split apart through fascism and nationalism. And revolutionaries have allowed their energies to be sapped in strategic deals and misplaced alliances. 'On the Concept of History' is Benjamin's reckoning with social democracy, Stalinism and bourgeois thought, none of which have been able to prevent the disaster of fascism. Social democracy had engaged in deals with the political establishment and with capital, just as the Communist Parties entered into a pact with Hitler. There is reason for despair – despair is not a result of Benjamin's tragic disposition, as Scholem and others suggested. It is objective. But the theses offer hope too, or at least they attempt to formulate a way of thinking that may be of use for a revived revolutionary practice. Benjamin is clear: 'The subject of historical knowledge is the struggling, oppressed class itself.'[53] Just as in the analysis of reproducible art, the accent is on the mass as active participants in their culture and history. And he adds that, in Marx, this last enslaved class is the avenger that completes the task of liberation in the name of generations of the downtrodden. Throughout the theses, the emphasis is on the intimate connection between struggle, historical practice, and knowledge, theory. Liberation can come only after breaking with some of the inherited modes of thinking the world in terms of automatic progress, crisis as exception and history as objective unfurling towards an ever-better future that never arrives – modes that could neither foresee nor prevent fascism.

It was just such heterodox thinking – rejecting Communist-Party orthodoxy, rejecting inherited scholastic modes of thinking, rejecting bourgeois analyses – that appealed to a number of Marxist (Trotskyist) thinkers in the UK in the 1980s and after. In the early 1980s, Benjamin's thinking was compared to that of Trotsky. Cliff Slaughter contended that of all the major writers on literature and art who have adhered to Marxism, only Walter Benjamin and Leon Trotsky remained true to the fundamental legacy of Marx.[54] Terry Eagleton's *Walter Benjamin or Towards a Revolutionary Criticism* (1981) attempted to draw some analogies between the literary and historiographical method of Trotsky and Benjamin.[55] This association is reprised very briefly in the conclusion to

52 Benjamin 2003, p. 393.
53 Benjamin 2003, p. 394.
54 See Slaughter 1980.
55 See Eagleton 1981.

his subsequent study, *The Ideology of the Aesthetic*, though not in the chapter on Benjamin, which, reflecting then dominant concerns, is titled 'The Marxist Rabbi'.[56] Some ten years later Esther Leslie made analogies between the two men in her study *Walter Benjamin: Overpowering Conformism*, not only in relation to prognoses and recommendations for art and history writing, but also in terms of a theory of experience.[57] Like Bensaïd and Löwy, Leslie's work joins in the debate over the meaning of Benjamin's final piece of writing, 'On the Concept of History'. Mike Wayne described this effort in a review on the website *Cultural Logic*:

> Leslie effectively recovers what many have read as Benjamin's disillusioned parting of the ways with Marxism, for the authentic revolutionary traditions of Bolshevism. The 'Thesis' is centrally concerned to critique the Stalinist Marxism which holds that there is an objective historical teleology in which the victory of the working class is guaranteed. And it is also concerned to critique Social Democracy which also assumed that historical progress and reform will unfold automatically within the parameters of capitalism. On the eve of the Second World War, these philosophies of history are thoroughly bankrupt. The struggle in the present is also, for Benjamin, a struggle to redeem the forgotten past of its misery, its broken hopes, its waste. Benjamin understands the past 'from the perspective of lost opportunities, now potentially viable.' This concept of redemption is one sense in which Benjamin mobilises the discourse of theology, which others have read as evidence of a burgeoning religiosity to replace his dying Marxism.[58]

A recent European-American contribution to Marxist theory has evoked Benjamin as part of its contemporary re-imagining of the revolutionary project. Michael Hardt and Antonio Negri's *Empire* quotes from Benjamin's 1931 vignette 'The Destructive Character'.[59] The poverty of experience obliges the barbarian to begin anew, that the new barbarian 'sees nothing permanent. But for this very reason he sees ways everywhere'. For Hardt and Negri, the 'new barbarians' ruin the old order through affirmative violence and they propose for the progressive nature of barbarism following the collapse of the

---

56 Eagleton 1990, p. 378.
57 Leslie 2000, pp. 228–34.
58 Wayne 2001.
59 Benjamin 1999b, pp. 541–2.

Soviet Union a migrant barbarian multitude – former 'productive cadres' who desert socialist discipline and bureaucracy in a bid for freedom.[60] Their barbarism manifests in modes of life – their bodies transform and mutate to create new posthuman bodies, fluid both in sexuality and gender ascription, cyborgish and simian, bodies that are 'completely incapable of submitting to command', and 'incapable of adapting to family life, to factory discipline, to the regulations of a traditional sex life'. There is a technological supplement to this. Hardt and Negri write: 'The contemporary form of exodus and the new barbarian life demand that tools become poietic prostheses, liberating us from the conditions of modern humanity.' And these protheses are, according to Hardt/Negri, in a Benjaminian spirit, those of the 'plastic and fluid terrain of the new communicative, biological, and mechanical technologies'. Hardt and Negri's Benjaminian barbarian is misconceived. This fluidity and self-modification, arguably, misapprehends Benjamin's 'positive concept of barbarism', for this relates to art's producers and consumers and is strategic and negational – that is to say it operates in contradictory relation to the points of tension, rather than setting up a parallel utopian existence. Benjamin's positive concept of barbarism has less to do with an effortless prosthetic use of technologies to modify bodies, flowing in the direction of capital's own unfolding and posthuman dreams of immortality. It has more to do with a scornful appropriation of technologies and the techniques they suggest for strategic purposes of representation in pursuit of collective liberation.

Conclusion

Marxism's relationship to Benjamin over the past forty years has been varied, complex and generative. Benjamin's own thinking accounts for this fertile process. One of Benjamin's enduring theoretical contributions involves the question of tradition, legacy, how things – specifically knowledge and the historical past – are handed down. He observed the ways in which the reception of objects or ideas is accented by the ruling political exigencies of the moment. For Benjamin, a historical materialist may be able to evade this pull of dominant ideology. This is what Benjamin meant by the task of the historical materialist being

60 Hardt and Negri 2000, p. 214.

to 'brush history against the grain'.[61] His argument is that historical materialists do not just go with the flow, accepting the superficial but convenient explanation. Rather, the historical materialist disturbs the pile, seeking and exposing the roots that join events and things to the structure that cradles or crushes them. Apart from providing a total understanding that does not separate out economics, politics, cultural form and so on, such a process also disturbs ways of telling history – brushing history itself against the grain, because it refuses to take it as something that is completed, closed, past. In this case, the pastness of Benjamin is impossible, and his contribution to current disputes in Marxism and beyond still ongoing.

[61] Benjamin 2003, p. 392.

Chapter Thirty

Critical Realism and Beyond: Roy Bhaskar's *Dialectic*

Alex Callinicos

For some twenty years now, critical realism – the body of philosophical doctrines and arguments developed by Roy Bhaskar – has served as a rallying point for radical theorists in the English-speaking world who wish to escape from empiricism without falling prisoner to postmodernism. By concentrating on Bhaskar's major work of the 1990s, *Dialectic*, which attempts a dramatic and ambitious extension of his earlier ideas, I seek to here offer an appraisal of his achievements and of their relevance to social theory.[1]

A realist epistemology

Bhaskar's project emerged fully formed in his remarkable first book, *A Realist Theory of Science* (1975). This took the form of an intervention in the debates among anglophone philosophers of science. The dominant empiricist model of science, in the

[1] Bhaskar 1993. All citations in the text are from this book. Andrew Collier provides an admirable introduction to Bhaskar's earlier work in Collier 1994, including a useful biographical sketch (pp. 262–3). An earlier version of the present paper was published in French in *Actuel Marx*, 16 (1994), and appeared in English as University of York, Department of Politics Working Paper No. 7. I am grateful to Mark Evans for all his help.

form elaborated by the Vienna Circle and its followers, was by the late 1960s under increasing critical pressure. The most influential controversies focused on the problem of scientific revolution: whatever their differences, Kuhn, Lakatos, and Feyerabend were agreed that the systematic replacement of one body of theoretical concepts by another could not be interpreted along empiricist lines. But an important debate developed around the concepts of causality and of scientific laws shared by the empiricists. These were lineal descendants of Hume's reduction of causation to constant conjunction: 'We have no other notion of cause and effect but that of certain objects, which have been *always conjoin'd* together, and which in all past instances have been found inseparable.'[2] The very influential analysis of causality developed, for example, by Donald Davidson, a philosopher whose work, in other respects, pulls away from empiricism, treats it as a relationship between events.

The claim, central to the Humean view, that causation involves no necessary connection between events, but depends merely on the fact that events of one type are 'always conjoin'd' with events of a second type, came under increasing attack in the course of the 1960s and early 1970s. Thus Bhaskar's doctoral supervisor Rom Harré argued that the Humean 'regularity theory' was unable to give an adequate account of the nature of scientific laws. Constant conjunctions observed in the past could be the result of mere accident. Scientific laws could only attain the genuine universality on which their law-like status depended if the connections they posited were the result of some 'natural necessity'. Developing ideas of Locke's, Harré sought to ground this necessity in the powers inherent in the nature of the material objects making up the natural world. A causal explanation necessarily involves ascribing to some thing or things the 'material liabilities' to bring about certain effects. This is not to explain the sleep induced by opium by its dormitive virtue, since the ascription of causal powers is an *a posteriori* hypothesis formulated on the basis of empirical investigation into an object's 'real essence'.[3]

Plainly, this analysis of causal powers implies that nature has a structure which is not necessarily visible on the surface of experience. Hence Andrew Collier calls Bhaskar's development of Harré's arguments 'depth realism'.[4]

---

[2] Hume 1970, p. 141.
[3] See, for example, Locke, *An Essay Concerning Human Understanding*, III.vi.a.
[4] Collier 1994, pp. 5–6.

Perhaps the decisive step he took beyond Harré was to distinguish between open and closed systems. The world, he argued, consists of 'generative mechanisms' – the structures which produce the events registered in the flux of human experience. Since these mechanisms are plural, they interact with each other. The interference of other mechanisms means that, in general, no mechanism has the effect which it would have on its own. A law-like statement ascribing causal powers to something involves a claim about the operation of a generative mechanism if it were left undisturbed. Scientific laws thus identify tendencies in the world. Since the working of mechanisms is usually disturbed, these tendencies are typically unfulfilled; nevertheless, the mutual interference of mechanisms has effects – in the shape of events – which scientific investigation can trace back to their inherent tendencies. The world is thus an open system, in which 'causal laws [are] *out of phase* with patterns of events and experiences'. Human intervention in nature, typically in the form of scientific experimentation, is usually necessary in order to isolate the conditions under which a specific mechanism can operate undisturbed. Another way of characterising this kind of artificial situation is to call it a closed system, i.e. one 'in which constant conjunctions occur'. Thus the constant conjunctions of events which Humeans claim are so common a feature of experience as to provide the basis of the regularities in which (they believe) scientific laws consist turn out to be exceptions from the normal course of nature, resulting from human practice itself:

> In a world without men there would be no experience and few, if any constant conjunctions, i.e. had they been experienced [,] Humean 'causal laws'. For both experiences and invariances (constant conjunctions of events) depend, in general, upon human activity. But causal laws do not. Thus in a world without men the causal laws that science has now as a matter of fact discovered would continue to prevail, though there would be few sequences of events and no experiences with which they were in correspondence. Thus, we can begin to see how the empiricist ontology in fact depends upon a concealed anthropocentricity.[5]

It thus begins to become clear why Bhaskar calls his theory realist. The world revealed by the scientific discovery of causal laws is 'a multi-dimensional

[5] Bhaskar 1978, pp. 33, 34, 35.

structure independent of man'. Any epistemology which seeks to give a philosophical account of the nature of this process of discovery presupposes an ontology in the sense of 'a schematic answer to the question of what the world must be like for science to be possible'. Empiricism and idealism alike deny this primacy of ontology over epistemology. They are thereby guilty of the 'epistemic fallacy', that is, they assume that 'statements about being can be reduced to or analysed in terms of statements about knowledge'. Bhaskar, by contrast, distinguishes rigorously between the transitive and intransitive dimensions of science. The former embraces 'the antecedently established facts and theories, paradigms and models, methods and techniques of inquiry available to a particular scientific school or worker': but 'the intransitive objects of knowledge...are the real things and structures, mechanisms and processes, events and possibilities of the world: and for the most part they are quite independent of us'.[6]

Bhaskar's realism implies that the intransitive dimension of science is ontologically prior to the transitive. Yet he seeks to justify this position by means of an analysis of human practice, and more specifically of scientific experimentation. This analysis focuses on the claim we have already encountered, that experiment consists in human intervention in the course of nature in order to make possible the constant conjunctions of events that the mechanisms postulated by scientific theories will produce if left uninterfered with. It follows not only that the Humean account of causation is incorrect – there must, as Bhaskar puts it, be an 'ontological distinction' between 'causal laws' and 'sequences of events', but that the mechanisms identified by well-corroborated theories operate even where human practice does not act to create closed systems:

> In short, the intelligibility of experimental activity presupposes that a constant conjunction is no more a necessary than a sufficient condition for a causal law. And it implies that causal laws operate in their normal way under conditions, which may be characterized as 'open', where no constant conjunction or regular sequence of events is forthcoming.[7]

[6] Bhaskar 1978, pp. 21–2, 28–9, 36, 44.
[7] Bhaskar 1978, p. 33.

This, however, amounts to an ontological claim, namely that, insofar as science successfully postulates causal laws, it has an intransitive dimension, consisting of mechanisms irreducible to the events which they help to generate and which we encounter in experience. And this presupposes, in turn, the possibility of a non-human world, i.e. causal mechanisms *without* invariances and experiences. The analysis of one human activity thus implies a particular account of the world, one which paradoxically highlights the independence of that world of all human activity. Bhaskar called his position 'transcendental realism' in part because of the analogy he sees between this argument and the transcendental arguments Kant uses to establish the objectivity of the categories of the understanding in the *Critique of Pure Reason*. Moreover, though he differs from Kant in arguing that the world exists independently of, but is accessible to human knowledge, Bhaskar agrees with him in treating that knowledge as 'a structure rather than a surface'. And there is also perhaps the feeling that Bhaskar has developed a position which avoids the extremes of empiricism and idealism, just as Kant sought to escape a choice between Hume and Leibniz. Thus, for transcendental realism, 'science is not an epiphenomenon of nature, nor is nature a product of man'.[8]

One crucial feature of the world presupposed by science, according to Bhaskar, is that it is stratified. The behaviour of a particular mechanism in general is to be explained by postulating the existence of another mechanism at work at a 'lower-order', more fundamental level of being. These mechanisms form strata. Strata in general have the property of emergence. That is, while each is rooted in the mechanisms operative at the lower level(s), it cannot be reduced to them. Every stratum has causal powers which can only be explained by theories specific to it.[9] This analysis does not merely serve to prohibit the reduction of 'higher-order' sciences to 'lower-order' ones such that of biology to physics, but helps ground Bhaskar's attempt to capture the specificity of the human sciences, developed chiefly in *The Possibility of Naturalism* (1979). As the book's title suggests, he is concerned to defend 'an essential unity of method between the natural and the social sciences'. Naturalism follows from the falsehood of methodological individualism. 'Society is both the ever-present *condition* (material cause) and the continually reproduced

[8] Bhaskar 1978, pp. 25, 35.
[9] See Collier 1994, Chapter 4.

outcome of human agency.' Social structures therefore cannot be reduced to the mere consequences of individual actions; on the contrary, these actions presuppose structures, and scientific inquiry is necessary in order to isolate the latter's workings. The analogy between the natural and human sciences is not, however, complete:

> Society...is an articulated ensemble of tendencies and powers which, unlike natural ones, exist only as long as they (or at least some of them) are being exercised; are exercised, in the last instance via the intentional activity of men; and are not necessarily space-time invariant.

The ontological distinction between generative mechanisms and the events they produce is thus only partially present in the human world, since society is 'a structure irreducible to, but present only in its effects'. It follows that social scientists cannot, through experimentation, create closed systems in which to test their generalisations. The human sciences are thus radically non-predictive. Furthermore, since social structures depend on intentional human activity, their investigation has an irreducible hermeneutic dimension involving the discovery of the reasons for individual actions.[10]

Much of the content of Bhaskar's philosophy of social science was not especially original. There are, for example, close parallels between his conception of 'the *duality* of structure', that is, its role as both the condition and outcome of practice, and Anthony Giddens's account of the 'duality of structure and action', developed independently at much the same time.[11] Bhaskar's version was, however, undergirded by a forcefully argued and genuinely original account of the nature of science itself. It was perhaps for this reason that critical realism (the name the combination of Bhaskar's 'transcendental realism' and his 'critical naturalism' in the social sciences gradually acquired) emerged as an intellectual tendency in the English-speaking world. Its attraction lay in the fact that it is authentically anti-empiricist – as much of *A Realist Theory of Science* is taken up with criticism of empiricist epistemologies as is devoted to elaborating Bhaskar's alternative – while vigorously insisting on the objectivity and knowability of the world at a time when various forms of scepticism were gaining ground in the social sciences thanks to the influence

---

[10] Bhaskar 1979, pp. 3, 43, 49, 50.
[11] Bhaskar 1979, pp. 43–4. An interesting comparison can be made with Giddens 1976, and Giddens 1979.

of Kuhn and Feyeraband on the one hand, and of Derrida and Foucault on the other. Critical realism won support especially among left-wing researchers in a variety of disciplines, making possible the regular meetings of the Standing Conference on Realism in the Human Sciences, and, more recently, of the conferences organised by Bhaskar's Centre on Critical Realism.

The diffraction of dialectic

It was plain from the start that Bhaskar is a philosopher of the Left. Themes from Althusser's writings are detectable in Bhaskar's earlier works. Thus the account of the transitive and intransitive dimensions bears a strong family resemblance to the distinction drawn in *Reading 'Capital'* between the thought object and real object of a science.[12] Similarly, Bhaskar's conception of social structure as irreducible to, but present only in, its effects recalls Althusser's concept of structural causality. Bhaskar indeed has acknowledged Althusser as 'the foremost *Marxist* influence' on *A Realist Theory of Science*, and described him as 'the best and most advanced Marxist in the philosophy of science'.[13] *Dialectic*, however, provided him with the opportunity to situate himself more generally with respect to the Marxist tradition.

Bhaskar's aim in this book is, however, considerably more ambitious – '[t]he dialectical enrichment and deepening of critical realism',[14] its development into a 'system of dialectical critical realism [which] constitutes a second wave of critical realism'.[15] This radical extension of Bhaskar's earlier arguments in effect takes as its starting point Marx's critique of Hegel. This does not mean that he simply reproduces Marx's arguments. Bhaskar highlights the peculiar role of the law of non-contradiction in Hegel, which acts as 'a norm he covertly accepts, while seeing it ubiquitously violated as the mechanism that powers his dialectic to its final glaceating repose'. Contradictions emerge only to cancel themselves in the Hegelian dialectic as opposites are transformed

> from positive contraries simultaneously present and actual...into negative sub-contraries now simultaneously actual and absent, but retained as

[12] See Collier 1994, pp. 52–4, for a discussion of the similarities and differences between Althusser's and Bhaskar's conceptions of science.

[13] Qu., Elliott 1987, p. 331 n. 6.

[14] Bhaskar 1993, p. 2.

[15] Bhaskar 1993, p. 301.

> negative presences in a cumulative memory store, as the dialectical reader's consciousness or the path of history moves on to a new level of speculative reason.

It is the experience, described in retrospect, of the rise and fall of successive contradictions, that constitutes the dialectical process for Hegel. Thus 'Hegelian dialectic...is never simultaneously dialectical and contradictory. The materialist dialectic is.'[16] 'Real dialectical contradictions' of the kind analysed by Marx involve the co-existence of aspects of a totality which are at once intrinsically related but *'tendentially mutually exclusive'*;[17] their resolution requires the intervention of practice to secure 'the non preservative negation of the ground' of this contradictory totality,[18] and not, as in Hegel merely the opposites being 'retrospectively redescribed as moments of a transcending totality', which amounts to their *'analytical reinstatement'*.[19]

The significance for Bhaskar of Marx's critique of Hegel is twofold. In the first place, it gives rise to 'the materialist diffraction of dialectic'[20]: 'Marx's critique of Hegel's philosophy of identity permits a plurality of dialectical configurations, topologies, perspectives and inscapes which it would [be] idle to suggest could be captured by a single formula.'[21] This leads Bhaskar to isolate what he calls 'Four Degrees of Critical Realism', but which are perhaps best seen as four dimensions of this diffracted dialectic, each with its own distinctive concepts, scientific applications, and philosophical problems. The first ('1M') is, roughly speaking, the domain of Bhaskar's original philosophy of science, involving concepts such as 'differentiation, change, alterity', and representing the moment of irreducible non-identity which Hegel sought unsuccessfully to efface. The second ('2E') is 'the narrowly dialectical moment', involving, inter alia, 'the ideas of negation, negativity, becoming, process, finitude, contradiction, development..., spatiality, temporality, mediation, reciprocity' employed in sciences such as cosmology and 'human geo-history'. The third ('3L') is concerned with 'totalizing motifs', the concepts exploring the connections between human beings' theoretical understanding of, and

16 Bhaskar 1993, p. 62.
17 Bhaskar 1993, p. 58.
18 Bhaskar 1993, p. 61.
19 Bhaskar 1993, p. 62.
20 Bhaskar 1993, p. 98.
21 Bhaskar 1993, pp. 173–4.

practical engagement in the world. That engagement itself is the object of the fourth dimension of Bhaskar's pluralised dialectic ('4D'), where 'we seek to achieve the unity of theory and practice *in practice*'.[22] Thus, '[a]t the beginning of this new dialectic, there is non-identity – at the end, open, unfinished totality,' a thorough disruption of the self-identity of Hegelian Spirit.[23]

This multiplication of dialectics, while it starts from Marx, takes Bhaskar well beyond him. Too often, Marx is too far from, or too close to, Hegel. Thus the latter's influence leads Marx into a rejection of ethical thought which serves 'to render him (and the majority of subsequent Marxists) impervious to the need for a William Morris-type moment of positive concrete utopianism to stand alongside Marx's negative explanatory critique' of capitalism.[24] At the same time, breaking with the Hegelian notion of a 'preservative dialectical sublation' which incorporates the cancelled moments of the process within the final totality leads to Marx's 'failure... to come to terms with the material... presence of the past (and, to a degree, of the intrinsic outside)'. Stalinism, in seeking to build socialism in one country, ignoring the material constraints imposed by 'global intradependence [sic] and the presence of the past', represented an extreme version of this failure. It can, therefore, 'be given Marxian credentials, however much Marx would have loathed the outcome'.[25]

Bhaskar remains nevertheless indebted to Marx in a second respect. The exposure by the young Marx in his *Critique of Hegel's Philosophy of Right* of the 'tacit complicity' between speculative idealism and classical empiricism provides Bhaskar with the leitmotiv of his own critique of the Western philosophical tradition from Parmenides and Plato onwards.[26] Much of *Dialectic* is devoted to an exposure of three mutually reinforcing errors which, in different forms, run through this tradition, and are responsible for its characteristic 'irrealism' (by which Bhaskar presumably means what is more conventionally called anti-realism, or idealism, the denial of the existence of a world independent of, but knowable by thought). The first we have already encountered, the 'epistemic fallacy', which by treating statements about being as statements about knowledge effects the reduction of ontology to epistemology. This

[22] Bhaskar 1993, pp. 8–9.
[23] Bhaskar 1993, p. 3.
[24] Bhaskar 1993, p. 345.
[25] Bhaskar 1993, p. 350.
[26] Bhaskar 1993, p. 88.

functions merely to cover the generation of an implicit ontology, 'actualism', which denies the existence of a stratified world of mechanisms, and reduces reality to the actual, that is, to experience and the events encountered in it. Closely related to this error is a second, that of 'ontological monovalence', 'the generation of a purely positive, complementing a purely actual, notion of reality', involving the denial of any place to negation; its effect is 'to erase the contingency of existential questions and to despatialize and detemporalize (accounts of) being'.[27]

Finally, there is 'the operation I have dubbed "primal squeeze", the elimination of the middle term of scientific theory or, more importantly, its intransitive object and ontological counterpart, natural necessity'. Neither empiricism nor idealism have a place for 'empirically controlled critical scientific theory', the former replacing it with 'naturalistically given sense-experience', the latter with 'parthenogetically self-generating philosophy'.[28]

Power and desire

Since philosophical errors apparently take so universal a form, that of this 'unholy trinity of irrealism',[29] the question naturally arises of whether there is anything common to the dialectical variants distinguished by Bhaskar. One can in fact identify two unifying factors, one broader than the other. The most fundamental dialectical category is that of 'real negation', 'real determinate absence or non-being'.[30] The existence of such an absence, however, is not a stable state of affairs, but provides the impulse to remove it. Thus 'dialectics depends upon the positive identification and transformative elimination of absences. Indeed, it just is, in its essence, the process of *absenting absence*.'[31] Real negation has, for Bhaskar, a privileged ontological status. Against the doctrine of ontological monovalence he insists that 'the negative has ontological primacy'.[32] Indeed, he tells us at the beginning of *Dialectic*, 'by the time we

27 Bhaskar 1993, pp. 4–5, 7.
28 Bhaskar 1993, p. 90.
29 Bhaskar 1993, p. 111.
30 Bhaskar 1993, p. 5.
31 Bhaskar 1993, p. 43.
32 Bhaskar 1993, p. 48.

are through, I would like the reader to see the positive as a tiny, but important, ripple on the surface of a sea of negativity'.[33]

I return below to the arguments Bhaskar provides in support of this claim. But consider first this apparent anomaly. If, as Bhaskar claims, '[n]on-being is a condition of possibility of being',[34] why is there a tendency to eliminate it? Whence the impulse to absent absence, if absence is ontologically prior to presence? The only answer he gives to this question is specific to the human world. In general, Bhaskar seems to regard the dialectic as operative in nature as well as in society. Indeed at one point he states that 'there is nothing anthropomorphic about the dialectic presented here'.[35] It is true that he also says 'there cannot be a global dialectics of nature (qua being), where some dialectical categories like negation will, while others like reflexivity will not, apply to it'.[36] The clear implication of his overall treatment is, however, that the dialectical category of negation does apply to the whole of being, physical as well as human: thus Bhaskar has quite a friendly discussion of Engels's often derided three dialectical laws.[37]

At the same time, however, the dialectic 'is built around a hard core' which 'could not apply in an entirely inorganic world'. This is 'the logic of freedom'.[38] The major premiss of Bhaskar's argument here seems to be 'the definition of dialectic as absenting absence'.[39] Its minor premiss is a specification of the concept of absence: 'any ill can be seen as a constraint and any constraint as the absence of a freedom'.[40] It follows that dialectic involves 'absenting most notably of constraints on desires, wants, needs and interests. Foremost among such constraints will be those flowing from power$_2$ relations'.[41] By 'power$_2$ relations' Bhaskar means those 'expressed in structures of domination, exploitation, subjugation, and control', as opposed to 'power$_1$', 'the transformative capacity analytic to the concept of agency'.[42]

33 Bhaskar 1993, p. 5.
34 Bhaskar 1993, p. 47.
35 Bhaskar 1993, p. 304.
36 Bhaskar 1993, p. 338.
37 Bhaskar 1993, pp. 150–2.
38 Bhaskar 1993, pp. 373–4.
39 Bhaskar 1993, p. 173.
40 Bhaskar 1993, p. 182.
41 Bhaskar 1993, p. 175.
42 Bhaskar 1993, p. 60.

Dialectic thus acquires an ethico-political dimension, and Bhaskar offers a variety of generalisations of the above argument whose aim is to allow us to 'go from *primal scream to universal human emancipation*',[43] that is, from the expression of the most elementary desires to the demand for an 'eudaimonistic society', in other words, 'a society oriented to the free development and flourishing of each and all, and of each as a condition for all'.[44]

Bhaskarian dialectic thus acquires an anthropological specification as the 'inner urge that flows universally from the logic of elemental desire (lack, need, want or desire). It manifests itself wherever $power_2$ relations hold sway'.[45] Crucial here is the assumption that 'absence is paradigmatically a condition for desire', since 'desire presupposes an absence, viz. of the intentional object, in Brentano's sense, of the desired'.[46] This is, of course, a familiar left-Hegelian conception of desire; its locus classicus is the dialectic of master and slave in the *Phenomenology*, or rather Kojève's interpretation of this dialectic, from which Lacan transposed it into psychoanalysis. Challenging all such anthropologies is Deleuze's and Guattari's great anti-dialectic of desire. The Lacanian treatment of desire as negative, as lack, is one of the main targets of *L'Anti-Oedipe*, which conceptualises desire instead as positive and productive. Yet, in *Mille Plateaux*, they confront a problem identical to one that faces Bhaskar's version of the dialectic. Despite their very different conceptions of desire, Deleuze and Guattari on the one hand, and Bhaskar on the other hand posit a conflict between desire and power. For the former, the deterritorialising impulse of desire bursts out of the confines of any given assemblage [*agencement*]; for Bhaskar, the dialectical drive – 'absenting constraints on absenting ills' – is 'implicit in the most rudimentary desires'.[47] This raises the question of the basis of the power-relations themselves: whence this tendency to confine or constrain desire? Deleuze and Guattari give no very satisfactory answer to this question. Bhaskar does not consider it all. Perhaps this is because there is no general answer to it. Maybe '$power_2$ relations' have a variety of causes, some of them historically specific. But if this is the case, it seems like a significant restriction on a theory whose universal ambitions are evident.

---

43 Bhaskar 1993, p. 180.
44 Bhaskar 1993, p. 264.
45 Bhaskar 1993, p. 299.
46 Bhaskar 1993, p. 242.
47 Bhaskar 1993, p. 382.

The temptations of transcendental philosophy

These difficulties are of the sort one is likely to encounter in any work displaying the ambition and intelligence that *Dialectic* does. They do not affect the fertility of Bhaskar's ideas or the breadth of his horizons. But the book has one more unexpected weakness, and one that is more serious than first appears. To speak frankly, it is abominably written. Neologisms and idiosyncratic uses of familiar terms proliferate till they form what verges at times on a private language. Arguments are illustrated by figures whose frequency and complexity obscure rather than instruct. And, all too often, Bhaskar's prose becomes clogged by what seems like the irresistible need to say everything, to add to some specific assertion references to connected considerations and qualifications till the original point is in danger of being lost. Perhaps this is a temptation of all dialectical thinking, which Bhaskar rightly sums up as 'the art of thinking the *coincidence of distinctions and connections*'.[48] But the danger of trying to say everything is that one ends up saying nothing.

Often, Bhaskar's dreadful prose does not succeed in obscuring the nature of his arguments. Sometimes, however, style does affect substance, and for the worse. For one thing, various subjects are merely touched on. For example, it is clear that Bhaskar has some extremely intriguing ideas about the nature of space and time, which are relevant both to important contemporary debates in cosmology and to social theory (hence his tendency to rebaptise Marxism as '[geo-]historical materialism').[49] Unfortunately, these ideas are presented only in a number of passages scattered through the book, and in so condensed a form that it is extremely hard to arrive at any very precise understanding of them. It is tempting to conclude that the topic of space and time were better dealt with in a much more systematic way, or omitted altogether.

Perhaps, from a strategic point of view, of more seriousness is the way in which many of Bhaskar's most important arguments are very brief. Bhaskar's attempt to show that the negative, in the sense of determinate absence, has ontological priority over the positive offers a particularly important example of this tendency to rush his arguments. In fact, a variety of different arguments are deployed in support of the priority of the negative over the positive. Many are interesting, for example, the claim that 'a world without voids (absences),

---

48 Bhaskar 1993, p. 180.
49 Bhaskar 1993, p. 87.

that is, a "non-clumpy" material object world...would be a world in which nothing could move or occur',[50] though this rather Epicurean thought seems more like an *a posteriori* generalisation from the development of physics than any sort of *a priori* truth. But consider the following, slightly earlier passage:

> the identification of a positive existent is a human act. So it involves the absenting of a pre-existing state of affairs, be it only a state of existential doubt. This may be taken as a transcendental deduction of the category of absence, and a transcendental refutation and immanent critique of ontological monovalence.[51]

QED. These three sentences make up the sum of this 'transcendental argument'. This is cause for concern, and not only because it looks as if Bhaskar is begging the question at issue by assuming that change is to be understood primarily as absenting. For it is merely one instance of Bhaskar's tendency to offer what he calls 'transcendental arguments', often of comparable brevity and for similarly controversial conclusions.

The nature of transcendental arguments has been well brought out by Charles Taylor:

> The arguments I want to call 'transcendental' start from some feature of our experience which they-claim to be indubitable and beyond cavil. They then move to a stronger conclusion, one concerning the nature of the subject or his position in the world. They make this move by a regressive argument, to the effect that this stronger conclusion must be so if the indubitable fact about experience is to be possible (and being so, it must be possible).[52]

Thus Kant's transcendental deduction proceeds by seeking to establish that the very possibility of conscious experience depends on the ability to treat individual impressions as states of a coherent and enduring self underlying experience, and that this in turn requires the application of the categories of the understanding, which transforms these impressions into the structured, enduring, and causally governed world of appearances. A transcendental argument is thus, as Taylor puts it, a chain of 'indispensability claims', each of which is *a priori* and 'not merely probable, but apodeictic'. It is the fact that

---

[50] Bhaskar 1993, pp. 45–6.
[51] Bhaskar 1993, p. 44.
[52] Taylor 1978/9, p. 151.

these claims concern experience that gives them these characteristics: 'this is held to give us an unchallengeable starting point. For how can one formulate coherently the doubt that we have experiences?'.[53] The indubitability of the starting point is in effect (and provided that each indispensability-claim is well made out and properly connected to the others in the chain) transferred to the conclusion.

Do Bhaskar's purported transcendental arguments have these properties? Surely not. Consider, for example, his most important transcendental argument, from the nature of experimental practice to the distinction between open and closed systems, and hence to the existence of generative mechanisms irreducible to human experience. The starting point – scientific experiment – lacks the required indubitability. For one thing, the kind of elaborate, theoretically-driven interference in nature characteristic of the modern sciences, is evidently not a universal feature of human existence. For another, Bhaskar's starting point is not even the actual experimental practice of working scientists but rather a particular *description* of that practice. Arguably, this description presupposes what Bhaskar seeks to prove: is not the distinction between open and closed systems implicit in the claim that experimentation produces sequences of events which do not naturally occur?[54] But, even if his argument is not circular, it is not transcendental in the required sense, since it starts from a particular description of scientific practice whose irreducible element of interpretation makes it, not indubitable, but disputable.

How damaging is this criticism for Bhaskar's project? It may not have much of an effect on the substance of his philosophy. Indeed, for what it is worth, I think much of what his critical realism – and indeed its recent dialectical extension – asserts is true. The deflation of its transcendental pretensions is, nevertheless, important for two reasons. First, it highlights the danger in the proliferation of quick-kill arguments from *a priori* premises to conclusions embodying substantive and controversial generalisations about the world that is such a distressing feature of *Dialectic*. Secondly, it draws attention to one striking feature of Bhaskar's philosophy since it first burst onto the scene

---

[53] Taylor 1978/9, pp. 159–60. Bhaskar sometimes shows he is aware of this feature of transcendental arguments: see, for example, Bhaskar 1993, p. 103. Collier, however, is not: see Collier 1994, pp. 20ff.

[54] See David-Hillel Ruben's critique of transcendental realism in Ruben 1977, esp. p. 101, and Bhaskar's reply in Bhaskar 1978, pp. 255–60.

in 1975. Although he claimed for philosophy only the modest role assigned it by Locke of serving as 'the under-labourer, and occasionally as the mid-wife, of science', in fact his development of *transcendental* realism involves quite a strong claim about what philosophy can establish about the world by *a priori* means.[55]

In *A Realist Theory of Science*, this takes the form of a philosophical demonstration of the existence of a stratified and structured world independent of humankind. *Dialectic* displays the same ambitions. Bhaskar defines 'dialectical arguments as transcendental arguments establishing, inter alia, ontological conclusions'.[56] It is clear that the most important of these conclusions concern the social rather that the physical world. Indeed, we are promised a sequel, *Dialectical Social Theory*, which will give an account of 'what a truly dialectical critical social realist social science would look like and of how it may come to ground naturalistically generated substantive criteria for a feasible society oriented to the concrete singularity of each as condition for the concrete singularity of all.'[57] This may imply, comfortingly, that some of Bhaskar's more compressed 'proofs' are in fact promissory notes that will be cashed out in full arguments sometime in the future.

But this passage also raises, more acutely, the question of Bhaskar's relationship to Marxism. The description just cited of the future emancipated society recalls, of course, Marx's famous reference in the *Manifesto* to communism as a society where 'the free development of each is the condition of the free development of all'. In this respect, the passage is fairly typical of Bhaskar's treatment of characteristically Marxian concepts and themes: fairly concrete and clear propositions are translated into more abstract, and, all too often, less perspicuous formulae. The problem here is not Bhaskar's substantive criticisms of Marx. Those cited above are specific enough, and merit serious debate in their own terms, but there is nothing especially new about them. More to the point, they do not in any very obvious way depend on the philosophical apparatus of dialectical critical realism. One does not, for example, have to sign up to Bhaskarian epistemology to think that Marx may have been wrong to have dismissed the utopian-socialist tradition.

---

[55] Bhaskar 1978, p. 10.
[56] Bhaskar 1993, p. 107.
[57] Bhaskar 1993, p. 370.

Yet Bhaskar plainly believes that embedding Marxism within critical dialectical realism will strengthen it substantially. The closest that he comes to an argument to support this belief is when he claims that Marx's critique of Hegel 'depends upon *epistemological materialism*, asserting the existential intransitivity and transfactual efficacy of the objects of scientific thought'.[58] He goes on to suggest that in Marx's mature thought the dialectic substituted for the realist epistemology that he needed but lacked.[59] But, even if we were to grant that *A Realist Theory of Science* was the necessary philosophical complement of *Capital*, it does not follow that either critical realism or its dialectical extension provides Marxism (or indeed any other social theory) with substantive content it would otherwise lack. The implication to the contrary present both in Bhaskar's reliance on transcendental arguments and in his followers' attempts to develop critical-realist 'approaches' to specific topics in or aspects of social theory is evidence of overinflated philosophical ambition.

More specifically, such an enterprise confuses the propositions that form the conclusions of philosophical arguments with what Lakatos called the heuristic of scientific research programmes.[60] Each research programme has its own set of theoretical guidelines defining the problems it seeks to address, its methods for approaching them, and possible strategies for overcoming anomalies. While philosophical reasoning – and, indeed, much looser metaphysical ideas – may help to inspire what goes into such a heuristic, the latter can in no way be deduced from the former. Whatever insights dialectical critical realism may offer scientific researchers, philosophical argument cannot substitute for the processes of theory-construction and empirical inquiry specific to individual sciences. The mistaken belief that it can seems likely to lead in the human sciences to a kind of decaffeinated Marxism in which all that is interesting and controversial in historical materialism is submerged amid a vague mass of speculation. A more consistent naturalism, which stressed more strongly than Bhaskar does the continuity between philosophy and the sciences and the former's dependence on the latter, could protect him from the extravagant claims for philosophy into which he is sometimes tempted,

58 Bhaskar 1993, p. 91.
59 Bhaskar 1993, p. 97.
60 Lakatos 1978, I.

and provide a more secure basis for the many valid insights and fertile ideas this challenging and original philosopher has to offer.

Addendum

This assessment of Bhaskar was written in 1994. One then could envisage various intellectual trajectories that might emerge from the stimulating shambles of *Dialectic*. But none could have predicted the course Bhaskar has actually followed. His most recent book *From East to West* is in two parts.[61] The first announces a further extension of critical realism – to 'transcendental dialectical critical realism'. This 'transcendental radicalization' involves in particular 'a new realism about transcendence and God'.[62] God is both transcendent and immanent: more specifically, 'he/she/it' is immanent in the finite human self. The roots of social oppression and alienation lie in alienation from the self: this more fundamental alienation is overcome when the self breaks loose from the attachments that bind it to particular desires and fears and imprison it in the cycle of reincarnation, and recognises its identity with God. The second part narrates fifteen of the lives passed by one such self, culminating, it seems, in Bhaskar himself, whose task is 'to reconcile and resynthesize the opposites: East and West, male and female, *yin* and *yang*, reason and experience, fact and value, mind and body, heaven and earth'.[63]

Bhaskar stresses the continuities between this astonishing turn taken by his thought and his earlier writings. Certainly old concepts are put to new uses. His distinction between the real and the actual – i.e. between the events made possible by causal mechanisms and those events encountered in experience – now allows him to extend the real to include 'deities and avatars . . . and angels' and 'the denizens of the astral and causal worlds, including discarnate souls'.[64] There is perhaps scope for the baffled reader to try and detect the sources of this turn in Bhaskar's earlier work – for example, the ambiguities noted above that are generated by his insistence on treating dialectic as both as universally operative and as 'the logic of freedom'. But there seems little profit in such a search. As with Althusser's murder of his wife (though, of course, with

[61] Bhaskar 2000.
[62] Bhaskar 2000, p. x.
[63] Bhaskar 2000, p. 149.
[64] Bhaskar 2000, p. 50.

far fewer dreadful human consequences), Bhaskar's discovery of Eastern religion cannot be deduced from the logic of his earlier philosophy but must have arisen from contingencies of his life into which it would be inappropriate to inquire. The most that one can say is that it has long been true that the critical realism movement around Bhaskar displayed certain unhealthy cult-like qualities: perhaps, in this respect, being helped to change consciousness.

The fact remains that we are confronted here with a major tragedy. A leading philosopher of the Left has committed intellectual suicide. Bhaskar claims now to be seeking 'an integration of some of the insights of the New Age and the New Left movements'.[65] But this is little consolation. He also adapts one of his old slogans – reclaiming reality – and now proposes both to '*reclaim* and *re-enchant reality*'.[66] But precisely what we do not need is any re-enchantment of contemporary reality but, rather, a brutally clear and stark critical analysis. Plainly, Roy Bhaskar will no longer be contributing to this enterprise. His new writings will find new readers – though they may be rather baffled by the unfamiliar references they contain to the philosophy of science and the dialectical tradition. Others will have to continue, as best they can, the philosophical project to which Bhaskar has made such an important contribution. Books such as *A Realist Theory of Science* and *The Possibility of Naturalism* will remain an important reference point. But Bhaskar will no longer be one of our company. He has taken a different path.

---

[65] Bhaskar 2000, p. 149.
[66] Bhaskar 2000, p. 5.

Chapter Thirty-One

Bourdieu and Historical Materialism

Jacques Bidet

Bourdieu has produced a conceptual system whose relationship with Marx's is enigmatic. It involves a similar terminology: capital, reproduction, classes, and so on. In often analogous terms, it analyses modern forms of domination, providing a critique of them that is emancipatory in intent. It thus displays a theoretico-political ambition which recalls that of a 'theory of *praxis*'. However, it realises it in a body of competing axioms – those of a 'general theory of practice'. So how are these two conceptual universes related to one another?

I shall not seek an answer to this question in Bourdieu's references to Marxism, which remain internal to his own problematic, but in a comparison between it and Marx's problematic. I shall advance the following thesis: Bourdieu takes over the 'generalist' ambition of Marxism, but in terms of a 'sociology' – a theory of *social relations* – not those of a 'historical materialism', whose distinctive feature is that it takes the complex of the relations between social relations and *productive forces* as its object. In this sense, it involves a regional programme as opposed to a *general* one, which neither possesses the same ambitions, nor contains the same risks, as the Marxist programme, and which cannot prompt either the same kind of examination or the same expectations.

The general programme has everything to learn from regional knowledge. And 'Marxism', in this sense, lives on 'sociology'. However, here I shall leave to one side Bourdieu's most valuable contributions – particularly his 'theory of the production of symbolic goods'. If it is legitimate to focus on the project's 'limits', on what it cannot offer, it is because it presents itself as a 'general' project – that is to say, as taking up a challenge in the face of which Marxism has supposedly proved deficient. I would like to show why things are not so simple. On the other hand, I also want make it clear that Bourdieu's work offers some remarkable contributions to the programme outlined by Marx and, specifically, to a materialist theory of modern society: not only various 'additions' to Marxism, but some crucial indications for its critique and revision.

I shall therefore examine how Bourdieu retranslates a number of Marx's concepts into a different space, whose specific properties I shall study. Ultimately, my standpoint is not that of a supposedly standard Marxism, but of the 'meta/structural' problematic, inscribed in a 'historical materialism', proposed in *Théorie générale*.

Bourdieu does not thematise 'capital' as a process in the manner of Marx: he understands it primarily as a differential endowment. In Bourdieu, the terminology of 'capital' and its 'reproduction', construed as a class relationship, clearly articulates a claim to impart a new meaning to the words. To Marxism, which allegedly offers a picture of modern society, its dynamics and contradictions, based exclusively on the concept of 'economic capital', Bourdieu counter-poses the existence of another factor, which he assigns the same epistemological status in this respect: 'cultural capital'. He thus proposes a map of 'the space of social classes' on the basis of these two components. On the ordinate, according to the *volume* of capital, we find the dominant above and the dominated below. On the abscissa, according to the *type* of capital, we have economic capital on the one hand and cultural capital on the other. A population – broken down according to profession (that is, by its link to the 'relations of production'),[1] to which a certain level of income and education is attached, as well as various overdeterminations such as sex, age, ethnicity, region, religion, and so on – is thus distributed in a 'space of class conditions', on the basis of which struggles between classes and class fractions can be understood.

---

[1] See Bourdieu 1984, pp. 106–7.

But Bourdieu also uses this terminology more widely: in general, 'capital' is the 'resource' specific to each field. Thus, we have a 'political capital', a 'religious capital', a 'sporting' or 'mathematical' capital, and so on. What is thus referred to is 'symbolic capital'. The social space is conceived as a complex of spheres of activity, whose specific stakes, although given in a struggle between partners, do not pertain to a mere relationship of force, but always to a legitimate relationship. In traditional societies, the 'credit' of the powerful is sustained by honourable behaviour and ostentatious expenditure. In modern society, each field possesses its own criteria of excellence, inherent in its distinctive rationality, which characterise a specific 'capital'.

However, this does not involve *relative* autonomy, since the highest 'legitimacy' is expressed in state law, which, among other things, sanctions the 'mechanisms' whereby legitimate titles are attributed and guaranteed and social positions defined. We are thus led to the Weberian treatment of law as belief, which could be related to a certain Marxism:

> law does no more than symbolically consecrate – by recording it in a form that renders it both eternal and universal – the structure of power relations among the groups and the classes that is produced and guaranteed practically by the functioning of these mechanisms.[2]

However, this cannot be reduced to the mere *de facto* legitimation of the issue of legitimacy, which will resurface in classical fashion as universalisability.

The notion of 'capital' thus serves several fluctuating purposes, which are sometimes intermingled (cultural capital, *qua* legitimating, is sometimes referred to as 'symbolic capital'). A highly resonant matrix nevertheless dominates, which distributes individuals into classes according to their capital, envisaged in the two 'patrimonial' components of property and culture. Capital is understood here as an endowment, as an *asset*, in the sense of John Roemer and Erik Olin Wright's analytical Marxism – as a *differential* endowment and, in this sense, as a relation. It remains to discover what connection it has with capital as a *process*, such as Marx constructed the concept.

What Bourdieu commonly understands by 'reproduction' is not, in Marxian fashion, the social process peculiar to a form of society that reproduces it. It is the 'renewal' of agents in their original social position, in as much as it reproduces the structure.

---

2 Bourdieu 1990, p. 132.

Marx analyses reproduction within the 'process of capitalist production'. The latter reproduces its *material* presuppositions, in terms of concrete factors of production and in terms of value; and its *social* presuppositions, which are the existence of a class tied to the condition of wage-labour and a class that owns the means of production, and hence the enduring cleavage between them, which defines this structural form. The latter possesses both its functional aspect and its contradictory aspect, which are developed throughout *Capital*. Reproduction thus conceived has external conditions of possibility: it implies the existence of superstructural institutions that ensure (in a class confrontation) implementation of the juridical, political, and ideological presuppositions of the production relation.

The reproduction analysed by Bourdieu involves neither the structure, nor even the superstructure, in Marx's sense of the terms. It is usually construed as a circular process: structures are internalised by agents in the form of *habitus* that govern their *practices*, which underly a *structural* order, itself a generator of *habitus*. We shall call this model HPSH.

The crucial moment is education, often identified as that of reproduction (see Bourdieu and Passeron's 1970 book of that title). *Habituses* are certainly 'structured and structuring dispositions', but their 'structuration' is not due exclusively to the structural context: under the spur of inter-generational family solidarity, it is encouraged by an active process of education. The school, in as much as it is a class school, takes over from the family in producing a differentiated culture, wherein everyone acquires the mastery of the conditions that are those of their class of origin.

The analyses of Bourdieu and his colleagues are of an impressive originality and power in this respect. They deal with culture as re-produced by education, the practices of educators, and the process of formation of differentiated aptitudes. They demythologise the ideology of natural gifts. They unmask the artifice by showing that the cultural arbitrary is unconscious; that education is oblivious of its own genesis; that the consecration of the elect derives its legitimacy from the fact that, superior titles only being accorded to those of the inheritors who most distinguish themselves in this process of distinction (following a series of cumulative tests), socially proclaimed excellence seems to be attributable their own person.

The differentiated reproduction of the range of *habituses*, which extends from various dominated *habituses* to various dominant *habituses*, thus in itself ensures the overall reproduction of a differentiated social space of aptitudes.

It reproduces *the social space itself* in its class complexity. Even if like does not exactly reproduce like, their diversity reproduces social diversity, and their distance social distance, which is domination.

Or, at least, it 'contributes' to it. In fact, it forms a pair with another process – that of 'economic reproduction', construed as the renewal of inheritance, which is the other component of endowment capital. Bourdieu thus discloses 'strategies of reproduction' – that is, of inter-generational renewal – of an inheritance of culture and wealth and, correlatively, of honour and power, whether on the terrain of ethnology (Kabyle peasantry) or sociology (major French employers).

This analysis of reproduction differs in two related respects from Marx's.

On the one hand, it does not involve – or not expressly, at any rate – the reproduction of the social *system*. The problematic of the 'field', deriving from the Weberian tradition, directs attention to the particularity of each 'sphere' (and to the relations, especially of homology, between them), rather than to the system as such, as a relation between its parts, in its functionality, its logic, its dynamics, and its contradictions. The concept of 'practice', whose distinctive object is indicated in its constitutive categories (stake, belief, *illusio*, struggle, preservation/subversion, specific investment, field effect), in its founding link with that of *habitus*, has as its horizon the field, in its 'relative autonomy', not the social system as a whole. Thus, the 'political field' is understood as the space of interaction between 'politicians', the 'mathematical field' as that between mathematicians, and so on.

On the other hand, *it exclusively concerns 'social relations'*, including those that Bourdieu characterises as 'relations of production', not the 'productive forces'.

Bourdieu's programme – the 'theory of practice' – is thus a 'sociology', which differs from a 'historical materialism', whose particular challenge is to link economy and history.

As is well known, what is at stake in theories of reproduction is an understanding of historical development. In the Marxian schema, simple reproduction is conceived as the condition of a process of social transformation referred to by the term expanded reproduction. Described as capable of reproducing itself, the structure 'capital' in fact contains the conditions of its self-development. It exists as such only in the conditions of competition for profit, which gives rise to capitalist concentration, technological progress, and so on. The concept of structure opens onto that of its history, to the point of its supposedly inevitable detonation.

The Marxian idea of reproduction is thus understood as a problematic of the relationship between 'relations of production' and 'productive forces':

> In the social production of their life, men enter into definite relations that are indispensable and independent of their will, relations of production which correspond to a definite stage of development of their material productive forces.... At a certain stage of their development, the material productive forces of society come into conflict with the existing relations of production.... From forms of development of the productive forces these relations turn into their fetters. Then begins an epoch of social revolution.[3]

Let us call this model PFRP. Each of its concepts poses numerous problems, which cannot be considered here. Let us simply note that this model is in no way a historical teleology: in itself, it announces no end; the transformation of the 'productive (-destructive) forces' does not form part of some grand project of *homo faber*; it comes to pass as a mixture of the intentional and the unintentional, whereby human beings are in history rather than making it. Let us note that its object is an analysis of the relationship between social physics and social dynamics and the issue of a conscious common intervention in this dynamic: the distinctive object of a 'theory of *praxis*'.

Bourdieu's programme lies outside such considerations. The horizon of his HPSP model is the repetition of the same. *History* only enters into it in roundabout fashion, by way of the category of 'conjuncture'. *Habituses* are called upon to operate in endlessly new conjunctures, different from those that constituted them, and hence with different structuring effects. But where do these conjunctures come from? The question seems to be tacitly transferred to the discipline of history (informed, obviously, by the 'theory of practice'). But what sort of science is involved? Is its object defined by that which escapes 'practice'?

The Marxist problematic of *praxis*, implied in the PFRP model, takes as its challenge thinking the relationship between history and *economy* in non-'economistic' fashion, the Marxian category of 'labour in general' articulating the question of its *socially-necessary time* and that of *social use-value* – that is to say, definition of its ends in terms of culture and identity. By contrast, the theory of 'practice' counter-posed to it by Bourdieu appears to be a pure science

[3] Marx and Engels 1969, pp. 503–4.

of social relations, which refers the economic to a different discipline. Is this a science of the productive forces? Obviously, Bourdieu understands that economics cannot be enclosed in the abstraction of the *homo economicus*, but must be integrated into the historical field of the social sciences. However, at the same time, he constitutes praxiology, science of practice as relation, science of social relations, into a 'general theory', for which the 'productive forces' constitute an external *environmental* datum. But how can we understand 'practice', in its capacity for self-distantiation – as human practice – outside of the dialectic between the claims of control and appropriation and the historically dynamic technical conditions over which they are asserted?

In another respect, however, Bourdieu's research goes beyond this framework. Thus, in his Kabyle ethnological studies, he shows how honour alone, symbolic capital, mobilises the productive-reproductive springs of the social system of production. More broadly, we observe that 'the space of class conditions' is that of *differential* endowments, differences in social power; and that the problematic of 'fields' thus defines a set of cleavages, stakes of social struggle, which, in their homology, mark out a general cleavage: a division between those who hold sway over the social world, monopolising the material and cultural means of this ascendancy, and those who do not. In this whole section of his work, and the research that it prompts (for instance, in *The Weight of the World*), Bourdieu powerfully analyses in its 'sociological' dimension – as a 'social relation' – the very process of 'capital': a process of appropriation/dispossession of places, times, jobs, knowledge, and signs. The issue of the 'productive forces' – of the relations between the intentional and unintentional at the general level of social practice – nevertheless remain in the background. They are not the object of Bourdieu's sociological analysis, which is not articulated with this object either. This represents a repression whose conditions and effects remain to be analysed.

Bourdieu thus operates at the intersection of the 'phenomenal' and the 'essence', in the sense Marx attributes to these terms in Capital.

Contrasting the *essence*, or the relationship between classes, with the *phenomenon*, or the relationship between individuals, Marx polemicises against 'vulgar' conceptions that claim to account for the historical process in terms of inter-individual relations, such as competition. In his view, the individual moment is certainly just as 'essential', but it is only conceived in the context of generally defined structures. And class condition is not measured by the comparative 'volume' of capital that individuals possess, but – a vast problem, obviously, which is irreducible to its juridical aspect – by the ownership or non-ownership of the means of production: the 'essential' cleavage of the class relation and class struggle in the PFRP context. The logic of surplus-value is imposed on individuals as the logic of their practice. But, at the same time, it governs the (productive-destructive) dynamic of the productive forces, which periodically renews – regardless of the intention of individuals, behind their backs – the overall stake of the class relation, the historical horizon of practice.

Bourdieu most certainly takes account of a context of 'class condition'. He accords epistemic priority to the objective moment of structure over the subject moment of practical aim. And he cannot be criticised for taking *individual* practice as his special object. Moreover, by comparison with Marx, having assimilated subsequent ethnological and sociological culture, he expands the field of analysis: what is at stake in practical confrontation is as much cultural capital as economic capital. The competition between pupils characterised by their family *habitus* and, in the inter-generational dimension, between families pertains to the same ('phenomenal') level of analysis as competition on the market. And, as we shall see, Bourdieu presses the analysis to the point where classes, fractions, and other groups emerge that confront one another in terms of interests, aims, and strategies. Methodologically speaking, however, the analysis is maintained at a level below the decisive point – the relationship between the productive forces and the relations of production: the place where the intentional and the unintentional, structure and tendency, 'capital' as process and as historicity, and hence the possibility of taking distance from it, coincide. Not that in Bourdieu the sociological data are not always considered in their historical singularity, studied in their context and evolution, or that historico-political concerns are not evident; they increasingly are. But what is missing is an appropriate conceptuality. The category of 'conjuncture' alone imparts some motion to the HPSH paradigm: a chance movement, which does not warrant any historical projection. In order to envisage a 'theory of practice', however, in addition to the construction of social spaces ('constructed' class versus 'mobilised' class, *passim*), we must also (whatever the risks) accept the need to 'construct' historicity, in the knowledge that the concept of event forms part of such a construction (what *can* happen in a given structural order?). The profound 'mobilisation' of classes can be conceived only from the standpoint of the motives and goals that they can give themselves in an understanding of the relationship between class relations and *productive forces*, grasped in its *longue durée*.

The distinctiveness and fertility of the 'theory of practice' is that it is practised at the intersection of the phenomenal and the essence in the sense given these terms by Marx. However, it fails to consider the 'essence' for itself – the structure and field of the tendencies and possibilities that belong to it. Without this, practice cannot be understood as *praxis* – that is to say, according to the requisite distance from the claims of the *doxa*.

Within these limits, however, Bourdieu makes the phenomenal the operator of an 'essential' relationship: he makes the struggle between agents in the field the operator of a class struggle.

The 'theory of practice' provides resources for reflecting on collective action. It highlights *class habitus*, interests, and strategies. It involves an interface between agents who can be characterised not only by their individual features, but also by their class situations and *habitus*. Thus, in the social institutions particular to each field, classes confront one another. These are instances of class. The homology of the different fields, which imparts the same unequal opportunities to class *habitus*, and thereby indefinitely reduplicates the relation of domination, gives the latter its consistency, its properly hegemonic capacity.

The theorisation of a cultural arbitrariness, and of its imposition as symbolic violence, defines cultural reproduction as the reproduction of a class relation. What is reproduced is a difference that contains the conditions of a domination. A dominant class monopolises higher forms of knowledge only in particular cultural modes that its members have internalised since early infancy, which schools exalt and retranscribe, and wherein it identifies its chosen ones, who always enjoy a head start and amass successive victories which ultimately designate them as holders of the titles to be conferred. This is all the more the case in that their economic condition has facilitated a climate of 'leisure', which alone makes possible the distant relation to culture distinctive of scholarly culture. Symbolic violence resides in this serene innocence of a class confrontation that is unaware of itself, inheritance passing itself off as natural excellence. There is no calculation in this: the masters themselves share the same common sense as to what is 'distinguished'.

In this sense, the theory of culture and education established by Bourdieu and his colleagues (without it being possible here for me to consider the contribution of each of them) is an essential contribution to historical materialism. Previous critical theories stressed the monopolisation of knowledge. The approach in terms of *habitus*, distinction, 'relation to culture', directs us towards a more radical critique of the system, which lays bare the 'cultural' mechanisms of social segregation and its legitimation. This is a legitimate reproduction, because it is concealed in the form of the success of the most 'gifted' – in fact, the most fortunate of the inheritors, those endowed with sufficient assets. And it is a 'statistical' reproduction, not an automatic one, filtered and sublimated by exams and competitions, which ensures reproduction of the system of positions. In this sense, Marx showed that *competition*, whereby the 'best prevail', obscures the fact that in the 'capitalist process of production', despite some capitalists disappearing and others emerging, the capitalist structure is reproduced, identical to itself. In *competition* between individuals, Bourdieu likewise reveals a class struggle.

The instances particular to the various fields are thus designated as class institutions. Bourdieu is repelled by 'apparatuses', which announce 'the worst kind of functionalism'.[4] But he admirably described the... 'machine' for classifying:

> the educational institution...is able to function like an immense cognitive machine, operating classifications that, although apparently neutral, reproduce pre-existing social classifications.[5]

The sociology of education is treated as a sociology of class power. Just as, according to Marx, exploitation is concealed beneath the wage exchange, so, according to Bourdieu, subjugation is concealed beneath the formal equality of institutions. On these presuppositions, the state that possesses a 'monopoly of legitimate symbolic violence'[6] is a class state.

In this respect, Bourdieu makes a powerful contribution to a general theory of modern society.

In fact, an approach in terms of a dual endowment of agents, whose limits we have noted above, is nevertheless pertinent. This (so it seems to me) must be related to the fact that in modern society the class-relation operates specifically through the two mediations of the *market* and *bureaucracy* (and,

---

[4] Bourdieu 1992, p. 74.
[5] Bourdieu 1996, p. 52.
[6] Bourdieu 1992, p. 70.

more generally, the organisation, in the sense given this term by institutional economics); and that, correlatively, the state, supreme operator of these two class factors and their interface, likewise guarantees *two sorts of titles*: those of 'private property' and those of 'competence' (in Bourdieu's socio-critical sense). On this dual terrain, Bourdieu complements Marx with Weber, in addition mobilising the Weberian categories of the sociology of religion in order to name the work of the state educational institution – a theologico-political junction.

It is, it seems to me, this duality of the domination of the modern human being, in as much as he is to all intents and purposes dominated as a 'free man', which is translated into that of endowment capitals, which locates social agents and social groups on the map of 'class conditions'. One of the strengths of the analysis is the construction of 'social qualification', in its antinomic tension between class cultural arbitrariness and 'autonomous' excellence – where 'autonomy' refers to exclusive submission to the universal criteria of science for science's sake and of art for art's sake, foreign to the values and embellishments of economic or political power. In this way, Bourdieu deciphers the whole set of public and private institutions that are actually capable of conferring 'titles' – that is to say, distinctions, whatever they may be, which have advantages, prerogatives, rights or recognition attached to them – as institutions of a class state, a site of class confrontation. Ambiguous 'qualifications' and 'skills', which are vectors of class domination.

As a result of this dualistic reference, Bourdieu's problematic, so it seems to me, has manifest affinity with an opinion widely diffused in political philosophy and political sociology, which regards the intertwined pair of the market/bureaucracy as the typical form of modernity. In *Théorie générale*, I have proposed an interpretation of it that I call 'meta/structural'. Accordingly, beyond the 'non-mediation' of speech, two mediations irresistibly unfold that are polar opposites and yet indissociable, defined by Marx as the *a posteriori* and *a priori* modalities of productive co-operation: the *market* and the *organisation* (bureaucracies, hierarchies, and so on), correlative to the competing claims of the so-called liberty of the Ancients and the so-called liberty of the Moderns – claims which are always-already 'converted into their opposite'. In fact, in capitalist modernity market and organisation, *productive forces* as social modes of co-operation, are factors which, in their complex imbrication, give rise to class relations, in as much as they are relations of production.

Because he excludes consideration of the 'productive forces' from his field, Bourdieu cannot adequately include the 'relations of production' in it either. Consequently, nor can he take the dualistic gap illustrated by the conjoint reference to two 'species of capital', the economic and the cultural, to its ultimate conclusions. Nevertheless, his thematic opens powerfully onto such a bi-polar vision of class domination in modern society, which is less one-sided than Marx's. (It will be observed that the notion of 'relational capital', often evoked as a third term, is deduced in meta/structural analysis from primary factors: 'mediations', whether market or organisational, are never disconnected from 'immediate' relations – particularly those generated by the family on the market ownership side of the equation, and by the school on the bureaucratic organisation side.) It is not that Marx did not possess an acute sense of bureaucratic domination (his whole critique of the state attests to it). But he lacked certain operative concepts to this end, which Bourdieu has helped to develop.

However, Bourdieu tends – in line, at least, with the resonance of his HPSH scheme – to go no further than a study of this process of reproduction outside of the process of production.

In fact, he apprehends this cultural-bureaucratic dimension – the 'state nobility' – in a privileged fashion, *starting from the educational institution* that produces the hierarchy of *habitus* and 'skills'. However, we cannot dispense with considering it *on the basis of the social process of production itself*, in that hierarchical production reproduces hierarchy, supposed delegation to the centre relegates the executants, endlessly renews the separation between rulers and ruled, analogous to that between owners and non-owners characteristic of the capitalist production process according to Marx. Thus are constituted the differences and distances that *give rise* to differentiated, hierarchical titles of 'qualification', which in turn overdetermine these hierarchical relations (but do not possess the character of *original* determinant attributed to them by the conceptual framework of 'inheritance'). These titles are produced by the state educational machinery, in the sense of class state, which guarantees them in the same way as property titles. Here, we are indeed dealing with two processes (market/organisation) that are linked in polar fashion in a single process, co-involved in the modern class-form.

The privilege Bourdieu accords education in social reproduction gives his theory its Durkheimian tonality. Regardless of whether he makes it the reproduction of a relation of domination (*à la* Weber), or a class domination (*à la* Marx), he cannot avoid elaborating his analysis at a remove from the 'essential' site: the process of social production as an articulation of relations of production and productive forces. What remains unsatisfying in Bourdieu's analysis is thus a fixation on the structures of *transmission* of (endowment) *capital*, whereas reproduction, in its cultural and economic dimensions alike, is immanent in the social process of *production* as a whole, which *is reproduced as a process that separates* those who, by their market pre-eminence (property) or organisational pre-eminence ('skill'), monopolise practical control over the means of production (of exchange, information, etc.), and those who are dispossessed of it.

This analytical shortcoming manifests itself in Bourdieu's difficulty in dealing with an 'economic field'. The very idea that such a 'field' exists, characterised by its 'particular form of interest' – 'economic interest' – and by a particular mechanism – the 'economic mechanism' – is precisely what Marx deconstructs in his critique of political economy, by exploding the ideological unity of a univocal purpose of economic activity: wealth. The very concept of 'capitalist mode of production' refers to the fact that the purposes of use-value (concrete wealth) and of profit (abstract wealth) are separated. It dissolves the doxical unity of the supposed specific resource – the 'value-peculiar-to-the-field' – to which the idea that 'the criterion of value is a stake in the struggle' makes only oblique reference.[7]

Even so, Bourdieu not only draws on important research in the sociology of work and specifically on 'domination in labour',[8] imperative for the programme of 'historical materialism', but demonstrates that he can contribute towards a better understanding of the relationship between sociology and economics. In *Les Structures sociales de l'économie* (2000), the notion of (economic) *field*, as turned against the individualist metaphysics and 'scholastic' abstraction of the neo-classical economists, and that of *habitus*, likewise in accord with various institutionalist traditions from Veblen to Commons, Chandler to Polanyi, demonstrate that they can be mobilised in an analysis of oligopolistic strategies and their struggles in the national space for control of the state. In this context, globalisation emerges as the constitution of a

[7] Bourdieu 1984b.
[8] See *Actes de la recherche en sciences sociales*, no. 114, 1996.

universal, de-statised economic field, under the dominance of finance capital and its speculative logic, awaiting new bodies that are capable of 'genuinely universal ends'.[9] Bourdieu's distinctive programme – an economic anthropology – thus tends to converge with that of the circumambient neo-Marxism. But it must then be combined with theoretical tools different from those generally employed by Bourdieu.

The HPSH approach tends to represent the social structure of 'power' (at the summit) on the basis of its supposedly homological relationship with the educational structure. For historical materialism, the 'productive forces' comprise both technical knowledge (in its dialectical link with various sciences), as the art of arranging mechanisms in nature, and social know-how, co-operative knowledge. In this sense, market and organisation pertain to the productive forces – 'limited' rationality, which equally qualifies these forces as 'destructive'. In as much as it is social, this rational know-how is inseparable from rules. Human beings do not co-operate except according to certain rules that 'impose themselves', in the antinomy of the dual sense of this term, or without invoking what is supposedly reasonable. These 'modes of co-operation' thus constitute the interface of the productive forces and the relations of production. They represent 'relations of production', but not in the full sense in which the of themselves constitute the specific class relations of a 'mode of production', as a self-reproducible class structure. Thus, the market and organisation do not play the same role in antiquity, in the 'feudal' mode of production, or in capitalism. If capitalist modernity is defined, as I have said, by the metastructural interference of the market and organisation, it is characterised by an essential bi-polar division, on the basis of which we can perceive not only general class confrontation, but also the bi-polarity of the dominant class – the recurrent potential cleavage between its two constitutive fractions, according to the two class factors (which are imbricated and intersecting, but conceptually distinct and connected) of property and 'qualification', both of them being arbitrary social endowments, whose titles are guaranteed by the state.

Yet this primary-polar cleavage within the dominant class, evoked in Bourdieu by way of the two forms of endowment capital, is, despite everything, relatively disqualified, in favour of a *second cleavage*, internal to the

---

[9] Bourdieu 2000, p. 280.

sphere of qualification: between *scientific-cultural* qualification, recognised in academic hierarchies, and *managerial* qualification, which is attached to economic and political power. This second (intra-cultural) cleavage, maintained by family *habitus*, has its guarantor and condition in the summits of the educational system, between the 'autonomous' pole of higher education (of the Écoles normales supérieures variety, site of art and knowledge) and its 'heteronomous' pole (of the École normale d'administration, Hautes études commercielles, or Sciences po variety, where the values of economic and political power prevail). It can be referred to the temporal/spiritual duality of the process of domination, to the dialectical tension between these spheres, characteristic of the exercise of power, particularly in the modern era. This gives rise to interesting investigations, which nevertheless intersect rather problematically with the supposed cleavage in the dominant class, often evoked by Bourdieu, between a 'dominant fraction', which holds economic power, and a 'dominated fraction', responsible for intellectual and cultural functions.

The problem is created by the supposed homology between the 'field of schools of power' and the 'space of power', and also with the 'social space' as a whole, such as it is illustrated, for example, in a series of diagrams that refer to one another.[10] In reality, the putative homology between the two spaces is highly suspect. In fact, only the summit comprises this cleavage between two cultural criteria (autonomous/heteronomous culture). This intra-cultural cleavage cannot be taken as reflecting the one I have referred to as 'essential', which results from the duality of the mediations, market and organisation – modern class-factors which, as such, govern 'the space of power' (the 'heteronomous' schools prepare people for functions combining knowledge-power that is as much commercial as organisational).

In short, it is important to discern within the dominant class a *primary* duality, based on the *metastructural antinomy* between two 'poles' (market intra-individuality/organisational centricity), or between two interfering 'fractions', one of them endowed with 'ownership capital' (market mechanism), while the other is endowed with 'qualification capital' (an organisational, bureaucratic mechanism peculiar to firms and administration in general); and a

10 See in Bourdieu 1996, pp. 267–8, diagrams 13, 'the social space' (which is based on Bourdieu 1984, pp. 128–9), and 14, 'the space of institutions of higher education' (which is itself clarified by diagram 3, p. 145).

second duality, corresponding to *the antinomy of domination*, which is cashed in the duality of qualification procedures between the school of power (its direct exercise, characterised as economico-political) which trains managers, and the élite schools, which form intellectuals, artists, and scientists. I therefore maintain – and this is not the place to argue the ins and outs of the thesis – that Bourdieu is not justified in superimposing these two cleavages. This superimposition in fact tends to represent society on the basis of the school; and its fate on the basis of the figure of the intellectual.

This leads to a Kantian teleological view of emancipation, which cannot take the place of reflection on the alternative opened up by Marx. This concept of domination, which can be referred to Weber (the capacity to make oneself obeyed), and which concentrates social power in a 'field of power' situated at the summit of society, translates into a concept of history and politics that gives the elite and its 'autonomous' fraction more than their due.

This privileged consideration of a division of labour between two types of the dominant – one set of them devoted to economic-administrative domination, the other to symbolic domination – is in fact the prelude to a certain philosophy of politics and history. Symbolic capital, whereby economic and political domination is ensured, assumes a legitimation that can only be performed by autonomous cultural institutions, with criteria independent of any temporal power. The only thing that can be acknowledged as legitimate is a form of rule devoted to society's universal interests. And Bourdieu's thesis is that there is a productive tension here: domination can only be exercised by denying itself; and this is an opportunity that must be grasped by the dominated.

This thesis is not unambiguous, for it oscillates between reference to those below, who cannot tolerate arbitrariness, and reference to the servants of autonomy, whose particular interest is supposedly the universal. It recalls Habermas's thesis on the virtues of the scientific community. But Habermas makes this exigency of universality a property of ordinary language (the 'illocutionary' proposition – that of the communicative relation in general – always presents a triple claim to truth, to justice, and to authenticity) – that is to say, of ordinary human beings, *natural* supports of this universality, and not a property of the particular category of scholars.

It is true that Bourdieu is not to be criticised for emphasising the emancipatory potential of knowledge and, in particular, of sociological knowledge.

In *Leçon sur la leçon*, he legitimately stresses that 'knowledge is emancipatory when it unveils operations that owe some of their efficacy to the fact that people are ignorant of them'.[11] The peculiarity of struggle in the scientific field is that victory is supposed to go to those who demonstrate the validity of their analyses and demonstrations. The excellence recognised in it is the capacity to produce the truth. The practice of sociology can thus 'help render us ever so slightly the masters and possessors of social nature',[12] by making us aware of all the forms of fetishism. And the text ends with the 'faith' of the sociologists in the 'emancipatory powers' of social science as a 'science of symbolic power capable of restoring to social subjects control over the false transcendencies that ignorance is forever creating and recreating'.[13] This Pascalian wager – more strictly formulated than the Kantian reason for hope, marked by liberalism – opens into a historical teleology that commits us to a self-emancipatory practice. It will be observed that it only involves a 'wager'. But we might ask if it does not grant the man of (social) science, in as much as his putative *particular* interest is the universal interest – wager within the wager – an exorbitant privilege.

Correlatively, in so far at least as it tends to restrict analysis to the *sociological* dimension of 'social relations', falling short of their relations to the 'productive-destructive forces' – the 'metabolic relationship' between humanity and nature referred to by Marx – it, unlike historical materialism, lacks an epistemological orientation towards a programme for a revolutionary alternative. This, it is true, poses more generally the question of a 'Marxist' sociology or economics (i.e. which can be referred to historical materialism), as regional disciplines by definition, compared with a 'general theory of *practice*', which is the true challenge of Marxism – thinking human finitude *in its infinite entirety*. We should not make groundless accusations against a 'general theory of practice' for not being historical materialism. We shall simply question it about the indications it gives of dismissing the project of historical materialism, while claiming that the only thing which is scientific and legitimate is a programme that is theoretically and politically less ambitious.

11 Bourdieu 1982, p. 20.
12 Bourdieu 1982, p. 33.
13 Bourdieu 1982, p. 56.

Chapter Thirty-Two

Deleuze, Marx and Revolution: What It Means to 'Remain Marxist'

Isabelle Garo

> 'I think Félix Guattari and I have remained Marxists.'[1]

Introduction

Against the lifeless backdrop of France's current intellectual scene – and considering the weighty silence that falls upon all those who dare to step outside the mould – Deleuze stands out as one of the last major writers, a creative philosopher, original, even subversive. In any case, he appears as a marginal academic figure, linked to anti-establishment left-wing movements of which he was, however, never an active militant. He always refused to disown May '68 as well as Marx and, right to the end, associated himself not so much with revolution as with a constant, stubborn apologia for what becoming-revolutionary is or could be, avoiding any backsliding and rejecting all totalisations. Up until the 1990s he claimed the necessity of 'resistance to the present',[2] and sang the praises of 'anger with the

[1] Deleuze 1995, p. 171.
[2] Deleuze and Guattari 1994, p. 108.

way things are',[3] but he was and remains a well-respected, even revered, philosopher; his lectures at Vincennes were always packed and the retail success of his books, however taxing or voluminous they may be, persists to this today.

For this reason, it would be misguided and superficial to oppose a nostalgic portrait of a generation of 'committed' writers, for the main part deceased – Foucault, Deleuze, Châtelet, Althusser, Castoriadis, Badiou, etc. – to the expanding desert of today's normalised academic thought, which has disowned Marx, reduced May '68 to a student carnival, made the word revolution sound ridiculous and obscene, and obliterated anything to do with the will for transformation or even anything that is merely critical, on a political and ideological level. On the one hand, the political commitment of the protagonists of that time was of a complex kind and marked a turning point, namely in its opposition to Sartre and the mode of intellectual commitment he embodied and theorised,[4] as well as by rejecting the Marxist doctrine upheld by the French Communist Party (PCF) and the repulsive image of Marxism projected by the 'socialist' states. On the other hand, we can observe the scattered signs of a renewed interest in the work of certain thinkers of this generation (particularly Deleuze and Foucault), an observation that is indeed incompatible with the notion of a definitively buried era and which testifies, rather, to a complex continuity, to a legacy that is paradoxical and problematic but nonetheless real.

Indeed, Deleuze's continued presence as a vital figure on the contemporary intellectual scene is almost surprising, as he gives rise to conferences, publications, special issues – not only to celebratory commentaries but also to a re-engagement with and a pursuit of his work, occasionally to a new form of activism, and to a relative but genuine academic re-assessment. This raises a

---

[3] Deleuze 1995, p. vii.

[4] From this perspective, the 1972 conversation between Deleuze and Foucault entitled 'Intellectuals and Power' presents itself as a political manifesto: theory is a praxis but 'local and regional, as you say: non-totalising', as Foucault replies to Deleuze (Deleuze 2004, p. 207). The Marxist or Marxist-inflected theme of the alliance between theory and practice is both maintained and rejected through the refusal of any global or totalising conception. Far less marked than Foucault's, Deleuze's political commitment basically came down to his involvement with the Groupe d'information sur les prisons (GIP) and to his support for the comedian Coluche's 1980 presidential campaign. On the other hand, the repudiation of traditional forms of intellectual commitment strikingly combines with a 'proletarian' phraseology. Thus, Deleuze concludes the interview as follows: 'every partial revolutionary attack or defence…connects up with the struggle of the working class' (Deleuze 2004, p. 213).

question: how are we to apprehend the fact that the current retreat from a certain mode of political commitment, the virtual waning of radical alternatives to capitalism, is accompanied by the continued project of another conception of politics or the political, for which May '68 represents the call or the beginning, for Deleuze as well as for others of his generation? Where is the break to be located and was there really a break in the first place? In other words, did Deleuze's conception of revolution emerge at the end of a trajectory where all revolutionary prospects had collapsed? Or, instead, during the process of the redefinition of revolution as micrological and micro- or infra-political? Or, at the beginning of a new historical sequence that cancels out these two diagnoses and suggests the need of breaking with the break of the 1960s?

In any case, the facile picture that traces our decadence back to '68 is definitely inappropriate,[5] even though it turns on its head the diagnosis of its fiercest attackers, such as Ferry and Renaut. Rather, what still needs to be considered is how such a complex and contradictory transition from one part of that generation to ours may have taken place, a transition that not only signals a break and a decline but just as much the ongoing collapse of theoretical-political Marxism since the mid-1970s, when the effects of a relentless struggle against its representatives combined with its growing sterility. This collapse is wholly compatible with the proliferation of the name 'Marx', and immediately led to a redefinition of the 'revolution', as Deleuze demonstrates in exemplary fashion. Thus, what should be grasped is a kind of dislocation. And this change of perspective is indeed related to the ingenuity of Deleuze's teeming *œuvre* and inseparable from the political and intellectual context in which it is inscribed.

There are many reasons for this: not just the ideological and political transformation from the 1960s to the 1990s, but also the irruption of an economic crisis that challenged the social compromise and a certain conception of state action and its reformist and regulating capacities. This was a brutal and lasting economic sea-change, marking the collapse of Keynesian social policies that proved incapable of averting it, but also the end of the Fordist interlude. Ultimately, this also signalled a crisis of Marxism itself: the

5 In a 1980 interview, Deleuze himself suggests such a reading, referring to the 'sterile phase' of the present, and setting it against the previous period: 'After Sartre. The generation to which I belong was, I think, a strong one (with Foucault, Althusser, Derrida, Lyotard, Serres, Faye, Châtelet, and others' (Deleuze 1995, p. 27).

fossilised preservation, or even the reworking by some, of a theoretical-political legacy and approach in any case failed to gain the popular support that would have at least enabled it to maintain its significance as an energising political intervention and the bearer of real prospects of change. In short, during this period everything conspired to make of 'Marx' a name that some considered repellent and others obsolete, but also a reference that would henceforth be necessarily philosophical, only allowing the virtues and weapons of his critique to re-emerge on a theoretical terrain.

Because Marxism did not remain on the theoretical-political ground, and proved incapable of re-conquering it, it gradually waned and found itself forcefully excluded from the realms of higher education and publishing. Yet this process was shadowed by the retention of a reference to Marx, accompanying an often underground reworking which was echoed in Deleuze's thought. However, Deleuze did not provide the conceptual tools for grasping the conditions and implications of such a reworking of Marx.

Yet the point is not to read Deleuze's *œuvre* only as an effect of its context, firstly because he was an actor in his own right, but also because his thought provides a truly original and complex way of engaging with Marx which in turn, and in a non-reductionist fashion, casts light on the wider context of the ideological and theoretical shift. Deleuze was born in 1925 and belonged to the generation that experienced the Liberation; he witnessed the radical changes affecting the social and political landscape, accompanying and participating in these transformations himself through analyses that severed any connection between theory and direct involvement in the workers' struggles.[6]

This is why, ultimately, when Deleuze uses the word 'revolution', it is less to be understood as an objective than as challenge to the term's very meaning. The word thus becomes a faint echo, a flickering reference – both maintained and sublimated – to the 1968 events alone, read not as a partial

[6] Félix Guattari, far more than Deleuze, kept up throughout his life an intense political activism: at first a Trotskyist and the leader of the oppositional group *Voie communiste* from 1955 to 1965, he participated directly in the anti-colonial struggles, then gave his support to Italian *autonomia*, founded the CINEL in 1977 to explore 'new spaces of freedom' and in the eighties joined the environmentalist movement, theorising 'ecosophy'. To this list, of course, we must add his anti-psychiatric action, namely his collaboration with Jean Oury at the La Borde clinic. The books he wrote with Deleuze are the ones that most saliently display a political dimension and maintain a revolutionary theme.

political failure, but as the successful substitution of becoming for history. 1968 thus appears as the closure, exhaustion and reorientation of the entirety of revolutionary history, assimilated to that which by its nature comes to a sad end.[7] 'They say revolutions turn out badly. But they're constantly confusing two different things, the way revolutions turn out historically and people's revolutionary becoming' – May '68 having been defined a few lines above as 'an irruption, of becoming in its pure state'.[8] This is why the Deleuzean question of revolution should be placed at the heart of this seismic shift: still rooted in the sinking ground of political commitment, (using Bergson, Nietzsche and Whitehead as well as Marx) Deleuze migrates to the correlatively re-emerging ground of a renewed metaphysical approach, as a henceforth postmodern thinker of flows as well as an icon of insubordination...

This is why the answer Deleuze gave to Toni Negri in 1990 deserves attention: 'I think that Guattari and I have remained Marxists'.[9] We must try to read this statement in a manner that preserves its full complexity, its ambiguity even. It is to Deleuze's credit that he never took Marxism for granted. But, in his works, the word never had a well-defined meaning (he is very much like Foucault in this sense). It often refers to a certain political and theoretical configuration behind which we can discern the presence of established political forces, notably the PCF, and a mode of involvement or comradeship, but of which nothing is said either. And it is a question of 'remaining'. For a thinker of becoming, remaining cannot be a very stimulating objective but, at most, a slightly disenchanted and necessarily sceptical stance. On reading the rest of Deleuze's statement, we learn that 'remaining a Marxist' also means that 'we think that any political philosophy must turn on the analysis of capitalism and the ways it has developed'.[10] In a way, a great deal has already been stated here, which testifies to Deleuze's profound loyalty towards a political past that is not explicated – and which, in this sense, cannot be a legacy. But it

---

[7] This diagnosis is restated and further developed in the video-interview *Abécédaire*: 'All revolutions fail. Everybody knows it, but people act as if this a new discovery. You have to be stupid!'. Deleuze indistinctly evokes the Soviet, English, American and (1789) French, Algerian revolutions. Further on, regarding May '68, he adds: 'I am a firm believer in the difference between History and Becoming! It was a becoming-revolutionary without a revolutionary future' ('G comme Gauche', in Deleuze and Parnet 1996).

[8] Deleuze 1995, p. 171.

[9] Ibid.

[10] Ibid.

also reveals a radical shift onto the terrain of 'political philosophy' – a project utterly foreign to Marx's – and a concern with what political philosophy can understand by revolution and what it may have to say about it.

I. Capitalism and flows

In order to further examine this question, it may be useful to consider the economic aspect of Deleuze's account of capitalism, and how it reveals the ontological underpinnings of his notion of revolution. Indeed, an ontology of flows and becoming surfaces here more clearly than anywhere else, even if it pervasively and deeply structures Deleuze's thought. But, even if Deleuze positions himself in terms of a study of what he calls production, he never offers an economic analysis as such. This is despite his frequent use of economic categories to which he confers a metaphorical meaning that is far wider and far more ambiguous than either their technical meaning or the Marxist definition with which they are frequently but allusively reconnected.

The reasons for this run deep. *Anti-Oedipus*, published in 1973, and *A Thousand Plateaux*, published in 1980 – the two parts of a single work entitled *Capitalism and Schizophrenia* – set out to define contemporary capitalism, expressly rejecting any dissociation between base and superstructure, or between an economic reality and the various social and individual dimensions that go along with it. This is a Marxist thesis if ever there was one! But the proclaimed rejection of the reductionist argument seems to conceal another tendential reduction of production to exchange, of politics to practices of state repression and control, of social contradictions to mechanical assemblages. This reduction is all the less visible in that it is coupled with the extension of the term 'production' to individual desire and the correlative multiplication of its occurrences. But, in this case, in contrast to the simplifications of doctrinal Marxism, the refusal to separate base and superstructure (i.e. to distinguish them) seems to culminate in the base crashing against the superstructure, in the flattening of reality onto its concept, of revolution onto '*revolution*', that is of politics onto 'political philosophy.'

In effect, opposition to the capitalist order abandons the themes of ideology, alienation and class struggle for that of desire. In spite of their affinity with Freudo-Marxism, Deleuze and Guattari reject Wilhelm Reich's analysis, which seems to maintain desire and social life as parallel and possibly overlapping instances. Neither Freud nor Marx then, nor Freud *and* Marx, but the simultaneous critique of both. What they want to think is rather a 'desiring production' or 'the coextension of the social field and desire'.[11] And it is precisely here that the singularity of a mode of conceptual invention that is just as much a philosophical style becomes apparent: because generating a coherence between desire and the social is by no means straightforward. And because the two concepts are not related through a common causality, their correlation requires a conceptual operator that metaphorises one and the other, and one through the other, thereby establishing the correspondence and synonymy that authorises the constant shift from one to the other. This operator is the notion of flow, which runs through Deleuze's work as a whole and tends to reduce any historical reality to a vital process and an exchange of energy.[12]

On the specific terrain of the economy – whether we are dealing with the ancient city, the Germanic commune, or the feud – the apologia of flows accompanies the explanation of capitalism as an 'emergence of decoded flows' against their previous coding.[13] It is a question of replacing an analysis in terms of determinate historical contradictions, that of Marx, with one in terms of parallel, generalised, and almost interchangeable lines of flight. All of a sudden, the political sphere in the guise of the state finds itself strangely separated out and opposed to commercial flows. If we pause on this point, we can register another theoretical consequence, which is truly staggering. For the only perspective that such an analysis of capital opens onto is that of a sustained and accelerated 'deterritorialisation' of the commercial flows of capital! In fact, if there are no contradictions, or class struggles as bearers of the prospect of another social and economic formation, we cannot but always remain with the flows, and with the sole alternative of either artificially blocking them or freeing them further.

The notion of deterritorialisation risks revealing itself to be, both ultimately and on the economic terrain, a synonym for deregulation, whose effects have nothing emancipatory about them. Nevertheless, it is precisely here that the theme of revolution re-emerges, in the most paradoxical fashion:

---

11 Deleuze and Guattari 1984, p. 30.

12 Alain Badiou uses Deleuze's notion of life as the focus of his critique of a political conception that is losing its specificity. On this question, see Thoburn 2003.

13 Deleuze and Guattari 1984, p. 222.

> But which is the revolutionary path? Is there one? – To withdraw from the world market, as Samir Amin advises Third World countries to do, in a curious revival of the fascist 'economic solution'? Or might it be to go in the opposite direction? To go still further, that is, in the movement of the market, of decoding and deterritorialisation? For perhaps the flows are not yet deterritorialised enough, not decoded enough, from the viewpoint of theory and a practice of a highly schizophrenic character. Not to withdraw from the process, but to go further, to 'accelerate the process', as Nietzsche put it: in this matter, the truth is that we haven't seen anything yet.[14]

Reading these lines, we are allowed to wonder if the apologia of flows does not converge above all with the most radical and anarchistic liberal thematics, namely those of someone like Hayek – despite the fact that Deleuze says nothing explicit about this matter, even if he clearly relies at times on the marginalist theory of neoclassical economics,[15] without ever asking himself about its compatibility with Marxian theses.

Thus the revolution is always the obverse of an essentially morbid statification, as if Deleuze's work functioned as an echo chamber of the gradual failure, at the cusp of the 1970s, of Keynesian policies of increased public spending, a failure which is not analysed but metaphorically referred back to the blockage, arrest and asphyxiation of that which lives and circulates: economic knowledge and the critique of psychoanalysis combine in an astonishing theory of flows and of what obstacles them, a new version of a dualism that lays claim to universal historical validity:

> The social axiomatic of modern societies is caught between two poles, and is constantly oscillating from one pole to the other. Born of decoding and deterritorialisation, on the ruins of the despotic machine, these societies are caught between the *Urstaat* that they would like to resuscitate as an overcoding and reterritorialising unity, and the unfettered flows that carry them toward an absolute threshold.... There is an oscillation between the

---

14 Deleuze and Guattari 1984, pp. 239–40.

15 Deleuze and Guattari 1987, pp. 437–440. Daniel Bensaïd reminds us that the project of replacing labour-value with 'desire-value' can first be found among the neoclassical authors, namely Léon Walras and Charles Gide (Bensaïd 2004, p. 283).

> reactionary paranoiac overcharges and the subterranean, schizophrenic and revolutionary charges.[16]

In a capitalism of flows, every prospect of planning is horrifying[17] and resonates with a martial socialism. But Deleuze does not pursue an analysis that would bring him manifestly too close to liberal theses on this subject, despite the fact that he says nothing explicitly about them. In the end, the only 'true' revolutions would remain at the level of the micro-economy that describes them, albeit situated on another terrain: they too would be micro, invisible, barely thinkable, as Deleuze insists in an interview with Toni Negri we have already alluded to. While the diatribe against the market is evident, Deleuze displays a certain pessimism and defines minorities by their power of invention: 'a minority is not a model, it is a becoming, a process'. The process has been displaced from the economic toward the political, understood in an extremely restricted sense and, in so doing, it has become singular, creative, and rare, more Nietzschean than ever: 'A people is always a creative minority, and remains one even when it acquires a majority'.[18]

Extending the analysis through the description of societies of control that replace disciplinary societies, following a distinction borrowed from Foucault, Deleuze affirms that the forms of resistance also change: 'Computer piracy and viruses...will replace strikes and what the nineteenth century called "sabotage"'.[19] It would be difficult to signify more clearly without stating it that neither directly productive work nor the working class or waged workers are any longer at the centre of the analysis or of the epoch. The interview concludes with the apologia for events irreducible to their conditions and with the creation of 'vacuoles of non-communication' as the only remotely concrete goal. The theme of revolution is revealed as lacking any possible anchor in an analysis of labour or social conflicts, and is transported toward mores and art, writing and philosophy. What is more, the retention of the revolutionary theme only serves better to highlight the collapse in the midst of which it continues to radiate, like a prospect which is decidedly more poetic than political.

---

16 Deleuze and Guattari 1984, p. 260.
17 Deleuze and Guattari 1984, p. 256.
18 Deleuze 1995, p. 173.
19 Deleuze 1995, p. 175.

II. Reading Marx with Nietzsche

Deleuzean ontology is here a thinking of becoming, of the *élan*, of life, which is considerably in excess to the question of the economy but both envelops and displaces it. Bergson and Nietzsche are its substantial allies. In the *Anti-Oedipus*, they are spoken of far more rarely than Marx and Freud. But the treatment reserved to Marx is of a very particular nature: never commented on as such, by an author who is nevertheless considered a master in the art of erudite and original, academic and unnerving reading. Reading Deleuze's most original works, it is as if, compared to other figures, the fantasmatic presence of Marx were the most constant one, and as if, at the same time, the proliferation of imprecise references and general propositions prohibited a systematic reading, an explicit analysis, a sustained critique. Looking more closely, the mention of Marx is the index of a twofold approach: on the one hand, he is an indisputable and affirmed guarantee, on the other, he is the occasion to recall misunderstandings, blockages and limits which are peremptorily asserted.

The relationship to Marx thus reveals itself to be extremely complex. The laudatory reference to Marx, which is an important aspect of Deleuze's thought at a time when Marx is pilloried by the *nouveaux philosophes* and his death is declaimed by Jean-Marie Benoist[20] is not devoid of courage, or, for this very reason, of political significance. But, rather than being linked to a specifically political stance, this significance largely stems precisely from the opposition to an external context which condemns any relationship to Marx. We must also add to this well-known position other remarks that briefly preceded it, but which are far more substantial and wholly different in tone. Thus, in the course of 28 May 1973, Deleuze elucidates the three differences that separate Guattari and him from what he calls 'Marxism'. The first difference is that 'Marxism poses problems in terms of need; on the contrary, our problem is posed in terms of desire'. The second concerns ideology : 'there is no ideol-

[20] In 1970, Jean-Marie Benoist published *Marx est mort*. In 1977, Bernard-Henri Lévy's *La barbarie à visage humain* (*Barbarism with a Human Face*) (in which Deleuze and Guattari are precisely fingered as Marxists) and André Glucksmann's *Les maîtres penseurs* (*The Master Thinkers*) appeared in its wake. Deleuze reacted vigorously and immediately to the operation of political and media promotion of the 'new philosophers', placing it in the context of the great fear elicited by the prospect of an electoral victory of the united Left, Communists included. This is a very fertile recontextualisation, but it remains limited in a sense, since it focuses on the short-term analysis of the presidential elections.

ogy, there are only statements that organise power'. And the third involves the characteristic double movement of Marxism, of recapitulation and development. Deleuze adds: 'I think that these three practical differences make it so that our problem has never been that of a return to Marx. Rather, our problem is that of forgetting, including the forgetting of Marx. Yet in forgetting some small fragments rise to the surface'.[21]

How can the affirmation that one has 'remained Marxist' be accompanied without contradiction by this strange assertion of the shipwreck of Marxism? In order to dispel this paradox, we must understand how 'remaining Marxist', rather than signifying the retention of a theoretical reference to be used and studied as such, is above all a political marker, in the restricted sense of the term, which functions in the rapidly changing period from the 1960s to the 1990s, and does so in a variable manner: having started as the synonym of an inscription in a philosophical field where the reference to Marx and to Marxism is constant or at least trivial, from the mid-1970s onwards, and even more in the 1990s, the assertive mention of an allegiance suddenly appears as the refusal of an abandonment or a repudiation, at the very time when these have turned into the ideological norm. In this respect, Deleuze and Guattari are among the rare intellectual figures of that moment who display a stubborn resistance to the spirit of the times, and their declarations of Marxism are to be understood as an unmitigated refusal to accompany this brutal change of direction and to follow the example of the cynical and liberal conversions of some ex-*soixante-huitards*.

But despite this refusal to become turncoats, Deleuze and Guattari's reference to Marx is far from indicating an adherence to any kind of Marxist tradition. And it is here that the memory of Marx, which sometimes resembles a kind of retinal after-image, can precisely and non-contradictorily coincide with his 'forgetting'. That a name and some concepts escape this forgetting only further illustrates the ebb, the general retreat of a conceptuality and of a certain definition of theoretical-political work, through the retention of the reference to the very one (Marx) who sought to push such a definition forward. This affirmation can rely on two aspects of Deleuze's thought. On the one hand, the way in which the mention of Marx's writings and concepts is carried out in his work, especially in *Capitalism and Schizophrenia*. On the

21 Deleuze 1973.

other, we indeed find in Deleuze a theory of forgetting, which elucidates this complex relationship to Marx.

With regard to forgetting, the Deleuzean conception of history draws on a very determinate source: Nietzsche, of course, who makes forgetting into a central and well-developed concept. It is obvious that the entire conception of desire draws on this reading, combined with that of Spinoza, in order to think the power and productivity of being, rejecting anything that smacks of a separation into stratified instances, of the division between superstructure and infrastructure (even if Marx speaks of base), of power opposed to desire. In so doing, Marx and Nietzsche become compatible, commensurable, not so much in light of the politics that they inspire (and Deleuze never envisages Nietzsche in terms of a form of commitment which was nevertheless quite real),[22] but because of their common taste for philosophy, the play of their shared ontologisation which evades their properly historical anchoring: compared to the one attributed to Marx, Nietzsche's metaphysics can thus appear as promising far more liberation and harbouring a far superior subversive charge.

It is through a metaphorical game of contrasts that Nietzsche – an analogical philosopher if there ever was one – allows Deleuze to turn Hegel into the foil of all the theories of life and power, which are grasped from the luminous perspective of desire and not on the terrain of the biologistic and reactionary vitalism that they nevertheless draw much of their inspiration from![23] It is the height of paradox – though obviously very seductive because of the apparently audacious anti-doxa that it carries – to view dialectics as a thinking of *ressentiment*, as the very philosophy of the unhappy consciousness which according to Deleuze represents for Hegel himself the tutelary figure of his entire *œuvre*. The care lavished on the reading of Nietzsche compares badly with the casualness with which the portrait of a reactive and ultimately nihilist Hegel is painted.

More generally, such an approach allows Deleuze to evade the fact that Hegelian negation is by no means a mysterious negating power aiming at dissolution, but determinate negation, a moment of the thing itself and therefore a principle of its concreteness. The consequence of the Deleuzean condemna-

---

[22] See the monumental study of Nietzsche by Domenico Losurdo (Losurdo 2003).
[23] On this point, see Steiner 2001.

tion is that the Marxian criticism of the Hegelian dialectic itself falls under the blows of a critique so devastating that it does not even seem necessary to stop and consider it. For Deleuze, it is Stirner who finally reveals himself as the one who leads the dialectic back to its proper place, that of a procedural sophistics. In Stirner, it is the ego that destroys everything: in this sense 'Stirner is the dialectician who reveals nihilism as the truth of the dialectic'.[24] His merit is to have understood that the dialectic ultimately refers only to the ego, and it is on this terrain that Marx intervenes in his turn:

> Marx elaborates his famous doctrine of the conditioned ego: the species and the individual, species being and the particular, social order and egoism are reconciled in the ego conditioned by social and historical relations. Is this sufficient? What is the species and *which one* is the individual? Has the dialectic found its point of equilibrium and rest or merely a final avatar, the socialist avatar before the nihilist conclusion? It is difficult to stop the dialectic and history on the common slope down which they drag each other. Does Marx do anything but mark the last stage before the end, the proletarian stage?[25]

There is no way around it, the dialectic is dragged into an overpowering cascade of negations, which makes it so that, whether subjective or objective, it succumbs to the self-destruction of which it is merely the unconscious and imprudent discourse.

III. Revolution, history, philosophy

Here again, the extremely general nature of Deleuze's words enables him to construct an anti-dialectical motif he can integrate anywhere, appearing regularly throughout his work and determining to a great extent his reading of Marx. As he writes: 'What I most detested was Hegelianism and dialectics'.[26] As a consequence, what should be performed is either a 'liberation of Marx from Hegel',[27] or a critique encompassing Freud, Marx, and the

[24] Deleuze 1983, p. 161.
[25] Deleuze 1983, p. 162.
[26] Deleuze 1995, p. 7.
[27] Deleuze 2004, p. 145. When confronted with an interlocutor surprised that no concessions are made for Hegel, while a conservative philosopher like Bergson is

bourgeoisie on account of their common conception of history. In the former case, Deleuze argues that Althusser has undertaken that task, while in the latter, his critique becomes so devastating that 'remaining a Marxist' no longer seems really feasible, except if it means remaining inane and slightly embittered. In fact, for Deleuze, there are two notions, distinct though profoundly entangled, that should be attacked: the notion of development, and that of memory. As Deleuze states:

> In Marxism, a certain culture of memory appeared right at the beginning; even revolutionary activity was supposed to proceed to this capitalisation of the memory of social formations. It is, if one prefers, Marx's Hegelian aspect, included in *Das Kapital*.[28]

Along with this astonishing 'capital' of revolutions, memory is again juxtaposed by Deleuze to the Nietzschean apologia of forgetfulness.

With obvious respect but concealed antagonism, Deleuze constantly stands close to Marx's work. We can read this in light not only of the relentless critique undertaken by Deleuze but also of that kinship which he simultaneously lays claim to and denies. This leads Deleuze to be far less interested in the texts of Marx than in producing a counter-thought, a counter-Marxism, that for fundamental theoretical and political reasons has nothing to do with an anti-Marxism or another Marxism. In that respect, 'remaining a Marxist' should mean constructing an analysis as close to Marx as possible but featuring a perpetual alteration of him, inventing other words and other concepts at all the nodal points of the Marxian analysis of capitalism. It is precisely at this level that Deleuze's equally contradictory and complex relationship with philosophy, politics, and the university becomes apparent.

Depending on the cases, Deleuze undertakes the explicit dismissal of certain cardinal notions ascribed to Marxism or elaborated by Marx, carries out a more nuanced but never quite accurate critique of other notions, or advocates

---

granted honours, Deleuze responds: 'Why not Hegel? Well, somebody has to play the role of traitor. What is philosophically incarnated in Hegel is the enterprise to "burden" life, to overwhelm it with every burden, to reconcile life with the State and religion, to inscribe death in life – the monstrous enterprise to submit life to negativity, the enterprise of resentment and unhappy consciousness. Naturally, with this dialectic of negativity and contradiction, Hegel has inspired every language of betrayal, on the right as well as on the left (theology, spiritualism, technocracy, bureaucracy, etc.)' (p. 144).

[28] Deleuze 2004, p. 277.

the removal without further ado of certain concepts – in particular *dialectics, materialism, alienation, class struggle, communism*. Such a dismissal and critique draw the lineaments of another philosophy and a completely different understanding of politics and revolution. Starting from as close as possible to Marx or a certain conception of Marxism, it aims at subverting its meaning by shifting, displacing, or upsetting statements deemed too impoverished or simple. There is nothing questionable as such in the approach itself except the silence it generates as regards the operations it carries out. But though it produces a singular form of theoretical invention – the hallmark of Deleuze's thinking is its undeniable richness – it can nevertheless be confronted with its own propositions, not only to the persistent declaration of Marxism, as we have seen, but to a certain definition of thought activity and its relation to practice, to a definition of philosophy, and hence also to a type of political commitment or non-commitment.

It is interesting to linger again upon the stylistic devices occasioning this specific theoretical invention and the basis for this displacement, in particular as far as Marx is concerned. As we have remarked, Deleuze's thinking often works through analogies, shifts, displacements, to such an extent that it results in a singular form of writing and a recognisable style, which are just as much a way of thinking. Deleuze does not construct a system but displaces, generalises and metaphorises, suggests and circumvents, alludes, surveys and aestheticises.[29] This produces the overall impression that staggering discoveries are at stake in his writing, particularly for all the texts using heavily 'Marxist' terms, as they become suddenly endowed with new brilliance and fascinating depth, at the same time as they await comprehension. Here and there, one comes across a Marxism that is easy to identify through key terms – which are less concepts than mere signals – yet the selfsame terms are immediately rendered unrecognisable and unprecedented by the incorporation of foreign concepts disrupting their ordinary and 'well-known' logic. In *Anti-Oedipus* for instance, we can read the following:

> In brief, the flows of code that are 'liberated' in science and technics by the capitalist regime engender a machinic surplus value that does not directly

---

[29] Perry Anderson notes that a distinctive trait of French thought lies in its literary virtuosity, which he sees as grounded in the rhetorical tradition conveyed by élite institutions – *khâgnes* and the *école normale* (Anderson 2005, pp. 19–20).

> depend on science and technics themselves, but on capital – a surplus value that is added to human surplus value and that comes to correct the relative diminution of the latter, *both of them constituting the whole of the surplus value of flux that characterizes the system*.[30]

If 'machinic surplus value' is considered as a theoretical innovation capable of offering a major and definite objection to the Marxian understanding of value, it requires greater elaboration; but if it represents an approximation, it provides a mere impression that the thinking underlying this kind of statement constitutes a powerful innovation.[31] Yet this merely claimed complexity, the wagered assertion of what had until then not been understood or even noticed – and above all not by Marx or 'Marxism' – creates the impression that the text is more literary than analytical, fraught as it is with flashy intuitions that neglect any patient argumentation, and moreover that the innovative pose sometimes replaces any rigorous construction.

Conclusion

What is philosophy? The whole of Deleuze's work seems obsessed with this question, insofar as its persistent classicism constantly verges on its own denial, and insofar as subtle referencing is presented as an invention and rediscovery: 'the concept itself abandons all reference so as to retain only the conjugations and connections that constitute its consistency' or also 'the concept is defined by its consistency, its endoconsistency and exoconsistency, but it has no *reference*: it is self-referential; it posits itself and its object at the same time as it is created'.[32] If such statements tackle the materialist question, for that very reason they also engage with the relation to politics, which surprisingly enough is remarkably absent in the late work *What Is Philosophy?*, which nevertheless contrasts philosophy with art and science. That is why for Deleuze revolution is primarily a concept, transferring the political question

---

[30] Deleuze and Guattari 1984, p. 234.

[31] Félix Guattari, who developed the notion of 'machinic surplus value', defines it as a generalised expense of energy that subsumes the Marxian analysis in terms of labour-time. Yet the analysis remains just as vague from the standpoint of its properly economic details.

[32] Deleuze and Guattari 1994, p. 90 and p. 22.

onto a metaphysical ground while still playing with its concrete resonances, and dramatising an ontological serenity through the distant but violent and blunt echoes that such a word stills carries in contemporary France. But we can go even further: in the end, the Deleuzean paradox proves to be rather a contradiction crossing his thought without really taking root in it, percolating through the whole spectrum of contemporary social, political, and ideological reality, and feeding back on it.

In fact, there is no question of accusing Deleuze of guilty renunciations. This would entail overlooking the extent to which the persistence of the theme of revolution in theory relies on the building of alternatives that go beyond theory. In that regard, his work should only be read through a breaking away from the notion of the autonomy of philosophical discourse and neutrality from the university institution where its teaching is located, margins included. The main achievement of Deleuze lies, in a sense, in maintaining an ambition to protest, along with a protest vocabulary, witness his frequent and positive references to Marx, despite the fact that he belongs to a time of crisis and reversal for Marxism. Forsaking the mummified certitudes of official Marxism and a grandiloquent leftism, he endeavours to keep open the perspective of a critique of capitalism and the refusal of all forms of conformism during a time when many contrary endeavours attempt to close the door, to exorcise the ghost of '68, and from then on, to define political commitment in terms of a kind of salon anti-totalitarianism and professional abhorrence of Marx – a real political commitment but one that allows no space for any alternative, hence blandly introduces itself as 'death of ideologies' and rejection of 'ideas of blood'.[33]

Nevertheless, the Deleuzean possible has never been a project and remains an abstract possibility of alternative life-choices.[34] In the exergue for *Negotiations*, Deleuze asserts that philosophy is not a power, and for that reason, 'philosophy can't battle with the powers that be', but should limit itself to a guerrilla warfare passing through each and everyone of us,[35] infinitely pushing off the horizon of a real historical overcoming. Is this a return to philosophical

---

[33] 'It should be admitted that the idea of socialism and communism has become an idea of blood', Pignon and Rigoulot 1982.
[34] See, on this particular point, Zourabichvili 1998, pp. 338–40.
[35] Deleuze 1995, p. vii.

Proudhonism?[36] At any rate, this analysis has met with huge agreement at all times both past and present. As mentioned earlier, this prognosis can be attributed, on the one hand to the history of French society since '68: its multifarious mutations, the complex movement of its struggles, the oscillations of consciousness on the part of its various actors, and the PCF's incapacity to understand the extent of '68, as well as its refusal to support the workers' protest beyond the mere dimension of trade unionism. On the other hand, there is also the parallel incapacity of leftist movements to take part in the construction of a hegemonic front, closing themselves into a form of activism without prospects. The right wing and the whole of the ruling class recovered much quicker and quite easily managed to rally a share of ex-leading figures of the student protest scene. Meanwhile, the CFDT was politically very active and evolving from different forms of reflections – particularly those produced within the framework of the journal *Esprit* – so it worked out the perspective of a self-managed 'second Left' so efficiently that it rapidly appealed to and recycled another layer of '68 actors in the framework of a 'new look' social democracy. The economic crisis that broke out at the beginning of the 1970s accelerated the process of political reconfiguration and enabled the progressive rise of neoliberal arguments and choices, changed the management of the critique of work, and saw a new mode of accumulation emerge. The *divine surprise* that saw the lightning break-up of the 'socialist' countries initiated a one-sided revision of the previous social contract, prior to the final assault on the state. The process has continued and has now accelerated, notwithstanding moments of powerful mobilisation and protest of which the most recent developments are the movement of 1995 and the victory for the No in the European constitutional treaty referendum, and this remobilisation has been strongly crippled by the crisis of the 'Left' and the ongoing reconfiguration of trade unions…

Those facts are well known and despite this excessively linear and incomplete summary, it appears to us that the continuity with the 1960s is simultaneously self-evident and complex. From this standpoint, the 'political philosophy' of Deleuze, which may seem outlandish at first sight, is in fact very significant element of a complex history, particularly the history and teaching of philoso-

[36] Marx dubbed Proudhon a 'living contradiction', in 'On Proudhon (Letter to J.B. Schweitzer)', Marx and Engels 1987.

phy in France – propounding and displacing contemporary political issues but failing to conceptualise precisely their nature because of its very powerlessness and vocation. Now, as to the actuality of Marx and relevance of the word 'revolution', Deleuze reconfigures its import and displaces its meaning to such an extent that they are no longer intended as instruments for apprehending the real and the ferments of current developments, but aim rather at accompanying their very political withdrawal in a faint nostalgia: they aim at being discursive events which are quite paradoxical considering that, in the end, the word 'revolution' resounds with the obsolescence of its global design, and that the reference to Marx coincides with the desertion of its fields of research and intervention. If the question of commitment is transformed, it is not thematised in any other way than under the banner of its most modest miniaturisation – alleged to be more efficient – producing a specific micropolitics of specific intellectuals. Work and its current transformations are no longer research objects, even if the questions of organisation and machines still touch on its deserted domain and disputed centrality. In that respect, while the role of the state is radically and quite precisely redefined according to a logic which is politically decisive to understand, it is only thought through the lines of a universal history, in which it is above all opposed to the market, precisely at the time when the ruling class resorts to this selfsame state to organise the dazzling expansion of the market!

Paradoxically enough, the maintained relation Deleuze entertains with Marx is the most helpful tool for perceiving the withdrawal of a certain conception of theoretical work that Marx promoted. Taking a philosophical and conceptual turn, the mention of Marx still breaks a stifling taboo, but it also marks the academic, editorial, mediatic, and political decline and rejection of a form of thinking which was meant to be significant, even in, or especially on the basis of its political consequences which were supposed to testify to its very efficiency. And it is this very paradox which turns out to be a lively contradiction: for the term 'revolution' expresses and persists in expressing this unity of a thought and its historical aim, beyond and despite all forms of conceptual mutation, because of the political force retained by its very naming. Even though an echo is not a concept, and even less so a project.

This is precisely where the ambiguity of the Deleuzean use of the word lies, on the ground of an unprovable unity between a theory in the making and a sought-out practice, well beyond what is said about it in the works of

Deleuze and Guattari: revolution is not a concept, also and mostly because it exceeds any form of conceptualisation, and because the word remains filled with a dialectic which proves to be ineliminable, whatever one may think. In that sense, maintaining a reference to Marx and to the word 'revolution', at the same time as the prospect of its concrete realisation is declining and collapsing, continues to designate its void but also its lack, to delineate its site and assert its urgency, to somehow maintain its actuality and prompt a revival which should not be merely philosophical, but must remain grounded in theory. After all, to extend the Deleuzean metaphor, we can remark that what keeps surfacing in this way, fragmentary and barely recognisable, continues to arouse curiosity and pointing at the directions that should be further explored! Deleuze may also be read in that perspective today.

Chapter Thirty-Three

Jacques Derrida, 'Crypto-Communist?'

Jason Smith

> We parted for personal and political reasons. Political reasons: more and more, he became a fellow-traveler of the Communist Party.
> – Philippe Sollers[1]

> It was very difficult not to join the Party. It was extremely difficult for someone on the Left (need I remind people that I've always been on the Left?) to be thought of only as a crypto-Communist or a fellow-traveler.
> – Jacques Derrida[2]

During the decisive month of what is still known only as 'May '68', Jacques Derrida was not 'on the barricades'.

To begin to understand Jacques Derrida's relation to Marx and the Marxist tradition, it is no doubt best to start not from the history of his textual engagements, strategic alliances and missed 'encounters' with a hardly homogenous movement taking place under the sign 'Marx', but with a concrete situation. I will come back to the texts, lots of them and soon. We should first listen to what Derrida says about his role in the most important political upheaval in

[1] Quoted in Clément 1995.
[2] Derrida 1993b, p. 199.

France since the Liberation. In a 1994 interview with Maurizio Ferraris given the title *A Taste for the Secret* (*Specters of Marx* had been published one year earlier), Derrida briefly recalled his attitude toward the opening moments of the revolt, initiated largely by students within the universities during the month of March. Derrida had reservations. This is not necessarily remarkable.[3] What is remarkable is the set of references – I do not say authorities – Derrida has recourse to in explaining his reticence. After reminding his interviewer that, 'rightly or wrongly, my heart was not "on the barricades"', he immediately tries to account for his disheartened response, one that suggests a participation without belonging to the movement (I was there, but my heart was not in it), by emphasising what he calls the 'rhetoric of spontaneity' ('the liberation from any sort of apparatus, party or union') marking much of the student movement:

> In 1968 I had the impression that the action of the students (*which was not that of the workers*) to provoke a revolution was unrealistic, and that it could have dangerous consequences.... What really bothered me was...the spontaneist eloquence, the call for transparency, for communication without relay or delay.... The mistrust with regard to all those things that I witnessed in 1968 corresponded not only to a philosophical-political position, but also what was already, for me, a kind of *crypto-communist inheritance*, namely the condemnation of 'spontaneism' in Lenin's *What Is to Be Done?* In rereading Lenin's texts recently, in an altogether different context, I rediscovered this critique of spontaneism.[4]

Not Marx, Lenin. This explanation would require a long, patient response, taking into consideration the pragmatics and the strategy of this utterance as much as its objective content. Let us recall two things, two contexts. Only a year before this interview, Derrida had just published *Specters of Marx*, his long awaited 'encounter' with Marxism (my own essay's sole task is to complicate this rather pat story), a book that itself represents an intervention within a very determined historical configuration (theoretical and politi-

---

[3] Indeed, a large segment of the French intellectual class had 'reservations' about the student movement or, at the very least, the students' tactics. Among Derrida's 'friends', many were not 'on the barricades': Philippe Sollers, Louis Althusser, Jean Genet, for example.

[4] Derrida 2001a, p. 50; my italics.

cal). The moment he recalls, however, is perhaps even more complex. Before 1971, and especially in the years 1968–71, Derrida's philosophical work is best understood not only as an autonomous practice – it will always be that, too often to the detriment of the work or its effects – but as triangulating between two other poles within the Parisian theoretical scene: a very close relationship with Philippe Sollers and the journal *Tel Quel*, and a more discreet, more clandestine tie (one that does not exclude antagonism) with the work of Louis Althusser. That is to say, two figures whose role in the events of May and in particular the initial student revolt were hardly enthusiastic. *Tel Quel*, at the time closely allied with the French Communist Party (PCF) and its cultural apparatus (this alliance would last until 1971), was not only reluctant to support the student movement without qualifications, but was also actively opposed to the interventions of the Union des écrivains and the Comité d'action écrivains-étudiants (which included Blanchot, Marguerite Duras, Robert Antelme and others). Althusser, once again in the hospital, was completely absent from the events.

What to make of Derrida's account? It is, in parts, indistinguishable from the official PCF line at the beginning of the events: isolation of students from workers ('not that of the workers'), this isolation in turn meaning the revolt might only be a 'provocation' that, precipitating a confrontation with the state, would function as a pretext allowing the Gaullists to crush legitimate opposition (popular support of the working masses) and strengthen their own hand. It is true that the Right secured a landslide victory in the June 1968 elections. It is undeniable, however, that this language is couched in what are very classical, orthodox 'Communist' terms.[5] The term 'unrealistic' is particularly jarring. On the walls of Paris one could read 'Soyons réalistes, demandons l'impossible!' – and who more than Derrida has, after Heidegger, Bataille and Blanchot, analysed the necessary inscription of the impossible within every ethico-political act or wager? What is an historical event if not the sudden suspension of the opposition between possible and impossible? Can there be an event if it can be accounted for by the objective conditions of

[5] It is, indeed, not far from the language of Georges Marchais's editorials in *L'Humanité*, general secretary of the PCF during the events of May, excluding considerations of tone.

an historical moment, if it can be deduced from the given relations of force in a determined, concrete situation?

If the language Derrida adopts in the first part of this citation can easily be assimilated to the phraseology of the Party – rendering him an 'objective ally' of the PCF against the student provocation – it is the second half of the passage that is more interesting. At issue is 'spontaneity' or rather, 'spontaneist eloquence' and the denunciation of institutions (like the party or unions). It is the *rhetoric* of spontaneity that Derrida dislikes most. Rhetoric: the elevation of spontaneity to the status of a value, an operation that conceals the divisions, stratifications, 'delays' and mediations at the heart of an immediate relation to self. For spontaneity is another name for the immediate presence to self of a subjectivity *in actu*, coinciding with itself in the vitality of its upsurge or its insurrection. It is another name for what Husserl called the 'living Present' of temporalisation, the 'absolute beginning' that – this is from Husserl's *The Phenomenology of Internal Time-Consciousness* – 'does not come into existence as that which is generated but through *genesis spontanea*'.[6] To this spontaneity Derrida opposes the notion of the *institution*. From his earliest work on Husserl, beginning in the early 1950s, 'institution' (or, in the language of Husserl and Heidegger, *Stiftung*) has signified nothing less than memory, relation, *trace* in general, the very possibility of history itself. It will be necessary to denounce, subject to critique, deconstruct even this or that given institution in the name, always, of an institution 'to come' – not in the name of an absence of mediation or representation, or in the name of 'direct' democracy.

Derrida does not invoke Husserl here. He invokes *Lenin*. And he invokes Lenin in order to emphasise a certain difference between the moment of narration (1994, just after *Specters of Marx*) and 1968, namely that today he is able to assume a 'crypto-communist inheritance' that a quarter of a century before still remained a secret, from Jacques Derrida most of all. What this means, what the term 'crypto-communism' means, is not at all clear here, nor should it be. It seems to be a name Derrida uses to designate or seal his own inability to account for or recount, in the language of political 'responsibility', just exactly what his relation to Marxism and 'communism' was or will have been.

---

[6] Husserl 1964, p. 131; quoted in Derrida 1967b, p. 93. Althusser contends that it is not the spontaneity of the masses that Lenin opposes, but rather the rhetoric (to use Derrida's word) or 'ideology of spontaneity.' This distinction would require a great deal of elucidation (Althusser 1969, p. 254).

Repression, denial, foreclosure? An 'incorporation' that, refusing to assimilate this inheritance, expels it inward to remain, encrusted and encrypted, as a foreign body within his work?[7] And what is the relation between this secret encounter with Marxism – secret even to Derrida himself – and Derrida's own characterisation of a communism 'to come', a New International, whose mode of existence or appearing is allied with the *secret* if not the conspiratorial secret society, 'a still discreet tie, almost secret...hardly public even if it is not clandestine'?[8]

The following pages are by no means meant to provide a definitive account of Derrida's relation to Marx and Marxism. To the contrary, they merely seek to establish and formalise some of the conditions – methodological, historical, philological, theoretical – within which such a discussion can begin to take place. Derrida was neither a Marxist, nor a communist, nor a member of the French Communist Party, nor even more generally a member of the 'movement' that emerged in 1968 and persevered until 1977–8. But this is not what is in question here. To be sure, a truly historical account of Derrida's philosophical and political trajectory, in particular from the years 1952 to 1976, would be able to establish any number of alliances, complicities and solidarities with the communist Left and, indeed, the French Communist Party, provided the complexity of the angles and the mediations are accounted for. To truly ask after the nature of Derrida's 'involvement' with Marxism would, however, require a discourse of a great deal more theoretical rigour, beginning with a critical reflection on the very terms in which the question is to be posed: what is an 'encounter'? What is an 'alliance'? What is a 'crypt', a 'secret?' What, or who, is Marx? What is the relation between Marxism and the French Communist Party?

What is a communist?

* * *

There is a practice specific to philosophical or theoretical discourse. Reading a text is not reducible to an analysis or explication; reading is first of all a practice or a strategy of *intervention*. This conception of philosophy is one Derrida shares with his longtime colleague and friend, Louis Althusser. It is an image

[7] On the difference between incorporation and introjection, and the idea of the 'crypt,' see Derrida's 'Fors', in Abraham & Torok 1986, pp. xi–xlviii.
[8] Derrida 1993, pp. 141–2.

of thought that compels us to recognise that the field of conceptual elaboration is always overdetermined politically, in the broadest sense of the term; as a result, the reading of a philosophical text must be characterised as a complex act insofar as it is structured by a series of decisions and wagers that can never be justified or accounted for by reasons internal to philosophy itself. This act that has no purely theoretical justification is therefore a political *prise de parti*, one that delimits and reframes a philosophical corpus on the basis of relations of force that cannot be said to simply belong to the immanent organisation of a given theoretical articulation. Derrida's text in particular requires this sort of intervention. Especially at a moment when, following his death in 2004, the fate of his text suddenly seems open to a kind of strategic appropriation or inflection that might retroactively reorient how we read his entire philosophical trajectory. Brutally put: now is the moment when it is suddenly possible to reinscribe Derrida into the space of what we might call, in the most general sense, a materialist conception of philosophy. Indeed, we might even consider the situation of Derrida's text as being roughly analogous to that of Hegel's after his death. There is a struggle and a divide, a war of appropriation over a signature and a legacy – an emerging fault between a right and left Derridianism. This requires not only a strategic conception of reading, but the willingness to submit this text to a certain naïveté and a certain violence. Such violence is perhaps the sole 'salvation' Derrida's text will know.

To begin such a reading, the first gesture required is to disperse the consensus that has developed around Derrida's relation to Marxism. This consensus takes the form of an historical scansion, organised around two dates: 1971 and 1993. The story, pat as it is, goes something like this. In the 1971 interview 'Positions', conducted by two members of a *Tel Quel* on the verge of passing from an alliance with the PCF to a very unorthodox Maoism, Derrida is pressured into explaining, openly and with precision, the relationship between deconstruction and dialectical materialism. Derrida's response suggests a possible articulation or 'ajointement', but one that cannot be 'immediately given' and is therefore 'still to come'.[9] Silence for two decades. Two decades of intense political polarisation, the Union of the Left and the Common Programmme, the humanist 'reaction' of the late 1970s, the final victory of the Socialists in 1981, the collapse of 'really existing socialism'. Then, in 1993, the

[9] Derrida 1972b, p. 85.

publication of the long-awaited encounter with Marxism and the specificity of the Marxist text in *Specters of Marx* – a book that is in fact highly ambivalent with regard to the history and promise of the dialectical-materialist tradition, as many 'Marxist' readers were to discover.

There is something to this story. But consider this: immediately after the publication of the 1971 interview, Derrida distances himself from *Tel Quel* at the very moment the journal breaks its alliance with the PCF. Meanwhile, Derrida develops a relationship with the PCF-aligned journal *Les Lettres françaises*, edited by Louis Aragon and Jean Ristat. With the end of *Les Lettres françaises* in 1973, Derrida begins to publish in *Digraphe*, edited by Ristat (who remains in the PCF today) and hosting many writers from *Tel Quel* (Jean Ricardou, Jean Thibaudet, Maurice Roche – for example) who chose not to break with the PCF. In 1974, Philippe Sollers denounced what he called the 'alignment of Derrida and his clientele with the positions' of the PCF, specifically 'concerning its position on the Union of the Left and the Common Programme'.[10] More important than these anecdotal and perhaps opportunistic – supposing we were to take Sollers seriously – engagements, however, are the series of seminars that Derrida gives over the course of 1972 to 1976. That is, in the four years *immediately after* his remark that an encounter with Marxism was 'still to come'. A partial summary of the content of these lecture courses, all of them housed in the archives at the University of California, Irvine, would reveal the following:

a) 1972–3, 'Religion and Philosophy,' consisting of eight sessions, of which the first two are devoted to Marx (28 pages). Though much of this course is devoted to Kant and Hegel, the analysis of these authors takes place within

10 'It is no coincidence that the party and the university have recuperated those among or around us who were the most reticent about Marxism as well as psychoanalysis' (Sollers 1974, pp. 136–7). Derrida was already suspected, in late 1971, of wanting a rapprochement with *La Nouvelle Critique* and, by extension, with the cultural wing of the PCF; now, no less than three months after the definitive break with Sollers and *Tel Quel* in January 1972, a special issue of the PCF-aligned journal *Les Lettres françaises* is devoted to Derrida was published. In the March 29–April 4, 1972 issue (issue 1429), Jean Ristat organised a group of 'hommages' to Derrida whose number included Barthes and Genet, among others. The issue appeared on the occasion of the publication of Derrida's *La Dissémination*, and it was understood by Sollers as, according to Forest, Derrida's being '"recuperated" by the PCF' (Forest 1995, p. 403). Perhaps in response to these homages gathered by Ristat, *Tel Quel*'s Bulletin d'informations du Mouvement de juin 1971 will respond in April 1972 with an 'O mage à Derrida'.

a Marxist framework. The first session of the course addresses Marx and the critique of religion in the third *1844 Manuscript*, *The German Ideology* and the IVth Thesis on Feuerbach. The second session is entirely concerned with what Derrida calls the 'religious analogy in Marx's discourse on ideology,' with particular attention paid to Marx's analysis of the genesis of the commodity-form in the famous section of the first chapter of *Capital* on the fetishism of the commodity and its 'secret'. Much of the analysis of the first chapter of *Capital* (on the 'secret' of the commodity-form and the matrix of ideology) found in this seminar is reproduced with only minor modifications twenty years later – in *Specters of Marx*.

b) 1974–5, 'GREPH (the concept of ideology in the French ideologues)'. This seminar, concerned with the history and structure of the 'institution' of philosophy in its particularly French configuration as well as the question of the 'right to philosophy' offers – despite its title – readings of Gramsci, Althusser and Marx. An entire session is devoted to an analysis of Althusser's essay on 'ideological state apparatuses' and in particular on the notion of 'reproduction', with particular emphasis on Althusser's contention that in 'mature' capitalist societies it is the 'educational ideological apparatus' that is 'dominant' (rather than the Church). The last two sessions (40 pages) are devoted to the relation between Marx and Destutt de Tracy (the French 'idéologue') as well as the relation between ideology and the division of labour.

c) 1975–6, 'Theory and Practice'. Almost the entire first half of this seminar – 4 sessions – is devoted to the relation between theory and practice in Marx (in particular in the 'Theses on Feuerbach') and the evolving status of this relation in the work of Louis Althusser. One session concerns Althusser's definition of theory, practice, theoretical practice and the 'Theory of practice' in 'On the Materialist Dialectic'; another two are devoted to a reading of Lenin's *What Is to Be Done?* and the 'new' definition of philosophy Althusser proposes in *Lenin and Philosophy*.

d) 1976, 'Seminar for GREPH on Gramsci' (one session).

If, then, it will be necessary in the coming years[11] to take these texts into consideration in order to evaluate the exact relationship Derrida's work maintains with the Marxist tradition, we must in turn de-emphasise, it seems to

[11] Éditions Galilée has recently begun the process of publishing Derrida's seminars. The English translations will appear with the University of Chicago Press.

me, the importance of *Specters of Marx* in this history as well. Not only because this text should no longer be understood as a belated – two decades, and not until the end of the 'really existing' Marxism of the Communist International – and disappointing rallying to the 'cause' of Marxism. To the contrary, it would be just as easy to read this text, as Derrida invites us to do at many points, as *open break* with the entire history of Marxism as such. In this text we read that the 'spirit' of Marxism that Derrida is evoking or conjuring up in *Specters* is to radically distinguished or demarcated from

> the body of Marxist doctrine, to its supposed systematic, metaphysical, or ontological totality (notably to its 'dialectical method' or to 'dialectical materialism'), to its *fundamental concepts* of labor, mode of production, social class, and consequently to the *whole history* of its apparatuses (projected or real: the Internationals of the labor movement, the dictatorship of the proletariat, the single party, the State, and finally the totalitarian monstrosity).[12]

What is most remarkable about *Specters of Marx* is, in fact, its articulation of the problem of justice in its relation – suspensive and conflictual, but not destructive – to law. But, for this very reason, *Specters of Marx* might best be read less as a performative intervention in the Marxist tradition and its 'fundamental concepts' than as a continuation of one of Derrida's most important texts, his 1989 essay 'Force de la loi', on Walter Benjamin's 'Critique of Violence': the first moment in Derrida's text when the 'contamination' between justice and law will be laid out.[13] This conflict will be at the heart of Derrida's work over the last fifteen years of his life, and will orient the vast majority of his conceptual work, be it on hospitality, cosmopolitanism, or 'democracy to come'. Rather than choosing to elaborate post-deconstructive mutations of those concepts belonging to what is called 'dialectical materialism' – labour, mode of production, the state, the party – Derrida brackets the entire system of Marxist categories in order to inscribe Marx's text itself into a problematic of justice that is never articulated in any satisfactory way in the language of Marx himself.

---

12 Derrida 1993a, pp. 145–6, my emphasis.

13 Derrida 1994. 'Force of Law' was originally presented, in a different form, at a colloquium at Cardozo Law School in October 1989, and was initially published in English in 1992.

These considerations, then, compel us to direct our attention to a phase of Derrida's career that precedes the two dates (1971, 1993) that normally punctuate the story of Derrida's relation to Marx. The remainder of this essay will pay particular attention to Derrida's earliest work on Husserl as well as his very complex relationship to Louis Althusser in the late 1960s. What follows, of course, in no way pretends to be conclusive. To the contrary, what is necessary today – for *us* – is to start over, to begin again and map out a strategic line in the coming war over the name 'Derrida'. Why, after all, would it be necessary to abandon an ally, perhaps only a fellow traveler, to the predations of Reaction?

* * *

On 23 June 1966, Louis Althusser gave a lecture at the École Normale Supérieure on what he called the 'theoretical conjuncture of current French philosophy'. Althusser wanted to draw a 'map' of the theoretical field that is a 'structure' as well as a battlefield, a configuration that is also a balance of power in which competing forces struggle for 'domination', he says, in an ideological and theoretical struggle. The map he draws, then, depicts a combat undertaken by Marxist theory (both the science of historical materialism and dialectical materialism, which has a 'scientific character' but is not, *strictu sensu*, a science)[14] in a war involving three theoretical formations and two fronts. On one front, a battle against the reactionary spiritualist tradition of philosophy among whose contemporary representatives number Paul Ricoeur and the recently deceased Merleau-Ponty. On the other, a battle against a 'critical and rationalist idealist' line that draws on Kantian and Husserlian resources but which also includes, Althusser says, a series of names that belong to what in France is called the 'epistemological' tradition, concerned with a critical examination of the foundation of the sciences, with a particular emphasis on the genesis and historicity of scientific institutions and practices. This group – including Cavaillès, Bachelard, Koyré and Canguilhem – also belongs to this idealist line, we are told, save one 'extremely important nuance'. Whereas they 'often attach themselves consciously [*par conscience*] to the tradition of critical idealism…an entire

---

[14] This text, 'Conjuncture philosophique et recherche théorique marxiste' (Althusser 1995, pp. 407–30), is clearly a transitional text between the first and second 'definitions' of philosophy.

portion of their work in fact leans in another direction'.[15] Two pages later, he will note that the work of this group holds certain 'keys' to 'our future', a future Althusser identifies with a 'new materialist problematic'. After specifying that the keys to this new materialist problematic will come from the actual practice if not the explicit, conscious philosophical theses of this group, Althusser concludes: 'this struggle poses strategic and tactical problems, in particular the problem of alliances in the theoretical and ideological struggle'.[16]

Althusser's lecture was meant for Marxist philosophers. But in the audience that day, according to one version of the manuscript, was a group that Althusser calls 'our philosopher friends who are non-Marxist, but interested in Marxism'. He then singles out one friend in particular who is in attendance: 'mon ami Jacques Derrida'. Althusser notes that Derrida is not there, however, only out of friendship. What is at stake is the possibility of an 'alliance' in the current theoretical and ideological struggle and, perhaps, a 'new materialist problematic'.

In a 'dialogue' with Élisabeth Roudinesco published almost forty years later, Derrida discussed his earliest work at the École Normale Supérieure on Husserl, focusing in particular on the historicity of the scientific or logicomathematical object. After Derrida sent a copy of his 1962 Introduction to Husserl's *Origin of Geometry* to Althusser, he received a response that indicated, according to Derrida, an interest in the possibility of an 'alliance' between a certain stratum of Husserlian phenomenology and Marxism:

> Like certain Marxists in his circle, or, on the other hand and in a different way, like Trân-Duc-Thao, [Althusser] perceived (strategically) a *possible*

---

[15] Althusser 1995, p. 416. Derrida, in his turn, will draw the same map: 'In the first years of my philosophical studies, when I began to read and write on Husserl, at the beginning of the 1950s, after the introduction of phenomenology by Sartre and Merleau-Ponty, I felt the need to pose the question of science, of epistemology, starting from phenomenology, what Sartre and Merleau-Ponty in a certain way never did. Consequently, I wrote my first essays on Husserl by orienting them towards question of scientific objectivity and mathematics: Cavaillès, Tran-Duc-Thao, and also the Marxist question' (Derrida 2003, p. 20). The language of the 'map' and its implied 'fronts' returns in Derrida's own description of his earliest work, the 1954 *mémoire* on Husserl's concept of genesis. Speaking of his interest in Thao and Cavaillès rather than Sartre and Merleau-Ponty: 'on the philosophical and *political* map starting from which, in the France of the 1950s, a student in philosophy tried to orient himself' (Derrida 1990, p. viii). Note that the philosophical and the political are here indissociable.

[16] Althusser 1995, p. 418.

> *alliance* between Husserl's transcendental idealism – notably in its genetic and epistemological dimension – and a new Marxist problematic. I wasn't far from thinking so myself, though in a different way.[17]

The language of this passage is notable for its proximity to that of Althusser in 1966. What is again proposed is a strategic 'alliance' that would articulate together a certain reading of Husserl emphasising questions of science (its foundations and origins, its genesis and its history) and the possibility of what is here called not a 'new materialist problematic' but a 'new Marxist problematic'. But it is important to emphasise that the status of this articulation is, in the last instance, political and strategic in nature, rather than philosophical. Whether the alliance is unwitting and, as one says, 'objective', determined by a unique political and philosophical conjuncture, or whether it is avowed, taking the form of a more or less secret 'conjuration' (as Derrida puts it in *Specters of Marx*), what governs such a relationship in the final instance is a convergence between two forces with no institutional or substantial links that, before the necessities of battle, enter into a complicity in which no ruse is off-limits.

Political and not philosophical – in the last instance. I insist upon the question of the 'alliance' because I want to underline in what sense Derrida's relation to Marxism in general – both dialectical materialism, Marxist philosophy, as well as the 'science' of historical materialism and the critique of political economy – *cannot* be understood. Trân-Duc-Thao's 1951 book *Phénoménologie et matérialisme dialectique* treats the relationship between Marxism and transcendental idealism in strictly philosophical and, indeed, dialectical terms: Marxism or dialectical materialism is nothing less than the 'solution' to the contradictions and antinomies that Husserl rigorously formulates throughout his work. Dialectical materialism is therefore the logical result of the internal

---

[17] Derrida 2001b, p. 170. The letter Derrida refers to in this interview has now been published, but seems to makes no reference to a 'possible alliance' between Husserl and Marxism. Cf. Mallet & Michaud 2004, pp. 109–10. Nevertheless, 'Lenin and Philosophy' will speak of an 'objective alliance' between Husserl and Lenin: '... Husserl, at that time Lenin's objective ally against empiricism and historicism – but only a temporary ally and one who could not meet him, for Husserl, as a good "philosopher," believed he was going "somewhere"' (Althusser 1971, p. 49). And yet, what is so remarkable about a text like 'Philosophy as Rigorous Science', published only three years after Lenin's *Materialism and Empiriocriticism*, is that Husserl wages war on both historicism *and* theoreticism.

contradictions of Husserlian idealism, a result that is at once the 'dépassement' of the transcendental problematic and both the completion and annulment of philosophy as such. Such a relation is described in the idiom of dialectical and speculative logic, a movement in which dialectical materialism emerges necessarily out of the objective contradictions of Husserl's own text. As a result, Thao can argue that the analyses undertaken in the generally unread second half of his book (what he calls the 'dialectic of real movement') take place 'entirely on the plane of dialectical materialism'. In his 1954 *mémoire* on the problem of 'genesis' in Husserl's philosophy, Derrida maintains that this definitive surpassing of Husserlian idealism has the odd effect of returning Thao to a pre-phenomenological metaphysics that is not rigorously dialectical enough, a worldly genesis founded on a concept of 'matter' that is 'not animated by the dialectic'.[18] The dialectical overcoming of the transcendental problematic results, then, in what Derrida calls a 'relapse [*retomber*]' that abandons the 'transcendental purity of the dialectic' revealed in the *practice* of Husserl's phenomenological descriptions (of temporalisation, intersubjectivity and the 'hyletic' layer of the sensible), if not in his theoretical formulations: 'We must reject Trân-Duc-Thao's conclusions which... after having gotten as close as possible to the transcendental purity of [Husserl's] dialectic, relapse into the difficulties posed by a "worldly" genesis and a materialist dialectic'.

In a certain sense, Derrida argues that Thao's method is *not dialectical enough*, because the logic or scheme of 'dépassement' is not a truly dialectical movement, a movement that is disclosed only through placing the dialectic itself between phenomenological brackets. The term 'purity' here – the word is almost a synonym for transcendental – indicates how much more complex, indeed, how much more dialectical the relation between transcendentality and the dialectical method is than the scheme presented by Thao.[19] The practice of phenomenological bracketing is never undertaken to disqualify or

---

[18] Derrida 1990, p. 32. Derrida 1990, p. 257 n. 8.

[19] This theme of the relation between the transcendental and the dialectical returns in *Glas*, specifically in the analyses of Hegel's 'sister' (Antigone, the sister, and his own). There he speaks of an 'element excluded from the system that assures the space of possibility of the system.... The transcendental has always been, strictly speaking, the transcategorial, what cannot be received, formed, terminated in any of the categories internal to the system. The vomit of the system. And if the sister, the relation brother/sister represented here the transcendental position, ex-position?' (Derrida 1981, p. 227).

'negate' a given philosopheme or category but to purify it or, in another philosophical idiom, to draw a line of demarcation internal to the term, staking out or re-marking a distance between the worldly and transcendental faces of the concept. This 'purity' of the dialectic that is more dialectical than dialectical contradiction itself (in its wordly, metaphysical or speculative form), is referred to in Derrida's Introduction to the *Origin of Geometry* as an 'authentic dialetic*ity*' that is a dialectic *between* the dialectical and the non-dialectical:

> The *dialecticity* of genesis...is precisely and abundantly described by Husserl at different levels, even though the word itself is never pronounced. We have seen how the 'activity' of consciousness at the same time precedes and comes after a passivity; that the movement of primordial temporalisation, the ultimate foundation of all constitution, was dialectical through and through; and that, as is the case with every authentic dialecticity, it was nothing but the dialectic between the dialectical – the indefinite, mutual and irreducible implication of protentions and retentions – and the non-dialectical – the absolute and concrete identity of the Living Present, universal form of all consciousness.[20]

Only a phenomenological method can arrive at this pure dialecticity, only the resources and techniques of the *epochè* can suspend the functioning of every worldly or determined mode of the dialectical in order to bring out an originary or authentic dialecticity.

If, in 1954, Derrida argues that Tran relapses into a pre-phenomenological, non-dialectical philosophy of matter, in 1962 Derrida will in turn sketch out the contours of what Althusser calls a 'a new materialist problematic'. Once again, it is question of purity, a question of drawing a front internal to a concept through a philosophical act: a single category divides in two. In a long footnote at the close of the Introduction, Derrida speaks of a 'pure materiality of the Fact' that would mark the absolute limit of phenomenological idealism – an idealism that always transforms the fact into an 'example' of an *eidos* rather than understanding it in its materiality and singularity – but would be accessi-

---

[20] Derrida 1962, pp. 157–8. The dialectical movement described here is therefore the dialectic between the dialectical – irreducible implication of traces – and the transcendental, the 'universal form' of the living present. In a text on Artaud from 1967, Derrida differentiates between the 'horizon of the dialectic' and the dialectic of a 'conventional Hegelianism' (Derrida 1967a, p. 364).

ble only by 'exhausting' phenomenological discourse and all of its techniques, methods, only by taking phenomenology to its own extreme and forcing it to indicate, silently, its threshold:

> But only a phenomenology can lay bare the pure materiality of the Fact, by passing to the limit of eidetic determination and by exhausting itself. Only such a phenomenology can avoid the confusion between pure facticity with one of its determinations.[21]

This materiality, what remains of matter after it has been purified or even 'purged' of every worldly or positivistic determination, would be a materiality that is dialectical and temporal through and through. Such is the project of the early Derrida: an examination of the history of a science in order to arrive a new concept of 'history' that insists on both a 'pure' dialecticity and a 'pure materiality of the Fact'. A new materialist and dialectical problematic, if not a dialectical materialism.

In the same year Derrida published his Introduction in which this labour on the notions of dialecticity and materiality is undertaken, Althusser published a text – the famous 'Contradiction and Overdetermination' – that attempts to locate the specificity of a properly materialist dialectic in its difference from Hegel's speculative logic. The target here is less Hegel, however, than a certain stratum of Marx's own discourse, namely the tendency to reduce the complexity of social antagonisms to mere manifestations (or 'expressions') of a simple, fundamental contradiction. This simplification of class antagonisms to the directness of frontal opposition corresponds to what Hegel, in the *Science of Logic*, called the 'sharpening' of difference, its refinement into the pointedness of sheer, frontal opposition, with none of the blunting effects of multiple conflicts and the obliquity of their interaction:

> Thinking reason, however, sharpens, so to say, the blunt difference of diverse terms, the mere manifoldness of representation, into essential difference, into opposition. Only when the manifold terms have been driven to the point of contradiction do they become active and lively towards one another,

---

[21] Derrida 1962, p. 169, note 1: 'Mais seule une phénoménologie peut dénuder la pure matérialité du Fait en se rendant au terme de la détermination eidétique, en s'épuisant elle-même. Seule elle peut éviter la confusion de la pure facticité avec telle ou telle de ses determinations.'

> receiving in contradiction the negativity which is the indwelling pulsation of the self-movement and spontaneous activity [*Lebendigkeit*].[22]

To this Hegelian logic of position and opposition, to this reduction of antagonism to the clean demarcation of a front, Althusser calls on Lenin's analysis of the 'extremely unique situation' of the 1917 revolution in order to develop a theory of overdetermined contradiction, the sudden merging of otherwise extremely differentiated social forces and class interests: that is, a theory of revolutionary rupture.

On a purely formal level, Althusser's philosophical strategy with regard to Hegel anticipates Derrida's own, particularly in the late 1960s and early 1970s. In a July 1971 interview with Jean-Louis Houdebine and Guy Scarpetta (published in *Promesses*, a satellite journal of *Tel Quel*), Derrida stresses that the 'conflictuality of *différance*' was first mobilised specifically, as was the case in Althusser, against the Hegelian determination of difference *as* contradiction.[23] Such a conflictuality is irreducible to opposition and therefore not prey to speculative or political mediation. It is a conflictuality that determines difference neither as contradiction and opposition, nor as a mere diversity of positions that are, as Hegel demonstrates, indifferent to one another and therefore not yet in conflict with one another.[24] Neither opposition nor mere diversity, the conflictuality of *différance* therefore takes place in 'almost absolute proximity to Hegel',[25] since the *distance taken* from the logic of contradiction does not result in another determination of difference, but its *over*determination (to use Althusser's term). There is, therefore, *nothing* that distinguishes *différance* from contradiction, no new determination grafted onto the term that would permit the difference between them to appear as such, no new predicate or mark allowing us to measure, from within the closure of the philosophical field, the distance taken from Hegel. The intervention here is political, not philosophical.

I emphasise this purely formal resemblance between the strategies of Derrida and Althusser's with regard to Hegel in order to bring into relief a

---

22 Hegel 1969, p. 442.

23 Derrida 1972b, p. 60.

24 Hegel 1969, pp. 418–24: 'the indifference' of the merely diverse. Of course, many of the critiques of Althusser's 'Contradiction and Overdetermination' accuse him of empiricism, another name for the indifferent difference of the merely multiple.

25 Derrida 1972b, p. 60.

decisive difference: by 1963, Derrida will no longer use the term 'dialectics' or its variant 'dialecticity'. On the one hand, it should be emphasised that the non-dialectisable conflictuality of *différance* must be considered in relation to the thematics of violence and of force that dominate Derrida's work in the 1960s. *Différance* is an economy of violence – even an 'économie-de-guerre'[26] – that, because it is a question of differentials of force, cannot be identified with the fundamentally logical category of 'contradiction'. *Différance* is, in short, *both more and less* violent, *more and less* conflictual than dialectical contradiction. If, at the level of philosophical analysis, the two operations are very similar, Althusser, working within the framework of the Communist Party and as a Communist in philosophy, must 'save the name' dialectics by isolating the singularity of the Marxist dialectic, purging it of non-Marxist elements that have grafted themselves onto Marxist theory. Derrida, in his turn, abandons the conceptual chain dialectics-position-opposition-contradiction. In the 1971 *Positions* interview, Derrida is asked by Jean-Louis Houdebine to explain the distance he has taken from the terms dialectic and contradiction. Asked whether a 'materialist *prise de position*' in philosophy does not necessarily require a commitment to the 'double motif of "matter" and "contradiction",' Derrida responds by arguing that '[the] conflictuality of *différance*...can be called contradiction only on the condition of *demarcating* it [la démarquer] by means of a long work on Hegel's contradiction...'.[27] In short, the Althusserian operation.

Houdebine's reference to a materialist *prise de position* is accompanied by a reference to Lenin and, implicitly, to Althusser's February 1968 text 'Lenin and Philosophy'.[28] I will conclude with this text and what I consider to be Derrida's relation to it, but, for the moment, it is necessarily to underline that in the years 1967–72, Derrida asserted that deconstruction is a strategic operation and a practice that is never neutral but, to the contrary, always *intervenes* in highly determined theoretical conjunctures in order to transform

[26] Derrida 1972a, p. 11. It cannot be emphasised enough the extent to which the reflection on difference Derrida undertakes in the 1960s is also a reflection on conflict, violence and even 'war' – the irreducibility of a violence that is the condition for phenomenality as such, an ontological or transcendental violence that is structural and therefore unavoidable.

[27] Derrida 1972b, pp. 60–1; my italics.

[28] Houdebine's explicit reference is to a much weaker text of Philippe Sollers, 'Lenin and Materialism', published in 1970 in the issue 43 of *Tel Quel*.

the 'conflictual and subordinating structure' within which it intervenes. This definition of philosophy as a practice of intervention is an Althusserian formulation. Indeed, it was between 1966 and 1968, at the very moment Althusser suggests a possible alliance between Marxist philosophy and Derrida, that a working group at the École Normale Supérieure that included Balibar, Macherey and Badiou among others began to develop this 'second' definition of philosophy that will be presented in 'Lenin and Philosophy'. To put it as crudely as possible, I would go so far as to say that, in these years and in this very complex and overdetermined theoretical conjuncture, Derrida's definition of deconstruction is Leninist. I am not even certain he would have, provided there were time and space allotted for all the reservations he would have proposed, simply rejected this formulation.[29] But the relation between these two strategies of intervention must be posed with more precision.

There are three moments in 'Lenin and Philosophy', that should be isolated if we are to address this question.

1) Most analyses of this text have not underlined the extent to which the notion of philosophy as a practice of intervention is modelled on the intervention of the analyst in the clinical practice of psychoanalysis. The relation between philosophy and politics is described as an economy of repression and 'denegation' (that is, *Verneinung*), whereby the political position of a philosophical thought is only allowed to appear in the form of a symptomatic denial and misrecognition. Such an economy or structure is analogous to the clinical structure of neurosis and its traits ('rumination', the priority of the question, the compulsive repetition of the same inversions of terms within a relative stable structure). The task of dialectical materialism is therefore identified with the analytic act – dialectical materialism is cast as 'cure' to philosophy's neurosis. Such an act on the part of the analyst or the philosopher takes the form not of a production of new knowledge or the introduction of novel interpretation, but a minimal and yet decisive *dislocation* of the prevailing relations in the structure. Lenin's definition of philosophy represents a

[29] In his 1975–6 Seminar 'Théorie et Practique', Derrida devoted an entire session (around 20 pages) to an analysis of Lenin's *What Is to Be Done?* In the same seminar, we also find a long discussion of Althusser's 'Sur la dialectique matérialiste'. These texts can be consulted at the UC Irvine Special Collections.

first, 'wild' analysis of the neurotic structure of philosophy, an intervention that 'fai[t] bouger quelque chose'.[30]

2) The second moment is the rather elegant formulation of the distinction between science and philosophy: the former 'unites', the latter 'divides'.[31] This distinction recalls Mao's demarcation of antagonistic contradictions from non-antagonistic contradictions, between philosophy as a practice of division – the one divides in two – and the mediation of non-antagonistic contradictions. Philosophy divides because it has no object and, therefore, no history. The sciences have a history: a moment of inauguration or *Stiftung*, the production of a new object and the opening of a field of research, the beginning of a history that is both fundamentally open, subject to enormous variations, inventions and discoveries, while always maintaining the unity of *a* history, since all of these discontinuities take place within the horizon determined by the structure of the object itself. Philosophy has no history precisely because it cannot rely on the consistency of the object of science to guarantee the open unity of its history, that is, the accumulation, capitalisation and constant 'progress' of a determined scientific field. In short, scientificity is always founded on a minimal consensus concerning the nature of the object one is discussing, a consensus or unity within which all debate, innovation, and the production of new predicates takes place. In turn, philosophy is the eternal enemy of discussion, debate and conversation, since these 'synthetic' activities, resulting in the production of new knowledges, require a consensus as their condition.

3) The entirety of 'Lenin and Philosophy' is an explication of this Mao-like slogan (science unites, philosophy divides), and the text's best-known formulations – philosophy defined as 'drawing a line of demarcation' and as the 'void of a distance taken' – will give a needed precision to this brutal distinction. What is necessary, then, is to define the *place* of philosophy in the

---

30 Cf. Althusser 1995, pp. 353–4: 'On appellera «pratique philosophique» (II) une pratique de la cure philosophique. Dans la «cure philosophique,» comme dans la «cure analytique», il s'agit de «faire bouger» quelque chose.... Cette pratique (II) a pour objectif la «guérison» de la névrose philosophique.... Lénine a «donné la parole» à l'inconscient philosophique.... Cure «sauvage», car Lénine a seulement appelé ce lieu par son nom...'.

31 Althusser 1971, p. 26. Is it strange that the first lines of the Genet column in *Glas* appear to cite the Maoist slogan 'one divides in two'? 'Ce qui est resté d'un Rembrandt déchiré en petits carrés bien réguliers, et foutu aux chiottes se divise en deux' (Derrida 1981, p. 1). The expression is repeated on several occasions throughout the book.

topological relation both to the sciences and the ideological struggle. Since philosophy has no object and therefore no history, it must be defined as the 'strange theoretical site where nothing happens' – that is, where no knowledge or historical acquisitions are produced and sedimented, nothing 'new' discovered or invented in the course of an open history. Philosophy's site is strange because it does not belong to the system of places and regions articulated in a specific theoretical conjuncture (or 'topique', as Althusser will sometimes say, using the Freudian term). As with the analytic act in the clinical practice of psychoanalysis, the philosophical act consists in a mere displacement of the relations between the elements of a constituted conjuncture, *tipping* the balance of power in one direction rather than another. Such an act can only be identified by the *trace* it leaves in the existing asymmetrical and hierarchical structure, since it appears only through its effects, through the displacement it forces. This is why philosophy is identified with the nothing, or a 'void,' and yet it has real effects: like Spinoza's 'cause', it is not only immanent in its effects, but is nothing outside them.

The concluding formulation Althusser hits upon is mysterious: philosophy is only the 'the simple fact of demarcation [*le simple fait de se démarquer*], therefore, the void of a distance taken [*le vide d'un distance prise*]'. It is important to note here that what is *prise* in this phrasing is not a punctual position, but a distance. What is designated is therefore not an act of positing or a thematically formulated position, but the movement of a spacing. This spacing or distancing – this *Ent-fernung* – is identified with the void precisely because nothing happens in this movement other than the 'se démarquer' of a philosophical concept, signifier or 'mark', in such a way the elements of given conjuncture are spaced in a novel configuration. Derrida, in his turn, describes the practice of deconstruction as an intervention that does not, as I have already underlined, remain neutral, but takes side in a specific theoretical conjuncture, a given 'violent hierarchy'. Being partisan in philosophy means choosing or taking one of the terms in the structure, using it as a lever of intervention to displace the given relations of force in a 'conflictual and subordinating structure'. Because philosophy has no language or object of its own, it must necessarily appropriate one of the already existing terms of the configuration and transform or dislocate the relatively stable existing relations of force. Philosophy, then, adds nothing to the already existing configuration of forces. It is nothing more than an act of leverage, a strategic appropriation that must seize one of the already constituted marks in order to 'immediately *demarcate* it [*pour l'en* démarquer *aussitôt*]',[32] that is, to perform an operation of 're-marking' or a 'double science' of the 'double mark'.[33]

At the close of his long interview with Houdebine and Scarpetta, Derrida defines what he has been calling deconstruction's 'practice of the *écart*' as a movement of spacing, a 'spacing that designates *nothing*, nothing that is, no presence at a distance [l'espacement *ne désigne* rien, *rien qui soit, aucune présence à distance*]'.[34] The question that I would like to pose is, then, simply this: where is the line of demarcation between this 'spacing [that] designates *nothing*' and the philosophical nothing that, according to Althusser, is not a position but a distance taken? Who will draw the line of demarcation between these two practices of spacing, between the demarcation and the strategy, the science – albeit double – of the 're-mark'?

32 Derrida 1972b, p. 81; my italics.
33 Derrida 1972a, p. 10.
34 Derrida 1972b, p. 107.

Chapter Thirty-Four

Foucault, Reader and Critic of Marx

Roberto Nigro

In the following pages, I would like to sketch out some directions for research. Rather than presenting a possible or impossible summary of Foucault's relationship to Marx's *œuvre*, I wish to suggest some signposts for future work. My hypothesis is simple. Foucault's work is marked from beginning to end by a confrontation with Marx. However, I suggest distinguishing between two levels: Foucault's *actual* confrontation with Marx and Foucault's *potential* confrontation with Marx. These two levels are not opposed to one another like night and day; nor they prompt musings on an opposition between what is the case and what one would like to be the case. I seek a basis for the development of the second level in the first, even if what is at issue is, in my opinion, to be found in the potential confrontation. I believe that by posing to Marx questions that derive from Foucault, and to Foucault issues that emerge from Marx, we can discover new aspects of the works in question and thereby discover new routes for *contemporary* reflection.

By way of introduction, I would like to clarify certain points. It is futile to imagine that Foucault's *œuvre* is traversed from one end to the other by a 'systematic' confrontation with Marx. This does not mean that it is impossible to envisage an effort to reconstruct, step by step, the *Auseinandersetzung* between Foucault and Marx (the German word seems to me to express what is at stake more clearly, since it retains the dual sense of comparison and confrontation). But we should also be aware that the roads which lead Foucault to Marx resemble labyrinths more than they do straight lines.

I shall summarise the issues involved in this confrontation in three points. First, it means asking how heavily Marx's work weighs in Foucault's. Secondly, we need to ask which Marx Foucault takes up in his analyses; what Foucault excludes from his work; and why he privileges one track rather than another. Thirdly, although Foucault's *œuvre* does not make it easy to distinguish between its author's struggle with Marx and his struggle with Marxism, it is preferable to differentiate the two. I believe that while Foucault acknowledge a kernel of Marxism in which Marx's discourse was also involved, he tried at various points in his work to position Marx at a remove from Marxism.

Throughout his philosophical career as well as his biographical trajectory, Foucault's confrontation with Marx and Marxism was twofold. He rejected Marxism *qua* knowledge inscribed in the rationality of the Western world and sought to show that this knowledge constructed a system of power that he could not but refuse. Any Marxism committed to the system of power was rejected by Foucault. Hence his unease over, and mistrust of, the Marxist discourse dominating his epoch, which appeared to him to be a reverse sign of the same power mechanism. It seems to me that the words accompanying his response to the question, 'What is to be put in place of the system?', clearly convey this orientation: 'I think that to imagine a different system actually still forms part of the system'.[1] If we regard Foucault's *œuvre* as an attempt not to seal thought up in a closed system, but to confront it with a kind of infinite supersession whereby it avoids the trap of identity, we can understand why, from a certain point onwards, he came to mistrust 'like the plague' any Marxism that turned into a system. For Foucault, it was a question of using Marx like a toolbox and not seeking the lost meaning or revealing the true meaning of Marx's words.[2] For him, as for us, interrogating Marx meant interrogating the 'matter' of his thought and taking all the risks involved in such an enter-

---

[1] 'Par-delà le bien and le mal', in Foucault 1994b, pp. 233–4.

[2] See 'Méthodologie pour la connaissance du monde: comment se débarrasser du marxisme', in Foucault 1994c, p. 611.

prise, including failure. For Marx is not to be read in order to mythologise him or to make him survive the test of time. Foucault worked to detotalise the image of Marx – which is a way of saying that he wanted to use Marx for certain purposes, without completely subscribing to him.

In reading Foucault's *œuvre*, we can see the extent to which Marx was a conceptual character with several masks for him. Marx is sometimes presented as a friend, sometimes as the enemy, and often as both at once. That is why if Foucault approaches Marx, he distances himself just as often, attributes masks to him, thinks with him without citing him, cites him in order to criticise him or those who would appear to be his followers, but who seem to Foucault to resemble his 'dreadful gnomes' – especially since he was troubled by his era's copious references to Marx. His modesty and mistrust of the overly familiar kept him from directly confronting Marx.

My aim is not to stage the possible confrontation between the authors in order to make them say what they did not say. I would like to examine what remained unsaid, positioning myself between what they did and did not say, so that they impel *us* to say what *they* could not say. The following pages do not claim to provide an exhaustive analysis. I sketch a series of stages, which proceed from the supersession of humanism and exclusion of Hegelianism to the confrontation with the Marx to whom Foucault refers – that is to say, the theoretician of the articulation of practices. In conclusion, I shall sketch the new theoretical concerns about Marxism that mark Foucault's work from the second half of the 1970s.

Nietzsche, Heidegger and Althusser: the supersession of humanism

In order to situate Foucault's theoretical debut, we must first of all return to Nietzsche and Heidegger and then consider the role played by the thought of Althusser. There are many reasons for this. Here I shall confine myself to a few formulations from these authors, so as to identify the limbo in which Foucault's reflection is situated.

If Nietzsche stressed the absolutely historical character of the human being,[3] Heidegger, taking up such meditations, sought to pose the ontological

[3] See Nietzsche 1997.

problem of history.[4] For him, an understanding of the essence of historicality leads not to an anthropology, but to an ontology. Thus, Heidegger abandons an analysis of man as man, proceeding to an ontological reflection on the mode of being of existence as *Dasein*. Subsequently, following the *Kehre*, Heidegger also abandoned this approach: he deliberately set aside any reference to the role of *Dasein* for an interpretation of being.[5] For him, understanding man comes round to understanding being. That is why, he tells us, *we are on a level where there is principally being*.[6] This way of thinking, going beyond any humanism, likewise abandons any category bound up with subjectivity and objectivity, for Heidegger does not pose the question of who man is, but how he remains in the opening of being that Heidegger calls his *ek-sistence*.[7]

By a different route, Althusser likewise contributed to the supersession of humanism. Taking up the issue of Marx's theoretical anti-humanism, he wrote:

> It is impossible to *know* anything about men except on the absolute precondition that the philosophical (theoretical) myth of man is reduced to ashes. So any thought that appeals to Marx for any kind of restoration of a theoretical anthropology or humanism is no more than ashes, *theoretically*.[8]

Althusser emphasised that, in rejecting the essence of man as a theoretical foundation, Marx expelled the philosophical categories of subject, empiricism, and ideal essence from all the domains where they held sway. He also stressed the displacement effected by Marx, when he replaced the old individuals-human essence pair by new concepts such as forces of production, relations of production, and so on.

It is not difficult to trace this starting from Marx's work. In the *Grundrisse*, Marx sketches an analysis that is increasingly focused on the relations of production and the productive forces. One senses a kind of fascination in him when he prepares to describe the mutual, many-sided dependence of indi-

---

[4] See Heidegger 1962, pp. 444–9.
[5] See Heidegger 1988.
[6] See Heidegger 1993.
[7] See Heidegger 1988. And See Schürhmann 1982, where readers will find a detailed analysis of Heidegger's trajectory before and after the *Kehre*.
[8] Althusser 1969, pp. 229–30.

viduals, 'indifferent to one another', which 'forms their social connection'. Marx shows that:

> The social character of activity, as well as the social form of the product, and the share of individuals in production here appear as something alien and objective, confronting the individuals, not as their relation to one another, but as their subordination to relations which exist independently of them and which arise out of collisions between mutually indifferent individuals.[9]

Marx is increasingly interested in the operation of the social mechanism and in its power.

Escaping Hegelianism: Foucault as follower of Nietzsche

We are very familiar with the importance that Foucault attributes to the reflections of these authors. At a time when he was in the process of distancing himself from Hegelianism and the many forms it can take, reading (among many others) Heidegger, Nietzsche and Althusser functioned as the only means of access to a quite different culture.[10]

From its inception, Foucault's thought enables us to think the connections between the problems posed by these authors. Although it does not have precisely the same theoretical concerns, it is situated in the same constructive space.[11] Foucault's first work bore the stamp of a reflection on rationality and

---

[9] Marx 1973, pp. 156–7.

[10] See 'Le retour de la morale', in Foucault 1994d, p. 703, where he claims that 'my whole philosophical development has been determined by my reading of Heidegger. But I recognise that it's Nietzsche who prevailed'. See also 'Structuralisme et post-structuralisme', in Foucault 1994d, pp. 431–8; 'Entretien with Michel Foucault', in Foucault 1994d, pp. 41–62; and 'Entretien avec Madeleine Chapsal', in Foucault 1994a, pp. 513–18, where he asserts: 'our task is to free ourselves definitively from humanism' (p. 514). I am not claiming to mark a direct filiation between these two intellectual currents and Foucault's reflections. Moreover, it is necessary to stress much more firmly than I can here the distinction between recourse to Nietzsche during the 1960s, when it was a question of escaping the dominant phenomenology of the time, and during the 1970s, when Nietzsche played a fundamental role in the confrontation with certain Marxist currents. See Ansell-Pearson 1991 and, on the subject of the relationship between Foucault and Heidegger, Dreyfus 1994.

[11] In order to avoid the idea that the links between these themes are produced in linear fashion in Foucault's work, I would like to refer to Pierre Macherey's article 'At the Sources of *Histoire de la Folie*'. The author analyses these Foucauldian beginnings very closely. Macherey bases his interpretation on the rectification that occurred between 1954 and 1962, when Foucault prepared to republish his book *Maladie mentale*

formed part of a field of complete renewal of perspectives on these general major themes.[12] Foucault's books – particularly *L'Histoire de la folie* or *Les Mots et les choses* – appeared

> at the beginning of the major controversies that marked a complete renewal in ways of thinking and writing inherited from the immediate post-war period, with the simultaneous problematization of narrative realism, philosophies of the subject, continuist representations, historical progress, dialectical rationality, and so on.[13]

Obviously, there were various stages in this phase of his intellectual development. Pupil of Hyppolite, Foucault had crossed the road that led from Hegel to Marx. He had immersed himself in psychological studies to such an extent that the label of psychologist stayed with him in academic circles until 1968. The philosophical problem of anthropology haunted his thought at the same time as the horizon of *Daseinanalyse* attracted his interest. Thus, when he wrote his first book, he became involved in a theoretical revolution that led him to reject any philosophy based on a concrete horizon of anthropological reflection on man. To this end, he had followed the critique of Binswanger and recognised that the project of anthropology must be capable of situating itself in opposition to all forms of psychological positivism which exhaust the significance of man in the reductive concept of *homo natura*. The supporting surface of anthropology had to be replaced in the context of an ontological reflection whose main theme was presence to being, existence, *Dasein*.

> After all, the man-being (*Mensch-sein*) is only the actual, concrete content of what ontology analyses as the transcendental structure of *Dasein*, of presence to the world.[14]

---

et personnalité under the new title of *Maladie mentale et psychologie*. Macherey shows how the reference to Nietzsche and Heidegger in the latter replaces references to young Marx in the former. He adds that 'by displacing the idea of a psychological truth of mental illness towards the idea of an ontological truth of madness, this rectification leaves intact the presupposition of a human nature, even if the latter arises from a poetic evocation instead of from a positive knowledge' (Macherey 1998, p. 92).

[12] See Macherey 1992, pp. iii–vi.

[13] Ibid.

[14] 'Introduction', in Foucault 1994a, p. 66.

Moreover, Foucault recognised that Nietzsche represents the point where any interrogation of man ends, for it is in the death of man that the death of God is consummated. Foucault wrote:

> The trajectory of the question *Was ist der Mensch?* in the field of philosophy reaches its end in the response which both challenges and disarms it: *der Übermensch.*[15]

Foucault posed the question of whether man, in his forms of existence, was the only way to arrive at man. This approach impeded any philosophical humanism, any philosophy based on a problematic of human nature.

These problems were to haunt Foucault's first attempt at a historical inquiry, which does not escape the literary fascination of the subject. *Histoire de la folie* is a work that can be read on several levels. Many questions run through it. Foucault queries the status accorded to the mad in European societies between the sixteenth century and the beginning of the nineteenth century. He asks how these strange characters – madmen – began to be perceived in a society. *Histoire de la folie* deals with a classic problem – the eternal debate between reason and unreason. This complex work is marked by a dual movement. On the one hand, Foucault reflects on the link between reason and unreason on the basis of literary or philosophical experiences. On the other, he reworks the concept of man in order to reflect on the historical relationship between reason and unreason. At the time of *Histoire de la folie*, Foucault assumed the existence of a species of living, voluble, visible madness that the mechanics of power and psychiatry had thereafter repressed and reduced to silence. This text, which ponders the power of exclusion, is not far removed from the meaning of the Nietzschean experience of tragedy. Just as, for Nietzsche, the deadly struggle between the Dyonisiac and the Apollonian ends with the death of tragedy, the power of darkness yielding to the light of Socratism, so for Foucault these nocturnal powers fade before the truth of the sun. And, as with Nietzsche, these beginnings were only a step on the path that led him to distance himself from any notion of depth. For Foucault, this beginning would only last for a while: he too would come to understand that madness (as Blanchot wrote) did not constitute a fundamental experience situated

---

[15] Foucault 2007c, p. 130.

'outside history, of which poets (artists) have been, and still can be, the witnesses, the victims or the heroes'.[16]

With these references, I am endeavouring to show how, via Nietzschean and Heideggerian critique, Foucault situated his examination at a considerable remove from any Marxism as well as any Hegelianism. Foucault's endeavour consists in detaching himself from any anthropological truth of man, of any dream of an end to history, which is the utopia of causal thought systems. For him, Nietzsche had 'burned for us... the intermingled promises of the dialectic and anthropology':

> He took the end of time and transformed it into the death of God and the odyssey of the last man; he took up anthropological finitude once again, but in order to use it as a basis for the prodigious leap of the superman; he took up once again the great continuous chain of History, but in order to bend it round into the infinity of the eternal return.[17]

Foucault's struggle with Marx takes shape as a rejection of the path pursued by a certain Marxism after Marx: it is a refusal of dialectical culture – a refusal whose high point is to be found in Nietzsche's intellectual experience. Nietzsche showed that the death of God signified the disappearance of man, since

> man and God had strange kinship relations, they were at once twin brothers and one another's father and son, so that, with God dead, man could not but disappear at the same time, leaving behind him the dreadful gnome.[18]

In Nietzsche's tracks, Heidegger likewise grasped the end of the dialectic, while trying to recover the fundamental relation to being in a return to Greek origins. Foucault also cites the examples of Russell, Wittgenstein, and Lévi-Strauss, in order to show how a non-dialectical culture has emerged in utterly distinct fields. He thus distances himself from an interpretation of Marx in which history seems to play a negative role. History

---

16 Blanchot 1986, p. 15.

17 Foucault 1970, p. 263. An important reference in the context of readings of Nietzsche is unquestionably Gilles Deleuze's *Nietzsche and Philosophy* (1962), which helped free people from dialectical thinking.

18 'L'homme est-t-il mort?', in Foucault 1994a, p. 542.

> augments the pressures of need, ... causes want to increase, obliging men constantly to work and to produce more and more, although they receive no more than what is indispensable to them to subsist, and sometimes a little less.... In this way the number of those maintained by History at the limit of their conditions of existence ceaselessly grows; and because of this, those conditions become increasingly more precarious until they approach the point where existence itself will become impossible... according to the Marxist interpretation, History, by dispossessing man of his labour, causes the positive form of his finitude to spring into relief – his material truth is finally liberated.[19]

The dialectic in a sense promises man that he will become an authentic, true man. It promises man to man. Freeing oneself from this culture means no longer reasoning in terms of morality, values, reconciliation. This means freeing oneself from a whole series of postulates that govern this discourse: releasing oneself from the sovereign subject and the concept of consciousness;[20] from that of the author and the idea of a continuous history. All these elements are interconnected:

> Continuous history is the indispensable correlative of the founding function of the subject: the guarantee that everything that has eluded him may be restored to him; the certainty that time will disperse nothing without restoring it in a reconstituted unity; the promise that one day the subject – in the form of historical consciousness – will once again be able to appropriate, to bring back under his sway, all those things that are kept at a distance by difference, and find in them what might be called his abode. Making historical analysis the discourse of the continuous and making human consciousness the original subject of all historical development and all action are the two sides of the same system of thought. In this system, time is conceived in terms of totalisation and revolutions are never more than moments of consciousness.[21]

---

19 Foucault 1970, pp. 260–1.

20 See 'What Is an Author?', in Foucault 1994a, pp. 789–820. On this subject, it is necessary to analyse the influence on Foucault of the works of Georges Bataille and Maurice Blanchot. See Warin 1994 and Prély 1977.

21 Foucault 1972, p. 12. See also 'Sur l'archéologie des sciences. Réponse au Cercle d'épistémologie', in Foucault 1994a, pp. 699–700.

Here Foucault is pondering the epistemological mutation in the concept of history which, he says, has yet to be completed. It is also important to stress that he dates the point at which this epistemological mutation began back to Marx. He emphasises that the theme of a global history has played a constant role since the nineteenth century: it involved 'preserv[ing], against all decentrings, the sovereignty of the subject, and the twin figures of anthropology and humanism'.[22] The role played by Marx was quite different, for Marx had decentred history through his historical analyses of the relations of production, economic determinations, and the class struggle. It had been necessary to anthropologise Marx, make him a historian of the totality, rediscover him as a proponent of humanism, in order to check the decentring he had effected – in the same way that people had been led to interpret Nietzsche in terms of transcendental philosophy and to reduce his genealogy to a search for the origin:

> All the treasure of bygone days was crammed into the old citadel of this history; it was thought to be secure; it was sacralized; it was made the last resting-place of anthropological thought; it was even thought that its most inveterate enemies could be captured and turned into vigilant guardians. But the historians had long ago deserted the old fortress and gone to work elsewhere; it was realised that neither Marx nor Nietzsche were carrying out the guard duties that had been entrusted to them.[23]

Towards a genealogy of the technologies of power

From the 1970s, Foucault's theoretical work shifted. According to him, as a result of circumstances and particular events, his theoretical interests changed. In particular, he was led to interest himself in the problem of prisons: 'This new preoccupation offered itself as a veritable escape from the lassitude I was experiencing in the face of literary matter.'[24] Throughout his career, Foucault never stopped reinterpreting his work. In the numerous interviews he gave, which double the size of his *œuvre*, he tried to identify the themes that were his theoretical concern as his research progressed. His retrospective

---

22 Foucault 1972, p. 12.
23 Foucault 1972, p. 14.
24 'Je perçois l'intolérable', in Foucault 1994b, p. 203.

glance is always situated at the level of the reflection that accompanies it. This means that he constantly tried to impart a new meaning to his work or to displace what was at issue in it. Although, in following Foucault, there is the risk of losing track of the breaks, the ruptures, the leaps that accompanied the development of his research, his interviews nevertheless indicate the emergence of certain concepts. Thus, he says that in the 1960s he had sought to retrace how

> a certain number of institutions, setting out to function in the name of reason and normality, had exercised their power over groups of individuals, in relation to forms of behaviour, ways of being, acting or speaking, constituted as anomaly, madness, illness, etc. At bottom, I'd constructed nothing other than a history of power.[25]

And it is in the same direction that his research continued during the 1970s. Let us add that Foucault subsequently came to regard the analysis of subjectivity as the thread that ran through his research:

> I instead sought to produce a history of the different modes of subjectivation of human beings in our culture; in this optic, I've dealt with three modes of objectification that transform human beings into subjects.[26]

Simplifying my reading, it seems to me that Foucault's theoretical output in the 1970s can be divided into two parts: the first, spanning the first half of the decade, concludes with the publication of *Surveiller et punir*; the second begins with the publication of *La Volonté de savoir*. The early 1970s witnessed an increased interest on Foucault's part in Marx's historical research. In his own way, he examines the genealogy of capitalism. When he tackles the issue of the penal system, he begins to take a growing interest in the control mechanisms created by modern society. In a new swing of the pendulum, he attends to institutions and practices that are, in a sense, situated below the threshold of expressivity. Foucault shows that from the beginning of the nineteenth century a whole series of institutions functioned on the same model, obeying the same rules – i.e. a mechanism of surveillance in which individuals were attached to a punitive, correctional, or sanitary apparatus. Hospitals,

---

25 'Entretien avec Michel Foucault', in Foucault 1994d, p. 82.
26 'Le sujet et le pouvoir', in Foucault 1994d, p. 223.

asylums, orphanages, colleges, approved school, factories, and so on formed part of a major social form of power that was established at the beginning of the nineteenth century, and which was doubtless one of the operating conditions of industrial, capitalist society.[27] Foucault stresses that capitalism was not able to function with a system of political power indifferent to individuals. He argues:

> There came a time when it was necessary for everyone to be effectively perceived by the eye of power. When, in the division of labour, there was a need for some people who were capable of doing this, and others who were capable of doing that; when there was also a fear that popular movements of resistance, or inertia, or revolt would emerge to disrupt this whole capitalist order that was in the process of being born, then a precise, concrete surveillance over all individuals was required....[28]

If Marx describes the West's economic take-off with reference to the processes that made capital accumulation possible, Foucault stresses the means of managing the accumulation of human beings, which made a political take-off possible with respect to traditional forms of power. The accumulation of human beings cannot be separated from the accumulation of capital. It would not have been possible to resolve the problem of accumulating human beings without the development of an apparatus of production capable both of maintaining and utilising them. Conversely, the techniques that made the cumulative multiplicity of human beings useful accelerated the dynamic of capital accumulation. At a less general level, the technological mutations in the apparatus of production, the division of labour, and the development of disciplinary processes were intimately related. Each rendered the other possible and necessary; each served as a model for the other.

Foucault demonstrates that the disciplines are techniques for ensuring the regulation of human multiplicities. They are enrolled in the task of making the exercise of power as cheap as possible and seeing to it that the results of this social power are pushed to maximum intensity and extended as far as possible, without failures or gaps. The aim of the disciplines is to increase

---

27 See 'Prisons et révoltes dans les prisons', in Foucault 1994b, p. 431.

28 'Le pouvoir, une bête magnifique', in Foucault 1994c, p. 374. See also 'L'impossible prison', in Foucault 1994d, pp. 20–43 and 'Les intellectuels et le pouvoir', in Foucault 1994b, pp. 306–15.

both the docility and the utility of all the elements of the system. This triple objective responds to a well-known historical conjuncture: the major demographical spurt of the eighteenth century and the growth of the apparatus of production. With respect to demographic expansion, the disciplines present themselves as an anti-nomadic procedure. They consist in a set of tiny technical inventions that made it possible to increase the utility of multiplicities by reducing the drawbacks of power. For Foucault, the real, corporeal disciplines constituted the substratum of formal, juridical liberties. Thus, he can assert that the Enlightenment, which discovered the liberties, also invented the disciplines. The extension of disciplinary methods forms part of a broad historical process: the development at approximately the same time of many other technologies – agronomic, industrial, economic. Among these technologies, according to Foucault, panopticism has been largely ignored. The history of the West is marked by the invention of systems of

> domination of an extreme rationality. It took a long time to arrive at this, and still more time to discover what lay behind it. A whole set of goals, techniques and methods falls within it: discipline reigns in schools, the army, the factory.

Foucault adds: 'The power of reason is a bloody power'.[29]

Foucault's research into disciplinary power, the society of control, the birth of the punitive society outline the genealogy of modern state power. By pinpointing a series of technologies for governing bodies and individuals, it indicates the emergence of the modern form of subjectivity. This intersects with the research pursued by Marx in *Capital*. In both cases, the genealogy of capitalist society is traced from viewpoints that are not mutually exclusive, but which are integrated in describing the process of accumulation of forces of production and forces of political power. Foucault claims that it was not until the nineteenth century that it was known what exploitation was, but there was still hesitation on the subject of power. He stresses that we know approximately who exploits, where the profit goes, through whose hands it passes, and where it is re-invested, whereas we are still ignorant of what power is. He states:

---

[29] 'La torture, c'est la raison', in Foucault 1994c, p. 395. It is clear that a detailed analysis of all these themes is to be found in one of the most important works written by Foucault, *Discipline and Punish: The Birth of the Prison* (1975).

> And Marx and Freud are perhaps insufficient to help us to know this extremely enigmatic thing – at one visible and invisible, present and hidden, invested everywhere – that is called power.[30]

Although the respective *œuvres* of Marx and Foucault can be used to reconstruct the genealogy of modern, capitalist, Western society, they cannot be superimposed. I believe that the Foucauldian reading of Marx contains points of interest, but also some lacunae. To read Marx, Foucault proposes an optic that accentuates some aspects of his own work – particularly those that revolve around the relations of force, class struggle, and violence that run through society. According to Foucault, Marx analysed the real functioning of power:

> It seems to me that we can find the basic elements of an analysis of this kind in a certain number of texts.... We can obviously also find them in volume one of *Capital*.... In the first instance, what we find there is that there is not *one* power, but several powers.[31]

Foucault's Marx describes the emergence of a social field through rules of pure immanence. All the elements that produce a social field are produced there themselves as they produce it. There is not a certain prior social order, which is applied to individuals from without. Relations of force, the class war, different technologies of production or power – these produce a social field that is not established once and for all. In this analysis, there is no trace of teleology. Everything develops beyond good and evil, without there being someone behind the curtain ultimately controlling the mechanism.

Foucault devotes himself to attending to the roar of battle that resounds throughout society. He is interested in grasping the different forms of government, ever changeable, that emerge on this terrain. But, contrary to Marx, he does not seek to grasp the difference in perspectives, values, ways of life, desires, of which each subject engaged in struggle is the bearer. Nor does he concentrate on analysing the possible forms, albeit incomplete, to which each battle might give rise. In history, he seeks neither hidden meanings nor possibilities, but the positive forms that crystallise in each epoch. A whole area, clearly present in Marx, involving the various and changing forms of social exploitation eluded him, even if he tried to encompass it and extend

---

30 'Les intellectuels et le pouvoir', in Foucault 1994b, p. 312.
31 'Les mailles du pouvoir', in Foucault 1994d, p. 186.

it through the analysis of the microphysical forms of power with which the social field is striated.

From technologies of government to technologies of the self

During the 1970s, Foucault's theoretical and political work was drastically altered by the issue of social change and the revolution in forms of existence. He tried to give a response to the questions posed by his age. That is why, starting from the second half of the 1970s, he began a new critique of Marxism and of possible readings derived from Marx's *œuvre*. In this respect, *La Volonté de savoir* is an emblematic text, for it represents the beginning of the development of a new critique of Marxism. It is important to stress that Foucault discovered a common epistemological root between Marxism and Freudianism and it was on this couple that he was subsequently to practise his critique. Balibar has written that, with this critique, Foucault wished radically to question the self-evidence and efficacity of a certain leftism or revolutionary utopianism.[32]

When Foucault works around the concepts of 'domination', 'direction', and 'government', while trying to define a theory of state apparatuses, his theoretical aim is to criticise the idea of a repressive society (dubbed, on several occasions, the Reichian hypothesis). His work had long had the aim of freeing the field of epistemology from any opposition between the true and the false, reality and illusion, the scientific and the non-scientific, the rational and the irrational. He sought to exclude the risk of regarding the concepts of domination, dominant ideology, and subjection as involving an opposition between illusion and reality. This did not mean that these notions had no meaning or value. But the problem had to be posed in terms of practices constituting domains, objects and concepts within which the oppositions between scientific and non-scientific, true and false, reality and illusion could take effect.[33] This had been true of his attempt to read Marx. In Freudo-Marxism he once again identified a risk. As Balibar has written:

---

32 See Balibar 1997.

33 See Michel Foucault, 'Du gouvernement des vivants': course at the Collège de France of 9.1.1980, in the Fonds-Foucault, library of IMEC, Paris, audio document C 62 (01) b 2127/995.

> Freudo-Marxism is an *inversion* of the values expressed by powerful institutional apparatuses. It inspires contestation in these apparatuses, struggles whose importance Foucault acknowledges. But the main thing for him is to ponder the extent to which they really break with the discursive formation that they denounce.[34]

Foucault's critique of the repressive hypothesis, which includes all the variants of Freudo-Marxism, in Reich as in Adorno or Marcuse, is elaborated at the same time as he retraces the genealogy of *raison d'état* at the beginning of the seventeenth century, by recourse to the concept and notion of government. The notion of government seems to him to be more operative than power, for it enables us to pinpoint the procedures that have made it possible to lead men, to rule them, without it being necessary to postulate a theory or representation of the state.

These analyses of governmentality, the art of governing human beings, and the genealogy of *raison d'état* were not pursued to their conclusion by Foucault.[35] His reflections on Freudianism, as well as the events that marked the end of the 1970s, led him to a closer consideration of the problem of technologies of the self – i.e. the set of subjective practices that shape subjects.

Foucault must have believed that tracing a genealogy of the forms of subjectivity might counterbalance the stress he had laid on the issue of the objective relations of power. The changes in aesthetic and political sensibility at the end of the 1970s definitely contributed to reinforcing his view that 'we must refer to processes that are much more remote if we want to understand how we allowed ourselves to be caught in the trap of our own history'.[36]

---

[34] Balibar 1997, p. 284.

[35] See Foucalt 2007a and Foucault 2007b for analyses of the objective technologies of power; and the continuation of the courses at the Collège de France from 1980 to 1984 as regards the analysis of technologies of the self. See Foucault 2005.

[36] '*Omnes et singulatim*. Vers une critique de la raison politique', in Foucault 1994d, p. 136.

Chapter Thirty-Five

Beyond the Crisis of Marxism: Gramsci's Contested Legacy

Fabio Frosini

1. Historicism, anti-historicism, post-historicism

Discussion and research on Gramsci have for a long time been a predominantly Italian issue, or rather a question intrinsic or mainly referring to the history of the Italian Communist Party (PCI). It has seemed obvious then, for a whole generation of studies on Gramsci, to link his legacy to the history of the party that he had helped to found. In turn, this has meant that studies dedicated to Gramsci always had a double register: historical reconstruction and political evaluation walked hand in hand, or rather historical reconstruction was always functional to a given idea of how to use Gramsci's thought in contemporary contexts. This line of interpretation has been characterised by highly distinctive periods, corresponding almost exactly to the various moments of Italian politics and culture. Yet, at least one unifying trait might be identified in the whole period running from the immediate postwar period until the dissolution of the PCI in 1991. This trait derives from the way in which Togliatti prsented, at least from 1949, the question of Gramsci's legacy as 'thinker and man of action',[1] that is, as a great intellectual – heir to the 'national' tradition of Bertrando Spaventa, Antonio Labriola and Benedetto Croce – who was *also* a Communist politician. The self-evidence of the link between being an intellectual and being a Communist was part of a precise political strategy of Togliatti's. It aimed to conquer the sympathy and support of Italian intellectuals without asking them to put into question their idealistic and historicist education. Historicism, in fact, worked paradoxically as a meeting point for differentiated philosophical positions; historicism understood, of course, in terms generic enough not to question the theoretical matrix of anyone. Gramsci's thought itself was thus reduced to a variation of Benedetto Croce's historicism.[2]

In this way, Togliatti achieved at least two things: first, he linked the name of Gramsci closely to the politics of his own party, and second, at the same time, allowed *non-Marxist* intellectuals to participate in the elaboration both of Gramsci's legacy and of the cultural politics of the PCI. The result is what I have called the unifying trait of all readings of Gramsci until the beginning of the 1990s: in the changing interpretations, there was always a remarkable incomprehension of the specific theoretical problem and the related question of a *Weltanschauung*. What remains alive and vivid of Gramsci is, on the one hand, the exemplary model of a communist fighter and, on the other, his ability to rethink Marxist schemata from a 'national' point of view, thus unshackling himself from doctrinal and 'ideological' approaches. Gramsci was thus duly entered into the 'chronicles of Italian philosophy',[3] becoming a key reference point in the 'national culture'.[4] It might thus be said that, by imposing a strongly anti-theoretical and ecumenical imprint on the 'official' reading of Gramsci, Togliatti fulfilled what Benedetto Croce had anticipated in his 1947 review of the *Letters from Prison* published by Einaudi when he wrote that 'as a man of thought he was one of us', in Joseph Conrad's sense, re-read in the light of a universal, 'cathartic' and 'lyrical' function of culture and history.[5]

[1] This is the title of an essay of 1949, now published in Togliatti 2001, pp. 131–50.

[2] On the 'Croceo-Marxisms' of the 1950s and 1960s see Rossi-Landi 1982, p. 115.

[3] This is the title of an influential work by Eugenio Garin 1955, with numerous later editions.

[4] See also by Garin 1958, pp. 3–14. By the same author, see also in the same direction Garin 1967, pp. 119–43; and Garin 1969, pp. 37–73. All these texts are now gathered together in Garin 1997.

[5] Croce 1947, p. 86. The expression 'one of us' is picked up with approval by Garin 1958, p. 9.

It might be said then that the common element that Gramsci's followers could not or would not put into question is precisely that universalistic function of intellectuals as ministers of truth, a perspective that loses sight of the link between partiality and truth so clearly identified in the *Notebooks* and consigns Gramsci's legacy wholly into the hands of 'official' high culture. It thus cannot come as a surprise if every radical movement of social and political struggle in Italy from the 1970s to the 1990s was fiercely alien and hostile to Gramsci, always taken as the official version of 'Gramscianism':[6] from the group of the *Quaderni Rossi* gathered around Raniero Panzieri, through the *operaismo* of the 1960s and the 1970s, to the Nietzscheanism of the movement of 1977,[7] there is a continuing incapacity to grasp the ontological radicality of the *Prison Notebooks*, namely the fact that they build on the double premise of the critique of every universalism and of the link between truth and politics, both elements that those movements discovered and elaborated with the aid of non-Marxist theoretical instruments first, and then later on with the aid of postmodernism.

These movements represent an instance of the more general crisis of historicism in Italy. Confronted with these phenomena, official 'Gramscianism' reacted in the first instance with a stubborn defence of the old approach (perhaps adequate to the rural Italy of the 1950s but gain a purchase in a more industrialised country), or with an attempt to update the old doctrine through the introduction of new topics. Among these were such themes as 'civil society' or 'Gramsci, theoretician of superstructures' (as in the workshop organised by the Istituto Gramsci in 1967 with the title *Gramsci and Contemporary Culture*);[8] the admission of a partial obsoleteness of Gramscian historicism (in reality: of the historicism of official Gramscianism) and an accompanying vindication of a 'return to Marx' on the basis of the old epistemological Marxism of Della Volpe, or of the new structuralist approach of Althusser;[9] or, finally,

6 This circumstance has been cleverly highlighted by Baratta 1987. Cf. in general Liguori 1996, pp. 172–8. See the update in Liguori 2005, pp. 7–36.

7 The case of Toni Negri, from the fierce anti-Gramscianism of 1973, pp. 77–83, to the affected recovery of Gramsci as anti-Stalinist fighter in the recent Negri 2005 is exemplary in this regard. On the period 1977–9, see Liguori 1996, pp. 195–7.

8 See Liguori 1996, pp. 138–43.

9 See Liguori 1996, pp. 107–9 and 132–8. Cf. Badaloni 1971. A valuable (and biased) reconstruction of these events can be found in the 'Introduzione generale' by Nicola Badaloni in Badaloni 1987, pp. 161–2.

a strong updating and correction of the historicist framework of Gramsci's thought in the light of new political and theoretical approaches.[10]

This slowly transforming picture collapsed into rapid disbandment during the 1980s, when the whole Communist and neo-communist movement in Italy, both parliamentary and extra-parliamentary, suffered a sudden retreat. The relation between Gramsci's legacy and the politics of the PCI was severed. This moment had been prefigured during the 1970s, with the complete exhaustion of historicism as a reference point, and the break-up of the triangle culture-party-intellectuals. In fact, the regular decennial workshop of the Istituto Gramsci was dedicated in 1977 to the topic 'Politics and History in Gramsci', stressing the politicological nature of Gramsci's discourse. The categories mostly used in the papers of the workshop were organic crisis, passive revolution, intellectuals, rationalisation, hegemony; all in relation to Gramsci's peculiar redefinition of the state and his related analyses of fascism and Americanism.[11] If we compare these studies with those from the previous decade, the focus of attention has moved from the (unique) historical process to the (various) ramified networks of the exercise of power, from the intellectual as bearer of a *Weltanschauung* to the intellectual as civil servant and professional (in the sense attributed by Weber); from civil society as the alternative to Marxist economism[12] to civil society as the structured ground where forces exert power. The result is an increased emphasis on the antithesis between Gramsci's conception and the idea of the state as the 'executive committee of the bourgeoisie'. The state is, rather, the concrete form in which society exists in all its articulations, in an intertwined relation between 'social' and 'political' which leaves no room for any instrumentalist or utilitarian conception.[13]

It is far too easy to note how this reading coincided with the politics of the 'historic compromise', on the basis of which the PCI was about to enter government. It is far more interesting to notice the *objective* character of this pas-

---

[10] From this point of view, Nicola Badaloni's passage from Badaloni 1962 to Badaloni 1975 and Badaloni 1988 is noteworthy: the topic of historicism remains always at the core of his approach, but it progressively breaks free from any reference to the humanist centrality of the 'subject' in historical transformations.

[11] Cf. above all de Giovanni 1977, pp. 221–57; Mangoni, 1977, pp. 391–438; Vacca 1977, pp. 439–80; Cerroni 1977, pp. 127–60; De Felice 1977, pp. 161–220; Buci-Glucksmann 1977, pp. 99–125; Bodei 1977, pp. 61–98.

[12] This was, in the final analysis, the sense of the famous paper of Bobbio 1969, pp. 75–100.

[13] This is the key topic of an important book by Buci-Glucksmann 1975 that anticipates the most important topics of the workshop of 1977.

sage: it announces indeed with great sensitivity the end of the Fordist cycle of 'progressivism', based on intervention, assistance and repression policies and centred on the dialectic of capital and labour; it opens the discourse on post-Fordist politics of internal control and of multiplication of work forms with the loss of the distinction between work and life.[14]

It is not coincidental that the Gramscian category of 'passive revolution' acquires a central role in the workshop of 1977, marking the passage from a conflictual model to another where conflict is constantly re-integrated by mechanisms of control and regulation. This passage was summarised and polarised a few years later (in 1984) by Leonardo Paggi in the introduction to his *Le strategie del potere in Gramsci*:

> It is the unforeseen development of the political struggle that urges Gramsci to rethink radically the Hobbesian problem of *order*, thus performing the most successful attempt up to date to liberate Marxism from a naively conflictualist model of interpretation; and from here stems the acknowledgement and acceptance that any social and power order can survive as long as agreement and consensus on a series of norms and values, common to various and contrasting social strata, manage to curb the dividing and disintegrating effects of social conflict.[15]

As we can see, the category of 'passive revolution' is here almost identified with that of 'hegemony'. The result is that the abandonment of the catastrophist model of the Third International – which is, in substance, the import of the category 'passive revolution'[16] – is read in the light of the *primacy of stability over instability*. 'The role of subjectivity', which in the young Gramsci was 'the determining element in the acceleration of the historical process', becomes 'the most important source of endurance of the old power structures'.[17]

But, in this way, the historical passage of the 1970s is overturned, because it becomes a mere occasion for the transformation of the parties of the workers'

---

[14] On this period see in general Fanini and Zanini (eds.) 2001.

[15] Paggi 1984, p. x. Paggi maintains, also theoretically, the substitution of philosophy with political science in his essay 'Da Lenin a Marx' in Paggi 1984 (but first published in 1974), pp. 427–98.

[16] See Q 15, 17, p. 1774; Q 15, 56, pp. 1818–19; Q 15, 62, p. 1827. References are from Gramsci 1977a, using the internationally accepted standards. Q (*Quaderno*) stands for the Notebook followed by the number of the notebook, followed by the number of the paragraph and of the pages according to the Italian critical edition.

[17] Paggi 1984, p. ix.

movement into parties of government, thus eliminating the *dialectics* between conflict and control that can be thought through the category of 'passive revolution'. In fact, the 'passive revolution' does not mark the passage from a conflictualist to a consensual model, but the resolution of the dichotomy between 'crisis' and 'stabilisation' in a conception in which policies of control (what we call today 'governance') and social conflict, persistence and transformation, or in Gramsci's words 'restoration' and 'revolution', might be *thought together*, without one term excluding the other.

This category, in short, has a completely different heuristic import; in fact, during the 1990s, in those places where capitalist modernisation has been most intense, a new reading of Gramsci has developed, focusing on the notions of passive revolution, the translatability of languages, hegemony and civil society. These notions are seen as the key elements in the analysis of widespread power and control. This analysis does not eliminate the issue of conflict though; it is re-presented on a different level and in a new form. The question of language, a key issue in the *Notebooks* as a now classic work by Franco Lo Piparo once argued,[18] is at the centre of numerous analyses of hegemony and ideology,[19] while 'the translatability of languages and national cultures' has been linked to hegemony,[20] and thus to politics and economy, that is, with praxis.[21] There is also extensive research on passive revolution that highlights its capacity to rethink the topic of revolution in the framework of the twentieth century.[22] There is no univocal nexus between crisis and revolution; on the contrary, crises are continuously re-absorbed into regulation mechanisms. But this does not mean that stability prevails over crisis; on the contrary, it means that crisis is generalised, that it becomes *inseparable* from the stability and the continuity of the capitalist market.[23] If the *Notebooks* are read in this way, abandoning any 'historicist' temptations, it means that they not only allow but indeed require a productive confrontation with anti-

---

18 Lo Piparo 1979.
19 See, for example, Ives 1998, pp. 34–51; Ives 2004b, and Ives 2005, pp. 455–68.
20 Cf. Tosel 1981, pp. 235–56, in particular pp. 235–45.
21 Cf. Frosini 2003b, pp. 29–38.
22 Cf. Vacca 1999; Burgio 2002, pp. 88–97; Voza 2004, pp. 189–207.
23 See Gramsci 1977a, Q 15, 5, pp. 1755–9, entitled 'Past and Present. The Crisis'.

dialectical approaches, such as those of Althusser or Foucault, that only few years ago seemed utterly incompatible with Gramsci.[24]

2. A worldwide Gramscian web

The decade of Gramscian studies between 1978 and 1986 has been called the 'low season'.[25] This critical misfortune is closely linked to the ultimate crisis of the unstable balance between communist politics, the politics of the intellectuals, and slowly declining Italian historicism. The workers' movement in Italy suffered a persistent historical defeat and the relationship between Gramsci's thought and the PCI was definitively terminated. This termination implied not only the lack of interest of Italian intellectuals regarding Gramsci. It coincides, in fact, with two vitally important events that cannot be neglected by anyone who considers Gramsci's legacy to be irreducible to the merely scholarly dimension or, conversely, simply to the life of a political party. The cycle 1978–86 is, indeed, the period in which the critical edition of the *Prison Notebooks*, finally published in 1975 after a long preparation,[26] started to produce its effects. This laid the basis for the resumption of Gramscian studies from the early 1990s until today. This resumption – and this is the second event that must be taken into account – is not only Italian, nor European: in fact, already during the 1980s – thanks especially to the critical edition and to a felicitous anthology in English[27] – Gramsci's thought experienced a worldwide diffusion. Among others, there were translations of the *Prison Notebooks* into English, Spanish and Portuguese (in addition to those into French and German). In an article published in 1987,[28] Valentino Gerratana noticed favourably the 'spontaneous' character of this propagation; Eric Hobsbawm remarked that Gramsci was one of the most known, read and studied Italian authors in the

---

[24] On Althusser, see Robelin 1992, pp. 85–95, and Finelli 1997, on Foucault see Balibar 1992, pp. 259–69; and Kouvelakis 1996, pp. 83–94.

[25] Liguori 1996, pp. 198–221.

[26] See Gerratana 1967, pp. 240–59; Gerratana 1970, pp. 455–76; Gerratana's Preface to Gramsci 1977a; *Rinascita/Il contemporaneo* 1975.

[27] Gramsci 1971b. And, later on, Gramsci 1995.

[28] Gerratana 1987, p. 5.

world;[29] and in 1989 the Foundation Istituto Gramsci of Rome organised a large international conference dedicated to studying this phenomenon.[30]

It is from this turning point that we have to come to terms with the good fortune of Gramscian studies, which is no longer only Italian. We refer, obviously, to studies about Gramsci but also more generally the ways in which the impulse arising from reading Gramsci has been variously valued and used in different contexts. *Los usos de Gramsci* is the title of a book by Juan Carlos Portantiero, who in 1981 discussed the ways in which Gramsci was read and adapted to the Latin-American context.[31] It would be equally correct to speak of the good fortune of Gramscian studies in the English and North-American cultures,[32] in the cultural studies promoted by Stuart Hall,[33] or in the use of 'subalternity', 'civil society' and 'hegemony' by the South-Asian subaltern studies group or by an author such as Gayatri C. Spivak,[34] and so on and so forth. It would be far too easy to note the approximate and frequently indirect character of the knowledge that these authors have of Gramsci. What really matters is the fact that, in a moment of crisis not only of Marxism but of the whole culture of emancipation, freedom and personal liberty, Gramsci is still being read, studied and translated all over the world. His categories have demonstrated a vitality that transcends his epoch and also his personal culture; and this turns Gramsci not only into a classical author of Marxism or of philosophy, but into a source of suggestions and perspectives for the critique of the contemporary world.

As for the rest, two further points should be underlined. First of all, since the end of the 1990s, there seems to be a resumption of Gramscian studies also in Italy. Secondly, on the international level, there is a gradual definition of quality standards for Gramscian studies that might help to refine critically the approach of neo-Gramscianism. This is an effect of the presence, also outside Italy, of prominent and influential scholars who represent reference points for

---

29 Hobsbawm 1987.

30 Righi (ed.) 1995 with essays by 27 scholars from 4 continents. See also Hobsbawm 1995.

31 Portantiero 1981. Portantiero had first given the title 'Los usos de Gramsci' to his introduction to the anthology Gramsci 1977b.

32 See, for example, Martin (ed.) 2002.

33 A fertile critical interaction with this current is represented by Baratta 2003, in particular pp. 181–5.

34 Spivak 1988, pp. 271–313. A re-assessment of the import and the limits of Gramsci for subaltern studies can be found in Buttigieg 1999, pp. 27–38.

the areas in which they live and work, namely, Carlos N. Coutinho in Brazil or Joseph A. Buttigieg in the United States. Buttigieg and Coutinho are members of the International Gramsci Society, an association founded in 1997 under the chairmanship of Valentino Gerratana, which brings together Gramscians from all over the world.[35] The resumption of Gramscian studies in Italy is also to be attributed, at least partly, to the activities of the IGS.[36] In 2000, this organisation initiated an on-going workshop on the lexicon of the *Prison Notebooks* and published in 2004 the first fruits of these labours: a volume that collects thirteen essays on key categories of the *Notebooks*, ranging from 'Americanism and Fordism' to 'Translation and Translatability'.[37]

3. Philology and politics

Another significant event of the 1980s was the publication in 1984 of Gianni Francioni's *L'officina gramsciana. Ipotesi sulla struttura dei «Quaderni del carcere»*.[38] Francioni, who had advanced some findings in the conference organised by the Istituto Gramsci in 1977,[39] arrived in his book at an ensemble reading of the *structure* of the *Notebooks* that makes the most of the critical edition of Gerratana, pointing out the main characteristics of Gramsci's method of work and trying to assign a date as precisely as possible to all the notes of the *Notebooks*. *L'officina gramsciana* opened a new season in Gramscian studies, a season in which Togliatti's approach to Gramsci was definitely cancelled. Togliatti, together with Felice Platone, had published the *Prison Notebooks* in six thematic volumes between 1948 and 1951.[40] It was a huge mediation: a mediation, first of all, between Gramsci's thought and Togliatti's, and, more generally, a mediation between Gramsci's thought and Italian culture.[41] This

35 See <www.italnet.nd.edu/gramsci>.

36 See <www.gramscitalia.it>.

37 Frosini and Liguori (eds.) 2004, with contributions by Giorgio Baratta, Derek Boothman, Giuseppe Cospito, Lea Durante, Fabio Frosini, Guido Liguori, Rita Medici, Giuseppe Prestipino, Pasquale Voza.

38 Francioni 1984. On the topics discussed in this chapter see in general Liguori 1999, pp. 217–32.

39 Francioni 1977, pp. 369–94.

40 Gramsci 1948; Gramsci 1949a; Gramsci 1949b; Gramsci 1949c; Gramsci 1950; Gramsci 1951.

41 Togliatti's correspondence regarding the first edition of Gramsci's *Letters from Prison* and the *Prison Notebooks* is now available in Daniele 2005.

mediation aimed to render the *Notebooks* immediately productive in the Italian culture and politics of the day, at the cost, however, of redefining the ensemble profile of the text. The text was thus ordered in categories that followed an acceptable and accredited taxonomy of knowledge, whereas Gramsci's work method consisted rather in calling that taxonomy into question.[42] Second, the text was treated as a complete work, finished and definitive. A certain level of elaboration of the text – that which was considered to correspond the most to the intentions of the author – was taken for publication while all the previous elaboration was cancelled from the published text. In fact, although Gramsci was tempted on several occasions to order the materials of the *Notebooks*, he never arrived at any definitive conclusion. It is thus only by re-opening the workshop of *Notebooks*, in their provisional quality as a work in progress, that we can understand not only their problematic character but also the whole innovative capacity of the thought that they capture.[43] Necessary to this re-opening was, of course, the publication of the critical edition, which *L'officina gramsciana* elaborated further and in greater depth. It has thus become possible to access the text with a diachronic and not systematic approach, which allows us to follow the formation and progressive definition of the analytical categories of Gramsci, through changes, second thoughts and sharp inversions.

On the basis of this historical turning point, the discussion about the structure of the *Notebooks* has turned almost immediately into a debate on the expediency of a new critical edition,[44] a debate that has concluded with the launch of the National Edition of the Works of Antonio Gramsci. This edition will publish together with the *Notebooks* all the writings preceeding Gramsci's imprisonment and Gramsci's correspondence.[45] This initiative, which must surely be welcomed, runs the risk of drawing attention away from the real

---

[42] This aspect was emphasised by Mordenti 1989, pp. 413–28; and more recently Mordenti 1996, pp. 553–629. See also Monasta 1985.

[43] Cf. Frosini 2000, pp. 108–20; Frosini 2003a, pp. 21–76.

[44] Cf. Francioni 1992, pp. 85–186 and Istituto Gramsci Informazioni 1992, pp. 69–84, with statements by Nicola Badaloni, Sergio Caprioglio, Giuseppe Vacca, Renzo Martinelli, Dario Ragazzini, Rita Medici, Lucia Borghese, Joseph A. Buttigieg, Luciano Canfora, Gianni Francioni, Leonardo Paggi, Michele Ciliberto, and Marcello Mustè.

[45] The 'Commission for the National Edition of the Works of Antonio Gramsci' was set up by a decree of the Ministry of Culture in December 1996. In 2007 the first volume of the *Notebooks* was published, which contain the *Translation Notebooks* (Gramsci 2007).

novelty of the discussion about the structure of the *Notebooks*. When it is stated, as it has been, that we must speak of Gramsci today as 'we speak of Plotinus',[46] philology is exchanged for a practice of neutralisation, scientific stringency for disengagement, the classical nature of Gramsci's thought for its non-actuality.[47] The discussion about the structure of the *Notebooks*, launched by the publication of the critical edition, has indeed the opposite value of combining these two moments, restoring the text in its full force to politics. This principle is valid, as we said before, regarding the discovery of the work-in-progress nature of the categories of the *Notebooks*; but it is also valid – and it is of no minor importance – in relation to the text as a whole, to its form and to its *literary quality*.

In an important essay dedicated to these issues,[48] the 'constitutive incompleteness' of the research presented in the *Notebooks*, the fact that they are '*by nature* [...] *un/terminable*', was seen as the unavoidable consequence of a writing that in an 'absolutely *and typically* twentieth-century' manner aspired to 'reflect wholly the world outside the prison and its problems'.[49] Philology thus re-opens the relationship between the texts and politics, between words and praxis: the formal consideration of the *Notebooks* sheds light on the leaning of the text towards what, in the *content* of the *Notebooks*, is thought of as irreducible to a merely 'theoretical' reflection. Maybe a global reading of Gramsci will be possible only if we manage to fully apprehend the unevenness between the text and the world, and the constitutive incompleteness of 'theory',[50] thus realising that this is not postmodernism, nor post-communism, but the way in which Gramsci resumes and radicalises Karl Marx's 'Theses on Feuerbach'.

4. Partiality and truth

A reconstruction of the discussion about Antonio Gramci and his legacy in more recent years must have the courage to assume a partial point of view. First of all, this partiality is determined, obviously and unavoidably,

---

46 Paggi, in Istituto Gramsci Informazioni 1992, p. 79.

47 See Gerratana 1997, pp. xi–xxvi.

48 Mordenti 1996. See also Mordenti 2007.

49 Mordenti 1996, p. 613.

50 See Buttigieg's Introduction, in Gramsci 1991, pp. lvi, lxxii–lxxvi; Wagner 1991 and Buey 2001, pp. 129–84.

by the preferences and limitations of the writer: preferences and limitations regarding both the ways of reading and the chosen topics within Gramsci's thought. It is also determined, almost mechanically, by the huge amount of critical literature on Gramsci, whose flow has increased in the last twenty years in a way that allows us to speak of a world-wide *Gramsci renaissance*.[51] But this partiality is particularly determined by a much more important reason, closely related to the nature of our subject matter: it springs unavoidably from the *nature* of Antonio Gramsci's thinking, which is both, contemporaneously and inseparably, theoretical and practical, philosophical and political. In this peculiar characteristic it encloses – and thus renders unavoidable – a capacity of division and of rupture that comes over again and again.

It must be noted that this peculiarity is due not only to the fact that Gramsci was a Marxist; nor does it depend mainly on the special emphasis that he put on the concept of 'praxis' as the centre from which the whole idea of a Marxist philosophy should be reconstructed. Marxism, in fact, has always been traversed by the relations between philosophy and politics, between the understanding of real processes and intervention in them, between the criticism of ideology and the science of history and politics. Yet only with Gramsci does this relation become the *point of view* from which one might explain both Marxism and any other philosophy. The urgency with which Gramsci insists in the *Prison Notebooks* on the 'unity of theory and practice' cannot be understood as a 'theoretical' standpoint (in the sense attributed to 'theory' in the 'Theses on Feuerbach'), but it must be rightly interpreted as the displacement of philosophy onto a new terrain, a terrain in which thought is always, structurally, a standpoint involved in a network of forces and theoretical-practical relations; the standpoint is conditioned by the network and, in turn, reacts upon it.

But this philosophical novelty cannot be separated from the biography of Gramsci, which in an absolutely original manner – compared to any other Marxist of the 1920s – conjugates political and theoretical work.[52] This is not a value judgement at all, but an empirical observation from which one must

[51] The *Gramsci Bibliography*, edited by John M. Cammett, Francesco Giasi and Maria Luisa Righi, now available on line (<http://213.199.9.13/bibliografiagramsci>), is constantly updated, and includes almost 16,000 titles.

[52] This peculiarity is underlined by Paggi 1970, pp. xlv–xlvi, where we find an illuminating confrontation between Gramsci's Leninism and that of Lukács.

start if we want to grasp what is really at stake when we discuss the legacy of Antonio Gramsci. It is well-known that in 1911 he entered the Faculty of Arts of the University of Turin, where he studied humanities with the intention of obtaining a degree in linguistics. But, already around 1917, his main activity was political journalism and the leadership of the local group of the Italian Socialist Party. In 1921 he took part in the foundation of the PCI, and from the outset he directed its journal. In 1924 he became Secretary General of the Party until his arrest in November 1926. The texts of this period – mostly articles and political documents – portray a young socialist intellectual who, stimulated by the most vivid cultural challenges of his time (among them, Benedetto Croce, and especially *Aesthetics as Science of Expression and General Linguistics*), becomes a prominent Communist leader, in touch with all the most outstanding politicians of the Third International, and finally imprinting on the Party he leads an original physiognomy that somehow mirrors the originality of his own personality.

Now, if we compare the 1914 writings to those of 1926, we can notice a decisive passage. The young socialist journalist thinks at first that 'philosophy' (which he mainly understands as secular immanentism) is on its own capable of becoming an instrument for liberating people from prejudices and forming a critical and independent mass point of view. It is, after all, an idealistic conception of the autonomous capacities of philosophy, as expansive and revolutionary. This conception sees philosophy as an independent power that might be 'invested' in life to modify it; and, in fact, Gramsci's activity from 1914 to 1918 might be characterised as a 'cultural' struggle to defeat the positivistic and mechanical *Weltanschauung* dominant in the socialist milieu and to replace it with a new philosophy of freedom, of history, of energy and will (in short, a mixture of Bergson, Sorel and Croce).[53] At the time, Gramsci is not at all interested in Marxism as defence of some orthodoxy (just think of his article 'The Revolution Against *Capital*'), but in what Marxism as philosophy might represent in the conquest of autonomy and historical subjectivity for the working class: philosophy is that specific 'power' capable of awakening consciousness and thus producing revolutionary action.

Yet these years are equally marked by another element, in strong opposition to the first one. The 'culture' that the proletariat has to make its own

---

53 On the young Gramsci's struggle for 'culture' see Garin 1969, pp. 38–55.

is not deemed by Gramsci to be a closed and definite doctrine, that has to be merely propagandised and imposed on consciousness. On the contrary, it is a principle of critical liberation whose propagation requires other means, which converge with workers' so-called 'spontaneity' and integrate it not in a mechanical but in a dialectical manner. All this is translated into an intense 'educational' activity, that Gramsci understands as a practice of collective discussion, the construction of spaces free from the hegemony of the dominant ideology, and the formation of new ideological relations between forces different from those of the capitalist bourgeoisie. From 1914 onwards, Gramsci dedicated himself to promote the setting up of various study and education groups: from the 'club of moral life' in 1917, to the 'school of culture' in 1919, or the institute of workers' culture in 1921, and the party school in 1925. It is clear from the denominations that, from 1917 to 1925, there are some changes in the framework of strong ideological continuity: a progressive radicalisation in relation to 'bourgeois culture', and a certain 'organisational' stiffening, both understandable in the context of the onset and first organisation of the international Communist movement, which rendered ideological dispute, especially against socialist reformism, much more acrimonious. In these years, we can find some passages in Gramsci modelled on the Bukharinian distinction between 'bourgeois science' and 'proletarian science'.[54] Yet it is important to notice something else: it is in these pages that we find the decisive passage to a new conception, for the moment only implicit, of the status of philosophy as *coinciding* with the organisation of 'human knowledge relations'. In other words, it is a reformulation of the status of philosophy in line with the unity of theory and practice, and it is to the explicit formulation of this conception and to the identification of its 'practical', that is, political consequences that Gramsci dedicates, after all, the *Prison Notebooks*.[55]

---

[54] As for example the following: 'Not an "objective study" nor a "disinterested culture" can find a place in our ranks; nothing that resembles the normally accepted education issues according to the humanistic, bourgeois conception of the school. We are a struggle organisation [...]. Study and culture are for us nothing but the theoretical awareness of our immediate and ultimate aims, and of the way to put them in action.' ('La scuola di partito', in Gramsci 1971a, pp. 49–50). Cf. Bucharin 1977, pp. 7–11.

[55] Cf. Q 10 II, 6iv, p. 1245: 'Reduction of all speculative philosophies to "politics", to a moment of historical-political life; the philosophy of the praxis conceives the reality of human relations of knowledge as an element of political "hegemony"'.

This is the passage to a much more complex conception of the relations between philosophy and reality, a conception in which politics – as *organisation* of practical and theoretical, material and ideological relations – becomes the *real* network for the existence of ideologies and thus philosophies, which are ideological products themselves, even if strongly rationalised and centralised. The first formulation of the notion of 'hegemony' in the period 1925–6 corresponds to this development: hegemony is the political organisation of ideology, the way to make ideological relations real, that is, effective.[56] And Marxism is outlined as the theory-practice of hegemony, in the sense that it is theoretically aware of the hegemonic character of every ideological reality. Consequently, it inserts itself in the ideological relations as a partial point of view, as a political force that works actively in the criticism of the dominant hegemony. This awareness causes the dichotomy orthodoxy/heterodoxy to lose all meaning in relation to Marxist theory. In the *Notebooks*, in fact, Gramsci writes:

> The concept of 'orthodoxy' must be renewed and reinstated to its real origins. Orthodoxy must not be sought in this or the other of Marx's disciples, in this or that trend linked to currents alien to Marxism, but in the concept that Marxism is enough in itself, it contains in itself all the fundamental elements, not only to construct a total conception of the world, a total philosophy, but also to give life to a total practical organisation of society, that is to become an entire, total civilisation.[57]

This reduction of orthodoxy to philosophical autonomy implies the vanishing of the issue itself, because orthodoxy does not have a content of its own but is identified with the *critical* attitude that derives, in turn, from the criterion of praxis, that is, from the way in which the unity of philosophy and politics is reflected in Marxist philosophy and determines its relation to truth. Ultimately, orthodoxy is the conscious partiality of the Marxist point of view, its conscious finitude.

These are, then, the reasons for the unavoidable partiality of the reconstruction of the debate about Gramsci. The various interpretations of Gramsci must be questioned, selected and judged on the basis of their capacity to bring to the

---

[56] See the essay 'Alcuni temi della quistione meridionale', written in 1926, in Gramsci 1971a, pp. 137–58.

[57] Q 4, 14, p. 435.

surface, from different points of view, the structural peculiarity of the point of view assumed by the philosophy of the praxis: the fact that the philosophy of the praxis is a 'philosophy-politics'. Gramsci writes that:

> In its theory, Marxism cannot be confounded or reduced to any other philosophy: it is original not only because it overcomes previous philosophies, but especially because it opens a completely new track, that is, it renews from end to end the way philosophy is understood.[58]

Gramsci does not have in mind a passage from philosophy to politics[59] (and, in fact, he rejects the idea that the eleventh thesis on Feuerbach should be read thus),[60] but a completely new way of thinking philosophically (and of thinking philosophy). If this is not duly taken into account in the interpretation of the *Notebooks*, they will certainly come out trivialised. If the *Notebooks* are read as if they were a 'book of philosophy' (a 'book' that, as we saw, was in fact *never written*) it is certain that the result would be the underlining of the feeble theoretical coherence of Gramsci's thought, or its *non-philosophical* character,[61] or its lineage to some school or another of the history of philosophy, in a vision of substantial continuity. When we consider the 'interpretations' of Gramsci, we must learn to notice the fact that a whole series of readings – that we might define as 'academic' – are fundamentally erroneous, and that nothing or almost nothing can be gained from them. Their evaluations might be negative or positive,[62] but they will always remain external to the dynamic of Gramsci's thought.

---

[58] Q 4, 11, p. 433.

[59] As Lepre 1978, pp. 28–9, understands on the basis of the interpretation of Lucio Colletti: Gramsci's Marxism would be then a no-longer-philosophy, 'transformation' of the world, and no longer 'reflection' on it.

[60] Cf. Q 10 II, 31, p. 1270: 'The 11th thesis: "Philosophers have only variedly interpreted the world; it is now time to change it", cannot be interpreted as a rejection of any kind of philosophy, but only as annoyance about philosophers and their "parrot-talking" and the energetic statement of a unity of theory and practice'.

[61] Cf. Colletti 1974, pp. 3–28, in particular p. 25, who reduces the *Notebooks* to 'a "sociological" study of Italian society'. The same opinion was expressed by Sasso 1991.

[62] See, simply as examples: Finocchiaro 1988; Kanoussi 1999, pp. 349–64; Kanoussi 2000, pp. 81–7; Sasso 2003, pp. 351–402.

Chapter Thirty-Six

Falling Short of Marx – Habermas

Jacques Bidet

Habermas occupies a significant, emblematic position today as the philosopher of social democracy. Defending a standpoint that is progressive and emancipatory, powerful and original, for many he represents the most plausible position following the putative collapse of Marxism. Because of the way in which he connects philosophy and social science, he continues the impulse of Frankfurt-school critical theory and, indeed, Marx's original ambition. And he fascinates the inheritors of a Marxism from which he has gradually distanced himself.

If we wish to understand the nature of this estrangement, a genealogical work is required that goes back to his first, explicitly *marxisant* writings and deciphers the original difference on the basis of which the divergences were to develop. Here I shall confine myself to trying to take the measure of the 'loss' that attaches to it. I believe myself to be fully authorised to do this in that I have set out in two books the immense interest of Habermas's work for a critique of Marxism and the stimulus he provides for its recasting.[1]

[1] See Bidet 1990 and 1999.

1968: *Towards a Rational Society/Knowledge and Human Interests*

Marx is constantly referred to in *The Transformation of the Public Sphere* (1962), which evokes the Marxian perspective of emancipation.[2] *Theory and Practice* in 1963 devoted a chapter to 'Marxism as Critique',[3] to the materialist thinker who inscribes his philosophy of *praxis*, revelation of man to himself as the subject of history, in the objective tendencies of the crisis of capitalist society. But the first genuinely original developments are to be found in two works published in 1968.

Many of Habermas's subsequent views are anticipated in *Toward a Rational Society*. In it, Weberian modernity is reviewed negatively *à la* Marcuse (technology is social domination) and inscribed in a dualistic reinterpretation *à la* Parsons, which counter-poses the 'institutional framework' or 'life-world' to 'sub-systems of rational-purposive action' (SSRPA). The latter, which emerged at the dawn of the neolithic age and took shape in 'traditional societies', become predominant in modernity, delegitimating the old body of beliefs and values. In the first – liberal – age of modern times, the ideology of market equality (formal right) still stood in their way. But in 'advanced capitalism', marked by state intervention and the fusion of science and technology, it becomes obsolete. Under the banner of a productivist ideology, the subsystems invade the whole field, depoliticising social existence. Habermas thus assigns himself the task of examining this technocratic legitimation, which can in fact only justify its scientific pretensions by positioning itself in the space of 'public, unrestricted discussion, free from domination' – that is to say, by comparing itself with a quite different 'conception of rationalisation', based on 'unrestricted communication'.[4]

However, the way in which Habermas constructs the problem to be resolved is open to question. By translating the pair 'productive forces/relations of production' into 'labour/interaction' not only does he strip the second term of its specific content, but he recasts the first term. In fact, he attributes to Marx the idea that

> the capitalist mode of production can be comprehended as a mechanism that guarantees the *permanent* expansion of subsystems of purposive-

[2] See Habermas 1989, pp. 12–19

[3] See Habermas 1988, pp. 195–252.

[4] Habermas 1971, pp. 118–20.

> rational action and thereby overturns the traditionalist 'superiority' of the institutional framework to the forces of production.[5]

In thus identifying 'labour' with 'rational-purposive action', Habermas operates a surreptitious conceptual revolution from the outset. For Marx's concept of labour does not apply to the one-sided adequacy of means to an end [*Zweckrationalität*], but to the bilateral relationship between end and means. Labour in general is not only abstract labour characterised by an 'economy of time' for a given end. It is also, and correlatively, concrete labour, with a view to a determinate use-value, where use assumes a *social norm*. Labour is a means gauged by an end, but which is 'stripped of meaning' only with respect to the meaning that it imparts to the end it pursues. It is a *rational* activity only with respect to an end that is posited as *reasonable*. And Marx's whole endeavour consists in showing how, in the conditions of capitalism, these two terms are dissociated, because its concrete purpose – its end as use-value – is threatened by the profit motive, which is the particular goal of capitalism, an 'abstract' purpose pursued for its own sake, whatever the consequences for humanity and nature – in other words, the effects in terms of use-value. Marx thus deconstructs the notion of 'purposive rationality', dismantling the ideological unity of the categories of 'production', productivity, or 'productive force'. Capitalist production is not 'production' *tout court*: *it is defined by a specific, contradictory tension between these two ends*. The concept of 'sub-systems of rational-purposive action' restores the ideological unity of the category of 'productive force', the artificial unity that was shattered by Marx's analysis. Habermas can thus attribute to 'labour', in as much as its quintessence is embodied in the commodity-form of the 'sub-systems of rational-purposive action', the burden that Marx makes capital as such bear, at the same time as he legitimates the market as the consummate form of productive rationality.

The Habermasian category of labour as purposive action certainly possesses a critical intention and significance. Paradoxically, however, it neutralises itself because it crystallises this social relation in terms of 'system', in accordance with an epistemological model adopted from the natural sciences. It thus refers to the epistemological horizon of the neoclassical economists, to the *homo oeconomicus* for whom (as we shall see) Habermas ultimately reserves

[5] Habermas 1971, p. 96.

a considerable role in his meta-theory. A public juridico-political instance, 'anchored' in the life-world, is certainly articulated with this systemics of economic practice. However, it remains external to the economic relation, whose operative concepts are developed autonomously, as the object of an economic science.

The Habermasian devaluation of the Marxian theory of labour is also apparent in his adoption of a fairly widespread, albeit erroneous and basically trivial, interpretation of the 'labour theory of value', which associates it with the idea of 'simple labour' as unit of measurement. Marx's problematic supposedly loses its relevance with the development of science and technology, which represent

> an independent source of surplus value, in relation to which the only source of surplus value considered by Marx, namely the labor power of the immediate producers, plays an ever smaller role.[6]

By dismissing the 'labour theory of value' (which, in reality, presupposes labour-power replete with knowledge, irreducible to the immediate relation of production), Habermas trivialises the theory of surplus-value, which consequently can no longer be invoked as a theory of extortion, since it lacks the analytical presuppositions; or, *a fortiori*, as a theory of abstraction (of 'bad infinity', of the drive, by accumulating profit, to amass endless power at the expense of humanity and nature), since this has already been attributed – which is a quite different thing – to the 'system of the economy' as such, to its historical 'rationalisation' as a sub-system of rational-purposive action.

In *Knowledge and Human Interests*, Habermas distinguishes between the philosophical themes of the young Marx and the substance of Marx's research (leading to *Capital*). On the one hand, Marx makes labour the transcendental category, 'world-constituting life activity': a positivist' conception that 'lacks precisely th[e] element of reflection [in the Fichtean sense] that characterises a critique' and constitutes a retreat to 'a frame of reference restricted to instrumental action.[7]

On the other hand, '[a]t the level of his material investigations...Marx always takes account of social practice that encompasses both work and inter-

---

[6] Habermas 1971, p. 104.
[7] Habermas 1978, pp. 28, 47.

action' and hence refers to the world of 'norms' and 'communicative action' – and this specifically in terms of 'class struggles' or of an interaction between subjects as classes directed towards 'discussion free from domination'.[8]

In reality, on the second point it is Habermas who attenuates Marx's problematic. For Marx, *labour is interaction*. His economy is political. In contrast, the sub-system of rational-purposive action is a Janus-faced concept, of Weberian stamp: on the socio-critical side, it evokes social domination; on the rational side, it takes over the liberal tradition of *homo oeconomicus*. Thus is heralded a critique of economics that will remain external to its object.

As for the 'philosophical conception', Habermas argues (repetitively) that Marx could have found the correct route in the young Hegel – through the 'dialectic of morality' set out in *The Spirit of Christianity and its Fate*, which culminates in reconciliation.[9] This is an unusual philosophical solution, which assigns Marx's dramaturgy of classes a horizon that is configured in terms of relations *between individuals*: the struggle for recognition. Not that this is to be rejected. But it is not applicable to the *class relation* as such. A different Hegelian figure – that of 'master and slave' – would have been more adequate. However, far from ending in reconciliation, it concludes with the redundancy of the master, with his abolition, representing the abolition of classes. Contrariwise, the 'dialectic of morality' terminates in mutual recognition, communication 'restored', between the classes – one of which, however, dominates the other.

Thus are foreshadowed the ambiguities of 'unrestricted communication'.

1973: *Legitimation Crisis*

Legitimation Crisis attests to the impact of Marxism in this phase. In order to analyse the 'crisis of advanced capitalism', Habermas looks to the Marxist concept of social formation for clarification, but…in the terms of Parsons and Durkheim. The problems of 'systems integration', of the regulation of self-regulating sub-systems, manifest themselves in a crisis of 'social integration': the consensus formative of normative structures is collapsing; society is becoming anomic…

[8] Habermas 1978, pp. 53, 55.
[9] See Habermas 1978, pp. 55–6.

Habermas registers the end of liberalism and increasing state intervention in the economy, in order to compensate for the economic weaknesses of the market. What is emerging is 'an altered form of production of surplus-value', which is based on the public sector of production, education, scientific research – 'a quasi-political wage structure which expresses a class of compromise', 'a growing need for legitimation of the political system, which brings into play demands oriented to use values' in competition with capital's needs for exploitation.[10]

This system, caught between the exigencies of *laissez-faire* and those of bureaucratic planning, is encountering a crisis of rationality. The economic having lost its autonomy, the contradiction between classes and the issue of legitimacy are transposed to the state, which confronts non-generalisable interests.[11] The old legitimations have ceased to be beyond dispute and 'the stabilization of validity claims can succeed only through discourse'.[12] But the political régime – a purely formal democracy that stimulates consumerism and a retreat into private life – no longer produces anything more than a exchange between benefits from above and mass loyalty.

This exercise in line with a Eurocommunist agenda, with which the author seems to be in broad agreement, would ultimately be rather banal, were it not for the fact that it ends with a third chapter that goes beyond the problematic of legitimation to legitimacy: 'truth'. Therewith emerges the *deontological* challenge, to which Habermas will devote detailed attention in much of his subsequent work. However, it will be noted that this critical problematic is immediately weakened by a different one, which is interwoven with it: an irreducible *functionalism*, whose key concept is 'compromise', which comes into play as soon as supposedly non-generalisable particular interests appear on the horizon.

---

[10] Habermas 1976, pp. 53, 55.
[11] See Habermas 1976, p. 70.
[12] Habermas 1976, p. 72.

1976: *A Reconstruction of Historical Materialism*

This work appeared in French in 1985 under the title *Après Marx* – a difference that illustrates the ambiguity of the enterprise: reconstruction or deconstruction? Neo-Marxism or post-Marxism?

The Weberian impulse remains decisive: historical development is construed as a process of 'rationalisation'. But Piaget's genetic psychology authorises a positive inflection: the hypothesis of a phylo-ontogenesis parallelism supplies the leitmotiv of the 'reconstruction'. This opens up a 'cognitivist' path to a prospect of communicative emancipation, which will subsequently take concrete form in a re-working of post-Wittgensteinian linguistics.

Firstly, the technical element of the productive forces cannot be regarded as the 'motor of social development':

> The development of...normative structures is the pacemaker of social evolution, for new principles of social organisation mean new forms of social integration; and the latter, in turn, first make it possible to implement available productive forces or to generate new ones, as well as making possible a heightening of social complexity.[13]

Habermas thus intertwines historical materialism and 'an internal history of spirit',[14] of individual and social reason, subjective and objective spirit, in accordance with the polarity of its modes of activity and institutional forms, in the unity of its cognitive and normative functions. This is a 'reconstruction' construed in accordance with the programme of the 'reconstructive sciences', whose object is a rational reconstruction of universal competences of a transcendental kind. The preservation of a Marxist vocabulary barely conceals the profound subversion of its content.

The productive forces/relations of production pair, constitutive of the *infrastructure*, thus acquires a quite different meaning. Here 'productive force' refers to the rational potential of the producers in a particular era. As for the economic 'relations of production', they are successively constituted by *kinship* in primitive societies, by domination (which means mainly the *state*)[15] in traditional societies, and by the *market* in capitalist society.

---

13 Habermas 1979, p. 120.
14 Ibid.
15 Habermas 1979, p. 144.

The *superstructure* is to be understood as the 'institutional core' that permits 'social [*soziale*] integration': '[b]y *social integration*, I understand, with Durkheim, securing the unity of a life-world through values and norms'.[16] A crisis occurs when this core proves incapable of solving 'the problems that confront the system'. For this crisis to issue in a superior form of society, it is not enough for the productive forces – 'the instrumental and strategic domain' – to develop. Also required is a process of education of the species 'in the dimension moral-practical consciousness'[17] – something only made possible by world visions that anticipate new relations of production. 'In the concepts of historical materialism this means that the dialectic of forces and relations of production takes place through ideologies.'[18]

Secondly, this reinterpretation of the Marxist topography goes hand in hand with a more fundamental reorganisation, which integrates the paradigm of historical materialism into an evolutionist matrix. The most important distinction counter-poses a logic and a dynamic. The *logic* of development, which involves the *stages* of evolution of the species, refers to the psychogenetic model. The *dynamic* of development, which is related to periodisation and the process of transition from one *epoch* to another, refers to historical materialism.

The *stages* are theorised by analogy with those described by genetic psychology: a pre-conventional stage, marked by a certain lack of distinction between the natural and social worlds; a conventional stage, in which people reason on the basis of common values and principles; and a post-conventional stage, where the latter become the main subject of controversy. *But the various dimensions of social existence* – the 'systems of action', the 'visions of the world', and 'juridico-moral institutions' – *do not materialise along with these stages of development*. It is only after the neolithic age, in 'archaic states', that conventional rationality comes wholly to govern institutions. And the post-conventional stage, which emerges in 'developed civilisations' marked by the expansion of universal religions and philosophy, within 'world views', is only fully established in the modern epoch. And it is to historical materialism that Habermas

---

16 Ibid.
17 Habermas 1979, p. 148.
18 Habermas 1979, p. 169.

looks for an understanding of the process which leads from one epoch to the next, in accordance with the aleatory paths of historical contingency.

We thus observe a tension between two approaches. The first employs a *combined mechanism* of two distinct paradigms: one for logic ('logical' *stages*, essential moments in the development of reason, or of the species); and the other for dynamics (modes of production, forming the sequence of 'historical' *epochs*, crucial landmarks in the history of humanity). The second tends to *characterise* epochs on the basis of the categories of evolutionary logic: systems of action, forms of identity, of identification and demarcation of the ego, types of world view, of law and morality.

The theory of evolution does not of itself provide the concepts of the forms peculiar to each epoch, or the principles of mutation. The categories of history retain their irreducible character:

> In its developmental *dynamics*, the change of normative structures remains dependent on evolutionary challenges posed by unresolved, economically conditioned, system problems and on learning processes that are a response to them. In other words, culture remains a superstructural phenomenon, even if it does seem to play a more prominent role in the transition to new developmental levels than many Marxists have heretofore supposed.[19]

However, in the end (so it seems to me), the categories of the 'logic of evolution' prevail over those of 'historical dynamics' (and the materialist theory of history). In effect, it is they that determine the substantive quality of the stages, of which they order the course and prescribe the ultimate term.

Thirdly, a Parsonian representation of society thus tends to supplant the Marxian topography. Societal [*gesellschaftliche*] integration is supposedly achieved according to the two modalities of social [*soziale*] integration, inspired by Durkheim, and systems [*systemische*] integration, illustrated in particular by Luhmann. One corresponds to the immediate solidarity of the 'life-world' and the other to the detour via the 'media' – the 'sub-systems' of money (market) and power (administration). Social antagonism is thus retranslated into the cleavage between two modes of integration and its supersession is announced in the irreversibility of evolution.

---

[19] Habermas 1979, p. 98.

It is the reversal triggered by the psychogenetic schema that will allow the operational deployment of the philosophico-linguistic schema and, as a result, the realisation of the Weberian schema of a general history as a process of rationalisation. Ontogenesis thus supplies the 'key' to phylogenesis.[20]

Habermas undermines the Marxian concept of the juridical, by endowing it with an immediately consensual tonality. The moment of social contradiction, which in Marx overdetermines (and counter-determines) the moment of functionalism, in this sense is attenuated by the prevalence of the notion of 'integration', as a general category of inter-individual relations in society: Marx revised in conformity with Durkheim. And, although Habermas occasionally indicates that he is fully aware of class domination, this tends to disappear to the margins of his account. Revealingly, the notion of domination is interchangeable with that of the state: Marx revised in line with Weber.

The operator of the transition from one paradigm to the other, from history to evolution, is the functionalism that makes social institutions 'functions' of existence, of its development: '

> Law and morality serve to regulate action conflicts consensually and thus to maintain an endangered inter-subjectivity of understanding among speaking and acting subjects.[21]

This is their 'specific function'. This is a recurrent theme, given vivid expression in Clausewitzian fashion: they represent 'the continuation of communicative action with other means'.[22] Marx, by contrast, postulates that they are (just as much) an inversion *into its opposite*, the free and equal discourse of exchange turning into the right – and violence – of exploitation. Habermas's critical functionalism situates historical materialism in an irenic perspective. He consigns violence to contingency, or at least subjects it to a 'logic of evolution' – that of the emergence of morality and law, which are not specifically a matter of relations between classes. The distinctive concepts of historical materialism – those of class domination and exploitation – only feature negatively, in the form of the 'problems confronting systems' and the legitimation they demand.

---

20 See Habermas 1979, p. 116.
21 Habermas 1979, p. 116.
22 Habermas 1979, p. 99.

Overlooking the negative, Habermas understands the mode of production of a society as that of the reproduction of its existence. Marx's analysis inscribed it within the limits of the reproduction of class relations, vectors of violence and death: mode of domination and of reproduction of this domination – mode of destruction.

1981: *The Theory of Communicative Action*

Here, Habermas reconsiders Marx analytically one last time, fixing an interpretation that will henceforth simply be presupposed.

He corrects the Weberian matrix of a modernity that has fragmented into autonomous spheres under the predominance of abstract rationality in two respects. He formalises it in three orders – science, law and morality, art – which he refers to three forms of rationality: truth, justice, and authenticity. And he lays a bridge between them by showing that they are in fact subject to the common schema of argumentation and hence, *de jure*, to a higher form of action: communicative action. The paradigm of *discourse*, of discursive intersubjectivity, whose guiding thread is furnished by reflecting on post-Wittgensteinian pragmatics, thus takes over from that of labour.

It is appropriate, however, to consider the treatment to which Habermas subjects the Marxian analysis of labour. The specificity of market relations supposedly consists in the fact that the use-value of commodities is 'transformed' into exchange-value and concrete labour is thereby 'transformed' into 'abstract labour'. This 'transformationist' formulation licences a surprising allocation of concrete labour to the theory of action and of abstract labour to systems theory:

> On the one hand, labor power is expended in *concrete* actions and cooperative relationships; on the other hand, it is absorbed as an *abstract* performance by a labor process that is formally organised for the purposes of valorisation. . . . as an *action* it belongs to the lifeworld of the producers, as a *performance* to the functional nexus of the capitalist enterprise and of the economic system as a whole.[23]

---

[23] Habermas 1987a, p. 335.

The peculiarity of the market, defined on the basis of the 'medium' of money, is that it 'does not in its very definition disadvantage anyone involved in his calculation of utility'.[24] In this systemic context, human beings maintain a purely instrumental, objectifying relationship, which 'reifies' the whole of personal and communal life. The 'pathologies' of modern society are therefore to be sought on the side of market abstraction.

In short, the market is the best and the worst of things. However, what is lacking here is a dialectical concept of the relationship between this best and this worst: that of the relationship between market and capital developed by Marx, which assumes precisely what Habermas rejects – the labour theory of value. In it value signifies expenditure of labour-power and the capitalist relationship is understood as appropriation, mobilisation, and consumption of labour-power and profit as an accumulation of abstract wealth, a power that is ceaselessly sought for its own sake.

It is not that Habermas is officially antipathetic to such a view of things. But his conceptualisation is conducted in terms that disarticulate and neutralise the relevant concepts of this 'political-economy'. One cannot assign concrete labour to the life-world and abstract labour to the economic 'system', for these two categories form a rational unity in the concept of the commodity. And the distinctively capitalist relationship is to be understood as an *internal* tension, *an immanent contradiction*, in this unity, and not (except by Biblical hyperbole) as some inconceivable 'transformation of one into the other'.

In place of a theory, Habermas offers us a 'critique' of capitalist society, on the basis of the categories of reification and alienation. These categories suit him precisely because they are disjunctive: human being or thing, the ego or its other, counterposable in the same fashion as life-world and systems-world. In this conceptual context at least, such a thematic is incapable of articulating a process of domination which is not that of an object over a subject, or a 'system' over agents, but of subjects (or classes) over one another. Habermas, who has worked so hard for the transition to inter-subjectivity, thus reverts to the subject-object paradigm that he rejects.

This objectification of the two 'sub-systems' separates economics and politics from one another in liberal fashion. And one cannot but be astonished at its consequences. *Legitimation Crisis* in 1973 advocated a public sector of 'pro-

---

[24] Habermas 1987a, p. 271.

duction of collective commodities'.[25] In reality, this position would sit ill with a general approach that identifies economy and market. *The Theory of Communicative Action* aligns itself with the idea of an '*indirect* form' and 'refracted mode' of state intervention.[26]

1985: *The Philosophical Discourse of Modernity*

Taking up the thread of his writings of 1968, Habermas situates Marx in the tradition of German philosophy, structured by the figure of the subject that realises itself in an object. For the 'philosophy of reflection', up to Hegel, the subject is constituted and becomes self-conscious in the works of culture. For the 'philosophy of *praxis*', which refers beyond Marx to 'Western Marxism' as a whole, the process of self-creation is realised through productive practice. However, this is supposedly a mere variant of the philosophy of the subject, certainly directed towards reversing the modern alienation of labour, towards a practical emancipation by a reversal in the labour-form, but, precisely as such, incapable of representing anything other than 'the purposive rationality of the acting subject', or a pure 'cognitive-instrumental rationality', doubled by the illusory dream of a revolution abolishing the 'functional subsystems' and absorbing the whole of social existence into 'the horizon of the life-world'.[27]

To György Markus, who objects that use-value contains 'the context of its use and the needs whose satisfaction it serves', is a 'social dimension' – and that productive *praxis* is thus mediated by norms that ground rights and obligations – Habermas believes he can respond as follows: this clearly demonstrates that what is required is 'a clear analytic separation between "technical" and "social" spheres', 'technical-utilitarian rules' and 'social norms'. And he concludes that 'practice in the sense of norm-governed interaction cannot be analysed on the model of the productive expenditure of labor power and the consumption of use-values'.[28] This is manifestly a misinterpretation, since what is at issue here is not the *consumption* but the *production* of use-values –

---

[25] Habermas 1976, p. 54.
[26] Habermas 1987a, p. 344.
[27] Habermas 1987b, pp. 65, 67.
[28] Habermas 1987b, pp. 79–81.

two distinct processes that are separated by the *social* (norm-governed, and so on) division of labour.

At the root of all this is always the same blind spot in the Habermasian perception of 'Marxism'. The concept of 'expenditure of labour-power' (which does not pertain to physiology, but to 'sociology') is not reducible to a monological relationship between a subject and the object he produces, for it calls up that of 'consumption of labour-power' by those who 'set to work' (interaction as a class relation) and the antagonistic context of the social motivations and 'reasons' of labour.[29] The technical and the social can certainly be distinguished analytically. But Habermas does not stop there: he makes the economy a 'sub-system' structured by a purely technical rationality, whose functional logic is that of the market (or money). He thus fictively *realises* this *analytical* distinction. He identifies as the culmination of the historical process of rationalisation, as the very stamp of modernity, the (alleged) fact that 'production' pertains to a purely systemic functionality, on which deliberation can only intervene from without. He thus goes back on Marx's essential contribution. The theory expounded in *Capital* ceases to make sense when the juridico-political parameters (liberty-equality-rationality of the exchangers dialectically opposed to the subordination-exploitation of wage-labour) are disjoined from the technical-economic element, which cannot be expressed outside of them. Such *technical* categories as those of 'socially-necessary labour-time' or 'value of labour-power' are determined in the 'class struggle' – a social category laden with normative subtleties. Contrary to Marx's anti-liberal and anti-positivist breakthrough, Habermas's conceptual intervention once again separates and disjoins economics and politics. Obviously, this does not mean that for him there is no relation between them, or even that politics does not in some sense have to govern economics. But he conceives the primacy of politics only within limits defined from the outset by the supposed relationship of *ontological exteriority*. The consequences of this epistemological option will emerge in full at the end of this trajectory, when Habermas comes to propose a politics.

[29] See Bidet 1999, pp. 211–12.

1992: *Between Facts and Norms: Contribution to a Discourse Theory of Law and Democracy*

In *Between Facts and Norms*, following other research focused on law and morality, from *Moral Consciousness and Communicative Action* (1983) to *Justification and Application* (1991), Habermas formulates his 'politics'. The public space of law is deployed therein as an intersection between the life-world and the functional sub-systems of economy and bureaucracy.

I have shown elsewhere that this theorisation of the media derives from Marx, who in the *Grundrisse* distinguished between two mediations: the market and the organisation. Marx can be criticised for burdening the latter with unfounded expectations. Nevertheless, he indicates the correct path when he shows how the market 'medium' is transformed into its 'opposite', into a class relation: the 'transformation of money into capital' – that is to say, of market relations into capitalist relations, or the 'transformation' of the *functional system* into a *class structure*.[30]

By comparison with Marx, Habermas represents a regression in that he anchors his reflection in the moment of the 'media', basically regarded as systemic and *functional*. The *structural* category of class is certainly not rejected; it even resurfaces from time to time, in allusive and euphemistic fashion. But it has lost its strategic position, as a result of the abandonment of the constitutive presupposition – the 'labour-use theory of value'[31] – without which the concepts of exploitation, class, reproduction, abstraction, and so on possess only an evanescent status. The Marxian thesis of class domination gives way to the idea that the 'functional powers', the 'social powers' of the market, administration, social organisations come to colonise the life-world, the model sociality. What disappears is the tragically realistic Marxian view of the social machinery that reproduces classes, placing some on top, and others at the bottom; of the fundamental juridical and symbolic violence which pertains to the class state – that is to say, the political field as a battlefield. With Habermas, the class struggle mutates into misunderstanding. Henceforth the point is to arrive at a 'good' understanding, not to change the world. *A critique of systemic effects replaces the critique of the effects of (class) structure*. It is therefore not fortuitous if the repressed question of social classes now figures

30 See Bidet 1999, p. 912ff.
31 See Bidet 1999, p. 232.

exclusively in the guise of the issue of the 'compromises' that they can reach between themselves.

The theory of compromise, which accedes within supposedly universally admissible limits to the purely strategic game of the capitalist actor, is in fact an essential part of the Habermasian solution to the crisis of politics. It is satisfied if the social partners, who differ in terms of power and influence, agree to submit to a procedural order based on an equal sharing of rationally argued discourse. This, it is true, involves practical, material, and cultural presuppositions, which define the status of the citizen. And it is clear that for Habermas (as for Rawls) legitimate action to establish such a status is not limited to using discourse. But the communicative critique limits what can be demanded to the requirement of communication and negotiation.[32] From the outset it abandons everything else to unprincipled 'compromise': without any other principle than that of pursuing a discourse of negotiation equally shared between the powerful and the rest. To show that this precisely involves a 'performative contradiction', which a universal pragmatics should not entertain, and that a quite different 'principle of universality' is needed, would require further explanation.[33]

1996: *The Inclusion of the Other*

It remains to evoke the many reasons why reading Habermas particularly recommends itself to those who partially recognise themselves in the Marxist tradition. On the one hand, and while it is true (as I have suggested) that it is at the cost of serious 'losses', Habermas is without a doubt the author who most resolutely takes up the 'encyclopaedic' programme of Marxism: that of rooting the political project in a coherent concept combining philosophical anthropology and social science. On the other hand, it is an understatement to say that he illustrates more clearly than Marxism has done traditionally the need for a positive conception of political democracy. As we can see from the dialogues that are taking shape with the Gramscian (Stefano Petrucciani), Lukácsian (György Markus), or Anglo-American traditions (notably via *New Left Review*), Habermas's account of the cleavages between law, morality and

[32] See Bidet 1999, p. 931.
[33] See Bidet 1999, p. 914.

ethics is of a kind to stimulate investigations that have emerged only slowly in Marxism – particularly as a result of the inadequacy of its concepts of the state, nation, and humanity. The theoretical reorganisation that he proposes, oriented towards the idea of communication as an experiment in which the triple imperative of truth, justice and identity is experienced, can be understood, or adopted, as the precise argument of communism. Habermas's last major work, *The Inclusion of the Other*, published in France in 1998 under the title of *L'intégration républicaine*, continues his earlier reflections on this terrain. The most innovative text concerns 'perpetual peace'. It certainly repeats shortcomings that were noted earlier – in particular, the lack of a properly materialist foundation for the political universalism it proclaims. The repression of the principle according to which 'the Earth equally belongs to everyone' – the implicit clause of the 'principle of discussion', since any discussion bears on a certain use of the world, which in the last resort concerns all human beings[34] – weakens his discourse, which euphemises the imperialist matrix. However, by demonstrating the ineluctable emergence of a supra-national public space and the embryo of a global state, Habermas opens up the prospect of a planetary citizenship, relay of the 'Internationals' and a challenge for the future.

---

[34] See Bidet 1999, p. 622.

Chapter Thirty-Seven

Fredric Jameson: An Unslaked Thirst for Totalisation

Stathis Kouvelakis

It is widely agreed that Fredric Jameson is the major Marxist theoretician in the English-speaking world today and also a key figure in the massive intellectual constellation dubbed 'postmodern'. How is it, then, that the impact of an *œuvre* characterised by a commentator of Perry Anderson's stringency as the 'culmination' of the Western-Marxist tradition,[1] has hitherto remained marginal in Continental Europe and utterly negligible in France? No doubt the answer is to be sought in the formulation of the question itself. Jameson's dual claim to fame in the English-speaking world, and especially the United States (his identification with Marxism as a reference and the postmodern as an object) is precisely what explains his lack of success in Continental Europe. In fact, Jameson established himself as a protagonist in intellectual debate on an international scale in the 1980s, at the point when Marxism was collapsing in its heartlands of Latin Europe and when, particularly in France, a violently anti-Marxist, revanchist neoliberalism was rife. As for the topic of postmodernism, which propelled Jameson towards a considerably

[1] Anderson 1998, p. 71.

wider public than the audience for Marxism, while the French dimension is essential (notably Lyotard and his *La Condition postmoderne*, published in 1979), it remained a predominantly anglophone and, more specifically, American debate.

In reality, the emergence of the 'Jameson phenomenon', whose break with the Occidento-centrism of earlier Marxism is not the least of its specificities,[2] represents one of the symptoms of the shift that Anderson signalled in the early 1980s as a reversal in the basic coordinates of the geopolitics of the theoretical field:

> the traditionally most backward zones of the capitalist world, in Marxist culture, have suddenly become in many ways the most advanced.[3]

So it as if the discrepancy of the past had been cancelled, with the most advanced zone of the capitalist world – especially the United States – coinciding for the first time in history with the appointed terrain of an 'emergent Marxism', in the academy at least.

Such a reversal, which obviously coincides with the reassertion of American economic and military hegemony across the planet, could not have occurred without a decisive impact on the configuration and, in a sense, the very texture of the Marxism in question – especially in its relationship to political practice and its 'exterior' in theory. Simplifying to the extreme, it may be said that, confirming a version of the law of uneven and combined development in theory, the preservation of an intransigent radicalism and professed continuity with the 'great tradition' of classical Marxism has been paid for by a fairly radical recasting of the lines of demarcation within the contemporary theoretical *Kampfplatz*. Far from being limited exclusively to Jameson, these tendencies nevertheless assert themselves with especial clarity in his work.

Indeed, it is difficult to hide the fact that this *œuvre* takes the form of a paradox – at least, we may wager that it might appear thus to non-anglophone readers, who are used to certain types of intellectual specialisation and division. Rather than the exposition of a doctrine or system, what we are dealing with in Jameson's case is the operation of a major interpretative

---

[2] See Anderson 1998, pp. 74–5. China and South-East Asia form a strategic part of Jameson's project, both as subject of study and as a site of reception of his work. See Hardt and Weeks 2000, p. 6.

[3] Anderson 1983, p. 24.

machine, capable of 'digesting' virtually anything, or alternatively, a sort of insatiable 'desire for theory', borne alone by a seemingly boundless syncretism, combined with an intellectual curiosity whose breadth is unmatched in the history of cultural studies. Jameson certainly situates himself resolutely within Marxism. Author of one of the first studies of Sartre published in the United States, some years later he offered a landmark introduction to the set of major authors in what he called the 'dialectical tradition'. In it, Sartre was to be found alongside Adorno, Benjamin, Marcuse Bloch, and Lukács – an unprecedented endeavour to link the French and German traditions.

Jameson's major work, *The Political Unconscious*, to which the following pages are devoted,[4] and which sets out his own version of Marxism in condensed form, significantly expanded this apparatus of filiation – and in 'truly scandalous' fashion from a European,[5] and even more so a French, perspective. It did so both *within* the Marxist tradition, via a confrontation and assimilation between the 'dialectical current' and the work of Althusser; and *outside it*, in the direction of what is referred to as French 'structuralism' and 'poststructuralism' in the anglophone world. And it extended even further, since in the book we find the main continental philosophical currents, from phenomenology (Heidegger and Husserl), from which Jameson adopts the concepts of 'being' and 'sedimentation', to psychoanalysis (especially Lacan), and the hermeneutic or interpretative 'models' that have been developed in the specific field of literary studies (Gadamer and Ricoeur, obviously, but also Frye and Greimas). 'His clear objective', as Jean-Jacques Lecercle has quite rightly observed, 'is to construct a tradition'[6] – as much (it might be added) as it is to open up the theoretical field, and more widely still American culture, to the whole Western critical tradition. Marxism has pride of place in this project, on condition that it is itself tirelessly resituated and reconceived

---

4 I have deliberately opted to approach Jameson by way of the foundation of his project which, notwithstanding various inflections, is highly consistent, rather than through a sectoral thematic, however important – especially as the main source of Jameson's recent celebrity. Moreover, as Sean Homer notes, 'the publication of *The Political Unconscious* clearly marks [his] arrival and the emergence of Jameson as a major theoretician in his own right': Homer 1998, p. 36.

5 Homer 1998, p. 62. William Dowling goes so far as to say, without any polemical intent, that the originality of Jameson's approach consists exclusively in this 'originality-in-synthesis': Dowling 1984, p. 14.

6 Lecercle 1987, p. 86.

in an ensemble that far exceeds it, but in which it is summoned to occupy a sovereign position.

A dialectical hermeneutic

As readers advance through the pages of *The Political Unconscious,* they have the impression not so much of working their way through a systematic conceptual exposition (despite the theoretical density of the first chapter, which takes up a third of the book), as of witnessing a dynamic *process*, an endeavour announced from the text's opening words as the imperative of *historicisation.*[7] It operates on textual/cultural objects, or rather on their *interpretation*. For the reception/reading of an object has 'always-already' occurred through a prism comprising a tangle of eminently historical interpretations, structures, and mental schemas: 'our object of study is less the text itself than the interpretations through which we attempt to confront and to appropriate it', given that 'texts come before us as the always-already-read'.[8] Jameson firmly rejects any approach confined to so-called 'formal' analysis, which would disregard the exigencies of 'self-reflection' – of explaining the standpoint of the subject in history and social practice:

> Every individual interpretation must include an interpretation of its own existence, must show its own credentials and justify itself: every commentary must be at the same time a metacommentary as well. Thus genuine interpretation directs the attention back to history itself, and to the historical situation of the commentator as well as of the work.[9]

This does not involve counter-posing Marxism to different models of interpretation (psychoanalysis, semiotics, structuralism, etc.), but means assigning the latter an indisputable but local validity, reserving for Marxism the status (defined by Sartre) of 'untranscendable horizon'. As a theory of history, Marxism is the ultimate meta-commentary, with history itself constituting the ultimate, untranscendable horizon of any interpretation and, consequently, any hermeneutic model. Historical materialism thus possesses resources that

[7] 'Always historicize! This slogan…[is] the one absolute and we may even say "trans-historical" imperative of all dialectical thought' (Jameson 1983, p. 9).
[8] Jameson 1983, pp. 9–10.
[9] Jameson 1988a, p. 5.

enable it to subsume 'such apparently antagonistic or incommensurable critical operations', thanks to its superior theoretical *fertility* ('the priority of a Marxist interpretative framework [will be argued] in terms of semantic richness'): it is the only one capable of rising to the totality, to the 'dialectical or totalizing, properly Marxist ideal of understanding'.[10]

The hermeneutic structure proposed, whose elaboration and aesthetic sophistication will already have been sensed by readers, is formed as an articulation between several levels of approach (or interpretative horizons) to an object or structured set of textual/cultural objects. If, before proceeding to a more detailed exposition, we had to summarise it in one sentence, without fearing oversimplification once again, we might say that the individual textual object (a novel, a tale, and so on) is initially grasped as a *symbolic act* in relation to a political-punctual conjuncture; in a second phase, as *part* (or *parole*) of a *collective class discourse* (or *langue*), which is ideological in character; and finally – the last stage of the analysis – as a complex *form* situated in history understood as a sequence and coexistence of a multiplicity of modes of production.

The first hermeneutic moment is one in which individual textual objects are perceived as so many imaginary/formal resolutions of real contradictions. The formal schemata in question designate so many extensions of the social into the formal/aesthetic field. By means of an internal analysis at the formal level, the interpreter's task is to bring out 'a determinate structure of still properly formal *contradictions*',[11] so as subsequently to arrive at their 'resolution', still by formal means that need to be situated in the political-historical horizon peculiar to this level. Hence there is no confusion with a superficial sociologism or historicism, which regards the textual object either as a duplication of reality (the celebrated 'reflection'), or as a mere reference to a 'context' that is still external to the object itself. Rather than 'context', Jameson prefers to speak of 'sub-text', defined as the immanence of the Real in language.[12] The point is to achieve a grasp of the *production* of aesthetic/narrative form from within; and such is the task that the category of ideological 'act' – the invention of imaginary/formal solutions to insurmountable social contradictions –

10 Jameson 1983, p. 10.
11 Jameson 1983, p. 77.
12 I shall return shortly to this function of the Real, where the upper case indicates the Lacanian reference.

is charged with: 'language manages to carry the Real within itself as its own intrinsic or immanent subtext'.[13]

This understanding of ideology, which assigns practices primacy over the categories of consciousness, makes it possible to clarify two pairs of notions that represent so many typical pitfalls for the use of this concept not only within the Marxist tradition, but also outside it, namely, 'imaginary/real' and 'solution/act'. The risk entailed by the first is a devaluation of the Imaginary as 'unreality'. Moreover, Marx was not a stranger to this, both in his underestimation of the ideological, assimilated to the *phantastich* and hence to the 'unreal', and in his lack of a theory of the imaginary.[14] Contrariwise, Jameson expands this conception of the constitutive role of the imaginary, which unquestionably owes much to the Lacanian tripartition between Imaginary/Real/Symbolic,[15] by investing the terrain of formal analysis (while refusing to remain enclosed in it), insofar as it can demonstrate that the 'literary or aesthetic act therefore always entertains some active relationship with the Real'.[16] But here the Real is to be construed as History – not that of the individual subject retraced by psychoanalysis, and still less a mere aggregate of empirical factors, but History in the upper case: the absent centre that eludes all representation, that can be grasped only through its effects, with which individual and collective *praxis* is forever colliding[17] – an obstacle that is all the more formidable when *praxis* claims to circumvent it.

The formal act thus reorders reality – now understood in the sense of empirically available, historically situated material – in a specific manner. The antinomies identified by an analysis of form prove to be the 'symptoms' of something more profound: in fact, as use of the Greimassian semiotic rectangle (an instrument revealing, in the chemical sense of the term, 'repressed or realised possibilities' among the set of combinations of a textual sequence) will establish, they define a 'closure' and 'limitation' that distinguish ideology.

---

[13] Jameson 1983, p. 81. The 'models' of such an approach cited by Jameson are Lévi-Strauss's analyses of the facial decorations of the Caduveo Indians in *Tristes Tropiques* and of the Oedipus myth in *Structural Anthropology*.

[14] See Labica 1987, pp. 22–34.

[15] See in this connection the essay 'Imaginary and Symbolic in Lacan', in Jameson 1988a, pp. 75–115. In the event, Lacan is also read through his redeployment by Althusser, especially in the concept of 'absent cause'.

[16] Jameson 1983, p. 81.

[17] 'History is what hurts': Jameson 1983, p. 102.

And these in turn must be reconceived as a projection of contradictions inhering in social relations.[18]

The second interpretative 'level' involves a displacement of the individual text, such as it has been regarded up to now, towards the collective discourse of which it is a constitutive part. The object will now be considered as the '*parole*' pertaining to a '*langue*' which is a 'class *langue*', an ideological code always defined 'as a function of social class'.[19] The minimal units of this language are 'ideologemes', furnishing material that systematised cultural discourses subsequently assume the task of reinvesting and transforming.

Here, however, things become complicated. The language in question cannot in fact be assimilated to any sign system, in as much as the concept of class that it brings into play is a relational concept from the outset, and even a very particular relational concept, since it asserts itself constitutively as a relation between *antagonistic* classes. As Bakhtin had already indicated,[20] the 'multi-accentuation' of the ideological sign under the impact of class struggle is precisely what makes it possible to think the historicity of a semiotic system. As a result, 'the very content of a class ideology is relational' and 'class discourse – the categories in terms of which individual texts and cultural phenomena are now rewritten – is essentially *dialogical* in its structure.' The Bakhtinian concept of the dialogical is 'essentially an *antagonistic* one', for 'the dialogue of class struggle is one in which two opposing discourses fight it out within the general unity of a shared code'.[21]

There are then two possibilities: either to foreground the dialogical character of the form and restore its antagonistic, subversive, political element (in line with the cited analyses of fairy tales by Ernst Bloch or of black slave religion by Eugene Genovese); or, on the contrary, to highlight the unity of the 'master-code' within which contradictions are inscribed, and which 'thus characterizes the larger unity of the social system', the cohesion of each mode of production. Thus, there is 'a cultural dominant or form of ideological coding specific to each mode of production'.[22] The thesis in fact requires reformulation if it is not to betray its author's intention and lapse back into an

---

18 See Jameson 1983, p. 83.
19 Ibid.
20 See Voloshinov 1973, pp. 83–98.
21 Jameson 1983, p. 84.
22 Jameson 1983, pp. 88–9.

exercise in classificatory typology that is scholastic and utterly sterile. Where, wonders Jameson, is Milton, for example, to be allocated: 'within a "precapitalist" or a nascent capitalist context'? Formulated thus, the question is virtually meaningless and contributes nothing to an understanding of this author and his *œuvre*. In reality, it must be recognised that

> every social formation or historically existing society has in fact consisted in the overlay and structural coexistence of *several* modes of production all at once, including vestiges and survivals of older modes of production... as well as anticipatory tendencies.

It follows that

> texts emerge in a space in which we may expect them to be crisscrossed and intersected by a variety of impulses from contradictory modes of production all at once.[23]

In order to transcend the unity of the master-code, which (let us recall) is not the framework, discovered at last, of a consensus, but the expression of the 'structural limitation' peculiar to ideology, it is necessary to take the ultimate step and proceed to the third level of the hermeneutic structure: that of 'cultural revolution' and 'the ideology of form'. Let us clarify something of what is at issue in these two notions, starting with the second. The ideology of form is defined as

> the determinate contradiction of the specific messages emitted by the varied sign systems which coexist in a given artistic process as well as in its general social formation.[24]

The coexistence of a multiplicity of sign systems refers to the insurmountability of the antagonism between the various modes of production or tendencies, communism not being a mode of production that is contained in germ in capitalist relations, but a dominated tendency internal to these relations – a mode of production 'to come', if one likes, thereby eluding, like the Real of History, any representation and any pre-constructed image.

For its part, the 'cultural revolution' is to be understood as an extended *process* immanent in each mode of production (or each determinate articula-

---

[23] Jameson 1983, p. 95.
[24] Jameson 1983, pp. 98–9.

tion between modes of production), and not confined exclusively to periods of 'transition' in the strict sense from one mode to another. This process constantly structures and transforms the values, discourses and *habitus* anchored in the everyday, continually shakes up the accumulated layers of the 'matrix ideology', through antagonisms between and within modes of production, through class struggle. Openly 'transitional' moments are thus included in cultural revolutions, which nevertheless exceed them, in the sense, for example, that the 'bourgeois cultural revolution' refers not only to the moment of the Enlightenment and the French Revolution, but to the much broader phenomenon referred to by Weber as the 'spirit of capitalism'. In this sense, they are only 'the passage to the surface of a permanent process in human societies, of a permanent struggle between the various coexisting modes of production'.[25]

An articulated combination of these three interpretative horizons, Jameson's construction represents an enterprise in 'totalisation' without equal in Marxism, and doubtless well beyond it, sustained by a tenacious project of 'transcendence' (in the abolition/preservation sense of *Aufhebung*) of the opposition between intra-Marxist and extra-Marxist theoretical traditions alike. Its 'master-narrative' doubtless represents the most significant challenge, at the level of theoretical elaboration at least, both to the 'end of grand narratives' proclaimed by the postmodernist current – one that is all the more significant in that it aims to incorporate the truth articulated by the latter – and to the critique of Hegel and the Hegelian-Marxist tradition initiated by Althusser.

The result of a prolonged confrontation with the theses of the master of the rue d'Ulm, *The Political Unconscious* ends up according them a pre-eminent position – the categories of the Hegelian tradition in Marxism retaining only a local validity – while subjecting them to the test that would doubtless have seemed least desirable to their author: inscribing them, as good Hegelian method dictates, in the 'dialectical tradition' with which they precisely intended to effect a break. The operation in fact has a dual thrust. On the one hand, it is the guiding concepts of the Althusserian deconstruction of Hegelian Marxism – for instance, 'overdetermined contradiction', 'history as a process without a subject or goal', 'structural causality', 'efficacy of an absent cause' – that to a large extent structure the 'concrete analyses' of literary texts

25 Jameson 1983, p. 97.

(Balzac, Gissing, Conrad, romance). In return, however, these same concepts are treated in historicist fashion, which leads to the conclusion that, far from being opposed, intra-modal analysis (roughly speaking, *à la* Althusser) and inter-modal sequence (roughly speaking, *à la* Hegel or Lukács) mutually presuppose one another. Yet the second can only be represented, or expounded, in the form – which is an empty form of *Darstellung* – of a teleologically oriented narrative, yielding a 'properly Marxian "philosophy of history"'.[26]

Seductive and audacious, inconceivable even within the co-ordinates of 'Western Marxism', such an undertaking not unnaturally poses problems. In particular, it may be wondered whether it does not simply reinstate the duality of diachrony and synchrony, re-establishing the prerogatives of 'meta-narrative' in its traditional form (continuist and pre-Hegelian, if one wishes) as a genesis and succession of various 'forms' – especially of literary forms, since it is essentially they that are at issue in *The Political Unconscious* – succeeding one another in a homogeneous, linear historical time.[27] Thus, throughout the book it is the possibility of presenting a 'genealogy' of the various literary genres examined (essentially romance and the novel) that is the real object of the exercise. To bring out these diachronic perspectives, Jameson adopts the Husserlian notion of 'sedimentation'. A literary form supposedly carries as such an ideological charge that persists (is sedimented), and which can coexist with other elements when this form is adopted in a new historical context. In Lecercle's judgement, Jameson's solution is 'clever', but 'not wholly convincing'. In his view, Jameson

> overestimates the continuity of literary forms, underestimates the rupture created by a change in historical conjuncture, and thus runs the risk of lapsing back into tradition building, which is a traditional form of intellectual history.[28]

---

[26] Jameson 1983, p. 33.

[27] See Jameson 1983, p. 139f.

[28] Lecercle 1987, p. 91. Jameson has himself disavowed the formulation of the 'succession of modes of production in history' as forming a single narrative, insisting on the fragmentary and discontinuous character of this 'narration' (See Kouvélakis and Vakaloulis 1994).

The dialectic, ultimate utopian horizon

'[A]ll ideology...including the most exclusive forms of ruling-class consciousness, is in its very nature Utopian',[29] Jameson claims, at the risk of provoking a scandal. This is so not despite – but precisely because of – its function in perpetuating class domination, because the latter consists in the affirmation of collective solidarity. In general, we have seen that since the 'organic solidarity' manifested by the 'collectivity' forms the 'essence' of the social relation, it appears logical to conclude that ideology – 'class consciousness' or 'group solidarity' – is by its very nature utopian, since utopia is itself simply the image of 'the ultimate concrete collective life of an achieved Utopian or classless society'.[30] 'Figurations' of an emancipated society, utopias are inherent in the representations secreted by any society shot through with class antagonism. And, if we accept that the ideologies of the dominant are not – or at least not necessarily, or even mainly – mirrors wherein they seek to flatter themselves but, above all, 'mirrors held up to the others, to the dominated',[31] then it must be concluded that, in order to succeed in its function, any ideological configuration necessarily incorporates elements of utopia, if only in an extremely debased form. To put it differently, any ideology is an ideology 'of the weak' to the precise extent that it 'reflects', in the Hegelian sense, the fact of their domination and the traumatic burden that it conceals. On this point, Jameson very pertinently recalls the analyses by Bloch and Adorno and Horkheimer of the utopian impulses present in even the most degraded forms of 'mass culture' or in an ideology as foul as anti-Semitism; and one might add to this Étienne Balibar's analysis of racism as a 'humanism'.[32]

However, like the ideology from which it is indissociable, and paradoxical as it might seem, utopia is above all a matter of practice; and it is in this sense that Jameson proposes to define the utopian text as a '*praxis*' of a particular type:

> It is possible to understand the Utopian text as a determinate type of *praxis*, rather than as a specific mode of representation, a praxis that has less to do with the construction and perfection of a someone's 'idea' of a

---

[29] Jameson 1983, p. 289.
[30] Jameson 1983, p. 291.
[31] Labica 1987, p. 115.
[32] See Balibar and Wallerstein 1991, pp. 63–4.

> 'perfect society' than it does with a concrete set of mental operations to be performed on a determinate type of raw material given in advance, which is contemporary society itself – or, what amounts to the same thing, on those collective representations of contemporary society that inform our ideologies just as they order our experience of daily life.[33]

Utopia discloses the ambivalence within collective practice in so far as it embodies a form of *praxis* which, in the very endeavour to assert itself as the allegory of a different social form, succumbs to representation and is in a way transformed into its opposite – into a mode of *neutralisation*, as opposed to resolution, of real contradictions.

The true object of the utopian narrative is therefore its avowed failure: the confession of a failure, individual and collective, to produce a vision of the Other, to 'overleap one's time' (to adopt Hegel's formulation). This is why the ultimate image of utopia – concrete vector (or presentable in narrative mode at least) of the spirit of communism, strict counterpart to the history experienced by humanity as a nightmare from which there is no escape – is duty bound precisely to abolish any representation internally, to break with representation. The name of this utopia-beyond-utopia is none other than the dialectic. But it in turn cannot, any more than can any other textual operator, elude the test of the historicist hermeneutic.

At a first level, the dialectic refers to a precise mode of intervention in the conjuncture, which is theoretical initially – directed against empiricism and the refusal of theory flaunted by 'the peculiar linguistic habits of the philosophers of the Anglo-American School who, working without books after the example of Socrates, turn their minds carefully inside out like old packets in order to see what practical examples may be found here'.[34] But it is also political, in as much as the dialectic is spurred on by the methodological imperative of totalisation, which registers the unrepresentable character of the totality in order tirelessly to relaunch the labour of historicising interpretation, to the point of producing those 'cognitive mappings' that are capable of removing the constraints which cause the present to stumble over its own internal possibilities. Such an imperative dictates struggling against the fragmentation of

[33] Jameson 1988b, p. 81.
[34] Jameson 1972, p. 207.

the dominated classes and their struggles imposed by late capitalism, especially in the North-American context, which is now partially converging with the dominant trends in Europe. More profoundly, however, the 'persistence of the dialectic' refers to its very status such as it appears in the light of the ultimate hermeneutic horizon that it discloses. Neither *a priori* method, nor universal science, the dialectic refers to 'the anticipation of the logic of a collectivity which has not yet come into being'[35] – that of the classless society embodied in human beings' struggle for their liberation.

The encounter between Jameson's project and the debate on postmodernity, which was in no sense either spontaneous or predetermined, is nevertheless inscribed in the precise point where the History revealed by the 'political unconscious' crosses history in the present and politics *tout court*. Is it conceivable that this endlessly expansive interpretative machine could not capture, and in a way regard as its greatest challenge, what is asserted precisely as its denial, its maximum point of resistance: the 'end of grand narratives', the collapse of historical meaning, the celebration of the superficial and ephemeral?

With the hindsight afforded by the passage of time, we can say that the wager has been won: Jameson's intervention in the fray of postmodernism, which has produced decisive and, in a sense, irreversible effects,[36] has indeed functioned as a tremendous relaunching of the theoretical project as a whole. The encounter with the 'cultural logic of late capitalism', as Jameson defines postmodernism, has rejuvenated this dialectical and historicist set of instruments and, at the very heart of the imperialist centre, won him an audience that is now comparable only with that of the major figures in the Western-Marxist tradition. That an event of this magnitude should have occurred even as the historical defeat of the mass movement for self-emancipation supervened to terminate the 'short twentieth century' (Hobsbawm) clearly indicates that the 'political unconscious' of our time is far from having produced all its effects.

---

35 Jameson 1983, p. 286.

36 It is no exaggeration to say that there is a before, and an after, the publication in 1984 in *New Left Review* of the essay on 'Postmodernism, or the Cultural Logic of Late Capitalism' (reprinted in Jameson 1991).

Chapter Thirty-Eight

Henri Lefebvre, Thinker of Urban Modernity

Stathis Kouvelakis

Henri Lefebvre's discovery of 'modernity' – a term he did not coin, but to the establishment of whose theoretical pedigree he made a significant contribution[1] – seems fully to confirm Fredric Jameson's thesis that modernity can only be perceived as such from an 'exterior' which is identified with a 'premodern enclave';[2] or, more precisely, as an enclave facing its imminent modernisation, the devastating effects of its absorption into a world which, in the space of a final instant, it can confront in the manner of the 'not yet'. In this sense, the primal scene, whose repetition and displacements punctuate the long course of Lefebvre's life and thought, is none other than that of the 'crucified sun' which he himself retraced in some justly famous pages of *La Somme et le reste*.[3] An urban adolescent on holiday in Navarrenx – the maternal village, embodiment of the traditional universe – and immersed in a rural world that is at once oppressive and communal, archaic

[1] See the pioneering endeavour of Lefebvre 1995. In particular, Lefebvre distinguished between modernity and modernism, the former referring to the self-reflexive moment of an epoch, while the latter constitutes its dominant cultural phenomenon. Modernity appears as the 'shadow' cast over bourgeois society by the failure of revolution, at once a compensatory substitute and the ineliminable trace of vanquished hopes.

[2] See 'Marxism and Modernism' in Jameson 1998.

[3] See Lefebvre 1989, pp. 251–66.

and festive, is gripped by a primal fear at the sight of a disc stamped with a cross erected on a monument at the side of a country path: it is the 'crucified sun'. And, via this allegory of religion's oppressive function, he comes to *feel*, rather than understand as such, the internal gulf constitutive of the traditional social order, which is in the process of disappearing. The trauma at the centre of it, Lefebvre will discover later, refers to the destruction of a life-experience that is older still – an ancient pagan, solar, festive tradition, shattered by feudal power and its austere official religion. However, they will never entirely be rid of this prior form, which will find refuge in the subterranean strata of social existence, rising to the surface during each interruption of its normal course: festivals, carnivals, popular revolts.

With the aid of the retrospective obviousness typical of biographical constructions, it would doubtless not be difficult to 'rediscover' in the shock created by the discrepancy between two contradictory orders of experience the thematic core which the subsequent *œuvre* will seek to unfold – especially that 'ambiguous, distrustful and fascinated, lucid and forewarned curiosity'[4] which Lefebvre brought to bear on a triumphant modernity. This curiosity underlay what Lefebvre himself referred to as a 'new romanticism'[5] – an unstable, ambivalent and, by that very token, productive mixture of nostalgia for the past and enthusiasm for novelty, of active rebellion and a desire for harmony and reconciliation.

This is what is reactivated and revived during the traumatic shock – an obvious repetition of the primal scene[6] – triggered by the construction, towards the end of the 1950s, of the new town of Mourenx alongside the Navarrenx of Lefebvre's childhood and adolescence: the reflection on space and the urban phenomenon has its source here – in the brutal intrusion of an aggressive

---

[4] Lefebvre 1989, pp. 258–9.

[5] See the final 'prelude' in Lefebvre 1995 (pp. 239–388), entitled 'Towards a New Romanticism?'.

[6] The violence transpires more clearly in the freer, more settled terms of an interview that long postdates the event, than in the contemporary analysis of it in the nevertheless decisive chapter 'Notes on the New Town' (1960), in Lefebvre 1995, pp. 116–26: 'at one point I saw a town being constructed, with extraordinary brutality: the town was decided in high places, the bulldozers arrived, the peasants were traumatised – it was a drama in the country: Mourenx. It was then that I got down to studying the urban phenomenon. I witnessed the creation of a new town on the spot' (Lefebvre 1983, p. 56).

modernity, effected by an anonymous and normalised 'machine for inhabiting', functional for the needs of capitalism and carefully planned from above by the postwar technocratic state. And this modernity coexists in the order of non-contemporaneity, which is constitutive of modern experience,[7] with the spatial sedimentation of a form of a communal, aesthetic existence that has endured for centuries. Even so, stresses Lefebvre, it is in the unprecedented experience generated by the impersonal, repetitive machinery of Mourenx, in the conflicts and expectations created in it, that the limited character of traditional existence can be dissolved and a horizon of genuine emancipation for the men and women of modern times opened up.

Emancipation through the urban experience

The everyday – the town – the urban – re-production – space: here, in approximate order, are the sequences of the enactment of emancipation, conceived by Lefebvre as the advent of 'total man',[8] the universal communion of individuals liberated from alienation. Yet this sequence is in no sense equivalent to a linear evolution. And while it is true that is *de jure* inscribed in a certain philosophy of history, it is predominantly as a general framework, an allegorical narrative of potential emancipation, which allows Lefebvre to revive a conceptual labour of constant historicisation and specification of the dynamic towards humanity's disalienation and totalisation.[9]

As regards the continual interest knowledge has in emancipation, the first thing to investigate is the pair *œuvre*/product, in as much as it expresses two aspects of 'production' – itself at the centre of social existence. Production, Lefebvre adamantly insists, must be understood in the 'broad sense' – that of a total *praxis*. It is not restricted to

> the activity that fashions things in order to exchange them. There are *œuvres* and there are products. Production in the broad sense (the self-production

[7] 'Notes on the New Town' begins with this sentence: 'A few kilometres from the tower blocks of the new town lies the sleepy old village where I live. Just a few minutes from my timeworn house, and I am surrounded by the derricks of a building estate without a past' (Lefebvre 1995, p. 116).
[8] On the theme of the 'total man', directly derived from a re-reading of the young Marx and Feuerbach, see Lefebvre 1968, pp. 148–66.
[9] See Lefebvre 2002, pp. 180–93 and Lefebvre 1991, pp. 76–7.

> of human beings] implies and includes that of ideas, representations, language.... Thus, production excludes nothing, nothing that is human.[10]

Production is an image of the 'concrete universal',[11] which finds the realisation of its internal purpose in the *œuvre* rendered transparent to conscious *praxis*.[12] Closer in this to the Promethean gesture than, for example, 'objectification' in the late Lukács,[13] production finds initial fulfilment in everyday life; then in the town – that *œuvre par excellence*[14] – which allows the *œuvre* to recapture its meaning;[15] and, finally, in space, synthesis of the *œuvre* and the product,[16] final figure of the totality.

This is where a second conceptual pair, directly connected with the previous one, comes in: the contradiction between use-value and exchange-value, invoked in order to provide a specifically Marxist anchorage for the 'grand narrative' of humanity's alienation and imminent emancipation. Towns and urban reality are an *œuvre*, for they pertain to use-value:

> exchange-value and the generalisation of commodities through industrialisation have dislocated towns and urban reality, refuges of use-value, germs of a potential predominance and revalorisation of use.[17]

This position, constantly reiterated,[18] has important consequences, particularly in the analysis of the contradictions peculiar to urban space: 'use resists stubbornly: ineliminably. The ineliminability of the urban centre plays a crucial role in the argument'.[19] Use, previously dominant in the immediate unity of the natural community, but negated by the predominance of commodity exchange, resurfaces thanks to the negation of its negation: in a 'form' that

---

10 Lefebvre 1972, pp. 41–2.
11 Lefebvre 1990, p. 15.
12 See Lefebvre 2002, p. 156.
13 The root of the difference between Lukács and Lefebvre is doubtless to be sought in the unequal weight they assign labour: basis of social being for the former, it is subordinate to aesthetic creation for the latter.
14 Lefebvre 1974, pp. 10–11.
15 Lefebvre 1973, p. 20.
16 'In and of itself, social space does not have all of the characteristics of "things" as opposed to creative activity. Social space *per se* is at once *work* and *product* – a materialisation of "social being"' (Lefebvre 1990, pp. 101–2).
17 Lefebvre 1974a, p. 14.
18 See, in particular, Lefebvre 1974a, pp. 86–9; Lefebvre 1974b, p. 30; and Lefebvre 1974c, p. 204.
19 Lefebvre 1974a, p. 135.

'cannot disappear'.[20] For it is a 'pure' form, totally autonomous from the 'content' of which it is the 'receptacle'.[21] Defined as 'meeting point, the site of assembly, simultaneity',[22] it 'generates' its own object:[23] a 'potential' object always orientated towards its fulfilment – urban society.

Use, whose reality is restored to us by this form with demiurgic properties, is defined with the help of a third pair, contained in the two preceding ones: art/work. Art is the ever living model of the active appropriation of reality through the production of *œuvres* – precisely artworks.[24] The adoption of the theme, dear to German idealism, of the 'realisation' of art through its fusion with life and everydayness must be understood in its opposition to the relativisation of work, regarded as an activity that produces, in the 'narrow' and 'reductive' sense, 'things'[25] or 'products'. An impersonal production, condemned to remain such, whereas the creation of 'oeuvres is unintelligible if it does not depend upon human subjects',[26] work is historically superseded by the universalisation of the urban form, which, before our very eyes, is taking over from industrialisation.

The sequence of the categories (*œuvre*/product, use/commodity, art/work) thus circumscribes a major dialectical sequence, which totalises the meaning of 'universal history' in these three moments. Alternatively put, this allegorical narrative deploys a possible narrative presentation of the transition 'from nature to abstraction',[27] and thence to the concrete universality of 'human plenitude', realised in the primitive community and doubly lost in the alienation and 'real abstraction' of the state.[28] At the very heart of the alienated present, it reveals the 'conception of, and desire for, a plenitude (finite and relative, but "total")' borne by 'urban rationality'.[29] Lefebvre, it is true, rejects the hasty identification of 'what is possible' with an 'eschatology' and rejects 'traditional finalism'.[30] History nevertheless unfolds in a temporal continuum,

20 Lefebvre 1974a, p. 86.
21 Lefebvre 1974b, pp. 159–60.
22 Lefebvre 1974b, p. 159; and See Lefebvre 1974c, p. 121.
23 Lefebvre 1974b, p. 164.
24 See Lefebvre 1974a, pp. 119, 139, 142; and Lefebvre 1990, pp. 128, 349.
25 See Lefebvre 1972, p. 75.
26 Lefebvre 1972, p. 75.
27 Lefebvre 1990, p. 110.
28 See Lefebvre 1991, p. 209.
29 Lefebvre 1974b, p. 100.
30 See, respectively, Lefebvre 2002, p. 73 and Lefebvre 1974b, pp. 93–7.

graphically represented by a spatio-temporal axis proceeding from origins to the End,[31] where the potential contained in the present at once assures us of the direction of this evolution and of the image of the future foreshadowed thus.[32] If the break is not a guaranteed certainty, but a 'possibility',[33] the historical narrative delivers up a 'meaning'[34] that allows us to see the urban 'on the move since the Origin, in the vicinity of the initial zero'.[35] The transcendence/realisation of this historicity culminates in the ultimately restored beautiful Totality which, under the auspices of the conscious mastery of social transparency, reunifies 'art, technique, knowledge', 'science and utopia, reality and ideality, conceived and lived'.[36]

As a result, urban society takes the form of a kind of *Aufhebung* (abolition/supersession) of the social relation as such. Its representation oscillates between 'the very concrete and positive idea of a history which has at last been orientated, directed and mastered by knowledge and willpower'[37] – that is to say, an image of collective control that issues in the disappearance of the political, assimilated to the withering away of the state[38] – and a communion between universal individuals ('total men') in the realm of 'enjoyment' and 'non-work'.[39] Thanks to the conjoint abolition of work, the state and politics, the creative freedom of Subjects, the Festival, and 'ludic centrality' unfold unchecked, recreating at a higher level the immediate unity of nature, everyday life, and enjoyment which was characteristic of the original Festival specific to rural communities.[40] It is no accident if we discover in the Navarrenx of Lefebvre's childhood, albeit in a form limited by an archaic social order, the same features this projection attributes to the emancipated society of the future: a quasi-monadological, organic unity (a seashell 'has slowly secreted

---

[31] See Lefebvre 1974a, p. 79.
[32] See Lefebvre 1974b, p. 35.
[33] Lefebvre 1973, p. 16.
[34] 'What is possible forms part of reality: it gives it its meaning – that is to say, its direction and orientation': Lefebvre 1974b, p. 64.
[35] Lefebvre 1974b, p. 165.
[36] Respectively, Lefebvre 1974a, p. 119 and Lefebvre 1990, p. 60.
[37] Lefebvre 2002, p. 73.
[38] This thesis is constantly reiterated. In addition to Lefebvre 1978, we might signal Lefebvre 1991, pp. 91–2; Lefebvre 1974c, p. 153; Lefebvre 1973, p. 29; and Lefebvre 1990, p. 416.
[39] See Lefebvre 1974b, p. 47; Lefebvre 1972, pp. 65–9; and Lefebvre 1973, p. 20.
[40] See Lefebvre 1991, p. 207.

a structure')[41] – a collective *œuvre* that integrates the functional and the aesthetic, a spatial diagram based on the non-separation of social sites and activities.

Lefebvre thus immerses us in the great romantic dream: the transcendence of the separations brought about by the triumph of bourgeois society as a fulfilment of the promises contained in the premodern past – the dream of a community of existence embodying the fusion of the aesthetic principle, the ludic principle, and the 'artistic' principle of subjectivation. This is a dream at the heart of modernity if, in accordance with Lefebvre's own suggestions, we understand the latter as the shadow cast by the experience of the failure of revolution. Moreover, this is why the 'prelude' that closes the *Introduction to Modernity*, tellingly entitled 'Towards a New Romanticism?', concludes, perfectly logically, with the founding gesture of any modernism: the appeal to a new avant-garde, whose portent is situationism.[42] What must be stressed is that this dream, like any other narrative subjected to equivalent narrative constraints, does not occur without ambiguities and aporias, which we must now try to explain.

The urban: a false promise?

In reality, the categories that govern Lefebvre's narrative are directly transposable (and, in fact, transposed) from one object to another – from the everyday to the urban, from space to globality, from one historical period and type of society to those that preceded, and those that will succeed, it. Foreign to the logic peculiar to a specific object of knowledge, they often seem to pertain to a particular type of discourse, wherein history is invoked only in order to illustrate a sequence of self-development of the concept: a philosophy of history, or rather (to take up a distinction of Lukács's),[43] *on* history. Concrete analyses will thus often be diverted towards roads without an exit, interrupting the exploration of fertile tracks that have previously been sketched. We shall examine more closely two sources of aporiae that directly affect the problematic of urban space: the opposition between use-value and exchange-value

---

[41] Lefebvre 1995, p. 116.

[42] See Lefebvre 1995, p. 343ff.

[43] Lukács makes it the distinguishing feature of the 'bad abstraction' of utopian narratives: See 'Moses Hess and the Problem of Idealist Dialectics' in Lukács 1972.

and the aetheteticisation of everyday life as the paradigm of an emancipated society.

To start with, what is involved in the 'contradiction between use-value and exchange-value'? And, furthermore, granted that we find ourselves in the context of commodity relations (where an exchange-value *and* a use-value therefore exist simultaneously), why is there a contradiction? After all, the commodity is a unity of exchange-value and use-value, the second referring to the material support required by the first. And this is what makes commodity exchange a rational activity: what is aimed at through the expenditure of labour-power crystallised in an exchange-value, itself possessed by an exchanger, is the utility of the product possessed by another exchanger. The general form of value – the universal equivalent (money) – ensures the adequate expression of values, the general exchangeability that provides access to all the use-values produced.[44]

There are, then, two options: either the town, pre-existing the domination of capitalist relations, is 'commodified' and thereby becomes an object of commodity exchange, which only possesses meaning on account of the *use* obtained from it. This is how things stand, for example, with the tourist-type consumption of rehabilitated urban centres, compensation in nostalgic mode for the destruction of the historic town.[45] Alternatively – the second option – the term 'use' refers to *something other* than the use obtained in the context of commodity exchange and in fact this is what Lefebvre suggests: not 'any use whatsoever, but a "qualitative" use, which is already social appropriation, and as such in contradiction with commodity logic'.[46] A use inherent in the 'second nature' fashioned by the urban,[47] which refers to the anthropological attributes posited by the two other conceptual pairs (the creative freedom of human beings designated by the oppositions oeuvre/product, art/work).

In this case, the pair use-value/exchange-value as defined by Marx (and independently of whether a 'contradiction' exists between the two terms) is manifestly inadequate, for it can only refer to the two indissociable aspects of

---

44 For an overall demonstration, see Bidet 2000, pp. 220–2.

45 'The urban centre thus becomes a high-quality consumer product for foreigners, tourists, people from the periphery, suburbanites. It survives thanks to this dual role: place of consumption and consumption of place': Lefebvre 1974a, p. 21. See also Lefebvre 1974a, p. 103.

46 See Lefebvre 1974a, p. 89 and Lefebvre 1974c, pp. 204–5.

47 Lefebvre 1973, p. 19.

one and the same social activity: commodity exchange. It has no pertinence as regards an 'external contradiction', which refers to the opposition between two antagonistic 'social logics': between commodity relations (with their dual aspect: use-value *and* exchange-value) and an alternative appropriation based on socialised use.

We now find ourselves faced with a crucial aporia in Lefebvre's categories, which affects his very definition of the urban. If the urban is, *in essence* (the term is by no means fortuitous), in contradiction with market and capitalist rationality, it is because it is posited as a *pure form*: encounter, assembly, simultaneity. The potential negation of distance it makes possible allows the 'deterioration of social relations' due, precisely, to 'distance' to be avoided.[48]

While 'creating nothing', the urban form makes 'everything flow', for 'nothing exists without convergence, proximity – that is to say, *relations*'.[49] No doubt. However, except in the immutable world of 'essences', the relations in question can be of any sort: slavery, exploitation, destruction or…emancipation. This is where use, 'qualitative', socialising use, intervenes. How is it, in turn, defined? Indeed, as we have just seen, in the same way as the 'urban form', by the same attributes and qualities.[50] Here we are caught in a circular form of reasoning with no way out: the ineliminability of the urban is based on use, which is itself equivalent to the urban form, the latter being what defines the urban as such.[51] This vicious circle is readily explained when we realise that the urban is assimilated to a form prior to any social determination, in so far as it is called upon to play the specific role in the sequence of universal history outlined earlier – that of embodying an image of the singular universal.

Let us now turn to Lefebvre's version of the aesthetic critique of capitalism and, more broadly, of alienated forms of social life. The resumption of the project of the 'realisation' of art in its reunification with the totality of social life is intended, among other things, to contest a reductive and 'productivist' vision (in the sense of centred on productive activities) of a future socialist

48 See Lefebvre 1974b, pp. 159–60.

49 Lefebvre 1974b, p. 158.

50 For example, 'some inhabitants reconstruct centres, use places in order to restore meetings, even if they are derisory. The use (use-value) of places, of moments, of differences, eludes the exigencies of exchange, exchange-value': Lefebvre 1974a, p. 86.

51 On this point, see Manuel Castells, who observes that Lefebvre thus cancels any causal relationship between the form (the town) and human creation (Castells 1975, p. 122).

society. Consequently, Lefebvre forms part of a rich romantic tradition, which is prevalent in classical Marxism, beginning with Marx himself. As is strongly suggested by certain famous passages in the *Grundrisse*,[52] art – a 'higher activity' and form of 'actually free labour', to adopt Marx's formulations – finds itself promoted to the rank of central, if not unique, activity in an emancipated society.

Now, once we search in the here and now for a real vector of this future kingdom of the artwork, it has to be observed that the constant and growing aestheticisation of capitalist relations tends very rapidly to surpass the seemingly most subversive cultural demands, by 'realising' them in its fashion. More than a mere 'recuperation', there is a deep cultural logic at work here, fed by a multiform staging of the everyday, which aims to displace and neutralise real contradictions through practices of passive, symbolically gratifying consumption of images and participation in the proliferating culture of the urban happening. 'Already the urban space affords city folk dynamism, the unforeseen, possibilities, and encounters. It is a spontaneous theatre, or it is nothing', wrote Lefebvre in 1968.[53] But the representation proposed is in great danger of being the generalised spectacularisation, the unchained phantasmagoria of the commodity fetish, offering city dwellers pushed towards the periphery enjoyment of the spectacle of their own dispossession of the city.[54] Lefebvre's optimism, which is not wanting in lucidity as to the real meaning of this 'nostalgic consumption', seems to be based on the socialising virtues attributed to the 'urban form'. However, the spectacle's assembly of atomised individuals pertains more to the solitude of modern crowds referred to by Baudelaire, than to the now vanished mode of socialisation of the old urban districts.

Lefebvre's attempts to furnish a positive representation, a 'realistic image', of the emancipatory potential of 'realised art' are scarcely convincing: the architecture of R. Bofill,[55] which some might find unduly neo-Mussolinian; or the Montréal universal exhibition in 1967, which is supposed to illustrate the 'ideal' – postmodernist *avant la lettre* – of the 'ephemeral city, a perpetual

---

[52] See Marx 1973.

[53] Lefebvre 1974a, p. 138.

[54] Readers might usefully refer to Walter Benjamin's analyses of Haussmanian Paris (already!) in Benjamin 1973, pp. 157–76.

[55] See Lefebvre 1974c, p. 270.

work by its inhabitants, themselves mobilised for and by this work'.[56] Was this 'magnificent city, where everydayness was reabsorbed into the Festival, where the urban transpired in its splendour',[57] anything more than one of those urban spectacles – organised, what is more, by an ultra-liberal municipality[58] – supported by major financial companies? The primacy accorded to the aesthetic seems (to paraphrase Walter Benjamin) closer to the aesethicisation of political practice than to the politicisation of aesthetics. Boffil's historicist pastiche and Montréal's 'urban ephemera' appear to be the illusory promises of an 'ideal' that the postmodern age will take charge of transforming into (sur)reality.

Was Lefebvre precisely a postmodernist *avant la lettre*? Obviously, it all depends on what is meant by the term, whose polysemy and capacity for confusion seem at first sight to afford its only possible definitions. If, however, we decide to opt for the intelligibility of the postmodern authorised by Jameson's intervention, might we conclude that Lefebvre's aesthetic ideal prefigures, in its ambiguities, the 'cultural logic' of late capitalism and its dehistoricised, multi-fragmented 'hyper-space'? On this point, a small backwards glance is required. As Lefebvre himself said and repeated, it was indeed the shock created by a certain modernism, combining extreme functionalism and the glorification of the state, notably at the level of the symbolic and urban monumentality, that prompted his interest in the urban phenomenon.

The predominance of this modernism has quite rightly been linked to the rise of a new social stratum – the 'technocrats' – that is the organic support of this voluntarist policy of intervention in town and country, which it would perhaps be appropriate to designate by the term 'spatial Keynesianism'. Lefebvre was liable to be attracted by certain aspects of the postmodernist critique of this modernism – for example, at an architectural level – which might recall his own thematic: critique of functional standardisation (blocks of council housing or towers *à la* Mies van der Rohe); rehabilitation of the symbolic and ludic function; and references to 'history' via 'quotations' from the past or vernacular traditions. Is he then to be regarded as a spokesman for the new petit-bourgeois strata, formed in the atmosphere of 1960s 'cultural protest',

56 Lefebvre 1974a, p. 139.
57 Lefebvre 1974b, p. 175.
58 See Castells 1975, p. 52.

eager for 'standing' and 'quality' consumption – especially of old stone – and who, following the breakdown of the Keynesian compromise, have taken over from the austere technocracy of the era of postwar reconstruction?

Lefebvre's indulgence towards an apologetic postmodernism, despite the 'culturalist' ambiguities of his analyses, in the main involves a misunderstanding. With their stress on the critical and utopian dimension of art, their fidelity to the exigency of truth posited by Hegelian aesthetics, his aesthetic options are profoundly modern. They are at the antipodes of the liquidation of historical depth, the blurring of spatial reference-points, the pure surface play that characterises postmodern 'hyper-space'.[59] As for the ludic dimension, Lefebvre's Festival is not reducible to any disabused, nihilistic nod, to the facilities of eclecticism, and to the vampirisation of the past. More profoundly, Lefebvre never abandoned the ambition of changing the world, swapping it, for example, for a change in the way in which the world is contemplated. If he emphasised the symbolic and aesthetic dimensions, he never separated them from real practices and appropriation, which affect the foundations of social relations. Thus, he was able to perceive, at least in part, the possibility of a recuperation by the dominant logic of elements – particularly cultural ones – that were supposed to contest it. The 'pseudo-Festival', he lucidly observed,

> only apparently leaves the everyday. It extends it by other means, by a sophisticated organisation that combines everything – advertising, culture, arts, games, propaganda, work regulations, urban existence…and the police keeps a watchful eye, supervises.[60]

A politics of the possible

Formulated in abrupt fashion, the thesis I propose to develop here is the following: Lefebvre's aporiae are not unproductive, in as much as his thinking about space retains a critical significance and an analytical fertility that render it still contemporary. As a preliminary to discussion of it, examination of this thesis requires an ideal reconstruction of the approach around a few key propositions. Such an exercise might seem disloyal to a thought which,

---

[59] See Jameson 1991, especially his analysis of the Bonaventure Hotel and other, more 'experimental' postmodern spaces (Jameson 1991, pp. 38–45, 96–129 and 154–80).
[60] Lefebvre 1992, p. 52.

opting for the virtues of the fragmentary and the 'informal', was wary of systematic exposition. It carries with it the risk of a certain over-simplification and compression of the development of Lefebvre's thinking. Since it nevertheless seems to me to be difficult to do without them, unless we are to restrict ourselves to a few generalities, I shall provisionally formulate the following hypotheses:

1) The town is an inscription on the ground of the fundamental social relations of a mode of production. Generally speaking, each mode of production produces a space that is peculiar to it: it is inscribed in space by combining varied spatial practices.
2) The production of space is not a passive reflection, external to social relations: it refers to a dimension, decisive because *constitutive*, of the processes of their overall reproduction, which is also, at the same time, the spatial reproduction of their contradictions.
3) Space, and especially urban space, thus constitutes the terrain where antagonistic social forces are deployed – a new front in the class struggle.
4) An issue in struggles, space is consequently a site of increasing intervention on the part of the instance which, through its regulation of conflicts, enables the re-production of the general conditions of class domination: the state and its apparatuses, particularly the apparatuses of the local state (town and country planning, regional councils, municipalities).
5) The process of production of space mobilises a set of spatial practices, of representations of space, and of imaginary relations (the spaces of representations) – or, in Lefebvre's terms, the 'perceptual', the 'conceptual', and the 'experiential'. Each level possesses its own effectivity within the totality formed by the fundamental relations of the mode of production and the spatial practices that are constitutive of them.[61]
6) The spatialisation of the contradictions of the mode of production opens up the question of possibilities: through a strategy and a politics contributing to the development of struggles for the social appropriation of space.

[61] This particularly sensitive issue lies behind all the readings that see to annex Lefebvre to a *theoretical* postmodernism. On this controversy, see Harvey 1989a, pp. 262–3 and Soja 1989, pp. 76–9. In French, readers can refer to the studies by Dear 1994 and Hamel and Poitras 1994.

7) Just as the production of space has been a key issue for the survival of capitalism, so the 'test of space' is unavoidable for any attempt at a revolutionary transformation of social relations. No transition is possible without a specific social practice – i.e. without the 'creative destruction' of state and capitalist centrality, without collective reappropriation of the town and space, and without a transformation in ways of living.

Needless to say, none of these propositions is self-evident. On one side, the technocratism and positivism that were dominant in urban thinking presented space as neutral, a mere framework and physical receptacle for human activities; and the political interventions that occurred there as rational and placatory. On the other, the Marxist vulgate, confined to economism and workerism, ignored urban and spatial problems, except from the reductionist standpoint of 'housing'. Moreover, the traditional organisations of the workers' movement proved enduringly incapable of investing these new sites of confrontation with capitalist and state practices.

The opening to the urban and space offered Lefebvre a productive exit from the project of the critique of everydayness, which he had undertaken since the morrow of the Liberation, and whose germ in fact dates back to the 1930s.[62] The paths opened up allowed him to leave behind the rather speculative and abstract accounts into which, announcing inquiries whose object is hard to make out, the second volume of the *Critique of Everyday Life* seemed to be getting bogged down. They also facilitated – and this is far from negligible for someone who always strove to inscribe his thought in an endeavour to renew Marxism – combining the research object with real political practices: those of the urban movements that developed in the wake of the struggles of 1968 in France and throughout the world.

Lefebvre's analyses unquestionably need to be resituated in the historical period that gave birth to them (1968–74): the final prosperous moments of intensive (Fordist) accumulation and an auspicious conjuncture for social struggle and critical theoretical production, especially of Marxism. Hence, inevitably, certain limits and a generally optimistic tone which, to say the least, seems dated now. The period that began towards the end of the 1970s, marked by a succession of defeats for the workers' movement, a retreat by the

---

[62] See Trebitsch 1991.

'new social movements', and the stabilisation of new modes of capital accumulation, would profoundly transform the landscape, especially the urban landscape.

The Keynesian city of the era of 'growth', with its technocratic myths and the austerity of its modern town planning, was succeeded by the 'entrepreneurial city',[63] adapted to the new economic, social and aesthetic environment of triumphant neoliberalism. The entrepreneurial city impelled a profound reorganisation of the internal space of towns. The recovery of urban centres revalorised by privileged fractions of the so-called 'middle classes' proceeded in tandem with the extension of impoverished zones, often with shifting borders, where the 'losers' of the new era were concentrated: a sub-proletariat of the 'excluded', popular and working-class strata (especially those issuing from 'minorities' or from 'immigration').

The gentrification of town-centres is to be related to the intensified forms of inter-urban competition: investment in 'culture' and sites of 'upmarket' consumption (the conference centres, cultural facilities, sporting complexes or business centres are now legion), and renovation of a built environment that was appreciating in value, aimed to satisfy the 'qualitative' aspirations of the 'new middle strata' (neo-bourgeoisie, higher fractions of the intellectual strata). But they also aimed to recreate a new form of 'urban cohesion', uniting the totality of inhabitants around the 'image' and the spectacle of – and in – the town. Given that the spectacle and the image proved weak, or at least insufficient, when it came to preserving 'social cohesion', multiform state intervention (conflict regulation and, where necessary, violent repression) proved indispensable for maintaining order, neutralising the threats and fears that haunted the postmodern town (criminality, riots, zones of informal economic activity, and so on).

This development continued certain broad trends in capitalist urbanisation highlighted by Lefebvre: the intensification of class segregation in space and the transfer of working-class and popular strata, and hence the increased spatial polarisation that accompanied the rise of the new intermediate strata, whose role in the formation of consumption norms and the social base of

63 On this point, we take up the arguments of Harvey 1989a, pp. 256–78; Harvey 1989b, pp. 141–97; and Soja 1989, pp. 157–89.

the dominant social bloc was already glimpsed.[64] The explosion of cultural politics certainly exceeded his predictions and even, as we have already suggested, 'realised' the aspiration to the aestheticisation of the everyday and the urban that he shared. This does not mean that he totally misjudged the ambiguities. From the consumption of the urban spectacle[65] to the recuperation of leisure[66] and the festival by culture and entertainment industry,[67] Lefebvre discerned a 'a contradiction, specific to this society, between *expulsion* (of whole groups towards the spatial, mental and social periphery) and *integration* (which remains symbolic, abstract and "cultural")'.[68]

By contrast, Lefebvre's theses on the growing role of state intervention in the spatial reproduction of the relations of domination were to be fully confirmed in the post-Keynesian era. In particular, they make it possible to understand why, despite its anti-statist rhetoric, neoliberalism in no way betokens 'less state', but the redeployment of forms of state intervention precisely under the impetus of the progressive dismantling of the institutional compromises of the previous period. More than ever, the state, whose decentralisation multiplies the modalities of its presence, ensures the unity and overall organisation of space,[69] articulates the varied and contradictory practices of the sphere of social reproduction.[70] And, above all, the state asserts itself by 'pacifying' the social field, by regulating its internal conflicts.[71] Its ideological function is crucial. The increasing institutionalisation of 'urban policy', notably by the creation of an urban ministry, accentuates two phenomena that Lefebvre had highlighted. State intervention is extended under the impact of a deepening in the contradictions of space: the contradiction between global space, produced at a world level by a capitalism that no longer has any borders, and the local space of accumulation of private capital.

The accentuation of class polarisation in space triggers repressive unification and control.[72] Added to this is the effect of fetishisation created by state

---

[64] Lefebvre 1973, p. 31.
[65] Lefebvre 1974a, p. 103.
[66] Lefebvre 1974c, p. 177 and 1973, p. 32.
[67] Lefebvre 1972, p. 135.
[68] Lefebvre 1973, p. 30.
[69] Lefebvre 1990, p. 378.
[70] Lefebvre 1973, p. 30.
[71] See Lefebvre 1978, pp. 259–62, 308–14.
[72] See Lefebvre 1972, p. 153 and Lefebvre 1978, pp. 308–10.

activity itself, which gives a 'spatial' appearance to problems attributed to something specific to 'towns' or, above all, its 'inner-city areas' as such, which is only a spatial expression of the dominant social relations. As Lefebvre firmly insists, the contradictions of space ultimately refer to something other than themselves.[73] To reduce them to a so-called 'spatial pathology', whose 'cure' is taken in hand by the state and its auxiliaries, simply conveys the function of naturalisation of social antagonisms, and hence of the preventive disorganisation of resistance, performed by the action of state apparatuses.

The seamless continuity of discourses and practices, during a succession of 'alternations' at the top in France throughout the last two decades, offers striking confirmation of the dual dimension assumed by the state's increased presence in and through the urban. Generally speaking, the key idea that runs through Lefebvre's writings – that the study of spatial configurations is a condition of any serious analysis of social relations and, thereby, of any attempt to transform them – has been amply confirmed by the recent development of post-Fordist capitalism. The fact that his proposals have been taken up and taken further by a significant number of Marxist and radical researchers, for the most part outside France,[74] is an unmistakable sign of their impact and fertility.

---

[73] 'Spatial practice regulates life – it does not create it. Space has no power "in itself", nor does space as such determine spatial contradictions. These are contradictions of society – contradictions between one thing and another within society, as for example between the forces and relations of production – that simply emerge in space, at the level of space, and so engender the contradictions of space' (Lefebvre 1990, p. 358).

[74] See Soja 1989, pp. 43–93 and *passim*.

Chapter Thirty-Nine

Kôzô Uno and His School: A Pure Theory of Capitalism

Jacques Bidet

Kôzô Uno (1897–1977) studied economics at Tokyo University, where several young teachers had already been won to Marxism. From 1922 to 1924, he stayed in Berlin and basically devoted himself to studying *Capital*. Appointed to teach political economy, on his return to Japan he abstained from the debate that opposed the Kôza and Rônô schools and was already looking for a basis to transcend it. He became wedded to the idea that Lenin's and Hilferding's works, focused on a determinate phase in the history of capitalism, were not situated on the same level as those of Marx. The latter not only referred to a different epoch, but posited a more theoretical object, seeking to construct the concept of a pristinely capitalist society. Arrested in 1938, Uno was freed in 1940. In 1947, he became professor of political economy at the Tokyo Social Science Institute, which had just been created. Now began the period of his most important publications. But it was only in the 1960s, with the decline of Stalinist influence, that he gradually established himself as the head of the most important Marxist school in Japan. And to this day his influence remains pre-eminent.

His most significant work, *Keizai Genron* (1964), was translated into English by Thomas Sekine in 1980 under the title *Principles of Political Economy: Theory of a Purely Capitalist Society*. A first version in two volumes (1950 and 1952) had already had a great impact.

Uno's particular conception of 'scientific socialism' led him to separate (the better to unite them) practice and science. The latter possesses its own criteria and objects. In order to develop, it has no need of an external 'viewpoint', not even that of the proletariat. It does not advocate socialism; it seeks to identify its conditions of possibility. Wholly devoted to this task, Uno did not regard himself as a 'Marxist' in the strong sense of the term implied by political engagement and activity, but as a simple man of science. No doubt this position must have made Marxism acceptable to the academic establishment. At the same time, it led to a rigorous theoretical project that would furnish the principles for an intervention in the most concrete, burning debates. On the basis of the 'international Marxism' of the first decades of the twentieth century and an enormous modern culture, Uno developed an independent line of research. As with contemporary avant-garde Japanese aesthetics, there is nothing exotic about it. Uno's initiative intersects with analogous concerns – both Hegelian-dialectical and epistemological – that emerged in Europe at the same time, among economists and philosophers alike. But it displays exceptional originality and coherence. The work is vast and continued in the research of a whole school. The present chapter concentrates exclusively on Uno's *Principles of Political Economy* – the only work translated into English – and relies on a few studies published in European languages. This indicates the modesty of my undertaking and signals possible misunderstandings in advance. But it is only appropriate that a dialogue with Japanese Marxism should be started.

Kôzô Uno's epistemological project

So far as I am aware, Uno is the only theoretician of significance (or at least the first, given that his followers have taken up the task) whose project was to reformulate the exposition of the 'theory of capitalist society' *in conformity with an adequate order of exposition*, with a necessary beginning, development, and end. Such was Marx's project in *Capital*. And we are better informed today of the theoretical reasons underlying his concern to introduce each of his concepts at the appropriate moment.[1] Their definition and significance are determined by the precise position they occupy in the exposition. Paradoxically, the task of attending to the requisite order of explanation has been left to the authors of manuals, to popularisers and teachers. Uno quite rightly defines it as essential. And his *Principles* are nothing other than a methodical version of *Capital*.

The need for such a project gradually became clear to Uno as a result of the discrepancies between Marxist discourses referring to different levels of analysis. Uno distinguishes between three theoretical levels.

The first is the *'theory of a purely capitalist society'*, dealt with by Uno's *Principles*. Marx's *Capital* provides the essential elements. But Uno aims to give his exposition an adequate form. He eliminates anything that does not pertain to a structural definition – everything that concerns the historical emergence and development of capitalism. He excludes anything that is not specifically economic in character. He articulates his exposition in line with a ternary logical form that manifestly refers to Hegel's *Logic*. In this framework, he positions each of the constitutive categories of the capitalist mode of production in its proper place.

The second level is the *'theory of stages of capitalism'*. Uno distinguishes between three epochs – mercantilism, liberalism, and imperialism – which are characterised as three moments in the development of the relationship between the forces and relations of production. This periodisation and its general spirit might seem traditional enough. However, Uno seeks to formulate its principle more rigorously. With each stage, a type of production and a form of capital capable of realising accumulation are combined. Corresponding to domestic production (for instance, of wool) is commercial capital; to the factory age (for example, cotton production), industrial capital; and to heavy industry (for example steel), finance-capital. After 1917, a new epoch begins, with the emergence of socialist societies that alter the internal course of capitalism.

The third level is *concrete history* – the history of particular societies, grasped in their specificity, their distinctive historical-cultural context, the sequence of their conjunctures.

[1] See Schwarz 1978.

The theory of purely capitalist society

Uno's theory of purely capitalist society is divided into three parts, each of which contains three sections: *Circulation* (or 1. *commodity*; 2. *money*; 3. *capital*); *Production* (or, 1. process of *production* of capital, 2. process of *circulation* of capital, 3. process of *reproduction* of capital.); and *Distribution*, or (1. *profit*; 2. *rent*; 3. *interest*).

As we can see, this tripartition differs from that proposed by Marx. While the categories are the those of *Capital*, they are subject to a reorganisation that sometimes alters their meaning appreciably.

Part One – 'Circulation' – corresponds to Parts One and Two of Volume One. But we note an alteration of the utmost importance: according to Uno, the category of labour-value, which *Capital* introduces straight away, can only be introduced in Part Two ('Production'). The first route from the commodity to capital therefore starts out from a strictly formal approach to value, defined as the 'homogeneity' of commodities, such as it manifests itself in the act of exchange. Uno endeavours to show that such a value implies its universal expression in money form; and he proposes an original version of the well-known path leading from the 'simple' form to the 'developed' form and the 'general' form. He defines the 'simple' expression of the value of a commodity in the use-value of another commodity as a 'subjective evaluation' on the part of its owner. Owners of commodities thus tend to express their value in the use-value of the various goods they desire, depending on what they are prepared to give in order to acquire them. The formation of a market assumes the supersession of this diversity of expression and the emergence of one commodity as universal equivalent, convertible into any other commodity that is desired. Such, schematically, is Uno's version of the genesis of money. It differs from that of Marx, the immediate object of whose analysis is the articulation of the 'form' of value with its 'substance': labour-value. Here we remain in the sphere of 'desire' and 'evaluation' – in short, of comparison between use-values.

From money we are led dialectically to capital – to merchants' capital first of all, which is simply the commercial use of the money-commodity, or 'buying cheap and selling dear'; and finally to industrial capital. It emerges that capital

> cannot secure a firm foundation for its value-augmenting activity unless it goes a step further...capital must produce a commodity of higher value than that which it has purchased.[2]

It remains to demonstrate how this is possible.

Part Two – 'Production' – corresponds to the rest of Volume One and to Volume Two of *Capital*.

Uno casts the argument in an original form: he derives the necessity of the category of labour-value from an analysis of the capitalist production process. In order for his labour-power to endure, the wage-earner must receive the equivalent of an output corresponding to the time required for its reproduction – for example, a wage of $3 representing six hours of work. For these $3 he *must* receive 6 hours' output from capitalists in the consumer goods sectors. If he received less, the employers of his branch would lose out, since they sell 6 hours' output at $3. In short, the coherence of the capitalist system assumes that products exchange according to the socially-necessary labour-time required for their production. Labour and capital mobility, characteristic of the industrial capitalist order, ensures that this is indeed the norm governing exchange.

Furthermore, Uno reorganises the content of Volumes One and Two. Thus, he expands the field of the section on reproduction. In it, he regroups the set of structural problems dealt with by Marx in Volume One: the issue of accumulation, he explains, cannot be considered earlier, because it assumes that the notions of fixed and circulating capital have been introduced (in the section on Circulation). Uno can thus conjointly tackle the issues of the organic composition of capital and relative overproduction as elements of cyclical crisis. In addition, he stresses the theoretical need to differentiate endogenous forms of overproduction from those bound up with the relationship between capitalism and other forms of society. As for the reproduction schemata, he believes that they are intended to 'show how the basic process of capitalist production can be formulated in terms appropriate to the social material basis common to all societies'.[3] Against theoreticians who derive capitalist crisis

---

2 Uno 1980, p. 15.
3 Itoh 1980, p. 137.

from a surplus of commodities, Uno maintains (and had done so since 1932) that these schemata cannot demonstrate the inevitability of crisis.

The third part – 'Distribution' – corresponds to Volume Three of *Capital*. Let us focus on two points.

Uno offers an especially rigorous analysis of the tendency for the rate of profit to fall. In particular, he once again shows how, in his analysis of 'counter-tendencies' to this law, Marx intermingled endogenous and other elements. Since the latter concern the relations between capitalist society and different types of society, they cannot pertain to the pure theory of capitalism.

Uno proposes an interpretation of cyclical crises in terms of overaccumulation of capital, in line with an approach that integrates the relations between employment, wages, profits, and interest.[4] During the expansionary phase, he explains, capitalists are impelled to engage not in innovation, but in extensive development, by employing new wage-earners – until the point when, as a result of the growing demand for labour, wages increase and eat into profits. There thus occurs a 'condition of excess capital', wherein the accumulation of additional capital yields no additional profit. The fall in the profit rate triggers an increase in interest rates. And it is only when the crisis has broken out that, in the depressive phase, new methods are introduced as a new surplus production develops. In his *Value and Crisis*, Makoto Itoh relies on an expanded version of this model.

Pure theory and real history

Uno's texts on the stages of capitalism and on contemporary society have not as yet been translated from the Japanese. However, we possess three works, very different in character, which give us some access to the more general views of the Uno school: the books by Itoh, Sekine and Albritton.

Robert Albritton's book *A Japanese Reconstruction of Marxism* (1986) is the only work currently available that presents Uno's theory in its various aspects and compares it with the different perspectives of 'Western Marxism' (Lukács, Althusser, Colletti).

The articulation between 'stages' and purely capitalist society is based on the idea that the latter defines a system in which the law of the market com-

[4] See Uno 1980, pp. 87–9.

pletely and directly governs production. In the first age of capitalism, capital's control over production is only indirect, because production is still that of the former domestic economy. In the age of liberalism, the model is fully realised, the light industrial production characteristic of it being fully attuned to the exigencies of a competitive market structure. With imperialism, it is the type of production that changes in the first instance: the need for sizeable fixed capital and heavy, long-term fixed assets calls for the establishment of 'finance-capital'. The law of the market retreats in the face of state intervention, which is protectionist and aggressive.

Albritton offers some clarification of the significance of the distinction between analytical levels. A study of petty-commodity production of cotton in Uganda at the beginning of the twentieth century[5] involves a careful distinction between what pertains to the general form of capitalist relations of production, the particular stage of its development (imperialism, with the partition of Africa, the establishment of a periphery, and so on), and the specific historical context (cultural, technical, etc.). Likewise with the study of crises. Highly distinct types of necessity attach to these three levels. The order of pure theory is that of strictly necessary relations – for example, between commodities and money, wages and surplus-value, value and production prices. At the level of stages, the 'material contingency' of particular forms of use-value intervenes. The necessity characteristic of real relations and the propositions that encapsulate them (for instance, between heavy industry and finance-capital) cannot be of the same kind. There is even less possibility of formulating necessary relations when dealing with a properly 'historical' study, which considers a singular phenomenon with its extra-economic dimensions and conjunctural situation.

We may add that for Albritton, as for Uno, Marx's theory is essentially valid for capitalism and that the notion of historical materialism as a 'science of history' based on the notion of 'mode of production' is explicitly rejected. In this extensive sense, Marxism is conceived as an 'enlightened ideology',[6] based on the only thing that merits the title of 'science' – the pure theory of capitalism.

To this general presentation Albritton adds a more personal contribution, concerning the conception of the superstructure in the pure theory. In

---

5 See Albritton 1986, pp. 122–4.
6 Sekine 1984, p. 4.

doing so, he takes up a project of Uno's, which neither he nor his successors accomplished.[7] This is a difficult undertaking, because if the market wholly regulates such a society, the state seems superfluous. Albritton believes he can resolve the problem by suggesting that the *Rechtsstaat*, mediator between legal subjects linked by contractual relations, corresponds to a 'purely capitalist society':

> [t]he capitalist state form must be derived from the legal subject posited by the circulation of commodities and not from the realm of production where class always lurks behind the factory walls.[8]

The state is said to manifest itself as a relation of domination at the level of the stages and history.

Professor at York University in Canada, Thomas Sekine (to whom Albritton refers constantly) is the principal mediator between the Unoist tradition and European and American Marxism. Translator of Uno, he has appended to the author's text a study of his epistemology. Moreover, he has published a monumental work, *The Dialectic of Capital* (1984 and 1986), whose 500 pages form a methodical commentary on the *Principles of Political Economy*. Sekine reformulates the theory in the language of modern mathematics and brings out its underlying Hegelian framework. To this day, Sekine's book is the standard reference on Uno's *œuvre* for Western readers. Its ambition is considerable. Sekine aims to show that Uno has strictly modelled the plan of his treatise on that of Hegel's *Logic* and to display this correspondence term by term: *Circulation = Being*, where: commodity = quality, money = quantity, capital = money. Then *Production = Essence*, where: production of capital = foundation, circulation of capital = appearance, reproduction = **[effectivity]**. Finally, *Distribution = Concept*, where price of production = subjective concept, profit-rent = objective concept, profit-interest = Idea.

Each point is argued at length by Sekine, who presses beyond to a third triadic level. There is nothing surprising about this bi-univocal correspondence, he explains, for *Capital* occupies the same place in Marx's theory as does the *Logic* in Hegel's. It deals with the concrete universal synthesised theoretically, as opposed to its historical empirical realisation. Only Marx replaces the Abso-

---

[7] See Mawatari 1985, p. 407.

[8] Albritton 1986, p. 154.

lute Subject by capital.[9] The difficulties seem to me to be legion here, arising not so much from Sekine's text, whose dialectical subtlety appears infinite, but (as we shall see) from Uno's own views on the nature of the adequate exposition of the theory.

Makoto Itoh's work *Value and Crisis* (1980) is quite different in style. The author, an economics professor at Tokyo University and one of the acknowledged leaders of the Uno school, offers an original account of crisis theory.

In a recent article by Matawari, readers will find a detailed balance-sheet of the research conducted and the results obtained by the Unoists.[10] Uno is credited with having reformulated a certain number of basic notions in an original fashion: measure of value, money, reproduction, price of production, credit, interest, crises. These indications stimulated a veritable research programme, on the basis of which a whole generation of authors has worked.[11] Study has also focused on the 'stages', intersecting here with a different problematic that emerged very early on in Japan and independently – that of 'world capitalism', according to which capitalism developed as a world system from the outset. But it is obviously the analysis of contemporary society that forms the ultimate object of this reflection. Tsutomu Ouchi's book, *State Monopoly Capitalism* (1970), of which a brief survey exists in English,[12] was at the centre of the discussion. It is based on the Unoist approach to crisis as a result of overaccumulation of capital, bound up with a fall in profits related to the increase in wages and lagging productivity. However, today this view is challenged from within the school itself.

Theory and dialectics in Kôzô Uno

Uno's theorisation, it seems to me, contains numerous problems. It has been amply discussed in Japan;[13] and it might be assumed that all the arguments have already been aired and that we are arriving at the discussion rather belatedly. Nevertheless, it seems to me to be useful to re-open it, for it refers

---

9 Sekine 1984, p. 35.
10 See Matawari 1985, pp. 407–8.
11 Matawari 1985, pp. 413–16.
12 See Ouchi 1982.
13 See Otani and Sekine 1987.

to some genuine problems in Marx's theory, which the solutions advanced by Uno, even when they have to be declined, serve to bring out.

The first difficulty stems from the plan of exposition of the 'pure theory'. Uno declares himself a supporter of a theoretical, not a historical, plan. He therefore dismisses the idea that the exposition should begin with 'simple commodity production', which has never existed as a system reproducing itself endogenously. For this reason, he prunes from Part One of *Capital* anything that relates to production, thus radicalising the approach of the *Grundrisse*, which starts from 'simple circulation' understood as the surface of capitalist society. As we have seen, Uno only broaches production (and labour-value) in his second part. In reality, however, it seems to me that he falls back into a different type of historico-logical approach, which leads 'dialectically' from commodity to money, to money hoarding, to commercial capital, and then to industrial capital. Or rather, the spring of this dialectic is, alternately, that of the discursive constitution of a given structure in its coherence (for instance, no commodity system without general equivalent) and that of a historical dynamic, wherein cumulative processes prepare the way for qualitative changes. Thus, the money amassed is available for a commercial purchase: 'money becomes capital'.[14] And this prepares the way for industrial capital, for capital can only ensure its own foundation by taking a 'further step', by producing a commodity of greater value than the one it purchased.[15]

This approach, which foregrounds structural description on the basis of a historicising suggestion, seems to me to be a regression compared with the one that Marx settles on in *Capital*, where the first moment tends to be defined as that of the market as structure of commodity *production in general* (not precapitalist). This point is crucial today.[16] We need to know whether the market, as relation of production, belongs specifically to capitalism and can only develop in capitalism; or whether, on the contrary, it constitutes a more general matrix, able to exist in a specific way in different types of society. The issue would be settled if it could be demonstrated that this concept of market can be developed in a categorially autonomous fashion. Uno closes this path: he 'dialectically' identifies the market form and capitalism.

---

14 Uno 1980, p. 12.
15 See Uno 1980, p. 15.
16 See Bidet 2000.

The second difficulty concerns the Unoist conception of the purely capitalist economy as an economy regulated exclusively by the market – that is to say, one in which individuals are 'moved' by the laws of the market, by impersonal relations of sheer self-interest, understood as purely objective relations between things. We would then have the capitalist valuing the worker as a means of production with its definite cost and productivity on one side, and the worker maximising his interest as a consumer on the other. The system as a whole would be 'self-determined' in the sense of 'self-regulating'.[17] Related to this is the reference to an abstract labour that is understood as impersonal and simple and, consequently, mobile.[18] The 'class struggle' would therefore be external to the theory of the purely capitalist society. In Uno's view, this pure theory can enlighten us on the eventuality, the inevitable character of class struggle, but the latter remains outside its field. It certainly defines exploitation as appropriation of the product of labour by the capitalist, but it takes it as an objective datum. Its own object is the description of the systematic relations connected with it – for example, the definition of the impact of a variation in one element on the system's other elements (such as the impact of a reduction in working hours on the profit rate). However, it might be that the significance of the concepts introduced by Marx stems from the fact that they are politico-economic in the strict sense: the 'socially-necessary labour-time' for production is itself determined in a social confrontation.

This definition of pure theory leads to a paradoxical articulation of the economic and the political. If the market regulates, there is no need for the state. Sekine goes so far as to write: 'The state clearly is an institution alien to capital.'[19] Albritton seeks a middle way that allots the determinations of the *Rechtsstaat* to the pure theory and those of the state as apparatus of domination to the theory of stages. This position is untenable. What Albritton understands as the *Rechtsstaat* is the set of juridico-political determinations inherent in commodity relations as such.[20] But the 'pure' theory of capitalism as a theory of capitalist exploitation implies that of a class state. In this sense, the contradiction between *Rechtsstaat* and class state must be posited as internal to a 'pure' theory.

---

[17] Albritton 1986, p. 40.
[18] See Uno 1980, p. 34.
[19] Uno 1980, p. 154.
[20] See Bidet 1987a and 1987b.

This difficulty leads to a final one: that of the articulation between pure theory and the theory of stages. An oscillation between two positions can be observed. Either there is a tendency to identify the situation defined by the pure theory with that realised by nineteenth-century liberalism, which in some sense is the classical phase. Or the pure theory is treated as the set of *necessary* relations internal to the capitalist structure as such. Defining pure capitalism by free competition conduces to the first interpretation; excluding class struggle to the second. As the latter hardly seems acceptable, we are led back to the first hypothesis, which attenuates the problematic of a 'pure' theory.

Whatever these uncertainties, it remains the case that Uno's enterprise reveals the urgency of various theoretical tasks, in respect of which the Marxist tradition exhibits many failings.

In the first place, there is the need to distinguish between the exposition of the general structure of capital and the exposition of the general history of capitalism. Marx certainly posited the principle of such a distinction, observing that the theory of capital was a precondition for the theory of its genesis ('primitive accumulation'). But a full study of the articulation of the two general problematics has not been carried out. It can only be conducted if the requirement of conceiving the structural totality on the one hand, and the historical totality on the other, as genuine theoretical objects (and not as mere raw material for paedagogical or encyclopaedic exposition) is accepted. In their way, this is what the schools of pure theory and 'world capitalism' do. This exigency is far from having been acknowledged in the Marxist tradition.

Secondly, there is the need for an adequate order of exposition, without which the categories remain undefined and the relations between the different structural levels (for instance, between market and capitalism) remain indeterminate.

Thirdly, we need an approach to the historical curve of the capitalist phenomenon starting out from its most 'profound' structural element: the market – with the conclusion (seemingly highly simplified by Uno) that what challenges the primacy of the market also puts capitalism itself in question.

Uno doubtless failed to meet any of these objectives satisfactorily. Yet he posed such problems in sufficient depth to inspire a re-elaboration of most of the major theoretical and historical themes of Marxism.

Chapter Forty

Raymond Williams

Jean-Jacques Lecercle

I

Raymond Williams's relationship to Marxism went through two phases, separated by a long interlude. The first was natural. It followed the contours of his class origins. Born in 1922 in a rural region of Wales, son of a Labour Party railwayman who was active in the 1926 General Strike (Williams describes this episode in his best novel, *Border Country*), his political engagement in the British workers' movement was, in a sense, natural. This phase culminated with his arrival at Cambridge University in 1939, where he joined the most active of the far-left groups, the Young Communists, and began his career in political and cultural journalism. In this period, Williams's Marxism was that of the Third International, determinist and dogmatic, and fed into a reductionist critique of the dominant liberal and reactionary trends in his discipline of literary studies. It was not long before Williams found these simplifications irksome. After the War, in which he served in field artillery, he did not renew his membership of the Communist Party of Great Britain, but remained loyal to his origins, becoming one of the British intellectuals from a working-class background viscerally attached to left-wing ideas – to their social origin. Politically, he was situated on the left of the labour movement. Intellectually, he was influenced by the school of literary criticism associated with the journal *Scrutiny* (around F.R. Leavis), which combined close reading with an attempt to reconstruct the canon on ethical bases (Leavis's best-known work was entitled *Revaluation*). The school was also concerned with popular culture (albeit in disapproving mode): Williams would remember this excursion off the beaten track.

The second phase began with the early 1960s. At the time, Williams was known as an historian and theoretician of culture. He studied literature not as a succession of great works – a canon – but as a cultural formation, determined by the history of the society in which it was inserted and determining it in return. This shift was of the greatest importance in that it subsequently gave rise to the discipline of 'cultural studies', of which Williams must be considered the creator. He was already the author of two authoritative works, *Culture and Society* (1957) and *The Long Revolution* (1961). These books contain references to Marxism, but somewhat in the fashion of a nostalgic passing acknowledgement. The situation changed radically towards the mid-1960s – a period in which British Marxism underwent a spectacular revival. First of all, because a core of indigenous Marxist historians began to produce outstanding works (for instance, E.P. Thompson, a friend of Williams, with his *The Making of the English Working Class* in 1963), but above all because on the ruins of the British Communist Party – abandoned after 1956 by the majority of its intellectuals – there arose a New Left, highly influential among intellectuals, whose organ was *New Left Review*. Thanks to this journal, resolutely internationalist in the cultural sphere, the British intelligentsia discovered Continental Marxism in its numerous varieties: courtesy of it, Lukács, Goldmann, Adorno, Gramsci, Althusser, and many others were translated and published. Williams participated in this development. He was a member of the editorial committee and wrote in the *Review*, whose positions he defended against the temptations of Anglocentric involution (from which Thompson, for example, was not immune: cf. his violent attack on Althusser). At the same time, he resumed political activity, and joined the Labour Party and the Campaign for Nuclear Disarmament. For Great Britain and its left-wing intellectuals (of whom Williams is archetypal), the 1960s (the 'swinging sixties') were prosperous years, both politically (election of a majority Labour government under Harold Wilson) and culturally (avant-garde theatre from Osborne to Pinter;

the Beatles; a prestigious cinema). Williams situated himself on the left of this Left: he resigned from the Labour Party because it was pursuing right-wing policies; in 1966, he participated in the solidarity campaign with Vietnam; and he was the editor of the *May Day Manifesto*, a political statement of the non-Communist radical Left. It was also in 1961 that he quit teaching in adult education (this professional experience nourished his theory of culture) and began to teach English literature at Cambridge University. There followed some classic academic studies, especially on theatre: *Modern Tragedy* in 1966, *Drama from Ibsen to Brecht* in 1968, and *The English Novel from Dickens to Lawrence* in 1970.

However, what marked Williams's work in this decade was a return to Marxism, but a return enriched by his reading of Goldmann, Althusser and Gramsci. The concepts of ideology and hegemony appeared in his writing and 'Marxified' his key concept of culture. A personal version of Marxism emerged, characterised by a form of humanism (his sympathy for Althusser reached a limit here) and a rejection of determinism (finding support in Goldmann and Gramsci, but also in Althusser, he rejected the vulgate of unlinear determination of the superstructure by the base): in short, a typically Anglo-American Marxism – that is, libertarian – stressing the capacity of agents to alter their conditions of existence, rather than social and cultural determinants. This Marxism, which is Williams's contribution to the tradition, ran counter to the dominant 'structuralist' version. Without slipping into a beatific humanism of the Garaudy variety, Williams, whose positions on this issue were close to Thompson's, emphasised the action of the individual subject against the constraints of structures, the imbrication of the personal and the political, and the central position of cultural and ideological formations in the social totality.

In the following decade, this conception of Marxism enabled Williams to make theoretical advances of major significance in two fields: that of culture (after *Communications* in 1962, *Television: Technology and Cultural Form* in 1973, *Keywords* in 1976, and *Culture* in 1981); and that of literary theory (*Marxism and Literature* in 1977 and *The Country and the City* in 1973). This is the respect in which Williams's *œuvre* matters to the Marxist tradition and has worn well with time. The last years of his life saw the publication of collections of articles (*Problems in Materialism and Culture* in 1980 and *The Politics of Modernism* in 1989), characterised, *inter alia*, by a robust defence of modernism and the avant-garde against the recent postmodernist wave. Raymond Williams died in 1988 at the age of 66.

2

Raymond Williams was, in the first instance, a theoretician of culture. In this area, his influence, combined with that of Richard Hoggart and the Centre for Contemporary Cultural Studies (CCCS) at Birmingham (directed for a time by another Marxist theoretician of culture, Stuart Hall), was immense. He paved the way for an entirely new discipline, in terms of subject-matter (para-literature, the media, fashion, popular arts) and methods (analysis of cultural formations, concerned not so much with works as their social conditions of production). And the shift that he thereby effected in return drastically altered his original discipline – literary studies – both in Great Britain and the United States (where his influence combined with that of Foucault to give birth to what is called 'cultural materialism' – a term coined by him). Textual and historical studies retreated in favour of 'critical theory' and new critical perspectives (feminist criticism, postcolonial criticism, gay criticism). Williams was not the only source of these developments, which drastically redrew the field (and sometimes provoked bewilderment). But his theory of culture was a major contributor to them.

This began with *Culture and Society*, seemingly a study in literary history, which opens with a famous account of the four modern senses of the word 'culture': (1) a state of mind (the fact of being 'cultivated'); (2) the intellectual development of society as a whole (people refer to 'high culture'); (3) the set of the arts (assigned to a ministry of the same name); and (4) a total way of life – material, intellectual, and spiritual (reference is made, for example, to the culture of the Dogon people). These four meanings do not represent an arbitrary slicing up of a semantic field: they sketch out a history, whose development in Great Britain from the end of the eighteenth century to the present is traced by Williams, in parallel with that of other keywords: 'industry', 'democracy', 'class'. Here we glimpse Williams's basic method, which is a historical semantics, painstakingly retracing the complex intellectual history of a society through that of its keywords. This first book, which was still Leavisite in inspiration, thus describes a British tradition, and still awards pride of place to T.S. Eliot (*Notes Towards a Definition of Culture*) and George Orwell, rather than to Marxism. A single chapter, entitled 'Marxism and Culture', discusses the Marxist theories of the 1930s, which have today sunk into oblivion (but it at least has the advantage of making amends for an injustice by devoting several pages to the Marxist aesthetician, Christopher Caudwell). In reality, it still reflects the sway of a certain idea of literature as the heart of culture (for Leavis, D.H. Lawrence's *œuvre* was the highest expression of high culture). The second book, *The Long Revolution*, pursued this path, but also effected the strategic displacement mentioned above. In it, culture is understood through the concept of *experience*. Culture is what determines and informs the experience of the subject; it is through experience that the subject appropriates culture, makes it living, and enriches it. Literature occupies an important place in this experience. By reading literary texts, my experience is constituted, in as much as it is not solipsistic but social, public and not private. But it is not the only site of experience and hence not necessarily the privileged form of culture. Like other forms of existence, it contributes to constructing human reality. In fact, there is in Williams an anticipatory echo of what would today be called constructivism (cf. Berger and Luckmann's *The Social Construction of Reality*, which likewise appeals to Marxism by way of the sociology of knowledge). '[A]ll our experience is a human version of the world we inhabit':[1] here we detect an echo of the phenomenologists' *Lebenswelt*.

But *The Long Revolution* also operates a strategic displacement, whereby Williams moves closer to classical Marxism and founds cultural studies. The second part of the book is devoted to an institutional history and critique, in the vein of the 'social history' in which the British excel. The chapter titles might seem banal today, but they were not at the time: the role of the educational apparatus; the history of the reading public; the popular press; 'Standard English' (this is the first appearance of what has become a rich linguistic tradition in Great Britain, proximate to Marxism – for instance, Fairclough's *Language and Power* – in which we hear Bourdieusian accents *avant la lettre*); the social history of the notion of the author, but also of dramatic forms. The third part is a historico-political analysis of the situation of Great Britain in the 1960s (a theme that at first sight pertains more to a Central Committee report than a treatise in literary history). We thus realise that we have graduated

---

1 Williams 1961, p. 34.

from the Leavisite concept of 'revaluation' to that of 'revolution' (in the conditions and means of cultural production), even if it is characterised as 'long', different social strata and cultural formations having their own peculiar history. We have shifted from analysing the *œuvre* and the intended meanings (the culture) of its author – that is to say, from literary history as a history of *œuvres* and movements, to that of institutions, of forms as embodiments of institutions, and of different types of medium: in short, to the analysis of the collective conditions of production of works. This continued with *Communications* and *Television*, where Williams, anticipating the discipline today known as media studies, places the media at the centre of the analysis – even if his analysis in *Communications* is now dated, for want of an explicit Marxist theorisation and undue reliance on American empiricist sociology.

In the final phase, when Williams was explicitly Marxist, the concept of culture remained at the centre of his concerns and was not conflated with that of ideology (despite the reproach by Terry Eagleton, the leading British Marxist literary critic). *Marxism and Literature* begins with a definition of the word 'culture' in terms of 'cultural materialism' – a category invoked in response to the aporiae of the reduction of superstructure to base – that is to say, as the name of a constitutive social process, producing general 'forms of life' that have a material origin, but in which the subject fashions the experience of his or her reality. The book proceeds to a programmatic description of a Marxist sociology of culture, whose key concept is 'structure of feeling', to which I shall return.

3

One aspect of Williams's *œuvre* is generally neglected. Yet it is essential, for it underlies all the others: the analysis of language. It is easy to see why it has been neglected. Williams was formed within a culture in which linguistics occupied a marginal position. He only read Saussure later and was distrustful of what he had read (he spoke of Saussurean reductionism). As for Chomsky, his influence had not yet made itself felt and this was to the advantage of Williams, whose implicit philosophy of language is at the antipodes of the Cartesian innatism and speculative psychology of faculties that underlines the cognitivist programme. Moreover, as is well known, the Marxist tradition long neglected the question of language, making do with endless quotations from *The German Ideology*, or from the solid good sense of the pseudo-Stalin (*Marxism and Linguistics*). At a time when the discipline was still very much in limbo, Williams therefore had to put together a *historical semantics* that seems to me still to be of the very greatest interest today.

The idea is simple. Language (or rather a natural language, in a historical conjuncture) is the sedimentation of the history and culture of the community of its speakers. It is a question not only of recognising that words have a history (etymology exists for that purpose), but of arguing that they are solidified history and that they help to make history. In linguistics, such a position will readily be taken to be reactionary. Formalism has triumphed, synchrony has been elevated to the status of a principle, and Saussurean *langue* is today regarded as a stock of rules, not of words. Williams, who pays no attention to linguistics (this is what distinguishes him, in literary criticism and outside it, from structuralism), proposes a philosophy of language that has a pedigree (for instance, in Horne Tooke, the Jacobin philosopher of language of the late eighteenth century – see his *Epea Pteroenta, or the Diversions of Purley*). For him, words are the embodiment of the collective experience that makes up a culture: it is through words that the subject constitutes her experience in so far as it is irreducibly individual (it is I who speak) and collective (I speak with the words of the tribe; I am therefore also spoken by them). In this respect, Williams's treatment of the concept of culture is revealing: he provides no stipulative definition of it. In truth, he provides no definition full stop. Instead, he describes the weaving of the historical threads that constitute its meaning. Williams's theory of culture is, in the first instance, an uncovering of the history of the word 'culture'.

This is why *Keywords* (whose sub-title is 'A Vocabulary of Culture and Society') is not a minor excursion in dictionary-writing, but the heart of Williams's theory of culture and society. (This insistence on the role of language, of vocabulary, is typical of postwar British culture – see, for example, the Wittgensteinians, for whom philosophical problems are basically grammatical problems.) He began the book as a terminological appendix to *Culture and Society*, which the publisher rejected for reasons of space. He only published it after much rumination in 1976, at the moment when his theory of culture had reached maturity. In it, he defined the specificity of his intervention in the theoretical discussion of the 1970s, in particular within Marxism, by defining his conception of historical semantics:

> The kind of semantics to which these notes and essays belong is one of the tendencies within *historical semantics*, where the theoretical problems are indeed acute but where even more fundamental theoretical problems must be seen as at issue. The emphasis on history, as a way of understanding contemporary problems of meaning and structures of meaning, is a basic choice from a position of historical materialism rather than from the now more powerful positions of objective idealism or non-historical (synchronic) structuralism. This is an exploration...not [of] a *tradition* to be learned, nor a *consensus* to be accepted, nor a set of meanings which, because it is 'our language', has a natural authority, but as a shaping and reshaping in real circumstances and from profoundly different and important points of view: a vocabulary to use, to find our own ways in, to change as we find it necessary to change it, as we go on making our own language and history.[2]

Here we are at the heart of Williams's thinking and we can understand why language plays such a crucial role in it. His overriding concern is the subject's capacity to alter her conditions of existence, to change the world, and hence to construct personal experience in, with, and against a collective experience. This is the natural situation of speakers appropriating the language in order to express their meanings in it.

This conception of language has immediate consequences for literary criticism. It allows Williams to expand the concept of style and to apply it outside the literary or even artistic field (something that has had an impact on cultural studies: cf. Dick Hebdige's *Subculture*). For Williams, style is not only the characteristic of an individual way of appropriating the language, but a collective form of *parole*, expressing the fact that, for generation after generation, the way speakers inhabit their language changes, with changing historical conditions of production of utterances. At the same time, each speaker, in the style of their generation, constructs her own style. As we can see, here style is another name for the place where the individual is articulated with the collective.

---

[2] Williams 1976, pp. 20–2.

4

Despite the displacement that gave rise to cultural studies (I am not sure that Williams would take pride in some of his American offspring), the privileged terrain of his reflection was literature. This is where he began and this is where, in his mature phase, he produced what is perhaps his masterpiece: *The Country and the City*. And this is where he developed his most celebrated concept – 'structure of feeling'.

We shall begin once again with the notion of style: the content of a collective style, which marks the historicity of language, is a 'structure of feeling'. It is there that subjects conduct their individual appropriation of the collective culture and this is where they construct their reality, in interaction with other subjects and with the institutions that constrain this construction. The structure of feeling is what constitutes the experience of the subject. The expression is deliberately paradoxical; it is the very embodiment of the paradox that I have already described and which is at the heart of Williams's thinking. Stage left, we have feelings, experienced by individuals, whose experience they constitute ('characteristic elements of impulse, restraint, and tone; specifically affective elements of consciousness and relationships: not feelings against thought, but thought as felt and feeling as thought: practical consciousness of a present kind, in living and inter-related continuity').[3] Stage right, we have structures, which have a collective existence, are embodied in the collective medium that is language, and which are therefore public, the object of relations and tensions, and intervene in the construction of relations of forces ('[w]e are... defining these elements as a "structure": as a set, with specific internal relations, at once interlocking and in tension').[4] The result is Williams's dialectic of the social and the individual, the private and the public:

> We are also defining a social experience which is still *in process*, often indeed not yet recognised as social but taken to be private, idiosyncratic, and even isolating, but which in analysis... has its emergent, connecting, and dominant characteristics, indeed its specific hierarchies.[5]

---

[3] Williams 1977, p. 132.
[4] Ibid.
[5] Ibid.

This is the concept that shapes *The Country and the City*, a history of English literature conceived as a *tradition* (a concept dear to Eliot, such as his 'Tradition and the Individual Talent' – but which is given a new content here: the series of structures of feeling): that of the relations between city and country. It is difficult to do justice in a few lines to this panorama, which analyses the sequence of works, genres and styles within the history of the social relations between country and city, from poems celebrating country houses that constitute English pastoral in the seventeenth century, up to the city of the 1930s, such as it appears in the novels of George Orwell (to whom Williams devoted a study in 1971). For there is in fact a literary reflection on the city in mid-century England, a Marxist version of which is to be found in the novels of Patrick Hamilton.

5

Experience, tradition, style, structure of feeling, culture: these are rather unusual Marxist concepts. They justify the description of Williams's *œuvre* as neo-Marxism. But he would doubtless have rejected it, for he was strict about principles. In any event, they have the great advantage of restoring centre-stage what Marxist analysis has habitually expelled to the margins: language, literature, and culture. And they furnish an original solution – one much more faithful to the sources than the reconstructions, inspired by methodological individualism, of Anglo-American analytical Marxism – to the problem of the relations between the individual and the collective, the personal and the political, the superstructural and the infrastructural. Since his death in 1988, Williams's reputation has certainly waned: a certain abstractness of style and conceptual imprecision account for this. He produced no systematic exposition of his thought that does not take the form of popularisation. Enthusiasts for cultural studies and cultural materialists, who owe him an enormous debt, have divested themselves of him as a historical figure, to whom it is enough to raise one's hat. It is normal for epigones to wish to kill the father. But it is him, with his venerable white beard, who will always hold the attention of the sculptor.

Notes on Contributors

Tony **Andréani** is professor emeritus of political science at the University of Paris-Saint-Denis. He is the author of *Le socialisme est (à)venir* (2 vols, Paris, 2001–2004).

Jacques **Bidet** is Professor Emeritus of Philosophy at the University of Paris-Nanterre. His recent publications include *Explication et reconstruction du 'Capital'* (Paris, 2004), *Exploring Marx's* Capital (Leiden, 2007) and, with Gérard Duménil, *Altermarxisme: Un autre marxisme pour un autre monde* (Paris, 2007).

Christopher **Bertram** teaches philosophy at the university of Bristol and was, until recently, the editor of *Imprints*. He is the author of *Rousseau and the Social Contract* (London, 2003).

Paul **Blackledge** teaches social and political theory at Leeds Metropolitan University. His recent publications include *Reflections on the Marxist Theory of History* (Manchester, 2006).

Alex **Callinicos** is Professor of European Studies at King's College London. His recent publications include *An Anti-Capitalist Manifesto* (Cambridge, 2003) and *Resources of Critique* (Cambridge, 2006).

Robert **Carter** teaches sociology at the University of Warwick. He is the author of *Realism and Racism: Concepts of Race in Sociological Research* (London, 2000) and, with Alison Sealey, of *The Limits of Language: Applied Linguistics as Social Science* (London, 2004).

Vivek **Chibber** teaches sociology at New York University. He is the author of *Locked in Place: State-Building and Late Industrialization in India* (Princeton, 2003).

Thomas **Coutrot** is a researcher at the DARES (Paris) and the author of *Capitalisme ou démocratie* (Paris, 2005).

Frédérick Guillaume **Dufour** is postdoctoral researcher in sociology at the Université du Québec à Montréal. He has been visiting scholar in international relations at Sussex University and at the Center for Social Theory and Comparative History (UCLA).

Gérard **Duménil** is senior researcher at the CNRS (France). His recent publications include *Capitalism Resurgent: Roots of the Neoliberal Revolution* (London, 2004, with Dominique Lévy).

Fabio **Frosini** is a researcher in philosophy at the university of Urbino. He is the author of *Gramsci e la filosofia. Saggio sui 'Quaderni del carcere'* (Rome, 2003) and the co-editor, with Guido Liguori, of *Le parole di Gramsci. Per un lessico dei 'Quaderni del carcere'* (Rome, 2004).

Isabelle **Garo** teaches philosophy in Lille. She is the author of *Marx, une critique de la philosophie* (Paris, 2003).

Jean-Marie **Harribey** teaches economy at the University of Bordeaux IV and is currently chair of ATTAC France. His recent publications include *La Démence sénile du capital: Fragments d'économie critique* (Bordeaux, 2004).

Rémy **Herrera** is a researcher at the CNRS (Centre d'Economie de la Sorbonne, University of Paris I, Panthéon-Sorbonne). He is coordinator of the World Forum for Alternatives (presided by Samir Amin).

Michel **Husson** is a researcher in political economy at the IRES in Paris. He is the author of *Les casseurs de l'Etat social* (Paris, 2003) and the *Le grand bluff capitaliste* (Paris, 2001).

Bob **Jessop** teaches sociology at the University of Lancaster. His recent publications include *The Future of the Capitalist State* (Cambridge, 2002) and *State Power* (Cambridge, 2007).

Jim **Kincaid** is a researcher in political economy. He edited the symposium on Christopher J. Arthur's 'The New Dialectic and Marx's *Capital*' in *Historical Materialism* 13/2 2005.

Stathis **Kouvelakis** teaches political theory at King's College London. He is the author of *Philosophy and Revolution. From Kant to Marx* (London, 2003) and the co-editor, with Sebastian Budgen and Slavoj Žižek of *Lenin Reloaded. Towards a Politics of Truth* (Durham, 2007).

Jean-Jacques **Lecercle** teaches linguistics and literature at the University of Paris-Nanterre. He is the author of *A Marxist Philosophy of Language* (Leiden, 2006).

Dominique **Lévy** is senior researcher at the CNRS (France). His recent publications include *Capitalism Resurgent: Roots of the Neoliberal Revolution* (London, 2004, with Gérard Duménil).

Neil **Lazarus** teaches English and comparative literatures at the University of Warwick. His recent publications include *Marxism, Modernity and Postcolonial Studies* (Cambridge, 2002) and the *Cambridge Companion to Postcolonial Literary Studies* (Cambridge, 2004).

Esther **Leslie** teaches political aesthetics at Birkbeck College (London). Her recent publications include *Walter Benjamin* (London, 2007).

Michael **Löwy** is an emeritus researcher at the CNRS and teaches at the EHESS. His recent publications include *Fire Alarm. Reading Walter Benjamin's 'On the Concept of History'* (London, 2006).

François **Matheron** teaches philosophy in Paris and is the editor of Louis Althusser's *Ecrits philosophique et politiques* (2 vols, Paris, 1994–1995).

Roberto **Nigro** teaches philosophy at Michigan State University and is the editor of Michel Foucault, *Anthropology from a Pragmatic Point of View* (Los Angeles, 2007).

Gérard **Raulet** teaches the history of ideas in Germany at the University of Paris Sorbonne. His recent publications include *Positive Barbarei. Kulturphilosophie und Politik bei Walter Benjamin* (Münster, 2004) and *Critical Cosmology. Essays on Nations and Globalization* (Lanham MD, 2005).

Jason **Smith** has taught at Occidental College and California Institute of the Arts, and currently teaches philosophy at the Art Center College of Design. He is working on a manuscript on Jacques Derrida.

André **Tosel** is Professor Emeritus at the University of Nice. His recent publications include *Etudes sur Marx (et sur Engels)* (Paris, 1996) and *Les marxismes du 20e siècle* (forthcoming in 2008).

Alberto **Toscano** teaches sociology at Goldsmith College (London). He is the author of *The Theatre of Production: Philosophy And Individuation Between Kant And Deleuze* (London, 2006).

Maria **Turchetto** teaches political science at the University of Venice and the editor of *Althusseriana,* the journal of the Italian Louis Althusser Association.

Rashmi **Varma** teaches postcolonial literatures and theory and feminist theory at the University of Warwick. Her most recent publications include the co-edited *McGraw-Hill Anthology of Women Writing Globally in English* (2007), and an essay on feminist theory and critical race studies in *The Cambridge Companion to Feminist Theory* (2006).

Jean-Marie **Vincent** (1934–2004) was Professor of Political Science at the University of Paris-Saint-Denis and the author of many books on the Frankfurt school and Marxism, including *Abstract Labour: A Critique* (New York, 1991).

Bibliography

Abraham, Nicolas & Maria Torok 1986, *The Wolf Man's Magic Word: A Cryptonomy*, trans. Nicolas Rand, Minneapolis: University of Minnesota Press.

Ackard, Patrick 1992, 'Corporate Mobilization and Political Power: The Transformation of U.S. Economic Policy in the 1970s', *American Sociological Review*, 57, 5: 597–615.

Actuel Marx 1997a, *Habermas, une politique déliberative*, Volume 24, Paris: Presses Universitaires de France.

Actuel Marx 1997b, *Marx, Wittgenstein, Arendt, Habermas*, Volume 25, Paris: Presses Universitaires de France.

Actuel Marx 2000, *L'hégémonie américaine*, Volume 27, Paris: Presses Universitaires de France.

Adorno, Theodor Wiesengrund 1973, *Negative Dialectics*, London: Routledge.

Aglietta, Michel 1979 [1976], *A Theory of Capitalist Regulation: The US Experience*, translated by David Fernbach, London: New Left Books.

Aglietta, Michel 1995, *Macroéconomie financière*, Paris: La Découverte.

Aglietta, Michel 1998, *Le Capitalisme de demain*, Paris: Note de la Fondation Saint-Simon.

Aglietta, Michel & Robert Boyer 1982, 'Une industrie compétitive en France et dans le monde', in *Une politique industrielle pour la France*, Paris: Ministère de la Recherche et de l'Industrie.

Ahmad, Aijaz 1992, *In Theory: Classes, Nations, Literatures*, London: Verso.

Albert, Michael & Robin Hahnel 1991, *The Political Economy of Participatory Economics*, Princeton: Princeton University Press.

Albiac, Gabriel 1998 [1997], 'Althusser, Reader of Althusser: Autobiography as Fictional Genre', translated by Christine Campbell, *Rethinking Marxism*, 10, 3: 80–9.

Albritton, Robert 1986, *A Japanese Reconstruction of Marxist Theory*, London: Macmillan.

Albritton, Robert & Thomas Sekine (eds.) 1995, *The Japanese Approach to Political Economy: Unoist Variations*, London: Macmillan.

Albritton, Robert et al. (eds.) 2001, *Phases of Capitalist Development: Booms, Crises and Globalization*, London: Palgrave.

Ali, Tariq 2006. *Pirates of the Caribbean: Axis of Hope*. London: Verso.

Allen, Theodor W. 2002, 'On Roediger's *Wages of Whiteness*', *Cultural Logic*, 4: 2.

Alquati, Romano 1962, 'Composizione organica del capitale e forza-lavoro alla Olivetti', *Quaderni Rossi*, 2: 63–98.

Alquati, Romano 1976, 'Università, formazione della forza-lavoro e terziarizzazione', *Aut aut*, 154.

Althusser, Louis 1966, 'Matérialisme historique and matérialisme dialectique', *Cahiers marxistes-léninistes*, 11: 90–122.

Althusser, Louis 1969a [1965], *For Marx*, translated by Ben Brewster, London: Allen Lane.

Althusser, Louis 1969b, 'How to Read Marx's *Capital*', *Marxism Today*, October: 302–5.

Althusser, Louis & Étienne Balibar 1970 [1965], *Reading 'Capital'*, translated by Ben Brewster, London: New Left Books.

Althusser, Louis 1971a, *Lenin and Philosophy and Other Essays*, translated by Ben Brewster, London: New Left Books.

Althusser, Louis, 1971b, 'Ideology and Ideological State Apparatuses', in Althusser 1971a.

Althusser, Louis 1972, *Politics and History: Montesquieu, Rousseau, Hegel and Marx*, translated by Ben Brewster, London: New Left Books.

Althusser, Louis 1976, *Essays in Self-Criticism*, translated by Graham Locke, London: New Left Books.

Althusser, Louis 1978, 'What Must Change in the Party', translated by Patrick Camiller, *New Left Review*, I, 109: 19–45.

Althusser, Louis 1979 [1977], 'The Crisis of Marxism', trans. Grahame Lock, in *Il Manifesto, Power and Opposition in Post-Revolutionary Societies*, London: Ink Links.

Althusser, Louis 1984, *Essays on Ideology*, translated by Ben Brewster and Graham Lock, London: New Left Books.

Althusser, Louis 1990, *Philosophy and the Spontaneous Philosophy of the Scientists and Other Essays*, translated by Ben Brewster et al., London: Verso.

Althusser, Louis 1991 [1977], 'On Marx and Freud', translated by Warren Montag, *Rethinking Marxism*, 4, 1: 17–30.

Althusser, Louis 1993 [1992], *The Future Lasts a Long Time* and *The Facts*, translated by Richard Veasey, London: Chatto & Windus.

Althusser, Louis 1994a, *Écrits philosophiques et politiques. Tome I*, Paris: Stock/IMEC.

Althusser, Louis 1994b, 'Marx dans ses limites', in Althusser 1994a.

Althusser, Louis 1994c, 'Lettre à Merab', in in Althusser 1994a.

Althusser, Louis 1995a, *Écrits philosophiques et politiques. Tome II*, Paris: Stock/IMEC.

Althusser, Louis 1995b, *Sur la reproduction*, Paris: Presses Universitaires de France.

Althusser, Louis 1996a, *Pour Marx*: Paris: La Découverte.

Althusser, Louis 1996b, *Psychanalyse et sciences humaines*, Paris: Le Livre de Poche.

Althusser, Louis 1996c [1993], *Writings on Psychoanalysis: Freud and Lacan*, translated by Jeffrey Mehlman, New York: Columbia University Press.

Althusser, Louis 1997 [1994], *The Spectre of Hegel: Early Writings*, London: Verso.

Althusser, Louis 1998, *Lettres à Franca*, Paris: Stock/IMEC.

Althusser, Louis 1999a [1995], *Machiavelli and Us*, translated by Gregory Elliott, London: Verso.

Althusser, Louis 1999b [1988], 'Machiavelli's Solitude', in Althusser 1999a.

Althusser, Louis 2003 [1995], *The Humanist Controversy and Other Writings*, London: Verso.

Althusser, Louis et al. 1996 [1965], *Lire 'Le Capital'*, Paris: Presses Universitaires de France.

Altvater, Elmar 1992, *Des Preis des Wohlstands, oder Umweltplünderung und neue Welt(un)ordnung*, Münster: Verlag Westfälisches Dampfboot.

Altvater, Elmar 1993 [1991], *The Future of the Market: An Essay on the Regulation of Money and Nature after the Collapse of 'Actually Existing Socialism'*, translated by Patrick Camiller, London: Verso.

Altvater, Elmar 1997, 'Les contradictions de l'économie politique libérale dans un monde de ressources naturelles fini. Coûts globaux de cette société industrielle', *Page 2*, 8–9: 23–39.

Altvater, Elmar & Birgit Mahnkopf 1999, *Die Grenzen der Globalisierung*, Münster: Westfälisches Dampfboot.

Amin, Samir 1974 [1970], *Accumulation on a World Scale: A Critique of the Theory of Underdevelopment*, translated by Brian Pearce, New York: Monthly Review Press.

Amin, Samir 1976 [1973], *Unequal Development: An Essay on the Social Formations of Peripheral Capitalism*, translated by Brian Pearce, Hassocks: Harvester Press.

Amin, Samir 1978 [1973], *The Law of Value and Historical Materialism*, translated by Brian Pearce, New York: Monthly Review Press.

Amin, Samir 1980 [1979], *Class and Nation Historically and in the Current Crisis*, translated by Susan Kaplow, London: Heinemann Educational.

Amin, Samir 1990 [1985], *Delinking: Towards a Polycentric World*, translated by Michael Wolfers, London: Zed Press.

Amin, Samir 1994 [1993], *Rereading the Postwar Period: An Intellectual Itinerary*, translated by Michael Wolfers, New York: Monthly Review Press.

Amin, Samir 1996, *Les défis de la mondialisation*, Paris: L'Harmattan.
Amin, Samir 1997. *Capitalism in the Age of Globalization: The Management of Contemporary Society*, New York: Monthly Review Press.
Amin, Samir, Giovanni Arrighi, André Gunder Frank, & Immanuel Wallerstein 1982, *Dynamics of World Crisis*, New York: Monthly Review Press.
Amin, Samir, Giovanni Arrighi, André Gunder Frank, & Immanuel Wallerstein 1990, *Transforming the Revolution: Social Movements and the World-System*, New York: Monthly Review Press.
Amin, Samir & Rémy Herrera 2000, 'El Sur en el sistema mundial en transformación', *Marx Ahora*, 10: 161–78.
Amin, Samir & Rémy Herrera 2005, 'Fifty Years After the Bandung Conference: Towards a Revival of the Solidarity Between the Peoples of the South?', *Inter-Asia Cultural Studies*, 6, 4: 546–56.
Anderson, Benedict 1991 [1983], *Imagined Communities: Reflections on the Origins and Spread of Nationalism*, Rev. edn., London: Verso.
Anderson, Perry 1966, 'Socialism and Pseudo-Empiricism', *New Left Review*, I, 35: 2–42.
Anderson, Perry 1972, 'Introduction to Glucksmann', *New Left Review*, I, 72: 61–7.
Anderson, Perry 1976, *Considerations on Western Marxism*, London: New Left Books.
Anderson, Perry 1979, *Lineages of the Absolutist State*, London: Verso.
Anderson, Perry 1980, *Arguments within English Marxism*, London: Verso.
Anderson, Perry 1983, *In the Tracks of Historical Materialism*, London: Verso.
Anderson, Perry 1992a, *A Zone of Engagement*, London: Verso.
Anderson, Perry 1992b, *English Questions*, London: Verso.
Anderson, Perry 1992c [1987], 'The Figures of Descent', in *English Questions*, London: Verso.
Anderson, Perry 1992d [1964], 'Origins of the Present Crisis', in *English Questions*, London: Verso.
Anderson, Perry 1993, 'Maurice Thompson's War', *London Review of Books*, 4 November: 13–17.
Anderson, Perry 1998a, 'Introduction', *New Left Review*, I, 229: i–v.
Anderson, Perry 1998b, *The Origins of Postmodernity*, London: Verso.
Anderson, Perry 2005. *La pensée tiède*. Paris: Seuil.
Andréani, Tony 1996, 'Un socialisme pour demain', in *Congrès Marx international*, Paris: Presses Universitaires de France.
Andréani, Tony 1999: 'Vers une issue socialiste à la crise du capitalisme', *Utopie critique*, 14.
Andréani, Tony 2004a, 'Les « modèles » du socialisme', *La Pensée*, 338: 73–93.
Andréani, Tony 2004b, *Le Socialisme est (a) venir*, Volume 2: *Les possibles*, Paris: Syllepse.
Andréani, Tony 2005, 'Socialisme et démocratie économique', *Utopie Critique*, 32: 59–74.
Andréani, Tony & Marc Féray 1993, *Discours sur l'égalité parmi les hommes. Penser l'alternative*, Paris: L'Harmattan.
Ansell-Pearson, Keith 1991, 'The Significance of Michel Foucault's Reading of Nietzsche: Power, the Subject, and Political Theory', *Nietzsche-Studien*, 20: 267–83.
Arato, Andrew & Paul Breines 1979, *The Young Lukács and the Origins of Western Marxism*, London: Pluto Press.
Archer, Margaret S. 1988, *Culture and Agency: The Place of Culture in Social Theory*, Cambridge: Cambridge University Press.
Arendt, Hannah 1963, *On Revolution*, London: Penguin.
Ariffin, Yohan 1996, 'The Return of Marx in International Relations Theory', *Economy and Society*, 25, 1: 127–34.
Arnason, Johann 1982, 'Prospettive e problemi del marxismo critico dell'Est Europeo', in *Storia del marxismo*, Volume 4, *Il Marxismo oggi*, edited by Eric Hobsbawm et al., Turin: Einaudi.
Aron, Raymond 1969, *D'une sainte famille à l'autre. Essai sur les marxismes imaginiares*, Paris: Gallimard.

Aronson, Ronald 1995, *After Marxism*, New York: The Guildford Press.
Arrighi, Giovanni 1970, 'Labour Supplies in Historical Perspective: A Study of the Proletarisation of the African Peasantry in Rhodesia', *Journal of Development Studies*, 3.
Arrighi, Giovanni 1978, *The Geometry of Imperialism*, London: New Left Books.
Arrighi, Giovanni 1994, *The Long Twentieth Century*, London: Verso.
Arrighi, Giovanni 1996, 'Capitalism and the Modern World-System: Rethinking the Non-Debates of the 1970s', American Sociological Association Meeting, New York.
Arthur, Christopher J. 1993, 'Hegel's *Logic* and Marx's *Capital*, in Moseley (ed.) 1993.
Arthur, Christopher J. 2002, *The New Dialectic and Marx's 'Capital'*, Leiden: Brill Academic Publishers.
Arthur, Christopher J. 2003, 'The Hegel-Marx Connection', *Historical Materialism* 11, 1: 185–94 and 195–8.
Arthur, Christopher J. & Geert Reuten (eds.) 1998, *The Circulation of Capital: Essays on Volume Two of 'Capital'*, London: Macmillan.
Artous, Antoine 1999, *Marx, l'État et la politique*, Paris: Editions Syllepse.
Assmann, Hugo & Franz Hinkelammert 1989, *A Idolatria do Mercado. Ensaio sobre economia e teologia*, San Paulo: Vozes.
Assmann, Hugo et al. 1980, *La lucha de los dioses. Los ídolos de la opresión y la búsqueda del Dios liberador*, San José (Costa Rica): DEI.
Assoun, Paul Laurent & Gérard Raulet 1968, *Marxisme et théorie critique*, Paris: Payot.
Aston, Trevor H. & Charles H.E. Philpin (eds.) 1985, *The Brenner Debate*, Cambridge: Cambridge University Press.
Babson, Steve 1995, *Lean Work: Empowerment and Exploitation in the Global Auto Industry*, Detroit: Wayne State University Press.
Backhaus, Hans-Georg 1997 [1968], *Dialektik der Wertform. Untersuchungen zur Marxschen Ökonomiekritik*, Freiburg: Ça ira.
Badoloni, Nicola 1962, *Marxismo come storicismo*, Milan: Feltrinelli.
Badaloni, Nicola 1971, *Il marxismo italiano degli anni Sessanta*, Rome: Editori Riuniti.
Badaloni, Nicola 1972, *Per il comunismo. Questione di teoria*, Turin: Einaudi.
Badaloni, Nicola 1975, *Il marxismo di Gramsci: dal mito alla ricomposizione politica*, Turin: Einaudi.
Badaloni, Nicola 1988, *Il problema dell'immanenza nella filosofia politica di Antonio Gramsci*, Venice: Arsenale Editrice.
Badaloni, Nicola 1987, 'Gramsci e l'espansione della democrazia', in *Letture di Gramsci*, edited by Antonio A. Santucci, Rome: Editori Riuniti.
Badiou, Alain 1982, *Théorie du sujet*, Paris: Seuil.
Badiou, Alain 1984, 'La figure du (re)commencement', *Le Perroquet*, 42: 1/8–9.
Badiou, Alain 1985, *Peut-on penser la politique?*, Paris: Seuil.
Badiou, Alain 1986, 'L'usine comme site événementiel', *Le Perroquet* 62-63: 1-6.
Badiou, Alain 1987, 'À bas la société existante! (1)', *Le Perroquet* 69: 1–3.
Badiou, Alain 1991, 'L'être, l'événement, la militance' (interview with Nicole-Édith Thévenin), *Futur Antérieur*, 8, available at: <http://multitudes.samizdat.net/L-etre-l-evenement-la militance.html>.
Badiou, Alain 1992, *Conditions*, Paris: Seuil.
Badiou, Alain 1999, *Manifesto for Philosophy*, translated by Norman Madarasz, Albany: SUNY.
Badiou, Alain 2001, *Ethics*, translated by Peter Hallward, London: Verso.
Badiou, Alain 2003, 'Philosophy and the "Death of Communism"', in *Infinite Thought*, edited by Justin Clemens and Oliver Feltham, London: Continuum.
Badiou, Alain 2004, 'Hegel and the Whole', in *Theoretical Writings*, edited by Ray Brassier and Alberto Toscano, London: Continuum.
Badiou, Alain 2005a, *Metapolitics*, translated by Jason Barker, London: Verso.
Badiou, Alain 2005b, 'The Triumphant Restoration', translated by Alberto Toscano, *positions: east asia cultures critique*, 13, 3: 659–62.
Badiou, Alain 2006, *Being and Event*, translated by Oliver Feltham, London: Continuum.

Badiou, Alain 2007, *The Century*, translated by Alberto Toscano, Cambridge: Polity.
Bahr, Ehrhard 1970, *Georg Lukács*, Berlin: Colloquium.
Bakker, Isabella & Stephen Gill (eds.) 2003, *Power, Production and Social Reproduction*, Basingstoke: Palgrave.
Balibar, Étienne 1974, *Cinq études du matérialisme historique*, Paris: Maspero.
Balibar, Étienne 1991, *Écrits pour Althusser*, Paris: La Découverte.
Balibar, Étienne 1992, 'Gramsci, Marx et le rapport social', in *Modernité de Gramsci? Actes du colloque franco-italien de Besançon. 23–25 novembre 1989*, edited by André Tosel, Besançon: Annales Littéraires de l'Université de Besançon.
Balibar, Étienne 1993, 'L'objet d'Althusser', in Lazarus (ed.) 1993.
Balibar, Etienne 1994, *Lieux et noms de la vérité*, Paris: Editions de l'Aube.
Balibar, Étienne 1995 [1993], *The Philosophy of Marx*, translated by Chris Turner, London: Verso.
Balibar, Étienne 1997, 'Foucault et Marx. L'enjeu du nominalisme', in *La Crainte des masses*, Paris: Galilée.
Balibar, Étienne & Immanuel Wallerstein 1991 [1988], *Race, Nation, Class: Ambiguous Identities*, translated by Chris Turner, London: Verso.
Balibar, Renée 1974, *Les Français fictifs*, Paris: Hachette.
Balibar, Renée & Dominique Laporte 1974, *Le Français national*, Paris: Hachette.
Banton, Michael 1988, *Racial Consciousness*, Harlow: Longman.
Banton, Michael 1998, *Racial Theories*, Cambridge: Cambridge University Press.
Banton, Michael 2000, 'Ethnic Conflict', *Sociology*, 3, 34: 481–98.
Baran, Paul & Paul Sweezy 1966, *Monopoly Capital*, New York: Monthly Review Press.
Baratta, Giorgio 1987, 'Liberiamo Gramsci', *Democrazia proletaria*, part I: n. 1; part II: n. 2.
Baratta, Giorgio 2003, *Le rose e i Quaderni. Il pensiero dialogico di Antonio Gramsci*, Rome: Carocci.
Bardhan, Pranab K. & John Roemer (eds.) 1993, *Market Socialism: The Current Debate*, Oxford: Oxford University Press.
Barker, Colin 1997, 'Some Reflections on Two Books by Ellen Wood', *Historical Materialism*, 1: 22–65.
Barrow, Clyde W. 1993, *Critical Theories of the state: Marxist, Neo-Marxist, Post-Marxist*, Madison: University of Wisconsin Press.
Bartelson, Jens 1995, *A Genealogy of Sovereignty*, Cambridge: Cambridge University Press.
Bartelson, Jens 2001, *The Critique of the State*, Cambridge: Cambridge University Press.
Bartolovich, Crystal 2002, 'Introduction: Marxism, Modernity and Postcolonial Studies', in *Marxism, Modernity and Postcolonial Studies*, edited by Crystal Bartolovich and Neil Lazarus, Cambridge: Cambridge University Press.
Beaud, Michel 1986, *Le Système national/mondial hiérarchisé*, Paris: La Découverte.
Beck, Ulrich & Edgar Grande 2004, *Das kosmopolitsche Europa. Wege in die Zweite Moderne*, Frankfurt am Main: Suhrkamp.
Becker Joachim & Werner Raza 2000, 'Theory of Regulation and Political Ecology: An Inevitable Separation?', *Économies et sociétes*, 11, 1: 55–70.
Beffa, Jean-Louis, Robert Boyer, & Jean-Philippe Toufutt 1999, *Les Relations salariales en France*, Paris: Note de la Fondation Saint-Simon.
Behrmann, Günter 1999, 'Zwei Monate Kulturrevolution', in *Die intellektuelle Gründung der Bundesrepublik. Eine Wirkungsgeschichte der Frankfurter Schule*, edited by Albrecht Clemens et al., Frankfurt am Main: Suhrkamp.
Beier, A.L. et al. (eds.) 1989, *The First Modern Society*, Cambridge: Cambridge University Press.
Bello, Walden 2004, 'Coming: A Re-run of the 1930s?', in *World Social Forum: Challenging Empires*, edited by. Jai Sen, Anita Anand, Arturo Escobar and Peter Waterman, New Delhi: Viveka Foundation.
Bellofiore, Riccardo & Nicola Taylor (eds.) 2005, *The Constitution of Capital: Essays on Volume One of Marx's 'Capital'*, London: Palgrave Macmillan.
Benjamin, Walter 1969, *Kommunistische Pädagogik, Spielzeug, Spielen, Kindertheater*, Berlin: Zentralrat der sozialistischen Kinderläden West-Berlin.

Benjamin, Walter 1973, *Charles Baudelaire, A Lyric Poet in the Era of High Capitalism*, London: New Left Books.
Benjamin, Walter 1974, *Proletarisches Kinder- Und Lehrlingstheater*, Köln-Nippes: APO-Raubdruck, Rote Maske.
Benjamin, Walter 1986, *Moscow Diary*, Cambridge, MA.: Harvard University Press.
Benjamin, Walter 1995a, *Gesammelte Briefe*, Volume 1, Frankfurt am Main: Suhrkamp,.
Benjamin, Walter 1995b, *Gesammelte Briefe*, Volume 2, Frankfurt am Main: Suhrkamp.
Benjamin, Walter 1995c, *Gesammelte Briefe*, Volume 3, Frankfurt am Main: Suhrkamp.
Benjamin, Walter 1995d, *Gesammelte Briefe*, Volume 4, Frankfurt am Main: Suhrkamp.
Benjamin, Walter 1995e, *Gesammelte Briefe*, Volume 5, Frankfurt am Main: Suhrkamp.
Benjamin, Walter 1999a, *Arcades Project*, Cambridge, MA.: The Belknap Press of Harvard University Press.
Benjamin, Walter 1999b, *Selected Writings: Volume 2, 2, 1931–1934*, translated by Rodney Livingstone and others, edited by Howard Eiland, Michael W. Jennings and Gary Smith, Cambridge, MA.: The Belknap Press of Harvard University Press.
Benjamin, Walter 2003, 'On the Concept of History', in *Selected Writings: Volume 4, 1938–1940*, translated by Edmund Jephcott and others, edited by Howard Eiland and Michael W. Jennings, Cambridge, MA.: The Belknap Press of Harvard University Press.
Bensaïd, Daniel 1990, *Walter Benjamin: sentinelle messianique. A la gauche du possible*, Paris: Plon.
Bensaïd, Daniel 1993, 'Les tourments de la matière', *Écologie et politique*, 7: 91–105.
Bensaïd, Daniel 1995, *La Discordance des temps*, Paris: Editions de la Passion.
Bensaïd, Daniel 1997, *Le Pari mélancolique: métamorphoses de la politique, politique des métamorphoses*, Paris: Fayard.
Bensaïd, Daniel 1999, *Qui est le juge?: pour en finir avec le tribunal de l'histoire*, Paris: Fayard.
Bensaïd, Daniel 2000, *Le Sourire du spectre*, Paris: Michalon.
Bensaïd, Daniel 2001a, *Les Irréductibles: théorèmes de la résistance à l'air du temps*, Paris: Textuel.
Bensaïd, Daniel 2001b, *Passion Marx, les hiéroglyphes de la modernité*, Paris: Textuel.
Bensaïd, Daniel 2001c, *Résistances: essai de taupologie générale*, Paris: Fayard.
Bensaïd, Daniel 2002, *Marx for Our Times: Adventures and Misadventures of a Critique*, translated by Gregory Elliott, London: Verso.
Bensaïd, Daniel 2003a, *Le nouvel internationalisme: contre les guerres impériales et la privatisation du monde*, Paris: Textuel.
Bensaïd, Daniel 2003b, *Un monde à changer: mouvements et stratégies*, Paris: Textuel.
Bensaïd, Daniel 2004, *Une lente impatience*, Paris: Stock.
Bensussan, Gérard 1985, 'Crises du marxisme', in Labica & Bensussan (eds.) 1985.
Bensussan, Gérard 2007, *Marx le sortant: Une pensée en excès*, Paris: Hermann.
Benton, Ted 1977, *Philosophical Foundations of the Three Sociologies*, London: Routledge & Kegan Paul.
Benton, Ted 1989, 'Marxism and Natural Limits: An Ecological Critique and Reconstruction', *New Left Review*, I, 178: 51–86.
Berger, Peter & Thomas Luckmann 1967, *The Social Construction of Reality*, London: Allen Lane.
Berggren, Christian 1992, *Alternatives to Lean Production: Work Organisation in the Swedish Auto Industry*, Ithaca: ILR Press.
Bernstein, Eduard 1961 [1899], *Evolutionary Socialism*, translated by Edith Harvey, New York: Schocken Books.
Bertram, Christopher 1988, 'A Critique of John Roemer's General Theory of Exploitation', *Political Studies*, 36: 123–30.
Bertram, Christopher 1990, 'International Competition in Historical Materialism', *New Left Review*, I, 183: 116–28.
Bertrand, Hugues 1979, 'Le régime central d'accumulation de l'après-guerre et sa crise', *Critiques de l'économie politique*, 7–8: 114–66.
Bertrand, Hugues, Robert Boyer, Bernard Guibert & Bruno Théret 1980, *Marx et la crise? Pour un débat entre 'marxistes empiriques'*, working paper.

Besnier, Bertrand 1976, 'Conrad Schmidt et les débuts de la littérature économique marxiste', in *Histoire du marxisme contemporain* 1976.

Bhabha, Homi K. 1991, 'A Question of Survival: Nations and Psychic States', in *Psychoanalysis and Cultural Theory: Thresholds*, edited by James Donald, New York: St. Martin's Press.

Bhabha, Homi K. 1994. *The Location of Culture*. London: Routledge.

Bhabha, Homi K. 2005, 'Foreword: Framing Fanon', in Frantz Fanon, *The Wretched of the Earth*, translated by Richard Philcox, New York: Grove Press.

Bhaskar, Roy 1978, *A Realist Theory of Science*, Hassocks: Harvester.

Bhaskar, Roy 1979, *The Possibility of Naturalism*, Brighton: Harvester.

Bhaskar, Roy 1989, *Reclaiming Reality: A Critical Introduction to Contemporary Philosophy*, London: Verso.

Bhaskar, Roy 1992, 'Dialectics', in Bottomore (ed.) 1992.

Bhaskar, Roy 1993, *Dialectic: The Pulse of Freedom*, London: Verso.

Bhaskar, Roy 2000, *From East to West: Odyssey of a Soul*, London: Routledge.

Bidard, Christian (ed.) 1984 'Systèmes de prix de production' (CNRS), 2–3, *Cahiers de la RCP*, University of Paris X–Nanterre.

Bidet, Jacques 1987a, 'Capitalisme-Marché-Socialisme', preface to Japanese and Spanish editions of Bidet 2000.

Bidet, Jacques 1987b, 'Place des catégories juridicopolitiques dans la théorie du mode de production capitaliste', *Socialism in the World*, 58: 69–86.

Bidet, Jacques 1988, 'Sur l'épistémologie du jeune Croce. A propos du débat Labriola/ Croce sur la valeur, 1896–1899', in *Labriola d'un siècle à l'autre*, edited by Georges Labica and Jacques Texier, Paris: Méridiens-Klincksieck.

Bidet, Jacques 1990, *Théorie de la modernité, suivi de Marx et le marché*, Paris: Presses Universitaires de France.

Bidet, Jacques 1992, 'Y-a-t-il une écologie marxiste?', *Actuel Marx*, 12: 96–112.

Bidet, Jacques 1995, *John Rawls et la théorie de la justice*, Paris: Presses Universitaires de France.

Bidet, Jacques 1999, *Théorie générale. Théorie du droit, de l'économie et de la politique*, Paris: Presses Universitaires de France.

Bidet, Jacques 2000 [1985], *Que faire du 'Capital'? Philosophie, économie et politique dans Le Capital*, Paris: Presses Universitaires de France.

Bidet, Jacques 2004, *Explication et reconstruction du 'Capital'*, Paris: Presses Universitaires de France.

Bidet, Jacques 2007 [1984], *Exploring Marx's 'Capital': Philosophical, Economic and Political Dimensions*, translated by David Fernbach, Leiden: Brill Academic Publishers.

Bieler, Andreas & Adam David Morton 2003, 'Globalization, the State, and Class Struggle: A "Critical Economy" Engagement with Open Marxism', *British Journal of Politics & International Relations*, 5, 4: 467–500.

Bieler, Andreas & Adam David Morton 2004a, 'A Critical Theory Route to Hegemony, World Order and Historical Change: Neo-Gramscian Perspectives in International Relations', *Capital & Class*, 82: 85–113.

Bieler, Andreas & Adam David Morton 2004b, 'Unthinking Materialism?', *British Journal of Politics and International Relations*, 6, 2: 238–41.

Bieler, Andreas & Adam David Morton 2001 (eds.), *Social Forces in the Making of the New Europe. The Restructuration of European Social Relations in the Global Political Economy*, London: Palgrave Macmillan.

Bin Wong, R. 1997, *China Transformed: Historical Change and the Limits of European Experience*, Ithaca: Cornell University Press.

Bischoff, Joachim 2003, *Entfesselter Kapitalismus*, Hamburg: VSA.

Blackburn, Robin 1995, 'The Black Jacobins and New World Slavery', in *CLR James: His Intellectual Legacies*, edited by Selwyn Cudjoe and William Cain, Amherst: University of Massachusetts Press.

Blackburn, Robin 1999, 'Le retour du collectivisme: la nouvelle économie politique des fonds de pension', *Mouvements*, 5: 90–107.

Blackledge, Paul 2002/3, 'Political Marxism: Towards an Immanent Critique', *Studies in Marxism*, 9: 1–20.

Blackledge, Paul 2004, *Perry Anderson, Marxism and the New Left*, London: Merlin.
Blackledge, Paul 2005a, 'Brian Manning: Historian of the People and the English Revolution', *Historical Materialism*, 13, 3: 219–28.
Blackledge, Paul 2005b, 'Freedom, Desire and Revolution: Alasdair MacIntyre's Marxist Ethics', *History of Political Thought*, 26, 4: 696–720.
Blackledge, Paul 2005c, 'Leon Trotsky's Contribution to the Marxist Theory of History', *Studies in East European Thought*, 57, 4: 1–31.
Blackledge, Paul 2006, *Reflections on the Marxist Theory of History*, Manchester: Manchester University Press.
Blanchot, Maurice 1986, *Michel Foucault tel que je l'imagine*, Montpellier: Fata Morgana.
Bloch, Ernst 1972, *Das Materialismusproblem. Seine Geschichte und Substanz*, Frankfurt am Main: Suhrkamp.
Bloch, Ernst 1978, *Atheismus im Christentum: Zur Religion des Exodus und des Reichs*, Frankfurt am Main: Suhrkamp.
Bloch, Ernst 1986 [1959], *The Principle of Hope*, 3 vols., translated by Neville Plaice, Stephen Plaice and Paul Knight, Oxford: Basil Blackwell.
Bloch, Olivier 1995, *Le Matérialisme*, Paris: Presses Universitaires de France.
Blum, William 2001, *Rogue State. A Guide to the World's Only Superpower*, London: Zed.
Bobbio, Norberto 1969, 'Gramsci e la concezione della società civile', in Rossi (ed.) 1969.
Bodei, Remo 1977, 'Gramsci: volontà, egemonia, razionalizzazione, Crisi organica e Stato in Gramsci', in Ferri (ed.) 1977.
Bois, Guy 1985, 'Against Neo-Malthusian Orthodoxy', in Aston & Philpin (eds.) 1985.
Bologna, Sergio 1972, 'Composizione di classe e storia del partitio alle origini de l'ouvrier de métier', in *Operai e stato. Lotte operaie e riforma dello Stato capitalistico tra Rivoluzione d'Ottobre e New Deal*, edited by Sergio Bologna et al., Milan: Feltrinelli.
Bonefeld, Werner & John Holloway (eds.), 1996, *Global Capital, National State and the Politics of Money*, Basingstoke: Macmillan.
Bonss, Wolfgang 1983, 'Empirie und Dechiffrierung von Wirklichkeit. Zur Methodologie bei Adorno', in *Adorno-Konferenz 1983*, in von Friedeburg & Habermas (eds.) 1983.
Bonss, Wolfgang & Axel Honneth (eds.) 1982, *Sozialforschung als Kritik. Zum sozialwissenschaftlichen Potential der Kritischen Theorie*, Frankfurt am Main: Suhrkamp.
Bordini, Luigi 1985, *O marxismo e a teologia da libertaçâo*, Rio de Janeiro: Editora Dois Pontos.
Bosteels, Bruno 2005a, 'Post-Maoism: Badiou and Politics', *positions: east asia cultures critique*, 13, 3: 575–634.
Bosteels, Bruno 2005b, 'The Speculative Left', *South Atlantic Quarterly*, 104, 4: 751–67.
Bosteels, Bruno 2005c, 'Can Change Be Thought? A Dialogue with Alain Badiou', in *Alain Badiou: Philosophy and its Conditions*, edited by Gabriel Riera, Albany: SUNY.
Bottomore, Tom (ed.) 1992, *A Dictionary of Marxist Thought*, Oxford: Blackwell.
Boullé, Jacques, Robert Boyer, Jacques Mazier, & Gaston Olive 1974, 'Le modèle Star', *Statistiques et études financières*, 15.
Bourdet, Yvon 1972, *Figures de Lukács*, Paris: Anthropos.
Bourdieu, Pierre 1982, *Leçon sur la leçon*, Paris: Éditions de Minuit.
Bourdieu, Pierre 1984 [1979], *Distinction: A Social Critique of the Judgement of Taste*, translated by Richard Nice, London: Routledge and Kegan Paul.
Bourdieu, Pierre 1990 [1980], *The Logic of Practice*, translated by Richard Nice, Cambridge: Polity.
Bourdieu, Pierre 1996 [1984], *The State Nobility: Grandes Écoles and Esprit du Corps*, translated by Lauretta Clough, Cambridge: Polity.
Bourdieu, Pierre 1998, *Les Structures sociales de l'économie*, Paris: Seuil.
Bourdieu, Pierre & Jean-Claude Passeron 1977 [1970], *Reproduction in Education, Culture and Society*, translated by Richard Nice, London: Sage.
Bourdieu, Pierre & Loïc Wacquant 1992, *Réponses*, Paris: Seuil.
Bowles, Samuel & Herbet Gintis (eds.) 1998a, *Recasting Egalitarianism: New Rules for Communities, States and Markets*, London: Verso.

Bowles, Samuel & Herbert Gintis 1998b, 'Efficient Redistribution: New Rules for Markets, States and Communities', in Bowles & Gintis (eds.) 1988a.
Bowles, Samuel, David Gordon & Tom Weisskopf 1984, *Beyond the Wasteland: A Democratic Alternative to Economic Decline*, New York: Anchor.
Bowles, Samuel & Tom Weisskopf 1999, 'David M. Gordon: Radical Political Economist and Activist (1944–1996)', *Review of Radical Political Economics*, 31, 1: 1–15.
Boyer, Robert 1978, 'L'évolution des salaires en longue période', *Économie et statistique*, 103: 27–57.
Boyer, Robert 1979, 'La crise actuelle: une mise en perspective historique', *Critiques de l'économie politique*, 7–8: 5–113.
Boyer, Robert 1986, *La Théorie de la regulation: une analyse critique*, Paris: La Découverte.
Boyer, Robert et al. 1987, *Aspects de la crise – Tome III: Les éeconomies au milieu du gué*, Paris: Plan/CEPREMAP.
Boyer, Robert, Alain Lipietz et al. 1977, *Approches de l'inflation: l'exemple français*, Paris: CEPREMAP.
Boyer, Robert & Jacques Mistral 1978, *Accumulation, inflation, crises*, Paris: Presses Universitaires de France.
Boyer, Robert & André Orléan 1991, 'Les transformations des conventions salariales entre théorie et histoire. D'Henry Ford au fordisme', *Revue économique*, 42, 2: 233–72.
Boyer, Robert & Yves Saillard 1995, *Théorie de la régulation: l'état des savoirs*, Paris: La Découverte.
Brand, Ulrich & Christoph Goerg 2003 *Post-fordistische Naturverhältnisse*, Münster: Westfälisches Dampfboot.
Braudel, Fernand 1979, *Civilisation matérielle, économie et capitalisme. XVe–XVIIIe siècle. vols 1-3*, Paris: Librairie Armand Colin.
Braudel, Fernand 1985, *La Dynamique du capitalisme*, Paris: Flammarion.
Braverman, Harry 1974, *Labour and Monopoly Capital: The Degradation of Work in the Twentieth Century*, New York: Monthly Review Press.
Brennan, Timothy 1997, *At Home in the World: Cosmopolitanism Now*, Cambridge, MA.: Harvard University Press.
Brenner, Neil 2004, *New State Spaces: Urban Restructuring and State Rescaling in Western Europe*, Oxford: Oxford University Press.
Brenner, Robert 1976, 'Agrarian Cass Structure and Economic Development in Pre-Industrial Europe', *Past & Present*, 70: 30–75.
Brenner, Robert 1977, 'The Origins of Capitalist Development: A Critique of Neo-Smithian Marxism', *New Left Review*, I, 104: 25–92.
Brenner, Robert 1978, 'Dobb on the Transition from Feudalism to Capitalism', *Cambridge Journal of Economics*, 2: 121–40.
Brenner, Robert 1982, 'The Agrarian Roots of European Capitalism', *Past & Present*, 97: 16–113.
Brenner, Robert 1983, 'World System Theory and the Transition to Capitalism: Historical and Theoretical Perspectives', in *Perspektiven des Weltsystems*, edited by Jochen Blaschke, Frankfurt am Main: Campus Verlag.
Brenner, Robert 1985a, 'Agrarian Class Structures and Economic Development in Pre-Industrial Europe', in Aston & Philpin (eds.) 1985.
Brenner, Robert 1985b, 'The Paradoxes of Social Democracy: The American Case' in *The Year Left*, edited by Mike Davis et al., London: Verso.
Brenner, Robert 1986, 'The Social Basis of Economic Development', in Roemer (ed.) 1986.
Brenner, Robert 1989, 'Bourgeois Revolution and the Transition to Capitalism', in Beier et al. (eds.) 1989.
Brenner, Robert 1990a, 'La base sociale du développement économique', *Actuel Marx*, 7: 65–93.
Brenner, Robert 1990b, 'Feudalism', in *The New Palgrave Marxism Economics*, edited by John Eatwell et al., London: Palgrave.

Brenner, Robert 1991, 'Economic Backwardness in Eastern Europe in Light of Developments in the West', in *The Origins of Backwardness in Eastern Europe*, edited by D. Chirot, Berkeley: University of California Press.

Brenner, Robert 1991a, 'The Soviet Union and Eastern Europe, Part 1', *Against the Current*, 27–31.

Brenner, Robert 1991b, 'The Soviet Union and Eastern Europe, Part 2', *Against the Current*, 40–5.

Brenner, Robert 1991c, 'Why is the United States at War with Iraq?', *New Left Review*, I, 185: 122–37.

Brenner, Robert 1993, *Merchants and Revolution*, Cambridge: Cambridge University Press.

Brenner, Robert 1996, 'The Rises and Declines of Serfdom in Medieval and Early Modern Europe', in *Serfdom and Slavery*, edited by M. Bush, Harlow: Longman.

Brenner, Robert 1997, 'Property Relations and the Growth of Agricultural Productivity in Late Medieval and Early Modern Europe', in *Economic Development and Agricultural Productivity*, edited by Amit Bhaduri and Rune Skarstein, Cheltenham: Edward Elgar.

Brenner, Robert 1998, 'The Economics of Global Turbulence: A Special Report on the World Economy 1950–98', *New Left Review*, I, 229, 1–264.

Brenner, Robert 1999a, 'Competition and Class: A Reply to Foster and McNally', *Monthly Review*, 51, 7, available at: <http://www.monthlyreview.org/1299bren.htm>.

Brenner, Robert 1999b, 'Reply to Critics', *Comparative Studies of South Asia, Africa and the Middle East*, 19, 2: 61–85.

Brenner, Robert 2000, 'The Boom and the Bubble', *New Left Review*, II, 2: 5–43.

Brenner, Robert 2001, 'The Low Countries in the Transition to Capitalism', in *Peasants into Farmers*, edited by Peter Hoppenbrouwers, Turnhout: Brepols.

Brenner, Robert 2003a, *Merchants and Revolution*, London: Verso.

Brenner, Robert 2003b, 'Towards the Precipice', *London Review of Books*, 6 February 2003.

Brenner, Robert 2004, 'New Boom or New Bubble?', *New Left Review*, II, 25: 57–100.

Brenner, Robert & Mark Glick 1991, 'The Regulation Approach: History and Theory', *New Left Review*, I, 188: 45–119.

Brenner, Robert & Christopher Isett 2002, 'England's Divergence from China's Yangzi Delta: Property Relations, Microeconmics, and Patterns of Development', *Journal of Asian Studies*, 61, 2: 609–62.

Bromley, Simon 2003, 'Reflection on Empire, Imperialism and United States Hegemony', *Historical Materialism*, 11, 3: 17–68.

Browne, Irene & Joya Misra 2003, 'The Intersection of Gender and Race in the Labor Market', *Annual Review of Sociology*, 29: 487–513.

Brubaker, Rogers 2004, *Ethnicity Without Groups*, Cambridge, MA.: Harvard University Press.

Brumlik, Micha & Hauke Brunkhorst (eds.) 1993, *Gemeinschaft und Gerechtigkeit*, Frankfurt am Main: Suhrkamp.

Brunkhorst, Hauke 1994, *Demokratie und Differenz. Vom klassischen zum modernen Begriff des Politischen*, Frankfurt am Main: Suhrkamp.

Brunkhorst, Hauke (ed.) 1998, *Einmischung erwünscht? Menschenrechte und bewaffnete Intervention*, Frankfurt am Main: Suhrkamp.

Bucharin, Nicolai. I. 1977, *Teoria del materialismo storico. Manuale popolare di sociologia marxista*, translated into Italian by Andrea Binazzi, Florence: La Nuova Italia.

Buci Glucksmann, Christine 1975, *Gramsci et l'Etat*, Paris: Fayard.

Buci-Glucksmann, Christine 1977, 'Sui problemi politici della transizione: classe operaia e rivoluzione passiva, Crisi organica e Stato in Gramsci', in Ferri (ed.) 1977.

Buck-Morss, Susan 1977, *The Origin of Negative Dialectics: Theodor W. Adorno, Walter Benjamin, and the Frankfurt Institute*, New York: Macmillan Free Press.

Buck-Morss, Susan 1989, *The Dialectics of Seeing: Walter Benjamin and the Arcades Project*, Cambridge, MA.: MIT Press.

Buey, Francisco F. 2001, *Leyendo a Gramsci*, Barcelona: El Viejo Topo.
Burbach, Roger & William I. Robinson 1999, 'The Fin De Siècle Debate: Globalization as Epochal Shift', *Science & Society*, 63, 1: 10–39.
Bürger, Peter 1983, *Zur Kritik der idealistischen Ästhetik*, Frankfurt am Main: Suhrkamp.
Bürger, Peter 1984 [1974], *Theory of the Avant-Garde*, translated by Michael Shaw, Manchester: Manchester University Press.
Burgio, Alberto 1999, *Modernità del conflitto. Saggio sulla critica marxiana del socialismo*, Rome: DeriveApprodi.
Burgio, Alberto 2000, *Strutture e catastrofi: Kant, Hegel, Marx*, Rome: Editori Riuniti.
Burgio, Alberto 2002, *Gramsci storico. Una lettura dei 'Quaderni del carcere'*, Bari: Laterza.
Burkett, Paul 1996, 'On Some Common Misconceptions about Nature and Marx's Critique of Political Economy', *Capitalism, Nature, Socialism*, 8, 3: 57–80.
Burkett, Paul 1999, *Marx and Nature: A Red and Green Perspective*, New York: St Martin's Press.
Burnham, Peter 1991, 'Neo-Gramscian Hegemony and the International Order', *Capital & Class*, 45: 73–93.
Burris, Val 1987, 'The Political Partisanship of American Business: A Study of Corporate Political Action Committees', *American Sociological Review*, 52, 6: 732–44.
Burris, Val 2005, 'Interlocking Directorates and Political Cohesion among Corporate Elites', *American Journal of Sociology*, 111, 1: 249–83.
Burris, Val & James Salt 1990: 'The Politics of Class Segments: A Test of Corporate Liberalism Theory', *Social Problems*, 37: 3: 341–59.
Buttigieg, Joseph A. 1999, 'Sulla categoria gramsciana di "subalterno"', in *Gramsci da un secolo all'altro*, edited by G. Baratta and G. Liguori, Rome: Editori Riuniti.
Cain, Glenn 1976, 'The Challenge of Labor Market Theories to Orthodox Theory: A Survey', *Journal of Economic Literature*, 14, 4: 1215–57.
Callinicos, Alex 1982, *Is There a Future for Marxism?*, London: Macmillan.
Callinicos, Alex 1983, *The Revolutionary Ideas of Karl Marx*, London: Bookmarks.
Callinicos, Alex 1987, *Making History*, First Edition, Cambridge: Polity.
Callinicos, Alex 1989, *Against Postmodernism*, Cambridge: Polity.
Callinicos, Alex 1991, *The Revenge of History*, Cambridge: Polity.
Callinicos, Alex 1993, *Race and Class*, London: Bookmarks.
Callinicos, Alex 1995, *Theories and Narratives*, Cambridge: Polity.
Callinicos, Alex 1996, 'Whither Marxism?', *Economic Political and Weekly*, January 27: 9–22.
Callinicos, Alex 1998a, 'Marxism and the Crisis of Social History', in *Essays on Historical Materialism*, edited by John Rees, London: Bookmarks.
Callinicos, Alex 1998b, 'The Secret of the Dialectic', *International Socialism*, 78: 93–103.
Callinicos, Alex 2000, *Equality*, Cambridge: Polity.
Callinicos, Alex 2004, *Making History*, Revised Edition, Leiden: Brill Academic Press.
Calvet, Louis-Jean 1964, *Linguistique et colonialisme*, Paris: Payot.
Campbell, Martha 1997, 'Marx's Theory of Money: A Defense', in Moseley & Campbell (eds.) 1997.
Campbell, Martha & Geert Reuten (eds.) 2001, *The Culmination of Capital: Essays on Volume III of Marx's 'Capital'*, London: Macmillan.
Candeias, Mario & Frank Deppe (eds.) 2001, *Ein neuer Kapitalismus?*, Hamburg: VSA.
Carchedi, Guglielmo 1977 *On the Economic Identification of Social Classes*, London: Routledge & Kegan Paul.
Carling, Alan 1991, *Social Division*, London: Verso.
Carter, Bob 2000, *Realism and Racism: Concepts of Race in Sociological Research*, London: Routledge.
Carver, Terell & Paul Thomas (eds.) 1995, *Rational Choice Marxism*, Basingstoke: Macmillan.
Castells, Manuel 1975, *Luttes urbaines*, Paris: Maspero.
Castells, Manuel 1977, *The Urban Question*, translated by Alan Sheridan, London: Edward Arnold.

Cerroni, Umberto 1977, 'Universalità e politica', in Ferri (ed.) 1977.

Chakrabarty, Dipesh 2000, *Provincializing Europe: Postcolonial Thought and Historical Difference*, Princeton: Princeton University Press.

Chakrabarty, Dipesh 2002, *Habitations of Modernity: Essays in the Wake of Subaltern Studies*. Chicago: University of Chicago Press.

Chesnais, François 1997, *La Mondialisation du capital*, Paris: Syros.

Chomsky, Noam 2001, *Rogue States: the Rule of Force in World Affairs*, London: Pluto.

Cingoli, Mario 1996, *Il secondo e il terzo libro del 'Capitale'*, Milan: CUEM.

Clark, Timothy J. 2003, 'Should Benjamin Have Read Marx?', *boundary 2*, 30, 1: 31–49.

Claussen, Detlev 1990, *Georg Lukács. Die Oktober Revolution und Perestroïka*, Frankfurt am Main: Lichterhand/Literaturvert.

Clément, Cathérine 1995, *Sollers. La Fronde*, Paris: Éditions Julliard.

Cliff, Tony 1988, *State Capitalism in Russia*, London: Bookmarks.

Coase, Ronald 1960, 'The Problem of Social Cost', *The Journal of Law and Economics*, 3, 1: 1–44.

Cockshott, Paul & Allin Cottrill 1993, *Towards a New Socialism*, Nottingham: Spokesman.

Cohen, Gerald A. 1978, *Karl Marx's Theory of History: A Defence*, Oxford: Clarendon Press.

Cohen, Gerald A. 1982a, 'Reply to Elster on "Marxism, Functionalism and Game Theory"', *Theory & Society*, 11, 4: 483–95.

Cohen, Gerald A. 1982b, 'Functional Explanation, Consequence Explanation and Marxism', *Inquiry*, 25: 27–56.

Cohen, Gerald A. 1988, 'Forces and Relations of Production', in *History, Labour and Freedom: Themes from* Marx, Oxford: Clarendon Press.

Cohen, Gerald A. 1989, 'On the Currency of Egalitarian Justice', *Ethics*, 99: 906–44.

Cohen, Gerald A. 1995, *Self-Ownership, Freedom and Equality*, Cambridge: Cambridge University Press.

Cohen, Gerald A. 1996, 'Self-Ownership, History and Socialism', *Imprints*, 1, 1: 7–25.

Cohen, Gerald A. 1997, 'Where the Action Is: On the Site of Distributive Justice', *Philosophy and Public Affairs*, 26, 1: 3–30.

Cohen, Gerald A. & Will Kymlicka 1988, 'Human Nature and Social Change in the Marxist Conception of History', *Journal of Philosophy*, 85, 4: 171–91.

Cohen, Marcel 1950, *Le Langage: structure et evolution*, Paris: Éditions Sociales.

Cohen, Marcel 1971, *Matériaux pour une sociologie du langage*, 2 vols., Paris: Maspero.

Cohen Margaret 1993, *Profane Illumination; Walter Benjamin and the Paris of Surrealist Revolution*, Berkeley: University of California Press.

Cohen, Robert S. & Marx W. Wartofsky (eds.) 1984, *Hegel and the Sciences*, Dordrecht: Reidel.

Cole, George D.H. 1951–61, *A History of Socialist Thought*, 5 vols., London: Macmillan.

Colletti, Lucio 1973 [1969], *Marxism and Hegel*, translated by Lawrence Garner, London: New Left Books.

Colletti, Lucio 1974, 'A Political and Philosophical Interview', *New Left Review*, I, 86: 3–28.

Colletti, Lucio 1975, 'Introduction', in Marx 1975.

Colletti, Lucio 1980, *Tramonto dell'ideologia*, Bari: Laterza.

Collier, Andrew 1994, *Critical Realism*, London: Verso.

Comninel, George 1987, *Rethinking The French Revolution*, London: Verso.

Comninel, George 2000, 'English Feudalism and the Origins of Capitalism', *The Journal of Peasant Studies*, 27, 4: 1–53.

Cooper, Fredrick 2005, *Colonialism in Question: Theory, Knowledge, History*, Berkeley: University of California Press.

Coriat, Benjamin 1994, 'La théorie de la regulation. Origines, spécificité et perspectives', in *École de la regulation et critique de la raison économique*, Paris: *Futur Antérieur*/ L'Harmattan.

Corradi, Cristina 2005, *Storia del marxismo in Italia*, Rome: Manifestolibri.

Coutrot, Thomas 1998, *L'entreprise néo-libérale, nouvelle utopie capitaliste?*, Paris: La Découverte.
Cowling, Mark & James Martin (eds.) 2002, *Marx's Eighteenth Brumaire. Post-Modern Interpretations*, London: Pluto.
Cox, Oliver Cromwell 1970 [1959], *Caste, Class and Race: A Study in Social Dynamics*, New York: Monthly Review Press.
Cox, Oliver Cromwell 1972, 'Race and Exploitation: A Marxist View', in *Race and Social Difference: Selected Readings*, edited by Paul Baxter and Basil Sansom, Baltimore: Penguin.
Cox, Robert W. 1976, 'On Thinking About the Future of World Order', *World Politics*, 28: 175–96.
Cox, Robert W. 1981, 'Social Forces, States and World Order: Beyond International Relations Theory', *Millennium*, 10: 2: 126–55.
Cox, Robert W. 1987, *Production, Power and World Order, Social Forces in the Making of History*, New York: Columbia University Press.
Cox, Robert W. 1993a, 'Gramsci, Hegemony and International Relations: An Essay in Method', in Gill (ed.) 1993.
Cox, Robert W. 1993b, 'Production and Security', in *Building a New Global Order: Emerging Trends in International Security*, edited by D. Dewitt, D. Haglund, and J. Kirton, Oxford: Oxford University Press.
Cox, Robert W. 2001, 'Structures sociales et autorité politique', in *Une société-monde? Les dynamiques sociales de la mondialisation*, edited by D. Mercure et al., Québec: Presses de l'Université Laval.
Cox, Robert W. & Michael G. Schechter 2002, *The Political Economy of a Plural World. Critical Reflections on Power, Morals and Civilization*, London: Routledge.
Cox, Robert W. & Timothy J. Sinclair 1998, *Approaches to World Order*, Cambridge: Cambridge University Press.
Croce, Benedetto 1947, 'Antonio Gramsci, Lettere dal carcere', *Quaderni della 'Critica'*, 8.
Cutler, Anthony 2002, 'Critical Historical Materialism and International Law: Imagining International Law as Practice', in *Historical Sociology of International Relations*, edited by Stephen Hobden and John M. Hobson, Cambridge: Cambridge University Press.
Cutler, Anthony et al. 1977–8, *Marx's 'Capital' and Capitalism Today*, 2 vols., London: Routledge.
D'Hondt, Jacques 1972, *De Hegel à Marx*, Paris: Presses Universitaires de France.
Dal Pra, Mario 1977, *La Dialettica in Marx*, Bari: Laterza.
Daly, Herman E. 1992, 'Il n'y a pas de croissance durable', *Transversales Science/Culture*, 13: 10–11.
Daniele, C. (ed.) 2005, *Togliatti editore di Gramsci*, Introduction by G. Vacca, Rome: Carocci.
Darder, Antonia and Rodolfo D. Torres 2004, *After Race: Racism After Multiculturalism*, New York: New York University Press.
Davidson, Neil 2003, *Discovering the Scottish Revolution*, London: Pluto.
Davidson, Neil 2005a, 'How Revolutionary were the Bourgeois Revolutions? Part I', *Historical Materialism*, 13, 3: 3–33.
Davidson, Neil 2005b, 'How Revolutionary were the Bourgeois Revolutions? Part II', *Historical Materialism*, 13, 4: 3–54.
Davies, Matt 1999, *The International Political Economy and Mass Communication in Chile: National Intellectuals and Transnational Hegemony*, New York: St. Martin's Press.
Davies, Matt 2005, 'The Public Sphere of Unprotected Workers', *Global Society*, 19, 2: 131–54.
De Brunhoff, Suzanne 1973, *La Monnaie chez Marx*, Paris: Éditions Sociales.
De Felice, Franco 1977, 'Rivoluzione passiva, fascismo, americanismo in Gramsci', in Ferri (ed.) 1977.

De Giovanni, Biaggio 1977, 'Crisi organica e Stato in Gramsci', in Ferri (ed.) 1977.

Dear, Michael 1994, 'Les aspects postmodernes de Henri Lefebvre', *Espaces et sociétés*, 76: 31–40.

Deléage, Jean-Paul 1992, *Histoire de l'écologie. Une science de l'homme et de la nature*, Paris: La Découverte.

Deléage, Jean-Paul 1993, 'L'écologie, humanisme de notre temps', *Écologie politique*, 5: 1–14.

Deleuze, Gilles 1973, 'Marx/désir-besoin/Faye/la monnaie/sur Baudrillard' (28 May 1973), in *Les cours de Gilles Deleuze*, available at: <www.webdeleuze.com>.

Deleuze, Gilles 1983, *Nietzsche and Philosophy*, New York: Columbia University Press.

Deleuze, Gilles 1995, *Negotiations*, New York: Columbia University Press.

Deleuze, Gilles 2004, *Desert Islands and Other Texts, 1953–1974*, New York: Semiotext(e).

Deleuze, Gilles & Félix Guattari 1984, *Anti-Oedipus: Capitalism and Schizophrenia*, London: Athlone.

Deleuze, Gilles & Félix Guattari 1987, *A Thousand Plateaus*, Minneapolis: University of Minnesota Press.

Deleuze, Gilles & Félix Guattari 1994, *What Is Philosophy?*, London: Verso.

Deleuze, Gilles & Claire Parnet 1996, *L'Abécédaire de Gilles Deleuze*, directed by Pierre-André Boutang, Paris: Vidéo Editions Montparnasse.

Delgado, Richard & Jean Stefancic (eds.) 1999, *Critical Race Theory: The Cutting Edge*, Philadelphia: Temple University Press.

Della Volpe, Galvano 1980 [1950], *Logic as a Positive Science*, translated by Jon Rothschild, London: New Left Books.

Demirovic, Alex 1999, *Der non-konformistische Intellektuelle*, Frankfurt am Main: Suhrkamp.

Denis, Henri, *L''économie' de Marx. Histoire d'un échec*, Paris: Presses Universitaires de France.

Derrida, Jacques 1962, 'Introduction', in Edmund Husserl, *L'origine de la géometrie*, Paris: Presses Universitaires de France.

Derrida, Jacques 1967a, *L'écriture et la différence*, Paris: Seuil.

Derrida, Jacques 1967b, *La voix et le phénomène*, Paris: Presses Universitaires de France.

Derrida, Jacques 1972a, *La dissémination*, Paris: Seuil.

Derrida, Jacques 1972b, *Positions*, Paris: Minuit.

Derrida, Jacques 1981, *Glas*, Paris: Denoël/Gonthier.

Derrida, Jacques 1990, *Le problème de la genèse dans la philosophie de Husserl*, Paris: Presses Universitaires de France.

Derrida, Jacques 1993a, *Spectres de Marx*, Paris: Galilée.

Derrida, Jacques 1993b, 'Politics and Friendship: An Interview with Jacques Derrida', in *The Althusserian Legacy*, edited by E. Ann Kaplan and Michael Sprinker, London: Verso.

Derrida, Jacques 1994, *Force de loi*, Paris: Galilée.

Derrida, Jacques 2002, *Marx and Sons*, Paris: Presses Universitaires de France/Galilée.

Derrida, Jacques 2003, *Sur parole*, Paris: Éditions de l'Aube.

Derrida, Jacques & Maurizio Ferraris 2001, *A Taste for the Secret*, trans. by Giacomo Donis, Cambridge: Polity.

Derrida, Jacques & Elisabeth Roudinesco 2001, *De quoi demain…*, Paris: Fayard.

Devine, Pat 1988, *Democracy and Economic Planning*, Cambridge: Polity.

Dews, Peter 1987, *Logics of Disintegration: Post-Structuralist Thought and the Claims of Critical Theory*, London: Verso.

Dimitrov, George 1935 'The Fascist Offensive and the Tasks of the Communist International in the Struggle of the Working Class against Fascism' available at: <www.marxists.org/reference/archive/dimitrov/works/1935/08_02.htm#s18>.

Dobb, Maurice 1963 [1946], *Studies in the Development of Capitalism*, London: Routledge.

Dockès, Pierre & Bernard Rosier 1983, *Rythmes économiques. Crises et changement social: une perspective historique*, Paris: La Découverte/François Maspero.
Doeringer, Peter & Michael Piore 1970, *Internal Labor Markets and Manpower Analysis*, Lexington: Heath.
Dostaler, Gilles 1985, *Un échiquier centenaire*, Paris/Montréal: La Découverte/Presses Universitaires de Québec.
Dowling, William 1984, *Jameson, Althusser, Marx: An Introduction to 'The Political Unconscious'*, London: Methuen.
Drainville, André 1994, 'International Political Economy in the Age of Open Marxism', *Review of International Political Economy*, 1, 1: 105–32.
Drainville, André 2002, 'Quebec City 2001 and the Making of Transnational Subjects', in *Socialist Register 2002 – A World of Contradictions*, edited by Leo Panitch and Colin Leys, London: Merlin.
Draper, Hal 1977–86 *Karl Marx's Theory of Revolution*, Volumes 1–3, New York: Monthly Review Press.
Dreyfus, Hubert 1994, 'Die Gefahren der modernen Technologie: Heidegger und Foucault', in *Pathologien des Sozialen. Die Aufgaben der Sozialphilosophie*, edited by Axel Honneth, Frankfurt am Main.: Fischer.
Droz, Jacques (ed.) 1972–8, *Histoire générale du socialisme*, 4 vols., Paris: Presses Universitaires de France.
Drucker, Peter 1993, *Post-Capitalist Society*, Oxford: Butterworth-Heinemann.
Du Bois, William E.B. 1939, *Black Folk Then and Now: An Essay in the History and Sociology of the Negro Race*, New York: Henry Holt.
Du Bois, William E.B. 1973 [1903], *The Souls of Black Folk*, New York: Kraus-Thomson.
Dubiel, Helmut 1978, *Wissenschaftsorganisation und politische Erfahrung*, Frankfurt am Main: Suhrkamp.
Dubiel, Helmut 1994, 'Ihre Zeit in Gedanken erfasst. Entwicklungsstufen kritischer Theorie', in Institut für Sozialforschung an der J.W. Goethe-Universität Frankfurt am Main, *Mitteilungen*, 4: 5–14.
Duménil, Gérard 1975, *La position de classe des cadres et employés. La fonction capitaliste parcellaire*, Grenoble: Presses Universitaires de Grenoble.
Duménil, Gérard 1978, *Le Concept de loi économique dans 'Le Capital'*, Paris: Maspero.
Duménil, Gérard 1980, *De la valeur aux prix de production*, Paris: Economica.
Duménil, Gérard & Dominique Lévy 1994, 'The Emergence and Functions of Managerial and Clerical Personnel in Marx's *Capital*', in *Bureaucracy: Three Paradigms*, edited by Neil Garston, London: Kluwer Academic.
Duménil, Gérard & Dominique Lévy 1996, *La dynamique du capital. Un siècle d'économie américaine*, Paris: Presses Universitaires de France.
Duménil, Gérard & Dominique Lévy (eds.) 1999a, *Le triangle infernal. Crise, mondialisation, financiarisation*, Paris: Presses Universitaires de France.
Duménil, Gérard & Dominique Lévy 1999b, *Costs and Benefits of Neoliberalism: A Class Analysis*, Paris: CEPREMAP-Modem.
Duménil, Gérard & Dominique Lévy 2001a, 'Periodizing Capitalism: Technology, Institutions, and Relations of Production', in *Phases of Capitalist Development: Booms, Crises and Globalisation*, edited by Robert Albritton, London: Palgrave.
Duménil, Gérard & Dominique Lévy 2001b, 'Brenner on Competition', *Capital & Class*, 74: 61–78.
Duménil, Gérard & Dominique Lévy 2002a, 'The Field of Capital Mobility and the Gravitation of Profit Rates (USA 1948–2000)', *Review of Radical Political Economy*, 12, 34: 417–36.
Duménil, Gérard & Dominique Lévy 2002b, 'The Profit Rate: Where and How Much Did it Fall? Did it Recover? (USA 1948–2000)', *Review of Radical Political Economy*, 12, 34: 437–61.
Duménil, Gérard & Dominique Lévy 2003 *L'économie politique marxiste du capitalisme*, Paris: La Découverte.
Duménil, Gérard & Dominique Lévy 2004 [2000], *Capitalism Resurgent: Roots of the*

Neoliberal Revolution, translated by Derek Jeffreys, Cambridge, MA.: Harvard University Press.
Duncan, C. 1983, 'Under the Cloud of Capital', *Science & Society*, 47, 3.
Dussel, Enrique 1982, 'Encuentro de cristianos y marxistas en América Latina', *Cristianismo y sociedad*, 74: 19–36.
Dussel, Enrique 1985, *La produccion teórica de Marx. Un comentario a los 'Grundrisse'*, Mexico: Siglo XXI.
Dussel, Enrique 1990, *El último Marx (1863–1882) y la liberación latinoamérica*, Mexico: Siglo XXI.
Dussel, Enrique 1993, *Las metáforas teológicas de Marx*, Estella: Verbo Divino.
Dussel, Enrique 2001 [1988], *Towards an Unknown Marx: A Commentary on the Manuscripts of 1861–63*, translated by Yolanda Angulo, London: Routledge.
Eagleton, Terry 1981, *Walter Benjamin or Towards a Revolutionary Criticism*, London: Verso.
Eagleton, Terry 1990, *The Ideology of the Aesthetic*, Oxford: Blackwell.
Eagleton, Terry 1991, *Ideology*, Verso: London.
Edwards, Richard, David Gordon & Michael Reich 1975, 'A Theory of Labor Market Segmentation', *American Economic Review*, 63, 2: 359–65.
Edwards, Richard, David Gordon & Michael Reich 1982, *Segmented Work, Divided Workers: The Historical Transformation of Labor in the United States*, Cambridge: Cambridge University Press.
Egan, Daniel 2001, 'The Limits of Internationalization: A Neo-Gramscian Analysis of the Multilateral Agreement on Investment', *Critical Sociology*, 27, 3: 74–97.
Ehrbar, Hans & Mark Glick 1986, 'The Labor Theory of Value and its Critics', *Science & Society*, 4: 464–78.
Eliot, Thomas S. 1947, *Notes Towards a Definition of Culture*, London: Faber.
Elliott, Gregory 1987, *Althusser: The Detour of Theory*, London: Verso.
Elliott, Gregory 2007, *Althusser: The Detour of Theory*, Reviesed Edition, Leiden: Brill Academic Publishers.
Elson, Diane 1988, 'Market Socialism or Socialization of the Market?', *New Left Review*, I, 172: 3–44.
Elster, Jon 1979, *Ulysses and the Sirens*, Cambridge: Cambridge University Press.
Elster, Jon 1980, 'Cohen on Marx's Theory of History', *Political Studies*, 28, 1: 129–35.
Elster, Jon 1982, 'Marxism, Functionalism and Game Theory', *Theory & Society* 11, 3: 453–82.
Elster, Jon 1983, *Sour Grapes*, Cambridge: Cambridge University Press.
Elster, Jon 1985, *Making Sense of Marx*, Cambridge: Cambridge University Press.
Elster, Jon 1986, 'Further Thoughts on Marxism, Functionalism and Game Theory', in Roemer (ed.) 1986.
Elster, Jon 1989, *Solomonic Judgements* Cambridge: Cambridge University Press.
Engels, Friedrich 1952, *Dialectique de la nature*, Paris, Éditions Sociales.
Engels, Frederick 1976 [1934], *Dialectics of Nature*, translated by Clemens Dutt, Moscow: Progress Publishers.
Engels, Frederick 1977, *Anti-Dühring*, translated by Emile Burns, Moscow: Progress Publishers.
Enzensberger, Hans Magnus 1970, 'Baukasten zu einer Theorie der Medien', *Kursbuch* 20: 159–86.
Escolar, Marcelo 1997, 'Exploration, Cartography and the Modernisation of State Power', *International Social Science Journal*, 151: 55–75.
Essed, Philomena 1991, *Understanding Everyday Racism: An Interdisciplinary Theory*, Newbury Park: Sage.
Estrin, Saul 1989, 'Workers' Cooperatives: Their Merits and their Limitations', in *Market Socialism*, edited by Julian Le Grand and Saul Estrin, Oxford: Clarendon.
Fadini, Ubaldo & Adelino Zanini 2001 (eds.), *Lessico postfordista. Dizionario di idee del mutazione*, Milan: Feltrinelli.
Fairclough, Norman 1989, *Language and Power*, London: Longman.

Fanon, Frantz 1968, *The Wretched of the Earth*, translated by Constance Farrington, New York: Grove Press.

Fausto, Ruy 1986, *Marx: logique et politique*, Paris: Publisud.

Fausto, Ruy 1996, *Sur le concept de capital: idée d'une logique dialectique*, Paris: L'Harmattan.

Fehér, Istvàn 1992, 'Lask, Lukács, Heidegger: The Problem of Irrationality and the Theory of Categories', in *Martin Heidegger. Critical Assessments*, Volume II, edited by Christopher Macann, London: Routledge.

Fenton, Steve 2003, *Ethnicity*, Cambridge: Polity.

Fenton, Steve 2007, 'Indifference Towards National Identity: What Young Adults Think about Being English and British', *Nations and Nationalism*, 13, 2: 321–39.

Ferguson, James 2006, *Global Shadows: Africa in the Neoliberal World Order*, Durham, NC.: Duke University Press.

Ferri, Franco (ed.) 1977, *Politica e storia in Gramsci*, two vols., Rome: Riuniti-Istituto Gramsci.

Fine, Ben et al. 1999, 'Addressing the World Economy: Two Steps Back', *Capital & Class*, 67: 47–90.

Fine, Ben, Costas Lapavitsas & Dimitris Milonakis 2000, 'Dialectics and Crisis Theory: A Response to Smith', *Historical Materialism*, 6: 133–7.

Finelli, Roberto 1987, *Astrazione e dialettica dal romanticismo al capitalismo*, Rome: Bulzoni.

Finelli, Roberto 1997, 'Introduzione. Una soggettività immaginaria', in Louis Althusser, *Lo Stato e i suoi apparati*, Rome: Editori Riuniti.

Finelli, Roberto 1998, 'Alcuni tesi su capitalismo, marxismo, e "post-modernità"', in *Capitalismo e conoscenza: l'astrazione del lavoro nell'era telematica*, edited by Lorenzo Cillario and Roberto Finelli, Rome: Manifestolibri.

Finelli, Roberto 2004, *Il parricidio mancato: Hegel e il giovane Marx*, Turin: Bollati Boringhieri.

Fineschi, Roberto 2001, *Ripartire da Marx. Processo storico ed economia politica nelle teoria del 'Capitale'*, Naples: La Città del Sole.

Fineschi, Roberto 2006, *Marx e Hegel. Contributi a una rilettura*, Rome: Carocci.

Finocchiaro, Maurice A. 1988, *Gramsci and the History of Dialectical Thought*, Cambridge: Cambridge University Press.

Fleurbaey, Marc 1993, 'Economic Democracy and Equality: A Proposal', in Bardhan & Roemer (eds.) 1993.

Foley, Duncan 1982a, 'Review of *Principles of Political Economy*', *Journal of Economic Literature*, 22, 2: 219–38.

Foley, Duncan 1982b, 'Value of Money, the Value of Labor Power and the Marxian Transformation Problem', *Review of Radical Political Economics*, 14: 37–47.

Forest, Philippe 1995, *Histoire de 'Tel Quel' 1960–1982*, Paris: Seuil.

Foster, John 1985, 'The Declassing of Language', *New Left Review*, I, 150: 29–45.

Foster John Bellamy 2000, *Marx's Ecology, Materialism and Nature*, New York: Monthly Review Press.

Foster John Bellamy 2002, *Ecology against Capitalism*, New York: Monthly Review Press.

Foster, John Bellamy 1999, 'Is Overcompetition the Problem?', *Monthly Review*, 51, 2, available at: <http://www.monthlyreview.org/699jbf.htm>.

Foucault, Michel 1961, *Introduction à l'anthropologie de Kant*, unpublished secondary thesis, Bibliothèque de la Sorbonne, Paris.

Foucault, Michel 1970 [1966], *The Order of Things*, London: Tavistock.

Foucault, Michel 1972 [1969], *The Archaeology of Knowledge*, translated by A.M. Sheridan Smith, London: Tavistock.

Foucault, Michel 1983, 'Um welchen Preis sagt die Vernunft die Wahreit?', interview with Gérard Raulet in *Spuren*, Hamburg; reprinted in *Dits et écrits*, Vol. IV, Paris: Gallimard 1994.

Foucault, Michel 1994a, *Dits et écrits. 1954–1988*, Volume One, Paris: Gallimard.

Foucault, Michel 1994b, *Dits et écrits. 1954–1988*, Volume Two, Paris: Gallimard.
Foucault, Michel 1994c, *Dits et écrits. 1954–1988*, Volume Three, Paris: Gallimard.
Foucault, Michel 1994d, *Dits et écrits. 1954–1988*, Volume Four, Paris: Gallimard.
Foucault, Michel 2004 *Sécurité, territoire, population. Cours au Collège de France, 1977–1978*, Paris: Seuil/Gallimard.
Foucault, Michel 2005, *Hermeneutics of the Subject. Lectures at the Collège de France 1981–1982*, edited by Frédéric Gros, London: Palgrave Macmillan.
Foucault, Michel 2007a, *Security, Territory, Population. Lectures at the Collège de France 1977–1978*, edited by Michel Senellart, London: Palgrave Macmillan.
Foucault, Michel 2007b, *The Birth of Biopolitics. Lectures at the Collège de France 1978–1979*, edited by Michel Senellart, London: Palgrave Macmillan.
Foucault, Michel 2007c, *Anthropology from a Pragmatic point of View*, translated and edited, with an Afterword and Critical Notes, by Roberto Nigro, Los Angeles: Semiotext(e).
Francioni, Gianni 1977, 'Per la storia dei *Quaderni del carcere*', in Ferri (ed.) 1977.
Francioni, Gianni 1984, *L'officina gramsciana. Ipotesi sulla struttura dei « Quaderni del carcere »*, Naples: Bibliopolis.
Francioni, Gianni 1992, 'Proposte per una nuova edizione dei *Quaderni del carcere*. (Seconda stesura)', in *IG Informazioni*, 2: 85–186.
Franco, Vittoria 1989, 'Introduzione', in Gyorgy Lukács, *La responsabilita sociale del filosofo*, Lucca: Maria Pacini Fazzi.
Frank, André Gunder 1967, *Capitalism and Underdevelopment, in Latin America*, New York: Monthly Review Press.
Frank, André Gunder 1972, *Lumpenbourgeoisie: Lumpendevelopment*, New York: Monthly Review Press.
Frank, André Gunder 1978, *Dependent Accumulation and Underdevelopment*, London: Macmillan Press.
Frank, André Gunder 1981, *Crisis in the Third World*, New York: Holmes & Meier.
Frank, Manfred 1989 [1983], *What Is Neostructuralism?*, translated by Sabine Wilke and Richard Gray, Minneapolis: University of Minnesota Press.
Frank, Manfred, Gérard Raulet & Willem van Reijen (eds.) 1988, *Die Frage nach dem Subjekt*, Frankfurt am Main: Suhrkamp.
Freedman, Francesca 1973, 'The Internal Structure of the Proletariat: A Marxist Analysis', *Socialist Revolution*, 26: 41–83.
Freeman, Alan 1996, 'Price, Value and Profit: A Continuous, General Treatment', in *Marx and Non-Equilibrium Economics*, edited by Alan Freeman and Guiglielmo Carchedi, Aldershot: Edward Elgar.
Friedeburg, Ludwig von & Jürgen Habermas (eds.), *Adorno-Konferenz 1983*, Frankfurt am Main: Suhrkamp.
Friedman, Milton 1962, *Capitalism and Freedom*, Chicago: University of Chicago Press.
Friedrichs, Jens 2001 'The Meaning of New Medievalism', *European Journal of International Relations*, 7, 4: 475–502.
Frosini, Fabio 2000, 'Il divenire del pensiero nei *Quaderni del carcere*', *Critica marxista*, 3–4: 108–20.
Frosini, Fabio 2003a, *Gramsci e la filosofia. Saggio sui 'Quaderni del carcere'*, Rome: Carocci.
Frosini, Fabio 2003b, 'Sulla "traducibilità" nei *Quaderni* di Gramsci', *Critica marxista*, 6: 29–38.
Frosini, Fabio & Guido Liguori (eds.) 2004, *Le parole di Gramsci. Per un lessico dei «Quaderni del carcere»*, Rome: Carocci.
Futur Antérieur 1993, *Sur Althusser. Passages*, Paris: L'Harmattan.
Futur Antérieur 1997, *Lire Althusser aujourd'hui*, Paris: L'Harmattan.
Gajano, Alberto 1979, *La Dialettica della merce*, Naples: Il Laboratorio.
Gaonkar, Dilip P. 1999, 'On Alternative Modernities', *Public Culture*, 11, 1: 1–18.
Garin, Eugenio 1955, *Cronache di filosofia italiana. 1900–1943*, Bari: Laterza.
Garin, Eugenio 1958, 'Antonio Gramsci nella cultura italiana', in *Studi gramsciani. Atti del convegno tenuto a Roma nei giorni 11–13 gennaio 1958*, Rome: Editori Riuniti-Istituto Gramsci .

Garin, Eugenio 1967, 'La formazione di Gramsci e Croce', in *Prassi rivoluzionaria e storicismo in Gramsci*, Rome: Quaderni di *Critica marxista*, 3.
Garin, Eugenio 1969, 'Politica e cultura in Gramsci (il problema degli intellettuali)', in Rossi (ed.) 1969.
Garin, Eugenio 1997, *Con Gramsci*, Rome: Editori Riuniti.
Garnier, Jean-Pierre 1994, 'L'écologisme ou la fétichisation de l'espace-temps', *Économies et Sociétés*, 6–7: 299–321.
Garo, Isabelle 2000, *Marx, critique de la philosophie*, Paris: Seuil.
Garroni, Stefano 1997, *Dialettica e differenza*, Naples: La Città del Sole.
Gattei, Giorgio 1982, 'Kozo Uno, *Principles of Political Economy*', *Il pensiero economico moderno*, 2.
Gellner, Ernest 1989, *Plough, Sword and Book*, Oxford: Blackwell.
Georgescu-Roegen, Nicholas 1971, *The Entropy Law and the Economic Process*, Cambridge, MA.: Harvard University Press.
Georgescu-Roegen, Nicholas 1995, *La Décroissance: entropie-écologie-économie*, Paris: Sang de la Terre.
Geras, Norman 1985, 'The Controversy about Marx and Justice', *New Left Review*, I, 150: 47–85.
Geras, Norman 1990, *Discourses of Extremity: Radical Ethics and Post-Marxist Extravagances*, London: Verso.
Gerratana, Valentino 1967, 'Punti di riferimento per un'edizione critica dei *Quaderni del carcere*', in *Prassi rivoluzionaria e storicismo in Gramsci*, Rome: Quaderni di *Critica marxista*, 3.
Gerratana, Valentino 1970, 'Sulla preparazione di un'edizione critica dei *Quaderni del carcere*', in Rossi (ed.) 1970.
Gerratana, Valentino 1987, 'Gramsci nel mondo', *Emigrazione*, 8–9.
Gerratana, Valentino 1997, 'Sulla "classicità" di Gramsci', in *Gramsci. Problemi di metodo*, Rome: Editori Riuniti.
Geschichte des Marxismus 1973, 2 vols., Frankfurt am Main: Suhrkamp.
Giddens, Anthony 1976, *New Rules of Sociological Method*, London: Hutchinson.
Giddens, Anthony 1979, *Central Problems in Social Theory*, London: Macmillan.
Giddens, Anthony 1981, *A Contemporary Critique of Historical Materialism*, London: Macmillan.
Gill, Stephen 1990, *American Hegemony and the Trilateral Commission*, Cambridge: Cambridge University Press.
Gill, Stephen 1995a, 'Globalization, Market Civilization, and Disciplinary Neoliberalism', *Millennium*, 24, 3: 399–423.
Gill, Stephen 1995b, 'Theorizing the Interregnum: The Double Movement and Global Politics in the 1990s', in *International Political Economy: Understanding Global Disorder*, edited by Bjorn Hettne, London, Zed Books.
Gill, Stephen 2000, 'Toward a Postmodern Prince? The Battle in Seattle as a Moment in the New Politics of Globalization', *Millennium*, 29, 1: 131-140.
Gill, Stephen 2003, *Power and Resistance in the New World Order*, London: Palgrave.
Gill, Stephen (ed.) 1993, *Gramsci, Historical Materialism and International Relations*, Cambridge: Cambridge University Press.
Gill, Stephen & David Law 1988, *The Global Political Economy. Perspectives, Problems and Policies*, Baltimore: John Hopkins University Press.
Gill, Stephen & James Mittelman (eds.) 1997, *Innovation and Transformation in international relations*, Cambridge: Cambridge University Press.
Gilloch, Graeme 1996, *Myth and Metropolis; Walter Benjamin and the City*, Cambridge: Polity.
Gilroy, Paul 1987, *There Ain't No Black in the Union Jack*, London: Hutchinson.
Gilroy, Paul 1993, *The Black Atlantic: Modernity and Double Consciousness*, London: Verso.
Gilroy, Paul 2001, *Against Race: Imagining Political Culture Beyond the Color Line*, Cambridge, MA.: Harvard University Press.
Godelier, Maurice 1986 [1984], *The Mental and the Material*, translated by Martin Thom, London: Verso.

Godelier, Maurice (ed.) 1978, *Sur les Sociétés précapitalistes – Textes choisis de Marx, Engels, Lénine*, Centre d'Études et de Recherches marxistes, Paris: Éditions sociales.
Göhler, Gerhard 1980, *Die Reduktion der Dialektik durch Marx*, Stuttgart: Klett-Cotta.
Goldberg, David T. 2002, *The Racial State*, Oxford: Blackwell.
Goldfield, Michael 1987, *The Decline of Organized Labor In the United States*, Chicago: University of Chicago Press.
Goldthorpe, John H. 2000, *On Sociology: Numbers, Narratives and the Integration of Research and Theory*, Oxford: Oxford University Press.
Gordon, David 1996, *Fat and Mean: The Corporate Squeeze of Working Americans and the Myth of Managerial 'Downsizing'*, New York: Martin Kessler Books and The Free Press.
Gorz, André 1978, *Écologie et politique*, Paris: Seuil.
Gorz, André 1990 [1988], *Critique of Economic Reason*, translated by Gillian Handyside and Chris Turner, London: Verso.
Gorz, André 1992, 'L'écologie politique entre expertocratie et autolimitation', *Actuel Marx*, 12: 15–29.
Gorz, André 1994 [1991], *Capitalism, Socialism, Ecology*, translated by Chris Turner, London: Verso.
Gotay, Samuel Silva 1985, *O pensamento cristão revolucionario na América Latina e no Caribe, 1969–73*, San Paulo: Ediçôes Paulinas.
Goux, Jean-Joseph 1973, 'Numismatiques', in *Freud, Marx: Economie et symbolique*, Paris: Seuil.
Goux, Jean-Joseph 1984 *Les monnayeurs du langage*, Paris: Galilée.
Gowan, Peter 2000, *The Global Gamble – America's Faustian Bid for World Domination*, London: Verso.
Graham, Laurie 1995, *On the Line at Subaru-Isuzu: The Japanese Model and the American Worker*, Ithaca: ILR Press.
Gramsci, Antonio 1948, 'Il materialismo storico e la filosofia di Benedetto Croce', in *Opere di Antonio Gramsci*, Volume 2, Turin: Einaudi.
Gramsci, Antonio 1949a, 'Gli intellettuali e l'organizzazione della cultura', in *Opere di Antonio Gramsci*, Volume 3, Turin: Einaudi.
Gramsci, Antonio 1949b, 'Il Risorgimento', in *Opere di Antonio Gramsci*, Volume 4, Turin: Einaudi.
Gramsci, Antonio 1949c, 'Note sul Machiavelli, sulla politica e sullo Stato moderno', in *Opere di Antonio Gramsci*, Volume 5, Turin: Einaudi.
Gramsci, Antonio 1950, 'Letteratura e vita nazionale', in *Opere di Antonio Gramsci*, Volume 6, Turin: Einaudi.
Gramsci, Antonio 1951, 'Passato e presente', in *Opere di Antonio Gramsci*, Volume 7, Turin: Einaudi.
Gramsci, Antonio 1971a, *La costruzione del Partito comunista. 1924–1926*, edited by Elsa Fubini, Turin: Einaudi.
Gramsci, Antonio 1971b, *Selections from the Prison Notebooks*, edited and translated by Quintin Hoare, London: Lawrence & Wishart.
Gramsci, Antonio 1977a, *Quaderni del carcere*, edited by Valentino Gerratana, 4 vols., Turin: Einaudi
Gramsci, Antonio 1977b, *Escritos politicos. 1917–1933*, by Juan Carlos Portantiero, Mexico City: Ediciones Pasado y Presente.
Gramsci, Antonio 1991, *Prison Notebooks*, edited by Joseph A. Buttigieg, translated by Joseph A. Buttigieg and Antonio Callari, Volume 1, New York: Columbia University Press.
Gramsci, Antonio 1993, *Grammatica e linguistica*, Rome, Editori Riuniti.
Gramsci, Antonio 1995, *Further Selections from the Prison Notebooks*, edited and translated by Derek Boothman, London: Lawrence & Wishart.
Gramsci, Antonio 2007, *Quaderni del carcere*, 1. *Quaderni di traduzioni (1929–1932)*, edited by Giuseppe Cospito and Gianni Francioni, Rome: Istituto della Enciclopedia Italiana.
Grassi, Enrico 1979, *L'esposizione dialettica nel 'Capitale' di Marx*, Rome: Basilicate.

Green, Pete 2005, 'Review of *The Culmination of Capital* edited by Martha Campbell and Geert Reuten', *Historical Materialism*, 12, 2: 249–67.
Grenier, Guillermo J. 1988, *Inhuman Relations: Quality Circles and Anti-Unionism in American Industry*, Philadelphia: Temple University Press.
Grey, Piers 2002, *Stalin on Linguistics and Other Essays*, Basingstoke, Palgrave.
Grundman, Reiner 1991, 'The Ecological Challenge to Marxism', *New Left Review*, I, 187: 103–20.
Gustafsson, Bo 1976, 'Capitalisme et socialisme dans la pensée de Bernstein', in *Histoire du marxisme contemporain* 1976.
Gutiérrez, Gustavo 1972, *Théologie de la liberation. Perspectives*, Bruxelles: Lumen Vitae.
Gutiérrez, Gustavo 1985, 'Théologie et sciences sociales', in *Théologies de la liberation. Documents et débats*, Paris: Éditions du Cerf.
Gwynne, Robert N. & Cristóbal Kay 1999, 'Latin America Transformed: Changing Paradigms, Debates and Alternatives', in *Latin America Transformed: Globalization and Modernity*, edited by Robert N. Gwynne and Cristóbal Kay, London: Arnold.
Habermas, Jürgen 1971 [1968], *Toward a Rational Society*, translated by Jeremy J. Shapiro, London: Heinemann.
Habermas, Jürgen 1972, 'Bewußtmachendeoder rettende Kritk – die Aktualität Walter Benjamins', in *Zur Aktualität Walter Benjamins*, edited by Siegfried Unseld, Frankfurt am Main: Suhrkamp, 174–223. [Translated into English as 'Consciousness-Raising or Redemptive Criticism: The Contemporaneity of Walter Benjamin': *New German Critique*, No. 17, Special Walter Benjamin Issue (Spring, 1979): 30–59.]
Habermas, Jürgen 1976 [1973], *Legitimation Crisis*, translated by Thomas McCarthy, London: Heinemann.
Habermas, Jürgen 1978 [1968], *Knowledge and Human Interests*, translated by Jeremy J. Shapiro, London: Heinemann.
Habermas, Jürgen 1979 [1976], *Communication and the Evolution of Society*, London: Heinemann.
Habermas, Jürgen 1983a, 'Einleitung zum Vortrag von Martin Jay', in von Friedeburg and Habermas (eds.) 1983.
Habermas, Jurgen 1983b, 'Die Verschlingung von Mythos und Aufklärung. Bemerkungen zur *Dialektik der Aufklärung* – nach einer erneuten Lektüre', in *Mythos und Moderne*, edited by Karl Bohrer, Frankfurt am Main: Suhrkamp.
Habermas, Jürgen 1985 [1980], 'Modernity – An Incomplete Project', translated by Seyla Benhabib, in *Postmodern Culture*, edited by Hal Foster, London: Pluto Press.
Habermas, Jürgen 1987a [1981], *The Theory of Communicative Action*, Volume Two, translated by Thomas McCarthy, Cambridge: Polity.
Habermas, Jürgen 1987b [1985], *The Philosophical Discourse of Modernity*, translated by Frederick Lawrence, Cambridge: Polity.
Habermas, Jürgen 1988 [1963], *Theory and Practice*, translated by John Viertel, Cambridge: Polity.
Habermas, Jürgen 1989 [1962], *The Structural Transformation of the Public Sphere*, translated by Thomas Burger with Frederick Lawrence, Cambridge: Polity.
Habermas, Jürgen 1995, 'Faktizität und Geltung. Ein Gespräch über Fragen der politischen Theorie', in *Die Normalität einer Berliner Republik*, Frankfurt am Main: Suhrkamp.
Habermas, Jürgen 1996 [1992], *Between Facts and Norms: Contributions to a Discursive Theory of Law and Democracy*, translated by William Rehg, Cambridge: Polity.
Habermas, Jürgen & Niklas Luhmann 1974 [1971], *Theorie der Gesellschaft oder Sozialtechnologie. Neue Beiträge zur Habermas-Luhmann-Diskussion*, Frankfurt am Main: Suhrkamp.
Hacking, Ian 2002, *Historical Ontology*, Cambridge, MA.: Harvard University Press.
Haldon, John 1993, *The State and the Tributary Mode of Production*, London: Verso.
Haldon, John 1997, *Byzantium in the Seventh Century*, Cambridge: Cambridge University Press.
Hallward, Peter 2003, *Badiou: A Subject to Truth*, Minneapolis: University of Minnesota Press.

Hamel, Pierre & Claire Poitras, 'Henri Lefebvre, penseur de la postmodernité', *Espaces et sociétés*, 76: 41–58.
Hardin, Garret 1968, 'The Tragedy of the Commons', *Science*, 162: 1243–8.
Hardt, Michael & Antonio Negri 2000, *Empire*, Cambridge, MA.: Harvard University Press.
Hardt, Michael & Antonio Negri 2004, *Multitude: War and Democracy in the Age of Empire*, New York: Penguin.
Hardt, Michael & Kathi Weeks 2000, 'Introduction', in *The Jameson Reader*, Oxford: Blackwell.
Harman, Chris 1974, *Bureaucracy and Revolution in Eastern Europe*, London: Pluto.
Harman, Chris 1982, *The Lost Revolution*, London: Bookmarks.
Harman, Chris 1984, *Explaining the Crisis*, London: Bookmarks.
Harman, Chris 1988, *The Fire Last Time*, London: Bookmarks.
Harman, Chris 1998, *Marxism and History*, London: Bookmarks.
Harman, Chris 1999, *A People's History of the World*, London: Bookmarks.
Harootunian, Harry 2000, *History's Disquiet: Modernity, Cultural Practice, and the Question of Everyday Life*, New York: Columbia University Press.
Harré, Rom & E.H. Madden 1975, *Causal Powers: A Theory of Natural Necessity*, Oxford: Blackwell.
Harribey, Jean-Marie 1997, *L'économie économe. Le développement soutenable par la réduction du temps de travail*, Paris: L'Harmattan.
Harribey, Jean-Marie 1998, *Le développement soutenable*, Paris: Economica.
Harribey, Jean-Marie 1999, 'La soutenabilité, une question de valeur(s)', Bordeaux: Centre d'économie du développement de l'Université Montesquieu.
Harrod, Jeffrey & Robert O'Brien (eds.) 2002, *Global Unions? Theory and Strategies of Organized Labour in the Global Political Economy*, London: Routledge.
Hartmann, Klaus 1972, 'Hegel: A Non-Metaphysical View', in MacIntyre (ed.) 1972.
Harvey, David 1989a, *The Urban Experience*, Baltimore: Johns Hopkins University Press.
Harvey, David 1989b, *The Condition of Postmodernity*, Oxford: Basil Blackwell.
Harvey, David 2003. *The New Imperialism*, Oxford: Oxford University Press.
Haug, Wolfgang Fritz 1974, *Vorlesungen zur Einführung ins 'Kapital'*, Köln: Pahl-Rugenstein.
Hausman, Daniel 1998, 'Problems with Supply-Side Egalitarianism', in *Recasting Egalitarianism*, edited by Bowles & Gintis (eds.) 1998.
Hebdige, Dick 1979, *Subculture: The Meaning of Style*, London: Methuen.
Hegedus, Andras 1976, *Socialism and Bureaucracy*, London: Allison & Busby.
Hegedus, Andras 1977, *The Structure of Socialist Society*, translated by Rudolf Fisher and revised by Peter Szente, London: Constable.
Hegel, Georg W.F. 1969, *Science of Logic*, translated by A.V. Miller, Atlantic Highlands: Humanities Press.
Hegel, Georg W.F. 1970, *Philosophy of Nature*, translated by A.V. Miller, 3 vols, Oxford: Oxford University Press.
Heidegger, Martin 1962 [1927], *Being and Time*, translated by John Maquarrie and Edward Robinson, Oxford: Blackwell.
Heidegger, Martin 1988, *Zur Sache des Denkens*, Tübingen: Niemeyer.
Heidegger, Martin 1993 [1947], 'Letter on Humanism', translated by Frank Capuzzi and Glenn J. Gray, in *Basic Writings*, London: Routledge.
Heinrich, Michael 2003 [1999], *Die Wissenschaft vom Wert*, Münster: Westfälisches Dampfboot.
Held, David 1980, *Introduction to Critical Theory*, Berkeley: University of California Press.
Heller, Agnes 1976 [1974], *The Theory of Need in Marx*, London: Allison and Busby.
Heller, Agnes 1979a, *On Instincts*, Assen: Gorcum.
Heller, Agnes 1979b, *A Theory of Feelings*, Assen: Gorcum.
Heller, Agnes 1980, *The Power of Shame*, Victoria: Bundoora.

Heller, Agnes 1982, *A Theory of History*, London: Routledge & Kegan Paul.
Heller, Agnes 1984, *A Radical Philosophy*, translated by James Wickham, Oxford: Blackwell.
Heller, Agnes 1990, *A Philosophy of Morals*, Oxford: Blackwell.
Heller, Agnes 1996, *An Ethics of Personality*, Oxford: Blackwell.
Heller, Agnes 1999, *A Theory of Modernity*, Oxford: Blackwell.
Heller, Agnes & Ferenc Fehér 1980, *Marxisme et démocratie. Au-delà du 'socialisme réel'*, Paris: Maspero.
Heller, Agnes, Ferenc Fehér & György Markus 1982, *Dictatorship over Needs*, Oxford: Blackwell.
Henry, Michel 1976, *Marx*, two vols., I. *Une Philosophie de la réalité*; II. *Une Philosophie de l'économie*, Paris: Gallimard.
Henry, Michel 1983, *Marx: A Philosophy of Human Reality*, translated by Kathleen McLaughlin, Bloomington: Indiana University Press.
Hering, Christoph 1979, *Der Intellektuelle als Revolutionär; Walter Benjamins Analyse intellektueller Praxis*, Munich: Wilhelm Fink.
Hill-Collins, Patricia 2000, *Black Feminist Thought: Knowledge, Consciousness, and the Politics of Empowerment*, London: Routledge.
Hill, Christopher 1958 [1954], 'The Norman Yoke' in *Puritanism and Revolution*, edited by Christopher Hill, London: Penguin.
Hill, Christopher 1975, *The World Turned Upside Down*, Harmondsworth: Penguin.
Hill, Christopher 2000 [1948], 'Marxism and History', in *Historians on History*, edited by John Tosh, London: Longman.
Hilton, Rodney (ed.) 1976, *The Transition from Feudalism to Capitalism*, London: New Left Books.
Himmelweit, Susan 1983, 'Marxist Economics in Japan', in Bottomore (ed.) 1983.
Hindess, Barry & Paul Hirst 1974, *Precapitalist Modes of Production*, London: Routledge.
Hindess, Barry & Paul Hirst 1977, *Mode of Production and Social Formation*, London: Routledge.
Hiromatsu, W. 1974, *The Philosophy of 'Capital'* (in Japanese), Tokyo.
Hirsch, Joachim 1995 *Der nationale Wettbewerbstaat. Staat, Demokratie und Politik im globalen Kapitalismus*, Berlin: Edition ID-Archiv.
Hirsch, Joachim 2005 *Materialistische Staatstheorie. Transformationsprozesse des kapitalistischen Systems*, Hamburg: VSA.
Hirschman, Charles 2004, 'The Origins and Demise of the Concept of Race', *Population and Development Review*, 30, 3: 385–415.
Histoire du marxisme contemporain 1976, Volumes 1–5, Paris: UGE-10/18.
Hobsbawm, Eric J. 1962, *The Age of Revolution*, London: Weidenfeld & Nicolson.
Hobsbawm, Eric J. 1975, *The Age of Capital*, London: Weidenfeld & Nicolson.
Hobsbawm, Eric J. 1978, 'The Historians' Group of the Communist Party', in *Rebels and Their Causes*, edited by Maurice Cornforth, London: Lawrence & Wishart.
Hobsbawm, Eric J. 1982, 'Il marxismo oggi: un bilancio aperto', in Hobsbawm et al. (eds.) 1978–82.
Hobsbawm, Eric J. 1987a, *The Age of Empire*, London: Weidenfeld & Nicolson.
Hobsbawm, Eric J. 1987b, 'Per capire le classi subalterne', in *Rinascita/Il Contemporaneo* 1987.
Hobsbawm, Eric J. 1990, *Echoes of the Marseillaise: Two Centuries Look Back on the French Revolution*, London: Verso.
Hobsbawm, Eric J. 1995, 'Introduzione', in *Gramsci in Europa e in America*, edited by Antonio A. Santucci, Bari: Laterza.
Hobsbawm, Eric J. 2004, 'History: A New Age of Reason', *Le Monde Diplomatique*, December.
Hobsbawm, Eric J. et al. (eds.) 1978–82, *Storia del marxismo*, 4 vols., Turin: Einaudi.
Hoffmann, Jürgen 2006, *Arbeitsbeziehungen im Rheinischen Kapitalismus. Zwischen Modernisierung und Globalisierung*, Münster: Westfälisches Dampfboot.

Hoggart, Richard 1957, *The Uses of Literacy*, London: Chatto & Windus.
Holloway, John 2002, *Change the World without Taking Power: the Meaning of Revolution Today*, London: Pluto.
Holz, Hans Heinz 1992, *Philosophie der zersplitterten Welt. Reflexionen über Walter Benjamin*, Bonn: Pahl-Rugenstein.
Homer, Sean 1998, *Fredric Jameson: Marxism, Hermeneutics, Postmdernism*, Cambridge: Polity.
Honneth, Axel 1991 [1985], *The Critique of Power: Reflective Stages in a Critical Social Theory*, translated by Kenneth Baynes, Cambridge, MA.: MIT Press.
Honneth, Axel 1995 [1994], *Desintegration. Bruchstücke einer soziologischen Zeitdiagnose*, Frankfurt am Main: Suhrkamp.
Honneth, Axel 1999 [1990], *Die zerrissene Welt des Sozialen*, Frankfurt am Main: Suhrkamp.
Hook, Sidney 1933, *Towards an Understanding of Karl Marx*, London: Victor Gollancz.
Hopkins, Terence & Immanuel Wallerstein 1982, *World-Systems Analysis Theory and Methodology*, Beverly Hills: Sage.
Horkheimer, Max 1947, *Eclipse of Reason*, Oxford: Oxford University Press.
Horkheimer, Max 1972 [1931], 'Die gegenwärtige Lage der Sozialphilosophie und die Aufgraben eines Instituts für Sozialforschung', in *Sozialphilosophische Studien*, Frankfurt am Main: Suhrkamp.
Horkheimer, Max 1996, *Gesammelte Schriften. Briefwechsel*, Volume 18, Frankfurt am Main: Suhrkamp.
Houlgate, Stephen (ed.) 1998, *Hegel and the Philosophy of Nature*, Albany: State University of New York Press.
Houston, David 1992, 'Is there a New Social Structure of Accumulation?', *Review of Radical Political Economics*, 24, 2: 60–7.
Howard, Michael C. & J.E. King 1989, *A History of Marxian Economics: Volume I, 1883–1929*, Princeton: Princeton University Press.
Howard, Michael C. & J.E. King 1992, *A History of Marxian Economics: Volume II, 1929–1990*, Princeton: Princeton University Press.
Huang, Philip 1985, *The Peasant Economy and Social Change in North China*, Stanford: Stanford University Press.
Huang, Philip 1990, *The Peasant Family and Rural Development in the Yangzi Delta, 1350–1988*, Stanford: Stanford University Press.
Hume, David 1970, *A Treatise of Human Nature*, Harmondsworth: Penguin.
Huntington, Samuel 1998. *The Clash of Civilizations and the Remaking of World Order* London: Touchstone.
Hurston, Zora N. 1991, *Their Eyes Were Watching God*, Urbana: University of Illinois Press.
Husserl, Edmund 1964, *The Phenomenology of Internal Time-Consciousness*, trans. James S. Churchill, Bloomington: Indiana University Press.
Husson, Michel 1996, *Misère du capital*, Paris: Syros.
Husson, Michel 1999, 'After the Golden Age: *Late Capitalism*', in *The Legacy of Ernest Mandel*, edited by Gilbert Achcar, London: Verso.
Husson, Michel 2000, *Six milliards sur la planète: sommes-nous trop?*, Paris: Textuel.
Ichida, Yoshihiko 1997, 'Temps et concept chez Louis Althusser', in *Futur antérieur* 1997.
Ilyenkov, Evald Vasilyevich 1977 [1974], *Dialectical Logic: Essays on its History and Theory*, translated by H. Campbell Creighton, Moscow: Progress Publishers.
Ilyenkov, Evald Vasilyevich 1982, *Dialectics of the Abstract and the Concrete in Marx's 'Capital'*, translated by Sergei Syrovatkin, Moscow: Progress Publishers.
Istituto Gramsci Informazioni 1992, 'Verbale della riunione del comitato di esperti del 3 luglio 1991', n. 2.
Itoh, Makoto 1980, *Value and Crisis: Essays on Marxian Economics in Japan*, London: Pluto Press.
Ives, Peter 1998, 'A Grammatical Introduction to Gramsci's Political Theory', *Rethinking Marxism*, 10, 1: 34–51.

Ives, Peter 2004a, *Gramsci's Politics of Language*, Toronto: University of Toronto Press.
Ives, Peter 2004b, *Language and Hegemony in Gramsci*, London: Pluto Press.
Ives, Peter 2005, 'Language, Agency and Hegemony: A Gramscian Response to Post-Marxism', *Critical Review of International Social and Political Philosophy*, 8, 4: 455–68.
Jameson, Fredric 1971, *Marxism and Form: Twentieth Century Dialectical Theories of Literature*, Princeton: Princeton University Press.
Jameson, Fredric 1972, *The Prison-House of Language: A Critical Account of Structuralism and Russian Formalism*, Princeton: Princeton University Press.
Jameson, Fredric 1981, The *Political Unconscious: Narrative as a Socially Symbolic Act*, Ithaca: Cornell University Press.
Jameson, Fredric 1984 [1961], *Sartre: The Origins of a Style*, New York: Columbia University Press.
Jameson, Fredric 1988a, *The Ideologies of Theory: Essays 1971–1986*, Volume One, *Situations of Theory*, Minneapolis: University of Minnesota Press.
Jameson, Fredric 1988b, *The Ideologies of Theory: Essays 1971–1986*, Volume Two, *The Syntax of History*, Minneapolis: University of Minnesota Press.
Jameson, Frederic 1990, *Late Marxism: Adorno, or, the Persistence of the Dialectic*, London: Verso.
Jameson, Fredric 1991, *Postmodernism, or the Cultural Logic of Late Capitalism*, London: Verso.
Jameson, Fredric 1993, 'Actually Existing Marxism', *Polygraph*, 6–7: 170–95.
Jameson, Fredric 1997, 'Five Theses on Actually Existing Marxism', in *In Defense of History: Marxism and the Postmodern Agenda*, edited by Ellen Meiksins Wood and John Bellamy Foster, New York: Monthly Review Press.
Jameson, Fredric 1998, *The Cultural Turn*, London: Verso.
Jameson, Fredric 2002, *A Singular Modernity: Essay on the Ontology of the Present*, London: Verso.
Janka, Walter 1981, *Schwierigkeiten mit der Wahreit*, Hamburg: Rowohlt.
Janka, Walter 1991, *Spuren eines Leben*, Berlin: Rowohlt.
Jarvis, Simon 1998, *Adorno: A Critical Introduction*, Cambridge: Polity.
Jauss, Hans Robert 1988, 'Das kritische Potential ästhetischer Bildung', in *Die Zukunft der Aufklärung*, edited by Jörn Rüsen, Eberhard Lämmert, and Peter Glotz, Frankfurt am Main: Suhrkamp.
Jay, Martin 1973, *The Dialectical Imagination: A History of the Frankfurt School and the Institute of Social Research, 1923–1950*, Boston: Beacon Press.
Jenkins, J. Craig & Craig M. Eckert 2000, 'The Right Turning Economic Policy: Business Elites and the New Conservative Economics', *Sociological Forum*, 15, 2: 307–38.
Jessop, Bob 1990, *State Theory: Putting the Capitalist State in its Place*, Cambridge: Polity.
Jessop, Bob 2002, *The Future of the Capitalist State*, Cambridge: Polity.
Jessop, Bob 2007, *State Power: A Strategic-Relational Approach*, Cambridge: Polity.
Johnson, Richard 1978 'Edward Thompson, Eugene Genovese, and Socialist-Humanist History', *History Workshop Journal*, 6, 2: 79–100.
Johnson, Richard 1980, 'Culture and the Historians', in *Working Class Culture*, edited by John Clarkem, London: Hutchinson.
Johnson, Richard 1981, 'Against Absolutism', in *People's History and Socialist Theory*, edited by Raphael Samuel, London: Routledge.
Jonas, Hans 1984 [1979], *The Imperative of Responsibility: In Search of an Ethics for the Technological Age*, translated by Hans Jonas with David Herr, Chicago: Chicago University Press.
Joos, Ernest 1993, *Lukács's Last Autocriticism: The Ontology*, Atlantic Highlands: Humanities Press.
Jorland, Gérard 1995, *Les Paradoxes du capital*, Paris: Odile Jacob.
Joseph, Jonathan 2006, *Marxism and Social Theory*, London: Palgrave Macmillan.
Kaiwar, Vasant 1992, 'Property Structures, Demography and the Crisis of the Agrarian Economy of Colonial Bombay Presidency', *Journal of Peasant Studies*, 19, 2: 255–300.

Kaiwar, Vasant 1993, 'The Limits of Techno-Malthusianism: A Rejoinder to Sumit Guha', *Journal of Peasant Studies*, 20, 3: 521–31.

Kalecki, Michael 1971, *Selected Essays on the Dynamics of the Capitalist Economy*, Cambridge: Cambridge University Press.

Kallscheurer, Otto 1986, *Marxismus und Erkenntnis in Western Europa*, Franfurt am Main: Suhrkamp.

Kanoussi, Dora 1999, 'La coerenza filosofica dei *Quaderni*', in *Gramsci e il Novecento*, edited by Giuseppe Vacca, Volume I, Rome: Carocci.

Kanoussi, Dora 2000, 'Gramsci e la filosofia europea del suo tempo', *Critica marxista*, 3–4: 81–7.

Kaye, Harvey 1992, *The Education of Desire*, London: Routledge.

Kaye, Harvey 1995, *The British Marxist Historians*, London: Macmillan.

Kelly, Brian 2001, *Race, Class and Power in the Alabama Coalfields, 1908–21*, Urbana: University of Illinois Press.

Kincaid, Jim 2005, 'A Critique of Value-Form Theory', *Historical Materialism*, 13, 2: 84–119.

King, Desmond & Mark Wickham-Jones 1995, 'Social Democracy and Rational Choice Marxism', in Carver & Thomas (eds.) 1995.

Kirk, Neville 1996, 'Class and the "Linguistic Turn" in Chartist and Post-Chartist Historiography', in *Social Class and Marxism*, edited by Neville Kirk, Aldershot: Ashgate.

Kirk, Neville 1997, 'History, Language, Ideas and Postmodernism: A Materialist View', in *The Postmodern History Reader*, edited by Keith Jenkins, London: Routledge.

Kleinknecht, Alfred, Ernest Mandel & Immanuel Wallerstein (eds.) 1992, *New Findings in Long Wave Research*, London: Macmillan.

Kolakowski, Leszek 1976–8, *Main Currents of Marxism*, 3 vols., Oxford: Oxford University Press.

Kolb, David 1986, *The Critique of Pure Modernity. Hegel, Heidegger and After*, Chicago: University of Chicago Press.

Kornai, Janos 1980, *Economics of Shortage*, North Holland: Elsevier.

Korsch, Karl 1973 [1931], 'Crise du marxisme', in *L'Anti-Kautsky, ou la conception matérialiste de l'histoire*, Paris: Champ Libre.

Kosík, Karel 1976 [1967], *Dialectics of the Concrete: A Study on Problems of Man and World*, translated by Karel Kovanda with James Schmidt, Dordrecht: D. Reidel.

Kouvélakis, Eustache 1996, 'Le postfordisme, une lecture à partir de Gramsci et Foucault', in *L'ordre capitaliste*, Paris: Presses Universitaires de France.

Kouvélakis, Eustache 2000, 'D'un congrès a l'autre: Marx fin de siècle', in *Marx 2000*, Paris: Presses Universitaires de France.

Kouvélakis, Stathis 2004, 'Marx et sa critique de la politique. Des révolutions de 1848 à la Commune de Paris, ou le travail de la rectification', available at: <http://semimarx.free.fr/article.php3?id_article=8>.

Kouvélakis, Eustache & Michel Vakaloulis 1994, 'Entretien avec Fredric Jameson', *Futur Antérieur*: 21, available at <www.multitudes.samizdat.net/article834.html>.

Kovel, Joel 1984, *White Racism: A Psychohistory*, New York: Columbia University Press.

Kovel Joel 2002, *The Enemy of Nature, The End of Capitalism or the End of the World?*, London: Zed Books.

L'Organisation politique 2001, 'Qu'est-ce que l'organisation politique', available at: <http://www.orgapoli.net/spip.php?article86>.

La Grassa, Gianfranco 1996, *Lezioni sul capitalismo*, Bologna: CLUEB.

La Grassa, Gianfranco 1998, *Movimenti progressivi: verso la ricostruzione di una teoria critica del capitalismo*, Milan: Punto Rosso.

La Grassa, Gianfranco 1999, *La tela di Penelope: conflitto, crisi e riproduzione nel capitalismo*, Pistoia: CRT.

La Grassa, Gianfranco 2005, *Gli strateghi del capitale: una teoria del conflitto oltre Marx e Lenin*, Rome: Manifestolibri.

Labica, Georges 1987, *Le Paradigme du Grand Hornu. Essai sur l'idéologie*, Paris: La Brèche.
Labica, Georges 1989, 'Le marxisme: orthodoxie et hétérodoxie. Pour un bilan critique', in *Encyclopédie philosophique universelle*, Volume 1, *L'univers philosophique*, Paris: Presses Universitaires de France.
Labica, Georges 2002, *Démocratie et révolution*, Paris: Le Temps des cerises.
Labica, Georges & Gérard Bensussan (eds.) 1985 [1982], *Dictionnaire critique du marxisme*, Paris: Presses Universitaires de France.
Labriola, Antonio 1934 [1899], *Socialism and Philosophy*, translated by Ernest Untermann, Chicago: Charles H. Kerr.
Labriola, Antonio 1966 [1896], *Essays on the Materialistic Conception of History*, translated by Charles Kerr, New York: Monthly Review Press.
Labriola, Antonio 1970 [1902], *Essais sur la conception matérialiste de l'histoire*, Paris: Gordon & Breach.
Labriola, Antonio 1975, *Lettere a Benedetto Croce, 1885–1904*, Naples: Istituto italiano per gli studi storici.
Lacher, Hannes 1999a, 'Embedded Liberalism, Disembedded Markets: Conceptualising the Pax-Americana', *New Political Economy*, 4, 3: 343–60.
Lacher, Hannes 1999b, 'The Politics of the Market: Re-Reading Karl Polanyi', *Global Society*, 13, 3: 313–26.
Lacher, Hannes 2002, 'Making Sense of the International System: Promises and the Pitfalls of Contemporary Marxist Theories of International Relations', in *Historical Materialism and Globalization*, edited by Mark Rupert and Hazel Smith, London: Routledge.
Lacher, Hannes 2003, 'Putting the State in its Place: The Critique of State-Centrism and its Limits', *Review of International Studies*, 29, 4: 521–41.
Lacher, Hannes 2005, 'International Transformation and the Persistence of Territoriality: Towards a New Political Geography of Capitalism', *Review of International Political Economy*, 12, 1: 26–52.
Laclau, Ernesto 1991, *New Reflections on the Revolution of Our Time*, London: Verso.
Laclau, Ernesto & Chantal Mouffe 1985, *Hegemony and Socialist Strategy*, London: Verso.
Lafont, Robert 1978, *Le Travail et la langue*, Paris: Flammarion.
Lakatos, Imre 1978, *Philosophical Papers*, 2 vols., Cambridge: Cambridge University Press.
Lange, Oskar 1938, 'On the Economic Theory of Socialism', in *On the Economic Theory of Socialism*, edited by Oskar Lange and Fred M. Taylor, Minneapolis: University of Minnesota Press.
Larrain, Jorge 2000, *Identity and Modernity in Latin America*, Cambridge: Polity.
Larsen, Neil 2005, 'Imperialism, Colonialism, Postcolonialism', in *A Companion to Postcolonial Studies*, edited by Sangeeta Ray and Henry Schwarz, Oxford: Blackwell.
Latouche, Serge 1986, *Faut-il refuser le développement?*, Paris: Presses Universitaires de France.
Lawler, James 1998, 'Marx as Market Socialist', in *Market Socialism: The Debate among Socialists*, edited by Bertell Ollman, London: Routledge.
Lazarus, Neil 2002, 'The Fetish of "the West" in Postcolonial Theory', in *Marxism, Modernity and Postcolonial Studies*, edited by Crystal Bartolovich and Neil Lazarus, Cambridge: Cambridge University Press.
Lazarus, Sylvain 2005, 'Dans quel temps de la politique sommes nous? (éditorial)', *Le Journal Politique*, 2, available at: <http://www.orgapoli.net/article.php3?id_article=57>.
Lazarus, Sylvain (ed.) 1993, *Politique et philosophie dans l'oeuvre de Louis Althusser*, Paris: Presses Universitaires de France.
Lazzarato, Maurizio & Antonio Negri 1992, 'Lavoro immateriale e soggettività', *DeriveApprodi*, 0: 31–7.
Leavis, F.R. 1936, *Revaluation*, London: Chatto & Windus.

Lebovici, Renée 1983, 'Shangaï et Gdansk', *Le Perroquet*, 29–30.
Lecercle, Jean-Jacques 1987, 'Le recit-maître de Fredric Jameson', *Actuel Marx*, 1: 84–93.
Lecercle, Jean-Jacques 2007, *A Marxist Philosophy of Language*, Leiden: Brill Academic Publishers.
Lecercle, Jean-Jacques & Denise Riley, *The Force of Language*, Basingstoke: Palgrave.
Lecourt, Dominique 1973, *Une crise et son enjeu. Essai sur la position de Lénine en philosophie*, Paris: Maspero.
Lefebvre, Henri 1966, *Le Langage et la société*, Paris: Gallimard.
Lefebvre, Henri 1968 [1940], *Dialectical Materialism*, translated by John Sturrock, London: Jonathan Cape.
Lefebvre, Henri 1972, *La Pensée marxiste et la ville*, Paris: Casterman.
Lefebvre, Henri 1973, *La Survie du capitalisme. La reproduction des rapports de production*, Paris: Anthropos.
Lefebvre, Henri 1974a, *Le Droit à la ville*, Paris: Seuil.
Lefebvre, Henri 1974b, *La Révolution urbaine*, Paris: Gallimard.
Lefebvre, Henri 1974c, *Espace et politique*, Paris: Seuil.
Lefebvre, Henri 1978, *De l'État*, Volume Four, Paris: 10/18.
Lefebvre, Henri 1983, 'Entretien avec Henri Lefebvre', *Villes en parallèle*, 7: 51–63.
Lefebvre, Henri 1989 [1959], *La Somme et le reste*, Paris: Méridiens-Klincksieck.
Lefebvre, Henri 1990 [1974], *The Production of Space*, translated by Donald Nicholson-Smith, Oxford: Blackwell.
Lefebvre, Henri 1991 [1947], *Critique of Everyday Life*, Volume One, translated by John Moore, London: Verso.
Lefebvre, Henri 1992, *Éléments de rythmanalyse*, Paris: Syllepse.
Lefebvre, Henri 1995 [1962], *Introduction to Modernity*, translated by John Moore, London: Verso.
Lefebvre, Henri 2002 [1961], *Critique of Everyday Life*, Volume Two, translated by John Moore, London: Verso.
Leff, Enrique 1986, *Ecologia y capital*, Mexico: UNAM.
Leff, Enrique 1999, 'On the Social Reappropriation of Nature', *Capitalism, Nature, Socialism*, 10, 3: 89–104.
Lenin, Vladimir I. 1964, 'On Slogans', in *Collected Works*, Volume 25, London: Lawrence & Wishart.
Lenin, Vladimir 1968 [1909], *Materialism and Empirio-Criticism*, in *Collected Works*, Volume 14, Moscow: Progress Publishers.
Lenin, Vladimir I. 1996, *Imperialism: the Highest Stage of Capitalism*, London: Pluto Press.
Lepre, Aurelio 1978, *Gramsci secondo Gramsci*, Naples: Liguori.
Lerner, Abba P. 1946, *The Economics of Control*, New York: Macmillan.
Leslie, Esther 2000, *Walter Benjamin: Overpowering Conformism*, London: Pluto.
Levine, Andrew & Erik O. Wright 1980, 'Rationality and Class Struggle', *New Left Review*, I, 123: 47–68.
Lidtke, Vernon L. 1976, 'Bernstein et les premises théoriques du socialisme', in *Histoire du marxisme contemporain* 1976.
Lie, John 1987, 'Reactionary Marxism: the End of Ideology in Japan?', *Monthly Review*, April: 45–51.
Liguori, Guido 1996, *Gramsci conteso. Storia di un dibattito 1922–1996*, Rome: Editori Riuniti.
Liguori, Guido 1999, 'Le edizioni dei *Quaderni* di Gramsci tra filologia e politica', in *Gramsci da un secolo all'altro*, edited by Giorgio Baratta and Guido Liguori, Rome: Editori Riuniti.
Liguori, Guido 2005, 'Gramsci conteso, dieci anni dopo', in Guido Liguori and Chiara Meta, *Gramsci. Guida alla lettura*, Milan: Unicopli.
Linebaugh, Peter 1991, *The London Hanged*, London: Allen Lane.
Lipietz, Alain 1979, *Crise et inflation, pourquoi?*, Paris: Maspero.
Lipietz, Alain 1982, 'The So-Called "Transformation Problem" Revisited', *Journal of Economic Theory*, 26, 1: 59–88.

Lipietz, Alain 1993, *Vert espérance. L'avenir de l'écologie politique*, Paris: La Découverte.
Lipietz, Alain 1994, 'De l'approche de la régulation à l'écologie politique: une mise en perspective historique', in *École de la regulation et critique de la raison économique*, Paris: *Futur Antérieur*-L'Harmattan.
Lipietz, Alain 1996, 'L'écologie politique et l'avenir du marxisme', in *Congrès Marx International. Cent ans de marxisme. Bilan critique et perspectives*, Paris: Presses Universitaires de France.
Lipietz, Alain 1998, 'Économie politique des écotaxes', in *Conseil d'analyse économique, Fiscalité de l'environnement*, Paris: La Documentation Française.
Lipietz, Alain 1999, 'Epargne salariale et retraites: une solution mutualiste', available at: <http://lipietz.net/spip.php?rubrique31>.
Lipietz, Alain 1999, *Qu'est-ce que l'écologie politique? La grande transformation du XXIe siècle*, Paris: La Découverte.
Lippit, Victor 1997, 'The Reconstruction of a Social Structure of Accumulation in the United States', *Review of Radical Political Economics*, 29, 3: 10–21.
Lo Piparo, Franco 1979, *Lingua, intellettuali, egemonia in Gramsci*, Bari: Laterza.
Looker, Robert 1988, 'Shifting Trajectories: Perry Anderson's Changing Account of the Pattern of English Historical Development', in *The Development of British Capitalist Society: A Marxist Debate*, edited by Colin Barker and David Nicholls, Manchester: Northern Marxist Historians Group.
Loren, Charles 1977, *Classes in the United States*, California: Cardinal Publishers.
Lorenzi, Jean-Hervé, Olivier Pastré & Joëlle Toledano 1980, *La Crise du XXème siècle*, Paris: Economica.
Losurdo, Domenico 2003, *Nietzsche, il ribelle aristocratico. Biografia intellettuale e bilancio critico*, Turin: Bollati Boringhieri.
Losurdo, Domenico 2006, *Controstoria del liberalismo*, Bari: Laterza.
Lowe, Lisa & David Lloyd 1997. 'Introduction', in *The Politics of Culture in the Shadow of Capital*, edited by Lisa Lowe and David Lloyd, Durham, NC.: Duke University Press.
Löwy, Michael 1979, *Georg Lukács. From Romanticism to Bolshevism*, translated by Patrick Camiller, London: New Left Books.
Löwy, Michael 1992, 'Benjamins Marxismus', *Argument*, 34: 557–62.
Löwy, Michael 1996, *The War of Gods: Religion and Politics in Latin America*, London: Verso.
Löwy, Michael 2001, *Walter Benjamin; Avertissement d'incendie – Une lecture des thèses 'Sur le concept d'histoire'*, Paris: Presses Universitaires de France. [Translated into English as *Fire Alarm: Reading Walter Benjamin's 'On the Concept of History'*, London: Verso, 2006.]
Löwy Michael (ed.) 2005, *Ecologie et socialisme*, Paris: Syllepse.
Lukács, Georg 1963, *Ästhetik. I. Die Eigenart des Ästhetischen, Gesamtausgabe*, Volumes 11 and 12, Luchterland: Darmstadt-Neuwied.
Lukács, Georg 1971, *History and Class Consciousness: Studies in Marxist Dialectics*, London: Merlin Press.
Lukács, Georg 1972 [1968], *Political Writings 1919–1929*, translated by Michael McColgan, London: New Left Books.
Lukács, Georg 1978, *Marx's Basic Ontological Principles*, translated by David Fernbach, London: Merlin Press.
Lukács, Georg 1980, *Labour*, translated by David Fernbach, London: Merlin Press.
Lukács, Georg 1983, *Georg Lukács: Record of a Life – An Autobiography*, translated by Rodney Livingstone, London: Verso.
Lukács, Georg 1984, *Zur Ontologie des gesellschaftlichen Sein, Gesamtausgabe*, Volume 13, Luchterland: Darmstadt-Neuwied.
Lukács, Georg 1990, *Prolegomeni all'ontologia dell' essere sociale. Questioni di principio di una ontologia oggi devenuta possible*, translated by A. Scarponi, Milan: Guerini.
Lukács, Georg 1991 [1958], *The Process of Democratization*, translated by Susanne Bernhardt and Norman Levine, Albany: State University of New York Press.
Lukács, Georg 2000, *A Defence of 'History and Class Consciousness': Tailism and the Dialectic*, London: Verso.

Luporini, Cesare 1974, *Dialettica e materialismo*, Rome: Editori Riuniti.
Lutz-Bachmann, Matthias (ed.) 1991, *Kritischer Materialismus*, Munich: Hanser.
Lutz-Bachmann, Matthias 1997, *Kritische Theorie und Religion*, Würzburg: Echter.
Lutz-Bachmann, Matthias & Gunzelin Schmid-Noerr (eds.) 1991, *Kritischer Materialismus. Zur Diskussion eines Materialismus der Praxis. Festschrift für Alfred Schmidt zum 60. Geburtstag*, Munich: Hanser.
Luxemburg, Rosa 1970 [1899], 'Reform or Revolution', in *Rosa Luxemburg Speaks*, edited by Mary-Alice Waters, New York: Pathfinder Press.
Lyotard, Jean-François 1984 [1979], *The Postmodern Condition: A Report on Knowledge*, translated by Geoff Bennington and Brian Massumi, Manchester: Manchester University Press.
Macey, David 2000, *Frantz Fanon: A Life*, London: Granta.
MacGregor, David 1996, *Hegel, Marx, and the English State*, Toronto: University of Toronto Press.
Macherey, Pierre 1979, *Hegel ou Spinoza*, Paris: Maspero.
Macherey, Pierre 1992, 'Foucault/Roussel/Foucault', in Michel Foucault, *Raymond Roussel*, Paris: Gallimard.
Macherey, Pierre 1998, *In a Materialist Way: Selected Essays*, translated by Ted Stolze, London: Verso.
Macherey, Pierre 1999, *Histoires de dinosaure*, Paris: Presses Universitaires de France.
MacIntyre, Alasdair 1998 [1958–9], 'Notes from the Moral Wilderness', in *The MacIntyre Reader*, edited by Kelvin Knight, Cambridge: Polity.
MacIntyre, Alistair (ed.) 1972, *Hegel*, New York: Anchor Books.
Maclean, B. 1981, 'Kôzô Uno's *Principles of Political Economy*', *Science & Society*, 45, 2.
Maler, Henri 1995, *Convoiter l'impossible. L'utopie avec Marx, malgré Marx*, Paris: Albin Michel.
Mallet, Marie-Louise & Ginette Michaud (eds.) 2004, *Jacques Derrida*, Paris: L'Herne.
Malthus, Thomas R. 1970 [1798], *An Essay on the Principle of Population*, Harmondsworth: Penguin.
Mandel, Ernest 1975 [1972], *Late Capitalism*, translated by Joris De Bres, London: New Left Books.
Mandel, Ernest 1995 [1980], *Long Waves of Capitalist Development: A Marxist Interpretation*, London: Verso.
Mangoni, Luisa 1977, 'Il problema del fascismo nei *Quaderni del carcere*', in Ferri (ed.) 1977.
Mann, Michael 1986 and 1993, *The Sources of Social Power*, 2 vols., Cambridge: Cambridge University Press.
Manning, Brian 1994, 'The English Revolution and the Transition from Feudalism to Capitalism', *International Socialism Journal*, 63: 75–87.
Manning, Brian 1997, 'A Muted Blast: Review of E.M. Wood & N. Wood's *A Trumpet of Sedition*', *Socialist Review*, 208: 28–9.
Manning, Brian 1999, 'The English Revolution: The Decline and Fall of Revisionism', *Socialist History*, 14: 40–53.
Marazzi, Christian 1994, *Il posto dei calzini: La svolta linguistica dell'economia e i suoi effetti nella politica*, Bellinzona: Casagrande.
Marcus, Laura & Lynda Nead (eds.) 1999, *The Actuality of Walter Benjamin*, London: Lawrence & Wishart.
Maréchal, Jean-Paul 1997, *Le Rationnel et le raisonnable. L'économie, l'emploi et l'environnement*, Rennes: Presses Universitaires de Rennes.
Markner, Reinhard 1994, 'Walter Benjamin nach der Moderne. Etwas zur Frage seiner Aktualität angesichts der Rezeption seit 1983', *Schattenlinien* 8–9: 37–47. (Online: <http://markner.free.fr/wbrezept.htm>).
Markus, György 1978, *Marxism and Anthropology*, Assen: Gorcum.
Markus, György 1986 [1971], *Language and Production: A Critique of the Paradigms*, Dordrecht: Reidel.
Martin, James (ed.) 2002, *Antonio Gramsci. Critical Assessments of Leading Political Philosophers*, 4 vols., London: Routledge.

Martinez-Alier, Juan 1992a, 'Valeur économique, valeur écologique', *Écologie politique*, 1: 13–39.
Martinez-Alier, Juan 1992b, 'La confluence dans l'éco-socialisme', in *L'idée de socialisme a-t-elle un avenir?*, edited by Jacques Bidet and Jacques Texier, Paris: Presses Universitaires de France.
Martinez-Alier, Juan & Klaus Schlupmann 1987, *Ecological Economics*, Oxford: Basil Blackwell.
Marx, Karl, 1964–72 [1905–10], *Theories of Surplus-Value*, 3 vols, transated by Emile Burns and Renate Sampson, Moscow: Foreign Languages Publishing House.
Marx, Karl 1973a [1856], 'Speech at the Anniversary of the People's Paper', in *Surveys from Exile*, London: Penguin.
Marx, Karl 1973b [1939], *Grundrisse*, translated by Martin Nicolaus, Harmondsworth: Penguin/*New Left Review*.
Marx, Karl 1975a, *Early Writings*, translated by Gregor Benton and Rodney Livingstone, Harmondsworth: Penguin/*New Left Review*.
Marx, Karl 1975b, 'Preface' to *A Contribution to the Critique of Political Economy*, in Marx 1975a.
Marx, Karl 1975c, *Contribution to the Critique of Hegel's Philosophy of Law*, in Marx and Engels 1975a.
Marx, Karl 1976–81 [1867], *Capital*, 3 vols, translated by Ben Fowkes and David Fernbach, Harmondsworth: Penguin.
Marx, Karl 1977, *Le Capital – Critique de l'économie politique*, Livre 1, Paris: Éditions Sociales.
Marx, Karl 1978, *Class Struggles in France*, in *Collected Works*, Volume 10, London: Lawrence & Wishart.
Marx, Karl 1981 [1894], *Capital: Volume Three*, translated by David Fernbach, Harmondsworth: Penguin/*New Left Review*.
Marx, Karl & Frederick Engels 1965, *The German Ideology*, London: Lawrence & Wishart.
Marx, Karl & Frederick, Engels 1969, *Selected Works*, Volume One, Moscow: Progress Publishers.
Marx, Karl & Frederick Engels 1976, *Collected Works*, Volume 3, London: Lawrence & Wishart.
Marx, Karl & Frederick Engels 1978, *On Colonialism*, Moscow: Progress Publishers.
Marx, Karl & Frederick Engels 1983, *Collected Works*, Volume 40, London: Lawrence & Wishart.
Marx, Karl & Friedrich Engels 1987, *Collected Works*, Volume 20: 1864–68, London: Lawrence & Wishart.
Masaryk, Tomas G. 1898, 'La crise scientifique et philosophique du marxisme contemporain', *Revue Internationale de Sociologie*, 6.
Matheron, François 1997, 'La recurrence du vide chez Louis Althusser', in *Futur Antérieur* 1997.
Matsuura, Tamotsu 1972, 'Marginalism in Japan', *History of Political Economy*, 4: 533–50.
Mayer, Tom 1994, *Analytical Marxism*, Beverly Hills: Sage.
Mazzone, Alessandro 2001 [1981], *Mega 2: Marx ritrovato*, Rome: Media Print.
McLennan, Gregor 1981, *Marxism and the Methodologies of History*, London: Verso.
McNally, David 1988, *Political Economy and the Rise of Capitalism*, Berkeley: University of California Press.
McNally, David 1999, 'Turbulence in the World Economy', *Monthly Review*, 51, 2, available at: <http://www.monthlyreview.org/699mcnal.htm>.
McNally, David 2001, *Bodies of Meaning*, New York: State University of New York Press.
McRobbie, Angela 1992, 'The *Passagenwerk* and the Place of Walter Benjamin in Cultural Studies; Benjamin, Cultural Studies, Marxist Theories of Art', *Cultural Studies*, 6, 2: 147–69.
Meaney, Mark E. 2002, *Capital as Organic Unity: The Role of Hegel's 'Science of Logic' in Marx's 'Grundrisse'*, Dordrecht: Kluwer Academic Publishers.

Mercier-Josa, Solange 1980, *Lire Hegel et Marx*, Paris: Éditions Sociales.
Mercier-Josa, Solange 1999, *Entre Hegel et Marx*, Paris: L'Harmattan.
Messner, Dirk 1998 *The Network Society*, London: Cass.
Mészáros, István 1970, *Marx's Theory of Alienation*, London: Merlin Press.
Mészáros, István 1972, *Lukács's Concept of Dialectic*, London: Merlin Press.
Mészáros, István 1986, *Philosophy, Ideology and Social Science*, Brighton: Harvester Wheatsheaf.
Mészáros, István 1995, *Beyond Capital: Towards a Theory of Transition*, London: Merlin Press.
Meyerson, Gregory 2001, 'Rethinking Black Marxism: Reflections on Cedric Robinson and Others', *Cultural Logic* 3, 2, available at: <http://clogic.eserver.org/3-1&2/meyerson.html>.
Miles, Robert 1982, *Racism and Migrant Labour*, London: Routledge & Kegan Paul.
Miles, Robert 1987, *Capitalism and Unfree Labour: Anomaly or Necessity?*, London: Tavistock.
Miles, Robert 1989, *Racism*, London: Routledge.
Miles, Robert 1993, *Racism After 'Race Relations'*, London: Routledge.
Milkman, Ruth 1997, *Farewell to the Factory: Auto Workers in the Late Twentieth Century*, Berkeley: University of California Press.
Miller, Christopher L. 1990, *Theories of Africans: Francophone Literature and Anthropology in Africa*, Chicago: University of Chicago Press.
Mitchell, Timothy J. 1991, 'The Limits of the State: Beyond Statist Approaches and their Critics', *American Political Science Review*, 85, 1: 77–96.
Mizruchi, Mark 1996, 'What Do Interlocks Do? An Analysis, Critique, and Assessment of Research on Interlocking Directorates', *Annual Review of Sociology*, 22: 271–98.
Mizuta, H. 1977, 'Il marxismo in Giappone', *Revista storica italiana*, 89, 2: 281–300.
Monasta, Attilio 1985, *L'educazione tradita. Criteri per una diversa valutazione complessiva dei 'Quaderni del carcere di A. Gramsci'*, Pisa: Giardini.
Moody, Kim 1988, *An Injury to All: The Decline of American Unionism*, London: Verso.
Moody, Kim 1997, *Workers in a Lean World: Unions in the International Economy*, London: Verso.
Mooers, Colin 1991, *The Making of Bourgeois Europe*, London: Verso.
Mordenti Raul 1989, 'Il Gramsci di Togliatti. Appunti per una filologia gramsciana', in *Modern times. Gramsci e la critica dell'americanismo*, edited by Giorgio Baratta and Andrea Catone, Milan: Diffusioni '84.
Mordenti, Raul 1996, '*Quaderni del carcere* di Antonio Gramsci', in *Letteratura italiana. Le Opere*, edited by Alberto Asor Rosa, Volume IV, 2, Turin: Einaudi.
Mordenti, Raul 2007, *Gramsci e la rivoluzione necessaria*, Rome: Riuniti.
Morley, David & Kuan Hsing Chen (eds.) 1996, *Stuart Hall: Critical Dialogues*, London: Routledge.
Morton, Adam David 2003a, 'Historicizing Gramsci: Situating Ideas in and Beyond Their Context', *Review of International Political Economy*, 10, 1: 118–46.
Morton, Adam David 2003b, 'Structural Change and Neoliberalism in Mexico: "Passive Revolution" in the Global Political Economy', *Third World Quarterly*, 24, 4: 631–54.
Moseley, Fred 1992, *The Falling Rate of Profit in the Postwar United States Economy*, New York: St. Martin's Press.
Moseley, Fred 1997, 'The Falling Rate of Profit and the Future of Capitalism', *Review of Radical Political Economics*, 29, 4: 23–41.
Moseley, Fred 1993 (ed.), *Marx's Method in 'Capital': A Reexamination*, Atlantic Highlands,: Humanities Press.
Moseley, Fred & Martha Campbell (eds.) 1997, *New Investigations in Marx's Method*, Atlantic Highlands: Humanities Press.
Moseley, Fred (ed.) 2005, *Marx's Theory of Money: Modern Appraisals*, London: Palgrave Macmillan.
Moulier Boutang, Yann 1992, *Louis Althusser. Une biographie*, Volume 1, Paris: Grasset.
Moulier Boutang, Yann 1997, 'L'interdiction biographique et l'autorisation de l'œuvre', in *Futur Antérieur* 1997.

Mugnai, Massimo 1984, *l mondo rovesciato: contraddizione e valore in Marx*, Bologna: Il Mulino.
Mulhern, Francis 1978, *The Moment of 'Scrutiny'*, London: New Left Books.
Müller, Jens Christian et al. 1994 *Der Staat in den Köpfen: Anschlüsse an Louis Althusser und Nicos Poulantzas*, Mainz: Decaton.
Münster, Arno 1998, *Le Principe 'discussion'*, Paris: Éditions Kimé.
Murphy, Craig N. 1994, *International Organization and Industrial Change. Global Governance since 1850*, Cambridge: Polity.
Murphy, Kevin 2005, *Revolution and Counterrevolution: Class Struggle in a Moscow Metal Factory*, Oxford: Berghahn.
Murray, Martin & Charles Post 1983, 'The Agrarian Question, Class Struggle and the Capitalist State in the United States and South Africa', *Insurgent Sociologist*, 11, 4: 37–56.
Murray, Patrick 1988, *Marx's Theory of Scientific Knowledge*, Atlantic Highlands: Humanities Press.
Murray, Patrick 1993, 'The Necessity of Money: How Hegel Helped Marx Surpass Ricardo's Theory of Value', in Moseley (ed.) 1993.
Murray, Patrick 2002, 'Reply to Geert Reuten', *Historical Materialism*, 10, 1: 155–76.
Nakano-Glenn, Evelyn 1999, 'The Social Construction and Institutionalization of Gender and Race: An Integrative Framework', in *Revisioning Gender*, edited by Myra Marx Ferree, Judith Lorber and Beth B. Hess, Thousand Oaks: Sage.
Napoleoni, Claudio 1973, *Smith, Ricardo e Marx*, Turin: Bollati Boringhieri.
Napoleoni, Claudio 1985, *Discorso sull'economia politica*, Turin: Bollati Boringhieri.
Naredo, José Manuel 1999, 'Quantifying Natural Capital: Beyond Monetary Value', *Conference of the Groupe Regards Critiques de l'Université de Lausanne*, 19–20 January.
Negri, Antonio 1973, 'Ultimo tango a Mirafiori. Note sul convegno del Gramsci', in *Aut aut*, 138: 77–83.
Negri, Antonio 1976, *Proletari e Stato. Per una discussione su autonomia operaia e compromesso storico*, Feltrinelli: Milan.
Negri, Antonio 1977, *La forma Stato*, Feltrinelli: Milan.
Negri, Antonio 1991 [1979], *Marx beyond Marx: Lessons on the 'Grundrisse'*, translated by Harry Cleaver, Michael Ryan and Maurizio Viano, London: Pluto Press.
Negri, Antonio 1997, 'Lettera dal Carcere di Rebibbia', 10/09/1997, text circulated on the internet.
Negri, Antonio 1997, 'Machiavel selon Althusser', in *Futur Antérieur* 1997.
Negri, Antonio 1999, 'Biopolitica e contropotere', *DeriveApprodi*, 18: 40–52.
Negri, Antonio 2005, *La differenza italiana*, Rome: Nottetempo.
Negt, Oskar & Alexander Kluge 1981, *Geschichte und Eigensinn*, Frankfurt am Main: Zweitausendeins.
Negt, Oskar & Alexander Kluge, 1993 [1972], *Public Sphere and Experience: Towards an Analysis of the Bourgeois and Proletarian Public Sphere*, translated by Peter Labanyi, Jamie Owen Daniel and Miriam Hansen, Minneapolis: University of Minnesota Press.
Neocleous, Mark 2003, *Imagining the State*, Maidenhead: Open University Press.
Nietzsche, Friedrich 1997 [1874], 'On the Uses and Disadvantages of History for Life', in *Untimely Meditations*, translated by R.J. Hollingdale, Cambridge: Cambridge University Press.
Nitzan, Jonathan & Shimshon Bichler 2002 *The Global Political Economy of Israel*, London: Pluto.
Nohra, Fouad 1997, *Théories du capitalisme mondial*, Paris: L'Harmattan/Forum du Tiers-Monde.
Nordhaug, Christian 2002, 'Globalisation and the State: Theoretical Paradigms', *European Journal of Development Research*, 14, 10: 5–27.
Nove, Alec 1983, *The Economics of Feasible Socialism*, London: Allen and Unwin.
Nozick, Robert 1974, *Anarchy, State and Utopia*, New York: Basic Books.
O'Connor, James 1992, 'La seconde contradiction du capitalisme: causes et conséquences', *Actuel Marx*, 12: 30–40.

O'Connor, James 1999, 'A Prolegomenon to an Ecological Marxism: Thoughts on the Materialist Conception of History', *Capitalism, Nature, Socialism*, 10, 2: 77–106.
O'Connor, Martin 1996, 'Cherishing the Future, Cherishing the Other: A "Post-Classical" Theory of Value', in *Models of Sustainable Development*, edited by Sylvie Faucheux, David Pearce and John Proops, Cheltenham: Edward Elgar.
O'Hanlon, Rosalind 2000, 'Recovering the Subject: Subaltern Studies and Histories of Resistance in Colonial South Asia', in *Mapping Subaltern Studies and the Postcolonial*, edited by Vinayak Chaturvedi, London: Verso.
Obispos Latinoamericanos 1978, *Los obispos latinoamericanos entre medellín y puebla*, San Salvador: Universidad Centroamericana.
Odum, Howard 1971, *Environment, Power and Society*, New York: Wiley-Interscience.
Offe, Claus 1984 [1972], *Contradictions of the Welfare State*, London: Hutchinson.
Okishio, Nobuo 1961, 'Technical Change and the Rate of Profit', *Kobe University Economic Review*, 7: 86–99.
Oldrini, Guido (ed.) 1979, *Lukács*, Milan: Mondadori.
Oldrini, Guido (ed.) 1981, *Il marxismo della maturità di Lukács*, Naples: Prisimi.
Ollman, Bertell 1993, *Dialectical Investigations*, London: Routledge.
Ouchi, Tsutomu 1983, 'Notes on the Theory of State-Monopoly Capitalism', *Annals of the Institute of Social Sciences*, 23, Tokyo University.
Overbeek, Henk 1990, *Global Capitalism and National Decline. The Thatcher Decade in Perspective*, London: Unwin Hyman.
Overbeek, Henk (ed.) 1993, *Restructuring Hegemony in the Global Political Economy: the Rise of Transnational Neoliberalism in the 1980s*, London: Routledge.
Paetzold, Heinz 1974, *Neomarxistische Ästhetik*, Dusseldorf: Schwann.
Paggi, Leonardo 1970, *Antonio Gramsci e il moderno principe. I. Nella crisi del socialismo italiano*, Rome: Editori Riuniti.
Paggi, Leonardo 1984, *Le strategie del potere in Gramsci. Tra fascismo e socialismo in un solo paese. 1923–1926*, Rome: Editori Riuniti.
Palmer, Bryan 1990, *Descent into Discourse*, Philadelphia: Temple University Press.
Panitch, Leo 1994, 'Globalization and the State', in Panitch et al., 2004.
Panitch, Leo 1996, 'Rethinking the Role of the State', in James H. Mittleman (ed.) *Globalization: Critical Reflections*, Boulder: Lynne Rienner Publishers.
Panitch, Leo et al. 2004, *The Globalization Decade, A Critical Reader*, London: Merlin Press.
Panitch, Leo & Colin Leys (eds.) 1998, *Socialist Register 1998: The Communist Manifesto Now*, London: Merlin.
Panzieri, Raniero 1994, *Spontaneità e organizzazione. Gli anni dei 'Quaderni Rossi' 1959–1964*, Pisa: BFS Edizioni.
Papi, Fulvio (ed.) 1983, *Dizionario Marx Engels*, Bologna: Zanichelli.
Parker, Mike & Jane Slaughter 1988, *Choosing Sides: Unions and the Team Concept*, Detroit: Labour Education and Research Project.
Parry, Benita 1987, 'Problems in Current Theories of Colonial Discourse', *Oxford Literary Review*, 9, 1–2: 27–58.
Parry, Benita 2004, *Postcolonial Studies: A Materialist Critique*, London: Routledge.
Pasolini, Pier Paolo 1972, 'Dal Laboratorio (Appunti *en poète* per una linguistica marxista)', in *Empirismo eretico*, Milan: Garzanti.
Passet, René 1996 [1979], *L'économique et le vivant*, Paris: Economica.
Pearce, David 1974, 'Economics and Ecology', *Surrey Papers in Economics*, 10.
Pêcheux, Michel 1982, *Language, Semantics and Ideology*, Basingstoke, Macmillan.
Pellerin, Hélène 2003, 'Crisis? What Crisis? The Politics of Migration Regulation in the Era of Globalization', in *Globalization. Theory and Practice*, edited by Gillian Young and Eleonore Kofman, London: Continuum.
Pellerin, Hélène & Henk Overbeek 2001, 'Neoliberal Regionalism and the Management of People's Mobility', in Bieler & Morton (eds.) 2001.
Perroquet 62–3: 1/4–6. English translation in *Prelom*, 8, available at: <http://www.prelomkolektiv.org/eng/08.htm>.
Perry, Matt 2002, *Marxism and History*, London: Palgrave.

Petitdemange, Guy 1985, 'Théologie(s) de la libération et marxisme(s)', in 'Pourquoi la théologie de la libération', supplement to *Cahiers de l'actualité religieuse et sociale*, 307.

Petrucciani, Stefano 1995, *Marx al tramonto del secolo: teoria critica tra passato e futuro*, Rome: Manifestolibri.

Peyrol, Georges (a.k.a. Alain Badiou) 1983, '30 moyens de reconnaître à coup sûr un vieux-marxiste', *Le Perroquet*, 29–30: 5–6. English translation in *Prelom*, 8, available at: <http://www.prelomkolektiv.org/eng/08.htm>.

Pfotenhauer, Helmut 1975, *Ästhetische Erfahrung und gesellschaftliches System: Untersuchungen zu Methodenproblemen einer materialistischen Literaturanalyse am Spätwerk Walter Benjamins*, Stuttgart: Metzler.

Phéline Christian 1975, 'Répartition primaire des revenues et rentabilité du capital (1954–1973)', *Statistiques et Études Financières*, 19.

Pignon, Dominique & Pierre Rigoulot 1982, 'La gauche schizophrène et la Pologne', *Les Temps Modernes*, 426.

Pigou, Arthur 1920, *The Economics of Welfare*, London: Macmillan.

Pinkard, Terry 1985, 'The Logic of Hegel's *Logic*', in *Hegel*, edited by Michael Inwood, Oxford University Press.

Pinkard, Terry 2000, *Hegel*, Cambridge: Cambridge University Press.

Podolinsky, Sergei 1880a, 'Le socialisme et l'unité des forces physiques', *La Revue socialiste*, 8: 353–65.

Podolinsky, Sergei 1880b, 'Le socialisme et la théorie de Darwin', *La Revue socialiste*, 3: 129–48.

Podolinsky, Sergei 1880c, 'Le travail humain et la conservation de l'énergie', *Revue internationale des sciences*, 5: 57–70.

Polanyi, Karl 1957 [1944], *The Great Transformation*, Boston: Beacon Press.

Pomeranz, Kenneth 2000, *The Great Divergence: Europe, China, and the Making of the Modern World Economy*, Princeton: Princeton University Press.

Portantiero, Juan-Carlos 1981, *Los usos de Gramsci*, Mexico City: Folios Ediciones [2nd. ed. Buenos Aires: Folios Ediciones, 1983; 3rd ed. Buenos Aires: Grijalbo, 1999].

Post, Charles 1982, 'The American Road to Capitalism', *New Left Review*, I, 133: 30–51.

Post, Charles 1995, 'The Agrarian Origins of US Capitalism: The Transformations of the Northern Countryside Before the Civil War', *Journal of Peasant Studies*, 22, 3: 389–445.

Post, Charles 1997, 'The Agrarian Revolution in the United States: The Development of Capitalism and the Adoption of the Reaper in the Antebellum US North', *Science & Society*, 61, 2: 216–28.

Postone, Moishe 1996, *Time, Labour and Social Domination*, Cambridge: Cambridge University Press.

Poulantzas, Nicos 1973, 'L'internationalisation des rapports capitalistes de l'État-nation', *Les Temps Modernes*, 319: 1456–500.

Poulantzas, Nicos 1975 [1974], *Classes in Contemporary Capitalism*, translated by David Fernbach, London: New Left Books.

Poulantzas, Nicos 1978, *State, Power, Socialism*, London: Verso.

Power, Nina 2005, 'What Is Generic Humanity? Badiou and Feuerbach', *Subject Matters*, 2, 1: 35–46.

Power, Nina & Alberto Toscano 2003, 'Think, Pig!: An Introduction to Badiou's Beckett', in Alain Badiou, *On Beckett*, edited by Nina Power and Alberto Toscano, Manchester: Clinamen Press.

Prakash, Gyan 1990, 'Writing Post-Orientalist Histories of the Third World: Perspectives from Indian Historiography'. *Comparative Studies in Society and History*, 32, 2: 383–408.

Préli, Georges 1977, *La Force du dehors. Extériorité, limite et non-pouvoir à partir de M. Blanchot*, Fontenay-sous-Bois: Recherches.

Prestipino, Giuseppe 2002, *Realismo e utopia: in memoria di Lukacs e Bloch*, Rome: Editori Riuniti.

Preve, Costanzo 1984, *La filosofia imperfetta: una proposta di ricostruzione del marxismo contemporaneo*, Milan: Franco Angeli.
Preve, Costanzo 1992a, *L'assalto al cielo: saggio su marxismo e individualismo*, Milan: Vangelista.
Preve, Costanzo 1992b, *Il pianeta rosso: saggio su marxismo e universalismo*, Milan: Vangelista.
Preve, Costanzo 1999, *I secoli difficili: introduzione al pensiero filosofico dell'ottocento e del novecento*, Pistoia: CRT.
Preve, Costanzo 2004, *Marx inattuale: eredita e prospettiva*, Turin: Bollati Boringhieri.
Preve, Costanzo 2007, *Storia critica del marxismo: dalla nascità di Marx alla dissoluzione de comunismo storico novescentesco*, Naples: La Città del Sole.
Prigogine, Ilya & Isabelle Stengers 1979, *La nouvelle alliance. Métamorphose de la science*, Paris: Gallimard.
Prigogine, Ilya & Isabelle Stengers 1984, *Order Out of Chaos*, London: Fontana.
Przeworski, Adam 1985, *Capitalism and Social Democracy*, Cambridge: Cambridge University Press.
Przeworski, Adam 1991, *Democracy and the Market*, Cambridge: Cambridge University Press.
Quiniou, Yvon 1989, *Problèmes du matérialisme*, Paris: Méridiens Klincksieck.
Raddatz, Fritz 1979, 'Die Kräfte des Rausches für die Revolution gewinnen. Der Literaturbegriff des preußischen Snobs und jüdischen Melancholikers Walter Benjamin', in *Revolte und Melancholie*, Frankfurt am Main: Suhrkamp.
Rancière, Jacques 1974, *La Leçon d'Althusser*, Paris: Gallimard.
Rancière, Jacques 1993, 'La scène du texte', in Lazarus (ed.) 1993.
Rancière, Jacques 1994, *The Names of History: On the Poetics of Knowledge*, Minneapolis: University of Minnesota Press.
Rancière, Jacques 1999, *Disagreement: Politics and Philosophy*, Minneapolis: University of Minnesota Press.
Raulet, Gérard 1988, 'Die neue Utopie. Die soziologische und philosophische Bedeutung der neuen Kommunikationstechnologien', in *Die Frage nach dem Subjekt*, edited by Manfred Frank, Gérard Raulet, and Willem van Reijen, Frankfurt am Main: Suhrkamp.
Raulet, Gérard 1989a, 'Stratégies consensuelles et esthétique post-moderne', *Recherches sociologiques*, 20, 2.
Raulet, Gérard 1989b, 'Ornament und Demokratie', *Kunstforum international*, 100: 342–53.
Raulet, Gérard 1998, 'Über eine Materialismusdebatte, die nicht stattfund', in *Kann Hoffnung enttäuscht werden?*, *Bloch-Jahrbuch 1997*, Tübingen: Talheimer.
Raulet, Gérard 1999a, 'Demokratie zwischen Ornament und Dissens. Zur Architektonik des Global Village', 8th Internationales Bauhaus-Colloquium, Weimar, October.
Raulet, Gérard 1999b, *Apologie de la citoyenneté*, Paris: Cerf.
Raulet Gérard (ed.) 1986, *Réification et utopie: Ernst Bloch et György Lukács. Un siècle après*, Arles: Actes Sud.
Raulet, Gérard & Jochen Hörisch 1992, *Soziokulturelle Auswirkungen moderner Informations- und Kommunitionstechnologien in der Bundesrepublik Deutschland und in Frankreich*, Frankfurt am Main: Campus.
Rawls, John 1971, *A Theory of Justice*, Oxford: Oxford University Press.
Raymond, Pierre (ed.) 1997, *Althusser philosophe*, Paris: Presses Universitaires de France.
Rebitzer, James 1993, 'Radical Political Economy and the Economics of Labor Markets', *Journal of Economic Literature*, 31: 1394–434.
Rees, John (ed.) 1998a, *Essays on Historical Materialism*, London: Bookmarks.
Rees, John 1998b, *The Algebra of Revolution: The Dialectic and the Classical Marxist Tradition*, London: Routledge.
Reich, Michael 1993, 'Radical Economics in Historical Perspective', *Review of Radical Political Economics*, 25, 3: 43–50.

Reich, Michael 1997, 'Social Structure of Accumulation Theory: Retrospect and Prospect', *Review of Radical Political Economics*, 29, 3: 1–10.
Reichelt, Helmut 1970, *Zur logischen Struktur des Kapitalbegriffs bei Karl Marx*, Frankfurt am Main: Europäische Verlagsanstalt.
Reichelt, Helmut 2001, *Zur logischen Structur des Kapitalbegriffs bei Karl Marx*, Freiburg: Ça ira Verlag.
Renault, Emmanuel 1995, *Marx et l'idée de critique*, Paris: Presses Universitaires de France.
Renton, David 2004, *Dissident Marxism*, London: Zed.
Rethinking Marxism 1998, *Rereading Althusser*, 10, 3.
Reuten, Geert 1989, 'Value as Social Form', in *Value, Social Form and the State*, edited by Geert Reuten & Michael Williams, London: Routledge.
Reuten, Geert 2000, 'The Interconnections between Systematic Dialectics and Historical Materialism', *Historical Materialism*, 7: 137–65.
Ricoeur, Paul 1986, *Lectures on Ideology and Utopia*, New York: Columbia University Press.
Righi, Maria Luisa (ed.) 1995 [1989], *Gramsci nel mondo, Atti del convegno internazionale di studi gramsciani, Formia*, Rome: Fondazione Istituto Gramsci.
Rinascita/Il contemporaneo 1975, *Gramsci: L'edizione critica dei 'Quaderni del carcere', n. 30* (with articles by Valentino Gerratana, Dino Ferreri, Eric J. Hobsbawm, Christine Buci-Glucksmann, Leonardo Paggi, Nicola Badaloni, Paolo Spriano, Giacomo Marramao).
Robelin, Jean 1989, *Marxisme et socialisation*, Paris: Méridiens Klincksieck.
Robelin, Jean 1992, 'Gramsci et Althusser: problèmes et enjeux de la lecture althusserienne', in *Modernité de Gramsci?*, edited by André Tosel, Besançon: Annales Littéraires de l'Université de Besançon.
Robelin, Jean 1994, *La Petite fabrique du droit*, Paris: Kimé.
Robelin, Jean 1998, *Les Sagesses de l'art*, Paris: Kimé.
Roberts, Marcus 1996, *Analytical Marxism: A Critique*, London: Verso.
Robinson, Joan 1962, *Essays in the Theory of Economic Growth*, London: Macmillan.
Robinson, William I. 2004, *A Theory of Global Capitalism*, Baltimore: Johns Hopkins Universty Press.
Rockmore, Tom (ed.) 1988, *Lukács Today: Essays in Marxist Philosophy*, Dordrecht: Reidel.
Roediger, David R. 1999, *The Wages of Whiteness: Race and the Making of the American Working Class*, London: Verso.
Roediger, David R. 2006, 'The Retreat from Race and Class', *Monthly Review*, 58, 1: 1–12.
Roemer, John 1981, *Analytical Foundations of Marxian Economic Theory*, Cambridge: Cambridge University Press.
Roemer, John 1982a, *A General Theory of Exploitation and Class*, Cambridge, MA.: Harvard University Press.
Roemer, John 1982b, 'New Directions in the Marxian Theory of Exploitation and Class', *Politics and Society*, 11, 3: 363–73.
Roemer, John 1982c, 'Exploitation, Alternatives and Socialism', *Economic Journal*, 92, 365: 87–107.
Roemer, John 1986, 'Should Marxists be Interested in Exploitation?', in Roemer (ed.) 1986.
Roemer, John 1992, 'Can There Be a Socialism after Communism?', *Politics and Society*, 3: 261–72.
Roemer, John 1994, *A Future for Socialism*, Cambridge, MA.: Harvard University Press.
Roemer, John 1995, *Theories of Distributive Justice*, Cambridge, MA.: Harvard University Press.
Roemer, John (ed.) 1986, *Analytical Marxism*, Cambridge: Cambridge University Press.

Roemer, John 1996 (ed.), *Equal Shares*, London: Verso.

Rorty, Richard 1998, *Achieving Our Country*, Cambridge, MA.: Harvard University Press.

Rorty, Richard 1999, 'Back to Class Politics', in *Philosophy and Social Hope*, London: Penguin.

Rosdolsky, Roman 1977 [1969], *The Making of Marx's 'Capital'*, translated by Pete Burgess, London: Pluto Press.

Rosenberg, Justin 1994, *The Empire of Civil Society. A Critique of the Realist Theory of International Relations*, London: Verso.

Rosenberg, Justin 1996, 'Isaac Deutscher and the Lost History of International Relations', *New Left Review*, I, 215: 3–15.

Rosenberg, Justin 2000, *The Follies of Globalization Theory*, London: Verso.

Rosenberg, Justin 2005, 'A Post-Mortem to Globalization Theory', *International Politics*, 42, 1: 2–74.

Rosenberg, Justin 2006, 'Why There is No International Sociology?', *European Journal of International Relations*, 12: 307–40.

Rosenberg, Justin with Alex Callinicos forthcoming, 'Uneven and Combined Development: The Social-Relational Substratum of "the International"?', *Cambridge Review of International Affairs*.

Rosenthal, John 1998, *The Myth of the Dialectic*, London: Macmillan.

Rosewarne, Stuart 1997, 'Marxism, the Second Contradiction and Socialist Ecology', *Capitalism, Nature, Socialism*, 8, 2: 99–120.

Rossi, Mario 1974, *Cultura e rivoluzione*, Rome: Editori Riuniti.

Rossi, Pietro (ed.) 1969, *Gramsci e la cultura contemporanea. Atti del convegno internazionale di studi gramsciani*, Volume I, Rome: Editori Riuniti-Istituto Gramsci.

Rossi, Pietro (ed.) 1970, *Gramsci e la cultura contemporanea*, Volume II, Rome: Editori Riuniti-Istituto Gramsci.

Rossi-Landi, Ferruccio 1982, *Ideologia. Per l'interpretazione di un operare sociale e la ricostruzione di un concetto*, Second edition revised and enlarged, Milan: Mondadori.

Rossi-Landi, Ferruccio 1983, *Language as Work and Trade*, South Hadley, Mass.

Rossi-Landi, Ferruccio 1990, *Marxism and Ideology*, Oxford: Oxford University Press.

Rousset, Pierre 1994, 'Biosphère, crise écologique et crise sociale', *Politis: La Revue*, 8: 81–4.

Ruben, David-Hillel 1977, *Marxism and Materialism*, Hassocks: Harvester.

Rubin, Isaac I. 1972 [1928], *Essays on Marx's Theory of Value*, translated by Milos Samardzija and Fredy Perlman, Detroit: Black and Red.

Runciman, Walter G. 1989, *A Treatise on Social Theory*, Cambridge: Cambridge University Press.

Rupert, Mark 1995, *Producing Hegemony: The Politics of Mass Production and American Global Power*, Cambridge: Cambridge University Press.

Rupert, Mark 2000, *Ideologies of Globalization: Contending Visions of a New World Order*, London: Routledge.

Rupert, Mark 2003, 'Globalizing Common Sense: A Marxian-Gramscian (Re)Vision of the Politics of Governance/Resistance', *Review of International Studies*, 29, 1: 181–98.

Saad-Filho, Alfredo 2002, *The Value of Marx: Political Economy for Contemporary Capitalism*, London: Routledge.

Sachs, Wolfgang & Gustavo Esteva 1996, *Des ruines du développement*, Montreal: Ecosociété.

Said, Edward W. 1979, *Orientalism*, New York: Vintage.

Said, Edward W. 1994, *Representations of the Intellectual*, London: Vintage.

Said, Edward W. 2004, *Power, Politics and Culture: Interviews with Edward W. Said*, edited by Gauri Viswanathan, London: Bloomsbury.

Salt, James 1989, 'Sunbelt Capital and Conservative Political Realignment in the 1970's and 1980's', *Critical Sociology*, 17: 145–65.

Samuel, Raphael 1980, 'British Marxist History', *New Left Review*, I, 120: 21–96.

Samuel, Raphael 1991, 'Reading the Signs', *History Workshop Journal*, 32, 3: 88–109.

Samuel, Raphael 1992, 'Reading the Signs: II. Fact-Grubbers and Mind-Readers', *History Workshop Journal*, 33, 2: 220–51.
Sandevince, Paul 1984a, 'La politique sous condition', *Le Perroquet*, 42: 1–3.
Sandevince, Paul 1984b, 'Les formes de conscience (Octobre 1980)', *Le Perroquet*, 42: 5–6.
Sandevince, Paul 1984c, 'La fin des références (May 1982)', *Le Perroquet*, 42, 1984.
Sartre, Jean-Paul 1968 [1960], *Search for a Method*, translated by Hazel Barnes, New York: Vintage Books.
Sasso, Gennaro 1991, 'Gramsci, troppo politico per essere filosofo', Interview by G. Lehner, in *Avanti!*, January 20–1.
Sasso, Gennaro 2003, 'Gramsci e l'idealismo (Appunti e considerazioni)', in *La Cultura*, 3: 351–402.
Saville, John 1977, 'The Radical Left Expects the Past to Do its Duty', *Labour History* 18, 2: 267–74.
Saville, John 1987, *1848: The British State and the Chartist Movement*, Cambridge: Cambridge University Press.
Saville, John 2003, *Memoirs from the Left*, London: Merlin.
Sayer, Andrew 2005, *The Moral Significance of Class*, Cambridge: Cambridge University Press.
Scheuerman, William E. 2004, *Liberal Democracy and the Social Acceleration of Time*, Baltimore: Johns Hopkins University Press.
Schmid-Noerr, Gunzelin 1988, *Metamorphosen der Aufklärung. Vernunftkritik heute*, Tübingen: Diskord.
Schmidt, Alfred 1965, 'Zum Verhältnis von Geschichte und Natur im dialektischen Materialismus', in *Existentialismus und Marxismus: eine Kontroverse zwischen Sartre, Garaudy, Hyppolite, Vigier und Orcel*, edited by Alfred Schmidt, Frankfurt am Main: Suhrkamp.
Schmidt, Alfred 1971a, 'Der strukturalistische Angriff auf die Geschicht', in *Beiträge zur marxistischen Erkenntnistheorie*, edited by Alfred Schmidt, Frankfurt am Main: Suhrkamp.
Schmidt, Alfred 1971b [1962], *The Concept of Nature in Marx*, translated by Ben Fowkes, London: New Left Books.
Schmidt, Alfred 1977a, *Studien über Materialismus (Schopenhauer, Horkheimer, Glücksproblem)*, Munich: Piper.
Schmidt, Alfred 1977b [1973], *Emanzipatorische Sinnlichkeit. Ludwig Feuerbachs anthropologischer Materialismus*, Munich: Hanser.
Schmidt, Alfred 1981 [1971], *History and Structure: An Essay on Hegelian-Marxist and Structuralist Theories of History*, translated by Jeffrey Herf, Cambridge, MA.: MIT Press.
Schmidt, Alfred & Werner Post 1975, *Was ist Materialismus?*, Munich: Kösel.
Scholem, Gershom 1976, *On Jews and Judaism in Crisis*, New York: Schocken Books.
Scholem, Gershom 1981, *The Story of a Friendship*, New York: New York Review of Books.
Schürmann, Reiner 1982, *Le Principe d'anarchie. Heidegger et la question de l'agir*, Paris: Seuil.
Schwarz, Bill 1982, '"The People" in History: The Communist Party Historians' Group, 1946–1956', in *Making Histories: Studies in History-Writing and Politics*, edited by Richard Johnson et al., Minneapolis: University of Minnesota Press.
Schwarz, Winfried 1978, *Die Strukturgeschichte des Marxschen Hauptwerkes*, West Berlin: DEB.
Schwarz, Yves 1988, *Expérience et connaissance du travail*, Paris: Messidor/Éditions Sociales.
Schwarz, Yves 1992, *Travail et philosophie: convocations mutuelles*, Toulouse: Octarès.
Schwarz, Yves 2000, *Le paradigme ergologique ou Un métier de philosophe*, Toulouse: Octarès.
Schweickart, David 1992a, 'Economic Democracy: A Worthy Socialism that Would Really Work', *Science & Society*, 56, 1: 9–38.

Schweickart, David 1992b, 'Socialism, Democracy, Market, Planning: Putting the Pieces Together', *Review of Radical Political Economics*, 24, 3–4: 29–45.
Schweickart, David 1993, *Against Capitalism*, Cambridge: Cambridge University Press.
Science & Society 2001–2, 'The Transnational Ruling Class Formation Thesis: A Symposium', 65, 4: 464–533.
Scott, David 1999, *Refashioning Futures: Criticism after Postcoloniality*, Princeton: Princeton University Press.
Scott, James 1998, *Seeing Like a State: How Certain Schemes to Improve the Human Condition Have Failed*, New Haven: Yale University Press.
Seel, Martin 1996a, *Ethisch-ästhetische Studien*, Frankfurt am Main: Suhrkamp.
Seel, Martin 1996b [1991], *Eine Ästhetik der Natur*, Frankfurt am Main: Suhrkamp.
Seel, Martin 1997 [1985], *Die Kunst der Entzweiung*, Frankfurt am Main: Suhrkamp.
Segesvary, Victor 2004, *World State, Nation States, or Non-Centralized Institutions? A Vision of the Future in Politics*, Lanham: University Press of America.
Sekine, Thomas 1975, 'Uno-riron: A Japanese Contribution to Marxian Political Economy', *Journal of Economic Literature*, 13, 3: 847–77.
Sekine, Thomas 1980, 'The Necessity of the Law of Value', *Science & Society*, 44, 3: 289–304.
Sekine, Thomas 1981, 'The Circular Motion of Capital', *Science & Society*, 45, 3: 288–305.
Sekine, Thomas 1982–3, 'The Law of the Market Value', *Science & Society*, 46, 4.
Sekine, Thomas 1984–6, *The Dialectic of Capital*, 2 vols., Tokyo: Yushindo Press.
Sekine, Thomas 1997, *An Outline of the Dialectic of Capital*, 2 vols., London: Macmillan.
Serequeberhan, Tsenay 1997, 'The Critique of Eurocentrism and the Practice of African Philosophy', in *Postcolonial African Philosophy*, edited by Emmanuel Chukwudi Eze, Oxford: Blackwell.
Sertel, Murat 1982, *Workers and Incentives*, North Holland: Elsevier.
Sève, Lucien 1980, *Une Introduction à la philosophie marxiste*, Paris: Éditions Sociales.
Sève, Lucien 1998, *Commencer par les fins*, Paris: La Dispute.
Sève, Lucien 2004, *Penser avec Marx aujourd'hui*, Volume 1, *Marx et nous*, Paris: La Dispute.
Sève, Lucien (ed.) 1998, *Sciences et dialectique*, Paris: La Dispute.
Sève, Lucien (ed.) 2005, *Émergence, complexité et dialectique: sur les systèmes non-linéaires*, Paris: Odile Jacob.
Shaikh, Anwar 1992, 'The Falling Rate of Profit as the Cause of Long Waves: Theory and Empirical Evidence', in Kleinknecht, Mandel & Wallerstein (eds.) 1992.
Shaw, Martin 2000, *Theory of the Global State. Globality as an Unfinished Revolution*, Cambridge: Cambridge University Press.
Shilliam, Robbie 2004, 'Hegemony and the Unfashionable Problematic of "Primitive Accumulation"', *Millennium*, 32, 1: 59–88.
Shohat, Ella & Robert Stam 1994. *Unthinking Eurocentrism: Multiculturalism and the Media*, London: Routledge.
Sivanandan, Ambalavaner 1981, 'From Resistance to Rebellion: Asian and Afro-Caribbean Struggles in Britain', *Race and Class* 23, 2–3: 111–52.
Sivanandan, Ambalavaner 1991, *A Different Hunger: Writings on Black Resistance*, London: Pluto Press.
Sivanandan, Ambalavaner 2006, 'Race, Terror and Civil Society', *Race and Class* 47, 3: 1–8.
Skirbekk, Gunnar 1974, 'Marxisme et écologie', *Esprit*, 440: 643–52.
Slaughter, Anne-Marie 2004 *A New World Order*, Princeton: Princeton University Press.
Slaughter, Cliff 1980, *Marxism, Ideology and Literature*, London: Macmillan.
Smith, Tony 1990, *The Logic of Marx's 'Capital': Replies to Hegelian Criticism*, Albany: State University of New York Press.
Smith, Tony 1993, 'Marx's *Capital* and Hegelian Dialectical Logic', in Moseley (ed.) 1993.

Smith, Tony 2000, *Technology and Capital in the Age of Lean Production: A Marxian Critique of the 'New Economy'*, Albany: State University of New York Press.
Smith, Tony 2003, 'On the Homology Thesis', *Historical Materialism*, 11, 1: 185–94.
Smith, Tony 2006, *Models of Globalisation: A Systematic Marxist Account*, Leiden: Brill Academic Publishers.
Sohn-Rethel, Alfred 1971, *Warenform und Denkform*, Frankfurt: Europa Verlag.
Sohn-Rethel, Alfred 1978, *Intellectual and Manual Labour*, Basingstoke, Macmillan.
Soja, Edward 1989, *Postmodern Geographies: The Reassertion of Space in Modern Critical Social Theory*, London: Verso.
Soldani, Franco 1994, *Il Cristallo e l'organismo. Natura del modo di produzione capitalistico*, Milan: Punto Rosso.
Sollers, Philippe 1974, 'Critiques', *Tel Quel*, 57: 127–37.
Sorel, Georges 1982, *La Décomposition du marxisme*, Paris: Presses Universitaires de France.
Spivak, Gayatri Chakravorty 1988, 'Can The Subaltern Speak?', in *Marxism and the Interpretation of Culture*, edited by Cary Nelson and Lawrence Grossberg, Urbana: University of Illinois Press.
Stalin, Joseph 1951, *Concerning Marxism in Linguistics*, London: *Soviet News*.
Ste Croix, Geoffrey de 1981, *The Class Struggle in the Ancient Greek World*, London: Duckworth.
Ste. Croix, Geoffrey de 1984, 'Class in Marx's Conception of History, Ancient and Modern', *New Left Review*, I, 146: 94–111.
Stedman Jones, Gareth 1983, *Languages of Class*, Cambridge: Cambridge University Press.
Stiegler, Barbara 2001, *Nietzsche et la biologie*, Paris: Presses Universitaires de France.
Stiglitz, Joseph 1993, 'Market Socialism and Neoclassical Economics', in Bardhan & Roemer (eds.) 1993.
Stroshane, Tim 1997, 'The Second Contradiction of Capitalism and Karl Polanyi's *The Great Transformation*', *Capitalism, Nature, Socialism*, 8, 3: 93–116.
Sugihara, Shiro 1983, 'Uno Kôzô', *Kodansha Encylopedia of Japan*.
Sung, Jung Mo 1989, *A idolatria do capital e a morte dos pobres*, San Paulo: Edições Paulinas.
Sung, Jung Mo 1995, *Teologia e economia*, Petropolis: Vozes.
Taylor, Charles 1975, *Hegel*, Cambridge: Cambridge University Press.
Taylor, Charles 1978/9, 'The Validity of Transcendental Arguments', *Proceedings of the Aristotelian Society*, 79: 151–65.
Taylor, Peter J. 1994, 'The State as Container: Territoriality in the Modern World System', *Progress in Human Geography*, 18, 3: 151–62.
Teeple, Gary 1983, *Marx's Critique of Politics, 1842–1847*, Toronto: University of Toronto Press.
Tertulian, Nicolas 1980, *Georges Lukács: étapes de sa pensée esthétique*, Paris: Sycomore.
Tertulian, Nicolas 1981, *Lukács. La rinascità dell'ontologia*, Rome: Riuniti.
Tertulian, Nicolas 1993, 'Georg Lukács et le stalinisme', *Les Temps Modernes*, 563: 1–45.
Teschke, Benno 1997, 'Review of Guy Bois's *The Transformation of the Year 1000*', *Historical Materialism*, 1: 96–202.
Teschke, Benno 1998, 'Geopolitical Relations in the European Middle Ages', *International Organization*, 52: 325–58.
Teschke, Benno 2001, 'The Non-Modernity of the Westphalian System of State: Dynasticism, Territoriality, Equilibrium', UCLA/Center for Social Theory and Comparative History.
Teschke, Benno 2002, 'Theorizing the Westphalian System of States: International Relations from Absolutism to Capitalism', *European Journal of international relations*, 8, 1: 5–48.
Teschke, Benno 2003, *The Myth of 1648. Class, Geopolitics and the Making of Modern International Relations*, London: Verso.
Teschke, Benno 2005, 'Bourgeois Revolution, State Formation and the Absence of the International', *Historical Materialism*, 13, 2: 3–26.

Texier, Jacques 1998, *Révolution et démocratie chez Marx et Engels*, Paris: Presses Universitaires de France.
Thoburn, Nicholas 2003, *Deleuze, Marx and Politics*, London: Routledge.
Thomas, Paul 1994, *Alien Politics: Marxist State Theory Revisited*, London: Routledge.
Thompson, Dorothy 1993, *Outsiders: Class, Gender and Nation*, London: Verso.
Thompson, Edward P. 1957, 'Socialist Humanism', *New Reasoner*, 1: 105–43.
Thompson, Edward P. 1958, 'Agency and Choice', *New Reasoner*, 5: 89–106.
Thompson, Edward P. 1976, *Whigs and Hunters*, Harmondsworth: Penguin.
Thompson, Edward P. 1978, *The Poverty of Theory and Other Essays*, London: Merlin.
Thompson, Edward P. 1980 [1963], *The Making of the English Working Class*, London: Penguin.
Thompson, Edward P. 1981, 'The Politics of Theory', in *People's History and Socialist Theory*, edited by Raphael Samuel, London: Routledge.
Thompson, Edward P. 1994 [1986], 'Agenda for Radical History', in *Persons and Polemics*, edited by Edward Thompson, London: Merlin.
Thompson, Willie 2000, *What Happened to History?*, London: Pluto.
Ticktin, Hilel 1998, 'The Problem Is Market Socialism', in *Market Socialism: The Debate among Socialists*, edited by Bertell Ollman, London: Routledge.
Togliatti, Palmiro 2001, *Scritti su Gramsci*, edited by Guido Liguori, Rome: Editori Riuniti.
Tomba, Massimiliano forthcoming, 'The Differentials of Surplus-Value', *Historical Materialism*.
Tooke, J. Horne 1993 [1786–1805], *Epea Pteroenta, or The Diversions of Purley*, London: Routledge.
Toscano, Alberto 2004a, 'Communism as Separation', in *Think Again: Alain Badiou and the Future of Philosophy*, edited by Peter Hallward, London: Continuum.
Toscano, Alberto 2004b, 'From the State to the World?: Badiou and Anti-Capitalism', *Communication and Cognition*, 37, 3/4: 199–224, also available at: <http://www.goldsmiths.ac.uk/csisp/papers/toscano_stateToWorld.pdf>.
Toscano, Alberto 2006a, 'Can Violence Be Thought? Notes on Badiou and the Possibility of (Marxist) Politics', *Identities: Journal for Politics, Gender and Culture*, 5, 1: 6–38.
Toscano, Alberto 2006b, 'The Bourgeois and the Islamist, or, The Other Subjects of Politics', *Cosmos and History: The Journal of Natural and Social Philosophy*, 2, 1–2: 15–38.
Tosel, André 1974, 'Le développement du marxisme en Europe occidentale depuis 1917. Histoire de la philosophie', in *Encyclopédie de la Pleiade*, Volume 3, Paris: Gallimard.
Tosel, André 1981, 'Filosofia marxista e traducibilità dei linguaggi e delle pratiche', in Bronislaw Baczko et al., *Filosofia e politica. Scritti dedicati a Cesare Luporini*, Florence: La Nuova Italia.
Tosel, André 1984, *Praxis: vers une refondation en philosophie marxiste*, Paris: Messidor/Éditions Sociales.
Tosel, André 1991, *L'Esprit de scission. Études sur Marx, Gramsci, Lukács*, Besançon: Annales Littéraires de l'Université de Besançon.
Tosel, André 1996, *Études sur Marx (et Engels). Vers un communisme de la finitude*, Paris: Kimé.
Touboul, Hervé 2004, *Marx, Engels et la question de l'individu*, Paris: Presses Universitaires de France.
Toussaint, Eric 1998, *La Bourse ou la vie: la finance contre les peuples*, Brussels: CADTM.
Tran Duc Thao 1973, *Recherches sur l'origine du langage et de la conscience*, Paris, Éditions Sociales.
Trebitsch, Michel 1991, 'Preface', in Lefebvre 1991.
Tronti, Mario 1971 [1966], *Operai e capitale*, Einaudi: Turin.
Tronti, Mario 1980, *Il tempo della politica*, Rome: Editori Riuniti.
Tronti, Mario 1998, *La politica al tramonto* , Turin: Einaudi.
Truffaut, François 1978, *Hitchcock*, London: Granada.

Turchetto, Maria 1999, *Lavoro impresa capitale: lezioni di storia del pensiero economico*, Saonara: Logos.
Turner, Graeme 1990, *British Cultural Studies*, Unwin Hyman: London.
UCFML 1983, 'Le Marxisme comme politique', *Le Perroquet*, 29–30: 1–3.
Uchida, Hiroshi 1988, *Marx's 'Grundrisse' and Hegel's 'Logic'*, London: Routledge.
Uno, Kôzô 1980 [1950–2], *Principles of Political Economy: Theory of a Purely Capitalist Society*, translated by Thomas Sekine, Brighton: Harvester.
Vacca, Giuseppe 1977, 'La "questione politica degli intellettuali" e la teoria marxista dello Stato nel pensiero di Gramsci', in Ferri (ed.) 1977.
Vacca, Giuseppe 1999, *Appuntamenti con Gramsci. Introduzione allo studio dei 'Quaderni del carcere'*, Rome: Carocci.
Vadée, Michel 1987, *Marx, penseur du possible*, Paris: Méridiens Klincksieck.
Van der Pilj, Kees 1984, *The Making of the Atlantic Ruling Class*, London: Verso.
Van der Pilj, Kees 1998, *Transnational Classes and International Relations*, London: Routledge.
Van der Pijl, Kees 2001–2, 'Globalization or Class Society in Transition?', *Science & Society*, 65, 4: 492–500.
Van der Pijl, Kees 2005, 'Gramsci and Left Managerialism', *Critical Review of International Social and Political Philosophy*, 8, 4: 499–511.
Van Parijs, Philippe 1981, *Evolutionary Explanation in the Social Sciences*, Totowa: Rowman and Littlefield.
Van Parijs, Philippe 1993, *Marxism Recycled*, Cambridge: Cambridge University Press.
Van Parijs, Philippe 1995, *Real Freedom for All*, Oxford: Oxford University Press.
Vanek, Jaroslav 1970, *The General Theory of Labour Managed Economics*, Ithaca: Cornell University Press.
Veca, Salvatore 1977, *Saggio sul programma scientifico di Marx*, Milan: Il Saggiatore.
Velho, Otavio Guilherme 1982, *Sociedade e agricultura*, Rio de Janeiro: Editora Zahar.
Vernadsky, Vladimir 1924, *La Géochimie*, Paris: Félix Alcan.
Vincent, Jean-Marie 1973, *Fétichisme et société*, Paris: Anthropos.
Vincent, Jean-Marie 1991 [1987], *Abstract Labour: A Critique*, translated by Jim Cohen, New York: St. Martin's Press.
Vincent, Jean-Marie 2001, *Un autre Marx*, Lausanne: Page 2.
Virdee, Satnam (forthcoming) 'Race, Class and the Dialectics of Social Transformation', in *Handbook of Race and Ethnic Studies*, edited by Patricia Hill-Collins and John Solomos, London: Sage.
Virno, Paolo 1990, 'Citazioni di fronte al pericolo', *Luogo commune*, 1: 9–13.
Virno, Paolo 2002, *Grammatica della moltitudine*, Rome: Derive Approdi.
Vivien, Franck-Dominique 1994, *Économie et écologie*, Paris: La Découverte.
Vivien, Franck-Dominique 1996, 'Marxisme et écologie politique, le rendez-vous manqué de Sergueï Podolinsky', in *Actualiser l'économie de Marx*, Paris: Presses Universitaires de France.
Voigt, Rudiger (ed.) 2000, *Abscheid vom Staat – Rückkehr zum Staat?* 3rd digital edition, available at: <www.staatswissenschaft.de>.
Voloshinov, Valentin N. 1973, *Marxism and the Philosophy of Language*, New York: Seminar Press.
Von Laue, Theodore 1987, *The World Revolution of Westernization: The Twentieth Century in Global Perspective*, Oxford: Oxford University Press.
Voza, Pasquale 2004, 'Rivoluzione passiva', in *Le parole di Gramsci. Per un lessico dei 'Quaderni del carcere'*, edited by Fabio Frosini & Guido Liguori, Rome: Carocci.
Vranicki, Predrag 1961, *Historija marksisma*, Zagreb: Naprijed.
Vygodskij, Vitali S. 1976, *Wie 'Das Kapital' enstand*, Berlin: Dietz Verlag [translated in English as V.S. Vygodski *The story of a great discovery. How Karl Marx wrote 'Capital'*, London: Abacus Press, 1974.]
Vygotsky, Lev S. 1962, *Thought and Language*, Cambridge, MA., MIT Press.
Wagner, Birgit 1991, 'Antonio Gramsci. La radicale provvisorietà del pensiero. Questione di metodo: Una rilettura del Quaderno 11', in *Il Manifesto*, November 6.

Wallerstein, Immanuel 1974–88, *The Modern World System, 3 vols*, New York: Academic Press.
Wallerstein, Immanuel 1983, *Historical Capitalism*, London: Verso.
Wallerstein, Immanuel 1991, *Unthinking Social Science: The Limits of Nineteenth-Century Paradigms*, Cambridge: Polity.
Warin, François 1994, *Nietzsche et Bataille. La parodie à l'infinie*, Paris: Presses Universitaires de France.
Watanabe, H. 1983, 'Logico-Genetical Approximation: The Analysis of the Unfolding of the Value Form', *Keisai Gaku*, 44, 4 and 45, 1.
Wayne, Mike 2001, 'Redeeming Walter Benjamin', available at: <http://clogic.eserver.org/3-1&2/wayne.html>.
Weisskopf, Thomas 1992, 'Towards a Socialism for the Future, in the Wake of the Demise of the Socialism of the Past', *Review of Radical Political Economics*, 24, 3–4: 1–28.
Weisskopf, Thomas E. 1993, 'A Democratic Enterprise-Based Market Socialism', in Bardhan & Roemer (eds.) 1993.
Wellmer, Albrecht 1985, 'Adorno, Anwalt des Nicht-Identischen', in *Zur Dialektik von Moderne und Postmoderne*, Frankfurt am Main: Suhrkamp.
Wells, David 1982, *Marxism and the Modern State. An Analysis of Fetishism in Capitalist Society*, Brighton: Harvester.
Werckmeister, Otto Karl 1992, 'Walter Benjamins 'Passagenwerk als Modell für eine kunstgeschichtliche Synthese', in *Frankfurter Schule und Kunstgeschichte*, edited by Andreas Berndt, Peter Kaiser, Angela Rosenberg and Diana Trinkner, Berlin: Dietrich Reimer Verlag.
Werckmeister, Otto Karl 1997, *Linke Ikonen. Benjamin, Eisenstein, Picasso – Nach dem Fall des Kommunismus*, Munich: Carl Hanser. [Translated into English as *Icons of the Left: Benjamin and Eisenstein, Picasso and Kafka after the Fall of Communism*, Chicago: University of Chicago Press, 1999.]
Wickham, Chris 1988, 'Historical Materialism, Historical Sociology', *New Left Review*, I, 171: 63–78.
Wiggershaus, Rolf 1994 [1986], *The Frankfurt School: Its History, Theories and Political Significance*, translated by Michael Robertson, Cambridge: Polity.
Williams, Michael (ed.) 1989, *Value, Social Form and the State*, London: Routledge.
Williams, Raymond 1958, *Culture and Society*, London: Chatto & Windus.
Williams, Raymond 1961, *The Long Revolution*, London: Chatto & Windus.
Williams, Raymond 1962, *Communications*, London: Penguin.
Williams, Raymond 1966, *Modern Tragedy*, London: Chatto & Windus.
Williams, Raymond 1968, *Drama from Ibsen to Brecht*, London: Chatto & Windus.
Williams, Raymond 1971, *Orwell*, London: Fontana.
Williams, Raymond 1973, *The Country and the City*, London: Chatto & Windus.
Williams, Raymond 1974, *Television: Technology and Cultural Form*, London: Fontana.
Williams, Raymond 1976, *Keywords*, London: Fontana.
Williams, Raymond 1977, *Marxism and Literature*, Oxford: Oxford University Press.
Williams, Raymond 1979, *Politics and Letters: Interviews with 'New Left Review'*, London: New Left Books.
Williams, Raymond 1981, *Culture*, London: Fontana.
Williams, Raymond 1989, *The Politics of Modernism*, London: Verso.
Willke, Helmut 1992, *Die Ironie des Staates*, Frankfurt am Main: Suhrkamp.
Wilson, Scott 1995, *Cultural Materialism*, Oxford: Blackwell.
Wissel, Jens 2007, *Die Transnationalisierung von Herrschaftsverhältnissen. Zur Aktualität von Nicos Poulantzas' Staatstheorie*, Baden-Baden: Nomos.
Witte, Bernd 1975, 'Benjamin and Lukács. Historical Notes on the Relationship Between Their Political and Aesthetic Theories', *New German Critique*, 5, 3–26.
Witte, Bernd 1992, 'Allegorien des Schreibens: Eine Lektüre von Walter Benjamins Trauerspielbuch', *Merkur*, 2, February: 125–36.
Wolff, Edward 1992, 'Structural Change and the Movement of the Rate of Profit in the USA', in Kleinknecht, Mandel & Wallerstein (eds.) 1992.

Womack, John, Daniel T. Jones, Daniel Roos 1990, *The Machine that Changed the World: Based on the Massachusetts Institute of Technology 5-Million Dollar 5-Year Study on the Future of the Automobile,* New York: Rawson Associates.
Wood, Ellen M. 1972, *Mind and Politics,* Berkeley: University of California Press.
Wood, Ellen M. 1978, 'C.B. Macpherson: Liberalism and the Task of Socialist Political Theory', in *Socialist* Register 1978, edited by Ralph Miliband and John Saville, London: Merlin Press.
Wood, Ellen M. 1981a, 'Liberal Democracy and Capitalist Hegemony: A Reply to Leo Panitch on the Task of Socialist Political Theory', in *Socialist Register* 1981, edited by Ralph Miliband and John Saville, London: Merlin Press.
Wood, Ellen M. 1981b, 'The Separation of the Economic and the Political in Capitalism', *New Left Review,* I, 127: 66–93.
Wood, Ellen M. 1984, 'Marxism and the Course of History', *New Left Review,* I, 147: 95–107.
Wood, Ellen M. 1985, 'The State and Popular Sovereignty in French Political Thought: A Geneology of Rousseau's 'General Will'', in *History from Below,* edited by Frederick Krantz, Oxford: Blackwell.
Wood, Ellen M. 1988, *Peasant-Citizen and Slave,* London: Verso.
Wood, Ellen M. 1991, *The Pristine Culture of Capitalism,* London: Verso.
Wood, Ellen M. 1992, 'Locke Against Democracy: Consent, Representation and Suffrage in the Two Treaties', *History of Political Thought,* 13, 4: 657–89.
Wood, Ellen M. 1994a, 'Radicalism, Capitalism and Historical Contexts: Not Only a Reply to Richard Ashcroft on John Locke', *History of Political Thought,* 15, 3: 323–72.
Wood, Ellen M. 1994b, 'From Opportunity to Imperative', *Monthly Review,* 46: 14–44.
Wood, Ellen M. 1995a, *Democracy Against Capitalism,* Cambridge: Cambridge University Press.
Wood, Ellen M. 1995b, 'Chronology of the New Left', in *Socialist Register* 1995, edited by Leo Panitch, London: Merlin Press.
Wood, Ellen M. 1995c, 'Rational Choice Marxism: Is the Game worth the Candle?', in Carver & Thomas (eds.) 1995.
Wood, Ellen M. 1996, 'Capitalism, Merchants and Bourgeois Revolution: Reflections on the Brenner Debate and its Sequel', *International Review of Social History,* 41: 209–32.
Wood, Ellen M. 1999a, *The Origin of Capitalism,* New York: Monthly Review Press.
Wood, Ellen M. 1999b, 'The Politics of Capitalism' *Monthly Review,* September 1999, 12–26.
Wood, Ellen M. 1998 [1986], *The Retreat from Class: A New 'True' Socialism,* London: Verso.
Wood, Ellen M. 2002, *The Origins of Capitalism. A Longer View,* London: Verso.
Wood, Ellen M. 2003, *Empire of Capital,* London: Verso.
Wood, Ellen M. & John Bellamy Foster (eds.) 1997, *In Defense of History,* New York: Monthly Review Press.
Wood, Ellen M. & Neal Wood 1978, *Class Ideology and Ancient Political Theory,* Oxford: Blackwell.
Wood, Ellen M. & Neal Wood 1997, *A Trumpet of Sedition,* London: Pluto.
Wood, Neal 1983, *The Politics of Locke's Philosophy,* Berkeley: University of California Press.
Wood, Neal 1984, *John Locke and Agrarian Capitalism,* Berkeley: University of California Press.
Wright, Erik Olin 1978, *Class, Crisis, and the State,* London: Verso.
Wright, Erik Olin 1985, *Classes,* London: Verso.
Wright, Erik Olin 1989, 'Rethinking, Once Again, the Concept of Class Structure', in *The Debate on Classes,* edited by Erik Olin Wright, London: Verso.
Wright, Erik Olin 1994, *Interrogating Inequality,* London: Verso.
Wright, Erik Olin 1997a, 'Reflections on Socialism, Capitalism and Marxism: An Interview with Erik Olin Wright', *Imprints,* 2, 2.
Wright, Erik Olin 1997b, *Class Counts,* Cambridge: Cambridge University Press.

Wright, Erik Olin 1998, 'Equality, Community and "Efficient Distribution"', in Bowles & Gintis (eds.) 1998.

Wright, Erik Olin, Andrew Levine, & Elliot Sober 1992, *Reconstructing Marxism*, London: Verso.

Yale French Studies 1995, *Depositions: Althusser, Balibar, Macherey and the Labor of Reading*, 88.

Young, Robert 1990, *White Mythologies: Writing History and the West*, London: Routledge.

Zeitlin, Jonathan & Philippe Pochet (eds.) 2005, *The Open Method of Co-ordination in Action: the European Employment and Social Inclusion Strategy*, Brussels: P.I.E.-Lang.

Ziltener, Patrick 2001, *Strukturwandel der europäischen Integration. Die Europäische Union und die Veränderung von Staatlichkeit*, Münster: Westfälisches Dampfboot.

Žižek, Slavoj 1998, 'Psychoanalysis in Post-Marxism: The Case of Alain Badiou', *The South Atlantic Quarterly*, 97, 2: 235–61.

Žižek, Slavoj 1999, *The Ticklish Subject*, London: Verso.

Zourabichvili, François 1998, 'Deleuze et le possible, de l'involontarisme en politique', in *Gilles Deleuze, une vie philosophique*, edited by Eric Alliez, Paris: Synthélabo.

Index